The Bristol and Gloucestershire Archaeological Society
Gloucestershire Record Series

Hon. General Editor

C. R. Elrington, M.A., F.S.A., F.R.Hist.S.
formerly General Editor of the
Victoria History of the Counties of England

Volume 11

The Original Acta of St. Peter's Abbey, Gloucester

THE ORIGINAL ACTA OF
ST. PETER'S ABBEY,
GLOUCESTER
C. 1122 to 1263

Edited, with an account of
the Scriptorium and its Scribes,
by
Robert B. Patterson
Professor of History, University of South Carolina

The Bristol and Gloucestershire Archaeological Society

1998

The Bristol and Gloucestershire Archaeological Society
Gloucestershire Record Series

© The Bristol and Gloucestershire Archaeological Society

ISBN 0 900197 47 1

British Library Cataloguing in Publication Data. A catalogue
entry for this book is available from the British Library.

Printed in Great Britain by J. W. Arrowsmith Ltd.

CONTENTS

TO ANNE ELIZABETH PATTERSON

PREFACE

The idea for an edition of the *acta* of St. Peter's Abbey, based on the massive collection of originals in Gloucesters Cathedral's muniments, was originally suggested to me by David J. H. Smith, the County and Diocesan Archivist and Honorary Secretary of the Bristol and Gloucestershire Archaeological Society. Preliminary archival surveying at Gloucester and other promising repositories, made possible by the Venture Fund of the University of South Carolina, revealed the project's potential. The wealth of hitherto unprinted charter evidence about the abbey, its priories, and its estates, and particularly about its scriptorium, made the proposal irresistible. So rich has been the harvest of secretarial and endorsement hands that financial constraints limit the illustration of each hand to one photograph rather than the ideal two.

Crown copyright material in the Public Record Office is reproduced by permission of the Controller of Her Majesty's Stationery Office. Permission to publish other transcripts and photographs of charters and endorsements has been generously granted by the Dean and Chapter of Gloucester, the Dean and Chapter of Hereford with the assistance of Canon John Tiller, the Dean and Chapter of Chichester, the Dean and Chapter of Rochester, the Dean and Chapter of Worcester, the Earl of Plymouth, Shropshire County Council, Gloucester City Council, the Trustees of the Berkeley Will Trust, the British Library, the Bodleian Library, Oxford, the Syndics of Cambridge University Library, the Principal and Fellows of Jesus College, Oxford, the National Library of Wales, and the Bristol Record Office.

Progress on the project has been greatly facilitated by grants for travel and photography from the Dean and Chapter of Gloucester Cathedral, the Friends of Gloucester Cathedral, the Bristol and Gloucestershire Archaeological Society, the Neil Ker Memorial Fund of the British Academy, the National Endowment for the Humanities (U.S.A.), the Southern Region Educational Board (Atlanta), the Research and Productive Scholarship Committee of the University of South Carolina, and my department through the agency of Peter W. Becker, the chairman. The provision of microfilms and photographs by the Gloucestershire Record Office, Hereford Cathedral Library, the Center for Research Libraries, and Professor William T. Reedy Jr. enabled me to study several large collections at a distance from their locations in the U.K. Also enormously helpful have been working facilities accorded to me by Worcester College, Oxford, and its librarian Joanna Parker, and the hospitality extended during my many archival visits by H. G. Pitt, James Campbell, John and Frances Walsh, Christopher and Jean Elrington, Brian and Alison Smith, Robert and Amanda Simpson, and Sir James C. Holt, and especially by my cousin Joseph P. Funke.

An array of archivists and librarians has also contributed to the completion of the project. In the forefront have been David J. H. Smith and his staff, Kate Haslem, Paul Evans, and Averil Kear, at the Gloucestershire Record Office and Canon John Tiller, Joan Williams, and Meryl Jancy at Hereford Cathedral Library. I am particularly indebted to Lowinger Maddison of Gloucester Cathedral Library; the staffs of the Students' Room of the British Library, of the Public Record Office, of the Bodleian Library, Oxford, and of the Historical Manuscripts Commission; also to Robert Bearman of the Shakespeare Birthplace Trust Library, Stratford-upon-Avon; R. S. Benedikz of the University of Birmingham Library; Penelope A. Bulloch of Balliol College Library, Oxford; Annette M. Burton and Susan Beckley of Glamorgan County Record Offices; Chris Butler of Corpus Christi College Library, Oxford; Gill Cannell of the Parker

Library, Corpus Christi College, Cambridge; R. J. Chamberlaine-Brothers of Warwickshire County Record Office; Sarah Cobbold of Jesus College Library, Oxford; Stephen Dixon of Rochester-upon-Medway Studies Centre; Christine Dowland of Gwent County Record Office; D. Wyn Evans of Exeter University Library; Suzanne Eward of Salisbury Cathedral Library; D. V. Fowkes of the William Salt Library, Stafford; Stephen Freeth of the Guildhall Library, London; Patricia Gill of West Sussex Record Office; Ruth Gosling of the Central Library, Birmingham; John Hardacre of Winchester Cathedral Library; Steven D. Hobbs of Wiltshire County Record Office; Linda H. Holderfield of the Thomas Cooper Library of the University Library of South Carolina; Canon Iain MacKenzie of Worcester Cathedral Libary; Mary McKenzie, Ruth E. Bagley, and Michael J. Hughes of Shropshire Record Office; D. J. McKitterick of Trinity College Library, Cambridge; Bernard Meehan and S. S. F. Ó Seanóir of Trinity College Library, Dublin; Richard Mortimer of Westminster Abbey Muniment Room and Library; Peter McNiven of the John Rylands Library, Manchester; Sheila Malloch of Canterbury Cathedral Library; John Owen and Janet Marx of Dyfed County Record Office; Martin Phillife of Keele University Library; Helen Powell of the Queen's College Library, Oxford; Margery M. Rowe, Paul Brough, and Tim Warmleighton of Devon County Record Offices; Alison Sproston of Gonville and Caius College Library, Cambridge; Graham C. G. Thomas of the National Library of Wales; William Voelkle of the J. Pierpont Morgan Library, New York; A. M. Wherry and Robin Whittaker of Hereford and Worcester Record Office; John S. Williams of Bristol Record Office; J. Joseph Wisdom of St. Paul's Cathedral Library, London; and P. N. R. Zutschi of Cambridge University Library;

I have also benefited from the advice of Mary G. Cheney, Eleanor Searle, Paul Hyams, Paul Brand, David Carpenter, Michael Gullick, Nicholas Vincent, Julia S. Barrow, Sir James C. Holt, Ann Geddes, Ralph W. Mathisen, and Michael Hare. The expertise of my editor Christopher Elrington has been invaluable. Ultimate responsibility for any errors must fall on my head.

As always, my wife Ruth has been my companion and support in this venture. It is with the greatest pleasure that I dedicate this work to my daughter in tribute to the doctorate which she earned through her scientific research.

ROBERT B. PATTERSON
The University of South Carolina
May 1998

ABBREVIATIONS AND BIBLIOGRAPHY

The place of publication is not given when it is London, Oxford, or Cambridge.

ASC	*The Anglo-Saxon Chronicle*, ed. Dorothy Whitelock, David C. Douglas, and Suzie Tucker (1961)
Anglo-Saxon Charters, ed. Sawyer	*Anglo-Saxon Charters*, ed. P. H. Sawyer (1968)
Annales de Burton	*Annales de Burton*, in *Annales Monastici*, ed. H. R. Luard, vol. i (Rolls Ser. 1864), 181–500
Annales de Dunstaplia	*Annales de Dunstaplia*, in *Annales Monastici*, ed. H. R. Luard, vol. iii (Rolls Ser. 1866), 1–420
Annales de Theokesberia	*Annales de Theokesberia*, in *Annales Monastici*, ed. H. R. Luard, vol. i (Rolls Ser. 1864), 41–180
Annales de Wigornia	*Annales Prioratus de Wigornia*, in *Annales Monastici*, ed. H. R. Luard, vol. iv (Rolls Ser. 1869), 353–564
Archaeologia	*Archaeologia or Miscellaneous Tracts relating to Antiquity* (published by the Society of Antiquaries of London)
B.C.M.	Berkeley Castle Muniments
BGAST	*Bristol and Gloucestershire Archaeological Society Transactions*
B.L.	The British Library
B.R.O.	Bristol Record Office
Baddeley, i	'Early Deeds relating to St. Peter's Abbey, Gloucester', ed. W. St. Clair Baddeley, *BGAST* xxxvii (1915), 221–34
Baddeley, ii	'Early Deeds relating to St. Peter's Abbey, Gloucester', ed. W. St. Clair Baddeley, *BGAST* xxxviii (1916), 19–46, and 'Further Early Deeds, Hitherto Unprinted, Relating to St. Peter's Abbey Gloucester', ed. idem, in ibid. 47–68
Barkly, 'Earlier House of Berkeley'	Henry Barkly, 'The Earlier House of Berkeley', *BGAST* viii (1883–4), 193–223
Barlow, *English Church*	Frank Barlow, *The English Church 1066–1154* (1979)
Barlow, *Thomas Becket*	Frank Barlow, *Thomas Becket* (Berkeley and Los Angeles, 1986)
Barlow, *William Rufus*	Frank Barlow, *William Rufus* (Berkeley and Los Angeles, 1983)
Barrow, *Hereford Episcopal Acta*	*English Episcopa Acta VII: Hereford 1079–1234*, ed. Julia Barrow (1993)
Bates, 'Abbey of St. Peter's'	David Bates, 'The Building of a Great Church: the Abbey of St. Peter's Gloucester, and its Early Norman Benefactors', *BGAST* cii (1984), 129–32
Binns, *Dedications*	Alison Binns, *Dedications of Monastic House in England and Wales 1066–1216* (Woodbridge, Suffolk, 1989)
Birch, *Catalogue of Seals*	*Catalogue of Seals in the Department of Manuscripts in the British Museum*, ed. W. de G. Birch, vol. i (1887)
Birch, *Penrice and Margam Manuscripts*	*A Descriptive Catalogue of the Penrice and Margam Manuscripts*, ed. W. de G. Birch, 1st ser. (1893), 4th ser. (1903)
Bishop, 'Notes on Cambridge Manuscripts'	T. A. M. Bishop, 'Notes on Cambridge Manuscripts I', *Transactions of the Cambridge Bibliographical Society*, 1 (1949–53), 432–41
Bishop, *Scriptores Regis*	T. A. M. Bishop, *Scriptores Regis* (1960)
Bishop and Chaplais, *English Royal Writs*	T. A. M. Bishop and Pierre Chaplais, *English Royal Writs to A.D. 1100* (1957)
Blair, 'Minster Churches'	John Blair, 'Secular Minsters in Domesday Book', in *Domesday Book: A Reassessment*, ed. Peter Sawyer (1985), 104–42
Bodl.	Bodleian Library, Oxford

Borough Charters   *British Borough Charters 1042–1216*, ed. A. Ballard (1913)

Brett, *English Church under*   Martin Brett, *The English Church under Henry I* (1975)
  Henry I

Brooke, *English Church and*   Z. N. Brooke, *The English Church and the Papacy* (reprinted
  the Papacy   edn. 1989)

Brooke, 'English Episcopal   C. N. L. Brooke, 'English Episcopal *Acta* of the Twelfth and
  Acta'   Thirteenth Centuries', in *Medieval Ecclesiastical Studies*, 41–
                                      56

Brooke, 'St. Peter of   C. N. L. Brooke, 'St. Peter of Gloucester and St. Cadog of
  Gloucester'   Llancarfan', in *The Church and the Welsh Border in the
                                      Central Middle Ages*, ed. D. N. Dumville and C. N. L. Brooke
                                      (Woodbridge, Suffolk, and Wolfeboro, N. H., 1986); printed
                                      earlier in *Celt and Saxon*, ed. Nora K. Chadwick (1963), 258–
                                      322

Brown, *Guide*   Michelle P. Brown, *A Guide to Western Historical Scripts to
                                      1600* (1990)

Burton, *York Episcopal Acta*   *English Episcopal Acta V: York 1070–1154*, ed. Janet E. Burton
                                      (1988)

CRR   *Curia Regis Rolls* (Public Record Office)
C.U.L.   Cambridge University Library
Cal. of MSS. of Dean and   Historical Manuscripts Commission [12], *Calendar of Manu-*
  Chapter of Wells   *scripts of the Dean and Chapter of Wells*, 2 vols. (1907–14)
Capes, *Hereford Charters*   *Charters and Records of Hereford Cathedral*, ed. W. W. Capes
                                      (Hereford, 1908)

Cart. Bristol   *The Cartulary of St Augustine's Abbey Bristol*, ed. David Walker
                                      (Bristol and Gloucestershire Archaeological Society, Record
                                      Ser. vol. x, 1998)

Cart. Glouc.   'Cartularium Monasterii S. Petri Gloucestriae', in *Historia et
                                      Cartularium Monasterii Sancti Petri Gloucestriae*, ed. W. H.
                                      Hart, 3 vols. (Rolls Ser. 1863–7)

Cart. Reading   *Reading Abbey Cartularies: British Library Manuscripts
                                      Egerton 3031, Harley 1708 and Vespasian E xxv*, ed. B. R.
                                      Kemp (Camden 4th ser. vols. 31, 33, 1986–7)

Cart. St. Mark's Bristol   *Cartulary of St. Mark's Hospital Bristol*, ed. C. D. Ross (Bristol
                                      Record Society vol. xxi, 1959)

Chaplais, *English Royal*   Pierre Chaplais, *English Royal Documents* (1971)
  Documents

Chaplais, *Essays*   Pierre Chaplais, *Essays in Medieval Diplomacy and
                                      Administration* (1981)

Chaplais, 'John de Branketre'   Pierre Chaplais, 'Master John de Branketre and the Office of
                                      Notary in Chancery, 1355–75', *Journal of the Society of
                                      Archivists* vol. iv (1971), 169–99; reprinted in Chaplais, *Essays*

Chaplais, 'The Making of the   Pierre Chaplais, 'The Making of the Treaty of Paris and the
  Treaty of Paris and the Royal   Royal Style', *English Historical Review* lxvii (1952), 235–53;
  Style'   reprinted in Chaplais, *Essays*

Chaplais, 'Seals and Original   Pierre Chaplais, 'The Seals and Original Charters of Henry I',
  Charters of Henry I'   *English Historical Review* lxxv (1960); reprinted with
                                      addendum in Chaplais, *Essays*

Chaplais, 'Westminster   Pierre Chaplais, 'The Original Charters of Herbert and Gervase,
  Charters'   Abbots of Westminster', in *A Medieval Miscellany for Doris
                                      Mary Stenton* (Pipe Roll Society, new ser. xxxvi, 1962), 89–
                                      110; reprinted with addendum in Chaplais, *Essays*

Chapuisat, 'Le chapitre   J.-P. Chapuisat, 'Le chapitre savoyard de Hereford au XIIIe
  savoyard de Hereford'   siècle', in *Congrès des Sociétés Savantes de la Province de
                                      Savoie*, new series 1, Actes du Congrès de Moutiers, 5 et 6
                                      Septembre 1964 (1966), 43–51

Chart. Chester	*The Charters of the Anglo-Norman Earls of Chester c. 1071–1237*, ed. Geoffrey Barraclough (Record Society of Lancashire and Cheshire, cxxvi, 1988)
Cheney, *English Bishops' Chanceries*	Christopher Cheney, *English Bishops' Chanceries 1100–1250* (Manchester, 1950)
Cheney, *Letters of Innocent III*	Christopher Cheney, *Letters of Pope Innocent III (1198–1216) concerning England and Wales* (1967)
Cheney, *Roger, Bishop of Worcester*	Mary G. Cheney, *Roger, Bishop of Worcester 1164–1179* (1980)
Cheney and John, *Canterbury Acta*	*English Episcopal Acta III: Canterbury 1193–1205*, ed. C. R. Cheney and E. John (1986)
Cheney and Jones, *Canterbury Acta*	*English Episcopal Acta II: Canterbury 1162–1190*, ed. C. R. Cheney and Bridgett E. A. Jones (1986)
Chew, *Ecclesiastical Tenants-in-Chief*	Helena M Chew, *English Ecclesiastical Tenants-in-Chief and Knight Service* (1932)
Chron. Evesham	*Chronicon Abbatiae Evesham ad Annum 1418*, ed. William Dunn Macray (Rolls Ser. 1863)
Clanchy, *From Memory to Written Record*	M. T. Clanchy, *From Memory to Written Record: England 1066–1307* (2nd edn. 1993)
Clark, *Cartae et alia*	*Cartae et alia Munimenta quae ad dominium de Glamorgancia pertinent*, ed. G. T. Clark, 6 vols. (2nd edn. Cardiff, 1910)
CloseR	*Close Rolls 1227–31* (Public Record Office, 1902)
Conway Davies, 'Ewenny Priory'	J. Conway Davies, 'Ewenny Priory: Some Recently Found Records', *The National Library of Wales Journal* iii (1943–4), 107–37
Cowley, *Monastic Order in South Wales*	F. G. Cowley, *The Monastic Order in South Wales 1066–1349* (Cardiff, 1977)
Cownie, 'Gloucester Abbey'	Emma Cownie, 'Gloucester Abbey, 1066–1135: An Illustration of Religious Patronage in Anglo-Norman England', in *England and Normandy in the Middle Ages*, ed. David Bates and Anne Curry (1994), 143–57
Crouch, 'Administration of the Norman Earldom'	David Crouch, 'Administration of the Norman Earldom', in *The Earldom of Chester and its Charters*, ed. A. T. Thacker, *Journal of the Chester Archaeological Society* lxxi (1991), 69–95
Crouch, *LEA*	*Llandaff Episcopal Acta 1140–1287*, ed. David Crouch (South Wales Record Society, 1988)
Darlington, *Cart. Worc.*	*The Cartulary of Worcester Cathedral Priory (Register I)*, ed. R. R. Darlington (Pipe Roll Society, new ser. xxxviii, 1968)
Davies, *Wales 1063–1415*	R. R. Davies, *Conquest, Coexistence and Change: Wales 1063–1415* (1987)
Davis, *Kalendar of Abbot Samson*	R. H. C. Davis, *The Kalendar of Abbot Samson of Bury St. Edmunds and Related Documents* (Camden 3rd ser. lxxxiv, 1954)
Davis, *Medieval Cartularies*	G. R. C. Davis, *Medieval Cartularies of Great Britain: A Short Catalogue* (1958)
Delisle, *BEC*	'Notes sur les chartes originales de Henri II, roi d'Angleterre et de Normandie, au British Museum et au Record Office', *Bibliothèque de l'École des chartes* lviii (1958), 272–314
Delisle, *Rouleau Mortuaire*	*Rouleau Mortuaire du B. Vital Abbé de Savigni contenant 207 titres écrits en 1122 dans differents églises de France et Angleterre*, ed. Léopold Delisle (Paris, 1909)
Delisle and Berger	*Recueil des actes de Henri II*, ed. Léopold Delisle and Élie Berger, vol. i (Paris, 1909)
Denholm-Young, *Handwriting in England and Wales*	N. Denholm-Young, *Handwriting in England and Wales* (Cardiff, 1964)

Domesday Book: Gloucester   *Domesday Book: Gloucestershire*, ed. and trans. John S. Moore (Chichester, 1982)

Drinkwater, 'Bromfield Priory'   C. H. Drinkwater, 'The Priory of Bromfield: A Royal Confirmation of Certain Charters to the Prior, etc.' *TSAS* 2nd ser. x (1898), 93–110

EAWD   *Episcopal Acts and Cognate Documents relating to Welsh Dioceses 1066–1272*, ed. J. Conway Davies, 2 vols. (Cardiff, 1946–8)

Ellis and Millen, *Catalogue of Seals*   *Catalogue of Seals in the Public Record Office: Monastic Seals*, vol. i, ed. Roger H. Ellis with plates by J. D. Millen (1986)

English Romanesque Art   *English Romanesque Art 1066–1200*, ed. George Zarnecki, Janet Holt, and Tristram Holland (1984)

Eyton, *Shropshire*   R. W. Eyton, *Antiquities of Shropshire*, including 'Bromfield' in vol. v (1857)

Fasti   *Fasti Ecclesiae Anglicanae 1066–1300*, vol. ii: *Monastic Cathedrals*, comp. D. E. Greenway (1971)

Finberg, *Charters of W. Midlands*   H. P. R. Finberg, *The Early Charters of the West Midlands* (Leicester, 1961)

Finberg, 'Early Charters of Glos.'   H. P. R. Finberg, 'The Early Charters of Gloucestershire', in Finberg, *Charters of W. Midlands*, 31–85

Finberg, 'Gloucester Abbey'   H. P. R. Finberg, 'The Early History of Gloucester Abbey', in Finberg, *Charters of W. Midlands*, 153–66

Florence of Worcester   *Florentii Wigorniensis Monachi Chronicon ex Chronicis*, ed. Benjamin Thorpe, 2 vols. (1848–9)

Foss, *Judges*   Edward Foss, *The Judges of England*, vol. ii (1848, reprinted edn. New York, 1966)

Franklin, 'Bodies in Medieval Northampton'   M. J. Franklin, 'Bodies in Medieval Northampton', in *Medieval Ecclesiastical Studies*, ed M. J. Franklin and Christopher Harper-Bill (Woodbridge, Suffolk, 1995), 57–81

Franklin, *Winchester Episcopal Acta*   *English Episcopa Acta VIII: Winchester 1070–1204*, ed. M. J. Franklin (1993)

GCH   *Glamorgan County History*, vol. iii: *The Middles Ages*, ed. T. B. Pugh (Cardiff, 1971)

G.C.L.   Gloucester Cathedral Library

GFAL   Adrian Morey and C. N. L. Brooke, *Gilbert Foliot and his Letters* (1965)

G.R.O.   Gloucestershire Record Office

Galbraith, 'Monastic Foundation Charters'   V. H. Galbraith, 'Monastic Foundation Charters of the Eleventh and Twelfth Centuries', *Cambridge Historical Journal* iv (1934), 205–22, 296–8

Gibbs, *Early Charters of St. Paul's*   *Early Charters of the Cathedral Church of St. Paul, London*, ed. Marion Gibbs (Camden 3rd ser. lviii, 1939)

Giraldi Cambrensis Opera   *Giraldi Cambrensis Opera*, ed. J. S. Brewer, vol. iv (Rolls Ser. 1873, reprinted edn. Wiesbaden, 1964)

Green, *The Government of England under Henry I*   Judith A. Green, *The Government of England under Henry I* (1986)

Guide to Seals   *A Guide to the Seals in the Public Record Office*, ed. Hilary Jenkinson (1954)

Gullick, 'The Illuminator of Gloucester'   Michael Gullick, 'The Illuminator of Gloucester', *English Manuscript Studies 1100–1700*, v (1995), 209–13

HBC   *Handbook of British Chronology*, ed. E. B. Fryde, D. E. Greenway, S. Porter, and I. Roy (Royal Historical Society, 1986)

H.C.L.   Hereford Cathedral Library

HRH   David Knowles, C. N. L. Brooke, and V. C. M. London, *Heads of Religious Houses in England and Wales 940–1216* (1972)

Hall, *Formula Book* — Hubert Hall, *A Formula Book of English Documents*, vol. i: *Diplomatic Documents* (1908)

..are, 'Gloucester as a Royal Centre' — Michael Hare, 'Kings, Crowns and Festivals: the Origins of Gloucester as a Royal Ceremonial Centre', *BGAST* cxv (1997), 41–78

Harvey, *Westminster Abbey and its Estates* — Barbara Harvey, *Westminster Abbey and its Estates in the Middle Ages* (1977)

Hector, *Handwriting of English Documents* — L. C. Hector, *The Handwriting of English Documents* (1966)

Hector, *Palaeography and Forgery* — L. C. Hector, *Palaeography and Forgery* (York, 1959)

Hemmeon, *Burgage Tenure* — Morley de Wolf Hemmeon, *Burgage Tenure in Medieval England* (Cambridge, Mass., 1914)

Herefordshire Place-Names — Bruce Coplestone-Crow, *Herefordshire Place-Names* (1989)

Heslop, 'Seals' — T. A. Heslop, 'Seals', in *English Romanesque Art*, 298–319

Hilton, *English and French Towns* — R. H. Hilton, *English and French Towns in Feudal Society* (1922)

Hilton, 'Gloucester Abbey Leases' — R. H. Hilton, 'Gloucester Abbey Leases of the Late Thirteenth Century', *University of Birmingham Historical Journal*, iv (1953–4), 1–17

Hilton, *West Midlands* — R. H. Hilton, *A Medieval Society: The West Midlands at the End of the Thirteenth Century* (1967)

'Historia' — 'Historia Monasterii S. Petri Gloucestriae', in *Historia et Cartularium Monasterii Sancti Petri Gloucestriae*, ed. W. H. Hart, 3 vols. (Rolls Ser. 1863–7), i, pp. 3–58

Hollister, 'St. Anselm on Lay Investiture' — C. Warren Hollister, 'St. Anselm on Lay Investiture', *Anglo-Norman Studies* x (1988), 145–58

Holt, 'Gloucester' — Richard Holt, 'Gloucester: An English Provincial Town during the Later Middle Ages' (University of Birmingham Ph.D. thesis, 1987)

Holt, 'Notions of Patrimony' — J. C. Holt, 'Notions of Patrimony', *Transactions of the Royal Historical Society*, 5th ser. xxxiii (1983), 193–220

Holt, 'The Revolution of 1066' — J. C. Holt, 'The Revolution of 1066', *Transactions of the Royal Historical Society*, 5th ser. xxxii (1982), 193–212

Holt and Mortimer — *Acta of Henry II and Richard I*, ed. J. C. Holt and Richard Mortimer (List and Index Society, special ser. xxi, 1986)

Hudson, 'Diplomatic and Legal Aspects of the Charters' — John Hudson, 'Diplomatic and Legal Aspects of the Charters', in *The Earldom of Chester and its Charters*, ed. A. T. Thacker, *Journal of the Chester Archaeological Society* lxxi (1991), 153–78

Hudson, *Land, Law, and Lordship* — John Hudson, *Land, Law, and Lordship in Anglo-Norman England* (1994)

Hudson, 'Life Grants of Land' — John Hudson, 'Life Grants of Land and the Development of Inheritance', *Anglo-Norman Studies* xii (1990), 67–80

Hurry, *Reading Abbey* — Jamieson B. Hurry, *Reading Abbey* (1901)

Hyams, 'The Charter as a Source' — Paul R. Hyams, 'The Charter as a Source for the Early Common Law', *Journal of Legal History* xii (1991), 173–89

Hyams, 'Warranty and Good Lordship' — Paul R. Hyams, 'Warranty and Good Lordship in Twelfth Century England', *Law and History Review* v (1987), 437–503

Jaffé, *Regesta Pontificum Romanorum* — Philippus Jaffé, *Regesta Pontificum Romanorum ab Condita Ecclesia ad Annum post Christum natum MCXCVIII*, vol. i (Leipzig, 1885)

James, *MSS. in Corpus Christi Coll. Libr.* — M. R. James, *A Descriptive Catalogue of the Manuscripts in the Library of Corpus Christi College, Cambridge*, 2 vols. (1912)

Jeayes — *Descriptive Catalogue of the Charters and Muniments in the Possession of the Rt. Hon. Lord Fitzhardinge at Berkeley Castle*, ed. I. H. Jeayes (Bristol, 1892)

John of Salisbury, *Historia Pontificalis*	*The Historia Pontificalis of John of Salisbury*, ed. Marjorie Chibnall (rev. edn. 1986)
John of Salisbury, *Letters*	*The Letters of John of Salisbury*, vol. i, ed. W. J. Millor, S. J. and H. E. Butler, rev. C. N. L. Brooke (1986)
John of Worcester	*The Chronicle of John of Worcester*, ed. J. R. H. Weaver (1908)
Johnson and Jenkinson	*English Court Hand A.D. 1066–1500*, ed. Charles Johnson and Hilary Jenkinson (1915)
K.C.C.	Kent County Council
Kealey, *Medieval Medicus*	Edward J. Kealey, *Medieval Medicus* (Baltimore and London, 1981)
Kemp, 'The Churches of Berkeley Hernesse'	B. R. Kemp, 'The Churches of Berkeley Hernesse', *BGAS* lxxxvii (1968), 96–110
Ker, 'Catalogue of Medieval Literary MSS.'	N. R. Ker, 'Catalogue of Literary Manuscripts in Gloucester Cathedral Library: Medieval Manuscripts', in *A Catalogue of Gloucester Cathedral Library*, ed. Suzanne Mary Eward ([Gloucester], 1972), 1–8
Ker, *English Manuscripts.*	N. R. Ker, *English Manuscripts in the Century after the Norman Conquest* (1960)
Ker, *MLGB*	*Medieval Libraries of Great Britain*, ed. N. R. Ker (1964)
Ker, 'William of Malmesbury's Handwriting'	N. R. Ker, 'William of Malmesbury's Handwriting', *English Historical Review* lix (1944), 371–6
Kimball, 'Frank Almoign'	Elizabeth Kimball, 'Tenure in Frank Almoign and Secular Service', *English Historical Review* xliii (1928), 341–53
Knowles, 'Abbatial Elections'	David Knowles, 'Essays in Monastic History 1066–1215, I: Abbatial Elections', *Downside Review* xlix (1931), 252–78
Knowles, *MOE*	David Knowles, *The Monastic Order in England* (1950)
Knowles and Hadcock	David Knowles and R. N. Hadcock, *Medieval Religious Houses in England and Wales* (1971)
LGCF	*The Letters and Charters of Gilbert Foliot*, ed. Adrian Morey and C. N. L. Brooke (1967)
Lally, 'Court and Household of Henry II'	John Lally, 'The Court and Household of King Henry II 1154–1189' (University of Liverpool Ph.D. thesis, 1969)
Leclerc, *Love of Learning*	Jean Leclerc, *The Love of Learning and the Desire for God*, trans. Catherine Misrahi (New York, 1982)
Letters of Lanfranc	*Letters of Lanfranc, Archbishop of Canterbury*, ed. Helen Clover and Margaret Gibson (1979)
List of Ancient Correspondence	*P.R.O. List and Index no. XV: List of Ancient Correspondence of the Chancery and Exchequer Preserved in the Public Record Office* (reprinted New York, 1963)
List of Sheriffs	*P.R.O. List and Index no. IX: List of Sheriffs for England and Wales* (rev. edn. New York, 1963)
Lobel, *Gloucester*	M. D. Lobel and J. Tann, *Gloucester*, in *Atlas of Historic Towns* vol. i (1969)
Loyn, 'Abbots of English Monasteries'	H. R. Loyn, 'Abbots of English Monasteries following the Norman Conquest', in *England and Normandy in the Middle Ages*, ed. David Bates and Anne Curry (1994), 95–103
Loyn, *Anglo-Saxon England*	Henry Loyn, *Anglo-Saxon England and the Norman Conquest* (1962)
Lunt, *Financial Relations of the Papacy*	William E. Lunt, *Financial Relations of the Papacy with England to 1327* (Cambridge, Mass., 1939)
MLWL	*Revised Medieval Latin Word-list*, ed. R. E. Latham (1965)
McDonald and Snooks, *Domesday Economy*	John McDonald and G. D. Snooks, *Domesday Economy* (1986)
McEvoy, *The Philosophy of Robert Grosseteste*	J. McEvoy, *The Philosophy of Robert Grosseteste* (1982)
Mason, *St. Wulfstan*	Emma Mason, *St. Wulfstan of Worcester* (1990)

Mayr-Harting, *Chichester Episcopal Acta* — *The Acta of the Bishops of Chichester 1075–1207*, ed. H. Mayr-Harting (Canterbury and York Society, 1964)

Medieval Town — *The English Medieval Town*, ed. Richard Holt and Gervase Rosser (1990)

Milsom, *Legal Framework of English Feudalism* — S. F. C. Milsom, *The Legal Framework of English Feudalism* (1976)

Moir, *Bromfield Priory* — Arthur Lowndes Moir, *Bromfield Priory and Church in Shropshire* (Chester, n.d.)

Monasticon — William Dugdale, *Monasticon Anglicanum*, ed. John Caley, Henry Ellis, and Bulkeley Bandinell, 6 vols. in 8 (1817–30)

Morey, *Bartholomew of Exeter* — Adrian Morey, *Bartholomew of Exeter, Bishop and Canonist* (1937)

Morgan, *Seals of Hereford Cathedral* — F. C. Morgan and Penelope E. Morgan, *A Concise List of Seals Belonging to the Dean and Chapter of Hereford Cathedral* (Hereford, 1966)

Mortimer, 'Charters of Henry II' — Richard Mortimer, 'The Charters of Henry II: What are the Criteria for Authenticity?', *Anglo-Norman Studies* xii (1990), 119–34

Mynors and Thomson, *Catalogue* — *Catalogue of the Manuscripts of Hereford Cathedral Library*, ed. R. A. B. Mynors and R. M. Thomson (Woodbridge, Suffolk, and Rochester, N.Y. 1993)

N.L.W. — National Library of Wales, Aberystwyth

Nicholl, *Normans in Glamorgan* — Lewis D. Nicholl, *The Normans in Glamorgan, Gower and Kidweli* (Cardiff, 1936)

OV — *The Ecclesiastical History of Orderic Vitalis*, ed. and trans. Marjorie Chibnall, vol. v (1975)

Orme, *English Schools* — Nicholas Orme, *English Schools in the Middle Ages* (1973)

Ortenberg, *English Church and the Continent* — Veronica Ortenberg, *The English Church and the Continent in the Tenth and Eleventh Centuries* (1992)

PNG — A. H. Smith, *The Place-Names of Gloucestershire*, 4 vols. (The English Place-Name Society, vols. xxxviii–xli, 1964–5)

P.R. — *Pipe Rolls: 5 Henry II* and *12 Henry II*, Pipe Roll Society vols. i (1884) and ix (1888)

P.R.O. — Public Record Office

Palaeographical Society — *Palaeographical Society*, ed. E. A. Bond and E. M. Thompson, 2nd ser. vol. i (1885)

Palmer, 'Origins of Property' — Robert C. Palmer, 'The Origins of Property in England', *Law and History Review* iii (1985), 1–50

Paris, *Chron. Maj.* — Matthew Paris, *Chronica Majora*, ed. H. R. Luard, 7 vols. (Rolls Ser. 1872–83)

PatR — *Patent Rolls 1225–32* and *Calendar of Patent Rolls 1232–47* (Public Record Office, 1903 and 1906)

Patterson, *EGC* — *Earldom of Gloucester Charters: The Charters and Scribes of the Earls and Countesses of Gloucester to A.D. 1217*, ed. Robert B. Patterson (1973)

Postles, 'Gifts in Frankalmoign' — David Postles, 'Gifts in Frankalmoign, Warranty of Land, and Feudal Society', *Cambridge Law Journal* l (1991), 330–46

Postles, 'Tenure in Frankalmoign and Knight Service' — David Postles, 'Tenure in Frankalmoign and Knight Service in Twelfth-Century England: interpretation of the charters', *Journal of the Society of Archivists*, xiii (1992), 18–28

RB — *The Rule of St. Benedict: Oxford, Bodleian Library, MS. Hatton 48*, ed. D. H. Farmer (Copenhagen, 1968)

Recueil des lettres anglo-francaises — *Recueil des lettres anglo-francaises*, ed. F. J. Tanquerey (Paris, 1916)

Regesta — *Regesta Regum Anglo-Normannorum*, ed. H. W. C. Davis, Charles Johnson, H. A. Cronne, and R. H. C. Davis, 4 vols. (1913–69)

Rot. Litt. Claus.   *Rotuli Litterarum Clausarum in Turri Londinensi asservati*, ed.
                               T. D. Hardy, i (1833)

S.R.O.   Shropshire Record Office

'Salop. Fines 1196–1211'   'Shropshire Feet of Fines A.D. 1196–1211', ed. W. K. Boyd,
                               TSAS 2nd ser. x (1898), 307–30

'Salop. Fines 1228–48'   'Shropshire Feet of Fines 1228–1248', ed. W. D. G. Fletcher,
                               TSAS 4th ser. vi (1916–17), 169–92

Salter, *Oxford Charters*   *Facsimiles of Early Charters in Oxford Muniment Rooms*, ed.
                               H. E. Salter (1929)

Saltman, *Theobald*   Avrom Saltman, *Theobald, Archbishop of Canterbury* (1956)

Sanders, *English Baronies*   I. J. Sanders, *English Baronies 1086–1327* (1960)

Southern, *Robert Grosseteste* R. W. Southern, *Robert Grosseteste* (2nd edn. 1992)

Stenton, *English Feudalism* F. M. Stenton, *The First Century of English Feudalism* (2nd edn.
                               1961)

Stenton, *Gilbertine Charters* *Transcripts of Charters relating to Gilbertine Houses*, ed. F. M.
                               Stenton (Lincoln Record Society xviii, 1920)

Stevenson   *Calendar of the Records of the Corporation of Gloucester*, ed.
                               W. H. Stevenson (Gloucester, 1893)

Stratford, 'Metalwork'   Neil Stratford *et al.*, 'Metalwork', in *English Romanesque Art*,
                               232–95

Swynnerton, 'Stanley St.   Charles Swynnerton, 'Stanley St. Leonards', *BGAST* xliv (1922),
  Leonards'   221–69

TSAS   *Transactions of the Shropshire Archaeological Society*

Tait, *The Medieval English* J. Tait, *The Medieval English Borough* (Manchester, 1936)
  Borough

Taxatio   *Taxation Ecclesiastica Angliae et Walliae . . . P. Nicholai IV*
                               (Record Commission, 1802)

Thompson, 'Free Alms   Benjamin Thompson, 'Free Alms Tenure in the Twelfth
  Tenure'   Century', *Anglo-Norman Studies* xvi (1994), 221–43

Thomson, *William of*   Rodney M. Thomson, *William of Malmesbury* (Woodbridge,
  Malmesbury   Suffolk, and Wolfeboro, N.H., 1987)

Thorne, 'English Feudalism   S. E. Thorne, 'English Feudalism and Estates in Land',
  and Estates in Land'   *Cambridge Law Journal* lxxv (1959), 193–209

Turner, *English Judiciary in* Ralph V. Turner, *The English Judiciary in the Age of Glanvill
  the Age of Glanvill*   and Bracton, c. 1177–1239* (1985)

Urry, *Canterbury*   William Urry, *Canterbury under the Angevin Kings* (1967)

VCH Glos.   *Victoria History of the Counties of England: Gloucestershire*,
                               vol. ii, ed. William Page (1907), including Rose Graham,
                               'Abbey of St. Peter at Gloucester', 'Priory of Leonard
                               Stanley', 'Abbey of St. Augustine, Bristol', and 'Hospital of
                               St. Margaret, Gloucester'; vol. iv, ed. N. M. Herbert (1988),
                               including N. M. Herbert 'Medieval Gloucester 1066–1547'

VCH Salop.   *The Victoria History of the Counties of England: Shropshire*, vol.
                               ii, ed. A. T. Gaydon (1973), including Marjorie M. Chibnall,
                               'The Priory of Bromfield'.

Valor Ecclesiasticus   *Valor Ecclesiasticus temp. Hen. VIII*, 6 vols. (Record
                               Commission, 1810–34)

Van Caenegem   R. C. Van Caenegem, *English Lawsuits from William I to
                               Richard I* (Selden Society cvi–cvii, 1990–1)

Verey, *Glos.: The Vale and the* David Verey, *Gloucestershire: The Vale and the Forest of Dean*
  Forest   (The Buildings of England, 1970)

Vincent, *Peter des Roches*   Nicholas Vincent, *Peter de Roches* (1996)

Vincent, *Acta of HenryII*   *Acta of Henry II and Richard I*, part 2, ed. Nicholas
  and Richard I   Vincent (List and Index Society, 1996)

W.S.R.O.   West Sussex Record Office

Walker, 'Earldom of Hereford Charters'	'Charters of the Earldom of Hereford, 1095–1201', ed. David Walker, in *Camden Miscellany*, xxii (Camden 4th ser. l, 1964), 1–75
Walker, 'Gloucester Charters'	'Some Charters Relating to St. Peter's Abbey, Gloucester', ed. David Walker, in *A Medieval Miscellany for Doris Mary Stenton* (Pipe Roll Society new ser. xxxvi, 1962), 247–68
Walker, 'Organization of Material in Medieval Cartularies'	David Walker, 'The Organization of Material in Medieval Cartularies', in *The Study of Medieval Records: Essays in Honour of Kathleen Major*, ed. D. A. Bullough and R. L. Storey (1971), 132–50
Walter Map, *De nugis curialium*	Walter Map, *De nugis curialium: Courtiers' Tales*, ed. and trans. M. R. James, rev. C. N. L. Brooke and R. A. B. Mynors (1983)
Warner and Ellis	*Facsimiles of Royal and Other Charters in the British Museum* i, ed. George F. Warner and Henry J. Ellis (1903)
Warner and Gilson	*Catalogue of Western Manuscripts in the Old Royal and King's Collections*, ed. George F. Warner and Julius P. Gilson, vol. i (1921)
Webber, 'Scribes and Handwriting'	Teresa Webber, 'Scribes and Handwriting of the Original Charters', in *The Earldom of Chester and its Charters*, ed. A. T. Thacker, *Journal of the Chester Archaeological Society* lxxi (1991), 137–51
Webber, *Scribes and Scholars*	Teresa Webber, *Scribes and Scholars at Salisbury Cathedral c. 1075–c. 1125* (1992)
Welander, *Gloucester Cathedral*	David Welander, *The History, Art, and Architecture of Gloucester Cathedral* (Stroud, Glos., and Wolfeboro, N. H., 1991)
Welsh, 'An Early Charter of Ewenny Priory'	R. E. Welsh, 'An Early Charter of Ewenny Priory', *National Library of Wales Journal* x (1957–8), 415–16
Westminster Abbey Charters	*Westminster Abbey Charters 1066–c. 1214*, ed. Emma Mason (London Record Society xxv, 1988)
Wightman, *The Lacy Family*	W. E. Wightman, *The Lacy Family in England and Normandy 1066–1194* (1966)
William of Malmesbury, *De Gestis Pontificum*	William of Malmesbury, *De Gestis Pontificum Anglorum*, ed. N. E. S. A. Hamilton (Rolls Ser. 1870, reprinted Wiesbaden, 1964)
William of Malmesbury, *De Gestis Regum*	William of Malmesbury, *De Gestis Regum Anglorum*, ed. William Stubbs, 2 vols. (Rolls Ser. 1887–9, reprinted Wiesbaden, 1964)
'Winchcombe Annals'	'Winchcombe Annals', ed. R. R. Darlington, in *A Medieval Miscellany for Doris Mary Stenton* (Pipe Roll Society new ser. xxxvi, 1962), 111–37

MANUSCRIPTS CITED

I. *Acta:*

Aberystwyth. National Library of Wales: Penrice and Margam Charters, nos. 19, 129, 132, 2800, 2802

Berkeley, Glos. Berkeley Castle Muniments: Select Charter no. 346

Bristol. Bristol Record Office: no. 3139 (238)

Chichester. West Sussex Record Office: Cap. I/17/84–87

Gloucester. Gloucester Cathedral Library:

Registers A and B

'Deeds and Seals', 10 vols.: i, nos. 3–7, 12, 13b–14, 18–21, 23, 25, 27–28, 30–32, 34–40, 42, 44, 47–50, 55, 57; ii, nos. 1–6, 12, 14–18, 20–21, 23–24, 28–30, 36; iii, nos. 1, 4–5, 8–9, 16, 19, 27–9; iv, nos. 1–10, 15–23, 26–28; v, nos. 2–14, 16–25, 27–28, 30, 33–34, 40, 42, 44;

vi, nos. 9, 11–12, 16, 18, 22, 24, 26, 28, 33, 39–40; vii, nos. 2–4, 6–11, 16–17, 20, 22, 26–27, 33, 35, 37–40; viii, nos. 2–3, 7–18, 20, 20(c)–(e), 21–23, 23(b), 25, ix, nos. 1–3, 5, 10–16, 18–20, 22–23, 25, 28, 31, 33–34, 36–38, 42; x, nos. 2, 4, 7–8, 20–22, 24, 27; xi, nos. 1–8, 24

Gloucester. Gloucestershire Record Office:

GBR/J1/85–86, 88, 115, 137, 147, 210, 243, 248, 272, 329, 355, 531

Microfilms MF 368 (Registers A and B); MF 1071, T.66 (Cartulary of St. Augustine's Abbey, Bristol); MF 1320 (G.C.L. 'Deeds and Seals'); MF 1383

Hereford. Hereford Cathedral Library: nos. 480, 490, 548, 575, 671, 725, 733–4, 740, 775–6, 778–80, 784, 788, 791, 796–800, 802, 838, 1166, 1168, 1170–1, 1323, 1387, 1411, 1511–13, 1519–20, 1525, 1582, 1602–9, 1614, 1628–30, 1632–3, 1635–8, 1641, 1644, 1651, 1655, 1662, 1665, 1668–9, 1672–8, 1735, 1737, 1833, 1893–4, 1897, 2174, 2178, 2185, 2196, 2201, 2292–3, 2295, 2297, 2299–2304, 2306–11, 2771, 2772

London. British Library:

Additional Charters 19606, 71309

Lord Frederick Campbell Charters XVIII–XVIII*

Cotton Charters XI.24, XVI. 38, XVII.3–4

Harley Charters 75.A.40, 75.B.3

Doubleday Casts of Seals D.7, E.740, XLIII.52–53, LXIII. 52–53, LXIII.60

London. Public Record Office:

C 115.K1/6679, C 115.K1/6681, C 115.K2/6683–6685, C 115.L1/6689, C 115.L2/6690 (Llanthony Cartularies)

C 150/1 (Gloucester Cartulary), C 150/2/[1]–[6]

CP 25/1/73/6, no. 54; CP25/1/73/7, nos. 84–85, 88, 100; CP 25/1/73/8, no. 116; CP 25/1/73/10, no. 170; CP 25/1/73/13. no. 250; CP 25/1/73/15, no. 278; CP 25/1/73/16, no. 303; CP 25/1/74/25, no. 557; CP 25/1/74/18, no. 329; CP 25/1/74/26, no. 570; CP 25/1/80/1, nos. 11–12; CP 25/1/80/6, nos. 76, 97; CP 25/1/80/7, no. 121; CP 25/1/80/12, no. 228; CP 25/1/193/2, no. 44; CP 25/1/193/3, no. 145; CP 25/1/284/18, no. 57

E 40/14281, 14555; E 42/308

SC 1/3 (151); SC 1/6 (18); SC 1/11, 41 (39)

Oxford. Bodleian Library: MSS. Charters Gloucs. a.1, nos. 5–7, 9, 20–23

Rochester, Kent. Kent County Council, Rochester upon Medway Studies Centre: DRc/T.660

Shrewsbury. Shropshire Record Office: 20/6/1–2

Worcester. Worcester Cathedral Library: B. 784

II. Manuscripts of Medieval Books

Cambridge. Corpus Christi College MS. 485
          Gonville and Caius College MS. 309
          Trinity College MSS. 75, 160–1, 166
          University Library MS. Kk.3.28

Dublin. Trinity College MS. 184

Gloucester. Gloucester Cathedral Library MS. 34

Hereford. Hereford Cathedral Library MSS. O.I.2, O.I.12, O.II.6, O.II.8, O.III.1, O.V.11, P.I.1, P.I.3, P.I.5, P.I.12, P.I.15–16, P.II.4

London. British Library: Cotton MSS. Domitian A.viii, Vespasian A.v; Harley MSS. 613, 627, 2659; Royal MSS. 2.C.xii, 5.A.xi, 10.C.vi, 11.D.viii, 13.C.v

New York. J. Pierpont Morgan Library: MS. 777

Oxford. Balliol College MS. 271
          Bodleian Library, MS. Bodl. 210; MS. Laud misc. 123; MSS. Jesus College 10, 43, 65
          Queen's College MS. 367

LIST OF PLATES

INTRODUCTION

The *acta* of this collection are the earliest original documentary survivors of Gloucester's post-Conquest literary culture.[1] They provide evidence of the abbey's administrative and proprietary history between the accession of the first Norman abbot Serlo (1072–1104) and the death of Abbot John de Felda (1243–63), arguably the most significant era in the nine-hundred-year monastic existence of St. Peter's.[2] Because they are originals, the *acta* also make it possible to study the development of the abbey's scriptorium, the mainstay of its literary culture, functioning as a secretariat soon after 1122/3, the earliest that any of the scriptorium's other original products can be precisely dated.[3]

The pre-Conquest history of St. Peter's is shadowy and riddled with uncertainties in part because house-preserved traditions are unsupported by adequate charter evidence.[4] To begin with, the monastery's very foundation charter has been shown by H. P. R. Finberg to be inauthentic; but among details which can be salvaged from this and other early charter evidence are its foundation possibly *c.* 679 by the ruler of the Hwicce, Osric, with the Mercian king Ethelred's assent, and a landed endowment which included among its earliest holdings a portion at what would become the Saxon *burh* of Gloucester.[5] The community, originally under the rule of abbesses, appears to have been intended as a refuge for royal and noble widows and as a facility for educating their children. Resident priests were to provide for the house's spiritual needs. According to the historical tradition preserved at St. Peter's, the monastery was abandoned for a time after the death of Eafe, the third abbess, in 767. Charter evidence, however, shows that the house remained intact, and at some point it

---

[1] Most of them still remain in the care of the Dean and Chapter in G.C.L. mounted in ten scrapbooks called 'Deeds and Seals' and in the small collection numbered 'Deeds and Seals' xi. Those which became dispersed for a variety of reasons following St. Peter's dissolution as a monastery under Henry VIII can be identified from their endorsements. Most of these found their way to Hereford Cathedral and are among the charter collection of H.C.L., possibly through the agency of Sir John Prise, given his well-known donations of Gloucester and St. Guthlac's books to Hereford (but against this view, see Walker, 'Gloucester Charters', 247). Other significant but smaller groups of dispersed *acta* are in the P.R.O., B.L., Bodl., S.R.O., and N.L.W.

[2] See below, pp. xxiii–xxxii. More than half have not heretofore been printed. Most of the printed ones are in *Cart. Glouc.* Among other significant collections (for all of which see the Bibliography above) are *LCGF*; Walker, 'Gloucester Charters'; Clark, *Cartae et alia*; Capes, *Hereford Charters*; Barrow, *Hereford Episcopal Acta*; and *Regesta*; of calendared texts, Baddeley i and ii; and Conway Davies, 'Ewenny Priory.' Suprisingly few appear in *Monasticon*. I have not included no. 14 in Walker 'Gloucester Charters', because of doubts about its apparent lack of relevance to the pre-1264 period (see ibid. 257 & n., 258). Also omitted is an illegible *actum* in Hebrew in G.C.L., 'Deeds and Seals', ii, no. 79, fol. 10. The principal collections of unprinted copies relevant to this edition are in ibid. Registers A and B.

[3] The literary *titulus* of 1122/3 which St. Peter's contributed to the Mortuary Roll of Abbot Vitalis of Savigny is the earliest product of the scriptorium which can be precisely dated: Delisle, *Rouleau Mortuaire*, titulus no. 85; Ker, *English Manuscripts*, 16, 34, Plate 14b; for similar letters, see Leclerc, *Love of Learning*, 176–7. For the evidence of earlier post-Conquest scribal activity, see below, p. xxiv and n. 27; some of the extant books produced at St. Peter's may antedate the *titulus*, but can be attributed only to the early twelfth century before *c.* 1125: see below, n. 32.

[4] e.g. comments in Brooke, 'St. Peter of Gloucester', 57 & n.; see *Anglo-Saxon Charters*, ed. Sawyer, nos. 70, 74, 77, 209, 1424, 1782.

[5] Finberg, 'Gloucester Abbey', 158–66; idem, 'Early Charters of Glos.' no. 1; *Anglo-Saxon Charters*, ed. Sawyer, no. 70.

became a college of secular priests.[6] St. Peter's apparently was not immediately affected by the tenth-century monastic reforms during the reign of King Edgar.[7] One of their effects was the subjection of England's most important monasteries to the spiritual direction of the bishops in whose dioceses they were located.[8] Evidence of their eventual impact upon St. Peter's becomes clear in the eleventh century. Wulfstan I, who held both the archbishopric of York and the diocese of Worcester, transformed the Gloucester community into a Benedictine house, and his later successor at Worcester and York, Ealdred, rebuilt the church in 1058. In the same year the bishop also installed Serlo's predecessor Wulfstan, a Worcester monk, as abbot.[9]

Ealdred's installation of Wulfstan was done with the assent of King Edward, which illustrates the relationship of both abbey and bishopric to the pre-Conquest Saxon theocratic church-state system. As has already been noted, St. Peter's fell under the spiritual authority of its bishop; but both abbots of important houses like St. Peter's and bishops were subject to the regalian rights of the king. As Frank Barlow has noted, monasteries like St. Peter's were royal *Eigenklöster*.[10]

Its ties to bishop and king did not bring prosperity to St. Peter's house in the late Saxon period. Indeed, its share of patronage from all sources was meagre.[11] In the abbey's view its community declined almost to the point of extinction. Ealdred archbishop of York and bishop of Worcester appropriated the abbey's estates at Barton by Gloucester, Northleach, Oddington, and Standish, apparently in connection with his rebuilding of the abbey church;[12] and by 1072 the community was impoverished and numbered only two monks and eight youths, apparently oblates.[13] In 1066 St. Peter's enjoyed an income of some £49 from estates in Gloucestershire, Worcestershire, Herefordshire, and Hampshire. While the monastery's version of its dire condition on the eve of the Norman Conquest may be exaggerated, the new Anglo-Norman regime did begin a dramatic change in the monastery's fortunes.[14]

---

[6] 'Historia', 7; Finberg, 'Gloucester Abbey', 158–64, where p. 161 gives the date 757. See also idem, 'Early Charters of Glos.' nos. 40–41, 45, 79–80. Binns, *Dedications*, 73, cites Finberg, 'Early Charters of Glos.' but seems strangely unaware of its implications.

[7] *VCH Glos.* ii. 53.

[8] Barlow, *English Church*, 177; Knowles, *MOE*, 31–57, esp. 45, 57; Loyn, *Anglo-Saxon England*, 243.

[9] G.C.L. MS. 34, fol. 3; 'Historia', 8–9; Florence of Worcester, i. 217. Knowles and Hadcock, 66, say that the house was refounded again before 1017; Binns, *Dedications*, 73–74. The date of 1022 claimed by the 'Historia' (p. 8) for Wulfstan's establishment of St. Peter's as a Benedictine house is unreliable; see Finberg, 'Gloucester Abbey', 165; Knowles, *MOE*, 70.

[10] *Florence of Worcester*, i. 217; Loyn, *Anglo-Saxon England*, 233, 241; Barlow, *English Church*, 177; Knowles, 'Abbatial Elections', 25; idem, *MOE*, Chap. 3, esp. p. 45.

[11] Finberg, *Charters of W. Midlands*, no. 163 for King Edward's paltry favour, half of a fishery at Framilode; see also ibid. no. 156.

[12] G.C.L., MS. 34, fol. 3; see also 'Historia', 9, 12. St. Peter's was critical of Ealdred's motives. Hare, 'Gloucester as a Royal Centre', 41–78, supports the hypothesis that Ealdred's building programme was motivated by a plan to make the abbey a setting for royal crown-wearings. The theory depends heavily, however, upon circumstantial evidence and deductive reasoning. Mr. Hare kindly made his article available in advance of publication.

[13] G.C.L., MS. 34, fol. 3b; 'Historia', 10; Knowles, *MOE*, 113, where it is claimed (p. 70) that the house ceased to exist some time after 1022; but see *VCH Glos.* ii. 53. At this time St. Peter's was considered an 'abbatia . . . pauperrima'(*Chron. Evesham*, 90; Mason, *St. Wulfstan*, 86, 126 & n., 131). According to William of Malmesbury, *De Gestis Pontificum*, 292, Serlo found no more than three monks at St. Peter's upon his arrival.

[14] For the growth in size of the monastic community, see below, at nn. 18 and 25.

In 1072, as part of his policy of introducing Norman and other continental monks as heads of English houses, on the advice of the royal chancellor Osmund, William the Conqueror appointed Serlo, a monk from Mont-St.-Michel and former canon of Avranches, to head Gloucester.[15] The king's opportunity was presented by the death in that year of Abbot Wulfstan on a pilgrimage to Jerusalem.[16] The pilgrimage, as Prof. David Bates has suggested, may well have been due to some crisis connected with Wulfstan's abbacy.[17]

Under Serlo the abbey virtually began a new life. He is credited with dramatically increasing the size of the all but non-existent community he had inherited – supposedly to 100 members.[18] The abbey's proprietary status also improved. As a part of William I's 'tenurial revolution,' the abbey and its estate became a tenancy-in-chief with the special privilege of exemption from military service.[19] The abbey's change in status also was accompanied by major increases in its estate and income which resulted in part from its success in attracting royal and baronial patronage; St. Peter's awarded credit for some of its early proprietary growth both to Serlo and to the house's first cellarer whom the new abbot appointed.[20] By the time of the Domesday survey of 1086 the abbey's assets in the adjacent borough of Gloucester had more than doubled from their pre-1066 level, and so had the value of the abbey's entire estate, to £99. In the 1090s the estate expanded from its Domesday-recorded four-shire base centered on Gloucestershire, into Buckinghamshire and Devonshire, and it further benefited from gifts in Breconshire, Glamorganshire, Pembrokeshire, and Cardiganshire.[21] By the time of Serlo's death in 1104 the estate's potential annual revenue, which can only be estimated on incomplete evidence, was over £138,[22] and the abbey's holdings in Gloucester then ranked it as the second largest mesne lord with 52 burgess-tenants. These households included some 260 of an expanding total population estimated at *c.* 3,000.[23] Nevertheless, prosperity must have come slowly. In the Domesday Survey, among English Benedictine abbeys and nunneries the annual income of St. Peter's ranked a poor fifth in the Severn Valley area and twenty-second in England.[24] When Bishop Samson of Worcester reflected about the state of the abbey in 1100, he considered that its endowments were not adequate to support a community of over 60 (as he calculated it) in 'due honour'.[25]

---

[15] G.C.L., MS. 34, fol. 3b; B.L., Cott. MS. Vesp. A.v, fol. 195v; 'Historia', 10–11; William of Malmesbury, *De Gestis Pontificum*, 292; Knowles, *MOE*, 106, 111–13; idem, 'Abbatial Elections', 255–6; Ortenburg, *English Church and the Continent*, 234, 243. For a recent discussion of this policy, see Loyn, 'Abbots of English Monasteries', 95–103.

[16] G.C.L., MS. 34, fol. 3; 'Historia', 9–10.

[17] Bates, 'Abbey of St. Peter's', 129.

[18] 'Historia', 13; the bishop assumed in 1100 that there were over 60 monks: below, n. 25; the community numbered only 50 monks in 1284: *VCH Glos*. ii. 56.

[19] Chew, *English Ecclesiastical Tenants-in-Chief*, 7–8; Knowles, *MOE*, 609, 612 & n.; William of Malmesbury, *De Gestis Pontificum*, 292–3, for his assessment of Serlo's contribution.

[20] See below, nos. 19, 28.

[21] G.C.L., MS. 34, fol. 4 & v; Brooke, 'St. Peter of Gloucester', 50–56, 58–61; Bates, 'Abbey of St. Peter's', 129–31; Cownie, 'Gloucester Abbey', esp. 145–53.

[22] Cownie, 'Gloucester Abbey', 152–3.

[23] 'Historia', 11, 13; *Domesday Book: Gloucester*, 10, 10; 10, 14, and Appendix, 'Evesham K', G1–4; Hilton, *English and French Towns*, 32; see also Lobel, *Gloucester*, 4; Bates, 'Abbey of St. Peter's', 129–30. On the issue of the borough's population growth, see Holt, 'Gloucester', pp. 16–20. McDonald and Snooks, *Domesday Economy*, 18, group Gloucester with towns of a population of more than 2,000 in 1086.

[24] Bates, 'Abbey of St. Peter's', 129; Knowles, *MOE*, Appendix VI, 702.

[25] *Cart. Glouc*. ii, no. 487.

To meet the literary and administrative demands of a Benedictine community, St. Peter's developed a scriptorium for the production of books and administrative *acta* which becomes visible around the first quarter of the twelfth century. Aside from liturgical books, the Rule required *lectio divina* at meals and at Compline and that each monk engage in daily and Lenten reading.[26] Some secretarial activity and a house-chronicle, no longer extant, seem to have been initiated even before Abbot Serlo's death.[27] The lost house-chronicle influenced John of Worcester and the later St. Peter's historians, Gregory of Caerwent and the compiler for Abbot Frocester, possibly the abbot himself.[28]

The abbey's developing Benedictine literary culture was fostered by Serlo's immediate successor Peter (1107–13), who contributed books for a library. Copyists and at least one 'librarian' who wrote contents-lists in the abbey's books were already at work by *c.* 1125.[29] Later, after a disastrous fire in 1122 which left only three Mass vestments and a few books, book production under the direction of the precentor was endowed by Gilbert Foliot (1139–48).[30] To judge from the extant remains of works attributable to the St. Peter's scribes, most of this activity seems to have involved copying borrowed texts of which a compendium of St. Augustine's works is a prime example.[31] Several scribes were major figures in this effort.[32] Perhaps one of them was the monk Gregory (d. 1157) whom the community remembered for his many literary contributions.[33] In addition, the library's holdings were augmented by donations and possible purchases.[34] These combined efforts produced a

---

[26] *RB*, Caps. xxxviii, xlviii, fols. 44–45, 52–54; on Benedictine literary culture, see e.g. Knowles, *MOE*, 487–560, and Leclerc, *Love of Learning, passim*.

[27] Brooke, 'St. Peter of Gloucester', esp. 56–60, argues persuasively for a chronicle maintained at St. Peter's under Abbot Serlo to record donations which were 'authenticated' by donors' *signa*. There also may be an element of truth in the story that Serlo warned King William Rufus by letters from Gloucester of a vision of his impending divine punishment: *OV*, 5: 286, 288; Barlow, *William Rufus*, 424, 428.

[28] Weaver, in *John of Worcester*, 6–7; Brooke, 'St. Peter of Gloucester', 58 & n., 65–66.

[29] Mynors and Thomson, *Catalogue*, 17 (MS. O.III.1), 66 (MS. P.I.3), 67 (MS. P.I.5).

[30] B.L., Cott. MS. Vesp. A.v, fol. 195v; *ASC*, a. 1122 (E); 'Winchcombe Annals', a. 1122; 'Historia', 13; *LCGF*, no. 288.

[31] Ker, *MLGB*, 91–92; H.C.L., MS. P.I.5; Webber, *Scribes and Scholars*, 51 & n. MS. books which can be attributed wholly or partially to the St. Peter's scribes prior to 1263 are B.L., Harl. MS. 2659; B.L., MS. Royal 11 D.viii; Cambr., Trinity Coll. MSS. 75, 160–1; Cambr. Univ. Libr., MS. Kk.3.28; New York, J. Pierpont Morgan Libr. MS. 777; Oxford, Jesus Coll. MSS. 10, 43, 65; Bodl., MS. Bodl. 210 and MS. Laud Misc. 123, and probably Cambr., Gonville & Caius Coll. MS. 309. Mynors and Thomson, *Catalogue*, 11, 14–15, 17, 65–68, 73, 76, 103, attribute sections of H.C.L., MSS. O.I.12, O.II.6, O.II.8, O.III.1, P.I.1, P.I.5, P.I.12, P.I.16, P.II.4, to the St. Peter's scribes; they consider H.C.L., MS. P.I.15 and Dublin, Trin. Coll. MS. 184 to be of Gloucester origin: ibid. 14, 66, 73, 76; and a hand of verses in H.C.L., MS. O.I.2, to have annotated MS. O.V.11 (ibid. 36). James, *MSS. in Corpus Christi Coll. Libr.* 439, attributes C.C.C.C. MS. 485 to St. Peter's. See also Thomson, *William of Malmesbury*, 70, 102. Rodney Thomson's article 'Books and learning at Gloucester Abbey in the twelfth and thirteenth centuries' in *Books and Collectors 1200–1700*, ed. James P. Carley and Colin G. C. Tite (1997) is also relevant but came to my notice only after this introduction was finished.

[32] See below, **Scribes 1, 2**; also the hand of H.C.L., MSS. O.II.8, ff. 1–33v, 34v a to line 13, 42b–65v, 74a, line 17–199v; P.I.1, fols. 1–16v; P.II.4, probably the main scribe of Jesus Coll. MS. 65, and B.L., Harl. MS. 2659, fols. 115–59, identified in Mynors and Thomson, *Catalogue*, 15, 76.

[33] B.L., Cott. MS. Vesp. A.v, fol. 199v; *GFAL*, 36 n., 80 & n.; he may have been the aged monk Gregory whom Walter Map knew there 1148 × 79: *De nugis curialium*, ii, p. 1.

[34] See e.g. B.L., Harl. MS. 627, fol. 8v, and Cambr., Trinity Coll. MS. 166, fol. 2v. Possibly some of Gloucester's pre-1300 books with '*ex libris*' inscriptions were also donations or purchases: e.g. B.L., MSS. Royal 2.C.xii, fol. 1, 10.C.vi, fol.1, and 13.C.v, fol. 2. H.C.L., MS. O.I.2, once belonged to Abbot Thomas of Bredon (1224–8), fol. ii verso: Mynors and Thomson, *Catalogue*, 5. B.L., MS. Royal

library collection with great Augustinian strength, which ranged from a copy of Archbishop Lanfranc's decretals to works of contemporaries such as Archbishop Anselm of Canterbury, Robert Pullan, Bernard of Clairvaux, Peter Lombard, and Hugh of St. Victor, and also included earlier European authors, Bede, Boethius, and Sidonius Apollinaris, and classical Seneca.[35] Some original work at Gloucester, as already indicated, probably dates from the time of Abbot Serlo. By the mid-twelfth century, more visible Gloucester authors, who probably included the hagiographer Osbern, were active. Abbot Gilbert Foliot (1139–48) is known to have produced a collection of sermons at the request of Haimo abbot of Bordesley;[36] and some time later the monk Benedict drew on Geoffrey of Monmouth's *History* in writing his *Life of St. Dubricius*. By about that time St. Peter's also had established a school which trained the likes of Gerald of Wales and possibly Walter Map.[37]

In 1089 Serlo began the construction of a new Romanesque abbey church, inspired by Norman models – possibly by Hereford cathedral as well – which was dedicated on 15 July 1100. By *c.* 1120 it included an east end, transepts, and nave.[38] Under Abbot Peter attention was given to the new abbey church's furnishings as shown by the magnificent Gloucester candlestick which has an inscription attributing the work's commission to the abbot and his community.[39] Serlo also established a distinguished reputation for the observance of the *opus Dei* at St. Peter's.[40] The account of Abbot Walter de Lacy's final illness and death preserved in the abbey's historical tradition provides glimpses of the community's observance of the *opus* and samples of its sacramental life.[41] The liturgical calendar, written at the abbey during the second half of the twelfth century and the early thirteenth, is an indication of the house's devotion to the cult of the saints among whom are represented local saints, Cyneburga, Arildis, Gundleus, and Guthlac.[42] St. Peter's, under Abbot William Godemon, also seems to have been one of the English houses where the new or revived feast of the Immaculate Conception of the Blessed Virgin was celebrated.[43] The calendar's entries also suggest that the community remembered in its prayers Abbot Serlo and possibly several other abbots on their obit days.[44] As early as 1077 Bishop Wulfstan of Worcester linked St. Peter's with four Benedictine houses in his diocese, Evesham, Pershore, Winchcombe, and Worcester, and two outside of it, Bath and Chertsey, into a confraternity devoted to promoting monastic ideals and prayer for the king, queen, and deceased

---

2.C.xii also may have belonged to Thomas of Bredon: see Warner and Gilson, i. 53. B.L., MS. Royal 5 A.xi with a twelfth-century '*ex libris*' inscription, but which I cannot attribute to a St. Peter's scribe at present, was also an acquisition acquired externally: ibid. fol. 2v. See also B.L., Cott. MS. Faustina C.I., fols. 66–93, Harl. MS. 613, fol. 204, and Cott. MS. Vesp. A.xiv, fols. 17–43v.

[35] Above, nn. 31, 34.

[36] *LCGF*, no. 7 & n.; *GFAL*, 69, 80 & n.

[37] *Giraldi Cambrensis Opera*, 4: 107; Walter Map, *De Nugis Curialium*, p. xv & n.; Orme, *English Schools*, 226; Knowles, *MOE*, 491 & n. There was a school in the town as early as the reign of Henry II, possibly of Henry I; perhaps this was the school to which Llanthony and St. Oswald's disputed the right of appointing the master: Orme, *English Schools*, 148–9, 170, 303; *VCH Glos.* ii. 314–20.

[38] G.C.L., MS. 34, fol. 4 & v; 'Winchcombe Annals', a.1100; Verey, *Glos.: the Vale and the Forest*, 198, 200, 202–8, 221–3; Welander, *Gloucester Cathedral*, 27–51, 61–75; on the possible influence of Hereford cathedral, see Mason, *St. Wulfstan*, 245.

[39] Stratford, 'Metalwork', 232 & no. 247; plates pp. 41, 73.

[40] *Letters of Lanfranc*, no. 54; see also below, no. 12; Crouch, *LEA*, no. 1.

[41] G.C.L., MS. 34, fol. 6v; 'Historia', 16–17.

[42] Bodl., MS. Jesus Coll. 10, fols. 1–6v; Ker, *MLGB*, 92; Welander, *Gloucester Cathedral*, 88–89. The calendar seems to have been given to St. Guthlac's Hereford.

[43] Bodl., MS. Jesus Coll. 10, fol. 6v; *Cart. Glouc.* i. 15; Knowles, *MOE*, 511 & n.

[44] Bodl., MS. Jesus Coll. 10, fol. 2; see also fols. 1v, 3.

members.[45] The abbey also came to be linked with several other somewhat similar networks, including the trans-Channel one sponsored by Savigny for Abbot Vitalis.[46]

Monks whose lives had been moulded by the quality of the abbey's Benedictine spiritual and intellectual life as early as 1085 began to gain preferment to abbacies which in time included Evesham, Cerne, Bruton, Malmesbury, Pershore, and Winchcombe;[47] Nicholas ap Gwrgent, a member of the community for 30 years, and Abbot Gilbert Foliot went on to bishoprics: Nicholas to Llandaff and Gilbert first to Hereford and then to London.[48]

Between 1072 and 1263 the community enjoyed to some degree the Benedictine ideal of free abbatial elections, which Pope Innocent III confirmed as one the house's liberties in 1201.[49] Some internal influence is suggested by the fact that Serlo's three successors, the priors Peter in 1104, William Godemon in 1107, and the chaplain Walter de Lacy in 1131, were from the house; but William's succession at least was secured by Henry I's appointment. Abbot William supposedly arranged Walter's election with the house's support.[50] The Cluniac Gilbert Foliot was elected by the community, but he had been nominated and was subsequently appointed by King Stephen in 1139, in part because of the influence which his cousin, Miles sheriff of Gloucester, enjoyed with the king. According to John of Salisbury, the Gloucester community hastily elected Hamelin the subprior to succeed Gilbert and obtained Simon bishop of Worcester's blessing of him as abbot to frustrate the plan of Foliot, when he became bishop of Hereford, to retain the abbacy as well. From Thomas Carbonel's election in 1179 successive elections were generally regarded by the abbey as canonical, and the succession of members of the house supports this: priors, Henry Blont, Thomas of Bredon, and Walter of St. John, respectively in 1205, 1224, and 1243; Henry Foliot, prior of Bromfield in 1228; and John de Felda, the precentor, in 1243. Other contemporary evidence, however, shows that these elections were subject to royal authority, which began with the king's licence to elect, following a petition from St. Peter's, and ended with royal ratification of the result.[51]

---

[45] Knowles, *MOE*, 161, 473 & n.; Darlington, *Cart. Worc.* p. xliv & n., no. 305; Barlow, *English Church*, 187; Mason, *St. Wulfstan*, 197–9.

[46] Barlow, *English Church*, 187–8; Mason, *St. Wulfstan*, 197–9; above, n. 3; see also *OV*, i, p. 86 & n. for inclusion of St. Peter's in the 'Liber Memorialis' of St.-Évroul.

[47] B.L., Cott. MS. Vesp. A.v, fols. 198, 199v–200v; *HRH*, 31, 37, 47, 55, 58, 79; 'Winchcombe Annals', a. 1085, 1095 & n., 1122, 1130, 1171, 1180.

[48] B.L., Cott. MS.. Vesp. A.v, fols. 198, 199, 200; 'Historia', 18–19; 'Winchcombe Annals', a. 1148, 1163; *HRH*, 53; Crouch, *LEA*, xiii–xiv; Gilbert had already been a monk at Cluny for some 17 years before coming to Gloucester as abbot: *GFAL*, 73, 76–104, and *passim*; *HBC*, 250, 258, 293; Barrow, *Hereford Episcopal Acta*, pp. xl–xli.

[49] *Cart. Glouc.* iii, no. 909, p. 3; for the correct date, see Cheney, *Letters of Innocent III*, no. 297. *RB*, Cap. lxiv, fols. 68v–69; Knowles, 'Abbatial Elections', 254 & nn. Brooke, *English Church and the Papacy*, 185, argued that St. Peter's escaped at least some of the authority of its Worcester diocesan by obtaining papal protection and confirmation of its privileges; there may be truth to this, but his source is more concerned with the abbey's proprietary interests (see Jaffé, *Regesta Pontificum Romanorum*, i, no. 7340, based on *Cart. Glouc.* ii. 47).

[50] *ASC*, a. 1113 (H), & xvii; 'Historia', 14; G.C.L., MS. 34, fol. 5; B.L., Cott. MS. Vesp. A.v, fol. 197, refers to William as prior; *HRH*, 52; John of Worcester, 30–31; below, n. 42; B.L., Cott. MS. Vesp. A.v, fol. 198; 'Winchcombe Annals', a. 1130, for William's transfer of authority to Walter. Brett, *English Church under Henry I*, 10, 104–5, has noticed the exceptional situation at Gloucester that Serlo's three successors were all members of the community, but he does not attribute this phenomenon to free election; he suggests, however, that Henry I mitigated his control of episcopal elections by consuting local opinion; see also Hollister, 'St. Anselm on Lay Investiture', 50–58.

[51] For these elections, see B.L., Cott. MS. Vesp. A.v, fols. 198v–201v; 'Historia', 15, 18–19, 23, 26 (Thomas of Bredon: '. . . in abbatem canonice electus . . ..'), 27 (Henry Foliot: '. . . successit . . .

During the twelfth century St. Peter's added a hospital in Gloucester for lepers and acquired a network of six dependent priories in Gloucestershire, Shropshire, Herefordshire, and Glamorganshire.[52] Continued acquisitions up to *c.* 1266 fleshed an urban-based estate of some 30 manors whose income by the end of the century made St. Peter's the richest of the Severn Valley monasteries.[53] By *c.* 1291 some £55 supposedly came from its rents in the borough of Gloucester.[54] Ambitious construction projects also continued. Significant additions were made to the abbey church and were celebrated by a formal rededication in 1239: the central tower in 1222, a lady chapel before the end of 1228, the nave vaulting in 1242, and the southwest tower between 1243 and 1263. In 1246 a new refectory was begun.[55] The abbey's wide-ranging development was not without problems. Its proprietary ambitions and successes led to numerous legal disputes with opponents ranging from the archbishops of York and William earl of Gloucester to its local Gloucester rival, Llanthony Secunda.[56] An array of financial burdens was relieved in part by borrowing funds and possibly by mortgaging property.[57] The abbey's ambitious building program must have been a major drain on its financial resources. Periodic visitation of Gloucester by monarchs, magnates, aristocracy, and royal officials, either at St. Peter's or at the suburban royal manor of Kingsholm, and royal and aristocratic patronage evidently encouraged the abbey to dispense hospitality to such visitors on a grand scale. Furthermore, the house became the target of royal fiscal exactions. Henry II levied a *donum* of 120 marks for his Toulouse campaign of 1159; and there were other burdens such as contributions to Richard I's ransom in 1194 and to King John's tallage of 1210.[58] Eventually this led to a debt of £3,000 under Abbot John de Felda which still stood at £1,500 at the accession of his successor Reginald de Homme in 1263. The former paragon of the rule also began to attract criticism for its elegant way of life. A visitation in 1242 by the abbey's diocesan Walter Cantilupe led to his cashiering the prior and other domestic officers. When financial assistance was sought from

incontinenter . . . unanimi assensu omnium fratrum in abbatem electus est . . . .' suggests free election, or at least one unanimously accepted by the community), 29 (Walter of St. John died before installation), 30 (John de Felda '. . . omnium fratrum electione praeficitur . . .'); *HRH*, 52–53. John's canonical election is supported by *Annales de Theokesberia*, 132. See also G.C.L., MS. 34, fols. 5–11; John of Salisbury, *Historia Pontificalis*, 48; 'Winchcombe Annals', a. 1139, 1148, 1179. For Gilbert Foliot's election and later plan to retain the abbey as bishop of Hereford, see *GFAL*, 76–79, 94 & n. For Knowles's use of circumstantial evidence to argue for internal influence in the choice of abbots see 'Abbatial Elections', 262, 266, 268–9, 274–5, and *MOE*, 395–401; see also *PatR 1225–32*, 188–9; *1232–47*, 390, 396, 407–8; *CloseR 1227–31*, 52; *Rot. Litt. Claus.* i. 619b, 621b, 646b.

[52] At various times in the twelfth century Gloucester had nine priories; see below, p. xxix; for the hospital originally called St. Sepulchre, see *VCH Glos.* ii. 121–2; Knowles and Hadcock, 273. While the house, located outside Northgate, was initially under the control of St. Peter's as founder and possessor of parochial rights over the new community, it did not function as a priory within the St. Peter's network. The abbey's influence seems to have been soon restricted to the hospital's chapel and the right of advowson. Initially this involved the abbey's control over the choice of the hospital's superior, since in the early years this was the chaplain.

[53] *Cart. Glouc.* iii. 35–213; see Hilton, *West Midlands*, 26, preferring the accuracy of monastic incomes reported in the *Valor Ecclesiasticus* of 1535 over the *Taxatio* of 1291. Hilton 'Gloucester Abbey Leases', 1–17, discusses the lease patterns of the non-urban sector of the estate.

[54] *Taxatio*, 231; *VCH Glos.* iv. 59.

[55] 'Historia', 25–30; Verey, *Glos.: The Vale and the Forest*, 198, 200, 205–8; Welander, *Gloucester Cathedral*, 97–122; *VCH Glos.* ii. 55.

[56] e.g. below, no. 105 & n.; see also nos. 104, 106–7 for early examples; 'Historia', 11–14, 16, 19, 25, 27–30; *Cart. Glouc.* ii, nos. 509–15; Patterson, *EGC*, no. 87; Crouch, *LEA*, nos. 11–14; *EAWD*, ii, nos. L.134–41; Brooke, 'St. Peter of Gloucester', 52–53; see also e.g. below nos. 104–7.

[57] e.g. below, nos. 243, 390 & n.

[58] *P.R. 5 Henry II*, 28; 'Historia', 23–24; *VCH Glos.* ii. 55; Knowles, *MOE*, 612 & n.

the bishop in 1251, he commanded the abbey to cease entertaining guests.[59] The status which certain aspects of the house's dramatic post-Conquest development had produced by 1263 was not without problems.

In St. Peter's view of its past, as expressed especially by its annals, the 'Historia,' written at the turn of the fifteenth century under the aegis of Abbot Walter Frocester, and possibly by him, heavy emphasis was placed upon proprietary themes.[60] Abbots from the era 1072–1263 were largely remembered for their acquisitions of land and revenue, their resolution of proprietary disputes, and the accumulation of privileges: Serlo,[61] Peter,[62] William Godemon,[63] Walter de Lacy,[64] Gilbert Foliot,[65] and Hamelin[66] were all credited with gains in estates or revenues; but particularly Serlo, for estates in Gloucestershire, Herefordshire, Hampshire, and Devonshire;[67] William Godemon, for land in and outside Gloucester;[68] Serlo and Hamelin, for the recovery of Abbot's Barton, Northleach, Oddington, and Standish from the archbishops of York.[69] Resolutions of lawsuits in favour of the abbey were memorialized, such as the already mentioned case between St. Peter's and the archbishops of York,[70] or thirteenth-century proprietary settlements with neighbour St. Oswald's Priory in 1218,[71] with Thomas of Berkeley in 1225 over Slimbridge,[72] with the canons of St. Augustine's Bristol over Lassington in 1241,[73] and with Thomas archdeacon of Gloucester in 1248.[74] Abbot Peter won the church of St. Peter Hereford in 1108 from Bishop Reinhelm of Hereford in one of the more bizarre and early examples. In a dispute over the right of burial of Ralph fitz Ansketill, an apparent benefactor of Gloucester's priory of St. Guthlac at Hereford, the bishop had forcibly made off with the body because he claimed that Ralph was a parishoner of the cathedral. When the *curia regis* judged that

---

[59] B.L., Cott. MS. Vesp. A.v, fol. 200; *VCH Glos.* ii. 55; Knowles, *MOE*, 369 & n.

[60] G.C.L., MS. 34, fols. 1–43v (mod. fol.); Ker, 'Catalogue of Medieval Literary MSS.' 5; the best text currently is unprinted, although a translation of it is in Welander, *Gloucester Cathedral*, Appendix XV, 597–648; Hart's edition of the St. Peter's cartulary in the Rolls Series is based upon the other texts; the same proprietary emphasis is found in the thirteenth-century chronicle of St. Peter's by the Gloucester monk Gregory of Caerwent, which survives only in a sixteenth-century transcript (B.L., Cott. MS. Vesp. A. v, fols. 195–203v); Prof. Brooke has shown that the chronicle based its account at least down to the twelfth century upon the same source as the 'Historia' used; Brooke, 'St. Peter of Gloucester', 51–52; and above, n. 33.

[61] G.C.L., MS. 34, fol. 4 & v; 'Historia', 12. Gregory of Caerwent was chiefly concerned with recording abbatial deaths and successions: B.L., Cott. MS. Vesp. A. v, fols. 195v, 196v–197, 198–200v, 201v–202.

[62] G.C.L., MS. 34, fol. 5; 'Historia', 13: Peter was remembered also for collecting books.

[63] G.C.L., MS. 34, fol. 5; 'Historia', 14.

[64] G.C.L., MS. 34, fol. 5v; 'Historia', 15: Walter's gains were remembered as acquisitions from his father and mother.

[65] G.C.L., MS. 34, fol. 6v; 'Historia', 18.

[66] G.C.L., MS. 34, fol. 7 & v; 'Historia', 19.

[67] G.C.L., MS. 34, fol. 4v; 'Historia', 12.

[68] G.C.L., MS. 34, fol. 5; 'Historia', 14.

[69] G.C.L., MS. 34, fols. 4v, 7; 'Historia', 11–12, 19; John of Salisbury, *Letters*, i, nos. 39 n., 42; Burton, *York Episcopal Acta*, Appendix I, no. 1. See the comment by William of Malmesbury, *De Gestis Pontificum*, 293, that Archbishop Thomas endowed St. Peter's with lands belonging to St. Oswald's Priory. The case was finally settled on 13 December 1157: *Cart. Glouc.* ii. 105–7.

[70] Hamelin finally settled the dispute with York by granting three estates to the archbishop: 'Historia', 19; *EAWD*, ii, no. L.141.

[71] G.C.L., MS. 34, fol. 9v; 'Historia', 25.

[72] G.C.L., MS. 34, fol. 10; 'Historia', 27, 114.

[73] 'Historia', 28–29.

[74] Ibid. 30.

Ralph's body should be restored to St. Peter's, Reinhelm offered Peter the church, minus the right of bell-ringing before the canons, in exchange for keeping Ralph, and the abbot accepted.[75] Furthermore, to supplement the 'Historia,' a Calendar of Donations was added like an appendix and listed the St. Peter's estates in alphabetical order along with the benefactors who gave them.[76]

Carefully noted were the donations which gradually created St. Peter's system of dependent priories. Ewyas Harold came by gift of Harold lord of Ewyas on the occasion of the dedication of Abbot Serlo's new church in 1100;[77] Kilpeck, from Hugh son of William in 1134;[78] Ewenny, in 1140 × 43 from Maurice de Londres;[79] St. Guthlac's Hereford, in 1143 from the unification of the church of St. Guthlac in the castle given by Roger de Port with the much earlier donation of St. Peter's church in the market by Hugh I de Lacy,[80] Leonard Stanley, from Roger III de Berkeley in 1146;[81] Bromfield, from the canons themselves, in 1155.[82] Other priories held only temporarily in the twelfth century were Cardigan and Llanbadarn Fawr.[83]

Some of the Calendar's entries and especially the cartulary copies and the surviving original texts of the *acta* reveal the patterns of patronage which were so influential in creating St. Peter's estate after the Conquest: donations and confirmations from the Anglo-Norman kings, their tenants-in-chief, and other members of the baronage,[84] from possible

---

[75] 'Historia', 13–14; *Regesta*, iii, no. 880; Brett, *English Church under Henry I*, 98; Franklin, 'Bodies in Medieval Northampton', 72–73. For disputes of burial rights at Gloucester between St. Peter's and Llanthony Priory and between the abbey on behalf of its priory at Ewenny and the bishop of Llandaff, see below, no. 105; *Cart. Glouc.* i, nos. II–IV, pp. lxxv–viii; ii, nos. 437–38; *LCGF*, nos. 42–45, 417; Cheney and John, *Canterbury Acta*, no. 506; *EAWD*, i, no. D.119; Franklin, 'Bodies in Medieval Northampton', 65–66, 73 & n., 74–75.

[76] G.C.L., MS. 34 includes both the history (fols. 1–24v) and the section entitled 'Hic incipiunt donationes omnium bonorum monasterii sancti Petri Glouc' tam temporalium quam spiritualium' (fols. 25–43v). Comparison of script, size of folios, and the arrangement of text of the two sections leaves no doubt that they were meant to form a single work; the text of the 'Historia' in several places (e.g. fol. 4) also mentions that supporting evidence is to be found in the calendar of donations below; see above, n. 60. 'Historia', i. 58–125; Gregory of Caerwent's chronicle, in its transcribed form, does not contain a calendar of donations; see above, n. 60.

[77] G.C.L., MS. 34, fol. 30v; 'Historia', 76; *EAWD*, i, no. D.141; Binns, *Dedications*, 71; *GFAL*, 84 n.; Brooke, 'St. Peter of Gloucester', 55.

[78] G.C.L., MS. 34, fol. 6; 'Historia', 91; Binns, *Dedications*, 76; *GFAL*, 84 n.

[79] 'Historia', 75–76; Binns, *Dedications*, 71, traces its evolution from church (1107 × 34) built by William de Londres to donation by Maurice de Londres for a priory (1140 × 48); *EAWD*, ii, nos. L.117–19; *GFAL*, 84 n.; Brooke, 'St. Peter of Gloucester', 56 & n.; G.C.L., MS. 34, fols. 30–34v places the foundation in 1141.

[80] G.C.L., MS. 34, fol. 33v; 'Historia', 84–87; *Cart. Glouc.* iii. no. 997; *EAWD*, i, nos. D.120, D.146; Barrow, *Hereford Episcopal Acta*, no. 21 & n.; Binns, *Dedications*, 75; *GFAL*, 84 n.; Brooke, 'St. Peter of Gloucester', 55 n.; Wightman, *The Lacy Family*, 173.

[81] G.C.L., MS. 34, fol. 41; 'Historia', 113; Binns, *Dedications*, 77; *GFAL*, 84 n. See below, no. 375 & n.

[82] G.C.L., MS. 34, fol. 7 & v; 'Historia', 66; Binns, *Dedications*, 65; *GFAL*, 84 n.

[83] 'Historia', in *Cart. Glouc.* i. 106; ii, nos. 547–57; *EAWD*, i, nos. D.79, D.98, D.186, D.197 Brooke, 'St. Peter of Gloucester', 55–56; Morey and Brooke, *GFAL*, 84 n.; Binns, *Dedications*, 67, 78.

[84] Donations to St. Peter's are well covered in *VCH Glos.* ii. 53–55, 72–73; *VCH Salop.* ii. 27–28; *GFAL*, 124–46; Brooke, 'St. Peter of Gloucester', 52–56, 58–65, 67–70; *LCGF*, 522; Bates, 'Abbey of St. Peter's', 129–31; Cownie, 'Gloucester Abbey', 143–55. For Wales see Conway Davies, 'Ewenny Priory', 109–27; Cowley, *Monastic Order in South Wales*, 15, 38, 166, 270; Davies, *Wales 1063–1415*, 142.

freeholders,[85] and Gloucester burgesses.[86] Mention is sometimes made of the motives of donors' monastic piety. Aside from the conventional desire for prayers for the souls of family members, lords, and monarchs,[87] some desired the monastic life itself and brought with them entry oblations;[88] others, enjoyment of confraternity,[89] maintenance,[90] burial,[91] or money to liquidate debts.[92] A gift might be made in thanksgiving for safe return from pilgrimage or crusade. Ralph of Abergavenny gave custody of half his land to the almoner until he returned from St. James of Compostella and if he did not, the land was to be God's and the abbey's.[93] The earmarking of revenues from donations for the care of the sick monks or almonries of St. Peter's also reveals appreciation for the monastic life and for the value of the abbey's service to the poor.[94] Donations were often made in the presence of the abbot and community and could involve a ritual act of conveyance such as when Robert Gernon placed his gift upon the altar with a knife.[95]

Various roles which the abbey filled as a landlord emerge from the charter evidence of properties which it purchased,[96] leased from other landlords,[97] and exchanged,[98] and from tenurial pleas involving it as plaintiff or defendant.[99] This is especially true of charters pertaining to the borough of Gloucester and its vicinity. There, aside from its status as a demesne landlord, acquisitions often made it a mesne tenant and landlord. Walter Bliss's grant of land in the girdlery obligated the abbey to a rent of 2s. to Richard Tirel.[100] Grants from Adam Esgar and from William le Breton made St. Peter's a tenant of, respectively, St. Oswald's Priory and of Llanthony priory.[101] Sometimes St. Peter's profited from burgesses' need for cash or to liquidate debts. Alexander Furbrich quitclaimed all right and claim to land by Alvingate 'in mea magna necessitate.'[102] A tenant, Adam son of Roger of Gloucester, granted and quitclaimed properties on the 'western street' and on Longsmith Street to St. Peter's in order to satisfy debts for rent and arrears in rent owed to the abbey.[103] Recovery of property from a tenant enabled the community to regrant it possibly under more favourable terms to a new tenant.[104] A transaction might in effect be the purchase of rent rather than of the property itself, [105] but acquisitions might equally come bound with rental

---

[85] e.g. below, nos. 205, 249.

[86] For possible examples see below, nos. 197, 199, 216, 277, and 'Historia', 82, 98.

[87] Ranulf II earl of Chester, confirmation of his sister's gift for the soul of husband: below, no. 201; Wimarc widow of John Franchevaler, for the salvation of her husband's soul, for William her son and all parents: below, no. 212.

[88] e.g. below, nos. 66, 100, 222; 'Historia', 60, 70, 79, 88–89, 93, 95, 112, 117–18; *RB*, cap. LIX.

[89] e.g. below, no. 231.

[90] 'Historia', 60, 106; see also below, no. 380.

[91] Below, no. 251; see 'Historia', 73; see also below, no. 31.

[92] e.g. below, nos. 214–15, 221, 230.

[93] Below, no. 195; 'Historia', 81.

[94] e.g. below, nos. 195, 198, 236, 238–9.

[95] Below, no. 52; see also nos. 247, 257; 'Historia', 106; see also below, nos. 31, 379–80.

[96] e.g. below, nos. 111–12, 194, 239; 'Historia', 65, 81, 94.

[97] e.g. nos. 140, 229–30, 256.

[98] Below, no. 44; 'Historia', 65, 74, 80, 88, 110, 112.

[99] e.g. below, nos. 104–7, 141, 149, 164, 166–7; see also above, p. xxvii; for an analysis based on the abbey's Cotswold estates in the 1260s, see Hilton, 'Gloucester Abbey Leases', 1–17.

[100] Below, no. 197.

[101] Nos. 198, 207.

[102] No. 213.

[103] No. 215.

[104] No. 206.

[105] No. 226.

obligations imposed by the burgesses granting them, whose deeds, issued to record transactions with St. Peter's as well as among themselves, show that they were following comparable economic strategies.

Many entries in the supplementary Calendar of the 'Historia' refer to charters on which they were based.[106] Others read like partial transcripts,[107] to such a degree that the supplement has been called 'an abstract of charters.'[108] Rightly has the style of history written at St. Peter's been classified as 'charter-chronicle.'[109] It was the means by which this great community, to adapt David Crouch's turn of phrase, preserved 'its . . . historical continuity.'[110] When authentic charter evidence to bolster some of its proprietary claims was lacking, St. Peter's even sponsored forgery.[111]

Abbot Serlo contributed to the abbey's administrative development by initiating the office of cellarer for one Odo, who became a monk in 1077.[112] Only under Serlo's successors, however, does the abbey's full monastic administrative system become visible, replete with a chapter and traditional Benedictine offices such as prior, cellarer, precentor, almoner, and sacristan.[113] Endowment of the abbey's principal monastic offices, which can be seen in progress at least as early as the abbacy of Gilbert Foliot (1139–48), ultimately produced the full-blown obedientiary system which is recorded in one of St. Peter's late medieval unprinted registers.[114] Complementing the house's monastic administration were other frequent bureaucratic members of seignorial households such as butler, chamberlain, and constable; lesser figures including the porter, cook, fisherman, and the sometimes undefined *minister* and *serviens*; and at the manorial level the bailiff.[115] In conjunction with the exercise of proprietary jurisdiction, there were various abbatial courts, and by c. 1250 a central exchequer.[116] Charter evidence, as has been noted, supported St. Peter's historical

---

[106] *Cart. Glouc.* i. 60, 64, 71, 73, 75, 78–79, 81, 82–84, 89, 92–94, 96–97, 100, 102, 104–5, 109–10, 113–14, 116–18, 120; Brooke, 'St. Peter of Gloucester', 52.

[107] *Cart. Glouc.* i. 61–62, 66, 68, 70–71, 81–82, 84, 86–87, 90–91, 96, 98–99, 103, 106, 108.

[108] Brooke, 'St. Peter of Gloucester', 52.

[109] Barlow, *English Church*, 198–9.

[110] Crouch, 'Administration of the Norman Earldom', 94.

[111] On the itinerant Westminster school forger who wrote no. 38 below for St. Peter's, see Bishop and Chaplais, *English Royal Writs*, pp. xxi–xxiii, and for his hand, Chaplais, 'Westminster Charters', 97 & n.; the standard account of forging for the abbey is *GFAL*, Chap. VIII, 124–46 & 266; see also Brooke, 'St. Peter of Gloucester', 60–64, 67–70; to the currently known list of Gloucester forgeries, which includes nos. 38, 40, 44, 390 below, may be added nos. 203–4; for Ewenny priory, nos. 15, 25–26; and for St. Guthlac's Hereford, no. 353.

[112] 'Historia', 11, 13. It may have been to this Odo along with another monk Hugh and the convent of St. Peter's that King Henry I confirmed two assarts in Chelworth (in Cricklade, Wilts.) apparently during the vacancy following Serlo's death in 1104: *Cart. Glouc.* i, no. 153; *Regesta*, ii, no. 673 & n.; on Odo's contributions see Cownie, 'Gloucester Abbey', 152.

[113] For early references, see Ker, *English Manuscripts*, Plate 14b (Walter prior, 1122 × 3); below, no. 247 (Simon sacristan, 1148 × 55); *Cart. Glouc.* i, no. 292 (almonry, 1121 × 47); below, no. 102 (cellarer, 1179 × 1205), 'Historia', 11, 13 (Odo, first cellarer professed 1077); *LCGF*, no. 288 (precentor, 1139 × 48); below, no. 387 (1203 × 14). For the chapter, 'Historia', 11–12 (1095).

[114] See *LCGF*, nos. 286, 288. *Acta* pertaining to St. Peter's obedientiary system are entered in G.C.L., 'Register B'.

[115] e.g. below, nos. 37 (Solomon porter, 1205 × 15), 70 (Godfrey cook, 1148 × 79), 71 (Ernesius, former chamberlain, 1155), 252 (*servientibus abbatis, c.* 1165 × 80); 102 (William bailiff of Standish, 1179 × 1205), 235 (Alexander butler, 1165 × 83), 195 (Morin *minister*, s. xii^ex); G.R.O., GBR/J1/118 (Gilbert baker, s. xii^ex, poss. before 1192); *Cart. Glouc.* ii, no. 783 (constable, 1148 × 79). For *servientes*, see Knowles, *MOE*, 439–41. Simon de aula *serviens* (1205 × 15) might be a steward (no. 37).

[116] A court held at Gloucester in the abbacy of Hamelin is indicated by *Cart. Glouc.* i, no. 11; see

tradition and reveal most of what can be known of its proprietary history. It also is a major source of information about the monastery's administration – in terms of indentifying offices and their incumbents, the chief one. But in no bureaucratic area is such evidence more crucial than in that of the abbey's secretarial administration, whose scribal staff, *modus operandi*, and range of activities emerge to such an extent from the original *acta* mostly written by anonymous scribes.

SCRIBES OF THE ST. PETER'S ACTA

I. *Abbatial Scribes*

The hand of **Scribe 1**, slightly left-leaning to perpendicular, has long been known from its identification by T. A. M. Bishop who recognized it in a spurious confirmation charter of King Stephen in favour of St. Peter's and in several books which belonged to the abbey's library.[117] It is an expert rounded and compact bookhand characterized by vertical compression, particularly in *d* and *s*.[118] The bowl of *h* and *m, n, u* can show signs of angularity as well, but inconsistently.[119] Ascenders of *b, d, h,* and *l* are clubbed.[120] Minims are finished with upwardly angled ticks to the right. Tailed-*E* and *e* for (*æ*) are crossed.[121] The scribe favoured a six-stroke *g* with closed tail;[122] his *S* often exhibits a partially or completely closed lower bowl fashioned by a sharply angled finishing stroke to the right.[123] Particularly noticeable are *puncti interrogativi* marks of punctuation in his books,[124] mostly footed 'gallows' paragraph/*nota* markings,[125] ampersands,[126] cup-shaped suspension signs,[127] *ct* and *st* ligatures,[128] 'biting' in *or*,[129] and his *notae* for -*us* and -*ur*.[130] His alphabet

---

also e.g. below, nos. 76–77, 101–3, 112, 117, 223–4, esp. 392. For the exchequer, see *Cart. Glouc.* iii. 105–8; Hilton, *West Midlands*, 72.

[117] Below, no. 44; C.U.L., MS. Kk.3.28; Cambr., Trinity Coll. MS. 75; Bishop, 'Notes on Cambridge Manuscripts I', 439. The status of no. 44 is discussed in Brooke, 'St. Peter of Gloucester', 61–64, 67–70, and in *GFAL*, 6 & n., 88, 125–27 & nn., 266; on Prof. Brooke's role in the exposure of this forgery, see *Regesta*, iii, no. 345 n.

[118] Below, no. 44, Plate II: *silua*, line 6; but the ascender of *d* generally is twice the height of minims; C.U.L., MS. Kk.3.28, Plate III, e.g. *dicendo*, line 2, *fuisse*, line 7, fol. 2.

[119] Below, no. 44, Plate II: *hida*, line 7; *Bertonam*, line 5; *dederunt*, line 4; C.U.L., Kk.3.28, Plate III: *mundo*, line 2, fol. 2. In his books, the bowl of *h* is rounded, but see *homines*, line 8, fol. 1.

[120] Below, no. 44, Plate II: *hida*, line 7; *de laci*, line 2; *obtinatu(m)*, line 3; Plate III: *habuit*, line 12, *sed, Uel*, line 10, fol. 2.

[121] Below, no. 44, Plate II: *r* in *rex*, line 2; *Ecclesie*, line 3. C.U.L., MS. Kk.3.28, Plate III: *om(n)ia*, line 5, fol. 2; *que*, line 5, fol. 1v.

[122] Below, no. 44, Plate II: *gloec(estrie)*, line 10; C.U.L., MS. Kk.3.28, Plate III: *intelligeres*, line 14, fol. 2 (closed); ibid. *theologie*, line 8, fol. 2v (open).

[123] C.U.L., MS. Kk.3.28, *Si*, line 10, fol. 1 (closed); ibid. *Surgens*, line 2, fol. 11 (open).

[124] C.U.L., MS. Kk.3.28, e.g. line 28, fol. 1v; line 5, fol. 3v. As has been noted, this mark is not restricted to punctuating direct questions: Denholm-Young, *Handwriting in England and Wales*, Plate 10 n.; Hector, *Handwriting of English Documents*, 47; Brown, *Guide*, 31.

[125] C.U.L., MS. Kk.3.28, line 21, fol.4 (footed); below, no. 44, Plate II, line 8 (footed); ibid. line 11 counting from lower left foot (unfooted and elongated form).

[126] Below, no. 44, Plate II, line 3; C.U.L., MS. Kk.3.28, Plate III, line 19, fol. 2.

[127] C.U.L., MS. Kk.3.28, below, Plate III, *uerbu(m)*, line 1, fol. 2; below, no. 44, Plate II, *c(on)firmaui*, line 3.

[128] C.U.L., MS. Kk.3.28, Plate III, *ct* in *facta*, line 13, *st* in *est*, line 3, fol. 2; below, no. 44, Plate II, *ct* in *predicte*, line 4; *st* in *castelli*, line 9 (counting from bottom right due to damage).

[129] Below, no. 44, Plate II, *angloru(m)*, line 2; C.U.L., MS. Kk.3.28, Plate III, *tempore*, line 6, fol. 2.

[130] Below, no. 44, Plate II, *Walteri(us)*, line 10, observation of *ur* not available due to damage; C.U.L., MS. Kk.3.28, Plate III, *us* in *intellect(us)* and *ur* in *emittit(ur)*, line 16, fol. 2.

included uncial and rustic capitals. Distinctive forms are *B*, *G*, *Q*, *g*, and the forms of *ct* ligature and footed 'gallows.' The scribe's forged charter has been dated to *c.* 1147/8. From what survives of his work, he was primarily concerned with book production for the St. Peter's library. In addition to the two works which Mr. Bishop discovered, Michael Gullick has recently found a Gospel of St. John in the J. Pierpont Morgan Library, but there may be still others.[131]

Charters written by **Scribe 2** establish his service to St. Peter's from the adminstration of Abbot Walter de Lacy at least to some point during the abbacy of Hamelin (1131 × 79);[132] and like the scribe of the spurious Cotton charter other evidence of his hand shows that he also was involved with the St. Peter's library. He wrote tables of contents in five books,[133] a compendium of patristic and canonical excerpts, possibly copied a Gospel, and began and occasionally corrected a collection of St. Augustine's works.[134] An endorsement of his on a charter which he wrote for a lay patron of St. Peter's is the earliest which can be attributed to an identified scribal hand.[135] One of the longer samples of his protogothic bookhand appears to have been written not later than *c.* 1174 because of its roundness and employment of tailed- *e*'s and the ampersand.[136] Scribe 2's elegantly rounded and slightly left-leaning to perpendicular script is a bookhand, occasionally adopting features of business hands by lengthening ascenders and adding descenders.[137] It employs abbreviation signs, ligatures, and biting in *or* virtually identical to those of Scribe 1. His easily identifiable paragraph/nota 'gallows' can be footed or unfooted.[138] Other distinguishing features are the six-stroke *g* with the thickened and occasionally straight cross-bar of the tail,[139] business-hand *s*,[140] *D*,[141] *R*,[142] and the form of tironian *et.*[143]

---

[131]   New York, J. Pierpont Morgan Library, MS. 777, fols. 59–76; letter to present editor from Michael Gullick dated 23 Feb. 1993; also noted by R. M. Thomson in Mynors and Thomson, *Catalogue*, 14; from my examination of extant books from St. Peter's, H.C.L., MS. P.I.3, fols. 21–68v, 69–93v, St. Augustine's *De vera religione* and *De gratia et libero arbitrio*, and B.L., MS. Royal 11.D.viii are the most likely candidates. This hand is akin to that of the St. Peter's *titulus* in the Mortuary Roll: Delisle, *Rouleau Mortuaire*, titulus no. 85; for a characterization of this hand see Ker, *English Manuscripts*, 34.

[132]   Below, nos. 59, 247, Plate IV; I am grateful to Michael Gullick for suggesting the association of no. 59 with this hand.

[133]   H.C.L., P.I.5, flyleaf (Ker, *English Manuscripts*, Plate 27a); see also the tables in ibid. O.III.1; B.L., Harl. MS. 2659; Bodl., MS. Jesus Coll. 43 (below, Plate V); Bodl., MS. Bodl. 210; see also Ker, *MLGB*, 91; idem, *English Manuscripts*, pp. xiii, 6 & n.; Mynors and Thomson, *Catalogue*, 17, 67.

[134]   H.C.L., O.I.12, fols. 34–75v, line 10, less fol. 48, line 6 to fol. 49, line 19; O.II. 6, fols. 1–48v; P.I.16, fol. 1, lines 1–8; corrections e.g. fols. 6, esp. 28v, 33v, 43v, 59, 66v, 86v; the tables and literary segments are noted in Mynors and Thomson, *Catalogue*, 11, 14, 17, 73. Michael Gullick has also attributed J. Pierpont Morgan Libr. MS. 777, fols. 4–23 to this hand.

[135]   Below, no. 247, Plate XLIIIc.

[136]   e.g. H.C.L., O.I.12 as in above, n. 134, *e* in *que*, *g* in *ligandi* and ampersand, line 21, fol. 34; *S* in *Si*, line 24, fol. 34v; Ker, *English Manuscripts*, 37–39.

[137]   e.g. *salute*, line 2, *r* in *proprio*, line 4, no. 247, Plate IV; they are absent in H.C.L., P.I.16, lines 1–8, fol. 1, and O.I.12, fols. 34–75v, line 10, as would be expected.

[138]   e.g. H.C.L., P.I.5, flyleaf: Ker, *English Manuscripts*, Plate 27a; MS. Jesus Coll. 43, fol. 1v, below, Plate V.

[139]   e.g. *religione*, H.C.L., O.III.1, line 3, fol. ii verso; ibid. O.I.12, *argutissime*, line 24, fol. 38v; *burgagio*, no. 59, line 2; *Rogeri(us)*, line 1, no. 247, Plate IV.

[140]   *heres*, below, no. 247, Plate IV, line 1; Bodl., Jesus Coll. MS. 43, Plate V, *Athanasii*, line 1, fol. 1v.

[141]   *De* in H.C.L., P.I.5, flyleaf, line 2; Bodl., Jesus Coll. MS. 43, Plate V, line 2.

[142]   *Rogeri(us)*, below, no. 247, Plate IV, line 1; VIDENTER in H.C.L., O.I.12., line 24, fol. 38v.

[143]   H.C.L., P.I.5, flyleaf, line 6: Ker, *English Manuscripts*, Plate 27a; below, no. 247, Plate IV,

Scribe 3 wrote bipartite chirographs for Abbot Hamelin.[144] His script is a slightly left-leaning to perpendicular protogothic bookhand. Ascenders are lengthened, but descenders are applied inconsistently.[145] The scribe employed the *ct*[146] and *st* ligatures,[147] and tironian *et* instead of ampersands. Tailed-*e* is absent. His two main forms of *g*,[148] *G*, *H*, *ct* ligature, 2-shaped signs for *ur*, and tironian *et* are distinctive.

One of the *acta* which **Scribe 4** wrote 1148 × 79 for the abbot and community records a confirmation to one of the St. Peter's tenants in 1155.[149] The scribe wrote in a book hand which incorporated a few of the more common features of business hands such as lengthened ascenders and descenders, albeit irregularly; and along with tironian *con*[150] and *et*,[151] he used *ct*[152] and *st*[153] ligatures. His slightly left-leaning script is compact, but words and lines are well spaced. The scribe's distinctive forms are the oval suspension signs,[154] tironian *et*, *D*,[155] *N*,[156] and the duct of the open tail of *g*.[157]

Scribe 5's *acta* written in the name of Abbot Hamelin and the St. Peter's community for different beneficiaries and also in a donor's name are excellent examples of a protogothic business hand. Ascenders of *b*, *d*, *f*, *h*, *l*, and *s* are not only lengthened but exaggerated,[158] and there are less prominent descenders; minims are angular. Tironian *et* is used in place of ampersands and tailed-*e* is abandoned. Ligatures, including *ct* and *st* forms,[159] 'biting' in *or*,[160] and especially various forms of abbreviation are stressed.[161] Although the script is compact, spacing is emphasized between words and lines. Calligraphic touches are evident

---

line 4.

[144] Below, no. 60, Plate VI, nos. 64, 66, all in favour of different beneficiaries; I am indebted to Michael Gullick for alerting me to this identification.

[145] e.g. *s* in *suo*, line 1, in *sigillo*, line 9; *r* in *transfer(r)et* and in *n(ost)ra*, line 6, no. 60, Plate VI; also *r* in *n(ost)ra*, line 4, *s* in *domus*, line 6, no. 64.

[146] *predictus*, line 5, no. 60, Plate VI; also *dictus*, line 3, no. 64.

[147] *festu(m)*, line 7, no. 60, Plate VI; also *restituetur*, line 7, no. 64; *prestitit*, line 5, no. 63; *p(re)stitit*, line 5, no. 66.

[148] *Ego*, line 1, no. 60, Plate VI; *gen(er)e*, line 10, no. 63; *Ego*, line 1, no. 66.

[149] Nos. 61, 71, ibid. for the 1155 issue. I am uncertain about the attribution of no. 65. As suggested to me by Michael Gullick, this could be a more formal version of the scribe's hand (letter of 22 June 1992). Note the corrected *d/q* and the abbreviation for *quod* in no. 61, Plate VIIa, lines 1, 4. This scribe also may have endorsed ibid. no. 71.

[150] *(con)uentione(m)*, no. 61, Plate VIIa, line 6; also *(con)uentu(m)*, no. 71, line 3.

[151] No. 61, Plate VIIa, line 1; also no. 71, line 1.

[152] *octo*, no. 61, Plate VIIa, line 3; *auctoritate*, line 8.

[153] e.g. *Magist(r)o*, no. 61, Plate VIIa, line 2; also *testes*, no. 71, line 6.

[154] e.g. *Ham(o)*, line 1, no. 61, Plate VIIa.

[155] *De*, no. 61, Plate VIIa, line 6; also *Durand(us)*, no. 71, line 11.

[156] *Nos*, no. 61, Plate VIIa, line 7; also *Nicolaus*, no. 71, line 8.

[157] e.g. *homagio*, no. 71, line 2; also *Sigar(us)*, no. 61, Plate VIIa, line 11.

[158] *b* and *s* in *abb(ati)s*, and *f* in *fut(ur)i*, line 1; *d* in *de* and *h* in *huic*, line 2, *l* in *australi*, line 4, no. 62, Plate VIII; also *f* and *l* in *fil(io)*, *h* in *tochi* and *d* and *s* in *duas*, line 1, no. 69. The scribe also wrote no. 222.

[159] e.g. *ti* in *fut(ur)i*, line 1, *ct* in *tactis*, line 6, *st* in *australi*, line 4, no. 62, Plate VIII; also *ri* in *reddiderit*, *ct* in *octo*, line 2, *st* in *posteru(m)*, line 6, no. 69.

[160] Ibid. *solidor(um)*, no. 62, Plate VIII, line 5.

[161] Suspension signs: dashes angling upward to the right, 7-shaped, and ovals; *notae* for *ur* and *us*; for examples see no. 62, Plate VIII, lines 1, 2, 4.

in the loops added to the tops of *s*.[162] It is an experienced hand, left-leaning, but not consistently; and some ascenders can be angled and bowed to the right.[163] Characteristic forms are a five-stroke *g* (formed by the diagonal stroke closing the tail drawn from right to lower left and overlapping the crosspiece of the tail, generally finishing with a sharp upward tick),[164] *G*,[165] and tironian *et*.

Scribe 6 served the administrations of Abbots Hamelin and Thomas Carbonel at some time between 1148 and 1205.[166] His hand is yet another bookhand modified for business purposes.[167] One of the examples of the scribe's work shows how he employed thin and mostly curving strokes to create descenders or to supplement them to create a decorated effect for his script.[168] The scribe used tironian *con* and *et* and *ct* and *st* ligatures.[169] The tail of *g*,[170] tall *s* especially drawn with a descender,[171] *q*,[172] and the form of tironian *et*[173] are distinctive.

Scribe 7's *acta* were written for St. Peter's and Abbot Thomas Carbonel (1179–1205),[174] and probably during this period the scribe acted as an archival endorser.[175] His is a boldly drawn, left-leaning formal business hand showing clear affinity to bookhand. Elongated ascenders of *b*, *d*, *h*, *k*, *l*, already finished with tick marks to the right, can also be notched at the top left so as to create a splayed effect.[176] The leftward and downward diagonal stroke into which the scribe transformed the comma of the semi-colon abbreviation for terminal *ue* accompanies other decorative finishing strokes which he added to the feet of minims.[177] The tail of *g* may be rounded or especially triangular[178] and it is the latter along with *A*,[179] *P*,[180] compressed *S*,[181] and oval suspension signs, which can be semicircular,[182] which are particularly indicative of his hand.

---

[162] *s(an)c(t)is* ibid. line 6.

[163] *bb* in *abb(a)s*, ibid. line 1; *ll* in *sigilli*, ibid. line 12.

[164] *ego*, line 1, no. 62, Plate VIII; line 1, no. 69; line 1, no. 222.

[165] *Gloesc'*, line 2, no. 62, Plate VIII; *Gloec'*, line 1, no. 69, line 2, no. 222.

[166] See below, nos. 70, 79. Michael Gullick alerted me to this identification (letter of 22 March 1993).

[167] The descender written over the original minim of the second *r* in *carpentario*, no. 70, Plate IX, line 2, is an excellent example.

[168] In no. 70, Plate IX, e.g. *m* in *Marie*, line 3, *terra*, line 2, *Hileb(er)to*, line 12.

[169] *(con)uent(us)*, line 1; *ct* in *p(re)dicte*, line 6; *st* in *prestitit*, line 12, no. 79; also *(con)ue(n)tus*, line 1; *ct* in *p(re)dicta(m)*, line 7; *st* in *sacriste*, line 2, no. 70, Plate IX.

[170] e.g. *contingat*, line 7 in no. 70, Plate IX.

[171] e.g. *solidos*, no. 79, line 6; also *ius*, line 6, no. 70, Plate IX.

[172] e.g. *que*, no. 79, line 4; also *q(u)am* in no. 70, line 1, Plate IX.

[173] e.g. no. 70, Plate IX, line 1.

[174] Nos. 86, 100.

[175] He endorsed no. 100, which he wrote for Abbot Thomas Carbonel; see also no. 74, Plate XLIIIi; possibly also no. 80.

[176] Respectively e.g. *Rob(er)t(us)*, no. 100, line 4; *d(e)i*, no. 86, Plate X, line 1; *toki*, no. 100, line 11; *Cap(e)llam*, no. 86, Plate X, line 2.

[177] e.g. *neque*, no. 100, line 6.

[178] Compare *g* in *gr(ati)a*, line 1 and in *sigilli*, line 9, no. 100, *Ego*, line 1, *sigilli*, line 4, no. 86, Plate X.

[179] *Abb(a)s*, line 1, no. 86, Plate X, line 1.

[180] *Pet(r)i*, ibid. line 1.

[181] *S(an)c(t)i*, no. 86, Plate X, line 1.

[182] e.g. *rat(u)m*, ibid. line 3.

Of **Scribe 8**'s *acta* only one was issued in the name of the abbot and community of St. Peter's (1179–1205), but all benefited St. Peter's in some way, so there is little doubt that he was an abbatial scribe.[183] Two of his products place his service in 1177 and possibly in 1178.[184] He wrote in an upright and undecorated bookhand, but exaggerated the length of ascenders and included equally exaggerated trailing headed *a*'s in his alphabet.[185] He employed tironian *et*, but not *con* or *ct* and *st* ligatures. Particularly indicative of his hand are the *ct* ligature,[186] *B*,[187] *R*,[188] *S*, and *U*.[189] With *S* the upper lobe is often stretched and the letter angled significantly to the left.[190]

Scribe 9, who was active in the service of St. Peter's at least between 1179 and 1205, wrote in an experienced upright business hand little removed from bookhand. His artificially added descenders are often easily visible.[191] He wavered back and forth between caroline and uncial *d*[192] and between *de* and *d'* for *de*.[193] The scribe used the tironian *notae* for *con* and *et*[194] and the *ct*[195] and *st*[196] ligatures. Tironian *con* and *et*, *g*,[197] tall *s*,[198] *G*,[199] and *R*[200] are distinctive.

The address clauses and beneficiaries of **Scribe 10**'s *acta* establish that he performed his secretarial duties as a member of the St. Peter's community during 1179 × 1205.[201] His left-leaning protogothic bookhand with its lengthened ascenders and added descenders is immediately recognizable.[202] The scribe employed *st* ligatures and 'biting' in *or*[203] and possibly *de*.[204] Distinctive features are *f* and *s* with straight and angled finishing strokes applied to the tops of their ascenders, *D*,[205] *T*,[206] and tironian *et* with a looped tail finished

---

[183]   No. 96 in the name of Abbot Thomas and the community; no. 36 by Richard archdeacon of Wilts.; H.C.L., no. 2771 by Richard Parvus. Cheney, *Roger, Bishop of Worcester*, 231, 259, 261–2, also recognized the same hand in no. 36 below and H.C.L., no. 2771, and speculated (p. 262 n.) that this hand might also have written a notification of Bishop Roger of a case which he had heard as a papal delegate (Cheney, *Roger, Bishop of Worcester*, no. 55).

[184]   Below, no. 36, H.C.L., no. 2771; for the dating, Cheney, *Roger, Bishop of Worcester*, 259, 261–2 & nn.

[185]   *absque*, no. 36, Plate VIIb, line 6; also *attestatione*, no. 96, line 6.

[186]   *p(re)dicta*, no. 36, Plate VIIb, line 5; also *Dilecto*, no. 96, line 1.

[187]   e.g. *Berkaleia*, H.C.L., no. 2771, line 11.

[188]   *Ric(ardus)*, below, no. 36, Plate VIIb, line 1.

[189]   e.g. *Uniu(er)sis*, no. 36, Plate VIIb, line 1.

[190]   Compare *Sal(utem)* and *Sciatis*, no. 36, Plate VIIb, line 1.

[191]   e.g. note the added descender on *r* in *arte(m)*, no. 90, Plate XI, line 11.

[192]   e.g. *eunde(m)*, line 4, and *q(uo)d*, line 1, no. 76.

[193]   e.g. *d(e)o*, line 4, *de* line 15, *d(e)* line 16, no. 90, Plate XI.

[194]   e.g. *et (con)uent(us)*, no. 90, Plate XI, line 1.

[195]   *(con)tradictione*, no. 90, Plate XI, line 6; also *octo*, no. 76, line 2.

[196]   e.g. *instauram(e)nto*, no. 90, Plate XI, line 5; also *custo*, no. 76, line 4.

[197]   *ego*, no. 90, Plate XI, line 1; also no. 76.

[198]   *abbas*, no. 90, Plate XI, line 1; also no. 76.

[199]   *Gloec'*, no. 90, Plate XI, line 1; also no. 76.

[200]   *Rob(erto)*, no. 90, Plate XI, line 15; also *Ric(ardo)*, no. 76, line 6.

[201]   Nos. 80–82, 92, 98; a formal version of this hand or a hand highly imitative of it is no. 99; note the *T* in *Thomas*, line 1, and tironian *et*, line 13; the decorated *T* in *.T.*, line 6, and *T* in *Testibus*, line 12, conform to the style in *Thomas*, line 1, no. 98.

[202]   e.g. *s*'s in *p(re)sentes*, no. 80, Plate XII, line 1.

[203]   e.g. *incisore*, no. 80, Plate XII, line 10.

[204]   *dei*, line 1, no. 81 may be an example.

[205]   *Dauid*, no. 80, Plate XII, line 10; no. 82; line 10.

[206]   e.g. *Thomas*, no. 80, Plate XII, line 1.

like a modern cursive *g* or *y*.

Very similar to the hand of the preceding scribe is the protogothic style of a contemporary, **Scribe 11**, who wrote a charter for Abbot Thomas Carbonel and recorded a layman's confirmation of a meadow to the abbot and monks.[207] His is an upright to slightly left-leaning business hand closely related to bookhand. The length of ascenders is exaggerated, while descenders are few. The script is compact and miniaturized. *D*,[208] *P*,[209] and tironian *et* are distinctive.

The hand of **Scribe 12**, who apparently wrote *acta* for Abbot Henry (1205–24) and his community, represents a style in transition between the prevailing business hand of the early thirteenth century and the more elaborate style of the next quarter century.[210] Decoration of capitals remains mostly simple as do the forms of minim letters. Even so, this scribe's slightly modified bookhand is acquiring the texture of the hand of the next quarter century, which favoured certain more complex letter forms and thickened suspension signs.[211] The script is a compact, slightly left-leaning, and miniaturized business hand only slightly removed from book hand. The adaptation is mostly achieved by exaggerating the length of ascenders; descenders are few.[212] Tops of *f* and *s* are often furnished with sharply angled downward strokes, but that of terminal *s* can be rippled.[213] Tops of *l* and of *L* can also be looped.[214] The bent-back arm of *d* and horizontal suspension signs are thickened.[215] Distinctive forms are *d*,[216] *g*,[217] *D*,[218] *G*,[219] *R*,[220] and the elaborate curved and straight suspension signs.[221] From the witness-lists of the scribe's *acta* it appears that at least one and perhaps all the transactions which he recorded for Abbot Henry Blont (1205–24) had occurred in the borough court.[222]

Scribe 13 wrote several chirograph grants for Abbot Henry (1205–24), of which both halves of one survive.[223] His script is an upright formal business hand, which can veer to the left or right, slightly modified from bookhand. The length of ascenders is exaggerated and

---

[207] Nos. 78, 256; see also no. 85.

[208] *Dura(n)d*, no. 256, Plate XIII, line 10; also *Drog(one)*, no. 78, line 17.

[209] *Pet(r)o*, no. 256, Plate XIII, line 9; also *Punteise*, no. 78, line 16.

[210] Nos. 120, 128; the partial text at the foot of no. 127 may be in this hand. See also no. 138.

[211] Particularly noticeable in bent-back *d*, e.g. *de*, no. 120, Plate XIV, line 1; also no. 128, line 1; and suspension signs with *gr(ati)a*, no. 120, Plate XIV, line 1; no. 128, line 1.

[212] *r* in *stabellario*, no. 120, Plate XIV, line 11 is the exception.

[213] e.g. *p(re)sentes*, no. 120, Plate XIV, line 1; also *Hiis*, line 8, no. 138.

[214] *Michaelis*, line 3, *Locum*, line 8, no. 120, Plate XIV; also *Le*, line 15, no. 128; *Locu(m)*, no. 138, line 6.

[215] e.g. *ad*, no. 120, Plate XIV, line 3; *de*, no. 138, line 2. Note that in no. 120, Plate XIV, both curved and straight suspension signs are used; in no. 138, they are all straight.

[216] e.g. *quod*, no. 120, Plate XIV, line 1; also nos. 128, 138.

[217] e.g. *ego*, no. 120, Plate XIV, line 1; nos. 128, 138, line 1.

[218] *Dauid*, no. 120, Plate XIV, line 10; no. 128, line 14; *Droco(ne)*, no. 138, line 9, has a slightly different form.

[219] *Glouc'*, no. 128, line 1; nos. 129, 138; compare with no. 120, Plate XIV, line 1.

[220] *Rei*, no. 120, Plate XIV, line 9; also *Ricardo*, no. 128, line 14; no. 138, line 8.

[221] e.g. *gr(ati)a*, line 1, and *t(er)ram*, line 2, no. 120, Plate XIV; also *gr(ati)a*, no. 128, line 1. As has been noted, the suspension signs of no. 138 are straight.

[222] The names of the Gloucester bailiffs, Richard Burgess and Maurice Durand, even lead the list of witnesses in no. 138.

[223] Nos. 115–16; see also no. 123.

descenders are added inconsistently.[224] All known examples of his work contain a tall *s* decorated with the papal 'coil' in the notification clause.[225] The scribe's distinctive forms are *e*,[226] *g*,[227] *v*,[228] and tironian *et*.[229]

Scribe 14 provides an excellent example of the early thirteenth-century dimunitive semi-cursive business hand which was widely used to about 1225.[230] There are ligatures such as *ri*,[231] *iu*,[232] *ui*,[233] *ur*,[234] in addition to *ct*[235] and *st*,[236] 'biting' in *pp*[237] in addition to the more usual *or*, and there is the occasional currently formed loop of *d*,[238] nevertheless the hand's indebtedness to bookhand is evident. Decoration of majuscules when employed involved only simple 'skeletonizing.' The tops of ascenders of *f* and tall *s* are sharply angled downward. Scribe 14 used tironian *con*[239] and *et*. *A*,[240] *R*,[241] *g* with closed or open tail and its duct,[242] and the form of tironian *et*[243] are distinctive.

Scribe 15's hand, found in several chirographs written for an Abbot Thomas, is another version of the transitional style described for Scribe 16 and thus can be attributed to the abbacy of Thomas of Bredon (1224–8).[244] It is a miniaturized, compact, slightly modified bookhand. The hand's thickened and looped suspension signs, 2-shaped signs for *ur*, tironian *et*, and *T* are distinctive.[245]

Scribe 16 wrote in the semi-cursive business hand in common use during the second quarter of the thirteenth century. He recorded transactions both by, and in favour of, St. Peter's during at least part of the abbacy of Henry Foliot (1228–43).[246] Among the hand's most visible signs are increased 'skeletonizing' of capitals, thickened suspension signs, and looping of bent *d*. His script is left-leaning, compact, and like at least one other contemporary colleague at St. Peter's he gave particular stress to minuscule *r* by elongating

---

[224] Compare *Elemosinam*, line 5, with *susscepit*, line 7, no. 115, Plate XV.

[225] e.g. *presentes*, no. 115 Plate XV, line 1; no. 116; also no. 123.

[226] e.g. *temp(or)e*, no. 115, Plate XV, line 5; also *De*, line 6, no. 123.

[227] e.g. *ego*, no. 115, Plate XV, line 1; also nos. 116, 123.

[228] e.g. *v(er)o*, no. 115, Plate XV, line 7; also *virorum*, no. 123, line 7.

[229] No. 123; no. 115, Plate XV, line 1.

[230] No. 18; nos. 121–2 (both halves of a bipartite chirograph); nos. 130, 391. No. 114 and the first of the endorsements of no. 391 also may be in this hand.

[231] *erit*, no. 121, Plate XVI, line 11; also no. 130.

[232] *diuiso*, no. 121, Plate XVI, line 16; also no. 130.

[233] *suis*, no. 121, Plate XVI, line 3; also no. 130.

[234] *mensurata*, no. 121, Plate XVI, line 5; also no. 130.

[235] *Octo*, no. 121, Plate XVI, line 6; no. 122.

[236] *p(re)stitit*, no. 121, Plate XVI, line 11; also no. 130.

[237] *app(re)ciatu(m)*, no. 121, Plate XVI, line 9; also no. 130.

[238] *Hocked(ai)*, no. 121, Plate XVI, line 4; also *totidem*, no. 130, line 7.

[239] *(con)cessim(us)*, no. 121, Plate XVI, line 2; also no. 130, line 1.

[240] *Abb(a)s*, no. 121, Plate XVI, line 1; also no. 130.

[241] *Ric(ardo)*, no. 121, Plate XVI, line 17; also no. 130.

[242] *Ego* and *gr(ati)a*, no. 121, Plate XVI, line 1; *g* in *Rog(er)o*, no. 130 is exceptional.

[243] No. 121, Plate XVI, line 1; also no. 130.

[244] Nos. 145, 147.

[245] e.g. the looped suspension sign in *t(er)m(in)is*, line 3, 2-shaped sign for *ur* in *uocat(ur)*, line 2, *et* line 1, *T* in *Thom(as)*, line 1, no. 145, Plate XVII; looped suspension sign in *annuatim*, line 3, 2-shaped sign for *ur* in *sec(ur)itatem*, line 11, *et*, line 1, *T* in *Thomas*, line 1, no. 143.

[246] Nos. 150–1, 159, 163; also no. 132; *acta* benefiting St. Peter's: nos. 208, 214 (mentioning Henry Foliot).

its arm. He also provided tops of *b*, *h*, *l*, and tall *s* with graceful rounded loops. Minim *g*,[247] *A*, *D*, and the forms of tironian *con* and *et*, and the 2-shaped sign for *-ur* are particularly distinctive.

A contemporary of Scribe 18, **Scribe 17** wrote two grants for St. Peter's, of which both halves of the bipartite chirographs survive, in a comparable style,[248] and like Scribe 18 he also accentuated *r*.[249] The script tends, however, to be more upright, of which this scribe's looped *d* is a good example.[250] The tail of his *g* also tends to be more semicircular.[251] Distinctive are the form of the 2-shaped suspension sign for *ur*,[252] tironian *et*,[253] *g*, *A*,[254] and decorated *S*.[255]

Scribe 18 served the administration of Henry Foliot (1228–43). He wrote in a formal upright business hand reflecting the style of *c.* 1225 × 50.[256] He also sought to create an overall decorative effect for his gracefully drawn script by means of thickened strokes, forking of ascenders, and the decorative treatment which he gave to suspension signs, superscript letters, and *notae* for *ur*. Distinctive forms are *g*[257] tironian *et*[258] and the *ct*[259] ligature.

Scribe 19 was a *scriptor* for St. Peter's during the abbacy of John de Felda (1243–63); several of his abbatial *acta* date from 1253 × 54.[260] His script is a slightly left-leaning, compact, and miniaturized business hand. It is reminiscent of the style commonly used during the first quarter of the century; but there is thickening of strokes, some 'skeletonizing' of capitals, forking at the tops of the ascenders of *b*, *h*, *k*, *l*, and *I*, and frequent looping of the arm of bent-back *d*. While the scribe employed several types of *g*, he overwhelmingly favoured one with a compact, closed, and sharply angled tail. This form, along with *A*, *Q*, decorated *R*, and tironian *et* are indicative of his hand.[261]

---

[247] e.g. *g* in *Ego*, line 1, *A* in *Abb(at)i*, line 5, *D* in *Diaconi*, line 4, *con* in *(con)tig(er)it*, line 12, *et, ur* in *Fut(ur)i*, line 1, no. 214, Plate XVIII; also *g* in *Ego*, *A* in *Abbas*, line 1, *D* in *Dauid*, line 13, *con* in *(con)uent(us)*, *et*, and *ur* in *fut(ur)i*, line 1, no. 163.

[248] Nos. 153–4, 155–6; he also wrote no. 302.

[249] e.g. *Henr(icus)* and *gr(ati)a*, no. 155, Plate XIX, line 1; no. 156.

[250] *d(e)i*, no. 155, Plate XIX, line 1; no. 156.

[251] e.g. *Ego*, no. 155, Plate XIX, line 1; no. 156.

[252] e.g. *Fut(ur)i*, no. 155, Plate XIX, line 1; *fut(ur)i*, no. 156.

[253] No. 155, Plate XIX, line 1; no. 156; no. 153; the scribe also employed a *nota* without a loop on its arm; e.g. no. 154, line 1.

[254] *Abb(a)s*, no. 155, Plate XIX, line 1; no. 156.

[255] *Sciant*, no. 155, Plate XIX, line 1; no. 156, or *Si*, no. 155, Plate XIX, line 9; no. 153, line 7.

[256] Nos. 20, 160, 165; the scribe also may have written no. 202.

[257] e.g. *Ego*, no. 165, Plate XXa, line 1; nos. 20, 160.

[258] No. 165, Plate XXa, line 1; nos. 20, 160.

[259] No. 165, *sectis*, Plate XXa, line 5; no. 20, *(con)fectu(m)*, line 9; no. 160, *Relicte*, line 2.

[260] Nos. 173, 175, 178, 184–6, 273. Other *acta* possibly written or influenced by this hand are nos. 21, 171, 176, 183.

[261] e.g. *g* in *reg(is)*, *A* in *Abb(a)s*, line 1, *Q* in *Q(ua)n(do)*, line 5, *R* in *Rog(er)o*, line 1, no. 186, Plate XXI; also *g* in *regni*, *A* in *Abb(a)s*, line 1, *Q* in *Q(u)ando*, line 6, *R* in *Rog(er)o*, line 11, no. 124.

II. *Scribes of* acta *benefiting St. Peter's*

Scribe 20: Royal **Scriptor xiii**, who was active 22 May 1127 × 39, wrote two of Henry I's extant originals for the abbey.[262]

A charter issued in the name of Rotrou count of Perche was begun by one scribe[263] and completed by another,[264] and the witness-list, written in the second hand, states that the deed was written by Walter de Maheruto (Mahéru?). His (**Scribe 21**'s), presumably, is the second hand. The scripts of both hands, bookhands, were contemporary with the known occurence-dates of the charter's witnesses, *c.* 1130 × *c.* 1154, and the hand of the charter's earlier of two endorsements places the execution of the deed to some time before *c.* 1170.[265] The first hand is English, to judge by the footings of the minims.[266] Various ligatures reveal the scribe's attempt to produce a business script. The second hand is continental, showing signs of English influence, to judge by the few feet finished with serifs or ticks.[267] The script, however, is also compatible with *c.* 1130 × *c.* 1154. Tironian *et, d,* and *e* are distinctive.

Scribe 22: Royal **Scriptor xvii** wrote a charter of King Stephen for St. Peter's between 1135 and 1139.[268]

Scribe 23: Between 1139 and 1161, Royal **Scriptor xiv** wrote one of Archbishop Theobald's charters benefiting the abbey's church at Newport (Mon.).[269]

Scribe 24: Another of King Stephen's charters from 1148 × 54 is in the hand of Royal **Scriptor xxii**.[270]

Scribe 25: Royal **Scriptor xxvii**, who is known to have been active in 1155 × 57, executed a charter of King Henry II for Leonard Stanley priory in January 1156.[271]

Scribe 26: Royal **Scriptor xxvi** executed a writ of Henry II on behalf of St. Peter's in 1155 × 58, possibly 1158.[272]

Scribe 27: Royal **Scriptor xl** wrote two *acta* benefiting St. Peter's during his period of known Chancery service *c.* 1163 × 87.[273]

---

[262] Nos. 39, 41. Bishop, *Scriptores Regis*, Plates V–V(d) & nn., XVII(a) & n. for descriptions of this hand; *Regesta* iii, pp. xiii–xiv; *Regesta* iv. 5–6, 12, 18–19, Plates V–XI & nn. for further examples and discussion of the scribe.

[263] Below, no. 248, Plate XXb, *Ego . . . per*, lines 1–2.

[264] Ibid. *illas . . . aldeburne*, lines 2–7.

[265] See no. 248.

[266] e.g. *s* and *l* in *consul; n*, and *s* in *monachis*, no. 248, Plate XXb, line 1.

[267] e.g. *l* and *r* in *liberas, e* in *eis*, no. 248, Plate XXb, line 4. Note also the spelling of *uuareuuic*, followed by *W* in *Walt(ero)*, line 5.

[268] No. 42. Bishop, *Scriptores Regis*, Plates VII(a) & n., XIX(a) & n. for the description of the hand; *Regesta*, iii, p. xv, no. 346, for the attribution; see also *Regesta*, iv, Plate XX(a) & n.

[269] Below, no. 385; Bishop, *Scriptores Regis*, no. S.28, Plate XVII(b) & n., for dating and the description of the hand. Ibid. 23–25; *Regesta*, iii, p. xiv; *Regesta* iv, 6–7, 11, 19–20, and Plates XIIa–XVII & nn. for further discussion.

[270] Below, no. 43; Bishop, *Scriptores Regis*, no. 224, 25, 32, and Plate XXII(b) & n.; *Regesta*, iii, p. xv; iv. 13–16, 18, Plates XXXIV–XXXVII & nn. for further discussion.

[271] Below, no. 366; Bishop, *Scriptores Regis*, no. 584, Plate XXVI (a) n. for description of the hand.

[272] Below, no. 49; Bishop, *Scriptores Regis*, no. 229, 15, 30, Plate XXV(b) & n. for discussion of the scribe and his hand.

[273] Below, nos. 46, 367; Bishop, *Sciptores Regis*, Plate XXXIV(a) & n., p. 30.

Scribe 28 can be credited with two *acta* recording confirmations by Henry II of Pomeroy (1165 × 1207) of gifts to St. Peter's made by his father Henry I (1123+ × c. 1165). The two must have been written about the same time since their witness-lists are almost identical.[274] The scribe wrote in a slightly left-leaning formal business hand characterized by boldly drawn vertical strokes. Tops of *f* and *s* are usually finished with angular curved ones, the feet of some minims and descenders with curved thin ones, in some cases constituting the descenders.[275] He used the *ct* ligature inconsistently.[276] Distinctive features are *g* with the angular 'tail' and duct,[277] tall and terminal short *s*,[278] two forms of *P*,[279] *R*,[280] and tironian *et*.[281]

A **Scribe 29**, who recorded leases granted to St. Peter's and to a Gloucester burgess and his wife in a hand of c. 1200 or even a decade earlier, can be placed within the abbacy of Henry Blont (1205–24).[282] He wrote in a slightly left-leaning formal business hand adapted from bookhand and decorated it with exaggerated tops to *F* and *G* and ascenders of bent-back *d*, letters such as *a* and *b* crossed with suspension signs, *tituli*, and papal 'coils'. Aside from the general appearance of his script his hand can be readily identified from his forms of tironian *et*[283] and addition of double or triple bowls to majuscule letters calling for respectively single or double ones.[284]

Large fragments of two charters recording notifications of a lay woman's quitclaims of right to St. Peter's reveal details of **Scribe 30**'s formal, perpendicular, business hand of the early thirteenth century. Loops added especially to lower case letters such as *h*, *l*, and *v*, and thickened suspension signs gracefully curving upward to the right are obvious calligraphic features. Distinctive letters are *d*, *g*, and *D*.[285] Since both charters specifically relate to proceedings in the St. Peter's court, there is little doubt that the two were the work of one of the abbey's scribes.

Although **Scribe 31** recorded a transaction of a Gloucester tenant, he also wrote a charter preserving the terms of a donation to St. Peter's made at the abbey in 1216.[286] He wrote in a calligraphic semicursive business hand. He decorated his text by adding loops and coils to ascenders of letters such as *b*,[287] *d*,[288] *l*,[289] *s*,[290] and *A*,[291] by exaggerating the arm of *F*,[292] by

---

[274] Below, nos. 254–5; Sanders, *English Baronies*, 106–7.

[275] In no. 254, Plate XXII, note *ss* in *imp(re)ssione*, line 11; in no. 255, note *s* in *sic(ut)* line 7, *f* in *fili(us)*, line 9.

[276] Compare *exactione* in no. 254, Plate XXII, line 7 with no. 255, line 8.

[277] *Ego*, no. 254, Plate XXII, line 1; also no. 255.

[278] In no. 254, Plate XXII, *sui*, line 8, *M(at)ris*, line 9; in no. 255, e.g. *suis*, line 4.

[279] In no. 254, Plate XXII, *Pomeria* and *Pom(er)ia*, line 1; in no. 255, *Pom(er)ia*, line 1.

[280] e.g. *Ric(ardo)* in no. 254, Plate XXII, line 13; also no. 255, line 14.

[281] No. 254, Plate XXII, line 1; also no. 255.

[282] Nos. 218, 293 (attested by Abbot Henry).

[283] e.g. *et* following *presentes*, line 1, no. 218, Plate XXIII; also no. 293.

[284] *Brackel'*, no. 218, Plate XXIII, line 4; also *Ricard(us)*, no. 293, line 1.

[285] e.g. *d* in *sec(un)d(u)m*, line 3, *g* in *Lege(m)*, line 3, *D* in *D(omi)no*, line 2, no. 223, Plate XXIV; *d*, in *Quod*, line 2, *g* in *Ego*, line 2, and *D(omi)ni*, line 1, no. 224.

[286] Nos. 246, 324.

[287] *testib(us)*, no. 246, Plate XXV, line 9; also no. 324.

[288] *ad*, no. 246, Plate XXV, line 1; also *q(uo)d*, no. 324.

[289] *millesimo*, no. 246, Plate XXV, line 2; also *videlicet*, no. 324, line 4.

[290] *quos*, no. 246, Plate XXV, line 1; also *p(re)sentes*, no. 324.

[291] *Abbatia*, no. 246, Plate XXV, line 2; also *Abb(at)i*, no. 324, line 5.

[292] *Fidelibus*, no. 246, Plate XXV, line 1; *Fut(ur)i*, no. 324.

thickening the tail of *g*,[293] and by using gracefully curved suspension signs.[294] Distinctive forms are *g, F, S,* and tironian *et.*[295]

Scribe 32 wrote in a style very similar to that of Scribe 19, but his hand is more finely drawn. *Acta* attributable to him benefiting St. Peter's contrast stressed and thickened shading of the upper portions of letters, particularly forked tops to ascenders, the shaft of bent-back *d*, the tails of long-tailed *a*'s, and suspension signs. Distinctive features of the scribe's hand are *g*,[296] the doubled form of *F*,[297] and *R*.[298]

While David Dunning and Walter Pain were bailiffs of Gloucester (*c.* 1228 × 40), **Scribe 33** recorded donations to St. Peter's by several laymen.[299] The hand is a compact, perpendicular, formal business hand. Gracefully thickened letters such as prominently forked *l* appear intermittently in words along with other calligraphic effects such as the graceful thickening of horizontal and vertical suspension signs. Distinctive are 2-shaped signs for *ur*,[300] tironian *et*, two forms of *g*,[301] *D*,[302] and the 9-shaped *-orum* compendium.

Scribe 34, who wrote a charter in favour of St. Peter's, also endorsed it, which establishes his membership in the community.[303] His script is an upright to slightly left-leaning bookhand modified principally by the addition of descenders to letters such as *f, r,* and *l*. His letter forms and suspension signs indicate that he was active in the early 13th century,[304] but short *s* was rendered in the style popular from the 1230s.[305] The distinctive *f*,[306] *A*,[307] and the elongated horizontal suspension signs ending with an upward loop establish the positive link between the secretarial scribe and the endorser.[308]

Two dated *acta* written by **Scribe 35** allow his career to be precisely placed between 29 Sept. 1248 and 28 Oct. 1259 × 27 Oct. 1260.[309] They also reveal how little a secretarial hand might change over roughly a decade. The hand is a very slightly left-leaning bookhand. The script is compact and miniaturized. Forking is a prominent feature of the ascenders of *b, h, k,*

---

[293] *Mucegros*, no. 246, Plate XXV, line 1; also *Ego*, no. 324.

[294] e.g. *Ric(ardo)*, no. 246, Plate XXV, line 10; also *annuati(m)*, no. 324, line 4.

[295] No. 246, Plate XXV, line 3. also no. 324, line 1.

[296] *Ego*, no. 239, Plate XXVI, line 1; also no. 211.

[297] *Foket*, no. 239, Plate XXVI, line 3; also no. 211, line 1.

[298] *Reddendo*, no. 239, Plate XXVI, line 10; also no. 211, line 5.

[299] Nos. 226, 261; the hand of no. 227 is very similar.

[300] *futuri*, no. 261, Plate XXVII, line 1; also no. 226.

[301] *Ego*, no. 261, Plate XXVII, line 1; also *Ego*, line 1, *gnet*, line 5, no. 226.

[302] *D(omi)no*, line 9, no. 261, Plate XXVII; also *Draperius*, line 6, *Dunni(n)g*, line 13, no. 226.

[303] No. 240 and endorsement, Plates XXVIII, XLIVg.

[304] e.g. *b, d, h, f*; note the simple notching at the tops of the ascenders of e.g. *b, h,* and *l*; even the elongated suspension sign lacks the thickness of the style of the 1230s and later: no. 240, Plate XXVIII.

[305] *Illas*, ibid. line 3.

[306] *(con)firmaui*, ibid. line 1; also *confirmat(i)o(n)is* no. 240v, Plate XLIVg.

[307] *Alicia*, no. 240, Plate XXVIII, line 1; *Alicie*, no. 240v, Plate XLIVg.

[308] *om(n)ib(us)*, no. 240, Plate XXVIII, line 1; also *Ioh(ann)is*, no. 240v, Plate XLIVg.

[309] Nos. 229–30.

l, and *I*. The scribe used several forms of *D*,[310] *P*,[311] *R*,[312] and *S*.[313] *A*,[314] *S* with the looped lower bow,[315] *g* with the compact and angular 'tail,'[316] and *v*[317] are distinctive.

Scribe 36, named Alan of Waldis, recorded a grant from Ralph of Willington to St. Peter's and the remission from his wife or widow of rent due from the land.[318] It is an expertly written example of the slightly modified bookhand which was commonly used for both business documents and books in the 1230s and 1240s. The compact script ranges from upright to slightly left-leaning. Forking of the usual ascenders, thickening of the diagonal stroke of bent back *d*, and *a* with its tailing-head looped,[319] are prominent features. The last, together with *d*,[320] *A*,[321] and tironian *et*[322] are distinctive.

The bureaucratic affiliation of **Scribe 37** is uncertain since of the two *acta* attributable to his hand one is in favour of St. Peter's and the other a private transaction. Circumstantial evidence suggests, however, that the scribe was a local Gloucester secular clerk or civilian. The *acta* appear to be products of the Gloucester hundredal court. The transactions which they record involved local Gloucester property, and their grantors and witnesses are local civilians and clerks not associated with St. Peter's.[323] Furthermore, the *acta* are written in a script appropriate to such a court, a semi-cursive business hand which reveals a most un-monastic haste.[324] The hand is compact and upright, but can veer from right to left. Ascenders are exaggerated, with those of *b*,[325] *h*,[326] and *l*[327] prominently forked. Thickened long-tailed *a*'s are stressed.[328] Descenders are are mostly 'spikes', and one of these is the exaggerated form of *r* which is prominent in the late thirteenth century.[329] This form along with *F* as *f* and *F*,[330] *g*,[331] and the form of tironian *et* with the looped top[332] are distinctive.

III. *Scribes of* acta *issued by tenants of St. Peter's*

Acta written by **Scribe 38** establish that he was active in the period 1200–*c*. 1228 at the Gloucester hallmoot.[333] The script is a slightly left-leaning and experienced compact formal

---

[310] *D(omi)no*, no. 229, Plate XXIX, line 12; also no. 230.

[311] e.g. *Philipp(us)* line 1, *Post*, line 8, no. 229, Plate XXIX.

[312] e.g. *Rog(er)i*, line 1, *Reddendo*, line 12, ibid.; also no. 230.

[313] *Sciant*, line 1, *Snedham'*, line 12, no. 229, Plate XXIX.

[314] *Abb(at)i*, ibid. line 2; line 11, no. 230.

[315] *Snedham'*, no. 229, Plate XXIX, line 12; also no. 230.

[316] *Rog(er)i*, no. 229, Plate XXIX, line 1; also *assignati*, no. 230, line 6.

[317] *videl(icet)*, no. 229, Plate XXIX, line 7; also *viginti*, no. 230, line 3.

[318] Nos. 275–6.

[319] e.g. *annuatim*, no. 276, Plate XXX, line 3; also *carta*, line 1, no. 275.

[320] e.g. *de*, no. 276, Plate XXX, line 1; also no. 275.

[321] *An(te)cessor(um)*, line 2, no. 276, Plate XXX; *Almar(ico)*, line 14, no. 275.

[322] e.g. no. 276, Plate XXX, line 1; also no. 275.

[323] Nos. 132, 238, 334.

[324] Examples of ligatures abound; see e.g. *li* in *solidis*, line 2, *in* in *p(er)tinentiis*, line 7, no. 238, Plate XXXI; also *ii* in *edificiis*, line 2, *ui* in *quiete*, line 5, no. 334.

[325] e.g. *abb(at)i*, no. 238, Plate XXXI, line 4.

[326] *hac*, ibid. line 1; also *Thome*, no. 334, line 3.

[327] e.g. *vel*, no. 238, Plate XXXI, line 5; also *lib(er)e*, no. 334, line 5.

[328] e.g. *hac*, no. 238, Plate XXXI, line 1; also no. 334.

[329] e.g. *t(er)re*, no. 238, Plate XXXI, line 2; also *t(er)ram*, line 2, no. 334.

[330] e.g. *confirmaui*, line 1, *Felde*, line 3, no. 238, Plate XXXI.

[331] *Ego*, no. 238, Plate XXXI, line 1; also no. 334.

[332] e.g. no. 238, Plate XXXI, line 1; also no. 334.

[333] No. 292; for the attestation by the (Gloucester) hallmoot, see no. 300.

business hand. It is decorated by various flourishes such as thickened and gracefully curving tails on *g* and *S*, descenders with finishing strokes angled to the right of the final minims of *m*,[334] and especially the crossing of the tailing head of *a* with the bent arm of *d* in *ad*.[335] The tops of ascenders, except those of tall *s*, are often finished with curving strokes to the right. The curving tops of *f* and tall *s* are crossed with a stressed stroke sharply angling downward.[336] Such letters, along with *m* and *ad* as described above and *g*,[337] are distinctive.

Several *acta* written in **Scribe 39**'s hand establish their writer as a borough clerk who recorded transactions in the Gloucester hundred court 1200 × *c*. 1228.[338] The script is a miniaturized, compact business hand adapted from book hand by lengthening ascenders and adding descenders; it can range from left- to right-leaning. The scribe's *g*,[339] *A*,[340] *R*,[341] and tironian *et*[342] are distinctive.

Philip clerk (**Scribe 40**) identified himself as the *scriptor* of two charters which recorded, respectively, a grant and a sale in the Gloucester hundred court 1200 × *c*. 1228.[343] He wrote in a compact formal upright business hand which may lean slightly to left or right with characteristics typical of the early thirteenth century such as the serifed footings on *f*, *l*, and *s*. His ascenders of these letters are disproportionately lengthened, often bowed slightly to the right; and the tops of *f* and *s* are sharply angled downward. Long-tailed *a* is similarly angled. He employed both tironian *con* and *et*.[344] Favoured abbreviation and suspension signs are wavy lengthened perpendicular and horizontal lines of which the latter are finished upward to the right. His *g* is five- or six-stroke with a closed tail variously formed.[345] An introductory *S* may be topped with a partial papal 'coil.'[346] Particular forms of *G*,[347] *R*,[348] and tironian *et* are distinctive.

Active in the early thirteenth century, **Scribe 41** wrote *acta* in a semi-cursive, upright to slightly left-leaning business hand which shows the influence of bookhand. The ascenders of his *b* and *l* can curve to the left and then to the right at the top. Distinctive features of his hand are *d*,[349] terminal *s* with curving descender,[350] *W*, and tironian *et*.[351]

---

[334] e.g. *illam*, no. 300, Plate XXXII, line 2; also *t(er)ram*, no. 292, line 4; note the treatment of tironian *con* on this line.

[335] e.g. *ad*, no. 300, Plate XXXII, line 4; see *ld* in *aldato*, no. 292, line 1.

[336] e.g. *p(re)sentes* and *fut(ur)i*, no. 300, Plate XXXII, line 1; also no. 292.

[337] e.g. *Ego*, no. 300, Plate XXXII, line 1.; also no. 292.

[338] Nos. 306, 316. The witnesses of both charters are all civilians except for Ernesius dean of Gloucester, who appears along with the bailiffs Helias Palmer and William Russel in no. 316.

[339] e.g. *Ego*, no. 316, Plate XXXIII, line 1; also no. 306.

[340] *Abbatie*, no. 316, Plate XXXIII, line 4; also *Alicie*, no. 306, line 1.

[341] *Rad(ulfi)*, line 1, no. 316, Plate XXXIII; *Rog(ero)*, line 9, no. 306.

[342] e.g. no. 316, Plate XXXIII, line 1; also no. 306.

[343] No. 286, Plate XXXIV; G.R.O., GBR/J1/138. As yet I am undecided about the attributions of ibid. nos. 248–50, 266, 269, 271, 273–4, 300–2.

[344] *et*, no. 286, Plate XXXIV, line 1; also G.R.O., GBR/J1/138; *consueui*, no. 286, Plate XXXIV, line 5; also *concessi*, GBR/J1/138, line 1.

[345] e.g. *ego*, no. 286, Plate XXXIV, line 8; also *Ego*, line 1., *mariagio* [sic], line 2, G.R.O., GBR/J1/138.

[346] *Sciant*, no. 286, Plate XXXIV, line 1; also G.R.O., GBR/J1/138.

[347] Compare *Galfridus*, line 1, with *Glouc(estrie)*, line 5, no. 286, Plate XXXIV.

[348] *Ric(ardo)*, line 11, no. 286, Plate XXXIV; also G.R.O., GBR/J1/138, line 7.

[349] e.g. *de*, no. 345, Plate XXXV, line 1; also no. 329.

[350] *suis*, no. 345, Plate XXXV, line 5; also *assignatis*, no. 329, line 4.

[351] No. 345, Plate XXXV, line 1; also no. 329.

The hand of **Scribe 42** is a finely drawn, left-leaning, semi-cursive business hand of the second quarter of the thirteenth century. Tops of ascenders are notched rather than forked and the forms of capitals remain simple. He was active between 1240 and 1265, but the preceding details suggest a date closer to 1240 than to 1265. His hand is characterized by exaggerated legthening of ascenders, the use of a form of coils on *f* and tall *s*, bowl-shaped tail of *g* and tail of the terminal *-us* compendium, and looping tops of *h, l, B,* and the left stroke of *v*. His *g*,[352] *N*,[353] and the *P*-shaped suspension sign are distinctive.[354]

Scribe 43, who was active at least *c.* 1228–40, was one of the most prolific clerks who served the Gloucester hundred court.[355] He wrote a very experienced, slightly left-leaning, modified book hand. Its air of elegance is enhanced by *tituli*, skeletonized *S*, tironian *con*, crossed and lined tironian *et*, and gracefully curved parallel suspension signs. His hand is immediately identifiable by its *g*[356] and by its decorated tironian *et*[357] and *con*.[358] The *nota* for *-ur* is also distinctive.[359]

Scribe 44 recorded land transactions in Gloucester's borough court where the proceedings he recorded might be attested by, among others, the bailiffs, and it is their attestations which place the *scriptor*'s service in 1258.[360] Some of his *acta* never found their way into St. Peter's muniments, which reinforces the classification of this scribe as a borough clerk.[361] The scribe wrote in the semi-cursive style of the 1230s and 40s with an upright hand which could angle slightly to left or right. Descenders are sharply pointed. Bent *d*'s with loops and forking of some ascenders are prominent. Biting with *ar*,[362] *a*,[363] *g*,[364] the doubled nota for *us*,[365] and the form of tironian *et*[366] are indicators of this hand.

Scribe 45 who recorded a grant of property made almost certainly in the Gloucester hundred in 1258 identified himself as William of Cokebury chaplain.[367] Cokebury's hand is another variation of a style in vogue at least from the 1230s until well after 1250. It is an upright bookhand modified for business purposes mostly by the lengthening of ascenders and their treatment by thickened strokes, and looping. Cokebury's thickenings often appear as elongated ovals.[368] Periodically his *f* and tall *s* are topped with strokes parellel to the base line.[369] Such forms along with tironian *et*[370] are distinctive.

---

[352] *ego*, no. 305, Plate XXXVI, line 1; also no. 283.

[353] *Notum*, no. 305, Plate XXXVI, line 1; also no. 283.

[354] *t(er)re*, no. 305, Plate XXXVI, line 2; *quiet(um)*, no. 283, line 2.

[355] No. 290 for the dates of his service. The scribe also wrote nos. 321, 347, and G.R.O., GBR/J1, nos. 223, 233, 239, 265, 283–5, 298–9, 318, 322, 325, 336, 348, 448; poss. GBR/J1/211, 237–8, 245.

[356] *ego*, G.R.O., GBR/J1/223, Plate XXXVII, line 1; also below, no. 321.

[357] G.R.O, GBR/J1/223, Plate XXXVII, line 1; also below, no. 321.

[358] *(con)cessi*, G.R.O., GBR/J1/223, Plate XXXVII, line 1; also below, no. 321.

[359] *fut(ur)i*, G.R.O., GBR/J1/223, Plate XXXVII, line 1; also below, no. 321.

[360] Nos. 298, 330; the scribe also wrote nos. 335–6.

[361] GBR/J1/308, 362.

[362] e.g. *argenti*, G.R.O., GBR/J1/362, Plate XXXVIII, line 7; *zonaria*, below, nos. 298, 330, line 4.

[363] e.g. *mea*, G.R.O., GBR/J1/362, Plate XXXVIII, line 2.

[364] *Ego*, G.R.O., GBR/J1/362, Plate XXXVIII, line 1; also below, no. 298.

[365] e.g. *defendem(us)*, G.R.O., GBR/J1/362, Plate XXXVIII, line 11; *sim(us)*, below, no. 330, line 5.

[366] e.g. G.R.O., GBR/J1/362, line 1; also below, no. 298.

[367] Below, no. 301; the exclusive composition of the witness-list by burghal personalities headed by Gloucester's bailiffs is the basis for attributing the transaction to the hundred court; and the identity of the bailiffs, William of Cheltenham and Roger Lenveyse, establishes the date (*VCH Glos.* iv. 372).

[368] For thickening, e.g. *d* in *dedi*, *h* in *hac*, line 1, *v* in *v(e)l*, line 3, *a* in *carte*, line 9; looping, e.g, *h* in *hac*, line 1, *s* in *scriptore*, line 9, *I* in *Iohanne*, line 8: no. 301, Plate XXXIX.

[369] e.g. *confirmaui* and *concessi*, no. 301, Plate XXXIX, line 1.

[370] e.g. ibid. line 1.

Scribe 46 wrote in a style of the mid-thirteenth century which was adaptable for book as well as documentary production. The witness-lists of his *acta* establish that he served the Gloucester hundred court *c.* 1228 × *c.* 1240.[371] Both halves of a chirograph which he wrote survive.[372] His script is an upright, miniaturized and compact semi-cursive business hand. Ascenders of *b*, *h*, *l*, and tall *s*, are often forked and/or looped.[373] The descender of *r* begins to be extended, as was common in the late thirteenth century.[374] Distinctive forms are *g*,[375] *A*,[376] *R*,[377] *T*,[378] and tironian *et*.[379]

The transactions and witnesses recorded by **Scribe 47** show that he was active in the vicinity of Yarkhill in Herefordshire.[380] His *acta* are written in another semi-cursive business hand of the mid-thirteenth century; but cursive elements are very prominent.[381] His script is miniaturized, compact, and left-leaning; looping of the tops of ascenders is common. The scribe's *g*,[382] *R*,[383] *nota* for suspended *-ur*,[384] and tironian *et*[385] are distinctive.

Scribe 48 recorded a disguised sale by a tenant of St. Peter's *c.* 1258 × 62.[386] He was a prolific burghal *scriptor* whose career can be placed between 1255 and 1269.[387] He wrote in an upright business hand. Introductory *S* is of two types.[388] Noticeable features of his script are some thickening in ascenders, forking, pronounced looping of *d*, and *g* with the tail a straight line parallel to the script line. Looped tironian *et*,[389] suspension signs,[390] *g*,[391] and superscript *a*[392] are distinctive.

IV. *Endorsement clerks*

As early as King Henry I's reign, an archive was initiated at St. Peter's to preserve *acta* which recorded such details as benefits which the abbey received from patrons, agreements to which the abbey was a party, or the terms of subinfeudations which St. Peter's itself

---

[371] Nos. 278–9, 318–19; *VCH Glos.* iv. 371.

[372] Nos. 318–19.

[373] e.g. see *bona*, line 1, *hac*, line 2, *voluntate*, and *presentes*, line 1, no. 318, Plate XL; also *Matildis*, *hac*, *confirmaui*, line 1, *pollicibus*, line 5, no. 278.

[374] e.g. *futuri*, no. 318, Plate XL, line 1; also *carta*, no. 278.

[375] *Ego*, no. 318, Plate XL, line 1; also no. 278.

[376] *Alano*, no. 318, Plate XL, line 19; also no. 278, line 12.

[377] e.g. *Regis*, no. 318, Plate XL, line 5; also *Retro*, no. 278, line 4.

[378] *Terra*, no. 318, Plate XL, line 4; also no. 278, line 3.

[379] e.g. no. 318, Plate XL, line 1; also no. 278.

[380] Nos. 326–7, 340.

[381] e.g. *suis*, *cuicumque*, line 4, *sui*, line 6, no. 326, Plate XLI; also *solidis*, line 2, *tenuit*, line 4, *cum*, line 6, no. 340.

[382] e.g. *Ego*, no. 326, Plate XLI, line 1; also no. 340.

[383] *Ricardus*, no. 326, Plate XLI, line 1; also *Radulfo*, no. 340, line 12.

[384] *Fut(ur)i*, no. 326, Plate XLI, line 1; also no. 340.

[385] No. 326, Plate XLI, line 1; also no. 340.

[386] No. 287.

[387] Ibid.; G.R.O., GBR/J1/545, 578; *VCH Glos.* iv. 372, for dating; the scribe also wrote GBR/J1/173, 207, 363, 373, 466, 510, 549, 566–7.

[388] *Sciant*, below, no. 287, Plate XLII, line 1; also e.g. G.R.O., GBR/J1/363.

[389] Below, no. 287, Plate XLII, line 1; also e.g. G.R.O., GBR/J1/207.

[390] *q(uo)d*, below, no. 287, Plate XLII, line 1; also e.g. G.R.O., GBR/J1/207.

[391] *Ego*, below, no. 287, Plate XLII, line 1; also e.g. G.R.O., GBR/J1/207.

[392] *assignati*, below, no. 287, Plate XLII, line 7; also e.g. *contra*, G.R.O., GBR/J1/207, line 12.

made. One of the king's charters recording a verdict of his court in favour of the abbey's possession of the manor of Coln Rogers is one of the earliest authentic originals to survive from St. Peter's muniments.[393] The abbey's documentary preservation was related to the increasing Anglo-Norman reliance of legal proceedings upon written evidence.[394] Abbot Gilbert Foliot has even become a bit notorious for having used forged evidence to gain the upper hand in the abbey's proprietary dispute with the archbishop of York over the possession of several manors.[395]

Gloucester scribes were closely associated with this archival development by helping to organize the abbatial charter collection. Individual charters were commonly stored folded, text inside, in thirds twice: first from top to foot, then sideways. So, first of all, to facilitate reference to their contents, Scribe 2 and others endorsed them with cryptic identifying descriptions on one of the external surfaces which remained visible after the folding process.[396] Secondly, as growth along with diversification of contents occurred, charters were stored in numbered chests (*capsule*) which were divided among several categories such as ecclesiastical and lay tenures, and the scribes added appropriate endorsements indicating the appropriate chest number and category to which the document belonged.[397] Ultimately, but beyond the scope of this study, Gloucester archival efforts created cartularies or registers to preserve copies of its *acta* against loss of or damage to the originals.[398]

Those associated with these scribal storage and organizational efforts can be considered the abbatial archive's 'filing clerks.' There are acute problems associated with the identification of such individuals. One involves establishing the identify of an individual endorsement hand. By definition, the texts on which to base palaeographical comparisons are short and mere similarities in scripts do not necessarily constitute proof of identity. Then there is the problem of determining when endorsers were active – certainly after the *acta* they endorsed were written, but how long after? An endorsement hand compatible with Stephen's reign appears on the charter of Henry I cited above and indicates one of the earliest 'filing' efforts.[399] An *actum* of Archbishop Theobald addressed to St. Peter's provides another.[400] A grant by writ from Earl Ranulf of Chester bears endorsements in several mid-twelfth century hands.[401] So far these and many other endorsers have yet to be identified, but from Henry II's reign on, the increasing involvement of these individuals has left two or more samples by which to indentify the following clerical hands.

Hand a. 1153; s. xii^2: nos. 201, 248 (Plate XLIIIa), 389; poss. no. 382.

Hand b. *c.* 1165 × 80; s. xii^2: nos. 201, 252 (Plate XLIIIb), 253.

Hand c/Scribe 2. 1148 × 55; s. xii^{med}: no. 247 (Plate XLIIIc).

Hand d/Scribe 4. 1148 × 79; s. xii^{med}: no. 61 (Plate XLIIId); poss. no. 71.

---

[393] Below, no. 39, datable to 22 May 1127: *Regesta*, ii, no. 1485; see also below, nos. 248, 389.
[394] On this process see Clanchy, *From Memory to Written Record*.
[395] *GFAL*, 124–5.
[396] e.g. below, nos. 201, 247–8, 389; see below **Hands a and b**.
[397] **Hands b** and **h** are prime examples; David Walker, 'Gloucester Charters', 250, long ago noted this trend; for the evidence of *capsule*, see below, pp. lix–lx.
[398] They are described in Davis, *Medieval Cartularies*, 51–52; see also Walker, 'Organization of Material in Medieval Cartularies', 133–4.
[399] No. 39; compare *Gileb' de Min'* e.g. with Warner & Ellis, no. 22, Salter, *Oxford Charters*, no. 64, or *Regesta*, iv, Plate XXXVb.
[400] Below, no. 384.
[401] Below, no. 201.

Hand e. 1148 × 79; s. xii^2: nos. 60 (Plate XLIIIe), 63–64, 66.

Hand f. 1205 × 24; s. xii^{ex} × s. xiii^{in}: nos. 65, 76, 114 (Plate XLIIIf), 139–40, 250; poss. no. 130.

Hand g. *c*. 1175 × 1205; s. xii^{ex} × s. xiii^{in}: nos. 75 (Plate XLIIIg), 87, 222, 309.

Hand h. 1197 × s. xiii^{in}; s. xii^{ex} × s. xiii^{in}: nos. 56, 72, 105 (Plate XLIIIh), 357; poss. nos. 38, 217, 246–7, 257.

Hand i/Scribe 7. 1179 × 1205; s. xii^{ex} × s. xiii^{in}: nos. 68, 74 (Plate XLIIIi), 100.

Hand j. Active 1179 × 1205+ and 1181+: nos. 89 (Plate XLIVa), 103.

Hand k. –1231; s. xii^{ex} × s. xiii^{in}: nos. 262 (Plate XLIVb), 263–6.

Hand l. 1228 × 43; s. xiii$^{med × ex}$: nos. 67, 73, 94–95 (Plate XLIVc), 98, 110, 115–18, 128, 144–5, 151, 163.

Hand m. s. xiii^{in}; s. xiii^{med}: nos. 110, 204, 242 (Plate XLIVd); see also no. 337.

Hand n. s. xiii^{in}; s. xiii^1: nos. 70, 131, 343 (Plate XLIVe).

Hand o/Scribe 17. 1228 × 43; s. xiii^1: nos. 132, 146 (Plate XLIVf), 154–6; poss. no. 147.

Hand p/Scribe 34. s. xiii^{med}; s. xiii^{med}: no. 240 (Plate XLIVg).

Hand q. *c*. 1259; s. xiii^{med}: nos. 181, 267 (Plate XLIVh), 268; poss. no. 203.

Hand r. 1258; s. xiii^{med}: nos. 219, 298, 330 (Plate XLIVi).

Hand s. xiii^{med}; s. xiii^{med}: nos. 326 (Plate XLIVj), 327; poss. nos. 94–95.

Hand t. *c*. 1225 × 40; s. xiii^{med}: nos. 62, 122, 146 (Plate XLIVk), 310.

DIPLOMATIC OF THE ABBATIAL CHARTERS

Charters issued in the names of the abbot and convent of St. Peter's conformed to a number of the general drafting trends in post-Conquest secretarial activities. To judge from St. Peter's earliest extant originals and copies, the community began to rely on forms of the writ-charter to record proprietary transactions about the same time as other Anglo-Norman lords increasingly did so, in the second quarter of the twelfth century.[402] The earliest extant abbatial originals and copy were issued during the abbacy of Walter de Lacy (1131–9),[403]

---

[402] Concerning the availability of original *acta* of religious communities after the second quarter of the twelfth century, see the comment of Pierre Chaplais, 'Westminster Charters', 90; the earldom of Chester's earliest extant original dates from 1130 × 40: Webber, 'Scribes and Handwriting', 140; the earliest originals from the earldom of Gloucester, 11 Jan. 1148 × 50 (Patterson, *EGC*, nos. 96, 179; ibid. no. 172 also may date from this period). See also Stenton, *English Feudalism*, 153; Clanchy, *From Memory to Written Record*, 54–56; Brooke, 'St. Peter of Gloucester', 58; Hudson, 'Diplomatic and Legal Aspects of the Charters', 162.

[403] Below, nos. 58–59; *Cart. Glouc.* i, no. 213; see also ibid. no. 135; ii, no. 571, which, although notifications of donations to St. Peter's, may have been written under the abbey's auspices; less certain is a donor's notification addressed to Abbot William in letter form: ibid. no. 189; Registers A & B contain no abbatial charter texts earlier than Gilbert Foliot's.

and multiple copies begin only with the abbacy of Gilbert Foliot (1139–48).[404] For the abbacies of Serlo through to William Godemon there are only *notitie* of grants and acquisitions recorded in St. Peter's charter-chronicle, the 'Historia,' a not uncommon device in England and Normandy, as Christopher Brooke has pointed out, for keeping track of proprietary acquisitions by beneficiaries.[405] Indeed, several of Gloucester's earliest originals and the earliest copy reveal some formulaic affinity to *notitie*.[406]

Like so many monastic communities, the form for its charters which St. Peter's preferred was the bipartite chirograph with a single turn-up for appending the abbot's seal *sur double queue*.[407] This documentary form consisted originally of duplicate texts of an agreement copied on a single parchment, between which the word *CYROGRAPHUM* or *CIROGRAPHUM* was usually written; then a cut, either straight or zig-zag, was made through the middle of the word. This provided the abbey and the other party involved with a copy, the cut end of which could be matched with the cut end of the abbey's copy as a test of authenticity in case of a dispute over the chirograph's terms.[408]

By the mid twelfth century abbatial charters were drafted to include current conventional diplomatic components, the superscription, address, dispositive, authentication, and witness clauses,[409] but warranty clauses, increasingly common in the thirteenth century, were rarely used.[410] Gloucester's practice of authenticating its *acta* by appended seals, at least from the time of Abbot Hamelin, was also in keeping with the contemporary view of the legal importance of sealed *acta* operative by the mid twelfth century.[411]

St. Peter's charters, like other private ones, generally were cast in the form of notifications.[412] Typically Gloucester's were introduced by the formula 'Sciant presentes et futuri quod . . .,' followed by the *intitulatio* and then by one or more dispositive subordinate

---

[404] *LCGF*, nos. 284–8; Gilbert's letters are not included in this edition because they survive only in copies (ibid. nos. 1–78).

[405] Above, p. xxiv & nn.; Brooke, 'St. Peter of Gloucester', 58. It is possible that even earlier charters were casualties of fires at Gloucester, especially that of 1122: B.L., Cott. MS. Vesp. A.v, fol. 197v; *ASC*, a. 1122; 'Winchcombe Annals', a. 1101, 1122; John of Worcester, 17 (1122); 'Historia', 12 (1102 for 1101?), 14–15 (1122); Finberg, *Charters of W. Midlands*, 11.

[406] Below, no. 59; see also no. 389; *Cart. Glouc.* i, no. 213; see also ibid. no. 135; ii, no. 571.

[407] e.g. below, nos. 67–68; for the popularity of the bipartite chirograph, see Chaplais, 'Westminster Charters', 90 & n.; some chirographs were sealed *sur simple queue*: e.g. below, no. 60.

[408] Surviving pairs are nos. 67–68, 83–84, 115–16, 121–2, 150–1, 153–4, 155–6, 157–8; see in general, Clanchy, *From Memory to Written Record*, 87–88.

[409] For Anglo-Norman royal charters, see *Regesta*, iv. 9; for comital *acta* see Patterson, *EGC*, 21–23; Hudson, 'Diplomatic and Legal Aspects of the Charters', 155–77; for episcopal charters, Cheney, *English Bishops' Chanceries*, 58–90; in general, Stenton, *Gilbertine Charters*, pp. xvii–xix, xxvii–xxxii.

[410] Below, nos. 18–19 (1205 × 24), 181 (1246 × 50), 187 (1254); but note the possible inability to warrant in no. 70 (1148 × 79); for the general trend, see Stenton, *English Feudalism*, 161 & n.; idem, *Gilbertine Charters*, p. xviii; Hyams, 'Warranty and Good Lordship', 455, 474–6; Hudson, *Land, Law, and Lordship*, 53.

[411] Below, no. 70. For this phenomenon as reflected by episcopal *acta*, see Brooke, 'English Episcopal *Acta*', 44, 52; in general, Clanchy, *From Memory To Written Record*, 310, 316; Bishop, *Scriptores Regis*, 2. For modern researchers, it may be necessary to establish the authenticity of seals from that of their charters: Chaplais, 'Seals and Original Charters of Henry I', 260–2; Mortimer, 'Charters of Henry I', 121. See below, nos. 91 & n., 95. For an exception to the practice, see no. 72.

[412] *LCGF*, 23.

clauses, the primary verb of which was usually in the perfect indicative or infinitive mood, most often the indicative.[413]

Concedere was the primary dispositive verb most heavily relied upon by the abbey in the period *c.* 1130–1263 and could be used to express an original grant, a regrant to an heir, and a confirmation.[414] It seldom appears, however, in the combination *dare et concedere* as was common in other landlords' charters for original grants and regrants, following *reddere et* for regrants, or preceding *et confirmare* for regrants and confirmations.[415]

St. Peter's abbatial charters also employed other diplomatic terms which became standard charter terminology during the twelfth century. One of the best examples is the phrase *in feodo et hereditate* which feudal landlords used in grants of heritable tenures owing some type of secular service, frequently military service. In Gloucester's abbatial charters, however, the phrase appears in connection with alienations owing secular but non-military service.[416] Frankalmoign terminology *in elemosinam* and variations such as *in perpetuam elemosinam* and *in puram et perpetuam elemosinam* abound in charters benefiting Gloucester from laymen.[417] Such grants were intended to obtain for donors spiritual benefits and often secular, non-military, services from ecclesiastical beneficiaries.[418] Among abbatial originals, however, such phraseology only survives in one charter, awarding a cleric his benefice in return for an annual rent.[419] Another difference between St. Peter's variations of the writ-charter and episcopal *acta* is the general absence of pious *arenge* from Gloucester's.[420]

Certain portions of charters issued in the names of the abbot and convent reveal that components of a house style were being developed by the abbey's secretarial personnel over the second half of the twelfth century. Originally superscription clauses did not employ uniform formulas.[421] *N. abbas totusque conuentus* was used under Walter de Lacy and apparently under Gilbert Foliot, who also seems to have employed several other forms.[422]

---

[413] As seen in the earliest extant abbatial original: no. 58.

[414] Original grants: e.g. nos. 60, 70 (1148 × 79), 127 (1205 × 24), 157 (1228 × 43); regrants to heirs, e.g. nos. 66 (1148 × 79), 96 (1179 × 1205), 102 (1179 × 1205), 114 (1205 × 24); see also nos. 37 (1205 × 15), 61 (1148 × 79); confirmations: e.g. nos. 79 (1179 × 1205), 160 (1228 × 43).

[415] Nos. 17 (1179 × 1205), 118 (1205 × 24); Galbraith, 'Monastic Foundation Charters', 296, for original gifts; for regrants and confirmations, see also Stenton, *English Feudalism*, 162; Thorne, 'English Feudalism and Estates in Land', 199, 202; Hudson, *Land, Law, and Lordship*, 72–77, 214. *Reddere, reddere et confirmare,* and *dare et reddere* were also used by other lords for regrants, but not in usual abbatial *acta*: Hudson, *Land, Law, and Lordship*, 72–77, esp. 75–76.

[416] e.g. below, nos. 61–63, and other references in the Index of Subjects; note the tenurial distinction involving the phrase in no. 71; Thorne, 'English Feudalism and Estates in Land', 202; Milsom, *Legal Framework of English Feudalism, passim,* esp. 176–82; Holt, 'The Revolution of 1066', 198–201; idem, 'Notions of Patrimony', 193, 196, 198, 215; Palmer, 'Origins of Property', 18–19, 23; Hyams, 'The Charter as a Source', 181, 184; Hudson, 'Life Grants of Land', 67–80; idem, *Land, Law, and Lordship,* Chap. 3, esp. pp. 90 & n., 91–97, 101–6, 176.

[417] e.g. below, nos. 47–48, 201, 389 and other references in the Index of Subjects.

[418] Kimball, 'Frank Almoign', 341–2, 350; Hudson, *Land, Law, and Lordship*, 90–91, 101; note the distinction drawn in idem, 'Life Grants of Land', 76; Thompson, 'Free Alms Tenure', esp. 225, 229–31 & nn., 235–9, 241; Postles, 'Tenure in Frankalmoin and Knight Service', 19–20, 24, 27–28; idem, 'Gifts in Frankalmoign', 333–4.

[419] Below, no. 86.

[420] Ths strongest case seems to be *diuine pietatis intuitu* in no. 37; see Cheney, *English Bishops' Chanceries*, 71–75; Barrow, *Hereford Episcopal Acta*, pp. lxxii–lxxxiii.

[421] The point has been made by David Walker, 'Gloucester Charters', 254.

[422] Below, no. 58; *LCGF*, nos. 285–8.

Walter also used a simple *Walt(erus) abbas*.[423] Under Hamelin two styles were favoured: variations of *ego Hamel' dei gratia abbas et conuentus sancti Petri Gloec'* and of *ego Hamel' dei gratia abbas et conuentus Gloec'*. A more standard formula emerged between the abbacies of Thomas Carbonel and John de Felda. The former of Hamelin's favoured styles became the basis of Carbonel's, and his successors departed from this formula mainly by substituting *Glouc'* for *Gloec'*.[424] Notification sections of dispositive clauses reflected this shared responsibility by wording such as *Sciant presentes et futuri quod*, followed by the plural form of the dispositive verb. The elements expressing joint authority reflect several influences. The Benedictine Rule mandated that abbots elicit counsel from their communities before taking important actions,[425] and there were canonical strictures against alienation of church possessions by bishops without the consent of their chapters.[426] One of the earliest and most explicit expressions of this notion of governance found among the St. Peter's extant originals, *concessu capituli sancti Petri Gloec(estrie)*, occurs in the sole surviving original issued in Walter de Lacy's name in which the first person singular form *concessi* is used;[427] abbatial seals, with a 'house' obverse and a personal abbatial counterseal on the reverse, reiterate the dualistic notion of governance.[428] Nevertheless, at St. Peter's the abbot's authority was diplomatically stressed at least from the time of Abbot Hamelin by combining *dei gratia*, an apparent borrowing of the popular episcopal style, with the abbatial title.[429]

Alienation charters by the abbot and convent provide the most ample and detailed evidence of formulaic development and creation of a house style. Such *acta*, as David Walker noted long ago, gradually acquired increased uniformity over the course of the twelfth century.[430] This is particularly true of charters written by St. Peter's for its local Gloucester burghal and suburban tenants.[431] Representative of their fully developed format is a grant of property by Abbot John de Felda (1243–63) and the convent to one John smith of Travel Lane.[432] The transaction was recorded in the form of a bipartite chirograph containing thirteen main subsections expressed in wording which was standard for such grants and placed in an order from which few such grants departed: 1) notification; 2) *intitulatio*; 3) dispositive statement of concession, including identification of the property, introduced by *concessimus*, etc.; 4) terms of tenure, generally *in feodo et hereditate*, introduced by *Tenendam . . .*; 5) specification of rent, *Reddendo inde nobis . . .* (or the like), often with due-date(s) for payment; 6) property measurements: *Predicta uero terra per uisum legalium uirorum mensurata . . .*; 7) property valuation, *Quando . . . predictus n. predictam terram a nobis recepit . . .*; 8) warranty against loss of the property's value if the tenant leaves, *Si uero aliquo casu emergente ipse uel heredes sui dictam terram reliquirent, simile edificium uel pretium nobis restituent*; 9) the tenant's oath of fealty to St. Peter's in respect to the payment of rent, *Idem uero iuramentum nobis prestitit, quod fidelis erit ecclesie nostre et maxime de reddendo redditu nostro . . . statutis terminis*; 10) the tenant's oath to protect the abbey from damages arising from the tenure and to accept restrictions on alienations, *Iurauit etiam quod nec artem nec ingenium exquiret vnde domus nostra per*

---

[423] Below, no. 58.
[424] e.g. nos. 60, 67, 78, 108, 144, 150, 171.
[425] *RB*, Cap. iii, fols. 11v–12; an early example in an original is no. 58; Knowles, *MOE*, 411–17.
[426] Hudson, *Land, Law, and Lordship*, 230–40.
[427] No. 58; see also esp. *LCGF*, nos. 286–7.
[428] See below, pp. lvi–lvii.
[429] Cheney, *English Bishops' Chanceries*, 63.
[430] Walker, 'Gloucester Charters', 254–5; see also Hilton, 'Gloucester Abbey Leases', 12.
[431] For formulaic application to lands elsewhere, see below, e.g. nos. 90, 171, 179.
[432] No. 173.

tenuram suam dampnum incurrat . et quod predictam terram neque uendet neque excambiet, neque in uadimonium ponet, neque alicui in feudum et hereditatem tradet, neque ad alium locum religionis transferet sine assensu et uoluntate nostra; 11) obligation of the tenant's heirs to renew the oath upon their succession: *Eandem securitatem nobis facient heredes sui cum singuli sibi succedent . . .*; 12) corroboration clause stating that the agreement was executed in the chirograph format and describing the sealing, *In cuius rei testimonium presens scriptum in modum cyrographi inter nos confectum est. Cuius unam partem sigillo ecclesie nostre munitam dicto N. tradidimus. Alteram uero partem sigillo ipsius roboratam penes nos retinuimus*; 13) a witness-list introduced by *Hiis testibus* with the names of witnesses in the ablative case.

Adoption of this format occurred in stages between the abbacies of Walter de Lacy and John de Felda. Contrary to a long-held view about freedom of sale at Gloucester, St. Peter's was particularly sensitive to guard against unauthorised alienations by its tenants.[433] Restrictions first appear in the lone extant original issued in Abbot Walter de Lacy's name (1130–39): *Uideat etiam ne eam alicui uendet nec in uadimonium mittat.*[434] Although the exact chronology is not clear, the abbacy of Hamelin (1148–79) seems to have been the time when the distinctive formulaic elements pertaining to property specification, terms and amount of rent, terms of tenants' oaths, and the chirograph subclause began to be adopted by the St. Peter's secretarial scribes.[435] The wording, however, in several of these deeds, while conveying the sense of their later formulaic counterparts, lacks their later generally uniform wording.[436] During the abbacy of Thomas Carbonel (1179–1205), measurement, property valuation, and warranty clauses, and the formulas providing for oaths of fealty to St. Peter's by grantees' heirs or successors make their initial appearance.[437] These oaths imposed by the abbey on its tenants, especially its urban ones, were in specified terms of feudal tenure, albeit of a manorial nature, and were no mere conventional phrases.[438] Under Thomas's successor, Henry Blont (1205–24), most of the original charters recording grants to the abbey's Gloucester tenants contain virtually the same clauses and formulaic wording as the sample cited above,[439] and the trend of uniformity continued during the abbacies of Thomas of Bredon (1224–28) and Henry Foliot (1228–43).[440] Finally, with virtual standardization of

---

[433] Hemmeon, *Burgage Tenure*, 112 & n., 184; elsewhere Hemmeon admitted that a lord's right of *retrait* may have existed at Gloucester, but he claimed that there was little evidence of it: 53–54 & n., 121 n.; in addition he recognized that restrictions on mortgaging were common with ecclesiastical lords, but did not mention St. Peter's as an example, 147. Tait, *The Medieval English Borough*, 101, is more cautious about the absence of restrictions on alienations by the tenants of lords other than the king in post-Conquest boroughs.

[434] No. 58. The abbey's restrictions on tenants' freedom to alienate their tenancies run counter to Hemmeon's belief in freedom of sale at Gloucester and provide examples in a town of major importance of an ecclesiastical lord restricting tenants' rights to mortgage; see Hemmeon, *Burgage Tenure*, 112 & n., 147; Hemmeon was apparently unaware of the abbey's restrictions on alienations in mortmain: ibid. 113 & n. For restrictions placed on tenants by Llanthony Priory in the early thirteenth century, see below, n. 459.

[435] See esp. nos. 60–64, 66–69.

[436] Esp. portions of clauses 10 and 12.

[437] Nos. 75, 78–79, 87–88, 93, 97, 99.

[438] Note the remark of Hemmeon, *Burgage Tenure*, 47, that 'in some of the baronial and ecclesiastical boroughs fealty had more of a feudal meaning or at least a feudal sound.'

[439] For the best examples see nos. 108,·111, 114, 119, 121–2, 129–30, 133–5, 137, 143; see also no. 20. Some of Henry Blont's charters do not use all of the clauses.

[440] For Thomas of Bredon, see nos. 144, 146–7; for Henry Foliot, nos. 152–9, 161–3.

the corroboration clause under John de Felda (1243–63), the formulaic development was completed.[441]

By the early thirteenth century, a few exceptions to the fully developed format may have resulted from careless scribal drafting.[442] Some diplomatic anomalies may be the work of alien scribes.[443] In other cases, special circumstances might require additional clauses such as an expression of *retrait féodal*.[444] 'Poor risk' tenants might need reminding of the abbey's right to repossess in the event of non-payment of rent;[445] potential brewers would be charged for the privilege;[446] and the absence of buildings on properties needed to be noted because of tenants' warranty obligations.[447] Nevertheless, major formulaic variations, especially those which coexisted with the dominant style of John de Felda's abbacy, suggest that drafting was not closely supervised.[448]

Unquestionably St. Peter's secretarial administration should be credited with developing a highly uniform house style; but the originality of this accomplishment is difficult to determine. In some cases Gloucester scribes applied legal notions and formulas which were in circulation. Some restrictions on alienations were common among *acta* of ecclesiastical lords. In a *conventio* of *c.* 1190 between Abbot Samson of Bury St. Edmunds and a tenant, the tenant is said to swear to preserve his monastic landlord from damages in the following terms: *iurauit etiam quod nec artem nec ingenium queret . . . per quod sanctus Ædmundus et conuentus ius . . . amittant aut in aliquo eis immimuatur aut super hoc uexeritur. . . .*[449] Corroboration clauses in the abbot's grants dating from the very early thirteenth century contain phrases relating to use of the chirograph format and sealing in terms similar to St. Peter's.[450] Richard son of Algar swore fealty in 1182 to St. Paul's London and to the terms of his lease.[451] Reading abbey could claim right of distraint for non-payment of rent roughly during the second quarter of the thirteenth century.[452] Ballard noted the frequency of warranty and sealing clauses in the charters of bishops and lay lords elsewhere.[453]

The formulas of the St. Peter's alienations were also used at Gloucester in *acta* of some of the abbey's tenants acting as mesne lords. Property belonging to Henry Kais which St. Peter's acquired was granted by Kais to Thomas of Evesham 1200 × *c.* 1228 in terms similar to abbatial *acta*.[454] Another example is a grant datable to *c.* 1228 × 40 from Alice daughter of Reginald Welbert to Hugh girdler, which contains among other comparable

---

[441] Nos. 172–8, 184–6, 188–9.

[442] e.g. clause 2 of no. 134; juxtaposition of parts of clause 7 of no. 131 and of parts of clause 10 of no. 110; and the use of *confecimus* instead of *confectum est* in clause 12 of no. 139.

[443] e.g. nos. 21, 392.

[444] No. 111; see Hemmeon, *Burgage Tenure*, 53–54 & n.; Hudson, *Land, Law, and Lordship*, 229 n.

[445] Below, nos. 172–3, 178.

[446] Nos. 143, 150–1, 153–6, 178.

[447] Nos. 113, 115–16, 120, 126, 128, 136; see also no. 131; for other examples of special clauses, see nos. 83, 119.

[448] For formulaic exceptions in John de Felda's charters, see e.g. the following clauses: notification: nos. 21, 392; superscription: nos. 21, 182, 187, 392; corroboration: nos. 179, 181, 183, 187–9, 392.

[449] Davis, *Kalendar of Abbot Samson*, no. 90; see also *Westminster Abbey Charters*, no. 236; Harvey, *Westminster Abbey and its Estates*, 118–19.

[450] Davis, *Kalendar of Abbot Samson*, nos. 147–8; see also Urry, *Canterbury*, e.g. nos. XXIX, XLI.

[451] Gibbs, *Early Charters of St. Paul's*, no. 220; see also *Westminster Abbey Charters*, nos. 288, 290, 294–5; Urry, *Canterbury*, no. XXXIII.

[452] *Cart. Reading*, nos. 502, 511; no. 512 dates from 1278.

[453] *Borough Charters*, i, p. xxiv.

[454] Below, no. 315. A charter of John of Great Witcombe and his wife Edith confirming land on Longsmith Street to Nicholas of Hereford does so to a lesser degree (no. 347).

sections the measurement, valuation, warranty, and sealing clauses of its monastic overlord.[455] One might suspect the influence of the monastic overlord's diplomatic practices in these cases, even though some at least, were recorded in the hundred court;[456] there is, however, evidence that a transaction of an abbatial tenant in the hundred could be relatively free of the diplomatic influence of St. Peter's.[457] St. Peter's-like clauses also appear in *acta* benefiting the abbey.[458]

Furthermore, there are cases of other Gloucester landlords who were not tenants of St. Peter's employing identical or very similar clauses in their alienations. Llanthony priory under Prior John (*c.* 1217–40) employed very similar clauses in several Gloucester and Bristol grants.[459] So too did Kingswood abbey and Richard son of Walter Kadifer in charters recording transactions in the borough court which occurred outside of the St. Peter's tenurial orbit.[460] A charter of Walter de Croili granting a messuage by the Cross in Gloucester and other properties restricted the tenant's right to subinfeudate them to a religious house.[461]

ABBATIAL SEALS

St. Peter's, like their contemporary lords and tenants, sought to ensure the authenticity of *acta* by the use of appended seals.[462] The earliest extant abbatial seal which can be dated with certainty is Hamelin's,[463] although there is apparent physical evidence for the use of an

---

[455] No. 344.

[456] No. 290 (*coram hundredo Glouc'*). Nos. 315, 344 (bailiffs' names first in the witness-lists).

[457] No. 320, a charter (1200 × *c.* 1228) of Isabel, daughter of Ralph Kechel, contains few of the distinguishing clauses except the warranty and sealing clauses and these do not use the exact wording of the St. Peter's formulas. No. 320 (*c.* 1199 × 1200) may be another example even though it is not certain from the witness-list that the transaction occurred in the Gloucester hundred.

[458] e.g. nos. 215 (s. xiii^med), 258 (*c.* 1225 × 50).

[459] P.R.O., C 115/K2/6683, Sect. V, no. 77 (e.g. *Que mensurata est per visum legalium hominum . . .; Quando . . . predictam terram cum edificiis a nobis receptam edificia super inuenta apreciata fuerunt pro octo marcis . et si contingat quod idem R. uel heredes sui dictam terram nobis resignare voluerint. de consimili edificio uel de viii marcas nobis respondebunt. . . . neque vendent neque escambient neque in vadimonium ponent neque alicui in feodum et hereditatem tradent neque ad alium locum religionis sine assensu nostro transferrent. . . . nobis iuramentum prestitit et heredes sui similiter facient.*); Sect. XIII, no. 3 (e.g. *Dictus . . . iuramentum nobis quod fidelis erit ecclesie nostre de redditu nostro statutis terminis . . . soluendo. et quod nec artem nec ingenium exquiret vnde domus nostra per tenuram suam dampnum incurrat.*); no. 4 (e.g. *Eandem vero securitatem quam idem . . . nobis fecit; facient nobis attornati sui singuli sibi succedentes.*) See also a charter of Nicholas Haym of Bristol: ibid. Sect. XIII, no. 7.

[460] B.C.M., Select Chs. nos. 139 [1200 × *c.* 1228], 189 [*c.* 1200], 310 [*c.* 1240 × *c.* 1265]; Jeayes, nos. 139, 189, 310. In Richard son of Walter Kadifer's charter for David Dunning (no. 139) especially note the clause, *Et ego Ricardus sepedictus affidaui quod nec queram artem uel ingenium per me uel per alium vnde predictus Dauid uel heredes sui sint aliquid perdentes uel dampnum incurrant de predicta terra.* In no. 189, note e.g. *Sepedictus . . . Rog(er)us . . . iurauit . quod non queret artem uel ingenium quo . . ..* In no. 310, note e.g. *fide media affidaui . quod non queram artem nec ingenium per me nec per aliquem alium vnde . . ..*

[461] P.R.O., C 115/K2/6683, Sect. II, no. 48, dated 1234 (*Habend' et tenend' . . . sibi et heredibus . vel cuicumque assignare voluerit; preter ad domum religionis . . .*).

[462] See in general Clanchy, *From Memory to Written Record*, 87–88, 308–17; Bishop, *Scriptores Regis*, 16–17 & nn.; *Guide to Seals*, 14–21; Cheney, *English Bishops' Chanceries*, 48–49.

[463] Below, no. 70. For an evaluation of H.C.L., no. A.541, see below, n. 479.

abbatial seal as early as Walter de Lacy.[464] It is evident that by the late twelfth century the abbey adopted a policy about how they were to be appended. *Acta* from the abbacy of Walter de Lacy, perhaps reflecting the earliest practice, were sealed *sur simple queue*, by attachment to a tongue which was created, possibly along with a wrapping tie, by one or two cuts made usually across the foot of a document.[465] There are possibly not more than two to six examples of the continued use of this method during the abbacies of Hamelin and Thomas Carbonel,[466] for in their time a new system became dominant and the writ-like method of sealing was reserved for letters.[467] Aside from the few exceptions just noted, after 1148 × 79 seals were appended *sur double queue*, usually by means of parchment tags inserted through slits in the feet of *acta*.[468] Most often the foot was strengthened by folding up a small portion of the foot to create a double-ply turn-up (*plica*) to better support the tag and seal, but there are quite a few cases of appending seals *sur double queue* without any turn-up.[469] Gloucester clerks also experimented with a method of reinforcing the tag's attachment still further. This involved passing the tag through three parallel cuts made in the turn-up. One end of the tag was first inserted through the top cut; then the projecting ends were pushed inward through the lower slit and then out through the third cut made along the fold of the turn-up. This technique was never used widely.[470] Even more exceptional was sealing by means of cords.[471]

In the case of bipartite chirograph-grants, the half provided to the abbey's tenants usually received the current abbot's seal,[472] and for virtually all of Hamelin's abbacy (1148–79) only that portion was sealed, as the authentication clauses specifically state.[473] Possibly under Thomas Carbonel (1179–1205), and almost certainly under his successors, Henry Blont and Thomas of Bredon, both copies generally were sealed, with the abbey's copy probably bearing the tenant's seal, even though the authentication formulas at this point in time might only state ambiguously that the chirograph bore the abbey's seal,[474] or that a sealed copy was given to the tenant without mention of sealing on the abbey's copy.[475]

---

[464] No. 58.

[465] No. 59.

[466] Nos. 60, 62–63, 66 (the physical evidence is not certain), 69, 96, 102.

[467] Nos. 124–5; Cheney, *English Bishops' Chanceries*, 49, noted that among episcopal *acta* use of sealing *sur simple queue* became reserved to administrative mandates toward the end of the twelfth century.

[468] Regarding these two methods, see Bishop, *Scriptores Regis*, 16–17; Cheney, *English Bishops' Chanceries*, 47–48.

[469] Nos. 68, 70, 73, 74 (also had a tie), 77, 85, 94–95, 114, 138; *Guide to Seals*, 15–16; Bishop, *Scriptores Regis*, 18 & nn.

[470] Nos. 17, 78, 99, 129, 357, 370–1, 392. See also nos. 92, 155 where the evidence is uncertain but likely.

[471] No. 112.

[472] This statement is based on the physical evidence of sealing on the *acta* and the wording of authentication formulas. There is evidence of sealing even on surviving halves with no mention of sealing in their authentication clauses. See below, n. 475. No. 61, which bears no sign of sealing, instead of being an exception, can be explained as the half retained by the abbey during the abbacy of Hamelin, when such copies were unsealed: e.g. no. 63.

[473] e.g. no. 60.

[474] For Hamelin, nos. 69–70; for Thomas Carbonel, e.g. esp. the two halves, nos. 80–81.

[475] Under Hamelin, no. 70; Thomas Carbonel, nos. 80–81; Henry Blont, esp. both halves, nos. 121–2; several of Henry's *acta* bear no sign of sealing: e.g. no. 132; for Henry Foliot, e.g. esp. both halves, nos. 157–8.

Some chirographs even make no mention of sealing.[476] Just beginning under Henry Foliot and becoming the rule under Abbot John de Felda the chirograph's clause stated that both halves were sealed.[477]

St. Peter's employed a two-sided seal. The obverse, as the commonly used legend 'Seal of St. Peter's of Gloucester' indicates, was the 'house' side. The same image was apparently used throughout the pre-1264 period and beyond: an enthroned frontal figure wearing a cloak or cope fastened by a pectoral clasp and holding a crosier in the right hand and an upraised book in the left. Speculation about the figure's iconographic identify has ranged from an abbot or St. Benedict to St. Peter. As T. A. Heslop has pointed out, using comparisons with other monastic seals and with a manuscript from Christ Church Canterbury, it is more plausibly an abbot or possibly St. Benedict, and similarity between the arrangement of the figure and that on a seal of Bishop Wulfstan of Worcester suggests a most plausible local influence.[478] Given that St. Peter's earliest charters date only from 1130 × 39, it is unlikely that an abbatial seal dates from as early as *c.* 1110, as apparently has been claimed.[479] In fact, the alleged examples, known only from the obverse side, bear striking resemblance to the obverse of Abbot Thomas Carbonel's seal, including its dimensions and legend.[480] So close is the resemblance that it appears likely that Thomas Carbonel merely continued to use Abbot Hamelin's obverse.

HAMELIN: wax, white, obverse: pointed oval; length unavailable; width 45 mm; an abbot or St. Benedict, enthroned facing front, in right hand a crosier; in left, an upraised book; legend: [ ]CI PET[ ]; reverse, a counterseal, oval, illegible.[481]

THOMAS CARBONEL: wax, white or green; obverse: oval, orig. *c.* 70 mm × 48 mm; an abbot or St. Benedict enthroned facing front wearing a cloak or cope fastened by a pectoral clasp; in right hand a crosier; in left, an upraised book; legend: +SIGILLV[']:SCI:PE[TRI:D]E GLOECESTRA; reverse: a counterseal: oval, an oval intaglio, *c.* 30 mm × 25 mm; beneath a tree a figure facing to right seizing a fawn by the hind legs; legend: +SECRETV.'THOME: ABBATIS: GLOEC'.[482]

---

[476] Some physical evidence of sealing in this category for Abbot Thomas is uncertain: nos. 76–77; but see nos. 94–95. For the abbacy of Henry Blont there is the evidence of sealing on both halves of nos. 115–16 and 121–2.

[477] Of the two examples deriving from the abbacy of Thomas Carbonel one is a *conventio* with the prior of Llanthony Secunda: see nos. 57, 152. All of the extant original chirograph-grants of Abbot John de Felda either bear seals or reveal evidence of having been sealed: e.g. nos. 177–8.

[478] e.g. Birch, *Catalogue of Seals*, no. 3192, p. 566; Welander, *Gloucester Cathedral*, 94, 96; Heslop, 'Seals', no. 350, p. 310; see also Ellis and Millen, *Catalogue of Seals*, M.340 & Plate 19.

[479] Morgan, *Seals of Hereford Cathedral*, A.541, p. 8, apparently followed by Heslop, 'Seals', no. 350, p. 310. Note the plaster cast with the same dimensions and almost identical legend in Birch, *Catalogue of Seals*, no. 3192, p. 566, labelled early twelfth century without explanation; see also ibid. no. 3193. The typescript of the Morgans' list of seals in H.C.L. identifies Birch no. 3192 as a cast of H.C.L., A.541: I am indebted to Miss Joan Williams, Librarian, H.C.L., for this information (letter of 23 Jan. 1996). Even if the obverse figure's Romanesque style was inspired by a model of *c.* 1110, as suggested by Heslop 'Seals', no. 350, p. 310, the seal's matrix need not be of this date.

[480] Heslop, 'Seals', no. 350, p. 310; above, n. 479; H.C.L., no. A.541 in its current damaged state measures 68 mm × 48 mm and its legend reads: +SIGILLV'.SCI.PET[RI DE] GLO[ECE]STRA; the B.L. cast, made from the then undamaged original measures 70 mm × 48 mm and bears the complete legend; see below, n. 482.

[481] Based on no. 70.

[482] Based on nos. 78, 82, 84; B.L., D[oubleday] C[asts], 7 and LXIII, 60, obverse, conform to these measurements exactly; their legends read +SIGILLV'.SCI.PET[RI D]E:GLOECESTRA (see Birch, *Catalogue*

HENRY BLONT: wax, white, green; obverse: pointed oval, orig. 67 mm (incomplete) × 37 mm (incomplete); an abbot or St. Benedict enthroned facing front wearing a cloak or cope held by a pectoral clasp; in right hand a crosier; in left, an upraised book; legend: +SI[GI]LLV:SCI[:] PETR[I GLOV]C[E]STRIE; reverse, a counterseal, pointed oval, 44 mm × 26 mm; an abbot in vestments standing to front; in right hand a crosier; in left, an upraised book; legend: +SECRETVM: ABBATIS:GLOVCESTRIE.[483]

THOMAS OF BREDON: seal not known to be extant.

HENRY FOLIOT: wax, green; very damaged; obverse: oval, *c.* 67 mm × *c.* 37 mm; upper torso of an abbot or St. Benedict with a crosier in his right hand, only portion extant; legend: +S . . . CESTRA; reverse: a counterseal, an oval 44 mm × 26 mm; a nimbed St. Peter or St. Benedict standing facing front in vestments; in right hand a crosier; legend: . . .RETUM . . .OVC. . .TRIE.[484]

JOHN DE FELDA: wax, white; obverse: oval; accurate meas. unavailable; an abbot or St. Benedict enthroned wearing a cloak or cope fastened by a pectoral clasp facing front; in right hand a crosier; in left, an upraised book; legend unavailable; reverse: a counterseal, pointed oval, 45 mm × *c.* 26 mm; a full standing St. Peter or St. Benedict, nimbed, in vestments; in right hand a crosier; in left, an upraised book; legend: [+]SECRETVM S. . . CES[T]RIE.[485]

SUMMARY: SECRETARIAL ADMINISTRATION OF ST. PETER'S

Before the end of the eleventh century elements of Benedictine literary culture developed at Gloucester. The earliest evidence suggests that from the first at least two products representative of such a literary culture, a charter-chronicle and abbatial letters, were produced by members of the community.[486] On the strength of surviving original in-house products – first books from the first quarter of the twelfth century, then charters from the second – the fact of in-house production is indisputable.[487] Describing this sponsorship in institutional terms at least for the first century of St. Peter's under Anglo-Norman rule is best accomplished by resorting to the usefully vague term scriptorium: not a well defined bureaucratic agency, but rather the in-house mobilization of monks with scribal training to satisfy various literary and documentary needs. One should not assume, however, that the

---

of Seals, nos. 3192, 3193; B.L., D.C., E. 740 (Birch, no. 3198), a cast of Thomas's counterseal, has the identical legend and measures 28 mm × 22 mm. In the legend of the counterseal *TH* of *Thome* are joined. D.C., XLIII, 52, a cast of a damaged obverse, has the same obverse image, but lacks the legend and reliable measurements (Birch, no. 3194).

[483] Based on nos. 18, 108, 111–12, 121. The reading of the counterseal's legend on no. 18 by Birch, *Penrice and Margam Manuscripts*, 1st ser., no. 129, p. 45, is faulty. The measurements for no. 18 recorded in Morgan, 'List of Seals', 8, should be disregarded; H.C.L., no. 1582 (below, no. 165) in ibid. also is mislabelled: its seal is appended to a charter of Henry Foliot. I am grateful to Miss Joan Williams, Librarian, for providing me with measurements and exact-size photographs which have made possible an accurate description of the counterseal (letter of 22 Feb. 1996); see also Birch, *Penrice and Margam Manuscripts*, 1st ser., no. 132, pp. 45–46.

[484] Based on no. 165.

[485] Based on nos. 174–5. A note on the back of B.L., D.C., XLIII, 53, a counterseal (Birch, *Catalogue of Seals*, no. 3194), attributes it to an Abbot John, but given the above evidence and the cast's different image, style, and legend, the abbot probably was not John de Felda; the cast is more likely to have been derived from a counterseal of Abbot John de Gamages (1284–1307).

[486] Above, pp. xxiii–xxiv & nn.

[487] Above, pp. xxiii–xxv, xxxii ff.

scriptorium was the exclusive source of production; the library certainly was stocked in part from external sources.[488]

The careers of Scribes 1 and 2 also show that in the early stages of the scriptorium's development scribal roles were undifferentiated, which resulted in scribes writing both literary works and *acta*, and such personnel wrote in bookhand or slightly modified versions.[489] It appears that during the abbacy of Hamelin (1148–79) some functional differentiation occurred. A clearly identifiable group of in-house secretarial scribes emerged, who, albeit with changing personnel, remained primarily responsible for executing business *acta* associated with the abbey's feudal and proprietary life. On occasion such personnel might write the charter-records of a patron's donations or possibly even record a land transaction by one of the abbey's tenants.[490] The scripts they used reveal emerging business hands,[491] but those of their successors continued to be influenced by training or experience with the hand of book-production.[492] The significant number of abbatial *acta* written in unidentifiable but similar hands shows that 'temporaries' also supplemented this group.

Of the scriptorium's core staff, at least six served during the abbacies of Hamelin and Thomas Carbonel,[493] three during Henry Blont's,[494] at least one during Thomas of Bredon's,[495] four, and possibly as many as eight, during Henry Foliot's,[496] and at least one, and possibly as many as six, during John de Felda's.[497] Some appear to have served under several abbots.[498] The fact that so many served exclusively under only one abbot suggests that they were intentionally recruited.

Around the mid twelfth century, the need to organize better its growing archive of benefactors' charters, and very soon to file copies of abbatial chirographs, produced another function for the abbey's business scribes, endorsing the stored folded documents for easier reference. These 'filing clerks,' as this personnel may be called, were sometimes the very individuals who had executed the texts which they endorsed, or they might be other members of the secretarial group, or even 'temporaries.' At least one of them engaged in several different literary activities.[499]

Endorsements by their very nature pose many problems for the palaeographical identification of hands, and a general complication is the fact that scribes could write in more than one hand.[500] The present editor has, however, found little evidence of stylistic variation in monastic deeds of this period. Calculating endorsers' chronologies must be

---

[488] Above, p. xxiv & n.; no. 20 was written by Glamorgan Scribe 26; no. 38, benefiting St. Peter's, was provided for the abbey by the Westminster forger.

[489] See e.g. Scribes 1 and 2.

[490] Scribes 3–6 for 1148–79; Scribes 6–19 subsequently; Scribes 2 (no. 247), 8 (no. 36 & H.C.L., no. 2771), 11 (no. 256), for abbatial scribes writing Gloucester patrons' charters; see nos. 208, 214; no. 202 is also a possible example.

[491] See for the early personnel Scribes 3–9, along with Scribes 1–2.

[492] See Scribes 10–13, 34.

[493] For Hamelin, Scribes 1–6; for Thomas Carbonel, Scribes 6–11.

[494] Scribes 12–14; see also Scribe 17.

[495] Scribe 15; other possibilities are Scribes 32, 34, 36, 37.

[496] Scribes 16–18, 33; also possibilities are Scribes 32, 34, 36, 37.

[497] Scribe 19; also possibilities are Scribes 32, 34, 35, 36, 37.

[498] Scribes 1, 2, 28, 33, 35, 37.

[499] Hand c/Scribe 2, Hand d/Scribe 4, Hand i/Scribe 7, Hand o/Scribe 17, Hand p/Scribe 34.

[500] Ker, 'William of Malmesbury's Handwriting', 371–6; Thomson, *William of Malmesbury*, 76–77, Plates 1–2; Chaplais, 'John de Branketre', 171.

based upon the vintage of their hands rather than on abbatial terms of office. This fact poses its own obstacle to accurate dating because hands could both anticipate the period when their styles were current, as well as survive beyond it. Nevertheless, after taking all the problematic factors into consideration, it may be suggested that by the mid twelfth century scribes were set to work writing endorsements, usually indicating the donor.[501] Over the second half of the twelfth century perhaps as many as five 'filing clerks' began to function before the end of Henry II's reign,[502] and these were succeeded by others over the period of this study, some of whom continued to serve in a secretarial capacity.[503] At least six were active late in the twelfth century and in the early thirteenth.[504] Three were engaged in 'filing' in the first half of the thirteenth century,[505] perhaps supplemented by some of the previous six and by at least some of the five clerks whose hands are datable to the period c. 1225–75.[506]

The charters produced by the scriptorium's personnel reveal especially its adoption of certain operational practices which constitute the best evidence for the professional quality of the monastery's secretariat. Bipartite chirographs became favoured forms for *conventiones* with other landlords like the prior of Llanthony Secunda and demesne tenants, particularly tenants in Gloucester.[507] Authentication of *acta* by two-sided seals appended *sur double queue* through single turn-ups became regular practice.[508] St. Peter's always used the same image on the obverse side, apparently to represent the community, but changed counterseals to distinguish the rule of incumbents from their predecessors'.[509]

Charters were drafted so as to employ commonly accepted formulaic components and terminology.[510] Especially in recording the details of grants to its tenants in Gloucester, the abbey's drafters developed set formulas which were applied so consistently as to suggest the adherence to an in-house formulary of some sort.[511] The point also receives some support from partial applications of the formulas in some of the abbey's rural manorial charters.[512] How original this diplomatic end product was is a question which at this point is unresolved, but the scriptorium may at the least be credited with creating from already known diplomatic elements a textual format which so far appears to be unique in the Gloucester region.[513] Contemporary with this diplomatic development, the scriptorium's 'filing clerks' used increasingly more descriptive endorsement terminology which included for 'filing convenience' the number of the case or chest (*capsula*) in which a charter was stored.[514] Both of these terminological developments occurred during the second half of the twelfth century, certainly during Thomas Carbonel's abbacy (1179–1205), and were fully

---

[501] See below, nos. 38, 201, 248, 384; Hand c: no. 247.

[502] Hands a–e, poss. f–g, i–j.

[503] Hand i /Scribe 7, Hand o/Scribe 17, Hand p/Scribe 32.

[504] Hands f, g, h, i, j, k.

[505] Hands m, n, o.

[506] Hands p, q, r, s, t.

[507] Above, p. xlix & n., pp. li–lii & nn.; e.g. below, nos. 57, 60, 65, 71.

[508] Above, p. lv & nn.

[509] Note how the obverse legend of Thomas Carbonel differed from that of Hamelin; how Henry Blont's counterseal differed from Carbonel's: above, pp. lvi–lvii. The inadequacy of the physical evidence of the extant seals prevents the claim that seals were changed at the accession of each new abbot.

[510] Above, p. l & nn.

[511] Above, p. li–lii & nn.; see in general, Cheney, *English Bishops' Chanceries*, 119–30.

[512] e.g. below, nos. 90, 171, 179; see also below, no. 391.

[513] Above, pp. liii–liv & nn.

[514] Above, p. xlvii & nn.

operational by the early thirteenth.[515] Such practices and the use of personnel with generally specified functions produced an administrative agency which is difficult to distinguish from so-called episcopal chanceries.[516] Hence it is fair to say that the original charter evidence from St. Peter's reveals the evolution of a functionally undifferentiated scriptorium into a monastic chancery.

THIS EDITION

The texts are arranged sequentially in the following groups: Bromfield Priory; Ewenny Priory; Ewyas Harold Priory; St. Peter's, Gloucester: England; St. Guthlac's Priory; Kilpeck Priory; Leonard Stanley Priory; and St. Peter's, Gloucester: Wales. Affiliation with the abbey and its major dependencies has been the criterion for the groupings, with one exception. The Welsh category has been devised to provide for the *acta* pertaining to non-prioral holdings like Llancarfan. Within each category, texts appear in the following order: royal; episcopal; monastic (St. Peter's; others); lay. *Acta* of laymen relating to the abbey and its priories are subdivided into transactions with the abbey/dependency and proprietary dealings between tenants.

Descriptive material which introduces each text includes a description and measurement of the document and any appended seal, transcriptions of medieval endorsements, and references to copies of the *acta* which are found in relevant cartularies, particularly the abbey's own late medieval registers, and to at least one modern printed version if such exists. Documentary measurements are of the length across the top and of the left edge unless otherwise indicated; measurements of oval seals are first by length, then width.

In transcribing the texts I have generally followed the system of the English Episcopal *Acta* series. This involves some alteration of capitalized and abbreviated forms found in the originals. I have, however, retained the tailed *e*, *u* and *v*, dotted *y* as *y*, the insular forms *Æ*, and thorn, and as much of the original punctuation as possible. *Christus* has been rendered as *Cristus*. Forms of the common endorsement *c'* or *caps'* has been extended to *c(apsula)* or *caps(ula)*, based on the use of *capsula* by an early fourteenth-century St. Peter's endorser;[517] *iustic'* to *iustic(iis)*. Abbreviated place-names have not been filled out; abbreviated personal names, other than those of donors or of the principals in a final concord are extended. In these two cases the personal names are extended with parentheses enclosing the extended parts. Names in the form of initials are not extended. Abbreviated place-names in adjectival form are fully extended. When I have been in doubt about an element of an extended word I have enclosed it in parentheses. Additions which have been made to the texts are indicated by brackets, and the reasons, unless obvious, are provided in commentaries or footnotes.

Dating

Most of these *acta* and all of their endorsements are undated, so palaeographical criteria have been major factors in establishing their dates. They have been particularly crucial in assigning dates based upon abbatial chronologies to *acta* issued in the names of Thomas, Henry, and John and their communities, because up to 1263 the names Thomas and Henry were each borne by two abbots, Thomas Carbonel (1179–1205) and Thomas of Bredon (1224–28), Henry Blont (1179–1205) and Henry Foliot (1228–43), while Abbot John de Felda (1243–63) was soon followed by John de Gamages (1284–1306). Thus, for example,

---

[515] Above, pp. xlvii & nn., liii & nn., Hands a–b, d–n.

[516] Cheney, *English Bishops' Chanceries*, 22–24, 26–27, 38–39, 40, 44–45, 55–56, 96–99.

[517] G.C.L., 'Deeds and Seals', iii, no. 23v, fol. 14v; on the problem associated with this word, see Walker, 'Gloucester Charters', 250 n.

acta of Thomas Carbonel can be distinguished at least provisionally from those of Thomas of Bredon because of the clear differences in style between the last quarter of the twelfth century and that of the 1220s.[518] Other factors need to be considered as well because scribes may utilize scripts which are anachronistic at a particular time for one reason or another; furthermore, the end of the abbacy of Henry Blont and the beginning of Henry Foliot's are divided by an interval of only four years. Precise chronologies are not known for the tenures of all of the abbots of St. Peter's because the evidence is either lacking or conflicting.[519] Consequently, when one or both of the dates of an abbot's tenure is involved with limiting the date of an *actum*, the years of his accession and/or his death are used. For chronologies of other officials and individuals, I have relied upon standard works of reference,[520] and, for witnesses in and around Gloucester, particularly upon Stevenson's *Gloucester Corporation Records* and Nicholas Herbert's list of Gloucester's bailiffs in his fine account of medieval Gloucester.[521] In addition to dating by limiting years (e.g., 1139 × 48) I have also used the designations employed by Dr. Michelle P. Brown in her *A Guide To Western Historical Scripts*, according to which a century year in Roman numerals followed by superscript *1, 2, in, ex* or *med*, stands respectively for the first or second half of the century, the first or final quarter, or the middle two quarters; and the turn of a century can be indicated by e.g. *c.* 1300 or by a Roman numeral combined with *in* and *ex*.[522]

---

[518] Compare e.g. G.C.L., 'Deeds and Seals', IV, no. 2, fol. 1, with ibid. I, no. 35, fol. 20.

[519] For Abbots Serlo (1072–1104), Peter (1107–13), William Godemon (1113–30), Walter de Lacy (1130–9), Gilbert Foliot (1139–48), Hamelin (1148–79), Thomas Carbonel (1179–1205), and Henry Blont (1205–24), see *HRH*, 52–53; *Regesta*, ii, no. 828; according to the 'Historia' of St. Peter's, Thomas of Bredon (1224–8) was elected on 31 August 1224 and was installed on 29 September (pp. 26–27); G.C.L., MS. 34, fol. 10, states that he was blessed on 22 September and installed on 29 September; the king knew of his election on 6 September and confirmed it on the 19th (*Rot. Litt. Claus.* i. 619b, 621b; see also 644b, 646b); another source claimed that he was blessed on 15 January 1224 and died simply in the year 1228 (*Annales de Wigornia*, 416; *Annales de Theokesberia*, 70); Gregory of Caerwent recorded 1224 for Thomas's succession and 11 May 1228 for his death (B.L., Cott. MS. Vesp. A.v, fol. 200v); Henry Foliot's election as Thomas's successor received the royal assent on 26 May 1228 (*PatR 1225–32*, 189); Henry died on 15 July 1243 ('Historia', 27–29; see also G.C.L., MS. 34, fol. 10v; B.L., Cott. MS. Vesp. A.v, fols. 200v, 201; *Annales de Theokesberia*, 70, 130; *Annales de Wigornia*, 435); the king approved John de Felda's election on 27 November 1243 (*PatR 1232–47*, 408); John was blessed on 6 December, was installed a week later, and died in 1263 (*Annales de Theokesberia*, 132; *Annales de Wigornia*, 435); according to the version of the 'Historia' in G.C.L., MS. 34, John died on 27 March 1263 (fol. 11); Walter of St. John was elected as Henry Foliot's successor, but died before his installation (G.C.L., MS. 34, fol. 11; 'Historia', 29; see also B.L., Cott. MS. Vesp. A.v, fol. 201v). For the obit days of Serlo, Walter de Lacy, and Thomas of Bredon, see also Bodl. MS. Jesus Coll. 10, fols. 1v., 2, 3.

[520] Notably *HRH*; *Fasti*; Sanders, *English Baronies*.

[521] In *VCH Glos.* iv.

[522] Brown, *Guide*, 2.

ORIGINAL ACTA OF
ST. PETER'S ABBEY,
GLOUCESTER

BROMFIELD PRIORY

1. *Notification by King Henry II of England that he has granted in alms prebends in Bromfield hundred to Bromfield Priory (Salop.); canons holding them could continue to do so for life; afterwards the prebends were to return to the priory. (1154 × 72) London.*

A. B.L. Cott. Ch. XVII.4 (189 mm × 268 mm); tag & seal missing; endorsements: Confirmatio regis .H. de Bre'feld' (s. xiii[in]); .B. i. (s. xv?); *Monasticon*, iv, no. 2, p. 555; *Palaeographical Society*, 2nd ser. i, no. 41; facsm. in ibid. and in Blair, 'Minster Churches', 129; **B**. P.R.O., C 150/1, fol. 208v; **C**. G.C.L., 'Reg. A', no. 26, fol. 16v; *Cart. Glouc.* ii, pp. 213–14; Delisle, *BEC* lxviii (1907), no. 27, p. 282; Bishop, *Scriptores Regis*, no. 360; Holt and Mortimer, no. 33.

.H. rex Anglorum et dux Normannorum . et Aquitanorum . et comes Andegavorum . archiepiscopis . episcopis . abbatibus . comitibus . baronibus . iustic(iis) . vicecomitibus . ministris . et omnibus fidelibus suis totius Angl'. salutem. Sciatis me pro salute anime mee . et antecessorum . et heredum meorum . dedisse . et carta mea confirmasse . ecclesiam meam sancte Marie de Bru'feld . cum omnibus pertinentiis suis . priori . et monachis ibidem deo seruientibus . tenendam de me et heredibus meis . in perpetuam elemosinam . integre . plenarie . honorifice . sicut meam dominicam capellam . et omnes prebendas . quas Fredericus clericus de Bureford . et Robertus Colemon de Pantesburi . et Edricus presbiter de Bru'feld [.] et Robertus presbiter de Feltuna . et alii canonici tenuerunt in Bro'feldehernesse tempore .H. regis aui mei . uel meo tempore. Scilicet omnes terras . et villas . de Hauerford . et de Dodinghopa . et de Esseford . et de Feltuna . et de Burhheia . et de Ledewich . et tres prebendas in Bru'feld . et tres in Halhtuna. Salua tamen tenura predictorum canonicorum quam diu uixerint . qui omnes has prenominatas terras . et villas . tenuerunt in elemosinam de predicta capella mea. Post mortem autem illorum, libere . et quiete . ab omnibus secularibus seruitiis . et exactionibus . et absque contradictione ullius . ad proprias usus . et dominium predicte capelle mee . et fratrum illius loci. reuertantur . cum omnibus libertatibus . et quietantiis . et liberis consuetudinibus . et regiis dignitatibus. Et volo . et firmiter precipio . ut custodiatis . et manuteneatis . et protegatis . omnes res . et possessiones suas . sicut meas dominicas . et proprias res . Ita bene . et in pace . ut nemini per ullum breue respondeant . de ulla terra quam teneant . uel aliquis per eos . nec ullo modo ponantur in placitum de tenemento unde habeant confirmationem carte mee . uel carte .H. regis aui mei. Et prohibeo ne ullus habeat communionem in nemoribus suis . nec in grauis . nec in moris . nec in herbagiis . nec in pratis . nec in aquis . nec in pasturis suis . nec usquam in tota terra sua . nec ullus in his predictis . aliquid capiat . nec inde se intromittat́ nisi licentia eorum . Testibus . Hilario Cicestrensi episcopo . Reinaldo comite Corn' . Willelmo comite Gloec' . Ricardo de Hum' constabularió apud London'.

This charter is the work of an unidentified royal scribe (Bishop, *Scriptores Regis*, no. 360). Pre-Conquest Bromfield church was a minster with 12 canons. It survived in this state, minus a prebend lost to secular appropriation, as a royal chapel until the above grant (Moir, *Bromfield Priory*, 10; Blair, 'Minster Churches', 127–31; see ibid. 130, for a map showing locations of the minster church and its prebends). In 1155 the canons, with the assistance of St. Peter's former abbot Gilbert Foliot, then bishop of Hereford, and with the assent of Archbishop Theobald, gave themselves as monks and their church to St. Peter's, becoming in the process another of the abbey's priories ('Historia', 19–20, 66); and Bishop Gilbert installed a monk from St. Peter's, Robert of Haseley, as prior (*LCGF*, no. 303; *VCH Salop.* ii. 27). The above charter was issued before the addition of *dei gratia* to the royal title in 1172/3, apparently May 1172, and it makes clear that the house's status as a royal chapel would continue (Bishop, *Scriptores Regis*, 19 & n.; Chaplais, *English Royal Documents*, 13; see no. 2).

2. *Confirmation by King Henry III of England of various rights awarded to Bromfield Priory by previous kings. 28 June 1258. Westminster.*

S.R.O., 52/7 (193 mm × 99 mm); seal on plaited pink cords, dark green wax, fragment, repaired; first seal; obverse (majesty side), round (*c.* 98 mm in diam.); the king seated on a throne to front, in his right hand an upraised sword, above his head a half-moon with ends pointing up between which is a five-pointed star; legend: . . . LI[1] . . . BERNIE; counterseal, round (*c.* 98 mm in diam.); equestrian figure to the right; shield held on left; legend: +HENRICV. . .VI (by right rear hoof of horse) . . .; endorsements: Confirmatio .H. Regis Anglie (s. xiii[ex]); B.i. (s. xv); Confirmatio prioratus de Bromfild (s. xv[ex] × xvi[in]).

H. dei gratia rex Anglie . dominus Hybernie . dux Normannie et Aquitannie . comes Andegauie . omnibus iusticiariis suis atque vicecomiti . et bayliuis suis de Solopssire salutem. Sciatis me inspexisse cartas illustrium regum Anglye sancti . scilicet Edwardi et uenerabilis Henrici aui mei . nec non et aliorum plurium regum Anglie quibus ipsi dederunt ac confirmauerunt omnes illas libertates . etiam cum regiis dignitatibus . vnde sicut expressius in illis cartis continetuŕ firmiter concedo. Et modis uolo omnibus quod ecclesia sancte Marie de Bromfeld que propria mea dominica capella est . gaudeat plenarie omni libertate sibi sic concessa. Set nec prior loci illius seu aliquis de suis hominibus . de aliquo tenemento respondeat́ nisi coram me. Et faciat dictus prior tam de boscis quam de terris quicquid uoluerit . sine impedimento alicuius. Datum sexto Kalendas Iulii . apud Westm' . Anno regni nostri .xl.° secundo.

See also *TSAS*, 2nd ser. 10 (1898), 93, for a transcript of a fifteenth-century copy of charters confirmed by Henry III in 1235.[2] The seal is Henry III's first (Birch, *Catalogue of Seals*, i, no. 100, pp. 15–16, and facsm. Plate II, 100).

[1] Read as II, but seems unlikely.
[2] The present editor is indebted to Miss Mary McKenzie, Assistant Archivist, Shropshire Record Office, for the location of this deed and reference to the transcript.

3. *Grant in fee and inheritance in the form of a chirograph by Abbot Henry and the convent of St. Peter's, Gloucester, to Walter de Capella of land held by Nicholas de Capella and lands at Felton (in Bromfield) to be held of Bromfield Priory for an annual rent 12s. per year. (1228 × 43)*

H.C.L., no. 1614 (201 mm × 182 mm); tag and seal missing; no endorsement; cal. in Baddeley i, no. 26, p. 232.

CYROGRAPHVM

Sciant presentes et futuri quod ego Henr(icus) dei gratia abbas et conuentus sancti Petri Glouc' concessimus Waltero de Capella et heredibus suis tres notatas terre et mesuagium cum gurgite in aqua de Corue cum omnibus pertinentiis quam Nicholas de Capella quondam tenuit . Et octo acras terre cum pertinentiis in campo de Felton . scilicet quatuor acras qui iacent iuxta Heihamstie tres ex vna parte ipsius semite . et vna ex altera . et duas que iacent inter terram Willelmi Blundi et terram regis vicinni sui . et duas que iacent in Caldemerse inter terram Willelmi filii Matildis et terram Nicholai de Felton . Et terram quam Willelmus monetarius tenuit cum mora adiacente . et aliis pertinentiis . in campo de Halecton' sub castro de Ludelawe. Tenenda et habenda de prioratu nostro de Bromfeld in feodo et hereditate libere et quiete . Reddendo annuatim sacriste de Bromfeld qui pro tempore fuerit . duodecim solidos pro omni seculari demanda et exactione ad duos terminos anni . medietatem ad festum sancti Michaelis . et aliam medietatem ad annuntiationem beate Marie. Pro hac autem concessione dedit nobis idem Walterus decem marcas argenti ad redditum emendum ad prioratum de Bromfeld et resignauit quoddam mesuagium ante capellam sancte Etheldride et quandam cruftam ante portam curie ulterioris Felton. Heredes uero predicti Walteri rationabile releuium priori de Bromfeld' facient cum singuli sibi succedent. Idem uero Walterus iuramentum nobis prestitit quod fidelis erit ecclesie nostre de soluendo redditu nostro plenarie statutis terminis . et quod nec artem nec ingenium exquiret vnde domus nostra per tenuram suam dampnum incurrat. Et quod predictas terras neque vendet neque escambiet . neque in vadimonium ponet nec alicui in feodum et hereditatem tradet . neque ad alium locum religionis transferet sine assensu nostro. Eandem securitatem facient nobis heredes sui cum singuli sibi succedent. In cuius rei testimonium presens scriptum in modumn cyrographi inter nos confectum est. Cuius vnam partem sigillo ecclesie nostre munitam dicto Waltero tradidimus. Alteram uero partem sigillo ipsius Walteri roboratam: penes nos retinuimus. Hiis testibus, Gerardo

Angeu(enens)i . Iordano de Ludeford . Roberto de Wodeton' . Henrico mil(it)e . Waltero scriptore . Drogone de Punteis . Iohanne Le Chamberlang' . Galfrido de Weston'. Willelmo de Berkelei . Roberto de Cuerne . Roberto de Halecton' . et multis aliis.

Walter *scriptor* was a frequent witness of St. Peter's *acta* and of those concerning the borough of Gloucester datable to *c.* 1200 × *c.* 1240 (Stevenson, nos. 89–90, 105, 107, 113–14, 131–3, 136, 148, 201, 210, 222, 235, 248, 259, 294–5, 304–5, 351, 375–6, 378–80). Walter received a grant of land on Castle Street, Gloucester, from the Brethren of the Hospital of St. Sepulchre *c.* 1200 (ibid. no. 107); two virgates of land which he held at Longford he gave to St. Peter's 1179 × 1205 ('Historia', 99); the proceedings which he attested often were the routine land transactions between burgesses in the borough court, but also could include some involving local monastic houses such as St. Peter's and St. Bartholomew's and St. Sepulchre and St. Margaret's hospitals.

4. *Final concord between Henry abbot of St. Peter's, Gloucester, and Robert de Wdeton' regarding 30 acres of land and 10 acres of wood with appurtenances in Bromfield. 14 June 1243. Westminster.*

P.R.O., CP 25/1/193/3, no. 145 (renumbered in pencil; formerly no. 146) (125 mm [left] × 205 mm [foot]); no endorsement; cal. in 'Salop. Fines 1228–48', 182–3.

C . . . R . . . R A . . . H . . . M

Hec est finalis concordia facta in curia domini regis apud Westm' . In octabis sancte Trinitatis anno regni regis Henrici filii regis Iohannis vicesimo septimo . Coram Roberto de Lexinton' [.] Rogero de Thurkelby [.] Iollano de Neuill' et Gilberto de Preston' iustic(iis) et aliis domini regis fidelibus tunc ibi presentibus . Inter Henricum abbatem sancti Petri Glouu' petentem per Thomam Maloyse positum loco suo ad lucrandum uel perdendum et Robertum de Wdeton' tenentem de triginta acris terre et decem acris bosci cum pertinentiis In Bromfeld' vnde placitum est inter eos in eadem curia. Scilicet quod predictus abbas recognouit et concessit totam predictam terram et predictum boscum cum pertinentiis esse ius ipsius Roberti. Habenda et tenenda eidem Roberto et heredibus suis de predicto abbate et successoribus suis et ecclesia sua predicta imperpetuum . Reddendo inde per annum tres solidos sterlingorum ad duos terminos . scilicet medietatem ad Annuntiationem beate Marie et aliam medietatem ad festum sancti Michaelis pro omni seruitio et seculari exacti[one. E]t[1] pro hac recognitione concessione fine et concordia? idem Robertus concessit pro se et heredibus suis quod idem abbas et successores sui decetero habeant liberam chaciam suam per omnes terras ipsius Roberti et heredum suorum in Wdeton' Onyber' et Walton' ad omnimodas bestias siluestres preterquam in prato ipsius Roberti et heredum suorum imperpetuum[.] Ita tamen quod non licebit eidem abbati uel successoribus suis in bladis uel pratis ipsius Roberti uel heredum suorum in predictis villis a die Pentcost(es) quousque blada illa et fena de prima falcatione fuerunt asportata querere nec aliquam bestiam querere nisi forte euenerit quod aliquam bestiam extra blada uel prata illa inuenerint[1] et tunc licebit eis illam bestiam per predicta blada et prata prosequi ad captionem illius bestie. Et similiter idem Robertus concessit pro se et heredibus suis quod idem abbas et successores sui habeant liberam piscariam suam per omnes aquas a(dia)centes in predictis maneriis de Wdeton' Oneber' et Walton'. Ita scilicet quod ubi terra ipsius abbatis iacet ex utraque parte predictorum aquarum. Idem abbas et successores sui habeant liberam piscariam suam sine aliqua communia[2] quam predictus Robertus uel heredes sui ibi exigere poterunt imperpetuum. Et similiter Robertus et heredes sui habeant liberam piscariam suam per omnes predictas aquas in predictis maneriis ubi terra predicti Roberti iacet ex utraque parte predictarum aquarum quietam sine aliqua communia quam predictus abbas uel successores suis exigere poterunt. Et preterea idem Robertus concessit pro se et heredibus suis et idem abbas pro se et successoribus suis quod ubi terra ipsius abbatis iacet ex una parte predictarum aquarum et terra predicti Roberti ex altera quod communissit piscaria in illis aquis ad predictum abbatem et successores suos et ad predictum Robertum et heredes suos imperpetuum. Et preterea Idem Robertus dedit predicto abbati duas marcas argenti.

.Salop.'

[1]   Hole in MS.
[2]   *commonia* in MS.

5. *Final concord between Elias prior of Bromfield and Robert son of Simon regarding a half hide in Bromfield. Wednesday 5 November 1208.*

P.R.O., CP 25/1/193/2, no. 44 (74 mm × 155 mm); no endorsement; cal. in 'Salop. Fines 1196–1211', 323–4.

C Y . . . O . . . R . . . P . . . V M

Hec est finalis concordia facta in curia domini regis apud Salop' . Die Mercur' proxima post festum Omnium Sanctorum . anno regni regis Iohannis x.°. Coram Radulfo de Ardern' . Willelmo de Albeny . Roberto de Berkelay . Vmfrido archidiacono Sarr' . Iohanne de Cest'. Her' de Pont'audem' . Ricardo de Musegros . Willelmo filio Ricardi . iustic(iis) . et aliis fidelibus domini regis ibidem tunc presentibus. Inter Elyam priorem de Bromfeld' . petentem. et Robertum filium Simonis tenentem . de dimidia hida terre cum pertinentiis . In Bromfeld' . vnde recognitio magne assise summonita fuit inter eos in prefata curia. Scilicet quod predictus prior recognouit totam predictam terram cum pertinentiis esse ius ipsius Roberti . Habendam et tenendam . sibi et heredibus suis de capitali domino . Ita quod predictus Robertus et heredes sui reddent predicto priori et ecclesie de Bromfeld' . et successoribus suis inperpetuum . vnam libram Turis per annum reddendam ad Natiuitatem beate Marie . pro omnibus ad predictum priorem uel successores suos pertinentibus.

Salop'Sir.'

6. *A* conventio *in the form of a chirograph between H(enry), prior, and the convent of St. Mary's, Bromfield, and Lord Walter de Lacy. (c. 1208 × 28)*

S.R.O., 20/6/2 (128 mm × 103 mm [right]); damaged; seal on tag, white wax, rubbed, chipped; obverse: round (*c.* 62 mm in diam.); a helmeted equestrian figure to right, shield held on left, in right hand an upraised sword; legend: . . . E . . . LACI; no counterseal; endorsement: Carta domini .W. de Lacy (s. xiii[ex]).

CYRO...UM

Sciant presentes et futuri quod ita conuenit inter .H. priorem et monachos sancte Marie de Bromfeld' . et dominum Walterum de Laci . super dampnis per duo molendina ipsius terris iamdicti prioris de Bromfeld' illatis. Quod idem Walter pro dampno quod molendinum suum de Corfua fecit terre prioris et monachorum . assignauit pro bono pacis in recompensatorem prioratui de Bromfeld' vnam acram terre in perpetuum possidendam . illam scilicet . quam Robertus clericus de Hagnetro tenuit apud Bromfeld'. Item pro dampno quod stagnum molendinum subtus castellum de Ludelaw' . fecit terre iamdictorum monacorum . assignauit idem Walter . vnum pratellum iuxta Corfua' prope Tameta' . quod iacet inter Corfua' . et terram prioris. Et si forsan contigerit quod absit . quod maius dampnum per predicta molendina terris emerserit. iamdictus Walterus uel heredes sui per uisum proborum hominum ad valentiam dampni . prioratui de Bromfeld' dampnum suum recompensabunt. Vt autem hec conuentio rata in perpetuum maneat et inconuulsam. presens cyrographum inter eos diuisum est . cuius alteram partem sigillo domini Walteri de Laci roboratam. prior de Bromfeld' penes se retinuit. Alteram uero partem iamdictus Walterus sigillo prioris penes se retinet confirmatam. Hiis testibus Milone Pichard . senescallo domini Walteri de Laci . Matheo de Tuc . magistro Rogero De Becch' . Achille fratre eius . Willelmo Monetario . Rogero filio Milonis . Hugone de Halton' . Hereueo de Chawerton' . Helya de Wnnecot' . Iordano de Vinea . Waltero Golfing'.

Henry Foliot became prior of Bromfield after *c.* 1208 and abbot of St. Peter's in 1228 after receiving royal assent on 26 May (*PatR 1225–32,* 189; *HRH,* 86). Walter de Lacy (d. 1242) succeeded to the honor of Weobley in 1190 (Wightman, *The Lacy Family,* 16; see also Sanders, *English Baronies,* 95).

7. *Chirograph between Alexander prior of Bromfield and Simon son of Robert of Bromfield regarding assarts at Mocktree in Bromfield. (1228 × 43)*

S. R.O., 20/6/1 (151 mm × 190 mm [foot]); seal on tag; dark green wax, round; obverse (32 mm in diam.); a cross with all arms of equal length perpendicular to each other, each ending in a three-pronged end; and at the centre of the cross pieces an *x* intersecting the right angles; legend: +SIGILL' SYMONIS:GERNUN; no counterseal; endorsement: Quedam compositio inter priorem de Bromfeld' et Simonem Gernon (s. xiii[ex]).

CIROGRAPHVM

Sciant presentes et futuri quod hec est finalis concordia facta inter Alexandrum priorem de Bromfeld et Symonem filium Roberti de Bromfeld de assartis in Mochtru ad villam de Bromfeld pertinente de quibus dictus prior implacitabat dictum Symonem per breue domini Regis apud Londonias. Scilicet quod dictus prior relaxauit omne clamium suum quod habuit uersus dictum Symonem de predictis assartis. Insuper dictus prior concessit Symoni et heredibus suis et hominibus suis communem pasturam et quietum pannagium in boscho suo de Mochtru et in campis de Bromfeld sicut antecessores sui habere consueuerunt. Similiter prior et homines sui habebunt communem pasturam et quietum pannagium in nemore dicti Symonis et in campis suis de Bromfeld sicut predecessores sui habere consueuerunt. Concessit etiam dictus prior Symoni et heredibus suis communem pasturam in haya sua que est in Mochtru de qua contentio mota fuit inter eos et liberum introitum et exitum per hayam et propriis porcis Symonis et heredum suorum quietum pannagium in haya. Homines autem dicti Symonis habebunt liberum introitum et exitum per dictam hayam tempore pannagii cum porcis et aueriis suis sine querela scilicet a festo sancti Michaelis usque ad festum sancti Martini. Ita etiam quod porci et aueria eorumdem hominum non facient moram in dicta haya ad pascendum. Reliquo autem tempore a festo sancti Martini habebunt communem pasturam in haya et extra omnibus aueriis suis exceptis capris siue haya clausa fuerit siue non. Concessum est etiam tam ex parte prioris quam ex parte Symonis quod dictus Symon et heredes sui possunt assartare et astrapare de nemore suo proprio quantumcumque uoluerint sine omni impedimento et contradictione dicti prioris uel successorum suorum. Idem etiam liceat dicto priori et successoribus suis de nemore suo. Pro hac autem assartorum relaxatione et quietaclamatione et dicta communa in prenominata haya habenda relaxauit dictus Symon dicto priori et suis omnes querelas quas habuit uersus priorem et homines suos. Dedit etiam dictus Symon deo et ecclesie beate Marie de Bromfeld et monachis ibidem deo seruientibus in liberam puram et perpetuam elemosinam sex acras terre sue de Bromfeld liberas et quietas ab omni seculari demanda. Scilicet unam acram que iacet inter bertonam de Bromfeld iuxta Fulesich . et tres acras in marisco que iacent continue . et duas acras in Miþengeslye proximas uolatui dicti prioris. Et ad maiorem rei securitatem et confirmationem finalis concordie inter priorem et Symonem facte . ego Henric(us) dei gratia abbas Glocestrie et eiusdem loci conuentus et Symon Gernun finali concordie assensum et fauorem prebentes scripto inter priorem et Symonem Gernun confecto in modum cyrographi diuiso sigilla nostra alternatim apposuimus. Hiis testibus . Roberto de Wdetun . Girardo langeuin . Hugone Anglico . Roberto Stantune . Willelmo Corebet . Ricardo de Mydelhope, Rogero de Furcis . et multis aliis.

Note the need for St. Peter's to ratify an *actum* of its Bromfield prior (see *VCH Salop.* ii. 28).

8. *Notification by William of Berkeley that he has granted to Bromfield Priory his land in Oakley and Halston (Salop.) for 40 marks received from the abbot and convent of St. Peter's, Gloucester. (s. xiii^{med})*

H.C.L., no. 480 (219 mm × 122 mm); seal on tag, white wax, chipped; obverse, oval ([orig. meas. of length unavail.; current] *c.* 37 mm × 21 mm [orig. width]); fleur-de-lis, Legend: + . . . WILELMI DE: BERKELEIA; no counterseal; endorsement: Carta Will(elm)i de Berkel' de terra de Akle (s. xiv[in]).

Sciant presentes et futuri quod Ego Will(elmu)s de Berkeleya pro salute anime mee et omnium antecessorum et successorum meorum dedi et concessi et hac presenti carta mea confirmaui prioratui de Bromfeld' et monachis ibidem deo seruientibus totam terram meam in villa de Acle cum omnibus edificiis meis. Illam scilicet quam tenui de Pagano de Acle faciendo predicto Pagano et heredibus suis debita seruitia et consueta sicut in cartis eiusdem Pagani continetur quas inde habui et predictis monachis ad maiorem securitate commisi. Dedi etiam et concessi et hac presenti carta mea confirmaui predictis monachis totam terram meam quam habui in villa de Haleshton' cum omnibus edificiis meis quam tenui de Roberto filio Radulfi . faciendo dicto Roberto et heredibus suis servitia debita et consueta secundum quod in cartis dicti Roberti continetur quas inde habui et monachis predictis ad maiorem securitatem commisi[.] Ita uidelicet quod predicti monachi habeant omnes predictas terras et omnia predicta edificia cum omibus pertinentiis suis in pratis, pascuis uiis semitis et omnibus aliis locis sine aliqua reclamatione et retentemento mei et heredum meorum adeo libere et quiete sicut ego predictas terras cum edificiis melius et liberius tenui uel tenere debui imperpetuum. Et ego uero Will(elmu)s et heredes mei predictas terras et predicta edificia cum omnibus pertinentiis suis predictis monachis warantizabimus. Pro hac autem donatione et concessione et warantizatione mea dederunt mihi predicti monachi de licentia et uoluntate abbatis et conuentus Glouc' quadraginta marcas premanibus de bonis ecclesie sue. In cuius rei testimonium presens scriptum sigillo meo sigillatum predictis monachis tradidi. Hiis testibus . Thoma de sancto Martino tunc senescallo abbatie Glouc' . Waltero scriptore . Drogone pincerna . Galfrido de Weston' . Iohanne de Bleched' . Nicholao clerico et aliis.

William of Berkeley announced himself as a tenant *in capite* of the abbot of Gloucester for land at Colethrop in one of his charters (G.C.L., 'Reg. B', no. 326).

9. *Notification by Robert son of Ralph of Halton that he has granted Bromfield Priory his land and rights in* Wulnroughale *(Salop.). (c. 1190 × 1220)*

B.L. Add. Ch. 71309 (209 mm × 104 mm); single turn-up; slit for tag; tag and seal missing; endorsement: Carta Rob(er)ti de Halctone de mora de Wolurenhale (s. xiii[ex]).

Sciant presentes et futuri quod ego Robertus filius Radulfi de Haleuctune assensu . et uoluntate heredum meorum pro salute anime mee . et omnium antecessorum meorum et successorum . dedi et concessi . et hac presenti carta mea confirmaui . in puram et liberam et perpetuam elemosinam deo et ecclesie sancte Marie de Bro'feld et priori et monachis ibidem deo seruientibus totam partem meam quam habebam in mora de Wulurenehale cum terra et herbagio.

Scilicet illam partem que iacet inter ueterem fossam . et ripam de Hemede in longitudine et latitudine. Tenendam et habendam in puram et liberam et perpetuam elemosinam sine omni reclamatione et communa mei uel heredum meorum. Concedo insuper ut predicti prior et monachi liberam habeant et plenariam potestatem assartandi in predicta mora . et omnia de illa facere sicuti eis melius et utilius uiderint expedire. Ego uero Robertus et heredes mei illam predictam moram priori et monachis sancte Marie de Bro'feld contra omnes homines et feminas warentizabimus . et ab omni seruitio seculari et exactione tanquam puram liberam et perpetuam elemosinam adquietabimus. Et ut hec mea donatio et concessio rata et inconuulsa inposterum permaneaṭ. eam presenti scripto sigilli mei inpressione munitoˊ. confirmaui. Hiis testibus . Roberto de Cuwerne . Simone Gernun . Waltero de Capella . Henrico mil(it)e . Pagano de Acleya . Gregorio sacerdote . Iohanne Clerico . et mvltis aliis.

The Halton family were lords of Oakley (Salop.); the moor granted to Bromfield was rendered *Wulroughale* by Eyton (*Shropshire*, v. 220, 222).

10. *Grant in the form of a chirograph of land at Felton (in Bromfield) for life by Thomas Louy to his brother Richard of the chapel of St. Etheldrida; 12d. to be paid to Thomas and 6d. to the prior of Bromfield annually. (s. xiii^2, poss. s. xiv^{in})*

S.R.O., 20/6/13 (89 mm × 164 mm [foot]); seal on tag through single turn-up; white wax, fragment (no details of any kind avail.); no medieval endorsement; attached to the tag by a knotted cord are two endorsement tags: 1) (held by knotted cord through a slit) reads: filia Thome Louy re[cepi]t^1 in plena curia istas duas cartas cum toto iure et clamio in quadam terra apud Feltone.(s. xiii^2); 2) strip appended by a tag through the knotted cord and then its ends sealed [stain and slight residue of indiscernible colour remains] is unreadable due to water damage.

C...OG...APH...M

Vniversis Cristi fidelibus ad quos presens scriptum peruenerit Thom(as) Louy salutem in domino sempiternam. Nouerit uniuersitas vestra me tradidisse et concessisse Ricardo de Capella sancte Eþeldride virginis fratri meo totam meam terram cum mesuagio et omnibus aliis pertinentiis suis quam habui in villa de Felton' ex dono magistri Philippi quondam coci conuentus sancti Petri Glouc' . habendam et tenendam de me et heredibus meis el assignatis ad terminum vite predicti Ricardi tantum. Reddendo inde annuatim michi et heredibus meis uel assignatis duodecim denarios in festis Annuntiationis dominice et sancti Michaelis pro equalibus portionibus et singulis annis in festo sancti Michaelis priori Bromfeld' qui pro tempore fuerit sex denarios pro omni seruitio ad me inde pertinente: Post decessum vero predicti Ricardi tota prefata terra cum mesuagio et omnibus aliis pertinentiis suis ad me et heredes meos uel assignatos meos plenarie reuertetur absque omni impedimento et iuris clamio heredum prefati Ricardi: In cuius testimonium rei presens scriptum in modum cyrographi inter nos confectum est: Cuius vnam partem sigillo meo signatam predicto

Ricardo tradidi: Alteram vero partem sigillo prefati Ricardi munitam penes me retinui. Hiis testibus Henrico mil(it)e [.] Willelmo filio Hugonis de Bromfeld' [.] magistro Alano Cementario [.] Henrico Monetario de Lodelawe [.] Waltero Kec [.] et multis aliis.

The similarity of the witness-lists of this and no. 11 suggests that they were issued on or near to the same occasion.

[1]   Remainder of word erased; recovered by ultra-violet light.

11. *Notification by Thomas Louy that he has granted his daughter Clarice the annual rent of 12d. which his brother owed him for land at Felton (in Bromfield); Clarice was to pay Thomas a clove and 6d. to the prior of Bromfield annually. (s. xiii^2; poss. s. xiv^{in})*

S.R.O., 20/6/14 (163 mm × *c.* 120 mm [right; damaged]); other meas. unavail.: seal and tag missing; mode of sealing unavail.; damage to turn-up; no visible endorsement.

Sciant presentes et futuri quod ego Thomas Louy . dedi . concessi . et hac presenti carta mea confirmaui Claricie filie mee et heredibus suis uel assignatis suis duodecim denarios anni redditus quos Ricardus de capella frater meus inde annuatim soluere tenetur in festis Annuntiationis dominice et sancti Michaelis pro equalibus portionibus pro terris mesuagio et omnibus aliis pertinentiis suis que tenet de me in villa de Felton' ad terminum vite predicti Ricardi tantum: Habendum et tenendum de me et heredibus meis uel assignatis meis predictum redditum duodecim denariorum cum omnibus pertinentiis suis predicte Claricie et heredibus uel assignatis suis ad terminum vite predicti Ricardi et post decessum ipsius Ricardi totam prefatam terram meam de Felton' cum mesuagio et omnibus aliis pertinentiis s[uis libere qui]ete[1] bene et in pace imperpetuum: Reddendo inde annuatim michi et heredibus meis uel assig[natis][2] meis vnum clauum gariofili(u)m[3] in festo sancti Michaelis et priori de Bromfeld' qui pro tempore fuerit annuatim sex denarios pro omnibus seruitiis et demandis ad me uel heredes meos inde pertinentibus. Et ego prefatus Thomas et heredes mei uel assignati mei totam prefatam terram cum mesuagio et omnibus aliis pertinentiis suis et cum prefato redditu ad terminum vite predicti Ricardi prefate Claricie et heredibus uel assignatis suis contra omnes mortales warantizabimus et quietabimus imperpetuum[.] In cuius rei testim[onium presenti][4] scripto sigillum meum apposui. Hiis testibus [.] Willelmo filio Hugonis[5] de Brom[feld' . . . fi]lio[6] Alani de eadem [.] Roberto de Morton' Henrico mil(it)e [.] Willelmo filio Petri de Bromfe[ld' .][7] et multis aliis.

See no. 10 & n.

[1]   Hole in MS.
[2]   Hole in MS.
[3]   Hole in MS.; exact reading uncertain.
[4]   Hole in MS.
[5]   *Hugones* in MS.
[6]   Hole in MS.   [7]   Hole in MS.

EWENNY PRIORY

12. *Confirmation by Uchtred bishop of Llandaff (Glam.) of grants of the churches of St. Bridget, St. Michael's Ewenny, and Colwinston (Glam.) for the foundation of a priory by Maurice de Londres. (1141 × 44; prob. s. xii^ex × s. xiii^in)*

W.S.R.O., Cap. I/17/84 (151 mm × 89 mm); tag for seal; seal missing; endorsements: Eweny (s. xiii); Utredus (s. xiv); Welsh, 'An Early Charter of Ewenny Priory', 415–16; Crouch, *LEA*, no. 1.

Vtred(us) dei gratia Landauensis episcopus omnibus sancte ecclesie filiis salutem in domino. Nouerit uniuersitas uestra quod nos ad instantiam magni uiri et bone memorie domini Mauricii de Lo[nd]oniis[1] donationes quas solempniter fecit in presentia nostra assensu nostro tam de ecclesiis quam de rebus a[d. . .pr]ioratum[2] suum de Eweni construendum auctoritate pontificali deuotissime confirmauimus [uidelic]et[3] ecclesiam sancte Brigide et ecclesiam sancti Michaelis de Eweni et ecclesiam de Colewinestune in usus proprios conuertendas monachis apud Eweni commorantibus ob fauorem et feruorem precla[r]e[4] et honeste et sancte religion[i]s[5] quam specialiter in monasterio Glouecesetrensi non sine magno fructu florere nouimus et gaudemus[6] de quo . . .[7] collegio sunt prefati monachi de Eweni quibus sicut predictus Mauricius in omnibus quicquid contulit et nos[8] eodem modo sicut in cartis suis continetur qua. . .itato[9] fortius presenti carta nostra corraborauimus sub pena excommunicationis districte inhibentes ne aliquis contra suam donationem vel hanc nostram confirmationem uenire presumat quod si quis prioratum predictum de diocesi mea uexare presumpsent maledictione dei omnipotentis et sancti Michaelis archangeli et beati Theleai tam in anima quam in corpore ferratur. Hec senten[tia] facta est apud Eweni in presentia domini Roberti comitis Gloucestrie et aliorum.

Many features of this text arouse suspicions about its authenticity. It begins by praising Maurice de Londres in terms usually reserved for the dead, although it is known that he lived well beyond the death of the supposed episcopal confirmer Uthred (d. 1148; H.C.L., no. 2295; Crouch, *LEA*, no. 1 n.; *GCH*, 632; Clark, *Cartae et alia*, i. 120). The text ends with a statement, preceded by a line-ending sign, which itself indicates that this is a copy. Then there is an almost total lack of punctuation, anachronistic tironian *et*s, and the prominence of 'biting'. When certain features of the script such as its lateral compression, periodic angularity of minims, and the ticking of some ascenders are also considered, the document appears unlikely to have been written before *c*. s. xii^ex at the earliest. Prof. Crouch implicitly defends the authenticity of this charter in *LEA*, no. 1 n. For the foundation of Ewenny see above, p. xxix. The founder Maurice de Londres, lord of Kidwelly, was also an honorial tenant of the earldom of Gloucester's Glamorganshire fee for the lordship of Ogmore (*GCH*, 24, 288). Grants by Maurice and Gilbert de Turberville to Ewenny Priory were confirmed by Earl Robert of Gloucester 1140 × 47 (Patterson, *EGC*, no. 68).

[1] MS. damaged; *Lo[nd]onis* in MS.
[2] MS. damaged; there is enough space for a short word between *ad* and *prioratum*.
[3] MS. damaged.   [4] MS. damaged.   [5] MS. damaged.   [6] *gaudamus* in MS.
[7] A single minim appears to be at the end of this stained portion of the MS., possibly a *d*.
[8] An erased letter occupies part of the space between *nos* and *eodem*.   [9] MS. damaged.

13. *Confirmation by Nicholas bishop of Llandaff of the gift of Colwinston church (Glam.) by Maurice de Londres to the church of St. Michael and the monks living there. (1148 × 66)*

B.L. Cott. Ch. XI.24 (285 mm × 172 mm); tag through one of two slits on turn-up; seal missing; endorsement: De Eweny (s. xiii); Clark, *Cartae et alia*, i, no. 127; Crouch, *LEA*, no. 8; cal. in *EAWD*, ii, no. L. 142.

C I R O G R A P V M:

.N. dei gratia Landauensis ęcclesię episcopus . omnibus successoribus suis canonice substituendis . et universis sanctę ęcclesię filiis . salutem.[1] Sciatis quoniam ego concedo et confirmo . donationem de ęcclesia de Colwinestuna quam Mauricius de Lundoniis fecit ęcclesię sancti Michaelis et monachis eiusdem ecclesie me presente et teste adhoc uocato. Hanc autem eclesiam sic dedit et cum omnibus scilicet pertinentiis suis libere et quiete in decimis et consuetudinibus . et nominatim terram duabus uiis et aque interiacentem que ab eadem ęcclesia ablata fuerat eidem ęcclesię reddidit et dedit. Facta autem hac donatione presentauerunt michi prefati monachi duas honestas personas . Willelmum[2] scilicet presbiterum[3] et Philipum . magistri . Radulfi filium quas ego prefate ęclesię . monachis et domino Mauricio hoc exigentibus et concedentibus inpersonaui . tali tamen pacto quod[4] marcam unam argenti ęclesię sancti Michaelis de Huggomora et monachis eiusdem ęcclesię singulis annis reddere debent dimidiam scilicet marcam in Annuntiatione sancte Marie . et alteram dimidiam marcam in festum beati Michaelis. Et si alter eorum mortuus fuerit⸴ alter marcam reddendo⸴ eandem ęcclesiam teneat . et post mortem istarum personarum⸴ prefata ęcclesia ęcleisę sancti Michaelis de Huggomora et monachis libera et quieta remaneat. Hiis testibus . Radulfo Landauensi ęcclesię . et magistro Iohanne canonicis. Eodem die disrationati sunt . Mauricius de Lundoniis . et monachi de sancto Michaele me presente decimas terre quam Ricardus latimarius de Willelmo de Lundoniis . et Mauricio eius filio tenuit et ita quod dominus Lefricus et Willelmus . et Iohannis filii sui⸴ clamauerunt eam quietam ęcclesię sanctę Brigidę . et monachis. His testibus . magistro Iohanne . et Radulfo de Lancarban . Isaac presbitero . Harnaldo . p(resbitero) Ricardi de Marcros . Gilleberto p(resbitero) . Oeno milite . Ris Walensi . Edwardo preposito .Willelmo Trauers . et Willelmo de Lancarban clericis[.]

The *actum* was written by Glamorgan Scribe 6 of a forthcoming study of the present editor's on the rise of secretarial bureaucracy in the lordship of Glamorgan. Ralph of Llancarfan may be the beneficiary of a grant by Abbot Gilbert Foliot in *Cart. Glouc.* ii, no. 652. For the dating see Crouch, *LEA*, no. 8 n.

---

[1] *Salutes* in MS.
[2] Added in an open space in a later and different hand.
[3] Also possibly added in a later hand.
[4] Possibly written by the later hand darkening the script of the earlier scribe.

14. *Confirmation by Nicholas bishop of Llandaff of the gift to Ewenny Priory of the rustic Godric and 40 acres from Simon de Turberville and confirmed by his brother Gilbert de Turberville. (1148 × 83; prob. 1148 × 79)*

H.C.L., no. 2306 (302 mm × 84 mm); fragment of tag through slit on foot; seal missing; endorsements: Confirmatio .N. episcopi de elemosina Gilleberti (s. xii^med). Eweny (s. xiv); facsm. and text in Conway Davies, 'Ewenny Priory', 133; Crouch, *LEA*, no. 10; cal. in *EAWD*, ii, no. L. 162.

.Nicholaus dei gratia Landauensi episcopus . uniuersis sancte ecclesie filiis salutem et benedictionem. Fraternitatem uestram non lateat dominum Gilebertum de Turberuilla concessisse ecclesie sancti Michaelis de Uggamora . et monachis ibidem morantibus illam donationem quam Simon frater suus illis donauerat in elemosinam . uidelicet quendam rusticum Godricum nomine fullonem . et quadraginta acras que iuxta illum habentur . et totam terram quam predictus Simon frater suus prefatis monachis dederat . in presentia mea et in presentia Maurici de Lund'[1] coram multis testibus. Dedit etiam eis pro anima fratris sui et pro animabus omnium antecessorum suorum . uiginti iiii^or acras apud Wicam . et ut abeant inperpetuum unum sumarium in nemore suo et eis ligna deferat . bis uidelicet singulis diebus in hierme . et ter singulis diebus in estate. Et haec omnia eis dedit et firmiter in elemosinam concessit . ut ea teneant libere et quiete ab omni terreno servitio. Et ut ista inperpetuum fuit et inconuulsa me illud ratum habere et sigilli mei attestatione confirmauisse non dubitetis. Quicunque igitur predicto[s] fratres in possessione predicta manutenuerit uel alicuius auxilii eis manum porrexerit dei benedictione et nostra repleatur. Et quicunque eis uim uel iniuriam de re predicta diabolo suadente intulerit perpetuo anathemati subscribatur. Hec carta facta est in presentia . Radulfi prioris et eorum monacorum qui eo tempore apud sanctum Michaelem fuerunt . et in presentia Iohannis filii Canor . et Adam canonici de Landaf . et Herberti clerici . et Basuini . et multorum aliorum.

The charter was written by Glamorgan Scribe 6, a member of Ewenny Priory; see above, no. 13 n. and Crouch, *LEA*, no. 10 n.

[1] *deund'* in MS.

15. *Alleged confirmation by Nicholas bishop of Llandaff of the previous confirmation by Bishop Uchtred in favour of Ewenny Priory. (1148 × 83; s. xiii^in)*

H.C.L., no. 2299 (161 mm × 36 mm); fragments of tongue and tie; seal missing; endorsement: .Eweny. (s. xiv); Crouch, *LEA*, no. 9; cal. in *EAWD*, ii, no. L.148; Conway Davies, 'Ewenny Priory', Appendix I, no. 8.

Nicholaus diuina gratia Landauensis episcopus.' omnibus filiis suis in Cristo in Landauensi diocesi gratiam et benedictionem. Sciatis nos inspexisse cartam bone memorie domini Utredi quondam Landauensis episcopi per quam ipse confirmauit elemosinam totam quam fecit Mauricius de Lond' . priori suo de Eweny et monachis ibidem commorantibus. Nos siquidem facimus tam precipimus ratum habentes et gratum eodem modo et in omnibus ut ipse͗. eadem auctoritate pontificali confirmamus . prohibentes districte ex parte dei et beati Theleai ne quis clericus et secularis super ista nostra concessione . dicto priori . aliqam molestiam inferre presumat. Et si quis fecerit͗. maledictione dei et nostra feriatur. Teste toto capitulo nostro.

Both its early thirteenth-century script and the wording of its text, from the address clause to the attestation form, mark the charter as a forgery. It was written by Glamorgan Scribe 13 (see no. 13 n.).

16. *Notification by Anselm bishop of St. David's regarding Ewenny Priory. (1231 × 47)*

H.C.L., no. 2303 (230 mm × 113 mm); fragment of tag through slit on foot; seal missing; endorsements: .Eweny. (s. xiv); Littera Anselmi Meneuensis episcopi (s. xv); cal. in Conway Davies, 'Ewenny Priory', Appendix I, no. 12, p. 131; *EAWD*, i, no. 546.

Omnibus sancte matris ecclesie filiis presentem cartam inspecturis uel audituris. Anselm(us) diuina miseratione Meneuensis episcopus salutem. Cum pro uariis negotiis ecclesiam Meneuensem contingentibus per prioratum de Eweni aliquotenus transactis et in dicto prioratu decenter receptis videns et ex relatu multorum audiens quod prior illius loci pauperibus Cristi atque hospitum receptioni ita instabat quod quasi vltra uires secusfunderet[1] in expensis faciendis . Volens eundem in hoc pio opere proseuerare cum plenius michi constaret eundem priorem beneficia ecclesiastica in episcopatu Meneuense debere habere a quibus annuas pensiones habebat et hoc per confirmationes predecessorum meorum͗. easdem pensiones percipiendas dicto priori et sui prioratui illo tenore confirmo et omni tali modo sicut episcopi Meneuenses prius confimauerunt. Scilicet ut de ecclesia de Ocstremua duas marcas percipiat donec illa vacauerit. Similiter de ecclesia de Carnewaylan . viginti solidos . de ecclesia de Penbrai decem solidos . de ecclesia de sancto Ysmaele duas marcas. Et cum dicte ecclesie vacauerint͗. tunc presentet idem prior nomine abbatis et conuentus Glouc' ydoneas personas vicarios faciendos in dictis ecclesiis ut ipsi vicarii Meneuensi episcopo de spiritualibus respondeant͗. et priori de Eweni de temporalibus. Habebit autem quisque vicarius in singulis illis ecclesiis honestas et sufficientes sustentationes. Set residuum in visum prefati prioris ad dictum prioratum sustinendum et transeuntibus maxime indigentibus largiendum conuertere. Et cum aliquo tempore ecclesia sancti Ysmaelis vacauit petiit memoratus prior consolidationem dicte ecclesie et ad vicarium ibidem faciendum Iohannem de sancta Brigida michi presentarit͗. Ita[2] ordinaui quod dictam Iohannem ad medietatem totius ecclesie vicarium institui. Hoc addito quod ille vicarius omnia opera illius ecclesie sustinebit tam ordinaria quam extraordinaria. Priorem uero de Eweni ad aliam medietatem canonice institui neque aliquid respondeat nisi de orationibus et elemosinis faciendis. Et ut in posterioribus temporibus de ista ordinatione nullus uertatur in dubium͗. huic presenti carte mee sigillum meum apposui[.] Hiis testibus . Abraham priore de Ketweli . W. Gabriele priore de Langunuth . Theodoro decano de Ketweli . Samsone vicario de Ocstremua . magistro Willelmo de Gobei . Iohanne Marscallo et aliis multis.

[1] Reading uncertain.
[2] *Ita* followed by an erasure or a stain obscuring one or two minims.

17. *Grant in fee and heredity in the form of a chirograph by Abbot Thomas and the convent of St. Peter's, Gloucester, of a messuage to Owen son of Herbert Lug to be held of Ewenny Priory for 16d. annual rent. In return Owen quitclaims any right he claimed in a meadow by Ewenny and in eight acres of arable at* Langelande. *(1179 × 1205)*

H.C.L., no. 2308 (159 mm × 136 mm); fragment of tag through three slits on foot; seal missing; endorsements: Eweny de laycis tenuris (s. xiv); c. E .ii. (s. xiv[med]); cal. in Baddeley i, no. 16, p. 229; Conway Davies, 'Ewenny Priory', Appendix I, B., p. 133.

CYROGRAPHUM

Sciant presentes et futuri quod ego Thomas dei gratia abbas et conuentus ecclesie sancti Petri Glouec' dedimus et concessimus Audoeno filio Hereberti Lug mesagium quod fuit [B]aldewini[1] de Ewenni cum octo acris de terra adiace[nte te]nenda[2] de prioratui de Eweni in feudo et hereditate libere et quiete ab omni seruitio pro sexdecim denariis [ad][3] festum sancti Michaelis et ad hockedai annuatim reddendis. Idem uero Audoenus abiurauit et quietum clamauit eidem ecclesie in perpetuum totum ius quod clamauit in prato quod iacet inter Carueldon et portam prioratus de Eweni et octo acris terre arabilis iuxta Langelande . et habebit idem Audoenus tantum pecunie in communi pastura eiusdem uille quantum pertinet ad tantum tenementum. Iurauit etiam idem Audoenus quod fidelis erit ecclesie de Eweni quod predictam conuentionem fideliter tenebit et quod nec artem nec ingenium exquiret. unde ecclesia sancti Michaelis dampnum incurrat. Quod quia ratum in inconuulsum manere uolumus presenti scripto sigilli nostri impressione munito diuiso inter nos cyrographo confirmauimus. His testibus . Roberto capellano de sancta Brigida . Adam capellano . Pagano de Turberuilla . Willelmo de Cantelupo . Osberno clerico . Thoma de Lond' . Iohanne de Lond' . Galfrido filio Nigelli . Rogero de Remni . Hugone de Vilers . Adam Norrensi . Will[elmo prep]osito[4] de Colewinestun', Roberto fratre suo . Ricardo BeauBos' . Philippo de Nouoburgo . Thoma clerico . [N]icholao[5] filio Briani . Waltero de Estenoure.

[1] Hole in MS.
[2] Hole in MS.
[3] Hole in MS.
[4] Hole in MS.
[5] Hole in MS.

18. *Grant in the form of a chirograph by Abbot Henry and the convent of St. Peter's, Gloucester, to the abbot and monks of Margam Abbey (Glam.) of the land in the fee of Llangewydd (Glam.) which William Scurlage gave to Ewenny Priory. (1205 × 24)*

N.L.W., P. & M. MS. no. 129 (91 mm [left] × 160 mm [foot]), **Scribe 14**; seal on tag, cream coloured wax stained brown; fragment, repaired; pointed oval (meas. unavail.); an abbot enthroned facing front wearing a cope or cloak held by a pectoral clasp; in left hand an upraised book; legend unavail.; counterseal; pointed oval (44 mm × 25 mm); an abbot in vestments standing to front, head uncovered; in right hand a crosier; in left, an upraised book; legend: +SECRETVM: ABBATIS:GLOECESTRIE; endorsement: H. abbas Sancti Petri de Gloevcest'e (s. xii^{ex} × s. xiii^{in}); Clark, *Cartae et alia*, ii, no. 517; cal. in Birch, *Penrice and Margam Manuscripts*, 1st ser. (1893), 44–45.

CYROGRAPHVM   CYROGRAPHVM (*inverted*)

Sciant tam presentes quam futuri quod ego Henr(icus) dei gratia abbas sancti Petri Gloucestr' et eiusdem loci conuentus . concessimus et hac carta nostra confirmauimus venerabilibus fratribus et amicis nostris abbati et conuentui de Margan . terram illam in feudo de Langewi quam Willemus Scurlagge dedit ecclesie sancti Michaelis de Eweni . ut habeant monachi de Margan predictam terram cum omnibus libertatibus et aisiamentis suis . liberam et quietam ab omni seruitio . consuetudine et exactione . reddendo inde annuatim duo solidos solummodo ecclesie sancti Michaelis de Eweni . ad terminum Pasche. Et nos predictam terram prefatis monachis contra omnes homines warantizabimus in perpetuum. In huius rei testimonium presens scriptum in modum cyrographi confecimus . Cuius unam partem sigillo ecclesie nostre munitam . predictis abbati et conventui de Margan tradidimus. Alteram uero partem sigillo eiusdem abbatis et conuentus de Margan roboratam. penes nos retenuimus. Hiis testibus . Adam priore . Thoma suppriore . Dauid tunc priore de Eweni . Gileberto de Ledebir' . Iohanne capellano de Eweni et multis aliis.

Prior David of Ewenny occurs 1205 × 24 (*HRH*, 89).

19. *Another copy of no. 18, in identical terms[1] but with differences in the the witness-list.(1205 × 24)*

N.L.W., P. & M. MS. no. 132 (83 mm [left] × 184 mm [foot]); seal on tag; fragment, cream coloured wax lacquered brown; pointed oval (meas. unavail.); partial image of an abbot seated to front holding a staff in right hand; legend unavail.; reverse; counterseal, fragment, pointed oval (meas. not avail.); partial image of an abbot standing facing front, lower portion of shaft of a staff held by right hand visible; in left hand, an upraised book; legend: . . . . ETVM:ABBATIS:GLOV . . .; endorsement: Carta abbatis Gloucest' de terra apud Langewi. (s. xiii^{in}); Clark, *Cartae et alia*, ii, no. 451; cal. in Birch, *Penrice and Margam Manuscripts*, 1st ser. (1893), 45–46.

Hiis . Testibus . Adam priore . Thoma suppriore . Dauid tunc priore de Ewen' . Gilleberto de Ledebir' . Gilleberto de Turberuill' . Waltero Luuel . Stephano clerico . Adam Wallense . et multis aliis.

[1] *tam* in line 1 of no. 18 is omitted.

20. *Grant in the form of a chirograph by Abbot Henry and the convent of St. Peter's, Gloucester, to Thomas of Hodenach of Goldland for 3s. annual rent payable to Ewenny Priory (Glam.). (1228 × 43)*

H.C.L., no. 2307 (98 mm [left] × 154 mm [foot]), **Scribe 18**; slit for tag on foot; tag and seal missing; endorsements: carta Thome de Hodeneth (s. xiii[in]); Corendon' (s. xiii[med]); cal. in Baddeley i, no. 29, p. 233; Conway Davies, 'Ewenny Priory', Appendix I, A., p. 133.

C . . . R O G R A P H V M

Sciant presentes et futuri quod Ego Henr(icus) dei gratia abbas et conuentus sancti Petri Glouc' concessimus Thome de Hodenach et assignatis suis totam terram illam de Goldelande quam Alexander prior noster de Eweny recuperauit super Alexandrum de Corendune. Tenendam de nobis sibi et assignatis suis libere et quiete ab omni exactione et demanda pro tribus solidis prioratui nostro de Eweny annuatim ad festum Sancti Michaelis persoluendis. Idem uero Thomas iuramentum nobis prestitit quod fidelis erit ecclesie nostre de reddendo redditu nostro statuto termino. Et quod nec artem nec ingenium exquiret unde prioratus noster de Eweny dampnum incurrat et quod predictam terram nullo modo sine assensu nostro alienabit. Eandem securitatem facient nobis assignati sui cum singuli sibi succedent. Et tam ipse quam assignati sui curiam nostram de Eweny cum liberis hominibus nostris sequentur. In cuius testimonium presens scriptum in modum cyrography inter nos confectum est. Cuius unam partem sigillo ecclesie nostre munitam eidem tradidimus. Alteram uero partem sigillo ipsius roboratam penes nos retinuimus. Hiis testibus . Iohanne Capellano . Thoma pincerna . Audoeno Lug . Iohanne Kandelam . Petro de veteri castello . et aliis.

The chirograph is the work of Glamorgan Scribe 26 (see no. 13 n.).

21. *Lease in the form of a chirograph from Abbot John and the convent of St. Peter's, Gloucester, to Master Henry of Llandaff of Tregoff manor (Glam.) for ten years at an annual farm of 18 marks, of which Henry paid 100 marks in advance for the first five years and part of the sixth, and was to pay the farm thereafter at Ewenny Priory; if he died within the term he might assign the issues of the manor. The abbey's cellarer was to hold the manorial court when he wished. If the manor fell into the earl's wardship Henry would be compensated. 29 September 1250.*

G.C.L., 'Deeds and Seals', vii, no. 26, fol. 15 (164 mm [left] × 212 mm [foot]); seal on tag, dark brown, possibly stained; rubbed; fragment, repaired; oval (meas. unavail.); obverse: image indiscernible; legend: +SI . . . ICI LA . . .; no counterseal; endorsements: de firma de Tregof; Caps(ula) .ii[a] de laicis tenuris (s. xiii[ex] × s. xiv[in]).

C Y R O G R A P H V M (*inverted*)

Omnibus Cristi fidelibus presens scriptum uisuris uel audituris. Ioh(ann)es dei gratia abbas Glouc' et eiusdem loci conuentus salutem in domino. Nouerit uniuersitas uestra quod hec est conuentio facta inter nos et magistrum Henricum de Land' . anno domini .m.° cc.° quinquagesimo . in festo sancti Michaelis. Videlicet quod idem magister Henricus soluet nobis annuatim decem et octo marcas sterlingorum pro [maneri]o[1] nostro de Treygof . quod ei tradidimus ad firmam dicto anno et dicto termino.[1] cum decimis garbarum et feni eiusdem uille . et omnibus aliis pertinentiis usque ad terminum decem annorum plene completorum. E quibus denariis pacauit nobis premanibus centum marcas argenti pro quinque primis annis . et decem marcas in sexto anno. In quo quidem anno soluet nobis octo marcas argenti que residue sunt de eodem anno in prioratu de Eweny ad Pascha . et deinceps annuatim in eodem loco usque at terminum suum plene completum . decem et octo marcas duobus terminis . videlicet medietatem ad festum sancti Michaelis . et aliam medietatem ad Pascha. Si uero de dicto magistro Henrico infra predictum terminum humanitus contigerit[1] licebit ei omnes prouentus dicti manerii assignare a prenominato festo sancti Michaelis . anno domini .m.° cc.° quinquagesimo . in decem annos continue sequentes . salua tamen nobis solutione decem et octo marcarum ab assignatis suis terminis predictis soluendarum. Quod nisi plenarie nobis soluerint[1] licebit nobis omnes prouentus dicti manerii nostri integre recipere absque alicuius contradictione uel calumpnia uel clamio assignatorum . executorum . uel legatariorum suorum. Idem uero magister Henricus iuramento prefato se obligauit . quod homines nostros cum iustitia tractabit . et quod nos conseruabit indempnes et ecclesiam nostram quo ad omnia dictum manerium nostrum contingentia. Eandem securitatem nobis facient assignati sui . si idem in fata decedat antequam de prouentibus illius manerii aliquod recipiant emolumentum. Quod si alique domus nostre aliqua forte indigeant emendatione[1] idem dictus magister uel sui assignati eas facient emendari . si per consilium et assensum celerarii nostri qui pro tempore fuerit[1] fiat . et quantum ad emendationem earum apposuerint[1] tantum per uisum legallium uirorum eis allocabitur. Preterea celerarius noster tenebit curiam nostram in dicto manerio quandocumque uoluerit . vt si que forte hominibus nostris illate fuerint iniurie[1] ipse faciat emendam. Et si aliquo casu contigerit quod garda illius manerii in manus comitis uel aliorum ceciderit[1] nos eundem magistrum uel suos assignatos indempnes conservabimus. Quia uero predictus Henricus totum manerium cum wareto ad predictum terminum sancti Michaelis a nobis recepit vna cum redditu et auxilio et omnibus aliis pertinentiis suis[1] eodem modo in fine decem annorum . ipse uel assignati sui totum predictum manerium cum wareto . redditu et auxilio . et omni melioratione superposita . et omnibus aliis pertinentiis suis[1] integre nobis relinquent. In cuius rei testimonium presens scriptum in modum cyrographi inter nos confectum est. Cuius unam partem sigillo ecclesie nostre munitam . dicto magistro Henrico tradidimus. Alteram uero partem sigillo ipsius roboratam[1] penes nos retinuimus.

For a later lease of the manor in similar terms see below, no. 392.

---

[1] Hole in MS.

22.   Conventio *between Ewenny Priory and Margam Abbey (Glam.); Ewenny concedo to Margam the tenement at Llangewydd (Glam.) which David Scurlage gave to the priory in alms in return for 2s. annual rent.. (c. 1156 × 93+; prob. c. 1180+)*

N.L.W., P. & M. MS. no. 19 (250 mm [left] × 132 mm [foot]; seal on tag; dark green wax, fragment: pointed oval (meas. unavail.); the prior of Ewenny facing left-front; in right hand a scroll; in left, a large book held to his side; legend: +SIGILLV . . . L':DE:VGGOMOR[1]; no counterseal; endorsement: Prioris de Oeweni (s. xii^{ex} × s. xiii^{in}); Clark, *Cartae et alia*, ii, no. 431; cal. in Birch, *Penrice and Margam Manuscripts*, 1st ser. (1893), 9.

:C Y R O G R A P H . . . M (*inverted*)

Sciant omnes tam presentes quam futuri quod hec est conuentio que facta est inter domum de Margan et ecclesiam sancti Michaelis de Oweni presidente monasterio de Margan domno Conano . abbate . et nontio Mauric(io) prioratus apud Oweni administrante. Scilicet quod ego Maur(icius) prior de Oweni dimitto et concedo in perpetuum . et hoc concilio et communi assensu fratrum et sociorum nostrorum monachorum nobiscum degentium . monachis et domui de Margan totum tenementum quod Willelmus Scurlagge nobis et ecclesie sancti Michaelis de Oweni in puram et perpetuam contulit elemosinam apud Lantgewi de libero tenemento suo. Per omnia sicut idem Willelmus nobis et domui nostre melius et liberius et integrius eandem dedit elemosinam in terris . et pasturis . et pratis . et communa pasture et ceteris aisiamentis terre et pheudi de Lantgewi nobis concessis et in elemosinam datis . sicut carta ipsius Willelmi testatur. Hec inquam omnia sine aliquo retenemento predicti monachi de Margan in perpetuum possidebunt . libere et quiete et sine omni seruitio et seculari exactione . reddendo nobis pro seruitio duos solidos . annuatim ad Pascha. Et quia carta prime donationis remansit in nostra custodia . nos de Oweni presentem conuentionem . et terram quam locauimus cum omnibus suis libertatibus monachis de Margan contra omnes in perpetuum warentizabimus. T(estibus) . Hugone et Osberno tunc monachis apud Oweni . Willelmo de Bedint' . et Godefrido monachis de Margan . Adam Capellano . Iordano conuerso de Margan . Waltero clerico de sancta Brigid' . Helia clerico . Rodberto de Gloecest' . Hereveio dapifero prioris.

The chirograph was written by Glamorgan Scribe 12 (see no. 13 n). Maurice prior of Ewenny occurs s. xii^2; Conan abbot of Margam, *c.* 1156 × 93+ (*HRH*, 89, 137). Llangewydd was a fee held of the earl of Gloucester's shire fee by the Scurlage family; before 1199 its then lord David Scurlage granted it to Margam Abbey; evidently the process was not completed until 1202 (Patterson, *EGC*, no. 137; see also ibid. nos. 139–40, 144–5, 147–9; *GCH*, iii. 32, 102; Nicholl, *Normans in Glamorgan*, 89, 132–4, 152).

[1] *E* appears on a tiny fragment of a seal, presumably this one, found in the box in which this *actum* is stored.

23. Conventio *in the form of a chirograph between Henry Le Holt and Bland his wife, formerly widow of Maurice Lugg, and John de Gamages prior of Ewenny. 12 March 1261.*

H.C.L., no. 2300 (206 mm [left] × 169 mm [foot]); seal on tag; white, formerly stained green; fragment, round (*c.* 33 mm in diam.); obverse, fleur-de-lis; legend: . . . E HOLTE; no counterseal; endorsement: .Eweny. de laycis tenuris (s. xiv); cal. in Conway Davies, 'Ewenny Priory', Appendix I, no. 9, p. 131.

CYROGRAPHVM

Hec est conuentio facta anno domini .M.CC.LX. die beati Gregorii pape inter Henr(icum) Le Holt(e) et Bland' vxorem suam quondam relictam Mauricii Lug' ex vna parte et dominum Ioh(annem) de Gamages priorem de Ewenny ex alteram. Videlicet quod dictus Henr(icus) et Bland' vxor sua assensu . et consensu . et etiam mera voluntate heredum suorum in legitima potestate sua tradiderunt ad firmam totam terram suam quam tenuerunt uel tenere debuerunt de feodo[1] prioris de Ewenny . et totam terram quam tenent uel tenere debent de domina de Hoggomor' cum omnibus pertinentiis . et omnibus inde prouenientibus . vna cum omnibus hominibus et tenentibus suis in villa de Ewenny manentibus. Videlicet Nicholao alba cum nouem acris terre arabilis et una acra prati . Hugone filio Sydonis cum nouem acris terre arabilis et .i. acra prati et duabus cottariis, scilicet Nony textore[2] cum mesuagio et curtillagio . et Alicia relicta Paynoti cum mesuagio et curtillagio . et redditu annuale quinque denariorum de domina Cecilia matre dicti Mauricii Lug' . Et si contigerit dictam Ceciliam interim infata decedere. quicquid de portione sua dictos Henr(icum) et Bland' contigerit. penes dictum priorem et prioratum de Ewenny sine dimunitione integre remanebit . usque in fine sex annorum proximorum subsequentium plenorum[3] completorum. Tenendam et habendam omnes dictas terras vna cum supradictis hominibus . et cottariis et tenementis suis et omnibus aliis . scilicet redditis . consuetudinibus . libertatibus . et omnimodis aliis interim inde prouenientibus . scilicet herieta . relevio . warda . et omnibus aliis consuetudinibus secularibus . et demandis que de dicta terra exeunt uel exire poterunt . libere quiete . pacifice . bene . et integre . sine omni conditione . cauillatione . dolo . et calumpnia et omni priuilegio . et iuris remedio per nos uel nostros inpetrato uel inpetrando tam canonico quam ciuili . usque in fine supradictorum sex annorum plenorum[4] completorum. Et si contigerit dominum Henr(icum) infra dictum terminum infata decedere quod absit. dicta Bland' fide media obligauit se iurisdictioni et coheritioni domini Landavensis episcopi . archidiaconi . officialis sive cuiuscumque alterius ordinarii qui pro tempore fuerint. quod sine strepitu iudiciali per censuram ecclesiasticam compellatur ad dictam firmam et conuentionem fideliter obseruandam . sin autem fine omni iuris remedio impetrato uel impetrando publice exq(u)icetur. Pro hac autem conuentione et firma fideliter et firmiter usque in finem supradictorum sex annorum plenor(um)[5] complet(orum) ut supradict(um) est tenend(a) et habend(a). dedit dictus prior dictis Henr(ico) et Bland' .xx. solidos esterlingorum iniug(re)ssum premanibus . et eisdem relaxauit .xvi. den(arios) annuos usque in finem termini prenominati . in quibus eidem priori et prioratui annuatim pro annuo redditu tenebantur. Et ipsi omnia supradicta ut prescriptum est . predictis priori et prioratui usque in fine termini prenominati. contra omnes mortales warantizabunt. Et ut hec conuentio et firma rata . stabilis . et inconcussa permaneat[1]. robur firmitatis et fidelitatis usque in fine termini prenominati obtineat[2]. presentibus scriptum inter partes in modo cyrographi confectis[3]. hinc inde sigilla sua alternatim apposuerunt. Hiis test(ibus) . domininis Iohanne pincerna . Willelmo de Wynton' . Daniele Syward' . Petro de veteri castro tunc constabulario de Oggemor' . Iacobo de Bonauill' tunc seruiente de comitatu . Thoma pincerna . Iohanne filio Candelemi . et multis aliis.

The lady of Ogmore referred to in the text was Hawisia daughter of Thomas de Londres (*GCH*, iii. 290; Nicholl, *Normans in Glamorgan*, 106).

[1] *fedo* in MS.
[2] *textit(ore)* in MS.
[3] *plenar(um)* in MS.
[4] *plenar(um)* in MS.
[5] *plenar(um)* in MS.

24. *Confirmation by Geoffrey de Mandeville, earl of Essex and Gloucester, of grants which Maurice de Londres made to St. Peter's, Gloucester, of the church of St. Michael and the vill of Ewenny with appurtenances.* *(1214 × 16)*

H.C.L., no. 2304 (181 mm × 179 mm); seal on tag; white wax, chipped; obverse: round (30 mm); a heart-shaped shield; legend: +SIGILL' GAL . . . MAUNDEVIL; no counterseal; endorsement: .Eweny. de laycis tenuris (s. xiv); Patterson, *EGC*, no. 93, facsm. ibid. Plate XXIIIa; facsm. in Conway Davies, 'Ewenny Priory', facing 132; cal. ibid. in Appendix I, no. 13, p. 132.

Galfrid(us) de Mandeuill' comes Essex' et Gloucestr' . H. Landauensi episcopo . et vicecomiti et ministris suis de Glamorgan et omnibus baronibus et hominibus suis Francis et Anglicis et Wallensibus Wallie salutem. Sciatis quod ego pro salute anime mee et comitisse Ysabelle uxoris mee et heredum meorum . et pro anima patris mei et antecessorum meorum concedo et confirmo elemosinam quam Mauricius de Lond' fecit in honore dei et sancti Michaelis et sancte Brigide deo et sancto Petro et monachis Gloucestr' . ecclesiam scilicet sancti Michaelis cum uilla de Eweni et pertinentiis suis et cum molendino sicut idem Mauricius illa liberius tenuit et ecclesiam sancte Brigide cum terris et decimis et omnibus pertinentiis suis sicut carta ipsius Mauricii et carte Willelmi heredis sui testantur. Saluo meo seruitio quod heredes eorum adquietabunt. Concedo etiam et confirmo eisdem monachis terram unam in uilla de Kenefeg in uico occidentali usque ad aquam nigram liberam et quietam ab omni consuetudine et seruitio[.] Concedo etiam priori et monachis de Eweni et seruientibus suis ut libere ab omni consuetudine et theloneo per totam terram meam Wallie ad usum suum ement et uendant. Hiis testibus Nicholao Poinz . Willelmo Blundo . Willelmo de Kaerdif . Gilberto de Turberuilla . Radulfo de Swinesheued . Herberto de Haweie . Ricardo Norrense . magistro Radulfo Mailoc . Thoma Pirun . et multis aliis.

The charter was written by the earldom of Gloucester's Scribe xxvii; Geoffrey became earl *iure uxoris* after he married Countess Isabelle in 1214 some time after 16 January (Patterson, *EGC*, 7–8, 20). Ralph Mailoc was a canon of Llandaff, who attested comital *acta*; Nicholas Poinz, William de Cardiff, Gilbert de Turberville, and Richard Norris were honorial tenants in Glamorgan (ibid. Index, s.vv.; Nicholl, *Normans in Glamorgan*, Index, s.vv.; Crouch, *LEA*, xii, nos. 49, 73).

25. *Alleged foundation charter of Ewenny Priory by Maurice de Londres. (1140 × 48; s. xiii^{in})*

N.L.W., P & M MS. no. 2800 (181 mm × 81 mm); tag for seal; seal missing; endorsements: Carta Mauricii de Lond' (s. xiii^{in}); Eweny de laycis tenuris (s. xiv); Clark, *Cartae et alia*, vi, no. 1621; cal. in Conway Davies, 'Ewenny Priory', Appendix III, pp. 135–36; *EAWD*, ii, no. L.119.

Notum sit omnibus domini diligentibus quod ego Maurici(us) de Lond' de uoluntate Adelais uxoris mee assensuque heredum meorum dedi et concessi et hac presenti carta mea confirmaui deo et beato Michaeli et sanctissime Brigide ad prioratum meum de Ewenni sustinendum priori meo de Hoggemora et fratribus in dicto prioratu deo deuote seruientibus ecclesiam sanctissime Brigide cum omnibus pertinentiis suis in puram et perpetuam elemosinam etiam cum eadem uilla ita libere et pacifice sicut aliqua elemosina melius potest possideri. Et habebunt homines dicti prioris illi scilicet de sancta Brigida communem pasturam a parte occidentali usque ad castrum de Hoggemora. Do etiam dicto prioratui ecclesiam sancti Michaelis de Ewenni cum terris et decimis ad eandem pertinentibus cum uilla de Ewenni et molendino de uado et siluula que est ad australem partem torrentis Alun. Et totam terram que est ex parte siluule a terra Roberti de Landefei usque ad pascua equorum domini. Et ex parte orientis totam terram de domo Edrici vicecomitis usque ad ripam Ewenni. Et centum acras quas habeo in feudo de ecclesia Thevkesburie[1] pro viginti solidis per singulos annos. Do etiam dicto prioratui ecclesiam sancti Michaelis de Colewinest' cum terris et decimis que ad illam pertinent. Do etiam ecclesiam de Haneduna et ecclesiam de Esegarest' cum omnibus que ad illas pertinent. Et omnes ecclesias de Carwathlan. Do etiam illis ecclesiam de Penbrei. Et ecclesiam de sancto Ismaele. Et ecclesiam de Landivailoc et omnes ecclesias terre mee quam modo habeo et quam adhuc adquiere potero. Do etiam dicto priori ut de nemore meo lignorum capiat sufficientiam absque alicuius calumpnia. Et capellam que est in nemore meo de Hoggemora. Cum autem prefate ecclesie predicto prioratui fuerint apropriate erit ibi conuentu ad minus tresdecim monachorum Gloucestrensis ordinis. Vt autem hec mea donatio iugiter perseueret . hoc presens scriptum meum sigillo meo communiui. Hiis testibus . Domino Vtredo Land' episcopo . Vrbano archidiacono . Pagano de ueteri castello . Goffrido de Chausi . Roberto de Cantulupo . Elia de Cantulupo . Oeno milite . Edwardo et Rogero armigeriis . Et Germano et Serlone ministris eiusdem loci . et aliis.

The St. Peter's Calendar of Donations attributes Ewenny's foundation by Maurice son of William de Londres to 1141; it adds that Maurice also gave St. Peter's the church of Oystermouth in Gower, the church of Pembrey, and the church of St. Ishmael 1139 × 48 with the confirmation of Archbishop Theobald ('Historia', 75–76). For the problem of Ewenny's foundation date see above, p. xxix & n.). Prof. Conway Davies did not question the authenticity of this charter ('Ewenny Priory', 109). The script is early thirteenth-century.

[1] *v* written over *o* in MS.

26. *Alleged charter of Maurice de Londres in favour of Ewenny Priory. (1148 ×
66; s. xiiiⁱⁿ)*

H.C.L., no. 2292 (111 mm × 96 mm [original meas.; currently as unfolded, 103 mm]);
endorsements: prima carta. ostandenda (s. xiii[2]); Eweny de laycis tenuris (s. xiv); facsm. in
Conway Davies, 'Ewenny Priory', facing p. 109, cal. Appendix I, no. 1, p. 129.

Maurici(us) de Lond' omnibus suis hominibus honoris de Vggom' salutem.
Sciatis me firmiter concessisse et hac carta mea confirmasse domino Bertranno
priori meo de Vggomor' et omnibus prioribus sibi succedentibus ut omne quod
tenent de me et heredibus meis tam libere teneant et pacifice ut nullus de meis
aliquid exigere possit preter orationes . sed habeat dictus prior cum monachis[1]
suis totum suum per se seperatur ut non liceat hominibus meis aliquid
communitatis exigere in terra dictorum monachorum nisi tamen de licentia
eorum. Sed uolo quod homines dicti prioris, illi, scilicet, de sancta Brigida,
communicent in illa duna mea que est ex parte occidentali uersus castrum meum
de Vggom'. Uolo etiam ut prefatus prior habeat omnes ecclesias de baronia mea
uidelicet ecclesiam sancte Brigide et ecclesiam de Colew'iston' et ecclesiam de
Egliskaynor . et similiter de Karwþathlan . de Penbray . de sancto Ysmaele . de
Landivayloc . ecclesias cum omnibus suis pertinentiis. Similiter de Hanedon' . de
Esgarston' ecclesias in Anglia. Et confirmo illas viginti quatuor acras uersus
Wica' a ponte riuuli alum scilicet . eo modo quo Gillebertus de Turb'uill' eis
dedit. Et fortiter prohibeo sub forsfactura decem librarum ne quis de meis dictos
monachos molestet super ista mea concessione. Hiis testibus . domino .N.
Landauensi episcopo . Willelmo de Lond' filio meo . Gilliberto de T'b'uill' .
Radulfo milite . Germano.

The charter was written by Glamorgan Scribe 13 whose approximately early thirteenth-century script betrays his forgery (see no. 13 n.).

[1] *manachis* in MS.

27. *Confirmation by William de Londres son of John Le Sor to St. Peter's,
Gloucester, of grants in alms made by Maurice de Londres, his grandfather
William, and Thomas de Londres, namely the church of St. Michael Ewenny with
the vill and appurtenances. (1223 × 50)*

N.L.W., P & M MS. no. 2802 (194 mm × 189 mm); tag for seal; wax stain on tag; seal
missing; written on tag just below foot *Carta bona*; endorsements: Confirmatio Willelmi
de London' (s. xiii[2]); .Ewenny. de laycis tenuris' (s. xiv[ex]); Clark, *Cartae et alia*, vi, no.
1621; cal. in Conway Davies, 'Ewenny Priory', Appendix III, p. 136.

Sciant presentes et futuri quod ego Willelmus de Londoniis filius Iohannis Le
Sor . concessi et confirmaui deo et ecclesie sancte Petri de Gloescestria et

monachis ibidem deo seruientibus in puram et perpetuam elemosinam omnes elemosinas quas Mauricius de Londoniis . et Willelmus auus et Thomas de Lond' dederunt prefate ecclesie. Scilicet ecclesiam sancti Michaelis de Eweni cum uilla de Eweni et omnibus pertinentiis cum prato et molendino et sequela sua. Concessi etiam quod omnes homines mei qui ibi uoluerint molere ibi moleant sine calumnia uel contradictione'. preter homines de Colowinestona. Concessi etiam illis'. ecclesiam sancte Brigide cum terris et decimis et omnibus pertinentiis suis. Et ecclesiam sancti Michaelis de Colowinestuna cum terris et decimis et omnibus pertinentiis suis . et sexaginta sex acras terre in eadem uilla. Similiter ecclesiam de Hanadune . et ecclesiam de Esegarestuna . et ecclesiam sancti Ismaelis . et ecclesiam de Penbrai. Similiter ecclesiam sancti Eslini de Carnewalan . et ecclesiam sancti Dauid . et ecclesiam sancti Iohannis in Carnewalan cum terris et decimis et omnibus pertinentiis suis . et capellam de Egleskeinn cum omnibus pertinentiis suis . Et omnes ecclesias mee terre quas modo habeo et ad huc perquirere potero. Similiter totam terram que est ex parte siluule de Aluuna usque ad pascua equorum domini[1] et ex parte orientis totam terram de domo Edrici uicecomitis usque ad ripam de Eweni . et centum acras terre in Bluntesduna. Concessi etiam et confirmaui predictis monachis decem et octo acras terre de feudo Ricardi de Landefei . et duas acras que fuerunt Stephani Marescot . et totam terram suam in Pitcota . et pro omnibus seruitiis ad predictam terram pertinentibus tam regalibus quam forinsecis ego et heredes mei respondebimus. Similiter piscarturam de Pencott cum loco hospitali super eundem fluuium . in Carnewalan . et totam terram quam Ricardus de Cantulupo possederat in Esegarest' . et totam terram de Suleham . aut escambium secundum quod ualet. Hiis . testibus Gileberto de Turb'uilla . Willelmo de Cantul' . Petro pincerna . Waltero Gundi . Dionisio Coco . Audono filio Hereberti . Ricardo Blundo . Iohanne sacerdote . Henrico camerario . Roberto Sem' . Hunfrido . Mauricio . Goffrido de Cored' . et multis aliis.

The identity of the donor, William de Londres, son of John Le Sor, is uncertain. Prof. Conway Davies, who believed that this charter was either the authentic original or a contemporary copy, has discussed the problem ('Ewenny Priory', 112–13 & n.); see also Nicholl, *Normans in Glamorgan*, 82–83, 105–6.

[1] Erasure in MS. at the terminal *i* of *domini*.

28. *Notification by Alexander son of William of Corendon that he has granted to Ewenny Priory all his land at Goldland with appurtenances, which he had recovered from the monks in the county court of Cardiff, in order to procure ornaments for the church. (1230 × 40?)*

H.C.L., no. 2302 (142 mm × 65 mm); fragment of tag through slit on turn-up; seal missing; endorsement: Carta Alexandri de Corond' (s. xiii[2]); cal. in Conway Davies, 'Ewenny Priory', Appendix I, no. 11, p. 131.

Sciant presentes et futuri quod ego Alex(ander) filius Willelmi de Corendun' pro salute anime mee et parentum meorum dedi et concessi et hac presenti carta mea confirmaui deo et ecclesie sancti Michaelis de Eweni et monachis ibidem commorantibus ad ornamenta eiusdem ecclesie inuenienda totam terram meam de Goldeland cum pertinentiis . illam scilicet quam recuperaui de predictis monachis in comitatu de Kairdif tenendam et habendam de me et heredibus meis siue[1] attornatis meis in puram et perpetuam elemosinam ita libere et pacifice sicut aliqua elemosina liberius et melius teneri potest . nichil inde michi uel successoribus meis reseruando . nisi tantum orationes. Sed ego et heredes mei uel noster attornatus pro omni seculari seruitio et demanda domino uel domine de Wggemorr' de cuius feudo est[.] respondebimus et contra omnes homines et feminas predictam elemosinam perpetuo warentizabimus. In huius rei testimonium hoc presens scriptum sigillo meo sic communiui. His testibus . domino Elya tunc Landauensi episcopo . Radulfo de nouo castro . Willelmo de Lameys tunc decano . Roberto de Cantilupo [.] Iohanne Wicario de sancta Brigida . Henrico Pinchu' . Ricardo Ingan . et aliis.

From the attestation of Bishop Elias of Llandaff, the notification was issued in 1230 × 40 (*GCH*, 693).

1 *sui* in MS.

29. *Notification by William Scurlage of his confirmation of the gift which his father made to Ewenny Priory of 24 acres at Llangewydd (Glam.). (1148 × 83)*

H.C.L., no. 2296 (180 mm × 83 mm [orig. meas.; now unfolded, 100 mm]); slit for tag on turn-up; tag and seal missing; endorsement: Confirmatio Will(elm)i Scurlag. (s.xiii[in]); cal. in Conway Davies, 'Ewenny Priory', Appendix I, no. 5, p. 130.

Sciant presentes et futuri quod ego Will(el)m(us) Scurlag pro salute animę meę et patris mei et omnium parentum meorum concedo et confirmo donationem patris mei Willelmi . scilicet . xxiiii.[or] acras terrę apud Landchewi quas dedit deo et ecclesię sancti Michaelis de Ewenni et monachis ibidem deo seruientibus in perpetuam elemosinam tenendam de se et heredibus suis libere et quiete ab omni terreno seruitio. Concedo etiam predictis monachis ut habeant communitatem omnium adeisamentorum totius terrę meę in paschuis et aquis et uiis et omnibus rebus ita liberam et quietam ab omni seruitio sicut illam prius pater meus eis dederat. Et ego et heredes mei adquietabimus supradictos monachos erga seculares dominos ab omnibus seruitiis et exactionibus. Quod ut ratum et inconuulsum permaneat[.] presenti scripto et sigilli mei munimine confirmo. His testibus Nicholao episcopo Landauensi . Willelmo diacono . Willelmo de Lund' . Roberto presbitero[1] . Benedicto . Ernaldo . Hugone . Hereberto presbiteris . Germano . Osberto . Roberto clerico . Alexandro milite . Baldwino . Rogero[2] . Ricardo filio Alfredi . Sauaro[3] . et aliis pluribus.

The charter was written by Glamorgan Scribe 7 (see no. 13 n.).

1 *cap(ellano)* added superscript apparently in the same hand.
2 *ioie* added superscript apparently in the same hand.
3 *aucupe* superscript in the same hand.

30. *Charter of Gilbert de Turberville confirming to Ewenny Priory a small meadow called* Leomeresham *that Hugh son of Elfric gave to the church. (1148 × 66)*

H.C.L., no. 2293 (170 mm × 81 mm); slit for tag on turn-up; tag and seal missing; endorsement: Confirmatio .G. de Turb'uilla de pratello de Leomeresham (s. xiii^{in}); cal. in Conway Davies, 'Ewenny Priory', Appendix I, no. 2, p. 129.

Notum sit tam presentibus quam futuris quod ego Gileb(er)t(us) de Turb'uilla concessi ecclesię sancti Michaelis de Vggom' et Bert'anno priori fratribusque ibidem deo seruientibus pratellum quod dicitur Leomeresham quod Hugo filius Elfrici predicte ecclesie dedit in elemosinam . liberum et quietum ab omni seruitio perpetuo possidendum . prefatusque prior dedit michi quoddam uexillum in recognitionem. Vnde quamquidem hoc semper ratum et inconuulsum consistere uolo✓. presenti scripto ac sigilli mei contestatione confirmo. His testibus . Thoma . Adam . monachis . Willelmo decano . Ernulfo . et Willelmo presbiteris . Germano clerico . Rannulfo . et pluribus aliis.

This charter was written by Glamorgan Scribe 7 (see no.13 n.). The Turbervilles were Glamorgan lords of Coety, a member lordship held of the lordship of Glamorgan as a serjeanty tenure (*GCH*, 23, 287); for Gilbert, see Patterson, *EGC*, nos. 68, 105, 135, and Nicholl, *Normans in Glamorgan*, 33–34.

31. *Grant of Gilbert de Turberville confirming to Ewenny Priory the donation which his brother Simon made of a rustic and 40 acres and adding for the soul of his brother 23 acres at* Wic. *(1148–79)*

H.C.L., no. 2295 (203 mm × 180 mm); seal on purple silk cords; purple wax, fragment, chipped; round (meas. unavail.); a helmeted equestrian figure to the right; reins and shield in left hand, in right hand a raised sword; no counterseal; endorsements: Carta Gileb(erti) fratris Symonis de Turberuill' (s. xiii^2); Carueldon (s. xiii^{ex} × s. xiv^{in}); cal. in Conway Davies, 'Ewenny Priory', Appendix I, no. 4, p. 130.

Sciant presentes et futuri quod ego Gislebert(us) de Turbeuilla concessi ecclesie sancti Michaelis de Ewenni et monachis ibidem commorantibus illam donationem quam Symon frater meus illis donauit in elemosinam uidelicet quendam rusticum nomine Godricum fullonem et quadraginta acras que iuxta illum habentur et totam terram de Caruelden quam idem Symon frater meus dedit prefatis monachis in presentia domini Nicholai Landauensis episcopi et in presentia Mauricii de London' coram multis testibus. Dedi etiam eis pro anima fratris mei et pro animabus omnium antecessorum meorum .xxiiii.^{or} acras apud Wicam . et ut habeant inperpetuum unum sumarium in nemore meo ad eundum propter ligna . duabus uidelicet uicibus singulis diebus in hieme et tribus uicibus singulis diebus in estate. Et hec omnia eis dedi et firme in elemosinam concessi . ut ea teneant libere et quiete ab omni terreno seruitio. Et ut ista inperpetuum firma sint et inconuulsa sigilli mei attestatione ea muniui . et coram testibus qui subscribuntur ecclesie sancti Michaelis et fratribus qui ibi commorantur in presentia domini Hamelini abbatis Gloecest'ie confirmaui. Me ipsum etiam in quocunque habitu uel loco decessero'. simul cum heredibus meis in predicta ecclesia sancti Michaelis'. sepeliendum facta super altare solempni oblatione concessi. His testibus . Helia de Boleu' . Roberto Sacerdote . Willelmo Sac(rista) . Randulfo uenatore . Drogone filio Alurici . Edwardo p(re)tore . Ricardo de Croilli . Rogero Mainardi . Germano clerico . Willelmo de Fluri . Cadiuor . Osberno de Cliue.

Mention of Abbot Hamelin dates the document.

32. *Grant of land at* Corendon *(Glam.) to Ewenny Priory by Gilbert de Turberville with the assent of his wife Agnes; the land was held of Gilbert by William of Corendon. (1210 × 19)*

H.C.L., no. 2301 (148 mm × 128 mm); tag for seal; residue of white wax on tag; seal missing; endorsements: Carta G. de Turb'eWill' (s. xiii^{in}); Carta C. de Turberuill' de terra Malemfant.(s. xiii^{in} × s. xiii^{med}); cal. in Conway Davies, 'Ewenny Priory', Appendix I, no. 10, p. 131.

Sciant presentes et futuri quod ego Gilebertus de Turberuilla assensu et uoluntate Agnetis vxoris mee et heredum meorum concedo et confirmo deo et ecclesie sancti Michaelis de Eaweni . et monachis ibidem deo seruientibus pro anima mea et vxoris mee et antecessorum et successorum meorum in perpetuam et puram elemosinam totam terram que fuit Malemfant in feudo de Corendona . quam Willelmus de Corendona tenet de me. Que scilicet iacet ab australi parte regalis vie in Corendona'. usque ad albam crucem'. super montem positam . Per easdem diuisas per eosdem terminos . sicut ille Willelmus de me et antecessorem eius de antecessoribus meis unquam melius et liberius tenuerunt . Preter nouem acras terre quas Philippus Hairun et Willelmus Kech . et Walterus eius frater et Edith Sparke tunc de Willelmo tenuerunt. Willelmus uero et heredes sui hanc predictam elemosinam predictis monachis contra omnes homines et feminas warantizabunt. Et pro omni seruitio seculari et exactione . michi et heredibus meis et omnibus hominibus respondebunt in omnibus. Hiis testibus . domino Thoma de London' . Willelmo de Cant' . Petro pincerna . et Iohanne filio eius . Ricardo de Landefei . Oeno filio Hereberti . Dionisio coco . Nicholao de Fluri . et multis aliis.

The Gilbert of this grant was the grandson of the previous Gilbert and attested several Gloucester comital *acta* of Countess Isabelle and Earl Geoffrey (see nos. 30–31; Patterson, *EGC*, nos. 93, 139–40, 148–49).

33. *Notification by letter patent from Henry de Turberville lord of Ogmore of his responsibility to pay Ewenny Priory 10 marks from the first proceeds of money from Ogmore (Glam.). 8 October 1237. Gloucester.*

H.C.L., no. 2310 (152 mm × 48 mm); tongue torn; tie and seal missing; endorsements: Eweny de laycis tenuris (s. xiii^{ex} × s. xiv^{in}); written across left foot (inverted), script in different hand: . . .en. Vicecom' . . . de stan. . . [1] (poss. s. xii^ex); cal. in Conway Davies, 'Ewenny Priory', Appendix I, D, p. 134.

Omnibus ad quorum notitiam littere presentes peruenerint Henr(icus) de Trubleuill' dominus Leuggemor' salutem in domino. Noueritis quod tenemur dilecto nostro patri in Cristo priori de Eweni in .x. marcis sterlingorum. ad soluendas illas de primis exitibus denariorum terre nostre de Uggemor' sibi uel successoribus assignatis. Si forte dictus prior nobiscum aliquam finem faciet de aliqua re. aliquo casu contingente . nos dictas marcas in fine dicto allaudabimus et sibi uel suis plenarie restituerimus. In cuius testimonium has litteras nostras eidem fieri patentes. Datum apud Glou'n' . Die Iouis post octabas sancti Michaelis . Anno domini .m.° cc.° xxx.° septimo.

Henry de Turberville married the de Londres heiress after the death of her husband Walter de Braose in 1234 and had died himself by 1240 (Conway Davies, 'Ewenny Priory', 126–7 & n.).

[1] Reading uncertain.

---

34. *Quitclaim of the right over the church of Llandyfodwg (Glam.) to St. Peter's, Gloucester, to support their brethren at Ewenny Priory by Enyr Vachan (Fychan), son of Enyr ab Wrgenn. (c. 1261)*

H.C.L., no. 2297 (228 mm × 136 mm); seal on tag, green wax, chipped, round (22 mm in diam.); an eight-point star or rosette; legend: . . . S'ENER VAH. . .; no counterseal; endorsement: carta Eyner Vackan de ecclesia de Landeuodok (s. xiii^med); cal. in Conway Davies, 'Ewenny Priory', Appendix I, no. 6, p. 130.

Sciant presentes et futuri quod ego Eneyr Vachan filius Eneri ab Wrgenn assensu et voluntate Neest vxoris mee et omnium heredum meorum dedi . et concessi . et hac presenti carta mea confirmaui . et quietum clamaui deo et ecclesie sancti Petri de Gloucest'ia et monachis ibidem deo seruientibus ad sustentatione fratrum suorum apud Ewe'ny commorantium totum ius quod ego et heredes mei habuimus . uel habere potuimus in ecclesia de Landewodoc . Cum terris . et decimis . et omnibus libertatibus ad dictam ecclesiam pertinentibus . ut eam habeant et teneant . pro me et heredibus meis . Ita libere . et quiete . sicut aliqua elemosina potest melius et liberius dari . vel possideri. Concessi etiam priori de Ewenny . et monachis ibidem commorantibus vt habeant omnia aisiamenta in terra mea . In boscis meis . et in pasturis meis . In viis . et semitis . In aquis . et omnibus locis . sine calumpnia . et contradictione mei . uel heredum meorum. Et tam ego quam heredes mei hanc predictam donationem . et quietam clamationem predictis monachis contra omnes homines et feminas imperpetuum warantizabimus. Vt autem hec mea donatio . et concessio . et quieta clamatio rata et stabilis permaneat presentem cartam sigilli mei impressione roboraui. Hiis testibus . domino Ricardo pyncerna . domino Iohanne pyncerna . domino Danyele Siwart . Thoma de Hodenet . Rogero Vachan . Willelmo Selikoc . et multis aliis.

35. *Grant of the church of Llandyfodwg (Glam.) to St. Peter's, Gloucester, for the support of Ewenny Priory by William son of Wrgenn. (s. xiii^{in}; from 1207)*

G.C.L., 'Deeds and Seals', v, no. 25, fol. 10 (190 mm × 165 mm); knotted fragment of cords for seal on foot through two slits; seal missing; endorsement: Carta .W. Wrgenni de ecclesia de Landewduch (s. xiii^{in}); cal. in Conway Davies, 'Ewenny Priory', Appendix II, no. 1, p. 135.

Sciant presentes et futuri quod ego Will(elmu)s filius Wrgeni assensu et uoluntate Guere uxoris mee et Oeni et Moreduth fratrum meorum et omnium heredum meorum dedi et confirmaui deo et ecclesie sancti Petri de Gloecest'ia et monachis ibidem deo seruientibus ad sustentationem fratrum suorum apud Eweni commorantibus commitandam in puram et perpetuam elemosinam ecclesiam de Landewduc cum omnibus pertinentiis suis . Et omne ius quod ego aut antecessores mei in predicta ecclesia umquam melius et liberius habuimus ut eam teneant i(m)perpetuum libere et quiete absque omnibus actionibus et demandis. Concessi etiam predictis monachis omnia aisiamenta in terra mea . in boscis meis et in pasturis meis in uiis et semitis in aquis et omnibus locis sine calumnia et contradictione. Et ut hec mea donatio et confirmatio rata et inconcussa permaneat presentem cartam sigilli mei i(m)pressione confirmaui. Hiis testibus . domino Gilleberto de Turb'uill' . Petro pincerna . Willelmo de Cantilupo . Radulfo decano de Landu . Nicolao de Leswrunu . Iohanne de sancta Brigida . Iohanne de Kenefeg capellano . Kenwrec filio Wian . Ada de Turberuill' . Madoco filio Goronu . Willelmo Turri . Iorouorth filio Wrgenni . Ricardo de Ingehan . Iohanne de Nategraue . Iuoro Gor . Willelmo de Landu . Ricardo de Westune . et multis aliis.

Gilbert de Turberville received seisin of his lordship in 1207 (Nicholl, *Normans in Glamorgan*, 34). For the identification of the church see Conway Davies, 'Ewenny Priory', 116 & n.

EWYAS HAROLD PRIORY

36. Compositio *between Richard archdeacon of Wiltshire and St. Peter's, Gloucester, regarding tithes of Robert of Ewyas from Clevancy (Wilts.). Richard was to enjoy the tithes for his life, rendering a pound of incense annnually to the prior of Ewyas; after his death, the tithes were to belong to St. Peter's, Gloucester. (1178?)*

H.C.L., no. 784 (202 mm × 116 mm), **Scribe 8** (below, Plate VIIb); seal on tag, white wax, rubbed; oval (*c*. 49 mm × 30 mm); a robed ecclesiastical figure facing front; legend: + SIGILLVM RIC. . RDI AR. . .DIACONI . . .IENSIS; no counterseal; endorsements: De decimis Roberti de Ewias de Cliua contra . . .[1] Ric(ardum) archidiaconum (s. xii^{ex}); Non indiget registrari (s. xiv^{ex} × s. xv^{in}); Walker, 'Gloucester Charters', no. 6; cal. in Baddeley i, no. 13, p. 228.

Universis sancte matris ecclesie filiis . Ric(ardus) archidiaconus Wiltesire salutem in domino. Sciatis quod talis compositio facta est inter me et monachos

Gloec' in presentia venerabilis domini nostri Rogeri Wigorniensis episcopi super decima dominii Roberti de Ewias de Cliua . quod ego in uita mea tantum eandem decimam de prefatis monachis tenebo reddens priori eorum de Ewias singulis annis unam libram incensi in Assumptione sancte Marie apud Gloec'. Post decessum autem meum . uel uite mutationem[1] predicta decima libera et quieta restituetur monachis Gloec' absque omni reclamatione alicuius. Quod quia ratum uolo et immutabile permanere[1] presenti scripto sigillum meum apposui. His testibus . Symone archidiacono . magistro Moyse . magistro Siluestro . magistro Iohanne de Paris . Will(el)mo Cantore.

The date for this actum appears to be 1178, based on Bishop Roger's known itinerary; its scribe also wrote H.C.L. no. 2771 (Cheney, *Roger, Bishop of Worcester*, 231, 262, 287). For the establishment of Ewyas as a priory of Gloucester, see above, p. xxix. Master Simon Lovel was archdeacon of Worcester from 1167/68 to 1189/90 (*Fasti*, ii. 105).

[1]   Damaged and illegible with ultra-violet light.

37. *Grant by Abbot Henry and the convent of St. Peter's, Gloucester, to the clerk Gerard of Pinkney of the church of St. Faith (Foy, Herefs.) with the appurtenances which belonged to their church of Ewyas as his predecessor William of Kilpec held it. (1205 × 15)*

H.C.L., no. 799 (164 mm × 147 mm); seal on tag, white wax, fragment; obverse, partial torso of seated figure wearing cope or cloak; reverse: fragment of a counterseal (below, Plate Ig): an abbot in vestments facing front; in right hand a staff or crozier; in left hand, an upraised book; legend: . . . ABBATIS GLOVCEST . . .; no medieval endorsement; Capes, *Hereford Charters*, p. 43; cal. in Baddeley i, no. 24, pp. 231–2.

Sciant presentes et futuri quod ego Henric(us) dei gratia abbas et conuentus sancti Petri Glouc' concessimus diuine pietatis intuitu dilecto clerico Gerardo de Pinkinni ecclesiam nostram de sancta Foa cum omnibus pertinentiis suis saluis antiquius portionibus ad ecclesiam nostram de Ewias de iure spectantibus tenendam sicut dominus Willelmus de Kilp' precentor Hereford' predecessor eius eam tenuit. In cuius rei testimonium presentem cartam sigillo ecclesie nostre munitam[1] ei tradidimus. Hiis testibus . magistro Hugone de Mapen' decano H'eford' . domino Willelmo precentore . domino Helya thesaurario . magistro Theobaldo . magistro Albinno . magistro Willelmo de La Rie . magistro Willelmo de Bergeuen' . canonicis Hereford' . Grente . Henrico de sancto Walerico . Iohanne coco . seruientibus domini episcopi Hereford' . Drogone pincerna . Salomone ianitore . Mauricio stabulario . Symone de aula . Galfrido de cellario . seruientibus domini abbatis Glouc' et multis aliis.

Hugh de Mapenore was dean of Hereford *c*. 1201–15 (Barrow, *Hereford Episcopal Acta*, pp. xlvi–xlvii). Harold of Ewias gave the church of St. Faith with a carucate and tithes from the mill as added endowment to his newly founded priory of St. Peter's, Gloucester, at Ewyas ('Historia', 76); see above, p. xxix.

GLOUCESTER ABBEY: ENGLISH POSSESSIONS

38. *Alleged writ-charter of King William 1 addressed to Wulfstan bishop of Worcester, William fitz Osbern, and all the king's barons and officers in Gloucestershire and Worcestershire: the king granted and confirmed to Abbot Serlo and the convent of St. Peter's, Gloucester, all the lands which Thomas archbishop of York unjustly held. (c. 1070; s. xii^{in})*

A. H.C.L., no. 1168 (200 mm × 107 mm); seal on tongue with tie, reddish brown wax, fragment, repaired; obverse: partial image of the king enthroned to front holding an upraised sword in right hand; legend: . . .O FATEARIS. E . . .NDE . . .; reverse: fragment, repaired; partial image of an equestrian figure to the right; in right hand the shaft of an upraised lance or standard extending to the ground; in the left, a shield and reins; legend: . . . ORMANNORVM . . .LLEL. . .; endorsements: Will(elmus) rex de Lech et Otintuna. et Stanedis. (s. xii^{in}); c(apsula) .viii.^{a} de laicis tenuris (s. xii^{ex} × s. xiii^{in}), poss. **Hand h**; **B**. P.R.O., C 150/1, fol. 167v; **C**. G.C.L., 'Reg. B', no. 221, p. 87; Capes, *Hereford Charters*, 2–3; *Cart. Glouc.* ii, no. 598; iii, no. 1006; cal. *Regesta*, i, no. 36.

Will(el)mus rex Anglorum. Wulstano episcopo Wigornie . et Willelmo filio Osberni . et omnibus baronibus et ministris suis de Gloecestra et de Wigrecestra scira͝. salutem. Sciatis me concessisse et reddidisse atque confirmasse deo et sancto Petro de Gloecestra et Serloni abbati et monachis eiusdem ecclesie omnes terras suas quas Thomas archiepiscopus Eboracensis iniuste tenebat . scilicet Læccie[1] . Ottintuna . Stanedis cum omnibus eisdem pertinentibus sic solutas et quietas͝. sicut ante me recognitum est easdem terras ad ecclesiam prefatam sancti petri de Gloecestra a sui principio pertinuisse . et eundum archiepiscopum nullum ius in illis terris habuisse. Quare uolo et firmiter precipio ut ecclesia prenominata de Gloecest' has supradictas terras cum omnibus sibi pertinentibus bene . et in pace . libere . et quiete . et honorifice teneat cum saca . et socna . et toll . et team . et infangendeof . et cum omnibus rectitudinibus . legibus . et consuetudinibus͝. quas eidem ecclesie nostra regia potestate concessi. Et defendo super hoc ne aliquis ei iniuriam uel torturam siue calumpniam faciat super forisfacturam meam. T(estibus) Lanfranco archiepiscopo . Gaufrido de Constantiis . et Roberto comite de Moretan'.

For the critique of this charter, the work of a Westminster Abbey forger, see *Regesta*, i, no. 36 n. and Bishop and Chaplais, *English Royal Writs*, pp. xxi–xxii & n. Dr. Chaplais identified twelve other fabrications, and possibly a thirteenth, by the scribe who wrote the above writ. They suggest the possibility that King Stephen's illegitimate son Gervase of Blois, abbot of Westminster, was their 'instigator' (ibid. pp. xii–xiii). Dr. Chaplais has since added another forgery to the scribe's credit ('Westminster Charters', 89–110).

According to the abbey's 'Historia', the estates in question were Northleach, Oddington, Standish, and Barton (Gloucester); supposedly they had been held for 39 years when Archbishop Thomas of York returned them on Palm Sunday 1095 beating his breast on bended knee in the monks' chapter in the presence of Abbot Serlo ('Historia', 11–12, 93; see Burton, *York Episcopal Acta*, Appendix I, no. 1; Bates, 'Abbey of St. Peter's,

Gloucester', 130; and above, p. xxviii). Only during the abbacy of Hamelin in 1157 was the controversy between the abbey and the archbishopric finally ended when the abbey granted to Roger Oddington, Condicote, and Cherington, £23-worth of land, and the archbishop renounced any claim to the other lands (*Cart. Glouc.* i, pp. 19, 105).

[1] Terminal *-cie* possibly added in a different hand.

39. *Notification by King Henry I that, resulting from a plea held in his court in which Gilbert de Miners claimed Coln Rogers from the convent of St. Peter's, Gloucester, it was determined that the manor had been given to the abbey; and this the king confirmed. (22 May 1127) Winchester.*

A. G.C.L., 'Deeds and Seals', vii, no. 3, fol. 2 and v (301 mm × 154 mm), **Scribe 20**; writ with tongue and tie missing; seal missing; endorsements: Gileb' de Min'. (s. xii[2]); contra Gileb(ertum) de Mineres (s. xii[med]); de Culna Rogerii (s. xii); c(apsula) .ii.[a] de laicis tenuris. (s. xii[ex] × s. xiii[in]); Registratur (14th cent.?); finis placiti pro carta regis de manerio de Culn' Rogeri. [:] .C. te[m]p(or)a(iu)m p(ar)te prima. (s. xiv[ex] × s. xv); **B**. P.R.O., 150/1, fol. 59–59v; **C**. C.U.L., i.2.3; William of Malmesbury, *De Gestis Regum*, ii. 521 n.; *Cart. Glouc.* i, no. 143; Bigelow, 135; Van Caenegem, no. 248; cal. in *Regesta*, ii, no. 1485; *EAWD*, i, no. D.67.

H. rex Anglorum . archiepiscopis . episcopis . abbatibus . comitibus . baronibus . vicecomitibus . et omnibus fidelibus suis Francis et Anglis totius Anglie. salutem. Sciatis . quia monachi de Gloecestria . et Gislebertus de Mineriis . in curiam meam uenerunt coram me . ad terminum inter eos positum de placito manerii . de Chulna . quod Gislebertus uersus eos . et abbatem suum clamabat. Et Adam de Portd . et Willelmus filius Odonis . coram me testificati fuerunt . quod ipsi affuerunt . ubi Rogerus de Gloec' manerium illud . ecclesie sancti Petri Gloecestr' . et monachis ibidem deo seruientibus . in elemosinam dederat . et ubi ego requisitione ipsius Rogeri . donationem illam eis concessi . Et inde isdem Gislebertus iudicium recusauit.[1] T(estibus) . Willelmo archiepiscopo Cantuarie . et Rogero episcopo Saresb'ie . et Willelmo episcopo Wintonie . et Bernardo episcopo de sancto Dauid . et Willelmo episcopo Exonię . et Vrbano episcopo de Glammorgan . et Gaufrido cancellario . et Roberto de Sigillo . et Milone Gloec' . et Henrico de Pordt . et Waltero de Amfreuilla . et Willelmo de Folia . et Rogero et Willelmo filiis Adami de Pordt . apud Wintoniam.

Coln Rogers, according to the St. Peter's Calendar of Donors, came from Roger of Gloucester in 1105 ('Historia', 69, 123). Henry I's charter granting Coln Rogers to St. Peter's is in *Cart. Glouc.* i, no. 142 and William of Malmesbury, *De Gestis Regum*, ii. 521. For the dating see *Regesta*, ii, no. 1485 n.

[1] **B** as printed in *Cart. Glouc.* ends here.

40. *Alleged writ of King Henry I or Henry II of England granting and confirming to the convent of St. Peter's, Gloucester, all its wood which pertains to its manor of Ruddle (in Newnham). (s. xiii[med])*

A. P.R.O., E 42/308 (151 mm × 111 mm); seal on tongue; tie: white wax, lacquered brown, edges broken; repaired; round (84 mm in diam.); obverse: king enthroned to front; raised sword in right hand; an orb topped with a cross in left hand; legend illegible [possible *N* above orb cross]; reverse: equestrian figure in hauberk to right, upraised sword in right hand, shield and reins held by left hand; legend: . . .A.DVX . . .; endorsements: Carta Henr(ici) regis[1] de Sudrugge bosco .s. sacriste Glouc' (s. xiii); Registratur (s. xiv^{ex} × s.xv^{in});[2] **B.** G.C.L., 'Reg. B', no. 64, p. 24; facsm. in Hector, *Palaeography and Forgery*, Plate 2; Hall, *Formula Book*, no. 18; Delisle, *BEC* 68 (1907), no. 63, p. 292; listed in Vincent, *Acta of Henry II and Richard I*, no. 74.

H. rex Anglie et dux Normannorum et Aquitannorum et comes Andegauorum . iustic(iis) . vicecom(iti) et omnibus balliuis suis de Gloucestria salutem. Notum sit omnibus me dedisse concessisse et ista carta mea firmiter confirmasse deo et sancto Petro et monachis meis Glouc' . totum nemus suum de Sudrugg' . quod pertinet ad manerium suum de Rudel' . ut habeant et teneant in bona pace et quiete et libere absque omni seruitio uel demanda . et ut liceat eis de predicto nemore capere quantum voluerint et wastare et omnino facere inde quidquid eis sederit et melius viderint expedire in usum et comodum ecclesie sue. Et fortiter prohibeo sub forisfactura .x.^{em} librarum ne quis de ministris uel forestariis meis ibidem aliquam habeat dominationem uel preceptum nisi tantum de venatione capienda si forsan illuc deuenerint. Et sit dictum nemus extra regardum et defensum nullusque super ista libertate a me dictis monachis concessa . molestiam uel grauamen inferre presumat quin per vicecomitem Glouc' statim corigatur[.] Et pro ista mea concessione uolo habere unum cereum iugiter ardentem ante maius altare beati Petri Glouc.' Teste Henr(ico) Wintoniensi episcopo apud Wintoniam.

The script and the royal title *rex Anglie* are thirteenth-century (Chaplais, *English Royal Documents*, 13). Although it is possible to make a case for Henry II as the supposed donor, based on some elements of the *intitulatio* and the attestation of Henry bishop of Winchester (for attributions, see Delisle, *BEC*, 68 (1907), no. 63, p. 292; Vincent, *Acta of Henry II and Richard I*, no. 74), the seal seems to be an example of Henry I's fourth and the charter appears to have been offered by St. Peter's as evidence of a grant to the abbey by Henry I in inquests in the thirteenth and the sixteenth centuries (Chaplais, 'Seals and Original Charters of Henry I', 265; *Cart. Glouc.* ii. 187; *Guide to Seals*, 31 & n.; see also Hall, *Formula Book*, nos. 18–19, 23; Hector, *Palaeography and Forgery*, 12–13).

[1] Determined with the aid of ultra-violet light.
[2] Hall mistakenly dated (p. 24) the hand of *Registratur* as 16th-cent.

41. *Writ of King Stephen of England granting St. Peter's, Gloucester, a small wood and two assarts with adjacent meadows at Chelworth in free alms. (1135 × 39) Burford.*

A. Bodl. MS. Charters Gloucester, a.1, no. 5 (201 mm × 61 mm), **Scribe 20**; tongue and tie; seal missing; endorsements: de h . . . g . . . stan[1] (s. xii^{med}); 2) De Chelewrd'[;] c(apsula) vii.a de laicis tenuris (s. xii^{ex} × s. xiii^{in}); Registratur (s. xv?); Carta prima de manerio. *Siluula*. et duabus assartis in Celeswor*þe* .*C.* temporalium parte 2.a (*c.* s. xv^{in});

B. P.R.O., C 150/1, fols. 60–60v, 209v; *Cart. Glouc.* i, no. 154; ibid. ii, no. 779; *Regesta*, iii, no. 351.

S. rex Anglorum . Rogero episcopo Saresbiriensi . et vicecomiti Wiltesc . et omnibus baronibus Wiltesc'. salutem. Sciatis me concessisse monachis de Gloec' . in manerio meo de Celeswrda . siluulam et ii. essarta . cum pratellis adiacentibus illis . in elemosinam et feodum . liberam et quietam . pro anima mea . sicut rex Willelmus auunculus meus concessit . et sicut rex Henricus testatur per cartam suam. Teste . Rogero cancellario . apud Buref'.

The limits for the writ's date are the king's accession and the arrest and death of Bishop Roger to whom the writ was addressed. *Stephanus rex* in a different hand (s. xii) appears on the obverse of the tongue.

[1] Reading uncertain.

42. Writ of King Stephen of England declaring that the money of St. Peter's, Gloucester, was to be free of toll and custom. (1135 × 41)

A. Bodl. MS. Charters Gloucester, a.1, no. 6 (201 mm × 60 mm), **Scribe 22**; fragments of tongue and tie; seal missing; endorsements: caps(ula) . . .de laicis tenuris[1] (s. xii$^{..ex}$ × s. xiii); de teloneo et omni consuetuetudine (s. xii[2]); Caps(ula) .xiiii. de laicis tenuris (s. xiii[2]); Registratur (s. xiv × s. xv^{in}); **B**. P.R.O., C 150/1, fols. 177v, 241; *Cart. Glouc.* ii, nos. 646, 889; *Regesta*, iii, no. 346; facsm. in ibid. iv, Plate XX (a).

S. rex Anglorum . iustic(iis) . et vicecomitibus . et baronibus . et ministris suis Francis et Anglicis'. salutem. Precipio quod tota pecunia sancti Petri Gloec' et abbatis et monachorum sit quieta de theloneo et omni consuetudine ubique uenerit. Et defendo quod non disturbetur iniuste'. super .x. libris foristactura[2] . Teste M . Gloec'.

The writ was issued between the king's accession and Miles of Gloucester's elevation to the earldom of Hereford by the Empress in 1141 (*Regesta*, iii, no. 346n.).

[1] Caption crossed out and partly unreadable.
[2] **B** as recorded in *Cart. Glouc.* ends *facturae meae. Hiis testibus.*

43. Writ of King Stephen confirming the exchange made by Abbot Gilbert with Walter son of Richard son of Pons of St. Peter's land at Glasbury (Herefs.) for Walter's land at Eastleach. (c. 1144) Oxford.

A. G.C.L., 'Deeds and Seals', vi, no. 24, fol. 12 (182 mm × 93 mm), **Scribe 24**; tongue torn from left foot; tongue and seal missing; endorsements: Confirmatio (s. xiv^{ex}?); Stephani regis de escambio de Estlech. (s. xii^{med}); c(apsula) .xii. de Laicis tenuris (s. xii$^{..ex}$ × s. xiii^{in}); C. te(m)p(or)al(ium). p(ar)t' p(rim)a.[1] (s. xiv^{ex}?; same hand as *Confirmatio*); **B**. P.R.O., C 150/1, fol. 93v; *Cart. Glouc.* i, no. 280; *Regesta*, iii, no. 360; facsm. in ibid. iv, Plate XXXIV (a); Bishop, *Scriptores Regis*, no. 224.

S. rex Anglorum . episcopis . iustic(iis) . et vicecomitibus et baronibus . et ministris . et omnibus fidelibus suis totius Angl''. salutem. Sciatis me concessisse escambium illud quod abbas Gislebertus et conuentus Gloecestr' fecerunt cum Waltero filio Ricardi de terra sua de Glasberia pro terra eiusdem Walteri de Estleche. Quare uolo et firmiter precipio quod monachi Gloecestr' predictam terram de Estlech' bene et in pace et libere et quiete teneant et habeant cum omnibus libertatibus et liberis consuetudinibus eidem terre pertinentibus . sicut idem Walterus eam illis concessit[2]. T(estibus) . R(oberto) episcopo Lincolniense . et Willelmo de Caisn' . et Iordan' filio Tesc' . apud Oxen'.

According to the St. Peter's Calendar of Donations, Bernard of Neufmarché gave Glasbury-on-Wye with all its appurtenances to the abbey in 1088 ('Historia', 80, 122). The text of the transaction Stephen confirmed, dated 1144, is in *Cart. Glouc.* i, no. 275; another version is in ibid. ii, no. 819; other relevant charters are in ibid. nos. 276–9. The exchange of land is summarized in the Calendar of Donations ('Historia', 80).

[1]   Reading uncertain.
[2]   **B** as printed in *Cart. Glouc.* ends here with *etc.*

44.   *Alleged general confirmation charter of King Stephen in favour of St. Peter's, Gloucester, contained in an inspeximus of Simon bishop of Worcester. 1138. (1146 × 48)*

A. B.L. Cott. Ch. XVII.3 (accurate meas. unavail.; *c.* 213 mm [top] × *c.* 425 mm [right]), **Scribe 1** (below, Plate II); text probably damaged from the Cotton Library fire of 1732; mounted flattened on a backing, but signs of a single turn-up; on the lower right there is a triangular pattern of slits, one above and two below, parallel to the edge of the foot, indicating cords may have been used to seal the document; endorsements: Confirmatio (s. xii[med]); Conf (s. xiii[in]); Symonis (s. xiii[in]?); Caps(ula) .i. de ecclesiasticis et laicis tenuris (s. xiii[med]); **B.** P.R.O., C 150/1, fols. 48–49v; **C.** G.C.L., Reg. A, p. 16v (incomplete); *Monasticon*, i. 551–2; *Cart. Glouc.* i, no. 127; *Regesta*, iii, no. 345 (text of Stephen's charter only).

[A]NNO AB INCARNATIONE DOMINI NOSTRI IH[E]SU CRISTI MILLESIMO CENTESIMO XXXVIII. Ego Steph(anu)s rex Anglorum anno regni mei tertio . Petitione Walteri de Laci . abbatis Gloec' . et quorundam obtimatum meorum concessi et confirmaui ęcclesię sancti Petri de Gloec' . terras . ecclesias et decimas et omnes donation[es] [qua]s [b]arones Anglię predictę ęcclesię dederunt . et antecessores mei reges . per suas cartas confirmauer[un]t. Scilicet . Bertonam . Stanedis . Lecce . Otintuna' . ¶ Manerium de Maismora cum silua et terris adiacentibus ex dono Henrici regis. ¶ Broctrop[´]. ex dono Aheline de Hibreio. ¶ Colna' sancti Andree et duos ratcnihctes . et unam ecclesiam cum una hida terrę . et unum molendinum . ex dono Rogerii de Gloec'. ¶ Ecclesiam sancti Petri de Herefort . cum prebendis . et terris . et decimis . et omnibus rebus quę ad ea[m] pertinent . ex dono Hugonis de Laceio. ¶ Escambium de orto mona[chorum] in quo turris Gloec' sedet . sicut Walteri(us) uicecomes eis lib[er]auit[. ¶ E]ccl[esi]am sancti Cadoci de Lan[carvan] cum terra que uocat[ur Treigof] ex dono Rodberti filii Hamo[nis. ¶] In Hantescira unam terram [que u]oc[at]ur Liteltuna . ex dono Hugonis de Portu. ¶ In Lincheolt[h] ex dono

Ernulfi de Hesdine. ¶ [Led]ene quam reddidit Walterius de Laceio. ¶ In
Deuenesci[ra Plu]mtreu᷈. ex dono Odonis filii G[a]melini . quam postea [a]bbas
Serlo excambiuit Nich[ol]ao de Pola [pro terra que] dicitur Alnodestun[a.] ¶
Clekangra᷈. ex dono Rogerii de Berchelai. ¶ In Herefortscire [unam] hidam apud
Aspretunam ex dono Rodberti Curci. ¶ In eadem prouincia unam hidam ex dono
Willelmi de Ebroicis. ¶ In Er[che]nefelt᷈. terram de Uesteuude de dono Walterii
de Gloec'. ¶ Unam terrulam apud Getinges de dono Iurici de Logis. ¶
Molendin[um] d[e F]ramalada quod Winebaldus de Badelona reddidit ecclesie.
¶ Cliffort᷈. de dono Rogerii [de Busel]eio. ¶ Rudefor[d]᷈. ex dono Henrici regis.
¶ Rudelai᷈. ex dono Radulfi Bloiht. ¶ Ecclesiam [de Eth]dorp cum decima
eiusdem uille . et terra presbiteri . et in eadem uilla un[um] molendinum cum
terra pertinente. [¶ Ecclesi]am de Chinemeresfort . cum decima et terra
sacerdotis. ¶ Ecclesiam de Nortuna cum quinque uirgatis [terre] et cum decima et
aliis rebus adiacentibus ex dono Ernulfi de H[esdine] et Emmeline uxoris eius. ¶
De[cimam C]estre]tone᷈. de dono Nigelli de Oilli. ¶ De dono Helie Giff[ard]
quandam partem silue cum tribus bo[rdariis.] ¶ De dono Patricii de Cadurcis
unam uirgatam terre in Chin[e]meresfort . liberam ab omnibus [rebus] exceptis
geldis meis et unam mansuram in mora nigri fossati similit[e]r liberam . et domos
Edrici prefecti [in mora] illa positas . et terram que ei pertinet . et decimam
pratorum [illius] uille . et unum molendinum cum [terra ei per]tinente . et
decimam duorum molendinorum ibidem . et unam [hidam] terre in Omenai de
feodo et co[ncessu] Pa[tri]cii. ¶ In eadem uilla dimid[iam] hidam quam Toui
tenuit [in] elemosina de rege Henrico. [¶ Glas]b'iam apud Brechennio cum terris
et [sil]uis et omnibus ad eam pertin[en]tibus . et totam decimam totius dom[inii
de Brechennio] scilicet . annone . pecorum . [c]aseorum uenationum [melli]s.
Insuper [etiam] eccl[esiam de Coure cum] tota dec[ima] illius parrochie [et ter]ra
ad ipsam ecclesiam pertinente . et una[m h]idam qu[e uocatur Be]che ex dono
Bernardi de No[u]o Mercato. [¶ E]cclesiam [sanc]ti Gunliu cu[m] terra et decimis
ei [pertinentibus] ex dono Willelmi regis. ¶ M[ol]endinum de dono Helie Giffart.
¶ Ecclesiam de Cerne [cum decima] ad eam pertinente . et ecclesiam sancte
Helene cum una uirgata terre ex dono Walterii uice[comitis.] Duo essarta cum
pratellis adiacentibus illis et siluulam in feodo meo de Celesuurda ex dono
Willelmi regis. ¶ Terram de Rugge quam Thomas de [sancto Iohanne] reddidit
predicte ecclesie. ¶ Dunt[e]sburna ex dono Ermeline uxor[is Walte]rii de Laceio.
¶ Unum molendinum cum uirgata terre adiacentis liberum et quietum ex dono
Willelmi d[e Auco.] ¶ Terram de Sotesora quam reddidit Rogerius de
Berchelai. ¶[1] Aquam que currit per abbatiam ex dono et concessu antecessorum
me[orum] regum. ¶ Ecclesiam sancti Petri que est in foro Norwiz ex dono
Willelmi regis senioris. ¶ Unam culturam [ter]re de Bulelega apud H. . .[2] et
decimam Willelmi de Buleliga ex dono eiusdem Willelmi. ¶ [Omne]m decimam
totius uenationis mee que capta erit in foresta prouincie Gloec' ex dono Henrici
regis. ¶ Ubicunque aliquid sibi uel ecclesie sue necessarium emerint uel
transierint absque ulla thelonei uel transitus redditione . liceat cum pace reme[are]
ex dono Henrici regis. ¶ Ubicunque euenerit capi piscem sturionem in piscaturis

suis sit eorum totus et integer . et hoc ex dono Willelmi regis. ¶ Totam terram eiusdem ecclesie esse quietam de carriagio et summagio et conductu . ex dono Henrici regis. ¶ Ecclesiam sancti Martini que est super Tamisia' apud Lundonia' et totam terram quam presbiter eiusdem ecclesie tenet solutam et quietam ab omnibus consuetudinibus et scotis ex dono Rannulfi Peurel[.] ¶ [Ecclesiam] sancti Guthlaci in Hereford' cum omnibus ad eam pertinentibus ex dono uener[abilis] fratris nostri Rodberti Her[efordensis episcopi. ¶ Ecclesiam de Wycesburie] et ecclesiam de Lauer[k]estoche ex dono Rodberti Gernun et assensu domini A. Lincolniensis [episcopi. ¶ Ecclesiam] sancti Leonardi de Stanleia cum omnibus ad ipsam pertinentibus. Capellam sancti Ioh[annis Baptis]te in silua [que] dicitur Basing [cum] omnibus ad eam pertinentibus. Ecclesiam de Nortuna cum omnibus ad ipsam pertinentib[us. ¶ Ecclesiam sancti [Iohannis Baptiste] de Gloec'[. ¶ Ecclesiam] sancti Paterni cum capellis et terris ad eam pertinentibus de dono Ricar[di] filii Gisleb[erti. ¶] Ecclesiam de [Teyntone et capellam de silua cum uirgata] terre. ¶ Ecclesiam d(e) Chilpeec cum terris et decimis et omnibus ad eam pertinentibus. ¶ [Ecclesiam sancti Michaelis de Ewyas cum] omnibus ad ipsam pertinentibus[.] insuper et decimas omnium maneriorum [Rodberti] de Ewias. ¶ Ecclesiam [sancti Michaelis de Huggemora] et sancte Brigide uirginis cum omnibus ad ipsas pertinentibus. ¶ Totam terram de manerio de[3] Estleche quam pro manerio Glasberie de [W]alterio de Cliffort excambierunt. ¶ Ecclesiam etiam de Quenintuna cum uirgata terre et decimis totius ville et aliis ad eam pertinentibus. ¶ Parrochiam etiam castelli Gloecestrie absque [alterius ecclesie participatione. ¶ Relique etiam ciuitatis] tam intra quam extra muros sicut eam tempore Wlstani Wigornensis episcopi et successoris eius [Samsonis habuerunt.] Vnam h[i]dam terre in Cumba ex dono Hugardi de Bascheruilla. ¶ Patri suo et domino Cantuariensi dei gratia episcopo totius Anglię primati T. Sim(on) Wigornensis ecclesię minister caritatis et obedientie famulatum. Quoniam plenum habeant firmamentum apostolica auctoritate confirmate donationes⸴ idcirco petitione dilecti fratris nostri G. abbatis Gloec' et fratrum eius sancte ecclesię sancti Petri Gloe' . cartas inspeximus⸴ et de his que in eis continentur . ueritatis testimonium sullimitati conscribimus . quatinus hec . et vestra si placeat. auctoritate confirmetis . et de hiis in apostolica testari presentia non dubitetis. Noverit igitur serenitas uestra . singula que in presenti carta regis Stephani subscripta sunt tam ipsius quam praedecessorum eius Catholicorum regum et episcoporum et uirorum et etiam nobilium donatione . ecclesię sancti Petri Gloec' concessa esse et eorum cartis similiter et sigillis confirmata. Valete.

The words in brackets have been supplied from the copy in B. This text has been demonstrated to be a forgery written about 1146 × 48 to fortify St. Peter's tenurial standing during the 'Anarchy' (*GFAL*, 125–7; *Regesta*, iii, no. 344 n.; Brooke, 'St. Peter of Gloucester', 67–70).

[1] *-ai* and ¶ are uncertain readings.

[2] Unreadable due to damage.

[3] Uncertain reading.

45. *Confirmation of the gifts from Bernard of Neufmarché to St. Peter's, Gloucester, by King Henry II. (1154 × 63) Rouen.*

A. H.C.L., no. 2185 (141 mm × 87 mm); tongue and tie removed; seal missing; no endorsement; **B**. G.C.L., 'Reg. B', no. 163, p. 57; Capes, *Hereford Charters*, 17–18; cal. in Baddeley ii, no. 39, p. 20; Holt and Mortimer, no. 129.

.H. rex. Anglorum . et dux Normannorum . et Aquitann' et comes Andegavorum . archiepiscopis . episcopis . comitibus . baronibus . iustic(iis) . vicecomitibus . ministris . et omnibus hominibus suis Anglie et Walie salutem. Sciatis me concessisse et carta mea confirmasse ecclesie sancti Petri et abbati et monachis Gloec' . omnes donationes et elemosinas quas Bernardus de Nouo Mercato . auus Henrici de H'eford' . et comes Rogerus frater eius assensu Walteri fratris eorum eis rationabiliter dederunt et concesserunt. Scilicet ecclesiam de Coure cum omnibus pertinentiis eius . et unam hidam que uocatur Beche. Quare uolo et firmiter precipio quod predicta ecclesia et monachi habeant et teneant hec omnia predicta bene et in pace et integre . et honorifice et plenarie cum omnibus pertinentiis suis . Sicut carta .H. aui mei et carta Henrici de H'eford' testatur. His testibus . Rotro Ebroicensi . Philippo Baiocensi . episcopis . Ricardo de Humete . constabulario . Man(nacero) Bis(et) . dapifer . Roberto de Dunstanuilla . apud Rothomagum.

A charter of Bernard of Neufmarché granting Glasbury-on-Wye to St. Peter's, Gloucester, is in G.C.L., 'Reg. B', no. 218, p. 83; charters of Bernard also relevant to this transaction are in *Cart. Glouc.* i, nos. 281–5; a variant of no. 281 is in ibid. iii, no. 912.

46. *Writ of King Henry II of England directing the sheriff of Herefordshire to protect the hide at Monkhide (in Yarkhill, Herefs.) of the abbot and convent of St. Peter's. (1154 × 72) Gloucester.*

A. P.R.O., E 40/A.14555 (154 mm × 59 mm), **Scribe 27**; tongue and/or tie torn off from left foot; seal missing. Endorsements: Hida (s. xii^{ex} × s. xiii^{in}); Registratur (s. xiv^{ex} × s. xv^{in}); **B**. P.R.O., C 150/1, fol. 222; **C**. G.C.L., 'Reg. B', no. 157, p. 55; *Cart. Glouc.* ii, no. 821; fascm. Bishop, *Scriptores Regis*, Plate III (c); ibid. no. 473; Holt and Mortimer, no. 130.

.H. rex Anglorum et dux Normannorum et Aquitanorum et comes Andegauorum. vicecomiti de Hereford'sira salutem. Precipio quod iuste deducas abbatem et monachos Gloec' de una hida terre de lahid' quam tenent. Et prohibeo ne ipsi in iniuste uexentur uel in placitum ponantur . aut in aliquas consuetudines quas facere non solebant tempore regis Henrici aui me. Et nisi fec[eritis][1] iustit(ius) meus faciat . ne amplius inde clamorem audiam pro penuria recti. Teste Widone decano apud Gloec'.

For the distinction between Monkhide and West Hide, see *Herefordshire Place-Names*, 215–16.

---

[1] MS. damaged.

47. *Writ of King Henry II of England confirming to St. Peter's, Gloucester, Monkhide (in Yarkhill) in Herefordshire which had been given by William Devereux. (1155 × 58) Winchester.*

G.C.L., 'Deeds and Seals', xi, no. 4 (165 mm × 68 mm); tongue and tie; seal missing; endorsements: De Hida (s. xiii^med); Carta Regis Henr(ici) de terra de Hyda [;] Registratur (s. xiv × s. xv^in); Bishop, *Scriptores Regis*, no. 228.

H. rex Anglorum . dux Normannorum . et Aquitannorum . et comes Andegauorum . archiepiscopis . comitibus . baronibus . iustic(iis) . vicecomitibus . et omnibus ministris et bailliuis suis Angl' salutem. Sciatis me concessisse . et hac carta mea confirmasse deo et ecclesie sancti Petri Gloec' . et monachis ibidem deo seruientibus terram quandam que uocatur Hida in H'efordsira . quam Willelmus de Ebroicis eis dedit in puram et perpetuam et liberam elemosinam. Quare uolo et firmiter precipio quod idem monachi habeant et teneant predictam terram cum omnibus ad eam pertinentibus integre . honorifice . pacifice . libere . et quiete . ab omni seruitio exactione . et consuetudine. Et prohibeo ne quis eis molestiam ut grauamen inde inferre presumat. T(estibus) . Thoma cancellario . Reginaldo comite Cornub' . et Mansero Biset . apud Wint'.

The charter's dating is established by the attestation of Thomas Becket as chancellor; of diplomatic interest is the absence of the phrase *gratia dei* from King Henry's title, the regular usage of which in *acta* issued by the Chancery occurred from 1172/73 and more likely from May 1172 (Bishop, *Scriptores Regis*, 8; Chaplais, *English Royal Documents*, 13). G.C.L., 'Reg. B', fol. v verso identifies the location of the land.

48. *Writ of King Henry II of England confirming Monkhide (in Yarkhill) in Herefordshire to St. Peter's, Gloucester; another version of no. 46. (1155 × 58) Winchester.*

A. G.C.L., 'Deeds and Seals', xi, no. 3 (147 mm × 83 mm); tongue and tie; seal on tongue, fragment (loose fragment in protective wrapper), white wax, round; obverse, image destroyed; orb with bird facing left on loose fragment; legend: . . .ILV. . .; reverse: image virtually destroyed; portion of upraised sword on loose fragment; legend: . . .T:COMI. . .; endorsements: De Hida (s. xiii^med); Carta regis Henr(ici) pro terra de Hyda [;] Registratur (s. xiv^ex × s. xv^in); B. G.C.L., 'Reg. B', no. 106, p. 37; Baddeley, 'Further Early Deeds', 48–49; Bishop, *Scriptores Regis*, no. 227.

H. rex Anglorum . et dux Normannorum . et Aquitannorum . et comes Andegauorum iustic(iis) vicecomitibus et omnibus bailliuis et ministris suis Angl' salutem. Sciatis me concessisse et hac carta mea confirmasse deo et ecclesie sancti Petri Gloec' . et monachis ibidem deo seruientibus terram quandam que uocatur Hida in H'efords' quam Willelmus de Ebroicis eis dedit in puram et perpetuam et liberam elemosinam. Quare uolo et firmiter precipio quod idem monachi habeant et teneant predictam terram cum omnibus ad eam pertinentibus integre et pacifice honorifice libere quiete ab omnibus seruitiis sectis exactionibus et omnibus aliis secularibus consuetudinibus. Et prohibeo ne quis eis inde molestiam aut grauamen inferre presumat contra cartam Willelmi de Ebroicis et Rogeri filii eius quas idem monachi inde habent⸴ super decem libris forisfacture. T(estibus) . Thoma cancellario . Regenaldo comite Cornubiense . Mansero Biset apud Winton'.

The text, which clearly expands that of no. 43, was arguably issued subsequent to it, but given the identical witness-list and place-date, probably soon after.

49. *Writ of King Henry II of England addressed to Earl Hugh and Countess Matilda of Chester: they were to cause the abbot and convent of St. Peter's, Gloucester, to receive without delay the revenue from Olney (Bucks.) and Tathwell (Lincs.) which Earl Ranulf II gave. (1155 × 58; 20 April 1158?) Worcester.*

A. H.C.L., no. 1170 (162 mm × 86 mm), **Scribe 26**; tongue and tie; seal on tongue, white wax, fragment, round (meas. unavail.); obverse: majesty side with crowned king seated to front with raised sword in right hand and orb, on which is perched a bird, in left hand; legend: +HENRICV. . .; reverse: helmeted equestrian figure to right, upraised sword in right hand; left hand holding shield and reins; legend: +HE. . . COMES:AN. . .; endorsements: Comiti Cestr' de Oldneia et Taddewella. (s. xii^{med}); c(apsula) .xv. de laicis tenuris. (s. xii^{ex} × s. xiii^{in}); Registratur (s. xiv^{ex} × s. xv^{in}); B. P.R.O., C 150/1, fol. 61; facsm. in Barlow, *Thomas Becket*, Plate 3; *Cart. Glouc.* i, no. 158; Bishop, *Scriptores Regis*, no. 229; Holt and Mortimer, no. 127.

.H. rex Anglorum et Dux Normannorum et comes Andegavorum .H. comiti Cestr' et M. comitisse . salutem. Precipio quod sine dilatione et iuste faciatis habere abbati et monachis de Gloec' redditus quos comes Ranulfus . eis dedit in molendinis de Oldneio et de Tadewella sicut carta sua testatur. Et displicet mihi quod hoc non fecistis sicut per alia breuia mea. Et nisi feceritis⸴ vicecomes mei uel iusticiarius faciat . ne inde clamorem amplius audiam pro penuria recti.[1] Teste Th(oma) cancellario apud Wigorn'.

[1] **B** as printed in *Cart. Glouc.* ends here.

50. *Letter from Otto cardinal deacon of St. Nicholas to the abbot and convent of Gloucester: he will promulgate their excommunication if the 81 marks promised for the papal subsidy has not been paid by the octave of the feast of St. Andrew. (19 November 1240) London.*

H.C.L., no. 1735 (177 mm × 79 mm); no turn-up and no provision for sealing; no endorsement; cal. in Baddeley ii, no. 42, p. 21.

Otto miseratione diuina sancti Nicolai in Carc'e Tull' diaconus cardinalis apostolice sedis legatus⸴ religiosis uiris abbati et conuentui Glouern' Wigornensis diocesis⸴ salutem in domino. Cum octoginta et unam marcas quas adhuc de subsidio domini pape soluere tenemini promis(er)itis soluere iam est diu propter quod quia non satisfecistis ad diem . suspensionis sententiam incurristis᷑. miramur quamplurimum quod eadem suspensione contempta᷑. de ipsa pecunia satisfacere non curatis. Ideoque uobis in uirtute obedientie districte precipiendo mandamus . quatinus usque ad octabam beati Andreę de ipso subsidio plenius satisfacere studeatis . alioquin cum tantum ecclesie Romane contemptum non possimus relinquere impunitum licet inuitii᷑. ex nutu in uos excommunicationis sententiam promulgamus . in quam incidatis ipso facto᷑. si usque ad diem predictam de ipso subsidio per nos non fuerit satisfactum. Rescribatis autem nobis quicquid inde duxistis faciendum. Datum Lond' .xiii. kalendas Decembrorum pontificatus domini Gregorio papę noui anno x°iiii.

The above text's reference to St. Peter's promised contribution to a papal subsidy refers to the levy Gregory IX imposed on the clergy of France and England to help finance his war against Frederick II. St. Peter's had failed to pay 81 marks it had pledged and was among those required to pay by 8 November 1240; Otto had extracted such pledged contributions from England's higher clergy, including abbots and priors of major houses, to the papal subsidy at Reading and London councils in 1240; they were required to pay at a later council held at London on 8 November or submit letters under their seals guaranteeing payment by 6 December (*Annales de Theokesberia*, 116; *Annales de Burton*, 257, 366; *Annales de Dunstaplia*, 154–5; Paris, *Chron. Maj.* iv. 10, 15, 35–37, 60–61; *Cal. of MSS. of Dean and Chapter of Wells*, i. 403; Lunt, *Financial Relations of the Papacy*, 145–7, 197–205). For political aspects of Otto's career in England and a query about his identity, see Vincent, *Peter des Roches*, 533, s.v.

51. Inspeximus *of William bishop of Hereford addressed to Richard abbot of Cirencester and Geoffrey prior of Llanthony Secunda. (c. 1189 × 24 December 1198; poss. c. 1189 × 1191)*

H.C.L., no. 1387 (181 mm × 88 mm); tongue stitched to foot; seal missing; endorsement: Berkeleye (s. xiii); Walker, 'Gloucester Charters', no. 13; Barrow, *Hereford Episcopal Acta*, no. 186.

W. dei gratia H'ef᷑ episcopus . venerabilibus et dilectis in Cristo fratribus .R. eadem gratia abbati Cirenc' . et .G. priori Lanton' . salutem. Litteras domni abbatis Glouc' . in hec uerba suscepimus. Venerabilibus dominis et amicis .W. dei gratia H'ef᷑ episcopo . et .R. eadem gratia abbati Cirenc' et .G. priori Lanton' . .T. eadem gratia abbas Glouc'. salutem . Mirari non sufficimus quo transactionem conditionaliter factam inter nos et abbatem et canonicos de Bristoll' super prebenda de Berkel' . diocesano episcopo et nobis iuste contradicentibus᷑. sigillis uestris confirmastis . maxime cum vos domine episcope sigillum vestrum tali confirmationi appositum apud Glouc' . habito consilio discretorum et honestorum uirorum ad nostram compositionem fregeritis. Vnde siquid inde postea factum est᷑ per obreptionem factum esse dionoscitur. Quia autem uidemus causam nostram in hoc periclitari . et id fieri in preiudicium iuris nostri᷑. ne id locum optineat . uel ius nostrum ledere possit᷑. presentiam summi pontificis appellauimus . rogantes si placet quatinus nobis et aduersariis nostris diem certum prefigatis . ut quod forte perperam et minus provide factum esse dinoscitur. vestra discretionem et communi consilio ad honorem uestrum et communis cause integritatem corrigatur. Honestius enim uidetur quod factum uestrum reuocetur prouisione et discretione propria. quam conhibitione et auctoritate summi pontificis. Valete in domino. ¶ Quia uero hec indiscreta precipitatio si doceri poterit . non solum nobis uerum etiam utrique uestrum per apposita nobisque ostensa prius[1] sigilla . inputari debet. uobis mandamus et tam nobis quam fame nostre consulimus . quatinus in primo ubi locum oportuniorem uideritis . nos tres conueniamus . communi consilio siquid in hac confirmatione precipitanter et altera parte reclamante attemptatum . est. celeriter in irritum reuocaturi . et utrique parti prout decet congrue satisfacturi. De die autem cum prouideritis. nobis significare curetis. Valete.

Geoffrey of Henlaw was prior of Llanthony Secunda *c.* 1189 × 1203 (*HRH*, 173); he granted land on Holy Trinity Lane, Gloucester, to Richard Mey *c.* 1200 (GBR/J1/91; Stevenson, no. 91). William bishop of Hereford died 24 December 1198 (*HBC*, 250). The dispute to which this charter pertains resulted from the churches of Berkeley Hernesse being given by four donors to three different monasteries, Gloucester, Reading, and Bristol, during the 1140s (see below, no. 367 & n.; Kemp, 'The churches of Berkeley Hernesse', 96–110; Barrow, *Hereford Episcopal Acta*, no. 186 n.). Dr. Kemp believes that the dispute was settled during the pontificate of Pope Clement III or soon after his death (*Cart. Reading*, i, no. 289 n.).

[1] Superscript.

52. *Letter of Bernard bishop of St. David's to Alexander bishop of Lincoln notifying that Robert Gernon gave the abbot and convent of St. Peter's, Gloucester, the churches of Wraysbury and Laverstoke (Bucks.), half of a mill, and half of its land. He attested that King Henry had confirmed the grant and that he had seen Queen Matilda lead Robert to the altar of St. Peter's where Robert placed his gift by means of a knife upon the altar. (22 July 1123 × 20 February 1148)*

A. H.C.L., no. 1511 (225 mm × 67 mm); fragment of tie; tongue torn away; seal missing; endorsements: De Wiretebi c(apsula) .iiii. de ecclesiasticis tenuris. (s. xii[ex] × s. xiii[in]); Bernardi episcopi (s. xiii[ex] × s.xiv[in]); Registratur (s. xiv[ex] × s.xv[in]); B. P.R.O., C 150/1, fol. 189v; *Cart. Glouc.* ii, no. 705; cal. in Baddeley i, no. 2, pp. 224–5; cal. in *EAWD*, i, no. D.144.

Venerabili domino .A. Lincoliensis ecclesię episcopo ceterisque dilectis in Cristo fratribus ecclesiarum totius Anglię tam prelatis quam subditis. Bern(ardus) ecclesię sancti David minister humilis . salutem in domino. Caritati uestre notum facimus . et quia ad presens uerbo non possumus scripto testamur. nos et presentes affuisse . hoc etiam uidisse et audisse quod Robertus Gernon dedit sancto Petro et Petro abbati de Gloec' et monachis eius ecclesiam de Wiretesb'ia . et ecclesiam de Lauerchestoche . et omnia quę ad easdem ecclesias pertinent . et dimidium molendinum . et medietatem terrę . quę ad illud pertinet. Hoc quidem uidimus et testamur. Scimus etiam quod rex Henricus donationem illam concessit et carta sua confirmauit. Vidimus etiam quod domina mea Matildis regina ipsum Robertum Gernon usque ad altare sancti Petri Gloec' conduxit . ubi ipse astante regina pluribusque aliis per cultellum super altare donationem illam confirmauit.[1] Valete.

This letter was written after the accession of the addressee Alexander bishop of Lincoln in 1123 and before the death of addressor Bernard of St. David's in 1148 (*HBC*, 255, 297). Robert Gernon's gift occurred in 1112; but Bernard did not become bishop of St. David's until 1115. A resolution of the chronological discrepancy has been suggested by Prof. Christopher Brooke, that the grant was made in 1111 and confirmed 1115 × 17 ('St. Peter of Gloucester', 53 & n.).

[1] **B** as recorded in *Cart. Glouc.* ends here.

53. *Confirmation by Simon bishop of Worcester to the church of Eastleach Martin of land and rights granted and confirmed by Gilbert abbot of St. Peter's, by the monks of Malvern, and by the parishioners of the church; those who shall have infringed upon what the bishop has confirmed have been publicly excommunicated. (1139 × 48)*

B.L., L.F.C. Charter XVIII.11* (208 mm × 85 mm); single turn-up; tag for seal; seal missing; no medieval endorsement.

Omnibus sancte matris ecclesie filiis. Sim(on) dei gratia Wigorniensis episcopus'. salutem. Ex commissi nobis officii solicitudine tenemur . ea que ecclesiis et diuinis locis collatione fidelium mancipantur . ut firmam stabilitatem forciantur'. episcopalis auctoritate diligentia roborare. Nouerit itaque modernorum uniuersitas . et in uenturis temporibus successura posteritas . quod in dedicatione ecclesie sancti Michaelis et beati Martini de Estlech que per ministerium nostrum dei intuitu et petitione delectorum filiorum .R. prioris et fratrum Maluern' celebrata est'. uenerabilis frater noster Gilebertus abbas Gloecestr' donauit eidem ecclesie unam uirgatam terre in campo de Vifhida cum pertinentiis suis in perpetuum libere et quiete possidendam. Concessit etiam cum terra quam dicta ecclesia ante dedicationem . habuerat omnem libertatem et plenariam communiam totius uille . tam in dominicis pasturis quam in omnibus aliis rebus . sicut Ricardus filius Puncii fratribus Maluern' concessit . quod ex carta eiusdem Ricardi quam inspeximus nobis innotuit. Monachi quoque Maluern' dederunt unam hidam terre quam habebant in campo de Sudthropa cum suis pertinentiis et cum omnibus libertatibus et consuetudinibus quas ipsi habebant in uilla de Estlech et eius pertinentiis. Preterea parochiani omnes concesserunt et super altare deposuerunt . cum omnibus decimis suis et obuentionibus uniuersa parochialia que ecclesiis debentur. Hanc siquidem predictorum donationem et concessionem in memorate ecclesie de Estlech possessione in perpetuum habendam auctoritate pontificali confirmantes'. omnes qui de prelibatis aliquid subtrahere uel inde quicquam infringre attentauerint'. publice excomunicauimus. Ut igitur ratum in perpetuum et inconuulsum perseueret'. presentis scriptiferiem sigilli nostri impressione communimus et publicẹ notioni commendamus. Testibus Gileberto abbate Gloec'. Ricardo archidiacono Gloec' . Patricio et Radulfo monachis Gloec' . Ernis[io] et Hugone monachis Malu' . Iohanne filio Frether' . Pagano . magistro Willelmo clericis episcopi . Osberto capellano . Rogero ianitor Malu'n' . Aldrei.[1]

For Richard archdeacon of Gloucester, see *Fasti*, ii. 107.

[1] Reading uncertain.

54. *Letter of Mauger bishop of Worcester addressed to A. dean of Gloucester prohibiting annual gifts from churches and chapels; within 15 days of receiving the letter the dean is to read it to the chapter of St. Peter's, Gloucester. (1200 × 12)*

H.C.L., no. 1833 (178 mm × 118 mm); no turn-up; no provision for sealing [a small hole and slight tear above next to last line, *c.* 10 mm above edge of foot might have been used for a small cord]; endorsements: Glouc' (s. xiii^{in}); Non registratur quia non indiget (s. xiv^{ex} × s. xv^{in}).

.M. dei gratia Wigorniensis episcopus dilecto in Cristo filio .A. decano Glouc' salutem gratiam et benedictionem. Cum ad hoc cura nobis sit credita pastoralis . ut in diocesi nostra erandicanda eradicemus . et plantanda plantemus . ad illa precipue erandicanda totis uiribus debemus inniti. que tam in iniuriam dei quam nostram . necnon et gregis nobis a deo commissi redu(n)dare indentur. Vnde quam cogniuimus prauam in archidiaconatu Gloec' uioleuisse consuetudinem . ex eo quod exiguntur de singulis ecclesiis et capellis annue prestationes que Strene uocantur . id de cetero fieri prohibentes . sententiam excommunicationis publice promulgauimus in omnes illos qui sex denarios qui in archidiaconatu Gloec' contra deum dari solebant nomine Strenarum . uel aliquid aliud uice earum amodo exigent . uel exsoluent . presertim cum Strenas dari. sanctorum patrum pagina detestetur. Quocirca tibi mandamus sub pena anathematis firmiter inhibentes . ne deinceps predictos sex denarios uel aliquid aliud uice eorum a personis seu capellanis de decanatu tuo exigere presumas. Sciturus pro cetero . quod si contra hanc prohibitionem nostram aliquid quod non credimus attemptaueris. in te tanquam in excommunicatum nostrum grauiter nec immerito animaduertemus. Mandamus igitur tibi districte precipientes . quatinus infra .xv. dies post susceptionem litterarum istarum quas in testimonium futurum tibi destinamus patentes. tuum co(n)uoces capitulum . et in eodem capitulo plenario hanc nostram s(ententiam) sollempniter denuntiare procures . prouisurus attentius . ut presentes littere huius mandati nostri memoriam plenius detinentes. pro assensum totius capituli in tuto loco fideliter reseruentur.

55. *Notification in the form of a writ by R(obert) of Burnham, dean of Gloucester, to the prior of Llanthony Secunda, the archdeacon of Gloucester,* *and the official of the bishop of Worcester, recording an agreement between William, rector of the church of Langley Marish and the prioress and nuns of Ankerwyke (Bucks.). 18 October 1224.*

A. H.C.L., no. 490 (168 mm × 54 mm); tongue and tie missing; seal missing; endorsement: De ecclesia de Langel(e)[;] Caps(ula) .iiii.[a] de ecclesiasticis tenuris. (s. xiii[ex]); **B**. P.R.O., C 150/1, fol. 191; *Cart. Glouc.* ii, no. 713 (text quoted in part).

Viris venerabilibus . priori de Lanton' iuxta Glouc' et archidiacono Glouc' et officiali domini Wigornensis .R. de Burneha' decanus salutem in domino. Noueritis quod hec est forma compositionis facte inter .W. rectorem ecclesie de Langel' et priorissam et moniales de Ancrewic . videlicet quod dictus .W. nomine ecclesie sue de Langel' de cetero percipiet omnes decimas minores et obuentiones et personales decimas[1] peruenientes[2] de terris et hominibus de assarto de P'stewic. Omnes homines iam dicti tam uiui quam mortui cum omni familia sua percipient in ecclesia de Langel' omnia sacramenta tam necessaria quam uoluntaria. Dicte autem moniales integre percipient decimas garbarum de dicto assarto soluendo singulis annis dicto .W. nomine ecclesie de Langel' nouem solidos ad duos terminos . Scilicet ad Annuntiationem beate Marie quatuor solidos et sex denarios et ad festum beati Petri quod dicitur ad uincula quatuor solidos et sex denarios. Et si prefate moniales dictos nouem solidos statutis terminis non soluerint. dictus .W. sine contradictione integre percipiet decimas garbarum de dicto assarto quousque dicte moniales de predictis nouem solidis eidem satisfecerint. Si autem de cetero contingat assartum iamdictum ampliari uel alibi nouum oriatur ecclesia de Langeleia integre percipiet omnes decimas portionis super excrescentis et cuiuslibet noui essarti. Capella de Alreburn' cum antiquis pertinentiis et antiquis libertatibus remanebit in statu in quo fuit ante dictam assartationem. Ita tamen quod capellanus qui pro tempore celebrabit in capella de Alreburn' nullum de parrochianis de Langel' neque de Prestewic admittet ad sacramenta uel sacramentalia in dampnum et preiudicium ecclesie de Langel'. Seruientes autem monialium qui pro tempore fuerint apud Alreburn' accedent tribus festis solempnibus scilicet ad Natale domini . ad Pascha . et ad Assumptionem beate Marie ad ecclesiam de Langel' facturi more aliorum parrochianorum. Facta est autem hec compositio anno ab incarnatione domini .m.°.cc.°.xx°iiii.° die beati Luce euangeliste. In porticu ecclesie de Langel' . Coram me . et Remundo de Huptone . et Helia tunc capellano de Langel' et Iuello capellano . et Hugone clerico . et Reginaldo clerico de Langel' et Gileberto de Ditone . et Hugone de Ditone . et Ricardo parcario . et Heruico seruiente domini de La'gel' . et Henrico de Bruera . et Iohanne de Bruera . et Ricardo Frend . et Henrico filio Hugonis La(m)bert . et multis aliis . Ad mandatum inde adhibitis mecum tribus capellanis discretis absolui priorissam de Ancrewic . recepta prius ab ea cautione inuentoria de parendo iuri coram uobis . Et in huius rei testimonium litteras meas patentes uobis transmitto.

On this dispute, see *Cart. Glouc.* ii, nos. 712–13.

---

[1] *personales decimas* superscript in the same hand.   [2] *peruenietes* in MS.

56. Notification in the form of a writ by David prior of Worcester attesting to proprietary rights of St. Peter's, Gloucester. (1143 × 45)

A. H.C.L., no. 1608 (172 mm × 84 mm); tongue and fragment of tie; white wax stain on tongue; seal missing; endorsements: De Lech. Otintun'. B'ton'.c(apsula) viii^a (s. xii^{ex} × s. xiii^{in}), **Hand h**; Stanedis; Registatur (s. xiv^{ex} × s. xv^{in}); **B**. P.R.O., C150/1, fols. 170–170v; **C**. G.C.L., 'Reg. B', no. 224, p. 88; *Cart. Glouc.* ii, no. 609 (different version); cal. in Baddeley i, no. 3, p. 225.

Omnibus sancte ecclesie filiis David prior Wigornie ueram in Cristo salutem. Quod religiosorum uirorum antecessorum meorum super calumpnia Eboracensis ecclesie aduersus Gloecestrensem certa relatione cognoui⸴ posteritati notum faciens . sub dei et districti iudicii timore testificor . Glocestrensis ecclesia . maneria ista . Lecche . Otintune . Bertune . continuæ a prima sui fundatione . Stanedis uero a post secuta comitis Beornulfi donatione possedit. Licet enim Ældredus archiepiscopus et postea successor eius Thomas . Lecce . Otintune . Stanedis . tenuerunt aliquandiu⸴ non[1] Eboracensis sed Gloecestrensis ecclesie tenuerunt[2]. Conuen(er)at namque inter Ældredum tunc Wigornensem episcopum . et Wilstanum abbatem Gloecest' . ut Aldredus cui hoc facilius erat quam abbati monasterium beati Petri in Glocest'ia redditibus uillarum istarum . Lecche . Otintune . Stanedis construeret et eas huius rex gratia[3] certo annorum numero teneret . nichilque interim de terris earundem absque abbatis notitia et uoluntate disponens⸴ finito tempore eas in nulla diminutas ecclesie restitueret . Bertona semper plenarie in dominio et potestate abbatis existente. Ældredus deinde factus Eboracensis archiepiscopus ante completum tempus decessit. Cui succedens in archiepiscopatu domnus Thomas predicta maneria tenuit. sicut dep(re)cessor ipsius tenuerat . et impleto tempore supradicto . se etiam in hoc ipso quod tenuerat recognoscens et in multorum audientia confitens deliquisse⸴ ecclesie beati Petri Gloec' ea sicut iustum erat restituit. Nuda ueritas est Eboracensem ecclesiam nichil amplius iuris in supradictis maneriis aliquotiens habuisse. In horum assertionem cum honestis uiris a quibus hec accepi . eram et ego meis temporibus si quando necesse fuisset⸴ ueritatis amore uel igniti ferri uel cuilibet alterius iudicii semper subire paratus examen . potuerit et post nos secure qui uoluerit quocumque modo sibi fuerit adiudicatum eorundem se probationi supponere.

For the date, see *HRH*, 83.

[1] Erasure.
[2] *tenuerint* in MS.
[3] Superscript.

57. Rental agreement in the form of a chirograph between Abbot Henry and the convent of St. Peter's, Gloucester, and Prior John and the convent of Llanthony Secunda concerning property near Southgate in Gloucester; the land was to be held of the priory in perpetuity by the almoner of St. Peter's for 4s. annual rent. (1205 × 24)

A. P.R.O., C 150/2/[6] (meas. 235 mm [left] × 184 mm [foot]); seal on tag, oval, white wax stained green, badly chipped; obverse: seated Virgin Mary and Child facing front; oval (meas. unavail.), legend illeg.; reverse: counterseal, oval (45 mm × 30 mm), image of a standing figure in full pontificals facing front, right hand holding a crozier, left hand raised in blessing ?; legend: + SIGILLV':PRIORIS LANTON:DE GLOVC. Endorsements: Carta prioris de Lantoney de quodam tenemento uersus portam australem (s. xiii[ex]); W (s. xiii[ex]?); Southgate (s. xiv); Ista carta vacatur ut[1] patet per qualem[2] compositionem; Registratur (s. xiv [ex] × s. xv[in]); **B**. G.C.L., 'Reg. B', no. 776, pp. 339–40; **C**. P.R.O., C 115/K.1/6681, Sect. 20, pt. 2, no. 54 (fol. 91); **D**. ibid. C 115/L.2/6690, no. 89.

C. . .R O G R A P H V M

Hec est conuentio facta inter H. abbatem sancti Petri Glouc' et eiusdem loci conuentum ex una parte . et I. priorem Lanton' iuxta Glouc' et conuentum eiusdem loci ex altera. Videlicet quod dicti prior et conuentus Lanton' iuxta Glouc' tradiderunt et concesserunt dictis abbati et conuentui sancti Petri Glouc' quandam terram suam in uilla Glouc' . illam scilicet que iacet infra portam australem inter terram Thome le taylur . et terram eorumdem monachorum quam Osbertus sacerdos dedit eis. Quam quidem terram elemosinarius sancti Petri inperpetuum de nobis tenebit nomine dictorum abbatis et conuentus. Quare uolumus quod dictus elemosinarius et successores sui habeant et teneant predictam terram de nobis libere et quiete inperpetuum . pro quatuor solidis nobis annuatim ad quatuor terminos soluendis pro omni seruitio . Videlicet ad festum sancti Michaelis . duodecim denariis . ad Natale domini duodecim denariis . et ad Annuntiationem beate Marie . duodecim denariis et ad Natiuitatem beati Iohannis Baptiste duodecim denariis. Predicta uero terra per uisum legalium uirorum mesurata tenet in fronte tres virgas ulnarias cum pollice interposito et dimidiam tribus pollicibus minus . In longitudine uero tresdecim uirgas ulnarias cum pollice interposito . Retro uero uersus portam australem tres uirgas ulnarias cum pollice interposito . Et tria quarteria cum pollice. Quando uero elemosinarius predictam terram a nobis recepit edificium suprapositum apreciatum est dimidiam marcam. Si uero aliquo casu emergente ipse vel successores ipsius qui pro tempore fuerint predictam terram nobis relinquere uoluerint . simile edificium aut precium nobis restituent. Ille elemosinarius in bona fide promisit quod fidelis erit ecclesie nostre . et maxime de redditu nostro plenarie reddendo statutis terminis . et quod nec artem nec ingenium exquiret unde domus nostra per tenuram suam dampnum incurrat. In cuius testimonium rei presens scriptum in modum cirographi inter nos confecimus cuius unam partem sigillo ecclesie nostre munitam predictis monachis tradidimus. Alteram uero partem sigillo ipsorum roboratam penes nos retenuimus. Hiis testibus . Ricardo burg' . Dauid Dunning . Waltero Hoch[3] . magistro Waltero Scriptore . Iohanne le draper . Drogo[ne][4] . Et multis aliis.

Two John of Hempsteads were successively priors of Llanthony Secunda c. 1217–40 (*HRH*, 173 & n.). The above text is the portion given by Llanthony to St. Peter's.

---

[1] Superscript.
[3] **B** ends here with *et aliis*.
[2] Reading uncertain.
[4] *Drogo* in MS.

58. *Grant in the form of a chirograph by Abbot Walter with the consent of the chapter of St. Peter's to Richard of Brecon of the land which Serlo the priest had held for 30s. rent per year; the tenant was to perform service due from the land to the king and was not to sell it or mortgage it. (1130 × 39)*

H.C.L., no. 1512 (165 mm × 45m); tongue cut off; endorsements: Contra Ricard(um) de Brechen' (s. xii; *c.* 1150 × 80?); de Bre eche Rich ar' (s. xiii²?); Walker, 'Gloucester Charters', no. 3; cal. in Baddeley i, no. 8, p. 226.

CYROGRAPHUM

Sciant presentes et futuri quod ego Walt(erus) abbas concessu capituli sancti Petri Gloec' concessi Ricardo de Brekenio terram que fuit Serlonis presbiteri ut omni anno inde .xxx. solidos reddat . et adquietat eam uersus regem. Et quamdiu ipse et heres suus censum bene reddiderint in pace teneant. Si uero reddere noluerint: recognoscant se monachi ad terram suam. Videat etiam ne eam alicui uendat nec in uadimonium¹ mittat. Istius conuentionis testes sunt Walt(erus) capellanus . Radulfus dapifer [.] Ingulfus ianitor.

¹ *uadimodium* in MS.

59. *Notification in the form of a chirograph of a grant made to Walter son of Bernard by Abbot William and the convent of St. Peter's, Gloucester. (1130 × 39; 1139 × 48)*

G.C.L., 'Deeds and Seals', ix, no. 15, fol. 7 (229 mm × 150 mm), **Scribe 2**; possible tongue removed from left top end; seal missing; endorsements: WALTERIUS CVM BARBA. (*c.* 1140 × 60); Caps(ula) .ii.a de ecclesiasticis tenuris (s. xiii^ex × s. xiv^in); Rodeford'[;] Pencombe. (s. xiii^ex); facsm. in Ker, *English Manuscripts*, Plate 16b.

Willelm(us) abbas totusque conuentus sancti Petri Gloecestrie concesserunt Walterio filio Bernardi cum barba .i. hidam terre in feudum apud Pencu'ba' . et .i. domum in burgagio Gloecestrie. Successor uero Will(el)mi abbatis scilicet Walteri(us) abbas postea dedit ipsi Walterio .i. uirgatam terre apud Rodefort . et ipse Walterius clamauit quietam terram et domum quam habebat in burgagio perpetualiter . et abiurauit super .iiii.^or euangelia calumpniam quam habebat interea quam pater suus tenuerat . fecitque inde hominium abbati. Ipse uero abbas et conuentus concesserunt ei corredium suum¹ unoquoque m(en)se² duobus diebus si uenerit . sibi et homini suo . et equo. Et pro seruitio terre quam habet in Her[e]fort sira seruiet in eadem sira quotiens cumque competenter summonitus fuerit . siue ad firmam eam tradat siue in dominium teneat. Similiter pro terra quam habet in Gloecestre sira faciat . seruiat uidelicet in eadem sira . uel solus aut cum abbate aut cum monachis ad corredium abbatis. Perget quoque semel in anno ad Lun[d]onia' . et Wintonia' . et ad sanctum Pat'nu'. Huius conuentionis testes sunt Walterius conestabulus . et Samson nepos eius . Rainaldus de Bechefort³ . Drogo Punheruis . Willelmus Brito . Walterius presbiter . Rogerius Castel . Wimundus . Willelmus et Ingulfus ianitor fratres eius . Fulco . Rogerius Caillewei . Goffridus filius Dauid . et .ii.° filii eius . Rogerius et Godefridus .

Ricardus filius Osberni . Nicholaus . et Grim . et Ingulfus . presbiteri . Willelmus de B'tona . Walterius Tochi et Haroldus prepositus . Hadulfus . Ouietus . et .ii.° filii eius . Sewoldus . et Rogerius . Ernulfus . Bihinde . Sewinus filius Goltstan . Steinerus. et[4] super hoc dominus abbas G. adauxit ei apud Rudeford .xii. acras[5] terre . et hoc annuente capitulo.

CIROGRAFIVM

[1] Superscript in same hand.
[2] Apparently for *merce*.
[3] Second *e* is superscript.
[4] This and the remaining text are in a different hand.
[5] *acros* in MS.

60. *Lease for his lifetime in the form of a chirograph by Abbot Hamelin and the convent of St. Peter's, Gloucester, of land by the bridge (at Gloucester) to Ernald son of Dunning and John his son for 3s. annual rent. (1148 × 79)*

G.C.L., 'Deeds and Seals', iv, no. 6, fol. 3 (189 mm × 92 mm), **Scribe 3** (below, Plate VI); tongue torn from left foot; seal missing; endorsements: Contra Ernaldum filium Dunningi. (s. xii[2]), **Hand e** (below, Plate XLIIIe); quarta Warda (s. xiii[ex]); Ioh' Ace (s. xiv); in via Ponte (s. xv)

CYROGRAPHVM

Sciant presentes et futuri quod ego Hamel(inus) dei gratia abbas . et conuentus Gloec' . concessimus Ernaldo filio Dunningi . et Iohanni filio suo terram nostram iuxta pontem que Thomas Wantarius tenuit . tenendam de nobis in uita sua tantum . pro tribus solidis per annum . tali tenore quod Ernaldus et Iohannes filius eius emendabunt domos eiusdem terre . et reedificabunt eas cum necesse fuerit de propriis sumptibus suis. Ipsi autem iuramentum prestiterunt quod fideles exsistent ecclesie nostre . nec artem uel ingenium exquirent quo per tenuram suam ecclesia nostra dampnum incurrat de predictis seldis . nec uendent eas nec excambient . nec in uadimonium ponent . nec ad alium religiosum locum uel personam transferent absque nostra permissione . et quod prenominatum censum fideliter persoluent . medietatem ad Hockedei . et medietatem ad festum sancti Michaelis. Post decessum autem eorum prefata terra cum omni melioratione apposita restituetur ecclesie nostre libera et quieta absque alicuius reclamatione. Quod quia ratum uolumus et inconuulsum permanere quamdiu ipsi predictum censum legitime reddiderint. partem huius cirographi sigillo ecclesie nostre munitam illi tradidimus . et alteram partem absque sigillo penes nos retinuimus.

Reference to Ernald's land in Gloucester is found in *Cart. Glouc.* i, no. 67. This half of the chirograph, unsealed and without a witness-list, was the abbey's file copy.

61. *Grant in fee and inheritance in the form of a chirograph by Abbot Hamelin and the convent of St. Peter's, Gloucester, of land (in Gloucester) to Rocelin son of Estrild for 8d. per annum. (1148 × 79)*

H.C.L., no. 788 (163 mm × 90 mm), **Scribe 4** (below, Plate VIIa); turn-up, but no provision for sealing; on inside face of outer leaf of turn-up *1a* is written in the same apparent hand as the charter text; endorsement: Roscelin' fil' Estrild. (1148 × 79), **Hand d/ Scribe 4** (below, Plate XLIIId); Walker, 'Gloucester Charters', no. 4; cal. in Baddeley i, no. 11, p. 227.

C I R O G R A P H U M : (*inverted*)

Sciant presentes et futuri quod ego Ham(elinus) dei gratia abbas Gloec' et conuentus eiusdem ecclesie concessimus Rocelino filio Estrildis terram quam eadem Estrild' . et Edmarus fullo tenuerunt de magistro Nicholao de sancto Oswaldo tenendam de nobis in feudum et hereditatem pro decem et octo denariis per annum . quas ipse Rocelinus et successores eius nobis reddent singulis annis ad festum sancti Michahelis . tali tenore quod nos eam adquietabimus de langabulo . scilicet sex denar(iis) et quod neque Rocelinus neque aliquis successorum eius transferet[1] eandem terram ad aliquem religiosum locum uel personam nec uendet . nec donabit nec excambiet eam sine nostra permissione. De ista conuentione fideliter et legitime tenenda. memoratus Rocelinus fecit nobis fidelitatem et iuramentum prestitit in capitulo nostro. Nos autem ut hec ipsa conuentio stabilis inter nos et firma permaneat. presentis eam cirographi et sigilli nostri auctoritate et testimonio confirmamus. Huius rei testes sunt . Rodbertus de sancto Michahele . Ricardus Hors . Siluester . Godefridus filius Esegari . Godefridus filius Thuri . Hugo filius Hawhulin[2] . Guaco Cocus . Leofwinus[2] Calueswombe[2] . Wlfei faber . H'arniet hachebutere . Osmundus Cais . Nicholas aurifaber . Sigarus ruffus . Hammelricus . Henricus filius Baldelwini[2] . Ernaldus filius Dunnig.

[1] *tranferet* in MS.   [2] The *w* is written in each instance as Old English wyn.

---

62. *Grant in fee and inheritance in the form of a chirograph by Abbot Hamelin and the convent of St. Peter's, Gloucester, to Bernard son of Ferin of two stalls in the stone house on the middle street* (medio vico) *(Gloucester) for 7s. annual rent. (1148 × 79)*

G.C.L., 'Deeds and Seals', iv, no. 16, fol. 7 (147 mm × 133 mm), **Scribe 5** (below, Plate VIII); tongue possibly cut from lower left foot; no slit for tag; no seal; endorsements: Contra Bernardum filium Farini (s. xii[ex]); .iii[a] Warda (s. xiii[2]), **Hand t**; sc(ribitur) (s. xiv[ex] × s. xv[in]); ; Elmer' ferrator'[;] Tertia Warda (s. xiv[1]); Registratur (s. xiv[ex] × s.xv[in]); in domo lapidea . . . Ioh. . . in ruta maccellu' (*c.* 1500?).

C Y R O G R A P H V M

Sciant presentes et futuri quod ego Ham(elinus) dei gratia abbas . et conuentus beati Petri Gloesc' . concessimus huic Bernardo filio Ferini . duas seldas tenendas de nobis in feudo et hereditate . quas habemus in domo lapidea in medio uico . affiniores ecclesie sancte Marie que est iuxta macellum . unam ex parte australi et alteram ex parte aquilonis . annua pensione septem solidorum . persoluendo unam medietatem ad hocchedei. et alteram medietatem ad festum sancti Michaelis. Ipse uero Bernardus tactis sanctis ewangeliis sacramentum prestitit quod fidelis erit ecclesie nostre . Nec quiret artem uel ingenium quo sciat ecclesiam nostram de tenura sua alienari . nec in aliquo detrimentum pati . Nec acceptas seldas alicui uendet quacumque necessitate urgente . sine permissu abbatis et conuentus . Nec excamniabit . Nec ad alium religiosum locum . uel personam transferet. Et quod in ipsis seldis postmodum restat emendandum⸝ propriis sumptibus Bernardus . emendabit. Vnde ut occasio litigandi in posterum succidatur⸝ cirographi testimonio predictum confirmamus . Alteram partem cirographi cum sigilli attestatione illi committentes⸝ et alteram absque sigillo penes nos retinentes. His testibus.

An example of a file copy. Reference to St. Mary's church and the Shambles locates the house in mid Westgate Street; cf. Lobel, *Gloucester*, 8.

63. *Grant in fee and inheritance in the form of a chirograph by Abbot Hamelin and the convent of St. Peter's, Gloucester, to Godwin fuller of half the land by the church of St. Thomas the Apostle (Gloucester), of which the other half was given to Richard fuller, for 40d. annual rent. (1148 × 79)*

G.C.L., 'Deeds and Seals', iv, no. 20, fol. 9 (213 mm × 88 mm [approx meas. since tongue cut from left foot]), **Scribe 3**; seal missing; endorsements: Contra Godwinum fullonem (s. xii[2]), **Hand e**; .ii.a Ward' (s. xiii[med]) sc(ribitur) (s. xiv[ex]); Registratur; Kingeshome (s. xiv[ex] × s. xv[in]).

CYROGRAPHVM

Sciant presentes et futuri quod ego Hamel(inus) dei gratia abbas . et conuentus Gloec' concessimus Godwino fulloni in feudo et hereditate medietatem terre iuxta ecclesiam sancti Thome apostoli . cuius alteram medietatem concessimus Ricardo fulloni⸝ tenendam de nobis pro .xl.[ta] denariis . per annum. Tali tenore quod et ipse . et heredes sui . emendabunt domos eiusdem terre . et reedificabunt eas cum opus fuerit . de propriis sumptibus suis . et quod nec dabunt . nec uendent . nec excambient . nec ad alium religiosum locum uel personam transferent eam absque nostra permissione . Nos autem adquietabimus eam de langabulo .iiii.[or] denariorum . aduersus archiepiscopum Eborac(ensem). Prefatus uero Godwinus iuramentum prestitit quod fidelis existet ecclesie nostre . et[1] quod annuum censum fideliter persoluet . scilicet .xx.[ti] denarios ad hockedei . et xx.[ti] denarios ad festum sancti Michaelis . et quod nec artem . nec ingenium exquiret quo per tenuram suam ecclesia nostra de predicta terra dampnum incurrat. Quam conuentionem quia ratam uolumus et inconuulsam permanere . quamdiu memoratus Godwinus et heredes sui annuum censum bene reddiderint⸝ eam sub presentis cirographi attestatione confirmamus . cuius partem sigillo ecclesie nostre munitam illi tradidimus . et alteram partem absque sigillo penes nos reseruamus. Hiis testibus . Willelmo albo sacerdote . Aluredo filio Brihtmeri[2] . Siluestro filio Willelmi filii Tudefled . God de horto . Gileberto genero Godwini.

[1] Superscript in MS.
[2] Possibly *Brihcmeri*: blot in ink.

64. Lifetime lease in the form of a chirograph by Abbot Hamelin and the convent of St. Peter's, Gloucester, of land by the Severn bridge (at Gloucester) to Walter Godheorte and Walter his son for ½ mark annual rent. (1148 × 79)

G.C.L., 'Deeds and Seals', iv, no. 7, fol. 3 (209 mm × 98 mm), **Scribe 3**, no turn-up; single slit on lower left foot; no tag or seal; endorsements: Contra Walterum Godheorte. et filium eius (s. xii²), **Hand e**; Terr' quond' P. le Taylur iiiia Warda (*c.* s. xiv^{ex}); in via ponte super Sabrina(m) (c. 1500?).

CYROGRAPHVM

Sciant presentes et futuri quod ego Hamel(inus) dei gratia abbas . et conuentus Gloec' concessimus Waltero Godheorte . et Waltero filio suo . domum[1] nostram iuxta pontem super Sabrinam . tenendam de nobis in uita sua tantum pro dimidia marcha argenti per annum . tali tenore quod idem Walterus et predictus filius suus emendabunt eam et reedificabunt cum necesse fuerit de propriis sumtibus suis. Ipsi autem iuramentum prestiterunt quod fideles existent ecclesie nostre nec artem uel ingenium exquirent quo per tenuram suam ecclesia nostra dampnum incurrat de predicta domo . nec uendent eam nec excambient . nec in uadimonium ponent . nec transferent ad alium locum religiosum uel personam . absque nostra permissione . et quod prenominatum censum fideliter persoluent . medietatem ad Hockedei . et medietatem ad festum sancti Michaelis. Post decessum autem eorum prefata domus cum omni melioratione apposita restituetur ecclesie nostre libera et quieta absque alicuius reclamatione. Quod quia ratum uolumus et inconuulsum permanere quamdiu ipsi prefatum censum legitime reddiderint. partem huius cirographi sigillo ecclesie nostre munitam illis tradidimus . et alteram partem absque sigillo penes nos retinuimus.

Possibly a file copy.

[1] *q(uandam)* erased before *domum.*

65. Grant in fee and inheritance of land at Choulton (in Lydbury North, Salop.) in the form of a chirograph by Abbot Hamelin and the convent of St. Peter's, Gloucester, to Hervey of Longfield for an annual rent of six shillings. (1148 × 79)

H.C.L., no. 1607 (172 mm × 140 mm), poss. **Scribe 4**; turn-up, but no provision for sealing; endorsements: Caurtuna (s. xii); contra Herueum de Langefeld (s. xii^{ex} × s. xiii^{in}), **Hand f**, Walker, 'Gloucester Charters', no. 5; cal. in Baddeley i, no. 112, pp. 227–8.

CIROGRAPHUM

Sciant presentes et futuri quod ego Hamel(inus) dei gratia dictus abbas et conuentus monachorum ecclesie BEATI PETRI Gloec' pro . . .ne[1] et amore illustris uiri Gaufridi de Ver . Concessimus Herueo de Langefeld . terram nostram de Cawertune in bosco et plano excepto prato quod est super ripam onie . et decima ipsius terre tenendam in fevdo et hereditate libere et quiete pro sex solidis . per annum . et accepimus inde homagium eius et fidelitatem . sub hac conditione quod si aliquis de predicta terra calumpniam nobis mouerit . consilium et auxilium fideliter ei prestabimus. Sed si forte derationata fuerit⸌. nullum escambium ei dabimus. Quod quia firmum esse uolumus⸌. presenti scripto et sigilli nostri auctoritate confirmamus. Huius rei testes sunt . Herebertus ianitor . Morin . Gaufridus camerarius . Willelmus Mansellus . Robertus de H'eford . Symon Brito . Walterus filius Seuari . Walterus constabularius . Walterus de Burt' . Iohannes des Mareis . Iohannes Flandrensis . Godefrei de Rudeford . Henricus Mustel . Snel de Longefeld . Hugo de camera . Randulfus . Seulfus faber . et Bernardus filius eius . Audoenus . Robertus de la Bertun'.

[1] Illegible due to stain on MS.

66. *Grant in fee and inheritance in the form of a chirograph by Abbot Hamelin and the convent of St. Peter's, Gloucester, to Richard fuller of half the land by the church of St. Thomas the Apostle (Gloucester). (1148 × 79)*

G.C.L., 'Deeds and Seals', iv, no. 15, fol. 7 (212 mm × 96 mm), **Scribe 3**; tongue apparently torn from lower left foot; no slit for tag; no seal; endorsements: Contra Ricardum fullonem (s. xii^2), **Hand e**; I . . . ii.a Warda. (*c*. s. xiii^{med}?); sc(ribitur) (s. xiv^{ex} × s. xv^{in}); Registratur (s. xiv^{ex}); Kyngeshome (s. xv?).

C Y R O G R A P H V M (*inverted*)

Sciant presentes et futuri quod ego Hamel(inus) dei gratia abbas . et conuentus Gloec' . concessimus Ricardo fulloni in feudo et hereditate medietatem terre iuxta ecclesiam sancti Thome apostoli . quam Gaufridus et Adam frater eius monachi nostri secum nobis dederunt . tenendam de nobis pro .xl.^{ta} denariis . per annum . Tali tenore . quod et ipse . et heredes sui emendabunt domos eiusdem terre . et reedificabunt eas cum opus fuerit . de propriis sumptibus suis . et quod nec dabunt . nec uendent . nec excambient . nec ad alium religiosum locum . uel personam transferent eam absque nostra permissione. Nos autem adquietabimus eam de langabulo .iiii.^{or} denariorum aduersus archiepiscopum Eboracensem. Prefatus uero Ricardus . iuramentum prestitit . quod fidelis existet ecclesie nostre . et quod annuum censum fideliter persoluet . scilicet .xx.^{ti} denarios . ad hockedei . et xx.^{ti}. denarios ad festum sancti Michaelis . nec artem uel ingenium exquiret . quo per tenuram suam ecclesia nostra de predicta terrra dampnum incurrat. Quam conuentionem quia ratam uolumus et inconuulsam permanere⸌. quamdiu memoratus Ricardus . et heredes sui annuum censum bene reddiderint⸌. eam sub presentis cirographi attestatione confirmamus . cuius partem sigillo ecclesie nostre munitam illi tradidimus . et alteram partem absque sigillo penes nos reseruamus. Hiis testibus[1] . Willelmo Albo sacerdote . God de Horto . Fulcherio de Horto . Aluredo conuerso . et Ricardo sage . Dauid diacono.

[1] The names of the witnesses were added by another contemporary hand in a different black (with tinge of brown) ink.

67. *Grant in fee and inheritance in the form of a chirograph by Abbot Hamelin and the convent of St. Peter's, Gloucester, of land by the castle ditch (Gloucester) to Wibert son of Tochi for 3s. annual rent. (1148 × 79)*

A. G.C.L., 'Deeds and Seals', iv, no. 18, fol. 8 (290 mm × 57 mm; possible tongue cut from left foot; slits for two tags on foot; seals missing; endorsements: Contra Wibertum (s. xiii^{med}), **Hand I**; castell' (s. xiii poss. s. xiii^{ex} in same hand as no. 68 endorsement *iuxta fossatum castelli*); Registratur (s. xiv); **B**. ibid. 'Reg. B', no. 675, pp. 292–3.

C Y R O G R A P H I U M

Sciant presentes et futuri quod ego Ham(elinus) dei gratia abbas et conventus sancti Petri Gloec' . concessimus Wiberto filio Thochi quamdam terram quam habemus iuxta fossatum castelli tenendam de elemosina in feudo et hereditate annua pensione trium solidorum . Quorum medietatem persoluet ad Hocchedei✓ et aliam medietatem ad festum sancti Michaelis. Idem uero Wibertus iurauit quod fidelis erit ęcclesię nostre nec quieret artem uel ingenium quo sciat ecclesiam nostram de tenuria sua alienari uel minui uel in aliquo detrimentum pati. Quod quia uolumus ratum haberi inposterum✓ hanc pactionem cyrographi testimonio confirmamus . Cuius alteram partem sigillo ecclesie munitam illi tradidimus . et alteram partem absque sigillo penes nos retinemus. Nec illam terram alicui uendet nec excambiet . nec ad alium locum uel personam transferet . sine nostra permissione.

68. *The other half of no. 67 in the same hand but without witnesses. (1148 × 79)*

G.C.L., 'Deeds and Seals', iv, no. 17, fol. 8 (65 mm × 289 mm, foot, meas. approx. due to damage); two slits, one above the other, for tag; no turn-up; endorsements: Contra Wibertum filium[1] Toki (s. xii), poss. **Hand i/Scribe 7**; iuxta fossatum castelli (s. xiii^{ex})[2]; Non Registratur quia duplex (s. xiv^{ex}–s. xv^{in}).

The scribe omitted tailed-*e* in this copy.

[1] *filu* in MS. [2] See no. 67, endorsement *castell'*.

69. *Grant in fee and inheritance in the form of a chirograph by Abbot Hamelin and the convent of St. Peter's, Gloucester, to Wibert son of Tochi of two stalls in the stone house on the middle street (Gloucester) for 8s. annual rent. (1148 × 79)*

A. G.C.L., 'Deeds and Seals', ii, no. 36, fol. 21 (340 mm; 338 mm [foot]; side meas. unavail. due to damaged edges), **Scribe 5**; tongue apparently cut from lower left edge; seal and tongue missing; endorsements: Contra Wibertum filium Tochi (s. xii^2; poss. s. xii^{med}); iii^a Warda (s. xiii^{med}); Registratur (s. xv^{in}?); 2.a selda apud domum lapideam in medio vico (*c*. 1500); **B**. ibid. 'Reg. B', no. 666, p. 289.

C Y R O G R A P H U M (*inverted*)

Sciant presentes et futuri quod ego Ham(elinus) dei gratia abbas . et conuentus sancti Petri Gloec' . concessimus Wiberto filio Tochi . duas seldas quas habuimus in domo lapidea in medio uico . vnam ex parte australi . et alteram ex parte aquilonis . tenendas de nobis in feudo et hereditate . Quamdiu debitum censum bene et absque uexatione reddiderit . Reddendo singulis annis . Octo solidos . Quatuor ad Hocchei´. et alios quatuor ad festum sancti Michaelis. Et preter ipsas seldas permisimus ei duas terras hereditarie tenendas que sunt uersus castellum . Quas Adam marescallus dedit ecclesie nostra . Dando annuatim .xx. et viii. denarios soluendos in terminis superius assignatis. Ipse uero Wibertus iurauit quod fidelis erit ecclesie nostre . Nec quiret artem uel ingenium qua sciat ecclesiam nostram de tenura sua alienari . uel in aliquo detrimentum pati . Nec iam dictas seldas uel terras alicui uendet . . . [1] nescessitate urgente . Nec excambiet . Nec ad alium religiosum locum uel personam transferet. Et quod postmodum[2] fuerit emendandum tam in seldis quam in subscriptis terris´. Wibertus de suo emendabit. Quod quia ratum uol[umus][3] haberi in posterum´. presenti scripto sigillum ecclesie nostre apponimus . et cirographum penes nos retinemus.

Apparently a file copy.

[1] MS. torn.
[2] A full stop is crossed out in the MS.
[3] MS. torn.

70. *Grant with freedom to grant and sell in the form of a chirograph by Abbot Hamelin and convent of St. Peter's, Gloucester, to William carpenter of land by Fulbrook (in Gloucester) for landgabel of 1¼d. a year. (1148 × 79)*

G.C.L., 'Deeds and Seals', iv, no. 19, fol. 9 (187 mm × 119 mm), **Scribe 6** (below, Plate IX); seal on tag: white wax, fragment, chipped; obverse (below, Plate Ia): oval (only width avail.; *c*. 45 mm); partial image of seated abbot or St. Benedict, facing front, crozier in right hand; an upraised book in left hand; legend: . . .CI PET. . .; reverse: counterseal indiscernible; endorsements: Contra Willelmum carpentarium (s. xiii[1]), **Hand n**; written on top reverse of tag: I Gar' (s. xiii?) de terra iuxta Foulbrok (s. xiii[med]); . . .[1] Warda (erased, s. xiii[med]); A (s. xiv).

CYROGRAPHVM

Notum sit omnibus tam presentibus quam futuris quod ego Hamel(inus) dei gratia abbas et conuentus monasterii sancti Petri Gloec' concessimus Willelmo carpentario terram que est iuxta Folebroc uicina[m] domui que quondam fuit Hereberti sacriste in excambio alterius terre que est ex altera parte ecclesie̦ beate Marie iuxta domum que quondam fuit Godefridi coqui nostri tenendam libere et quiete pro uno denario . et uno quadrante . de langabulo . et ita propriam ad dandum et uendendum´. sicut illa fuit quam suscepimus ab eo . et insuper marcam illi dedimus pro melioratione domorum quas suscepimus ab illo cum prefata terra. Gillebertus autem filius Beniami(ni) omne ius suum si quod habuit in eadem terra clamauit quietum coram nostro hundredo [.] Et si contingat aliquo casu ut non possit warantare nobis predictam terram´. illa terra quam ei tradidimus ad nos reuertetur . et afforabitur ex utraque parte melioratio apposita . et si quid de melioratione alterio parti superfuerit aut nobis scilicet aut illi´. pretium integre reddetur. Et si nos non poterimus warantare illi excambium nostrum.[1] faciemus illi eodem modo. Quod quia ratum esse uolumus.[1] diuiso inter nos cyrographo unam partem penes nos retinuimus alteram apposito sigillo nostro illi tradidimus. His testibus Ricardo sacerdote de sancta Trinitate . Petro de Pirituna . Helia de Filtuna . Willelmo diacone . Hileberto diacone . Hernaldo filio Dunning [.] Hereberto portario . Maurino . Roberto de Bertuna . Ricardo filio Beattis . Willelmo blancpein, et aliis multis.[2]

[1] Erasure.   [2] From *Beattis* the witness-list is covered by the turn-up.

71. *Grant in the form of a chirograph of a half virgate by Abbot Hamelin and the convent of St. Peter's, Gloucester, to Gilbert son of Richard Chamberlain for 5s. annual rent and not in fee, but at the pleasure of the abbot and convent. 1155.*

H.C.L., no. 1673 (137 mm × 103 mm), **Scribe 4**; possible turn-up now folded down flat, but no slit for tag; no evident provision for sealing; endorsement: Gilebertus filius Ricardi Camerarii. (s. xii[2]), poss. **Hand d/Scribe 4**; cal. in Baddeley i, no. 9, pp. 226–7.

CIROGRAPHUM

Notum sit presentibus et futuris quod Ham(elinus) dei gratia abbas Gloec' et conuentus eiusdem ecclesie anno ab incarnatione domini .m.°c.lv. Suscepto prius homagio Gisleberti filii Ricardi Camerarii de dimidia uirgata terre que ante patri suo per conuentum concessa fuerat in hereditate concesserunt eidem Gisleberto aliam dimidiam uirgatam tenendam pro quinque solidis per annum non in feudum uel hereditatem sed ex gratia et in misercordia quanto tempore voluerunt[1] abbas et conuentus. Huius rei testes sunt . Ingulfus et Grim presbiteri . et Helyas Giffard . et Robertus et Alardus de Sida nepotes eiusdem Helie . Wazo . et Radulfus Picardus . Iohannes de Piritona . et Edricus de Cors[2] . Nicolaus prepositus . et Ernietus achepotere . Willelmus le peiteuin . et miles Henrici de pomeria . Iohannes de Mareis[3] . Walterus Caperun . Willelmus Walensis . Nigellus filius Artur[i] . Willelmus de Dene et Galfridus frater eius et Walterus de Boxcliue . et Ernesius quondam camberarius abbatis . Durandus de Bristoue et Aschitillus de Lilletona.

The Helias Giffard of the witness-list is likely to have been the individual of this name who joined the St. Peter's community *c.* 1163 ('Historia', 69, 117; ii. 158); in 1157 he attested with his son Helias Archbishop Roger of York's *compositio* with St. Peter's, Gloucester (*Cart. Glouc.* ii, no. 597). His son Helias succeeded to his lands as early as 1162 and fined for them in 1165–6 ('Historia', ii. 157, 160; *P.R. 12 Henry II*, 79); and the son Elias died 1190–1 (Dugdale, *Baronage*, i. 500; Stevenson, 71 n.).

[1] *voluerit* in MS.
[2] terminal letter overstruck with *s*?   [3] The bowl of *d* in *de* is partially erased.

72. *Chirograph between Abbot Thomas and the convent of St. Peter's, Gloucester, and Osb(ert) of Droitwich (de Wiz) and his brothers regarding the plea between them over their tenant William. (1179 × 98; poss. 1180 × 98)*

H.C.L., no. 1520 (117 mm × 172 mm); no provision for sealing; endorsements: Contra Osbertum de Wiz' (s. xii^{ex} × s.xiii^{in}), **Hand h**; Caps(ula) .xiii. de Laicis tenuris (s. xiii^{ex}); Registratur (s. xiv^{ex} × s. xv^{in}); Walker, 'Gloucester Charters', no. 9, facsm. Plate XXII facing p. 262; cal. in Baddeley i, no. 22, pp. 230–1; *EAWD*, i, no. D.270.

C I R O G R A P H V M (*inverted*)

Forma concordie facte inter . Th(omam) et conuentum Gloec' . et Osebertum de Wiz . et fratres suos super placito quod uersabatur inter eos . pro homine suo . Willelmo. H(oc) est O . et frater suus .H. in presentia domini .P. Meneuensis episcopi . et aliorum plurium . Die lune proxima ante festum sancti Iohannis Babtiste coram dicto abbate comparuit . et se iurare cum uiris sexaginta legitimis obtulit. Hoc quod intulit homin[i] suo Willelmo in dedecus domini abbatis non fecisse et se plenum rectum facere homini suo . Willelmo . super uulnere quod ei intulerat . Salinam u(ero)[1] et totam terram de Wiz quam de dicto abbate petebat quietam clamauit . et precipue assarta . et quindecim selliones terre . de quibus uestituras asportauit . et ipsas uestituras reddere compromisit . tali pacto quod si ipse posset facere constare domino abbati absque breui . et placito . et iuramento . quod ipse de terra sua aliquid occupauerit id ei prefatus abbas restitueret. Apellationem uero quam ipse .O. et fratres sui mouerunt contra Iohannem Crispum[2] de .lx. marcas quas petebant . consentiente fratre suo .H. ex toto remisit . Quod si frater suus .R. facere recusaret . iam dicti fratres .O. et H. fratrem suum R. cum domino abbate toto nisu suo super querelis quas habet dominus abbas . aduerus eum . inpetrare non desistent. Super expensis . et laboribus . quos in his agendis dominus abbas pertiderit . pro uoluntate satis dicti abbatis satisfacere prenominatus .O. conpromisit . et super his coram iustic(iis) domini regis . aput Wigornia' . qui tunc aput Gloec' regalia tractabant negotia . cirographum diuidere . vel modo dicto cuncta in curia sua aput Gloec' . que dicta sunt peragere . si forte contineret iusticias iam dictas . aput Wigornia' non conuenire. Omnia uero ut dicta sunt iurauit ipse .O. et frater suus .H. et hoc prosequendi plegios inuenit firmiter et sine omni dolo tenere. Si hoc agendi illis . a iustic(iis) detur permissio. Quibus peractis dominus abbas . dicto O. et fratribus suis . de homine .W. tenere compromisit . Si quid haberent aduersus eum de iure obicere. Huius autem rei testes sunt hii . Petrus Menevensis episcopus . Rogerus de B'chelai . et fratres eius . Oliverus . et Philippus . Mahelus de Tornit' . Alexander pincerna . Robertus de B'ton' . et filius eius Robertus . et multi alii. Huius uero rei plegii et testes sunt hii ex parte Oseberti . Willelmus de Mo'strew' . Ricardus de Baggi'eden' . Reginaldus de Cirencest' . Adam de Blacheneie . et plures alii.

The limits for the charter's date are indicated by mention of Peter bishop of St. David's. For the date, possibly Monday after the feast of St. John the Baptist 1180 × 98, see Walker, 'Gloucester Charters', 263 n.

---

[1] There is a small hole in the MS.; reading uncertain.
[2] The editor is indebted for this reading to Miss Meryl Jancy.

73. *Grant in fee and inheritance from Abbot Thomas and the convent of St. Peter's, Gloucester, to John Bay of empty land [in Hare Lane, Gloucester] to be held of the almonry for 2s. annual rent. (1179 × 1205)*

A. G.C.L., 'Deeds and Seals', ix, no. 2, fol. 1 (195mm × 67mm); no turn-up; slit for tag between third and second to last line of text; tag and seal missing; endorsements: Contra Iohannem Bai (s. xiii^{med}), **Hand I**; De terra quam Rogerus Yue dedit nobis. (s. xiii^{ex} × s. xiv^{in}); Registratur (s. xiv^{ex} × s. xv^{in}); B. G.C.L., 'Reg. B', no. 449, p. 199.

Sciant presentes et futuri quod ego Thomas dei gratia abbas et conuentus ecclesie sancti Pet(r)i Gloec' concessimus Iohanni Bai illam uacuam terram quam Rogerus Yue dedit nobis tenendam de elemosinario nostro in feudo et hereditate pro duobus solidis annuatim . His terminis reddendis . medietate ad Hoched(ai) et medietate ad festum sancti Michaelis . et ipse eandem terram propriis sumptibus edificabit. Idem uero Iohannis iuramentum nobis prestitit . quod fidelis erit ecclesie nostre de soluendo reditu nostro plenarie . Et quod predictam terram neque uendet . neque escambiet . neque in uadimonium ponet . neque ad alium locum religionis transferet sine assensu nostro . Et quod nec artem neque ingenium exquiret'. unde domus nostra per tenuram suam dampnum incurrat. Quod quia ratum et inconuulsum manere uolumus . presenti scripto sigilli nostri impressione munito confirmauimus. His testibus . Rogero capellano de sancto Iohanne . Roberto filio Botild . Roberto Asse . Hugone filio Ernged . Willelmo Hawi . Waltero filio Ioelis . Willelmo de Botint' . Haþw' palmario . Willelmo Thurreb' . Alexandro seruiente elemosinarii.

For the location of this property see no. 74, endorsement.

74. *Another copy of no. 73, but not the other half of the chirograph. The witness-list has slight differences. (1179 × 1205)*

G.C.L., 'Deeds and Seals', ix, no. 25, fol. 11 (190mm × 84mm); tongue cut or torn from left foot; no turn-up; slit for seal on foot, tag and seal missing; endorsements: Contra Iohannem Bai (s. xii^{ex} × s. xiii^{in}), **Hand i/Scribe 7** (below, Plate XLIIIi); In H'lone de terra quam Rogerus Yue dedit nobis (s. xiii^{ex} × s. xiv^{in}); Non registratur quia duplex (s. xiv).

CYROGRAPHUM

Sciant presentes et futuri [*etc.*] His testibus Rogero capellano de sancto Iohanne . Roberto filio Botild,[1] Roberto Asse . Hugone filio Ernget . Willelmo Hawi . Waltero filio Ioelis . Willelmo de Botint' [.] Haþew(ino) palmario [.] Will(elmo) Thurreb'erd . Alexandro seruiente elemosinarii[.]

---

[1] **B** ends with *Rob(erto) filio Botild' et aliis.*

75. *Grant in fee and inheritance in the form of a chirograph by Abbot Thomas and the convent of St. Peter's, Gloucester, to William Cubleine of an external stall beside one in their stone house in the middle of the market (Gloucester) for 3s. 6d. annual rent. (1179 × 1205)*

G.C.L., 'Deeds and Seals', viii, no. 11, fol. 6 (173mm × 78mm [approx. meas.]); slit for tag on lower right corner of foot parallel to right edge; tag and seal missing; endorsements: Contra Cubleine (s. xii^{ex} × s. xiii^{in}), **Hand g** (below, Plate XLIIIg); iiia Warda (s. xiii^{med}); Registratur (s. xiv^{ex} × s. xv^{in}); .sc(ribitur) (s. xiv^{ex} × s. xv^{in}); in domo lapidea in medio foro (s. xv^{ex}).

C Y R O G R A P H U M: (*inverted*)

Sciant presentes et futuri quod Ego Thomas dei gratia abbas et conuentus ecclesie sancti Petri Gloec' . concessimus Willelmo Cubleine exteriorem seldam preter unam in domo nostra lapidea que est in medio foro . tenendam de nobis in feudo et hereditate pro tribus solidis . et .vi. denariis . annuatim reddendis duobus terminis . Vna scilicet medietate ad festum sancti Michaelis . et alia medietate ad Hokedai. Idem uero Willelmus iuramentum nobis prestitit quod fidelis erit ecclesie nostre . et quod predictam terram neque uendet . neque escambiet . neque in vadimonium ponet . neque ad alium locum religionis transferet . sine assensu nostro . Et quod nec artem nec ingenium exquiret unde domus nostra per tenuram suam dampnum incurrat. Heredes autem sui cum singuli sibi succedent similem nobis facient cautionem. Quod quia ratum et inconuulsum manere uolumus´ presenti scripto sigilli nostri impressione munito confirmauimus. His testibus Ricardo de sancta Trinitate . Henrico sacrista . Roberto filio Toui . Edwino piscario . Radulfo Aurifabro . Willelmo Arcuario . Alexandro Tilemon . Codw' Horn . Willelmo burg' . Adelelmo.

76. *Lifetime lease in the form of a chirograph by Abbot Thomas and the convent of St. Peter's, Gloucester, of a stall and a half by the cobblery in the stone house at the cross (Gloucester) to John Doforme for 8s. annual rent. (1179 × 1205)*

G.C.L., 'Deeds and Seals', viii, no. 10, fol. 5 (*c.* 186mm [irregular edge] × 77mm), **Scribe 9**; no turn-up; possible slit for tag on left end of foot; tag and seal missing; endorsements: Contra Iohannem Doforme (s. xii^{med} × s. xiii^{in}), **Hand f**; versus suteriam de domo lapidea (modern).

C Y R O G R A P H U M

Sciant presentes et futuri quod ego Thomas dei gratia abbas Gloec' et conuentus eiusdem loci concedimus Iohanni Doforme unam seldam et dimidiam uersus sutoriam de domo lapidea ad crucem pro octo solidis annuatim ad duos terminos scilicet ad Hokedai et ad festum sancti Michaelis. Hanc autem concessionem concedimus predicto Iohanni habendam omnibus diebus uite sue. Et ut rata et firma fiat eam presenti scripto et testium subscriptione confirmamus. Predictus uero Iohannes seldam suam de custo suo emendabit. Idem uero Iohannes dedit nobis ad introitum duos solidos. Predictam uero seldam liberauerunt eidem Iohanni Paganus monachus et Robertus ianitor tunc magistri coram hundredo nostro[.] Hiis testibus . Ricardo clerico . Waltero Hut . Henrico caluo . Ricardo filio Iordani . Waltero Kadifer . Giliberto filio   Radulfi [.] Benedicto cordeuanario . Ricardo rufo. Hernisio presbitero[1] . Ricardo filio Ernisii . Henrico mercennario . Ada filio Gladwini.

[1]   *presbiter* in MS.

77. *Lifetime lease in the form of a chirograph by Abbot Thomas and the convent of St. Peter's, Gloucester, to Robert Farrier of the anterior front and a stall by the furriery of the stone house at the cross (Gloucester) for 2s. annual rent. (1179 × 1205)*

G.C.L., 'Deeds and Seals', viii, no. 7, fol. 4 (191 mm × 74 mm); possible slit perpendicular to lower left end of foot; tag and seal missing; endorsements: Contra Robertum ferur. (s. xii[2]); Hered' Sandon'[;] tertia warda (s. xiv); Versus parmenteriam in domo lapidea ad crucem (s. xv[ex]).

Sciant presentes et futuri quod ego Thoma dei gratia abbas Gloec' et conuentus eiusdem loci concedimus Roberto Le ferur totam frontem anteriorem et unam seldam uersus parmenteriam de domo lapidea ad crucem pro viginti quatuor solidis reddendo nobis illos ad duos terminos . scilicet ad Hockedai . et ad festum sancti Michaelis. Hanc autem concessionem concedimus . predicto Roberto habendam omnibus diebus uite sue. Et ut rata et firma fiat́. eam presenti scripto et testium subscriptione confirmamus. Predictus autem Robertus seldas suas de custo suo emendabit. Idem uero .R. dedit nobis de introitu duos bisantios. Predictas uero seldas liberauerunt eidem .R. Paganus monachus et Robertus ianitor tunc magistri coram toto hundredo. Hiis testibus Ricardo clerico . Waltero Hut . Henrico caluo . Ricardo filio Iordani . Waltero Kadifer . Gilleberto filio Radulfi . Benedicto Cordewenario [.] Gibelot filio Osberti . Ricardo ruffo [.] Ernisio presbitero . Richemanno filio Enisii . Henr[ico] mercennario . Ada filio Gladwini.

CIROGRAPHV'

78. *Lifetime lease in the form of a chirograph by Abbot Thomas and the convent of St. Peter's, Gloucester, of two stalls in their stone house by St. Mary's church (Gloucester) to William Feragu for 10s. annual rent. (1179 × 1205)*

G.C.L., 'Deeds and Seals', viii, no. 2, fol. 2 (134 mm × 154 mm), **Scribe 11**; seal on tag; white wax, fragment, chipped, repaired; oval (meas. not avail.); obverse: upper torso of an abbot or St. Benedict facing front holding a crozier in right hand and an upraised book in the left; legend, partly unavail. and partly illegible; reverse: counterseal; an intaglio, oval (*c*. 27 mm × 15 mm); a figure to the right seizing a fawn by the hind legs; legend: . . . SECRETV':THOME: ABBATIS:GLOEC. . .; endorsements: .iii.ᵃ Warda (s. xiii^med); Registratur (s. xiv^ex × s. xv^in); Scriptum Will(elm)i feragu (s. xiv^ex); 2. selide in domo lapidea iuxta ecclesiam beate Marie (c. 1500?) .i.G. (uncertain date).

CYROGRAPHUM:

Sciant presentes et futuri quod ego Thomas dei gratia abbas . et conuentus sancti Petri Gloec' . concessimus Willelmo Feragu duas seldas in domo nostra lapidea . que sunt propinquiores ecclesie beate Marie . quarum una est ex parte australi . altera ex parte aquilonari . tenendas de nobis tantum in uita sua . Pro decem solidis . nobis annuatim persoluendis . duobus terminis . Medietate scilicet ad Hockedai . et alia medietate ad festum sancti Michaelis. Quando autem memoratus .W. memoratas seldas a nobis recepit⸴ edificia superposita appreciata sunt decem solidos. Si uero aliquo casu emergente . prefatas seldas reliquerit⸴ similia nobis edificia . aut pretium restituet. Post decessum autem ipsius . predicte selde cum omni melioratione superposita . ad nos libere . et sine reclamatione suorum reuertentur. Idem uero .W. iuramentum nobis prestitit quod fidelis erit ecclesie nostre . de soluendo redditu nostro plenarie . et quod nec artem nec ingenium exquiret unde domus nostra per tenuram suam dampnum incurrat . et quod predictas seldas neque uendet neque escambiet . neque in uadimonium ponet . neque ad alium locum religionis transferet . sine assensu nostro. Quod quia ratum et inconuulsum esse uolumus . presenti scripto sigilli nostri impressione munito⸴ diuiso inter nos cyrographo⸴ confirmauimus. His testibus . Roberto de Twiggeword . capellano . Ænaldo de Cutelbern . Waltero Cadiuor . Ricardo burg' . Petro . Henrico . fratribus eius . Ricardo filio Iordani . Iohanne le draper . Waltero scriptore . Drogone de Punteise . Philippo Carbonel . Durando de Hauuilla . et multis aliis.

The witness Richard burgess was one of Gloucester's most prominent citizens. He appears frequently as principal or witness in mostly local borough records from *c*. 1175 × 90 to *c*. 1240. Between *c*. 1200 and *c*. 1228 he served as one of Gloucester's bailiffs. Following an appointment in 1228 by King Henry III as his principal officer in the borough, Richard bore the title mayor of Gloucester for some eight years *c*. 1228 × 40 (*VCH Glos*. iv. 31 & nn., 371; *Medieval Town*, 154 & n.). He appears in this capacity in a dispute between burgesses and St. Peter's over common rights at Maisemore in 1236 (*Cart. Glouc*. iii, no. 983); see also ibid. ii, no. 566.

79. *Grant in fee and inheritance in the form of a chirograph by Abbot Thomas and the convent of St. Peter's, Gloucester, to William son of Godric of the land between the two bridges of Gloucester which Richard burgess gave to William by charter and his seal in the hundred before witnesses. (1179 × 1205)*

A. G.C.L., 'Deeds and Seals', iv, no. 2, fol. 1 (138 mm × 176 mm), **Scribe 6**; possible fold for turn-up at foot; no turn-up and no slit for seal; seal missing; endorsements: contra Will(elmu)m filium Godrici (s. xii^ex); inter duos pontes Glouc'; Infirmarie (s. xiii²); inter pontes [;] Registratur (s. xiv^{ex}–s. xv^{in}); **B**. P.R.O., C 150/1, fol. 95v; **C**. G.C.L., 'Reg. B', no. 1074 (1073), p. 466; *Cart. Glouc.* i, no. 290.

CIROGRAPHUM (*inverted*)

Sciant presentes et futuri . quod ego Thom(as) dei gratia abbas Gloec' et conuentus monachorum sancti Petri concessimus Willelmo filio Godrici tenendam de ecclesia nostra in feudo et hereditate terram inter duos pontes Gloec' . quam prius emptam de Ernisio filio Wulfwini. Ricardus burgeis tradidit . . .[1] eidem Willelmo sub carta et sigillo suo in hundredo coram testibus et postea dedit eam capelle sancte Brigide que est in cella infirmorum monachorum Gloec' . saluo iure dicte Willelmi et conuentione sub qua Ricardus eam concesserat eidem Willelmo . Scilicet quod inde reddet predicte capelle singulis annis tres solidos et tres denarios . Medietatem ad festum sancte Michaelis et medietatem ad Pasca. Et nos adquietabimus ipsam terram de langabulo duorum denariorum et unius oboli ad Hochdai erga regem de cuius feudo est. Edificia uero que fuerunt in predicta terra quando Willelmus recepit eam de Ricardo. fuerunt appreciata per uisum legalium hominum uiginti solidos. Vt si forte domus aliquo casu deciderent . uel deteriores fierent . uel Willelmus conuentionem non posset tenere uel nollet. reddet nobis terram et domos quales eas recepit. aut pretium. De qua uidelicet conuentione fideliter seruanda . Willelmus ex parte sua prestitit nobis cautionem . et in eadem terra ius ecclesie nostre conseruabit illesum et inte(grum)[2] pro posse suo . nec aliquo modo transferet eam uel ad alium religiosum locum sine assensu nostro uel personam . nec per se nec per alium artem exquiret nec ingenium . quo de predicto tenemento detrimentum ecclesia nostra uel impedimentum incurrat. Nos autem ex parte nostra sub cirographo presentem ei cartam ecclesie nostre sigillo tradidimus confirmatam[3]. His testibus Willelmo de Botintuna . Helya Celueswombe [.] Roberto de la Bertuna[4] . Galfrido de Lilletuna . Willelmo de Bromiard' . Iohanne de Mareis . Willelmo de Gloec' . Nicholao de Rudes . Rannulfo stabulario . Bernardo fabro . Nicholao filio Wlfiard et Rogero fratre ipsius . Roberto filio Faremon et Waltero fratre ipsius . Aluredo fullone et Simone filio eius . Willelmo filio Unenad et Thoma filio eius . et multis aliis.

[1]   Ink blot, possible crossing out of two minims.
[2]   Parchment patched and word(s) illegible.
[3]   **B** as printed in *Cart. Glouc.* ends here with *etc.*
[4]   **C** ends here with *et aliis.*

80. *Grant in the form of a chirograph by Abbot Thomas and the convent of St. Peter's, Gloucester, of land in the old castle (Gloucester) to Helias palmer to be held of the almonry for 5s. payable annually to the almonry. (1179 × 1205)*

A. G.C.L., 'Deeds and Seals', v, no. 17, fol. 7 (63 mm [left] × 131 mm [foot]), **Scribe 10** (below, Plate XII); two slits for tags, one along the right edge, the other at the foot; no turn-up; seal missing; endorsements: Contra Helyam palmarium (s. xii^{ex} × s. xiii^{in}); vetus castellum (s. xiii^{ex}); Registratur (s. xiv^{ex} × s. xv^{in}); **B**. ibid. 'Reg. B', no. 677, p. 293.

CYROGRAPHUM

Sciant presentes et futuri quod ego Thomas dei [gratia] abbas et conuentus sancti Petri Gloec' . Concessimus Helye palmario terram illam que iacet iuxta terram Wimundi . et terram Petri I(n)gan in ueteri castello tenendam de elemosinaria nostra in feudo et hereditate . sibi et heredibus suis in perpetuum . pro quinque solidis . annuatim elemosinarie nostre duobus terminis persoluendis . Medietate ad Hockedai . et alia medietate ad festum sancti Michaelis. Idem uero Helyas iuramentum nobis prestitit quod fidelis erit ecclesie nostre de soluendo redditu nostro plenarie . et quod predictam terram . neque uendet neque escambiet neque in uadimonium ponet . neque ad alium locum religionis transferet sine assensu nostro . et quod nec artem nec ingenium exquiret unde domus nostra per tenuram suam dampnum incurrat. Quod ut ratum et inconuulsum permaneat'. presenti scripto . sigilli nostri impressione munito'. diuiso inter nos cyrographo . confirmauimus. His testibus . Waltero Cadiuor . Ærnaldo cutelb(u)ri[1] . Willelmo Brutun . Mauricio filio Esgari[2] . Alexandro filius eius . Thoma palmario . Dauid incisore . Waltero scriptore et multis aliis.

[1] **B** ends here with *et aliis.*
[2] *filio . Esgari* in MS.

81. *Another copy of no. 80, with differences in the witness-list. (1179 × 1205)*

G.C.L., 'Deeds and Seals', v, no. 18, fol. 7 (130 mm × 71 mm), **Scribe 10**; slit for seal; no turn-up; tag and seal missing; endorsements: Contra Helia(m) palmariu(m) (s. xii?); in ueteri castelo. (s. xii[2]); Non registratur quia duplex (s. xiv).

His testibus, Waltero Cadiuor . Ærnaldo Cutelb(u)ri . Willelmo Brutun . Dauid i(n)cisore . Thoma palmario . Waltero scriptore . Mauricio filio Esgari . et multis aliis.

This is one half of a bipartite chirograph which replicates the text of the preceding grant (no. 80). It is not the other half of that document, because the remaining portions of the letters which form *cyrographum* are the same; while the texts of the two *acta* are identical, the order of the names in the witness-lists is slightly different and the name Alexander son of Maurice son of Esgar, found in the witness-list of no. 80, is missing from that of no. 81.

82. *Another copy of no. 80, with differences in the witness-list. (1179 × 1205)*

G.C.L., 'Deeds and Seals', xi, no. 5 (129 mm × 80 mm), **Scribe 10**; seal on tag, green wax, chipped, repaired, oval (orig. *c.* 69 mm × *c.* 48 mm); obverse: an abbot or St. Benedict wearing a cope or cloak fastened by a clasp, seated, facing front; in right hand a crosier?, in left, an upraised book; legend: . . .LLV:SCI:PE. . .T. . .; obverse, a counterseal; oval (30 mm × 25 mm); a figure facing to the right seizing a fawn by the hind legs; legend: +SECRETV.' THOME ABBATIS GLOE. . .; endorsement: Elie palmar' (s.[xii] ex × s. xiii[in]); Baddeley, 'Some Further Deeds', pp. 50–51.

His testibus . Waltero Cadiuor . Ærnaldo Cutelb'n . Willelmo Brutun . Dauid incisore . Thoma palmario . Ricardo filio Iordani . Roberto diuite . Waltero Paris . Ricardo filio Ricardi burg' . Waltero scriptore . et multis aliis.

This may be the extant half of yet another text of this grant, having significant differences between its witness-list and those of the preceding two (nos. 80–81); it lacks the names of Maurice son of Esgar and Alexander his son (missing in no. 81) and adds the names of Walter Paris, Richard son of Jordan, and Robert the rich (missing in nos. 80–81); it is possible that it is the upper half of one of the two.

83. *Grant in fee and inheritance in the form of a chirograph by Abbot Thomas and the convent of St. Peter's, Gloucester, to Henry mercer of land at Newland (Gloucester) for 4s. annual rent; the right of inheritance was limited to his heirs born of his legitimate wife. (1179 × 1205)*

A. G.C.L., 'Deeds and Seals', iv, no. 28, fol. 13 (157 mm × 113 mm); no turn-up; tag cut from foot; seal missing; endorsements: Contra Henricum mercatorem (s. xii^{ex} × 1224 × 28+); neulo'd' (xiii^{med}), **Hand s**; Registratur (s. xiv^{ex} × s.xv^{in}); B. G.C.L., 'Reg. B', no. 524, pp. 230–1.

CYROGRAPHUM (*inverted*)

Sciant presentes et futuri quod ego Thomas dei gratia abbas et conuentus sancti Petri Gloec' concessimus Henrico mercatori terram illam que iacet inter terram que fuit Thoui et terram Gileberti Cornarii apud Neoweland'[1] tenendam de elemosinaria nostra in feudo et hereditate . sibi et heredibus suis si de legitima uxore heredes habuerit . pro iiii.^{or} solidis annuatim reddendis duobus terminis . Medietate ad Hochedai . et medietate . ad festum Sancti Michaelis. Si autem prenominatus Henricus nullum de legitima uxore heredem habuerit . et uxor eius eum superuixerit . ipsa iam dictam terram teneat quamdiu sine uiro uixerit . et post mortem eorum tota prefata terra cum omni melioratione apposita sine omni reclamatione suorum nobis quieta remanebit. Idem uero Henricus iuramentum nobis prestitit quod fidelis erit ecclesie nostre de soluendo redditu nostro plenarie . et quod nec artem nec ingenium exquiret . unde domus nostra per tenuram suam dampnum incurrat . et quod prefatam terram neque uend[et]^2 . neque excambiet neque in uadimonium ponet . neque ad alium locum religionis transferet sine assensu nostro. Quod quia ratum et inconuulsum manere uolumus . diuiso inter nos cyrographo sigilli nostri impressione munito. confirmauimus. His testibus Iohanne decano Gloec' . Adam clerico[3] de Brodona . Waltero Hut . Waltero Cadivor[4] . Willelmo de la Bare . Waltero Thochi . Symone de Cellario . Philippo Carbonel . Nicolao de Rudes . Durando de Hauuilla . Ricardo de Caresi . Gaufrido de Liletona . Adam Boterel [. Willelmo Bromia]rd'[5] . Willelmo de Badmintona.

A grant of Abbot Thomas in favour of Gilbert *cornator* is in G.C.L., 'Reg. B', no. 526, p. 231. This charter (as well as ibid. no. 527 on p. 232) shows that at one stage, the Gloucester suburban hospital which came to be called St. Sepulchre and still later St.

Sepulchre and St. Margaret's, was an abbatial foundation. Another of Abbot Thomas's charters reveals that St. Sepulchre was a separate corporate tenant (*Cart. Glouc.* i, no. 79).

[1] The *w* is written as Old English wyn.   [2] MS. damaged.   [3] **B**. ends here with *et aliis*.
[4] *Chadiuor* in no. 84.   [5] MS. cut out here; text reconstructed from no. 84.

84. *The other half of no. 83.*

P.R.O., C 150/2/[2] (152 mm × 144 mm); seal on tag, white wax stained green, right edge chipped off; obverse (below, Plate Ib): oval (length *c.* 70 mm; width unavail.); a seated abbot or St. Benedict facing front, wearing a cloak or cope fastened by a centre clasp; crozier in right hand, a book upraised in left hand); legend: + SIGIL. . .E GLOECESTRA; reverse: counterseal (below, Plate Ic), oval (28 mm × 22 mm); a figure facing to the right seizing a fawn by the hind legs; legend: + SECRETV' THOME ABBATIS GLOEC'; endorsements: Henricus mercator (s. xiii^{med}); Non registratur quia duplex (s. xiv^{in}).

85. *Lifetime lease in the form of a chirograph by Abbot Thomas and the convent of St. Peter's, Gloucester, of two stalls in their stone house in the middle of the market (Gloucester) to William of Hereford for 10s. annual rent. (1179 × 1205)*

G.C.L., 'Deeds and Seals', viii, no. 8, fol. 5 (145 mm × 143 mm); no turn-up or evidence of fold at foot; slit for tag at lower left corner of foot; tag and seal missing; endorsements: Contra Willelmum de Hereford' (s. xii); due solid[. . .][1] in domo lapidea (*c.* 1500).

C Y R O G R A P H U M (*inverted*)

Sciant presentes et futuri quod ego Thomas dei gratia abbas et conuentus sancti Petri Gloec' . concessimus . Willelmo de Hereford' . duas seldas in domo nostra lapidea in medio foro . quas Willelmus Boui . et Adþelam Sutor tenuerunt . vnam scilicet ex parte australi . et aliam ex parte aquilonari . tenendas de nobis tota uita sua . pro decem solidis . annuatim nobis reddendis . duobus terminis . Medietate uidelicet ad Hockedai . et alia medietate ad festum sancti Michaelis. Et post eius decessum . predicte selde . cum omni melioratione superposita . ad nos libere et quiete et sine reclamatione suorum reuertentur. Idem uero W. iuramentum nobis prestitit quod fidelis erit ecclesie nostre de soluendo redditu nostro plenarie . Et quod nec artem nec ingenium exquiret . unde domus nostra per tenuram suam dampnum incurrat . Et quod prefatas duas seldas . neque uendet neque escambiet . neque in uadimonium ponet . neque ad alium locum religionis transferet sine assensu nostro. Quod ut ratum et inconuulsum permaneat . presenti scripto . sigilli nostri munimine roborato . diuiso inter nos cirographo . confirmauimus. Hiis testibus . Ricardo Ruffo . Ricardo Burg' . Waltero Cadiuor . Ricardo filio Iordani . Alexandro Druebred . Ricardo filio Willelmi . Willelmo Brutuna . Waltero Toki . Samsone de Clifford . Mauricio marescallo . Rogero Gos . et multis aliis.

[1] Terminal letter illegible.

86. *Grant in alms in the form of a chirograph by Abbot Thomas and the convent of St. Peter's, Gloucester, to Walter clerk, son of Walter Hut, of the chapel of Matson for 10s. annual rent. (1179 × 1205)*

A. G.C.L., 'Deeds and Seals', v, no. 28, fol. 12 (152 mm × 83 mm), **Scribe 7** (below, Plate X); foot torn away from slit for tag; tag and seal missing; endorsements: Mattesdon' (s. xiii^{med}?); Registratur (s. xiv?); **B**. ibid. 'Reg. B', no. 1135 (1136), p. 501.

CYROGRAPHUM

Notum sit omnibus quod ego Thomas dei gratia abbas et conuentus sancti Petri Gloec' . concessimus in puram elemosinam Waltero clerico filio Walterii Hut capellam nostram de Mattresduna sub annua pensione decem solidorum. Quod quia ratum et inconuulsum manere uolumus . diuiso inter nos cyrographo sigilli nostri impressione munito´ confirmauimus. Idem uero Walt(erus) iuramentum nobis prestitit quod fidelis erit ecclesie nostre de soluendo redditu nostro plenarie . et quod nec artem nec ingenium exquiret . unde domus nostra per tenuram suam dampnum incurrat.

A file copy of this chirograph.

87. *Grant in fee and inheritance in the form of a chirograph by Abbot Thomas and the convent of St. Peter's, Gloucester, of a tenure in Gloucester by Holy Trinity Church to William Hwidbread for 10s. annual rent. (1179 × 1205)*

G.C.L., 'Deeds and Seals', i, no. 38, fol. 21 (156 mm × 101 mm); no provision for sealing; endorsements: Contra Willelmum Witbrad (s. xii^{ex}), **Hand g**; iiiia Warda (s. xiii^2; poss. s. xiii^{ex}); Th de Bernwade (s. xiv^{in});[1] iiii^a Warda iuxta ecclesiam Tr(i)nitat(is) (s. xiv^{in}); Registratur (s. xiv^{ex}–s.xv^{in}).

CYROGRAPHUM

Sciant presentes et futuri quod ego Thom(as) dei gratia abbas et conuentus monsterii sancti Petri Gloec' . concessimus Willelmo Hwidbread terram iuxta ecclesiam sancti Trinitatis que est inter terram Walterii Sauonarii . et Arnaldi textoris . Tenendam de nobis in feudo et hereditate sibi et heredibus suis pro decem solidis annuatim reddendis . medietate ad festum sancti Michaelis . et medietate ad Hockedai. Ipse autem Willelmus iuramentum nobis prestitit quod fidelis erit monasterio nostro de soluendo redditu nostro plenarie . Et quod predictam terram neque uendet neque excambiet neque in uadimonium ponet . neque ad alium locum religionis transferet sine assensu nostro . Et quod nec artem nec ingenium exquiret unde domus nostra per tenuram suam dampnum incurrat. Successores autem sui cum singuli sibi succedent . similem nobis facient securitatem. Quod quia ratum mànere uolumus et inconuulsum presenti scripto et sigilli nostri munimine diuiso inter nos cyrographo roboramus. His testibus .

Ricardo de sancta Trinitate . et Milone fratre eius sacerdotibus . Henrico sacrista . Edwino piscario . Amis fratre eiusdem Willelmi [.] Roberto portario . Waltero Toki . Roberto Testard.

¹ Reading uncertain with ultra-violet light.

88. *Grant in fee and inheritance in the form of a chirograph by Abbot Thomas and the convent of St. Peter's, Gloucester, to Nicholas son of Sevar Irishman of land in Bride Lane (Gloucester) for 40d. annual rent. (1179 × 1205)*

G.C.L., 'Deeds and Seals', v, no. 21, fol. 8 (169 mm × 128 mm); no turn-up; no provision for sealing; tag and seal missing; endorsements: Contra Nicholaum filium Sevari. (*c.* 1200); .sc(ribitur) (s. xiv^ex–s. xv^in); .ii.^a Warda (*c.* s. xiii²); De terra in Brydelone quam tenet abbas de Haylys ex opposito¹ Alwinegate iuxta domum Iohannis Saunders existente i' . . . redditus iiis .iiiid (s. xv^ex).

CYROGRAPHUM

Sciant presentes et futuri quod ego Thomas dei gratia abbas et conuentus sancti Petri Gloec' concessimus Nicholao filio Seuari Hiberniensis terram illam in Bridelone que fuit Sewardi Wonnarri que scilicet terra iacet inter terram que fuit Radulfi Bremel et terram Roberti King . Tenendam de nobis in feudo et hereditate sibi et heredibus suis pro quadraginta denariis annuatim persoluendis . Duobus terminis . Medietate ad Hock(edai) . et medietate ad festum sancti Michaelis. Predicta uero terra per uisum legalium uirorum mesurata habet in fronte autem⸴ xii.^cim uirgas ulnarias et unam quarterium . Retro uero⸴ xi.^cim uirgas ulnarias et dimidiam . In profunditate autem⸴ xxx^ta viii.^to uirgas ulnarias uno quarterio minus. Idem uero Nicholas iuramentum nobis prestitit quod fidelis erit ecclesie nostre de soluendo redditu nostro plenarie . et quod terram illam neque uendet neque excambiet . neque in uadimonium ponet . neque ad alium locum religionis transferet sine assensu nostro . et quod nec artem neque ingenium exquiret⸴ unde domus nostra per tenuram suam dampnum incurrat. Quod quia ratum et inconuulsum manere uolumus diuiso inter nos sigilli nostri impressione munito confirmauimus. His testibus . Waltero Kadiuor . Helia palmario . Waltero sapiente . Roberto Toli . Roberto Botild . Waltero Cornubiense . Eluredo fabro . Waltero Toki . Waltero scriptore . Willelmo th[u]t'² it'.

¹ Reading uncertain.
² *u* is an uncertain reading with ultra-violet light; ink blot or stain covers initial letters.

89. *Lifetime lease in the form of a chirograph by Abbot Thomas and the convent of St. Peter's, Gloucester, of a mill at Barton (by Gloucester) for 12s. annual rent to Geoffrey of Matson. (1179 × 1205)*

H.C.L., no. 1674 (111 mm [left] × 130 mm [foot]); at present folded flat with no turn-up, but fold across the foot makes a turn-up likely; no provision for sealing; endorsements: Contra Galfridum de Mattresdon'. (s. xii^{ex} × s. xiii^{in}), **Hand j** (below, Plate XLIVa); Bertona (s. xiv^{in}?); cal. in Baddeley i, no. 19, p. 230.

C Y R O G . . . A P H V M

Sciant presentes et futuri quod ego Thom(as) dei gratia abbas et conuentus sancti Petri Gloec' concessimus Galfrido de Matresdon' molendinum nostrum de Bertona quod Robertus de Bertona tenuit . cum omnibus pertinentiis scilicet una crofta que iacet pro tribus acris et preterea cum una acra terre et uno mesagio . tenendum de nobis terram in uita sua libere et quiete ab omni seruitio pro duodecim solidis nobis annuatim quatuor terminis persoluendis . scilicet in festo sancti Andree tribus solidis . In Annuntiatione beate Marie tribus solidis . in festo sancti Iohannis Baptiste tribus solidis . in festo sancti Michaelis tribus solidis. Post decessum uero memorati .G. memoratum molendinum cum omni melioratione superposita ad nos reuertetur. Idem uero .G. iuramentum nobis prestitit quod fidelis erit ecclesie nostre de soluendo redditu nostro plenarie . et quod nec artem nec ingenium exquiret . unde domus nostra per tenuram suam circa predictum molendinum dampnum incurrat. Quod quia ratum esse uoluimus presenti scripto sigillo nostro munito diuiso inter nos cirografo confirmauimus. Hiis testibus Waltero Toki . Philippo Carbonel . Willelmo Ianitore . Galfrido de Lilet' . Roberto de Croilli . Mauricio de Snedha' . et Ricardo fratre eius . et multis aliis.

90. *Lifetime lease in the form of a chirograph by Abbot Thomas and the convent of St. Peter's, Gloucester, of Sheldon (Devon) to Richard de Mucegros for 5 marks annual rent. (1179 × 1205)*

H.C.L., no. 1606 (163 mm × 138 mm), **Scribe 9** (below, Plate XI); tag for seal; seal missing; endorsements: Carta reddita de Selden'; c(apsula) .vii.^{a} de laicis tenuris. (s. xii^{ex} × s. xiii^{in}); vacant. (s. xiii^{2}); Baddeley i, no. 14, p. 228.

C Y R O G R A P H U M (*inverted*)

Notum sit omnibus quod ego Thomas dei gratia abbas et conuentus ecclesie sancti Petri Gloec' concessimus Ricardo de Muchegros Seldene uillam nostram tenendam de nobis in uita sua tamen pro quinque marcis argenti . His terminis annuatim reddendis . Ad festum Omnium Sanctorum duas marcas et dimidiam . Ad Pentecost(em) duas marcas et dimidiam. Cum autem eundem Ricardum deo disponente mori uel uitam mutare contigerit. predicta uilla cum omni melioratione in domibus siue in terris ab eo apposita . et cum instauramento quod cum ea suscepit sine omni suorum reclamatione et contradictione nobis remanebit. Instauramentum autem tale est boues octo singuli appreciati .iii. sol(idos) . et .vi. d(enarios) . vacca una appreciata .iii. sol(idos) . Orreum plenum auena in occidentali parte euacuatum a superiori parte quattuor pedes . vna plaustrata siliginis^{1} . vna carruca.. Idem uero Ricardus iurauit nobis et istos

plegios iuuenit . Robertum de Botint' . Petrum de Pirit' . Walterum filium Wib' .
Iohannem de Pert' . Adam de Paris quod fidelis erit ecclesie nostre . et quod
predictum censum statutis terminis legitime reddet . Et nec artem nec ingenium
per se uel per alium exquirit[1] unde domus nostra de prefata uilla dampnum aut
impedimentum incurrat. Et ut hec conuentio inuiolabiliter obseruetur presenti
cyrographo cuius alteram partem sigillo nostro munitam predicto .R. tradidimus .
Alteram uero partem sigillo eiusdem .R. roboratam penes nos retinuimus[.] hinc
inde confirmata est. His testibus . Waltero de lariuere . Willelmo Danzel .
Roberto de Bekef' . Ricardo de Bekef' . Waltero de Paris . Roberto ianitore .
Waltero Toki . Iohanne des Mareis . Roberto Testard . Gaufrido de Lilletuna .
Adam Boterel.[2]

[1] *sigilinis* in MS.
[2] Covered by turn-up.

91. *Agreement between Thomas abbot of St. Peter's, Gloucester, and Richard*
parson of Norton regarding the church of Norton; Richard was to pay an
annual pension of 100s. (1179 × 1205)

H.C.L., no. 1632 (138 mm × 124 mm); fragment of tag; seal missing; endorsements:
Contra Ricardum personam de Nort' (s. xii[2]); Non indiget registrari (s. xiv); cal. in
Baddeley i, no. 20, p. 230.

C Y R O G R A P H U M (*inverted*)

Notum sit omnibus quod talis concordia facta est inter . Thom(am) abbatem
Gloec' et Ricardum personam de Norton' super ecclesiam de Norton'. Idem
Ricardus iuramentum prestitit quod fidelis erit predicto Thome abbati et
conuentui Gloec' de centum solidis eis annuatim soluendis nomine pensionis de
prefata ecclesia . et quod nec artem . nec ingenium exquiret . unde ecclesia sancti
Petri Gloec' per tenuram suam de iam dicto redditu dampnum uel impedimentum
incurrat . Et quod nec per se . nec per alium predicte ecclesie sancti Petri
impedimentum[1] erit . quominus a domino Lincoliensi predicti redditus
confirmationem adquirat . et quod pro[2] posse suo ius supradicte ecclesie contra[3]
Willelmum filium Alani manutenebit. Predictus uero Th. abbas Gloec' predicto .
Ricardo sicut clerico suo in manutenendo iure suo suum prestabit patrocinium. In
cuius rei testimonium presens scriptum sigillorum suorum appositione diuisa
inter eas cyrographo confirmatum est. His testibus . Iohanne decano Gloec' .
magistro Adam de Longedon' . Iacobo[4] de sancto Oswaldo . et Ernisio . et
Henrico de sancta Maria sacerdotibus . magistro Rogero de Culna . Willelmo de
Mortuo mari . Willelmo de Dunia clericis . Æmaldo filio Cutell' . Waltero
Kadiuor . Rogero taillur . Symone de cellario . Phillippo Carbonel . Nicolao de
Rudes [.] Willelmo pincerna abbatis . Durando de Hauuill'.

[1] *impedimento* in MS.
[2] Superscript.
[3] *fil'* erased.
[4] The scribe corrected the third letter from *b* to *c*.

92. *Grant in fee and inheritance in the form of a chirograph by Abbot Thomas and the convent of St. Peter's, Gloucester, to Peter de vallo of land by the old castle (Gloucester) for 20s. payable to the almonry annually. (1179 × 1205)*

A. G.C.L., 'Deeds and Seals', v, no. 16, fol. 7 (138 mm × 83 mm), **Scribe 10**; no turn-up; two slits for single tag; tag and seal missing; endorsements: Contra Petrum de vallo (s. xiii^{med}); vetus castellum (s. xiii^{ex}); Registratur (s. xiv^{ex} × s. xv^{in}; poss. xv^{in}); **B**. ibid. 'Reg. B', no. 679, p. 294.

CYROGRAPHUM

Sciant presentes et futuri quod ego Thomas dei gratia abbas et conuentus sancti Petri Gloec' . concessimus Petro de uallo terram quandam apud uetus castellum que iacet inter terram Roberti fratris eiusdem Petri et terram Helie palmarii . tenendam de elemosinaria nostra in feudo et hereditate sibi et heredibus suis in perpetuum . pro viginti denariis . annuatim elemosinarie nostre persoluendis duobus terminis . Medietate ad Hockedai . et alia medietate ad festum sancti Michaelis. Idem uero Petrus iuramentum nobis prestitit quod fidelis erit ecclesie nostre de soluendo redditu nostro plenarie . et quod predictam terram neque uendet neque escambiet . neque in uadimonium ponet . neque ad alium religionis transferet sine assensu nostro . et quod nec artem nec ingenium exquiret . unde domus nostra per tenuram suam dampnum incurrat. Quod ut ratum et inconuulsum permaneat . presenti scripto sigilli nostri impressione munito diuiso inter nos cyrographo confirmauimus. His testibus . Adam Berce . Roberto fratre eiusdem Petri[1] . Reginaldo lul[2] . Heli palmario . Will(elm)o þurbern . Reginaldo Fader . et multis aliis.

[1] **B** ends here with *et aliis.*
[2] Reading uncertain with ultra-violet light.

93. *Grant in fee and inheritance in the form of a chirograph from Abbot Thomas and the convent of St. Peter's, Gloucester, to Walter son of Peter then bailiff of Gloucester of the land next to Holy Trinity church (Gloucester), which Roger furbisher had held, for 15s. annual rent. (1179 × 1205).*

G.C.L., 'Deeds and Seals', i, no. 13[b], fol. 8 (97 mm [right] × 196 mm [foot]); slit for seal; tag and seal missing; endorsements: Contra Walterium filium Petri (s. xii^{ex}); iiii^{a} Warda iuxta ecclesiam Trinitatis (s. xiv^{in}); Ric' le Wise (s. xiv^{in}); Registratur (s. xiv^{ex} × s. xv^{in}).

C : YROGRAPHVM:

Sciant presentes et futuri quod ego Thom(as) dei gratia abbas et conuentus sancti Petri Gloec' . concessimus Walterio filio Petri tunc preposito Gloec' terram que fuit Rogeri furbarii que est iuxta ecclesiam sancti Trinitatis . Tenendam de nobis in feudo et hereditate pro .xv. solidis annuatim . Medietate ad Occhedai . et medietate ad festum Sancti Michaelis. Ipse autem Walterius iuramentum nobis prestitit in capitulo nostro quod fidelis erit monasterio de soluendo redditu nostro plenarie . Et quod predictam terram ad alium locum religiosum non transferet . Insuper nec artem nec ingenium exquiret⸴ unde domus nostra per tenuram suam dampnum incurrat. Successores autem sui cum singuli succedent . similem nobis facient cautionem. Quod quia ratum manere uoluimus et inconcussum⸴ presenti scripto et sigillo monasterii nostri . diuiso inter nos cyrographo communimvs. Hiis testibus[1] . Ricardo Coffin . Ernaldo filio Cutelberii . Waltero cild[2] . Durando parmentario . Reginaldo filio Reginaldi . Rogero burgeis . Rogero filio Mahaut . Roberto filio Selewine . Helia Calueswambe . David filio Seuare . et multis aliis.

[1] Erasure creating blank space.   [2] *clid* in MS.

---

94. *Grant in fee and inheritance in the form of a chirograph by Abbot Thomas and the convent of St. Peter's, Gloucester, to Reginald hooper of land (in Gloucester) for 4s. 6d. annual rent payable to the almoner. (1179 × 1205)*

A. G.C.L., 'Deeds and Seals', ix, no. 3, fol. 1 (113 mm × 125 mm); no turn-up; slit for tag on foot; tag and seal missing; endorsements: Contra Reginaldinum circulatorem (s. xiii[ex]), **Hand l**; I. Bay. Zonaria[1] (s. xiii[med]?), poss. **Hand s**; Registratur (s. xiv[ex] × s. xv[in]); B. ibid. 'Reg. B', no. 448, p. 199.

:C Y R O G R A P H U M: (*inverted*)

Sciant presentes et futuri quod ego Thomas dei gratia abbas et conuentus sancti Petri Gloce' . concessimus Reginaldo circulatori unam terram de terra que fuit Rogeri Iue . illam scilicet que est inter terram quam Galfridus de Pomerai tenet de nobis . et terram quam Iohannes Bay tenet de nobis . de eadem terra . tenendam de nobis in feoudo et hereditate illi et heredibus eius inperpetuum . pro quatuor solidis . et .vi. denariis . annuatim helemosinario nostro reddendis duobus terminis . Medietate ad Hockeday . et medietate ad festum sancti Michaelis. Prefatus uero Reginaldus iuramentum nobis prestitit quod fidelis erit ecclesie nostre de soluendo redditu nostro plenarie . et quod terram illam non uendet . neque excambiet . neque in uadimonium ponet . neque ad alium locum religionis⸴ transferet . sine assensu nostro . et quod nec artem neque ingenium exquiret⸴ unde domus nostra per tenuram suam dampnum incurrat. Quod quia ratum et inconuulsum manere uoluimus diuiso inter nos cyrographo in pleno hundredo nostro confirmauimus⸴ His testibus . Symone de celario tunc existente p(re)tore nostro .W. Rossello[2] .W. sapiente . Roberto filio Botild . Iohanne Bay . Alexandro Tilemon . Nicholao Cornubiense . Roberto Mollepain . Garino hopare. Waltero scriptore . Gileberto Gondric . Willelmo Chachepol . et pluribus aliis.

[1] Reading uncertain.   [2] **B** ends with *W. Rosello et aliis.*

---

95. *Another copy of no. 94. (1179 × 1205)*

G.C.L., 'Deeds and Seals', iii, no. 27, fol. 15 (113 mm × 124 mm); slit for tag at foot; no turn-up; tag and seal missing; endorsements: Contra Reginaldum circulatorem (s. xiii[ex]), **Hand l** (below, Plate XLIVc); Herlon' inter Bay et Pomeray (s. xiii[med]), poss. **Hand s**; Non Registratur (s. xv).

This is a verbatim copy of no. 94 except that it omits the phrase *in pleno hundredo nostro* before *confirmauimus*. These two *acta* are not halves of the same chirograph since they both bear at the top the same inverted cut lettering of *CYROGRAPHUM*.

96. *Grant in the form of a chirograph by Abbot Thomas and the convent of St. Peter's, Gloucester, to Richard burgess of land by the basilica of St. Mary in the market (Gloucester), formerly held by Geoffrey furrier and later by Richard's mother, for 6s. annual rent. (1179 × 1205)*

G.C.L., 'Deeds and Seals', viii, no. 12, fol. 6 (267 mm × 111 mm), **Scribe 8**; tongue missing from left foot; tongue and seal missing; endorsements: Contra. Ricardvm bvrgensem. (s. xii[ex]); Marie Graslone (*c.* 1230?); iii[a] Warda (s. xiii[ex]); sc(ribitur) (s. xiv[med]).

C Y R O G R A P H U M (*inverted*)

Notum sit presentibus et futuri quod ego .Th. dei gratia dictus abbas et conuentus Gloec' concessimus dilecto amico nostro et fratri Ricardo burgeis . et heredibus suis quandam masuram terre iuxta basilicam sancte Marie in foro quam Gaufridus parmentarius tenuerat . et post ipsum´ Matildis Euri(n)god mater eiusdem Ricardi. Ipse uero .R. et heredes sui soluent nobis sex solidos annuatim. Nos autem adquietabimus eam aduersus regem de langabulo .xii. denariis. Hiis testibus . Ricardo presbitero de sancta Trinitate . Waltero filio Petri . Barone . Henrico sacrista . Willelmo burgeis . Rogero burgeis . Baldewino herre . Roberto de B'tona. Quod quia ratum volumus et inconuulsum permanere presentem cartam cyrographi attestatione roboratam sigilli nostri appositione muniuimus.

97. *Grant in fee and inheritance in the form of a chirograph by Abbot Thomas and the convent of St. Peter's, Gloucester, of land (in Gloucester?) to Robert mercer for 18d. annual rent. (1179 × 1205)*

G.C.L., 'Deeds and Seals', ix, no. 12, fol. 6 (128 mm × 104 mm); slit for tag on turn-up; tag and seal missing; endorsements: Contra Robertum mercatorem (*c.* s. xiii[in]); Registratur (s. xiv?).

C Y R O G R A P H U M (*inverted*)

Notum sit omnibus quod ego Thomas dei gratia abbas et conuentus sancti Petri Glouc' concessimus Roberto mercatori quandam partem de terra que fuit Regenilde de la roche tenendam de elemosinaria nostra in feudo et hereditate illi et heredibus suis i(m)perpetuum pro xviii denariis annuatim reddendis . duobus terminis . Medietate ad hockedai et medietate ad festum sancti Michaelis. Predicta uero terra per uisum legalium uirorum mensurata´ habet in latitudine .xi. uirgas ulnarias et unum pedem . In longitudine uero .xxi uirgas ulnarias et unum pedem. Predictus uero Robertus iuramentum nobis prestitit quod redditum nostrum prefatis terminis fideliter persoluet . et quod nec artem neque ingenium exquiret*. unde domus nostra per tenuram suam dampnum incurrat. Quod quia ratum et inconuulsum manere uolumus*. diuiso inter nos cyrographo in pleno hundredo nostro confirmauimus. His testibus . Symone de cellario . Waltero Kadiuor . Henrico le mercer . Roberto filio Botild . Waltero sapiente . Waltero scriptore . Roberto de orto . Willelmo Thurebern' . et multis aliis.

For the possible location of this property see *Cart. Glouc.* i, no. 758.

98. *Grant in fee and inheritance in the form of a chirograph by Abbot Thomas and the convent of St. Peter's, Gloucester, to Robert de vallo of land at the old castle (Gloucester) to be held of the almonry for 12d. payable annually to the almonry. (1179 × 1205)*

A. G.C.L., 'Deeds and Seals', v, no. 19, fol. 7 (137 mm × 69 mm), **Scribe 10**; two slits for tags on foot, one above the other; tags and seals missing; no turn-up; endorsements: Contra Robertum de uallo (s. xiii^{med}), **Hand I**; Vetus castellum (s. xiii^{ex}); Registratur (s. xiv^{ex} × s. xv^{in}); **B**. ibid. 'Reg. B', no. 678, p. 293.

CYROGRAPHUM (*inverted*)

Sciant presentes et futuri quod ego Thomas dei gratia abbas et conuentus sancti Petri Gloec' concessimus Roberto de uallo terram quandam apud uetus castellum que iacet iuxta terram Petri fratris eiusdem Roberti . tenendam de elemosinaria nostra in feudo et hereditate sibi et heredibus suis in perpetuum . pro duodecim denariis annuatim elemosinarie nostre persoluendis . duobus terminis . Medietate ad Hockedai . et alia medietate ad festum sancti Michaelis. Idem uero Robertus . iuramentum nobis prestitit quod fidelis erit ecclesie nostre de soluendo redditu nostro plenarie . et quod predictam terram neque uendet . neque escambiet neque in uadimonium ponet neque ad alium locum religionis transferet sine assensu nostro . et quod nec artem nec ingenium exquiret . unde domus nostra per tenuram suam dampnum incurrat. Quod ut ratum et inconuulsum permaneat . presenti scripto sigilli nostri impressione munito confirmauimus. His testibus . Waltero Cadiuor . Adam filio Walteri[1] . Petro fratre eiusdem Roberti . Helia palmario . Reginaldo Fader . et multis aliis.

[1] **B** ends here with *et aliis.*

99. *Grant in fee and inheritance in the form of a chirograph by Abbot Thomas and the convent of St. Peter's, Gloucester, to Thomas limner of land by the castle gate (Gloucester) for 6d. annual rent. (1179 × 1205)*

G.C.L., 'Deeds and Seals', v, no. 8, fol. 3a (133 mm × 124 mm), poss. **Scribe 10**; seal on tag; white wax, fragment, repaired; obverse: oval (meas. unavail.); an abbot or St. Benedict seated facing front, a crozier in right hand; legend chipped away; reverse: counterseal: oval (*c.* 32 mm × *c.* 22 mm); image indiscernible; legend: . . . SECRETV' . . .E

ABBA. . .; endorsement: iiii.ᵃ Warda (s. xiii²); facsm. in Gullick, 'The Illuminator of Gloucester', 210.

CYROGRAPHUM

Sciant presentes et futuri quod ego Thomas dei gratia abbas et conuentus sancti Petri Gloec' concessimus Thome illuminatori . terram quandam ante portam castelli . tenendam in feudo et hereditate sibi et heredibus suis . pro sex denariis singulis annis ad festum sancti Michaelis sacristarie nostre persoluendis. Ipsa uero terra coram uiris legalibus mensurata . habet in latitudine quatuor uirgas ulnarias cum pollice interposito . In longitudine uero octo uirgas ulnarias cum pollice. Idem uero .T. iuramentum nobis prestitit quod fidelis erit ecclesie nostre de soluendo redditu nostro plenarie . et quod nec artem nec ingenium exquiret . unde domus nostra per tenuram suam dampnum incurrat . Et quod predictam terram neque uendet neque escambiet . neque in uadimonium ponet . neque ad alium locum religionis transferet´. sine assensu nostro. Quod quia ratum esse uolumus . presenti scripto sigilli nostri impressione munito . diuiso inter nos cyrographo confirmauimus. His Testibus . Willelmo sacrista seniore . Willelmo iuniore . Willelmo Albon . Alexandro sacrista . Willelmo þurbern . Rogero Brond . et multis aliis.

Thomas *illuminator* appears in several early Gloucester *acta* (Stevenson, nos. 86 [*c.* 1190], 120 [*c.* 1210], 195 [*c.* 1220], 266, 271 [*c.* 1230]; a Henry *illuminator* and his son Thomas attest a local charter *c.* 1210 (ibid. no. 118); the chronological overlapping of this evidence with the charter above heightens the possibility that this Thomas son of Henry was the same as the beneficiary of the above charter. Furthermore, as the charter shows, Thomas sought to acquire property near land which Henry *illuminator* held on a little street (*in vicolo*) by the castle (ibid. no. 120). At the least the above evidence places two and (if it is assumed that Thomas son of Henry also was an *illuminator*) possibly three *illuminatores* in the castle district about the first decade of the thirteenth century. Henry's property may have been on Walkers Lane where Adam *circulator* was his neighbour (ibid. no. 119). For the significance of the evidence about Thomas within the context of illuminators, see Gullick 'The Illuminator of Gloucester', 209–13, to whom the present editor is grateful for supplying him with an offprint.

100. *Grant in fee and inheritance in the form of a chirograph by Abbot Thomas and the convent of St. Peter's, Gloucester, to Robert son of Toli of the land (in Gloucester) which Leueward gave to the abbey with himself, for 10s. annual rent. (1179 × 1205)*

G.C.L., 'Deeds and Seals', i, no. 14, fol. 8 (165 mm × 104 mm), **Scribe 7**; slit for seal, no turn-up; tag and seal missing; endorsements: Contra Robertum filium Toli (s. xii²), **Hand i/Scribe 7**; iiiia Warda (s. xiiiᵉˣ); Registratur; .iiii.ᵃ Warda iuxta ecclesiam Trinitatis (*c.* s. xivᵉˣ).

CYROGRAPHUM

Sciant presentes et futuri quod Ego Th.¹ dei gratia abbas et conuentus sancti Petri Gloec' . concessimus Roberto filio Toli terram quam Leuewardus secum dedit domui nostre que iacet inter terram Radulfi aurifabri . et terram Willelmi Burgeis . tenendam de nobis in feudo et hereditate pro decem solidis annuatim reddendis duobus terminis . medietate ad Hochedai . et medietate ad festum sancti Michaelis. Idem uero Robertus iuramentum nobis prestitit . quod fidelis erit ecclesie nostre de soluendo redditu nostro plenarie . et quod predictam terram neque uendet . neque excambiet . neque in uadimonium ponet . neque ad alium locum religionis transferet sine assensu nostro . et quod nec artem nec ingenium exquiret . unde domus nostra per^2 tenuram suam dampnum incurrat. Quod quia ratum et inconuulsum manere uolumus^1. diviso inter nos cyrographo sigilli nostri impressione munito . confirmamus. His testibus Iohanne tunc decano Gloec' [.] Godefrido de Culna sancti Eilwini et Thoma de Sancto Nicolao sacerdotibus . Ærnaldo filio Cutelbern . Ricardo Burgeis . Waltero Hut . Rogero taillur . Willelmo Burgeis . Waltero Toki . Roberto Ianitore . Roberto Testard . Phillipo Carbunel . Willelmo de Bromiard . Radulfo aurifabro . Godefrido albo.

1 Superscript in the same hand.
2 Reading uncertain because of stain.

101. *Grant in fee and inheritance in the form of a chirograph by Abbot Thomas and the convent of St. Peter's, Gloucester, to Walter the wise of land on the bank of the Severn river (at Gloucester) for 12d. annual rent. (1179 × 1205)*

A. G.C.L., 'Deeds and Seals', v, no. 20, fol. 8 (151 mm × 112 mm); no turn-up; slit for tag on foot; tag and seal missing; endorsements: Contra Walterum sapientem (s. xiii^{med}); super ripam Sabrine iuxta castellum (s. xiii^{med}); Registratur (s. xiv^{ex} × s. xv^{in}); B. ibid. 'Reg. B', no. 676, p. 293.

CYROGRAPHVM

Sciant presentes et futuri quod ego Thomas dei gratia abbas et conuentus sancti Petri Gloec' concessimus Waltero sapienti terram nostram quam Edricus super ripam Sabrine nobis dedit tenendam de nobis in feudo et hereditate illi et heredibus eius inperpetuum pro xii. denariis . Annuatim reddendis . Duobus terminis . Medietate ad Hokedai . et medietate ad festum sancti Michaelis. Predictus uero Walterus iuramentum nobis prestitit quod fidelis erit ecclesie nostre de soluendo redditu nostro plenarie . et quod terram illam [neque uen]det^1 neque excambiet neque in uadimonium ponet neque ad alium locum religionis transferret sine assensu nostro . et quod nec artem neque ingenium exquiret$^.$ unde domus nostra per tenuram suam dampnum incurrat. Quod quia ratum et in conuulsum manere [uo]lumus^2 d[iui]so^3 in[ter n]os^4 cyrographo in pleno hundredo nostro confirmauimus. Hi[s testibus]^5 . Symone de celario . Ernaldo Cutelb(urn) . Alexandro Tilemon . Roberto Mullepain^6 . Waltero scriptore . et [mu]ltis^7 aliis.

1 Text blotted out by stain.   2 Text blotted out by stain.   3 Text blotted out by stain.
4 Text blotted out by stain.   5 Text blotted out by stain.
6 B omits the name of Alexander Tilemon and ends here with *et aliis*.   7 Text blotted out by stain.

102. *Grant in the form of a chirograph by Abbot Thomas and the convent of St. Peter's, Gloucester, to William son of William, formerly bailiff of Standish, of half a virgate in Standish and for the sustinence of his mother and family 20 acres for his life, for 6s. annual rent. (1179 × 1205)*

H.C.L., no. 1675 (145 mm × 101 mm); tongue for seal torn away from left foot; seal missing; endorsements: De Stanedis; (s. xii^{ex}); De Stanedis; (s. xii^{ex}); Non registratur quia non indiget (s. xiv^{med.}?); cal. in Baddeley i, no. 18, pp. 229–30.

C Y R O G R A P H V M (*inverted*)

Notum sit tam presentibus quam futuris quod ego Th. dei gratia abbas et conuentus sancti Petri Gloec' concessimus Willelmo filio Willelmi quondam prepositi nostri de Stanedis dimidiam virgatam terre in Stanedis pro decem solidis . quam pater suus tenuit simili pacto . et preterea concessimus ei pro amore dei ad sustentationem matris et familie sue viginti acras de dominio ipso in uita sua⸌. pro sex solidis . quas pater suus tenuit ad similem censum. Si autem uxorem duxerit uiuente matre sua⸌. edificabit sibi domos super predictam dimidiam virgatam et mater sua si uoluerit quam diu uiuet manebit in domibus quas pater iam dicti Willelmi edificauit super prescriptam terram de dominio nostro. Matre uero sua mortua idem Willelmus transferet domos illas de terra dominii nostri et equabit eas solo. Sed terram ipsam de dominio scilicet prefatas viginti acras⸌. tenebit in uita sua. Sed post mortem suam nullus suorum reclamabit aliquid iuris in illis viginti acris. Ipse autem preter predictas censas operabitur nobis unam aratam in hieme . Alteram in quadragesima . Tertiam ad waretu(m) . et faciet bederipam. et dabit don(a) abbatis cum ceteris hominibus. Hanc autem conuentionem confirmauimus[1] ei presenti carta et sigillo monasterii nostri diuiso inter nos cirographo. His testibus . Siluestro cellarario⸌. Willelmo Giffardo⸌. Ricardo de Horslega⸌. monachis . Godefrido Sacerdote . Ricardo burgeis . Galfrido camerario . Roberto filio Roberti de B'tuna . Roberto albo . Willelmo sacrista . Waltero Thochi . Galfrido de Lilletuna. et toto allimoto de Stanedis. Pro hac autem concessione dedit nobis quinque marcas et unam vncia aur[i].[2]

[1] *ui* superscript apparently in the same hand.
[2] The text may have continued further, but the remaining portion of the charter, which apparently formed a tongue and possibly a tie, is torn away.

103. *Grant in fee and inheritance by Abbot Thomas and the convent of St. Peter's, Gloucester, in the form of a chirograph to Hugh chapman of land (in Gloucester?) which Pain Cordwainer held before he became a monk; the land to be held for an annual rent of ½ mark and was not to be alienated outside the tenant's family. Second week of May, 1181.*

H.C.L., no. 1672 (154 mm × 122 mm); no turn-up and no provision for sealing; endorsement: Contra Hugonem Chepman. (s. xii^{ex} × s. xiii^{in}), **Hand j**; cal. in Baddeley i, no. 15, pp. 228–9.

C Y R O G R A P H V M

Sciant presentes et futuri. quod ego Thom(as) dei gratia dictus abbas ecclesie sancti Petri Gloec' . et conuentus monachorum eiusdem loci . concessimus Hugoni chepman . terram quam Paganus Corduanarius tenuit de nobis antequam fieret monachus . Tenendam in feudum et hereditatem pro dimidia marca per annum quam diu censum bene et integre reddiderit . tali conuentione quod nec ipse nec heredes eius transferent ea ullo modo ad aliquem locum religionis . uel ecclesiam uel personam extra progeniem suam sine licentia et assensu nostro. Et reddent inde fideliter consuetudines que ad eam pertinent . et predictum censum singulis annis . medietatem ad festum sancti Michaelis . et medietatem ad Hokedei. In huius autem rei testimonium et confirmationem tradidimus eidem Hugoni sub sigillo sancti Petri. partem unam huius cyrographi . aliam uero partem retinuimus penes nos . anno ab incarnationem domini millesimo . centesimo . octogesimo . primo . secunda septimana mensis Maii. Hiis testibus . Roberto . . .tori[1] de Bert' . Gaufrido de Liliton' . Iordano de Sudwic' . et hundredo nostro.

[1] Reading uncertain with ultra-violet light; it may be *Roberto pistori.*

104. *Final concord between Hodierna widow of William son of William the reeve and the abbot of Gloucester (Thomas) concerning Hodierna's free tenement of 20 acres in Standish; the tenement is to remain to the abbey, which grants half a virgate to Hodierna. 2 May 1189. Gloucester.*

A. Bodl. MS. Charters Gloucester, a. 1, no. 7 (165 mm × 85 mm); endorsements: Contra Odiernam de Standhediss (s. xii[ex]); Caps(ula) .viii. de laicis tenuris. (s. xiii[ex]); Stanedis; Registratur (s. xiv[ex]); **B.** G.C.L., 'Reg. B', no. 258, p. 105.

Hec est finalis concordia facta in curia domini Regis apud Gloc' . anno regni regis .H. secondi .xxx°.v.[to] die Martis proxima post festum apostolorum Philippi et Iacobi . Coram Radulfo de Arden . Willelmo filio Alani . Willelmo filio Stephani . Mauricio de Bercal' . Toma Noel . Hugone Pantulfo . magistro Roberto de Saloperia . Roberto de Hasele . Nicolao Britone . iustic(iis) regis . et aliis fidelibus domini Regis ibi tunc presentibus . Inter Odiernam que fuit uxor Willelmi filii Willelmi prepositi . et abbatem de Gloc' . de libero tenemento ipsius Odierne in Stanedis . scilicet . .xx. acris terre unde recognitio summonita fuit inter eos in curia regis. Scilicet quod abbati de Gloc' et conventui eiusdem loci . remanet in perpetuum totum predictum tenementum quietum de predicta Odierna . et heredibus suis. Et pro hac concordia predictus abbas et predictus conuentus concesserunt predicte Odierne . et heredibus suis in perpetuum tenendam .i. dimidiam virgatam terre cum pertinentiis in Standis scilicet illam dimidiam uirgatam quam Willelmus uir Odierne tenuit . ita integre possidendam . sicut Nicolas molendinarius et Willelmus portmon . tenuerunt die concordie . et hanc per liberum seruitium .viii. solidorum per annum pro omni seruitio quod ad abbatem pertinet et conuentui.

105. Conventio *in the form of a chirograph between Abbot Thomas and the convent of St. Peter's, Gloucester, and Geoffrey prior of Llanthony Secunda about the burial of parishioners. 11 July 1197.*

A. P.R.O., C 150/2/[3] (193 mm × 101 mm); seal on tag, white wax, chipped, oval (originally *c.* 69 mm × 50 mm); obverse: seated Virgin and child to front, arms outstretched; legend: . . .LVM . . .APIT : DE : LAN. . .; reverse: counterseal, oval (57 mm × 33 mm); a seated figure to front; legend: + SIGILLVM GALFR. . . PRIORIS.LANTONIE; endorsements: De compositione inter nos et canones Lant' de sepulturis; c(apsula) .iii. de laicis tenuris (s. xii^{ex} × s. xiii^{in}), **Hand h** (below, Plate XLIIIh); Lonton' (s. xiii^{ex}); Registratur (s. xiv^{ex} × s. xv^{in}); B. G.C.L., 'Reg. A', no. 131, pp. 95–96; C. P.R.O., C 115/K2/6683, Sect. I, no. 66; D. Ibid. C 115/L2/6690, Sect. I, no. 8; *Cart. Glouc.* i, no. IV, pp. lxxvii–lxxviii (from B).

C Y R O G R A P H U M (*inverted*)

In honore sancte atque indiuidue Trinitatis . et gloriose virginis Marie . et beatorum apostolorum Petri et Pauli . anno dominice incarnatione millesimo . centesimo . nonagesimo . septimo . Die translationis sancti Benedicti facta est hec conuentio inter Thomam abbatem et conuentum sancti Petri Gloec' . et Gaufridum priorem et conuentum Lanton' . quod si aliquis de parochianis monachorum[1] . scilicet ecclesie beate Marie ante portam abbatie . et sancti Iohannis Baptiste . et aliarum ecclesiarum cimiteriis carentium in villa Gloec' sitarum apud Lantoniam[2] duobus uel tribus presentibus in extrema uoluntate sepulturam elegerit. canonici hoc ipsum monachis denuntiabunt . et ita libere et pacifice licebit canonicis ipsum recipere. Similiter si aliquis de parochianis canonicorum Lanton' in villa Gloec' . scilicet ecclesie beate Marie infra portam australem . et sancti Audoeni extra muros ciuitatis apud ecclesiam beati Petri duobus uel tribus presentibus in extrema uoluntate sepulturam elegerit. monachi hoc ipsum canonicis Lant' denuntiabunt . et ita libere et pacifice licebit monachis ipsum recipere. Ita quidem quod si uel monachos[3] uel canonicos in tali electione contigerit esse presentes . intuitu caritatis eligentem monebunt . ut ecclesiam in[4] qua recedit siue monachorum[5] siue canonicorum in aliquo beneficio[6] respiciat. De capella autem castelli conuenit inter eos quod si quis de castello penes sanctum Petrum sepulturam sibi eligere uoluerit. liberum sit monachis eum recipere. Similiter si penes Lanton' sepiliri uoluerit. canonici eum libere recipiant . Nullis priuilegiis uel aliis scriptis hinc inde impetratis uel impetrandis huic amicabili compositioni in posterum preiudicantibus. Quod ut ratum et inconuulsum in eternum permaneat . sigillis vtriusque ecclesie diuiso inter eos cyrographo hinc inde confirmatum est. Hiis testibus . R. abbate Winchecu'b' . Baldewino Wac tunc constabulario Gloec'[7] . Henrico thesaurio Lond' . Iohanne decano Gloec'[8] . A. de Langedon' . Godefrido de Lant' . Nichilao de Wlfrunhamton' . Roberto Folet . Roberto Grosseteste . Iohanne Burgeis . magistris.

This agreement was confirmed in a charter of John bishop of Worcester, and in turn by Hubert Walter archbishop of Canterbury (*Cart. Glouc.* ii, nos. 437–38). The text of an earlier settlement between Llanthony, Margaret de Bohun, and St. Peter's, Gloucester, dated 6 July 1192 is in P.R.O., C 115/K2/6683, Sect. I, no. 70; *Cart. Glouc.* ii, no. 436. The witness Robert Grosseteste *magister* was the famous Aristotelian scholar who after 1192 was a member of the household of William de Vere bishop of Hereford until de Vere's death in 1198 (Southern, *Robert Grosseteste*, 66; also ibid. (2nd edn. 1992), pp. lvii, 66–67 & nn..; cf. McEvoy, *The Philosophy of Robert Grosseteste*, 4–6). The presence of known members of the Hereford episcopal *familia*, Godfrey of Llanthony, Nicholas of Wolverhampton, and Henry Banastre, along with Grosseteste is compelling evidence of this identification. The bishop of Hereford retained an interest in Llanthony, which had originally been founded in his diocese (Barrow, *Hereford Episcopal Acta*, p. xxxix, no. 150 n. & *passim*; *GFAL*, 275; *LCGF*, no. 259 n.).

1   *monacorum* in **A**.
2   *Lontoniam* in **A**.
3   *monacos* in **A**.
4   *a* changed to *i*.
5   *monacorum* in **A**.
6   *b(e)nficio* in MS.
7   **A** ends here with *et aliis*.
8   **C** ends here with *et aliis*.

106. *Final concord between Thomas abbot of St. Peter's, Gloucester, and Eva of Byford concerning a fourth part of a mill in Byford (Herefs.). 11 September 1199. Hereford.*

P.R.O., CP 25/1/80/1, no. 12 (158 mm [foot] × 85 mm [right]); no endorsement.

CYROGRAPHUM

Hec est concordia facta in curia domini regis apud H'eford' die Sabbati proxima post Natiuitatem sancte Marie a[n]no[1] regni regis Iohannis primo coram Alano abbate Teokesbir' . Henr' archidiacono[2] Stafford' . Simone de Pateshill' . Iohanne de Gestliges . Ricardo Flandrense . Willelmo de Faleis' iustic(iis) et aliis baronibus domini regis tunc ibi presentibus [.] Inter Thom(am) abbatem Glouc' petentem . Et Eua(m) de Boiford' tenentem . De quarta parte vnius molendini cum pertinentiis in Boiford' vnde placitum fuit inter eos in prefata curia . Scilicet quod predicta Eua recognouit predictam quartam partem illius molendini cum pertinentiis esse ius predicti abbatis. Et pro hoc fine et concordia et recognitione predictus abbas concessit predicte Eue et heredibus suis predictam quartam partem illius molendini tenendam de se et successoribus suis inperpetuum . per liberum seruitium quinque solidorum per annum pro omni seruitio scilicet ad festum sancti Michaelis triginta denariorum . et ad Annuntiationem sancte Marie triginta denariorum.

Hereford' .

1   Text rubbed here.
2   *Arched(iacono)* in MS.

107. *Final concord in the form of a chirograph between Roger (V) of Berkeley and Thomas abbot of St. Peter's, Gloucester, concerning the advowson of the church of Doddington. 8 November 1203. Gloucester*

H.C.L., no. 1519 (63 mm [right] × 116 mm [foot]); no provision for sealing; endorsement: Finalis concordia inter nos et Rogerum de Berkeley pro ecclesia de Dodinton. D. temporalium parte 2ᵃ (c. s. xivᵉˣ); cal. in Baddeley i, no. 23, p. 231.

C Y. . .O. . .A P H U M

Hec est finalis concordia facta in curia domini regis apud Glouc' in octabo Omnium Sanctorum anno regni regis Iohannis .v.° coram .W. de Cantelup' . Simone de Pateshull' . Henrico de Nor'h't . Ricardo de Seing' iustic(iis) et aliis fidelibus domini regis ibidem tunc presentibus . Inter Rog(erum) de B'kelai petentem et Thomam . abbatem Glouc' deforciantem de aduocatione ecclesie . de Doddinton' cum pertinentiis vnde recognitum assisa ultime presentationis summonitum fuit inter eos in prefata curia . Scilicet quod predictus Rogerus recognovit predictam aduocationem cum pertinentiis esse ius ipsius abbatis et ecclesie sancti Petri de . Glouc' et eam remisit et quietam clamauit de se et . heredibus suis predicto abbati et successoribus suis . et eccelsie sancti Petri de Glouc' in perpetuum. Et predictus abbas intuitu caritatis dedit predictam ecclesiam ad petitionem ipsius Rogeri Waltero clerico de Bannebir' . Tenendam ipsi Waltero tota uita sua nomine persone . Et post decessum ipsius Walteri predictus abbas intuitu caritatis conferet uni clerico ydoneo predictam ecclesiam ad petitionem predicti Rogeri uel heredum suorum qui eam tenebit tota uita sua nomine persone.

This is the lower right portion of a tripartite chirograph. The second half of the word [CYRO]GRA[P]HU[M] is written down the left-hand side.

108. *Grant in fee and inheritance in the form of a chirograph by Abbot Henry and the convent of St. Peter's, Gloucester, to Ærnaldus of Butterley of land outside their garden (by Gloucester) for 4s. annual rent payable to their almoner. (1205 × 24)*

G.C.L., 'Deeds and Seals', viii, no. 3, fol. 2 (92 mm [left] × 202 mm [foot]); seal on tag, white wax, chipped, rubbed, fragment; obverse: oval (meas. unavail.); partial torso of an abbot or St. Benedict facing front wearing a cope fastened by a pectoral clasp, an upraised book in the left hand; legend unavail.; reverse: a counterseal, pointed oval (length unavail.; width 29 mm); an abbot standing to front; in the right hand a crozier; in the left an upraised book; legend: . . .RETVM A. . .TI. . .V. . .STRI. . .; endorsements: extra ortum (s. xiiiᵉˣ?); Arnaldus de Butterleya. (s. xiii²?); subelemosinaria (s. xiv).

C Y R O G R A P H U M : (*inverted*)

Sciant presentes et futuri quod ego Henr(icus) dei gratia abbas et conuentus sancti Petri Glouc' . concessimus Ærnaldo de Buterleia terram nostram extra ortum nostrum . Illam scilicet quam Rannulfus tenuit . Tenendam de nobis in feudo et hereditate sibi et heredibus suis pro quatuor solidis elemosinario nostro annuatim persoluendis . ad duos terminos . Medietate ad Hockedei . et alia medietate ad festum sancti Michaelis. Predicta uero terra per uisum legalium virorum mesurata: habet in fronte decem et septem uirgas ulnarias cum pollice interposito . In medio: quindecim virgas ulnarias[1] cum police interposito . Retro᷄. decem virgas ulnarias[2] cum pollice interposito . In profunditate᷄. sexaginta tres virgas ulnarias cum pollice interposito. Quando uero predictus Æmaldus predictam terram a nobis recepit᷄. edificium superpositum appreciatum est viginti solidos. Si autem aliquo casu emergente ipse vel heredes sui prefatam terram nobi reliquerint᷄. simile edificium aut pretium nobis restituent. Idem uero Æmaldus iuramentum nobis prestitit᷄. quod fidelis erit ecclesie nostre de soluendo redditu nostro plenarie statutis terminis . Et quod nec artem nec ingenium exquiret . vnde domus nostra per tenuram suam dampnum incurrat . Et quod predictam terram neque vendet . neque escambiet nec in vadimonium ponet . nec alicui in feudum et hereditatem tradet . neque ad alium locum religionis transferet sine assensu nostro. Eandem securitatem facient nobis heredes sui cum singuli sibi succedent. In cuius rei testimonium᷄. presens scriptum sigillo ecclesie nostre munitum . diuiso inter nos cyrographum᷄. ei tradidimus. Hiis testibus . Ricardo ruffo . Ricardo filio Iordani . Ricardo Burgeis' . Ricardo filio Willelmi . Radulfo de Tuddeham . Ada Walense . Waltero Scriptore . Salomone Ianitore . Helya camerario abbatis . Drogone pincerna . Mauricio stabulario . Helya de Paggeham . et multis aliis.

[1] *ulnaru'* in MS.
[2] *ulnaru'* in MS.

109. *Grant in fee and inheritance in the form of a chirograph by Abbot Henry and the convent of St. Peter's, Gloucester, of land on the west corner of Christchurch Lane opposite Holy Trinity Church (Gloucester) to John Le Cellere for 5s. annual rent. (1205 × 1224)*

G.C.L., 'Deeds and Seals', v, no. 11, fol. 4 (196 mm × 99 mm); slit for seal; tag and seal missing; endorsements: Gerlone p'or Bartholea;[1] another endorsement illegible with ultra-violet light.

CYROGRAPHUM

Sciant presentes et futuri quod ego Henric(us) dei gratia abbas et conuentus sancti Petri Glouc' concessimus Iohanni le Cellere terram nostram que iacet in occidentali cornerio de Cristechirchelane ex opposito ecclesie sancte Trinitatis [.] Habendam et tenendam de nobis in feodo et hereditate pro quinque solidis nobis et successoribus nostris annuatim soluendis duobus terminis videlicet duos solidos et sex denarios ad Hock(edai) et duos solidos et sex denarios ad festum sancti Michaelis[.] Predicta uero terra per visum legalium virorum mensurata continet in fronte inter tenementum nostrum ex parte occidentali et Chistechirchelane ex parte orientali tres virgas vlnarias cum pollice interposito et vnum [qu]arterium[.] In profunditate continet xi.^{cim} virgas vlnarias cum police interposito[.] Idem uero Iohannes iuramentum nobis prestitit quod fidelis erit ecclesie nostre de soluendo redditu nostro plenarie statutis terminis et quod nec artem nec ingenium exquiret vnde domus nostra per tenuram suam dampnum incurrat et quod predictam terram neque vendet neque excambiet neque in vadimonium ponet neque alicui in feodo et hereditatem tradet nec ad alium locum religionis transferet sine assensu nostro[.] Eandem securitatem facient nobis heredes sui cum singuli sibi succedent[.] In cuius rei testimonium presens scriptum sigilli ecclesie nostre munitum diuiso inter nos cirographo ei tradidimus[.] His testibus Iohanne decano Glouc' [.] Willelmo Hut [.] Hugone Euruget et multis aliis.

¹ Reading *p* 'or *Bartholea* uncertain.

110. *Grant in fee and inheritance in the form of a chirograph by Abbot Henry and the convent of St. Peter's, Gloucester, of land by the castle (in Gloucester) to Philip Cloche for 20d. annual rent payable to the almoner. (1205 × 24)*

A. G.C.L., 'Deeds and Seals', v, no. 12, fol. 4 (85 mm [left] × 223 mm [foot]); slit for tag on turn-up; tag and seal missing; endorsements: Contra Philipum Cloche (s. xiii^med), **Hand I**; vetus castellum (s. xiii^ex); Registratur (s. xiv^ex × s. xv^in); **B**. ibid. 'Reg. B', no. 681, p. 294.

C Y R O G R A P H [U M] (*inverted*)

Sciant presentes et futuri quo ego Henr(icus) dei gratia abbas et conventus sancti Petri Glouc' concessimus Philippo Cloch(e) quandam terram apud vetus castellum que iacet inter terram Roberti fratris Petri de vallo et terram Helye palmarii tenendam de elemosinaria nostra in feudo et hereditate sibi et heredibus suis in perpetuum pro viginti denariis annuatim elemosinarie nostre persoluendis . duobus terminis . Medietate ad Hockedai et alia medietate ad festum sancti Michaelis. Idem vero Philippus iuramentum nobis prestitit quod fidelis erit ecclesie nostre de soluendo reditu nostro plenarie et quod predictam terram neque vendet neque excambiet neque in vadimonium ponet neque ad alium locum religionis transferet sine assensu nostro et quod nec artem nec ingenium esquiret; vnde domus nostra per tenuram suam dampnum incurrat[.] Quod ut ratum et inconcussum permaneat presenti scripto sigilli nostri inpressione munito diuiso inter nos cyrografpho confirmauimus. His testibus . Willelmo de Radigge . Iohanne Cloch'¹ . Willelmo Algar . Martino Budde [.] Daniele piscario . Waltero de Radleie . Ricardo filio Katerine . Iohanne gode [.] Ada ferario et multis aliis.

¹ **B** ends here with *et aliis.*

111. *Grant in fee and inheritance in the form of a chirograph by Abbot Henry and the convent of St. Peter's, Gloucester, to Ralph Craft baker of two pieces of land in Holy Trinity Lane (Gloucester), one from the tenement of Llanthony Secunda, the other from the abbey's fee, for 8s. annual rent . (1205 × 24)*

G.C.L, 'Deeds and Seals', i, no. 6, fol. 4 (137 mm [left] × 135 mm [foot]); seal on tag, white wax, fragment, chipped; obverse: oval (meas. unavail.); partial image of an abbot or St. Benedict seated facing front, a cloak or cope fastened by a pectoral clasp; a crozier in right

hand; an upraised book in the left; legend chipped away; reverse: counterseal (43 mm ×
28 mm); a full-standing image of an abbot facing front; in right hand a crook or crozier;
legend: + SECRETV. . .STRIE; endorsement: scriptum Radulphi Craft de terris et tenementis
versus ecclesiam sancte Trinitatis (s. xv?).

. . .Y R O G R.. . .PH. . .M (*inverted*)

Sciant presentes et futuri quod ego H(e)nric(us) dei gratia abbas et conuentus sancti
Petri Glouc'r' concessimus Radulfo Craft pistori . duas terras nostras in viculo sancti
Trinitatis . vnam scilicet de tenemento Lanthon' . et aliam de feodo nostro . illas
scilicet que iacent inter terram Alexandri Tilemon . et seldas que tendunt versus
magnam rutam quas emimus de Willelmo Bretun . Tenendas de nobis et habendas in
feodo et hereditate sibi et heredibus suis libere et quiete pro octo solidis nobis
annuatim pro omnibus seruitiis ad duos terminos persoluendis . Medietate ad
Annuntiationem beate Marie'. et alia medietate'. ad festum sancti Michaelis. Terra
uero de predicto tenemento Lant' . per visum legalium uirorum mensurata'. habet in
fronte'. duas uirgas ulnarias cum pollice interposito uno quarterio minus . In
profunditate decem uirgas ulnarias'. cum pollice interposito. Altera uero terra de
feodo nostro'. habet in longitudine decem et septem uirgas ulnarias'. cum pollice
interposito . In latitudine decem virgas ulnarias . cum pollice interposito. Quando
autem predictus Radulfus terras a nobis recepit'. edificia super posita appreciata erant
tres marcas. Si uero aliquo casu emergente ipse uel heredes sui prefatas terras nobis
reliquerint'. simile edificium aut pretium nobis restituent. Et si fortasse ipse uel
heredes sui predictas terras uendere uoluerint'. erimus propinquiores quam aliquis
alius'. ad illas emendas. Idem vero Radulfus iuramentum nobis prestitit quod fidelis
erit ecclesie nostre de soluendo redditu nostro plenarie statutis terminis . et quod nec
artem nec ingenium exquiret . vnde domus nostra tenuram suam dampnum incurrat .
et quod predictas terras non escambiet. nec ad alium locum religionis transferet'. sine
assensu nostro. Eandem securitatem facient nobis heredes sui'. cum singuli sibi
succedent. In huius rei testimonium presens scriptum sigillo ecclesie nostre
munitum'. diuiso inter nos cyrographo'. ei tradidimus. Hiis testibus . Ricardo
Burgens' . Mauricio filio Durandi . Willelmo Bretun . magistro Waltero scriptore .
Drogone pincerna . Henrico Le bel . et multis aliis.

112.   *Grant in fee and inheritance in the form of a chirograph to Gilbert of
Eldersfield by Abbot Henry and the convent of St. Peter's, Gloucester, of a parcel of
land between the bridges of Gloucester which they bought from Juliana, widow of
John, with a road extending to the river Severn; the rent was to be $^1/_2$ mark payable
annually to the master of the works. (1205 × 24)*

P.R.O., C 150/2/[5] (145 mm × 212 mm); seal on cords, white wax stained green, chipped;
obverse (below, Plate Id): oval (original meas. unavail.); an abbot or St. Benedict seated facing
front with a cloak or cope secured by a clasp; in the right hand a crozier; in the left an open
book; legend: . . .ILLV. . . SCI PETR. . . ; reverse (below, Plate Ie): counterseal; oval (44 mm ×

27 mm); an abbot standing in full pontificals to the front, a crozier in the right hand, a book in the left; legend: + SE. . .RETVM ABBATIS GLOVCESTRIE; no medieval endorsements.

C. . . R O G R A P H. . .M

Sciant presentes et futuri quod ego Henric(us) dei gratia abbas et conuentus sancti Petri Glouc' concessimus Gileberto de Eldesfeld' illam partem terre inter pontes Glouc' quam emimus de Iuliana relicta Iohannis cum uia extendente usque ad ripam Sabrine . Illam scilicet que iacet inter capitale mesuagium dicte Iuliane et terram abbatis Theok' . tenendam et habendam de nobis sibi et heredibus suis in feodo et hereditate . libere et quiete . pro dimidia marca magistro operis ecclesie nostre qui pro tempore fuerit annuatim persoluenda . Scilicet medietate ad Pascham et alia medietate ad festum sancti Michaelis. Predicta uero terra per visum legalium uirorum mensurata habet in fronte sex uirgas ulnarias et unum quarterium cum pollice interposito . Retro uero quinque uirgas ulnarias et tria quarteria cum pollice interposito . In profunditate uero octo uirgas ulnarias et dimidiam cum pollice interposito. Quando uero predictus Gilebertus dictam terram a nobis recepit⸴ edificium superpositum apreciatum erat quinque marcas. Si uero predictus Gilebertus uel heredes sui aliquo casu emergente predictam terram relinquerint⸴ simile edificium uel pretium nobis restituant. Idem uero Gilebertus iuramentum nobis prestitit quod fidelis erit ecclesie nostre . et maxime de reddendo redditu nostro plenarie statutis terminis . Et quod nec artem nec ingenium inquiret vnde domus nostra per tenuram suam dampnum incurrat . Et quod predictam terram neque uendet . neque excambiet . neque in uademonium ponet . neque alicui in feodum et hereditatem tradet . neque ad alium locum religionis transferet sine assensu nostro. Eandem securitatem facient nobis heredes sui cum singuli sibi succedant. Et dictus Gilebertus et heredes sui curiam nostram sequentur. In cuius rei testimonium presens scriptum in modum cyrographi inter nos confecimus . cuius unam partem sigillo ecclesie nostre munitam dicto Gileberto tradidimus . alteram uero penes nos retinuimus. Hiis testibus . Hugone Cissore . Galfrido de Weston' . Roberto filio Cecil' . Reginaldo Hadde . Radulpho tinctore . Willelmo Walense . Nicholao clerico . et multis aliis.

113. *Grant in fee and inheritance in the form of a chirograph by Abbot Henry and the convent of St. Peter's, Gloucester, to Henry of Elmore of land in Kingsholm (by Gloucester) for 3s. annual rent. (1205 × 24)*

G.C.L., 'Deeds and Seals', iii, no. 29, fol. 16 (152 mm [left] ×127 mm [foot]); no slit on foot; no seal; endorsements: Contra Henricum de Elmou'e. (s. xiii[in]); ii Warda. (s. xiii[med]); sc(ribitur) (s. xiv[ex] × s. xv[in]); Registratur (s. xiv[ex] × s. xv[in]); Hvngeshome (s. xv?).

C. . . R O GRA P H U M

Sciant presentes et futuri quod ego Henric(us) dei gratia abbas et conventus sancti Petri Glouc' concessimus Henrico de Elmovre terram nostram versus aulam regis .

illam scilicet que iacet propinquior terre Ricardi de Sobbire tenendam de nobis in feudo et hereditate sibi et heredibus suis pro tribus solidis nobis annuatim persoluendis ad quatuor terminos . Videlicet ad festum sancti Michaelis nouem denariis . Ad festum sancti Andree nouem denariis . In Annuntiatione beate Marie. nouem denariis . Et in Natiuitate sancti Iohannis Baptiste nouem denariis. Predicta vero terra per visum legalium uirorum mensurata. habet in fronte duodecim virgas ulnarias cum pollice interposito . Retro. totidem . In longitudine vero se extendit usque ad fossatum gardini Petri de aula regis. Quando autem predictus .H. predictam terram a nobis recepit. nullum edificium superpositum fuit. Idem vero Henricus[1] iuramentum nobis prestitit quod fidelis erit ecclesie nostre de soluendo redditu nostro plenarie statutis terminis . et quod nec artem nec ingenium exquiret . vnde domus nostra per tenuram suam dampnum incurrat . et quod predictam terram neque uendet . neque escambiet . nec in vadimonium ponet . nec alicui in feudum et hereditatem tradet . neque ad alium locum religionis transferet. sine assensu nostro. Eandem securitatem facient nobis heredes sui cum singuli succedent. In huius rei testimonium presens scriptum sigillo ecclesie nostre munitum diuiso inter nos cyrographo. sepedicto Henrico tradidimus . Hiis testibus . Ricardo Burgens' . Henrico fratre eius . magistro Waltero scriptore . Drogone de Ponteis' . Mauricio Marescallo . Henrico le bel . et multis aliis.

[1] Har(oldus) in MS.

114. *Grant in fee and inheritance in the form of a chirograph by Abbot Henry and the convent of St. Peter's, Gloucester, of land by the Severn bridge (Gloucester) to Walter son of Walter Godheorte for an annual rent of 7s. (1205 × 24)*

G.C.L, 'Deeds and Seals', iv, no. 4, fol. 2 (126 mm [left] × 152 mm [foot]), poss. **Scribe 14**; single slit for tag on lower left foot; no turn-up; tag and seal missing; endorsements: contra Walterum Godheorte (s. xiii[in]), **Hand f** (below, Plate XLIIIf); iiii.[a] Ward' (s. xiii[med]); vasta[;] prior sancti Barth' tenet in perpetuum (s. xiii[2]); P. Taylour[1] (s. xiii[ex]?); Nunc tenet Henricus Hause alias dictus de refectorio (s. xiv[ex] × s. xv[in]); In magna[2] platea usque pontem (s. xiv × s. xv[in]?).

C Y R O G R A P H' C Y R O G R A P H' (*inverted*)

Sciant presentes et futuri quod ego Henr(icus) dei gratia abbas et conuentus sancti Petri Glou' concessimus Waltero filio Walteri Godheorte terram nostram iuxta pontem super Sabrinam . Illam scilicet quam pater suus de nobis tenuit . tenendam de nobis in feudo et hereditate sibi et heredibus suis . reddendo inde nobis annuatim septem solidos ad quatuor terminis . Videlicet ad festum sancti Michaelis. viginti et unum denarium . Ad Natale domini. viginti et unum denarium . In Annuntiatione beate Marie. viginti et unum denarium . et in Natiuitate sancti Iohannis Baptiste. viginti et unum denarium. Quando uero predictus Walterus filius Walteri predictam terram a nobis recepit. edificium superpositum . appreciatum fuit. Si autem aliquo casu emergente ipse uel heredes sui prefatam terra nobis reliquerint. simile edificium uel pretium nobis restituent. Idem uero Walterus iuramentum nobis prestitit quod fidelis erit ecclesie nostre de soluendo redditu nostro plenarie statutis terminis . et quod nec artem nec ingenium exquiret unde domus nostra per tenuram suam dampnum[3] incurrat . Et quod predictam terram neque uendet neque escambiet nec in vadimonium ponet . nec alicui in feudum et hereditatem tradet . neque ad alium locum religionis transferet sine assensu nostro. Eandem securitatem facient nobis heredes sui[.] cum singuli sibi succedent. In cuius rei testimonium[.] presens scriptum sigillo ecclesie nostre munitum diuiso inter nos cyrographo[.] predicto Waltero tradidimus. Hiis testibus . Ricardo Burgeis . Ricardo filio Willelmi . Henrico Burg' . Reginaldo de Breken' . Dauid Dunning . Adam Walense . Salomone Ianitore . Symone de Aula . Galfrido de Cellario . Henrico Le Bel . Waltero de Mora . et multis aliis.

Geoffrey de Cellario attested a grant by Henry son of Philip of Hacholte *c.* 1210 as the abbot of Gloucester's bailiff (Stevenson, no. 129).

[1] Reading uncertain.
[2] Reading uncertain.
[3] *dapnum* in MS.

115. *Grant in fee and inheritance in the form of a chirograph by Abbot Henry and the convent of St. Peter's, Gloucester, of land in Castle Street (Gloucester) to Hugh Guiun for 32d. annual rent payable to the almoner. (1205 × 24)*

A. G.C.L., 'Deeds and Seals', v, no. 22, fol. 9 (138 mm [left] × 130 mm [foot]), **Scribe 13** (below, Plate XV); slit for tag on turn-up; tag and seal missing; endorsements: Contra hugonem Guiun (s. xiii[med]), **Hand I**; castell' (s. xiii[ex]); Registratur (s. xiv[ex] × s. xv[in]); **B**. ibid. 'Reg. B', no. 680, p. 294.

C Y R O G R A... . H U M

Sciant presentes et futuri quod ego [.]H[.] dei gratia abbas et conuentus sancti Petri Glouc' . concessimus Hugoni Guiun . terram nostram in vicolo castelli illam scilicet que iacet inter terram Roberti nigri et terram Tome Toli . Tenendam de nobis in feudo et hereditate . illi et heredibus eius inperpetuum . pro xxx.[a] duobus denariis . annuatim elemosinario nostro qui pro tempore fuerit persoluendos duobus terminis . Medietatem . ad Hock(edai) et medietatem ad festum sancti Michaelis. Quando vero predictus .H. predictam terram de nobis suscepit nullum edificium super eandem recepit. Predicta uero terra per uisum legalium uirorum mensurata . habet in fronte autem .vii.[tem] uirgas ulnarias . cum pollice . Retro uero vii.[tem] uirgas ulnarias . et iii.[a] quarteria cum pollice . In profunditate .xx.[ti] uirgas ulnarias cum pollice. Idem uero H. iuramentum nobis prestitit quod fidelis erit ecclesie nostre de soluendo redditu nostro plenarie . statutis terminis . et quod terram illam neque uendet neque escambiet nec in uadimonium ponet nec alicui in feudum et hereditatem tradet neque ad alium locum religionis transferet sine assensu nostro. Eandem securitatem facient nobis heredes suis cum singuli sibi succedent. Quod quia ratum esse uolumus diuiso inter nos cyrografo confirmauimus. His testibus . Ricardo Burgense . Ricardo rufo[1] . W[.] scriptore . R. Guiun . R. de horto . W. de Abilade et multis aliis.

[1] **B** ends here with *et aliis.*

116. *The other half of no. 115.*

G.C.L., 'Deeds and Seals', v, no. 23, fol. 9 (171 mm [left] × 131 mm [foot]), **Scribe 13**; slit for tag on turn-up; tag and seal missing; endorsements: Contra Hugonem Guiun (s. xiii[med]), **Hand I**; in viculo castelli (s. xiii[in]); Non registratur quia duplex (modern?).

This text differs from no. 117 only in minor instances of spelling.

117. *Grant in fee and inheritance in the form of a chirograph by Abbot Henry and the convent of St. Peter's, Gloucester, of land on Feet Lane (probably Alvin Street, Gloucester) to John Hackebon for 5s. annual rent payable to their almonry. (1205 × 24)*

A. G.C.L., 'Deeds and Seals', ix, no. 11, fol. 6 (166 mm × 103 mm); in remaining portion of turn-up at left foot, a slit through turn-up for tag; tag and seal missing; endorsements: Contra Iohannem Hakesbon (s. xiii[ex]), **Hand I**; in Fetelon' (s. xiii[med]); Registratur (s. xiv[ex] × s. xv[in]); **B**. ibid. 'Reg. B', no. 562, p. 245.

CYROGRAPHVM

Sciant presentes et futuri quod ego Henr(icus) dei gratia abbas et conuentus sancti Petri Glouc' concessimus Iohanni Hackebon terram nostram in Fetelone . illam scilicet que iacet iuxta terram Mauricii Marescalli tenendam de nobis in feudo et hereditate illi et heredibus suis pro quinque solidis elemosinario nostro annuatim persoluendis duobus teminis . Medietatem ad Hocked(ai) . et medietatem ad festum sancti Michaelis. Predicta uero terra per uisum legalium uirorum mensurata habet in fronte autem xli. uirgas ulnarias[1] et tria quarteria cum pollice interposito . In medio quinque uirgas et tria quarteria cum pollice . Retro uero .xv. uirgas ulnarias cum pollice. et dimidiam . In profunditate centum . et xxxviii. uirgas cum pollice. Predictus uero Iohannes iuramentum nobis prestitit quod fidelis erit ecclesie nostre de soluendo redditu nostro plenarie predictis terminis . Et quod nec artem neque ingenium exquiret unde domus nostra per tenuram suam dampnum incurrat . Et quod terram illam nec uendet . Neque excambiet . Neque in uadimonium ponet . Neque ad alium locum religionis transferet . Neque alicui alio in feudum tradet sine assensu nostro. Quod quia ratum esse uolumus . diuiso inter nos cyrographo in pleno hundredo nostro confirmauimus. Hiis testibus . Iohanne Andreu . Mauricio Marescallo . Roberto de orto[2] . Willelmo Cutelappe . Roberto Feutrer . Iohanne clerico . magistro Waltero scriptore . Helia Godmon . et multis aliis.

The scribe added the names of the witnesses in a light brown ink after *testibus*; down to *testibus* the script was in a dark brown ink. Since there is a slit for a tag on the left side portion of the turn-up and the right side has been torn away, it is likely that the chirograph bore a second seal appended right of centre to the foot.

[1] *uirgam ulnariam* in MS.
[2] **B** ends here with *et aliis.*

118. *Grant in fee and inheritance by Abbot Henry and the convent of St. Peter's, Gloucester, to William Hackespone of land in Kingsholm (by Gloucester) for 10d. annual rent. (1205 × 24)*

G.C.L., 'Deeds and Seals', i, no. 32, fol. 18 (122 mm [left] × 167 mm [foot]); tag and seal missing; endorsements: Contra Willelmum hakespon' (s. xiii^{med}), **Hand I**; versus aulam regis (s. xiii^{med}); Registratur (s. xiv^{ex} × s. xv^{in}).

C I R. . .G R A.. . .H. . .M (inverted)

Sciant presentes et futuri quod ego Henric(us) dei gratia abbas . et conuentus sancti Petri Gloucest'ie . dedimus et concessimus Willelmo Hakespone unam terram ad avlam regis que fuit Willelmi þurbren tenendam et habendam de nobis illi et heredibus suis in feudo et hereditate libere et quiete . Reddendo annuatim elemosinario nostro .x. denarios . medietatem ad Hocked(ai) et medietatem ad festum sancti Michaelis. Predicta uero terra iacet iuxta terram Æmaldi Walensis . et media est inter terram quam Walterus filius Willelmi þureberti . et terram quam mater ipsius Walteri que uxor erat predicti Willelmi tunc tenuerunt. Predictus uero Walterus filius sepedicti Willelmi qui heres fuit predicte terre ipsam terram assensu et concessione matris sue . et fratris sui senioris Willelmo Hackespone et heredibus suis uendidit et concessit . cum omnibus pertinentiis pro xiiii. solidis . ipsum Willelmum Hackespone in omnibus instituendo . et se ipsum in omnibus eliminando. Predicta vero terra per uisum legalium hominum mensurata in fronte habet octo uirgas ulnarias et dimidiam . In longitudine uero . lxvi. virgas ulnarias et dimidiam . A medietate uero usque ad partem preteriorem .xi. uirgas ulnarias. Willelmus uero Hackespone iuramentum prestitit quod fidelis erit de redditu persoluendo et quod terram illam nec uendet . Nec escambiet . Nec in uademonium ponet . Nec ad aliam domum religionis transferet sine nostro assensu . Nec artem nec ingenium inquiret . vnde per tenuram suam dampnum incurramus. Et quia hanc concessionem ratam esse uolumus . et permanere eam cirographo inter nos diuiso confirmauimus. Hiis testibus . Waltero scriptore . Roberto de orto . Rogero Budel . Ricardo Noreis . Æmaldo Walense . Nicholao breugerio . Thoma Cornubiense . Waltero episcopo . Willelmo Dickil . Gocelino permunterio . Waltero filio Gocelini . et aliis.

119. *Grant in fee and inheritance in the form of a chirograph by Abbot Henry and the convent of St. Peter's, Gloucester, to Henry baker of land outside Alvingate (Gloucester) for 7s. 6d. annual rent. (1205 × 24)*

A. G.C.L., 'Deeds and Seals', v, no. 33, fol. 15 (103 mm [left] × 181 mm [foot]); seal on tag, white wax, fragment, chipped; repaired; obverse: oval (meas. unavail.); partial image of an abbot or St. Benedict seated facing front, an upraised book in the left hand; legend unavail.; reverse: counterseal: pointed oval (length unavail.; width, 26 mm); partial image of an abbot in full pontificals facing front, the lower portion of a crozier in the right hand; legend: . . .ETV' ABBAT. . . GLOVCEST. . .; no endorsement; **B.** ibid. 'Reg. B', no. 458, pp. 202–3.

CIROGRAPHUM CIROGRAPHUM (*inverted*)

Sciant presentes et futuri quod ego Henricus dei gratia abbas et conventus sancti Petri Glouc' concessimus Willelmo pistori terram nostram extra Aluenyathe[1] contra portam curtillagii nostri . illam scilicet que iacet inter terram Mauricii marescalli ex una parte et terram Nicholai de infirmaria ex parte altera . Tenendam et habendam de nobis in feudo et hereditate . sibi et heredibus suis pro septem solidis et sex denariis . nobis annuatim ad quatuor terminos reddendis . Videlicet ad Annuntiationem beate Marie viginti duobus denariis et obolo . ad festum sancti Iohannis Baptiste viginti duobus denariis et obolo . ad festum sancti Michaelis viginti duobus denariis et obolo . ad festum sancti Andree viginti duobus denariis et obolo. Predicta uero terra per visum legalium virorum mensuratá. habet in fronte viginti septem virgas ulnarias et dimidiam et unum quarterium [cum][2] pollice interposito . In medió. viginti virgas ulnarias et dimidiam . [cum] pollice interposito . In extremo . decem et octo virgas ulnarias et unum quarterium [cum] pollice interposito . In profunditate uero centum et viginti sex virgas ulnarias et vnum quarterium et dimidium quarterium . cum pollice interposito. Quando uero predictus Willelmus predictam terram a nobis recepit́. edificium superpositum appreciatum est unam marcam . Et si aliquo casu emergente ipse aut heredes sui dictam terram nobis reliquerint . simile edificium aut pretium nobis restituent. Predictus uero Willelmus iuramentum nobis prestitit . quod fidelis erit ecclesie nostre de soluendo redditu nostro plenarie statutis terminis . et quod nec artem nec ingenium exquiret́. vnde domus nostra per tenuram suam dampnum incurrat . et quod predictam terram neque vendet nec excambiet nec in vadimonium ponet . nec alicui in feudum et hereditatem tradet nec ad alium locum religionis transferet . sine assensu nostro . nec aliquod edificium in dicta terra proprius portam curtillagii nostri eriget . postquam ibidem vero prius edificium construi solet. Idem iuramentum faciet nobis heredes suí. cum singuli sibi succedent. In cuius rei testimonium presens scriptum sigillo ecclesie nostre munitum diuiso inter nos cirographó. eidem tradidimus. Hiis testibus . Waltero scriptore . Dauid Dunning[3] . Adam Croc . Drogone pincerna . Henrico Le Bel . Henrico de Bares . Waltero de Mora . Nicholao de infirmaria . Mauricio marescallo . et multis aliis.

[1] Reading uncertain.
[2] *cum* omitted in this and the next two measurements.
[3] **B** ends here with *et aliis.*

120. *Grant in fee and inheritance in the form of a chirograph by Abbot Henry and the convent of St. Peter's, Gloucester, to Walter Hoic of land by the cemetery wall (Gloucester) for 18d. annual rent. (1205 × 24)*

G.R.O., GBR/J1/210 (69 mm [left] × 168 mm [foot]), **Scribe 12** (below, Plate XIV); seal on tag; white wax; fragment; rubbed (meas. and image unavail.); no endorsement; cal. in Stevenson, no. 210.

C...ROGRAPHUM CYROGPHUM (*inverted*)

Sciant presentes et futuri quod ego Henric(us) dei gratia abbas et conuentus sancti Petri Glouc' . concessimus Waltero Hoch . terram nostram . que iacet iuxta murum cimeterii nostri . inter terram Iohannis de Gosedich et terram Iohannis Gode . Tenendam et habendam de nobis in feodo et hereditate sibi et heredibus suis . pro decem et octo denariis . ad duos terminos anni inde nobis annuatim persoluendis . Medietate ad festum sancti Michaelis . et alia medietate ad Hockedai. Predicta uero terra mensurata per visum legalium uirorum habet in fronte . nouem uirgas ulnarias . et dimidiam . Retro⸍ totidem . In profunditate uero⸍ continet viginti duas uirgas ulnarias . et dimidiam. Quando uero predictus Walterus . predictam terram de nobis recepit . nullum edificium superpositum. Idem uero Walterus iuramentum nobis prestitit quod fidelis erit ecclesie nostre . de soluendo redditu nostro plenarie statutis terminis . Et quod nec artem . nec ingenium exquiret vnde domus nostra per tenuram suam dampnum incurrat . Et quod predictam terram neque uendet neque excambiet . neque in vadimonium ponet . neque in feodum et hereditatem tradet . neque ad alium locum religionis transferet sine assensu nostro. Eandem securitatem facient nobis . heredes sui . cum singuli sibi succedent. In cuius rei . testimonium . presens scriptum . sigillo ecclesie nostre munitum⸍ diuiso inter nos cyrographo ei tradidimus. Hiis testibus . Ricardo Burg' . Dauid Dunning . Willelmo de Sanford . Waltero scriptore . Drogone pincerna . Henrico Le Bel . Mauricio stabellario et multis aliis.

121. *Grant in fee and inheritance in the form of a chirograph by Abbot Henry and the convent of St. Peter's, Gloucester, of land on Castle Street (Gloucester) to William Lorimer for 4s. 4d. annual rent. (1205 × 24)*

G.C.L., 'Deeds and Seals', vii, no. 9, fol. 5 (110 mm [left] × 133 mm [foot]), **Scribe 14** (below, Plate XVI); seal on tag; white wax, worn and chipped; obverse: oval (length unavail.; width *c.* 42 mm); an abbot or St. Benedict seated facing front, a cope held by a pectoral clasp, a crozier in the right hand, an upraised book in the left; legend, illegible; reverse: counterseal; pointed oval (length unavail.; width 27 mm); a standing figure in full pontificals, a crozier in right hand; legend: . . .IE.; endorsements: .iii.[a] Warda (s. xiii[med]); ex opposito . . .[1] Sprot (s. xiii); Registratur (s. xiv[ex] × s. xv[in])[;] sc(riptum) Willelmi lorim(er)[;] Castellone (s. xiv[ex]).

CYROGRAPH... .CYROGR... (*inverted*)

Sciant presentes et futuri quod ego Henr(icus) dei gratia abbas et conuentus sancti Petri Gloucestr' concessimus Willelmo Le Lorimer terram nostram in vico castelli que iacet inter terram Thome de Euesham' et terram Sibille tenendam de nobis in feodo et hereditate sibi et heredibus suis pro quatuor solidis et quatuor denariis . nobis annuatim persoluendis ad duos terminos . Medietate ad Hocked(ai) et alia medietate ad festum sancti Michaelis. Predicta uero terra per visum legalium virorum mensurata⸍ habet in fronte decem virgas vlnarias et dimidium quarterium . cum pollice interposito . Retro⸍ octo virgas vlnarias . cum pollice interposito . In medio⸍

decem virgas vlnarias cum pollice interposito . vno quarterio minus . In profunditate'. quindecim virgas vlnarias cum pollice interposito . vno quarterio minus. Quando uero predictus .W. predictam terram a nobis recepit'. edificium superpositum appreciatum est viginti solidos. Si autem aliquo casu emergente ipse uel heredes sui prefatam terram nobis reliquerint'. simile edificium aut pretium nobis restituent. Idem uero .W. iuramentum nobis prestitit quod fidelis erit ecclesie nostre de soluendo redditu nostro plenarie . statutis terminis . et quod nec artem nec ingenium exquiret'. vnde domus nostra per tenuram suam dampnum incurrat . et quod predictam terram neque uendet neque escambiet nec in vadimonium ponet . nec alicui in feudum et hereditatem tradet . neque ad alium locum religionis transferet'. sine assensu nostro. Eandem securitatem facient nobis heredes sui'. cum singuli sibi succedent. In huius rei testimonium'. presens scriptum sigillo ecclesie nostre munitum diuiso inter nos cyrographo ei tradidimus. Hiis testibus . Ricardo Rufo . Ricardo Burg' . Ricardo filio Willelmi . Henrico Burg' . Iohanne Draperio . Wilelmo Russel . Waltero scriptore . Salomone Ianitore . Mauricio stabulario . Helya de Paggeh' . et multis aliis.

[1] Illegible with ultra-violet light.

122. *The other half of no. 121.*

G.C.L., 'Deeds and Seals', vii, no. 37, fol. 21 (101 mm [left] × 137 mm [foot]), **Scribe 14**; slit on foot for tag; tag and seal missing; endorsements: Contra Willelmum lorimer' (s. xiii^{in}); .iiii^a Warda (s. xiii^{med}), **Hand t**; Caps(ula) .xviii. de laicis tenuris (s. xiii^{ex} × s. xiv^{in}); Non registratur quia duplex (s. xiv^{med}).

123. *Grant in fee and inheritance in the form of a chirograph by Abbot Henry and the convent of St. Peter's, Gloucester, to Ralph Mazon and Alice his wife of land in Newland (by Gloucester) for 3s. 2d. annual rent. (1205 × 24)*

A. G.C.L., 'Deeds and Seals', v, no. 5, fol. 3 (150 mm [left] × 142 mm [foot]), **Scribe 13**; torn; glued on page so that lines are misaligned; slit for tag; tag and seal missing; endorsements: Contra Radulfum Mazonem (s. xiii^{med}); apud Neula'd' (s. xiii × s. xiv); apud Newlond redditus iii. . . iid (s. xiv × s. xv).; Registratur (s. xiv?); **B**. ibid. 'Reg. B', no. 523, p. 230.

C . . R O G R A P H U M

Sciant presentes et futuri quod ego Henricus dei gratia abbas et conuentus sancti Petri Glouc' concessimus Radulfo Mazoni et Alice vxori eius terram nostram apud Neulande illam scilicet que iacet inter terram Willelmi de L[a] Barre et terram quam Turstinus Faber tenuit . tenendam de nobis in feudo et hereditate sibi et heredibus suis pro tribus solidis et duobus denariis annuatim elemosin[ario] nostro qui pro tempore [f]uerit persoluendis duobus terminis . Medietate ad Hok(edai) . et medietate ad festum sancti Michaelis. Si uero contigerit quod de seruitio suo h'eamus ad faciendum pro uno d(enario) et corradio suo nobis s[eru]iet[1][.] Predicta uero terra per uisum legalium uirorum mensurata˙. habet in fronte .xix. uirg[a]s ulnarias et dimidiam cum pollice interposito . In profunditate .xx. uirgas ulnarias cum pollice interposito. Idem uero Radulfus iuramentum nobis prestitit quod fidelis erit ecclesie nostre de soluendo redditu nostro plenarie˙. statutis terminis et quod nec artem nec ingenium ex[qu]iret unde domus nostra per tenuram suam dampnum incurrat . et quod predictam terram neque uendet . neque escambiet . nec in uadimonium ponet . nec alicui in feudum et hereditatem tradet . neque ad alium locum religionis transferet˙. sine assensu nostro. Eandem securitatem facient no[bis] heredes sui cum singuli sibi succedent. Quod quia ratum esse uolumus[2] presenti scirograffo inter nos diuiso confirmauimus. His testibus . Ricardo Rufo . Ricardo [et] Henrico Burg'[3] . Waltero scriptori . et multis aliis.

Missing portions of the damaged text have been supplied from **B**.

[1] MS. damaged, reading uncertain.

[2] *uolim(us)* in MS.

[3] The names of Richard and Henry Burgess are missing from **B**.

---

124. *Letter in writ-form from Abbot H(enry) to H(ugh) de Neville, excusing his failure to answer a summons. (1205 × 24; poss. 1228 × 43)*

P.R.O., SC 1/11, 41 (39) (132 mm × 44 mm); tongue cut or torn from left foot; seal missing; no endorsement; *Cart. Glouc.* i, pp. lxxviii–lxxix.

Karissimo domino et amico digne diligendo .H. de Neuill' . suus .H. diuina permissione dictus abbas Glouc' . salutem et in quantum mundi hoc permittunt aduersa˙. deuotas orationes et obsequia. Ad multiplices gratiarum actiones dilecte domine uobis tenemur . eo quod in cunctis agendis nostris et maxime in placitis que ad nos pertinent[1] penes iustitiam uestram cui semper admixta est pietas humilem auditum et salubre consilium et finem a uobis accipimus affectatum . parati benignitati uestre cum tempus accepimus oportunum . in quantum possumus condigne respondere. Sed valde pertimescimus . ne occasionem iracendi et hominibus nostris nocendi uobis prebeamus˙. quum ad presens coram uobis sicut summoniti sumus . non comparemus. Precamur igitur dilectionem uestram quatinus pro deo et humili nostre petitionis obtuitu absque indignatione et mala uoluntate nos habeatis si placet excusatos. Tot enim tribulationes et tot negotia cotidie nobis emergunt quod sine maximo dampno a domo nostra nos elongare non possemus. Cum autem contigerit uos partibus nostris appropinquare˙. per auxilium dei uobis occurremus . et beneplacitum uestrum pro possibilitate nostra,[2] faciemus. Bene et diu in domino valeat.

This letter is dated *c.* 1229? and attributed to Abbot Henry Foliot in *List of Ancient Correspondence*, 154, but the script is more appropriate for the abbacy of Henry Blont.

[1] *et maxime in placitis que ad nos pertinent* superscript in the MS. in the same hand.

[2] Superscript in the MS. in the same hand.

125. *Letter in writ-form from Abbot H(enry) of St. Peter's, Gloucester, to R(alph) de Neville dean of Lichfield, on behalf of a friend accused of robbery at Archenfield (Herefs.). (1205 × 24)*

P.R.O., SC 1/6 (18) (154 mm × 32 mm); tongue cut or torn from left foot; seal missing; no endorsement.

Uenerabili viro in Cristo suo karissimo domino .R. de Nouill' . decano Lichefeld' . H. dei gratia abbas Glouc' salutem et tam[1] deuotum quam debitum in Cristo famulatum. Grates uobis referimus multiplices pro beneficiis nobis vestris gratia a vestra serenitate collatis . profitentes in perpetuum uobis merito nos esse obligatos. Confidentes autem de liberalitate vestra rogamus vos quanto possumus affectu et desiderio quatinus consilium vestrum et auxilium cuidam amico nostro familiarissimo prestare dignemini . vt pacem habeat super eo quod implacitatur de roberia aput Vrchenefeld' in Wallia facta[2] quando guerra maior fuit . Tamen facientes ut devoti vobis teneamur deuotiores . esse in perpetuum. Valete.

[1] Superscript in the MS.
[2] Superscript in the MS.

126. *Grant in fee and inheritance in the form of a chirograph by Abbot Henry and the convent of St. Peter's, Gloucester, of land in Kingsholm (by Gloucester) to William de Oswestry for 3s. annual rent. (1205 × 24)*

G.C.L., 'Deeds and Seals', v, no. 10, fol. 4 (58 mm [left] × 177 mm [foot]); no turn-up; no provision for sealing; endorsements: Contra Willelmum de Oswaldestre de terra uersus aulam regis (s. xiii[in]); ii.[a] Warda (s. xiii[med]); Registratur (s. xiv[med]); sc(ribitur) (s. xiv[med]); Kyngeshome (s. xv[in]).

C Y . . . O G . . . A P H U M

Sciant presentes et futuri quod ego H(e)nric(us) dei gratia abbas et conuentus sancti Petri Glouc' concessimus Willelmo de Oswaldestre terram nostram versus aulam regis . Illam scilicet que iacet propinquior terre eiusdem Willelmi quam tenet de Petro de Aula Regis . tenendam de nobis in feudo et hereditate sibi et heredibus suis pro tribus solidis annuatim persoluendis ad quatuor terminos . In festo sancti Michaelis nouem denarios . In festo sancti Andree᷄ nouem denarios . In Annuntiatione beate Marie nouem denarios . Et in natiuitate sancti Iohannis Baptiste nouem denarios. Predicta vero terra per visum legalium virorum mensurata᷄ habet in fronte duodecim virgas ulnarias cum pollice interposito . Retro᷄ totidem . In longitudine uero se extendit usque ad fossatum gardini Petri de aula regis. Quando uero predictus W. predictam terram a nobis recepit᷄ nullum edificium superpositum fuit. Idem vero .W. iuramentum nobis prestitit quod fidelis erit ecclesie nostre de soluendo redditu nostro plenarie statutis terminis . et quod nec artem nec ingenium exquiret vnde domus nostra per tenuram suam dampnum incurrat . et quod predictam terram . neque uendet neque escambiet . nec in vadimonium ponet . nec alicui in feudum et hereditatem tradet . neque ad alium locum religionis transferet'. sine assensu nostro. Eandem securitatem facient nobis heredes sui'. cum singuli sibi succedent. In huius rei testimonium presens scriptum sigillo ecclesie nostre munitum diuiso inter nos cirographo'. sepedicto .W. tradidimus. Hiis testibus . Petro de aula regis . magistro Waltero scriptore . Drogone pincerna . Waltero de mora . Simone de cellario . Henrico le Bel . et multis aliis.

127. Lifetime lease in the form of a chirograph by Abbot Henry and the convent of St. Peter's, Gloucester, to Walter Palmer of land between the two bridges (at Gloucester) for 2s. annual rent. (1205 × 24)

G.C.L., 'Deeds and Seals', iv, no. 5, fol. 2 (83 mm [left] × 123 mm [foot]); no turn-up; slit for tag on foot; a diagonal slit on lower left foot; tag and seal missing; endorsements: Contra Walterum Palmarium (s. xiii): poss. in same hand; Contra Walterum Palmarium (s. xiii^{med}); quarta Warda vac' (s. xiii^{ex}); Greffre[1] et I. de Hope (s. xiv^{in}?); inter duobus pontibus (c. 1500).[2]

CYROGRAPHUM

Sciant presentes et futuri quod ego Henricus dei gratia abbas et conuentus sancti Petri Glouc' concessimus Waltero Palmario seruienti nostro quandam terram inter duos pontes . illam scilicet quam Roger et Edid Slane uxor eius nobis dederunt . tenendam de nobis terram in uita sua pro duobus solidis nobis annuatim persoluendis duobus terminis . Medietate ad Hockedai'. et alia medietate ad festum sancti Michaelis. Predicta uero terra per uisum legalium uirorum mensurata habet in fronte septem uirgas ulnarias cum pollice interposito . Retro uero nouem uirgas ulnarias et unum quarterium cum pollice interposito. Predicta terra cum omni melioratione superposita post decessum predicti Walteri absque omni suorum reclamatione ad nos libere reuertetur. Idem uero Walterus iuramentum nobis prestitit . quod fidelis erit ecclesie nostre de soluendo redditu nostro plenarie . et quod nec artem nec ingenium exquiret per se uel per alium unde domus nostra per tenuram suam dampnum incurrat. Quod quia ratum uolumus permanere'. presens scriptum sigilli nostri impressione munitum diuiso inter nos cyrographo'. ei tradidimus. Hiis testibus . Rogero filio Cecilie . Willelmo filio Katerine . Gilleberto pistore . Ansketillo fabro . Reginaldo de Breckenian . Salomone Portario . Mauricio marescallo . Helya medico . Waltero scriptore . et multis aliis.

Sciant presentes et futuri quod ego Henricus dei gratia abbas et conuentus sancti Petri Gloec'[3]

Walter Palmer's land referred to above is mentioned in a charter of the keeper of the Hospital of St. Bartholomew datable to c. 1230, granting land which the hospital received by gift of William son of Katherine (Stevenson, no. 288).

[1] Reading uncertain.

[2] Another endorsement has been erased and is illegible.

[3] This partial text is not in the hand of the text above. Apparently another scribe began a new text on the strip of parchment before realizing that there was not enough space at the foot for a seal to be appended. When this became apparent the scribe stopped writing and the parchment was cut. The text which this scribe completed has yet to be located.

128. *Grant in fee and inheritance in the form of a chirograph by Abbot Henry and the convent of St. Peter's, Gloucester, to Robert de Roei of land in* magna ruta *(Westgate St.) at the bridge (Gloucester) for 8s. annual rent. (1205 × 24)*

G.C.L., 'Deeds and Seals', iv, no. 3, fol. 2 (101 mm [left] × 155 mm [foot]; orig. with turn-up folded *c.* 91 mm × 155 mm), **Scribe 12**; two slits for a single tag in centre of foot; a single slit on lower left corner of foot; tags and seals missing; endorsements: Contra Robertum de roei (s. xiii^{med}), **Hand I**; iiii.^{a} Warda (s. xiii^{med}); Marger(ia) breua (*c.* 1230); in magna ruta apud pontem (s. xv^{ex}).

C Y R . . G . . A P H U M : C Y R O G R A P U M (*inverted*)

Sciant presentes et futuri quod ego Henric(us) dei gratia abbas et conuentus sancti Petri de Glouc' concessimus Roberto de Roey . terram nostram . in magna ruta apud pontem . illam scilicet que iacet inter terram Thome Ouenat ex vna parte . et vicum qui dicitur Pukelana ex altera . Tenendam et habendam de nobis in feodo et hereditate sibi et heredibus suis . pro octo solidis inde nobis annuatim ad quatuor terminis anni. persoluendis . duobus solidis ad festum sancti Michaelis . et duobus solidis ad Natale domini . et duobus ad Hockedai . et duobus solidis ad festum sancti Iohannis Baptiste. Predicta uero terra mensurata per visum legalium virorum habet in longitudine viginti [et] vnam uirgam ulnariam et vnum quarterium . cum pollice interposito iuxta Pukelana' . Item in longitudine iuxta terram Thome Ouenat . viginti septem uirgas ulnarias . et dimidiam et duos pollices . cum ostio quinque pedum . In fronte de latitudine tresdecim uirgas ulnarias . cum pollice interposito . vno quarterio minus . Retro de latitudine . versus terram archidiaconi tresdecim uirgas ulnarias . et vnum quarterium et dimidium . cum pollice interposito. Quando uero predictus Robertus predictam terram de nobis recepit. nullum edificium fuit superpositum. Idem vero Robertus iuramentum nobis prestitit quod fidelis erit cclesie nostre de soluendo redditu nostro plenarie statutis terminis . Et quod nec artem nec ingenium exquiret vnde domus nostra per tenuram suam dampnum incurrat . Et quod predictam terram neque uendet neque excambiet neque in vadimonium ponet neque in feodum et hereditatem tradet . neque ad alium locum religionis transferet sine assensu nostro. Eandem securitatem facient nobis heredes sui cum singuli sibi succedent. In cuius rei testimonium presens scriptum sigillo ecclesie nostre munitum . diuiso inter nos cyrographo . ei tradidimus. Hiis testibus . Ricardo Burg' . Dauid Dunning . Willelmo de Sanford . Mauricio Durand . Waltero scriptore . Drogone pincerna . Henrico Le Bel . Mauricio stabollario et multis aliis.

129. *Grant in fee and inheritance in the form of a chirograph by Abbot Henry and the convent of St. Peter's, Gloucester, of land on Castle Street (Gloucester) to Roger farrier for 26d. annual rent. (1205 × 24; poss. 1228 × 43)*

A. G.C.L., 'Deeds and Seals', vii, no. 8, fol. 4 (86 mm [left] × 172 mm [foot]); fragment of tag for seal; seal missing; endorsement: Carta de terra in vico Castelli (s. xiii^med); glued to foot a parchment fragment on which is written *Castell lone* (s. xv); **B.** ibid. 'Reg. B', no. 1053 (1052), p. 456.

CYROGRAPHVM (*inverted*)

Sciant presentes et futuri quod ego Henr(icus) dei gratia abbas . et conuentus sancti Petri Glouc' . concessimus Rogero marescallo . terram nostram in uico Castalli quam Adam Walensis nobis dedit . illam scilicet que iacet inter terram eiusdem Rogerii ex una parte . et rutam regis ex altera parte . Tenendam de nobis in feudo et hereditate sibi et heredibus suis pro uiginti sex denariis . nobis annuatim persoluendis ad duos terminos . Medietate ad Hocked(ai) . et alia medietate ad festum sancti Michaelis. Predicta uero terra per uisum legalium uirorum mensurata . habet in fronte . sex uirgas ulnarias et dimidiam . cum pollice interposito . Retro . totidem . In profunditate . totidem. Quando uero predictus Rogerus predictam terram a nobis recepit . edificium superpositum appreciatum est dimidiam marcam. Si autem aliquo casu emergente predictus Rogerus predictam terram reliquerit . simile edificium aut pretium nobis restituet. Iuramentum etiam prestitit nobis dictus Rogerus . quod fidelis erit ecclesie nostre de soluendo redditu nostro plenarie statutis terminis et quod nec artem nec ingenium exquiret . unde domus nostra per tenuram suam dampnum incurrat . Et quod predictam terram non uendet neque escambiet neque in uadium ponet neque ad alium locum religionis transferet sine assensu nostro. Idem iuramentum facient nobis heredes sui . cum sibi singuli succedent. In huius rei testimonium presens scriptum sigillo ecclesie nostre munitum diuiso inter nos cyrographo . ei tradidimus. Hiis testibus . magistro Waltero scriptore . magistro Thoma de Slotr'[1] . Henrico bel . Mauricio marescallo . Adam Lebret . Waltero de Mora. et multis aliis.

The text of a final concord dated 25 Henry III (1241) between Abbot Henry Foliot and a Roger farrier concerning Upleadon is in *Cart. Glouc.* i, p. 383; a variation is in ibid. ii, no. 830.

---

[1] **B** ends here with *et aliis.*

130. *Grant in fee and inheritance in the form of a chirograph by Abbot Henry and the convent of St. Peter's, Gloucester, to Roger Seli of land outside Ailesgate (Eastgate, Gloucester) for 32s. annual rent. (1205 × 24)*

G.C.L., 'Deeds and Seals', i, no. 21, fol. 12 (111 mm [left] × 125 mm [foot]), **Scribe 14**; no evidence of sealing; endorsements: Contra Rogerum Seli (s. xiii^in), poss. **Hand f**; .iii Warda (s. xiii^med?); Henricus le Draper (s. xiii^ex); Registratur; Extra Ailesgate (s. xiv^ex).

CYROGRAPH...M CYROGRAP' (*inverted*)

Sciant presentes et futuri quod ego Henr(icus) dei gratia abbas et conuentus sancti Petri Glouc' concessimus Rogero Seli terram nostram extra Æilesgete . que iacet inter terram Alexandri Kentwin(e) . et[1] terram Ricardi textoris tenendam de nobis in feudo et hereditate sibi et heredibus suis pro triginta duobus denariis . nobis annuatim persoluendis . ad duos terminos . medietate ad Hocked(ai) et alia medietate ad festum sancti Michaelis. Predicta uero terra per visum legalium virorum mensurata habet in fronte octo virgas vlnarias cum pollice interposito . vno quarterio minus . In medio. septem virgas ulnarias et dimidiam cum pollice interposito . Retro. totidem . In profunditate. viginti nouem virgas vlnarias cum pollice interposito. Quando uero predictus Rogerus predictam terram a nobis recepit. edificium superpo[s]itum appreciatum est duas marcas. Si autem aliquo casu emergente ipse uel heredes sui prefatam terram nobis reliquerint . simile edificium aut pretium nobis restituent. Idem uero .R. iuramentum nobis prestitit quod fidelis erit ecclesie nostre de soluendo redditu nostro plenarie statutis terminis . et quod nec artem nec ingenium exquiret; vnde domus nostra per tenuram suam dampnum incurrat . et quod predictam terram neque uendet neque escambiet . nec in vadimonium ponet nec alicui in feudum et hereditatem tradet . neque ad alium locum religionis transferet sine assensu nostro. Eandem securitatem facient nobis heredes sui cum singuli sibi succedent. In cuius rei testimonium. presens scriptum sigillo ecclesie nostre munitum diuiso inter nos cyrographo. predicto Rogero tradidimus. Hiis testibus . Ricardo Rufo . Ricardo Burg' . Ricardo filio Willelmi . Willelmo Russel . Henrico Burg' . Iohanne Draperio . Waltero scriptore . Salomone Ianitore . Drogone le Butiller . Waltero de La more . Waltero de Chandos et multis aliis.

[1] The tironian *et* is repeated in the MS.

131. *Lease for two lives in the form of a chirograph by Abbot Henry and the convent of St. Peter's, Gloucester, to Walter Slep of land on Sater Lane (Gloucester) for 2s. annual rent. (1205 × 24)*

G.C.L., 'Deeds and Seals', vii, no. 27, fol. 16 (158 mm [left] × 117 mm [foot]); tag for seal; seal missing; stain and residue of white wax on tag; endorsements: Carta Walteri Slep (s. xiii[1]), **Hand n**; Goffridus clericus[;] iii[a] varda vacat (s. xiv[med]); A (s. xiii).

C...ROGRAPHUM

Sciant presentes et futuri quod ego Henr(icus) dei gratia abbas et conuentus sancti Petri Glouc' concessimus Waltero Slep terram nostra in Satereislon' quam Willelmus clericus dedit nobis tenendam de nobis tantum in vita sua et in uita vnius heredis quam uoluerit . pro duobus solidis nobis annuatim persoluendis ad duos terminos . Medietate ad Hocked(ai) . et alia medietate ad festum sancti Michaelis. Heres uero illius triginta denarios post decessum predicti Walteri quamdiu uixerit nobis persoluet ad predictos terminos. Post decessum uero illorum prefata terra ad nos cum omni melioratione superposita sine reclamatione alicuius heredum suorum libere reuertetur. Predicta autem terra per visum legalium virorum mensurata᷄ habet in longitudine tredecim virgas vlnarias cum pollice interposito . In profunditate᷄ septem virgas vlnarias in uno capite cum pollice interposito . In alio capite nouem virgas vlnarias tribus pollicibus minus. Edificium nostrum superpositum fuit᷄ quando predictus .W. predictam terram a nobis recepit. Idem uero .W. iuramentum nobis prestitit quod fidelis erit ecclesie nostre de soluendo redditu nostro plenarie statutis terminis . et quod nec artem nec ingenium exquiret; vnde domus nostra per tenuram suam dampnum incurrat . Et quod predictam terram neque uendet . neque escambiet . nec in vadimonium ponet . nec alicui in feudum et hereditatem tradet . neque ad alium locum religionis transferet᷄ sine assensu nostro. Eandem securitatem faciet nobis ille quem heredem suum constituerit᷄ cum sibi succedet. In cuius rei testimonium presens scriptum sigillo ecclesie nostre munitum diuiso inter nos cyrographo᷄ ei tradidimus. His testibus . Ricardo Burg' . Iohanne Ruffo . Dauid Dunning . Iohanne le Draper . Salomone Portar(io) . Waltero de Mora . Hugone de Bramton' et multis aliis.

Walter Slep attested a local charter datable to *c.* 1210 (Stevenson, no. 137).

132. *Grant in fee and inheritance in the form of a chirograph by Abbot Henry and the convent of St. Peter's, Gloucester, of land at the brook near Morin's mill (by Gloucester) to Gilbert Sumer for 3s. annual rent. (1205 × 24)*

G.C.L., 'Deeds and Seals', x, no. 21, fol. 16 (102 mm [left] × 190 mm [foot]), **Scribe 37**; damaged and stained; turn-up, but no slit for tag; no evident provision for sealing; endorsements: Contra Gilebertum Sumer (s. xiii[1]), **Hand o/Scribe 17**; magister operr' ten[et?][1] (s. xiv); . . .[2] ot'estrete (modern?).

. . . Y R O . . . P H . . . M

Sciant presentes et futuri quod ego Henr(icus) dei gratia abb[as et conuentus sancti Petri Gl]ouc'[3] concessimus Gilberto Sumer terram nostram de Broc uersus molendinum Morini . illam scilicet que iacet inter terram Walteri de . . .[4] et venellam que uocatur Smalelone . Tenendam et habendam de nobis in feodo et hereditate sibi et heredibus suis pro tribus solidis nobis annuatim persoluendis ad duos anni terminos . videlicet medietatem ad festum sancti Michaelis . et aliam medietatem ad Annuntiationem beate Marie. Predicta uero terra per uisum legalium uirorum mensurata᷄ habet in fronte quindecim uirgas ulnarias et dimidiam et unum quarterium cum pollice interposito . In longitudine᷄ centum et quinque uirgas ulnarias cum pollice interposito . Retro᷄ sexdecim uirgas ulnarias et tria quarteria cum pollice interposito. Idem uero Gilebertus iuramentum nobis prestitit quod fidelis erit ecclesie nostre de soluendo redditu nostro plenarie statutis terminis . et quod nec artem nec ingenium exquiret unde domus nostra per tenuram suam dampnum incurrat . et quod predictam terram neque vendet neque excambiet neque in vadimonium ponet nec alicui in feodum et hereditatem tradet . neque ad alium locum religionis transferet sine assensu nostro. Eandem securitatem facient nobis heredes suis cum singuli sibi succedent. In cuius rei testimonium presens scriptum sigillo ecclesie nostre munitum diuiso inter nos cyrographo'. ei tradidimus. Hiis testibus magistro Waltero scriptore . Dauid Dunning . Willelmo de Sanford [.] Ricardo de Bredon' . Galfrido de Weston' . Benedicto[5] . et Alexandro filio Turstani . et aliis.

See no. 136 for mention of Roger Morin, which allows the brook to be located.

[1] The terminal letter is apparently *n*, but the reading of this letter is not certain due to a fold in the MS.
[2] Hole in MS.
[3] Entire section of MS. destroyed.
[4] Part of destroyed area.
[5] The names of witnesses from Richard of Bredon to Alexander son of Turstin are largely covered by the turn-up.

133. *Grant in fee and inheritance in the form of a chirograph by Abbot Henry and the convent of St. Peter's, Gloucester, of land by Feet Lane (probably Alvin Street, Gloucester) to Wido Tailor for 4s. 8d. annual rent payable to their hosteler. (1205 × 24)*

A. G.C.L., 'Deeds and Seals', ix, no. 1, fol. 1 (130 mm [left] × 157 mm [foot]); tongue torn from left foot; seal missing; endorsements: Contra Widonem le taillur (s. xiii[in]); tenementum in Vetelone (s. xv[ex] × s. xvi[in]); Registratur (s. xv); **B**. ibid. 'Reg. B', no. 407, p. 177.

C Y R O G R A P H U M (*inverted*)

Sciant presentes et futuri quod ego Henricus dei gratia abbas et conuentus sancti Petri Glouc' concessimus Widoni Le taillur terram nostram iuxta Vetelone . Illam scilicet que iacet iuxta terram Ricardi Mogge . quam Walter scriptor dedit hostilarie nostre . tenendam de nobis in feudo et hereditate sibi et heredibus suis pro quatuor solidis et octo denariis hostilario nostro qui pro tempore fuerit'. annuatim persoluendis ad duos terminos . Medietate ad Hockedei et alia medietate ad festum sancti Michaelis. Predicta uero terra per uisum legalium uirorum mensurata'. habet in fronte autem octo virgas vlnarias et vnum quarterium cum pollice interposito . Retro'. octo virgas vlnarias cum police interposito . In profunditate'. quadraginta et vna virgas vlnarias cum pollice interposito. Quando uero predictus .W. predictam terram a nobis recepit'. edificium superpositum apreciatum est tres marcas. Si autem aliquo casu emergente ipse uel heredes sui prefatam terram nobis reliquerint'. simile edificium aut pretium nobis restituent. Idem uero .W. iuramentum nobis prestitit quod fidelis erit ecclesie nostre de soluendo redditu nostro plenarie statutis terminis . et quod nec artem nec ingenium exquiret unde domus nostra per tenuram suam dampnum incurrat . et quod predictam terram neque uendet neque escambiet nec in vadimonium ponet . nec alicui in feudum et hereditatem tradet . neque ad alium locum religionis transferet sine assensu nostro. Eandem securitatem facient nobis heredes sui'. cum singuli sibi succedent. In cuius rei testimonium presens scriptum sigillo ecclesie nostre munitum diuiso inter nos cyrographo'. ei tradidimus. Hiis testibus . Ricardo Burg' . Henrico Burg' . Iohanne Draperio . magistro Waltero scriptore[1] . Henrico Le Bel [.] Mauricio stabulario . et multis aliis.

[1] **B** ends here with *et aliis.*

134. *Grant in fee and inheritance in the form of a chirograph by Abbot Henry and the convent of St. Peter's, Gloucester, of a stall in the cobblers' quarter (Gloucester) to Walter of Tewkesbury for 8s. annual rent. (1205 × 24)*

G.C.L., 'Deeds and Seals', viii, no. 9, fol. 5 (122 mm [left]; foot, irregular edge; 97 mm [right]); possible slit for tag perpendicular to left edge of foot; tag and seal missing; endorsements: Contra Walterum de Theok' (s. xiii[in]); : iii[a] Warda (s. xiii[med]); Registratur[;] In Sutaria (s. xiv[ex]); sc(ribitur) (s. xiv[med]).

CI RO GRA PHUM

Sciant presentes et futuri quod ego H(e)nric(us) dei gratia abbas Glouc' et conuentus sancti Petri Glouc' concessimus Waltero de Theokebir' seldam nostram in Sutaria illam scilicet que iacet inter seldam Ricardi Dubelday ex una parte . et seldam Willelmi Vlger' altera pa[rte][1] tenendam de nobis in feudo et hereditate sibi et heredibus suis pro octo solidis nobis annuatim ad quatuor terminos persoluendis . In Natiuitate sancti Iohannis Baptiste duobus solidis . In festo sancti Michaelis . duobus solidis . In Natali⸍ duobus solidis . et ad Hocked(ai) duobus solidis. Predicta uero terra per visum legalium virorum mensurata⸍ habet in fronte duas virgas ulnarias cum pollice interposito . Retro⸍ totidem . In longitudine vero decem uirgas cum pollice interposito. Quando autem predictus Walterus predictam terram a nobis recepit⸍ edificium superpositum appreciatum est unam marcam. Si uero aliquo casu emergente ipse uel heredes sui prefatam terram nobis reliquerint⸍ simile edificium aut pretium nobis restituent. Idem etiam .W. iuramentum nobis prestitit quod fidelis erit ecclesie nostre de soluendo redditu nostro plenarie statutis terminis . et quod nec artem nec ingenium exquiret vnde domus nostra per tenuram suam dampnum incurrat . et quod predictam seldam neque uendet . neque escambiet . nec in uadimonium ponet . nec alicui in feudum et hereditatem tradet⸍ neque ad alium locum religionis transferet⸍ sine assensu nostro. Eandem securitatem facient nobis heredes sui cum singuli sibi succedent. In huius rei testimonium presens scriptum sigillo ecclesie nostre munitum diuiso inter nos cyrographo⸍ sepedicto .W . tradidimus . Hiis testibus. Ricardo Burg' . et Henrico fratre eius . Dauid Dunning . Ricardo filio Willelmi . Waltero scriptore . Henrico Le Bel . Ma[uric]io[2] marescallo . et multis aliis.

Both Henry burgess, the likely brother of Richard burgess, and David Dunning, a wine merchant and important Gloucester landholder, served as bailiffs of Gloucester, respectively,

1200 × *c.* 1228 and 1200 × *c.* 1240 (Stevenson, no. 132; *VCH Glos.* iv. 22, 371–2). David Dunning's local social and political importance is reflected by the frequency of his appearances as a witness in local Gloucester *acta*.

¹ A stain or ink-blot covers this area.
² A stain or ink-blot covers this area.

135. *Grant in fee and inheritance in the form of a chirograph by Abbot Henry and the convent of St. Peter's, Gloucester, to Thomas palmer of a stall in the Cordwainery (Gloucester) for 14s 6d. annual rent. (1205 × 24)*

G.C.L., 'Deeds and Seals', ii, no. 20, fol. 11 (99 mm [left] × 166 mm [foot]); seal on tag; white wax, fragment, repaired (meas. unavail.); obverse: partial figure of an abbot or St. Benedict seated facing front; in the right hand a crozier; in the left an upraised book; legend illegible; reverse: counterseal: fragment of a standing figure facing front, a crozier in the right hand; legend: . . .ET. . .STRIE; endorsement: iii.ª Warda (s. xiii^{ex.}?).

C Y R O G R A PH . . .M

Sciant presentes et futuri quod ego Henr(icus) dei gratia abbas et conuentus sancti Petri Glouc' concessimus Thome palmario seldam nostram in Cordianar' illa scilicet que est inter seldam Simonis de Fetel' ex vna parte . et seldam Iohannis Hackebon(e) ex altera . Tenendam de nobis in feudo et he[r]editate sibi et heredibus suis pro quatuordecim solidis et sex denariis ad quatuor terminos nobis annuatim persoluendis . videlicet tribus solidis et septem denariis et oboluḿ. ad Natale domini . tribus solidis et septem denariis et oboluḿ. ad Hocked(ai) . tribus solidis et septem denariis et oboluḿ. ad festum sancti Iohannis Baptiste . tribus solidis et septem denariis et oboluḿ. ad festum sancti Michaelis. Predicta uero selda per visum legalium virorum mensuratá. habet in fronte duas virgas ulnarias cum pollice interposito . et duos pollices . Retró. totidem . In profunditaté. quatuor virgas vlnarias et vnum quarterium cum pollice interposito et tres pollices. Quando uero predictus Thomas predictam seldam a nobis recepit́. edificium superpositum appreciatum est vnam marcam. Si autem aliquo casu emergente ipse uel heredes sui prefatam seldam nobis reliquerint́. simile edificium aut pretium nobis restituent. Idem uero Thomas iuramentum nobis prestitit quod fidelis erit ecclesie nostre de soluendo redditu nostro plenarie statutis terminis . et quod nec artem nec ingenium exquiret; vnde domus nostra per tenuram suam dampnum incurrat . et quod predictam seldam neque uendet neque escambiet . nec in vadimonium ponet . nec alicui in feudum et hereditatem tradet . neque ad alium locum religionis transferet́. sine assensu nostro. Eandem securitatem facient nobis heredes suí. cum singuli sibi succedent. In cuius rei testimonium presens scriptum sigillo ecclesie nostre munitum diuiso inter nos cyrographó. ei tradidimus. His testibus . Ricardo Burg' . Ricardo Ruffo . Henrico Burg' . Dauid' Dunning . Waltero scriptore . Waltero de mor' . Hugone de Bramton' . et multis aliis.

136. *Grant in fee and inheritance in the form of a chirograph by Abbot Henry and the convent of St. Peter's, Gloucester, to Turstin fuller of land by the mill of Roger Morin pertaining to the abbey's barton (by Gloucester) for 3s. 2d. annual rent. (1205 × 24)*

G.R.O., GBR/J1/147 (133 mm [left] × 145 mm [foot]); seal on tag; white wax; fragment; obverse: partial torso of a seated figure; reverse: illegible; legend not avail.; no endorsement; cal. in Stevenson, no. 147.

C Y R O G R A P H U M (*inverted*)

Sciant presentes et futuri quo ego Henr(icus) dei gratia abbas et conuentus sancti Petri Glouc' . concessimus Turstino fulloni terram nostram uersus molendinum Rogeri Morin . que pertinet ad bertonam nostram . Illam videlicet . que iacet inter terram Henrici filii Hunfridi et terram Mauricii Durand . tenendam de nobis in feudo et hereditate sibi et heredibus suis . Reddendo nobis inde singulis annis tres solidos et duos denarios ad quatuor terminos . Videlicet ad festum sancti Michaelis'. nouem denarios et obolum . Ad Natale domini'. nouem denarios et obolum . In Annuntiatione beate Marie'. nouem denarios et obolum . Et in Natiuitate sancti Iohannis'. nouem denarios et obolum. Predicta uero terra per visu legalium virorum mensurata'. habet in fronte'. decem et octo virgas vlnarias et minus quarterium cum pollice interposito . Retro'. decem et octo virgas vlnarias et tria quarteria cum pollice interposito . In Longitudine'. quinquies viginti et decem et septem virgas vlnarias cum pollice interposito. Idem autem Turstinus nullum edificium a nobis recepit cum predicta terra. Idem uero Turstinus iuramentum nobis prestitit quod fidelis erit ecclesie nostre de soluendo redditu nostro plenarie statutis terminis . et quod nec artem nec ingenium exquiret vnde domus nostra per tenuram suam dampnum incurrat . Et quod predictam terram neque uendet neque escambiet . nec in vadimonium ponet . nec alicui in feudum et hereditatem tradet . neque ad alium locum religionis transferet sine assensu nostro. Eandem securitatem facient nobis heredes sui'. cum singuli sibi succedent. In huius rei testimonium'. presens scriptum sigillo ecclesie nostre munitum'. diuiso inter nos cyrographo'. predicto Turstino tradidimus. Hiis testibus . Iohanne Rufo . Iohanne de Gosedich . Iohanne Draperio . Rogero Morin . Waltero Blundo . Eynulfo Le feutrer . Drogone Le Butiler . Salomone Ianitore . Waltero de Mora . et multis aliis.

137. *Grant in fee and inheritance in the form of a chirograph by Abbot Henry and the convent of St. Peter's, Gloucester, to Warin smith of land on the lane to the castle (Gloucester) for 28d. annual rent. (1205 × 24)*

G.C.L., 'Deeds and Seals', ix, no. 16, fol. 7 (91 mm [left] × 152 mm [foot]); no turn-up; slit for tag at left foot; hole for possible cord or tag at centre of foot; tag(s) and seal(s) missing; endorsements: Contra Warinum fabrum (s. xiii[in]); .iiii.[a 1] Warda (*c.* s. xiii[med]); Registratur (s. xiv?); Castellene (modern?).

CYROGRAPHVM:

Sciant presentes et futuri quod ego Henric(us) dei gratia abbas et conuentus sancti Petri Glouc' . concessimus Warino fabro terram nostram in viculo uersus castellum quam Cr(ist)oforus clericus de nobis tenuit . tenendam de nobis in feudo et hereditate sibi et heredibus suis pro viginti et octo denariis nobis annuatim persoluendis duobus terminis . medietate ad hokedaí. et medietate ad festum sancti Michaelis. Predicta uero terra per uisum legalium uirorum mensuratá. habet in fronte octo virgas ulnarias et dimidiam cum pollice interposito . Retró. totidem² . In profunditaté. quadraginta virgas ulnarias et dimidiam cum pollice interposito. Quando uero predictus .W. predictam terram a nobis recepit́. edificium superpositum appreciatum est dimidiam marcam. Si autem aliquo casu emergente ipse uel heredes sui nobis prefatam terram reliquerint́. simile edificium aut pretium nobis restituent. Idem uero .W. iuramentum nobis prestitit quod fidelis erit ecclesie nostre de soluendo reditu nostro plenarie statutis terminis . et quod nec artem nec ingenium exquiret vnde domus nostra per tenuram suam dampnum incurrat . Et quod predictam terram neque uendet neque excambiet neque in vadimonium ponet . nec alicui in feudum et hereditatem tradet . neque ad alium locum religionis sine assensu nostro transferet. Eandem autem securitatem facient nobis heredes suí. cum singuli sibi succedent. In cuius rei testimonium presens scriptum sigillo ecclesie nostro munituḿ. diuiso inter nos cyrographo ei tradidimus. His testibus . Roberto le Riche . Ricardo rufo . Ricardo filio Iordani . Waltero scriptore . Ricardo Burgeis . Ricardo filio Willelmi Burgeis . Iohanne draperio . Henrico Burgeis . Salomone lanitore . Helia medico . Mauricio stabulario . et multis aliis.

¹ Reading uncertain with ultra-violet light.
² Superscript in the same hand.

138. *Grant in fee and inheritance in the form of a chirograph by Abbot Henry and the convent of St. Peter's, Gloucester, to William del bailli of land by the old castle (Gloucester) to be held of the almonry for 12d. annual rent. (1205 × 24; poss. 1228 × 40)*

A. G.C.L., 'Deeds and Seals', v, no. 13, fol. 5 (82 mm [left] × 168 mm [foot]), **Scribe 12**; no turn-up; slit for tag; tag and seal missing; endorsements: Contra Willelmum del Bayli (s. xiii^med); vetus castellum (s. xiii^ex); Registratur (s. xiv^ex × s. xv^in); **B**. ibid. 'Reg. B', no. 682, pp. 294–5.

CYROGRAPHUM

Sciant presentes et futuri quod ego Henric(us) dei gratia abbas et conuentus sancti Petri Glouc' . concessimus Willelmo del bailli terram quandam apud vetus castellum . que iacet iuxta terram Petri fratris Roberti de uallo . tenendam de elemosinaria nostra in feudo et hereditate sibi et heredibus suis in perpetuum . pro duodecim denariis . annuatim elemosinarie nostre persoluendis . Medietate ad Hockedai et alia medietate ad festum sancti Michaelis. Idem vero Willelmus iuramentum nobis prestitit quod fidelis erit ecclesie nostre de soluendo redditu nostro plenarie statutis terminis . et quod predictam terram neque uendet neque escambiet neque in vadimonium ponet . neque ad alium locum religionis transferret sine assensu nostro et quod nec artem nec ingenium exquiret . vnde domus nostra per tenuram suam dampnum incurrat.[1] Quod ut ratum et inconcussum permaneat . presenti scripto sigilli nostri inpressione munito . diuiso inter nos cyrographo . confirmauimus. Hiis testibus . Ricardo burg'nsi . et Mauricio Durant tunc prepositis[2] . magistro Waltero scriptore . Drocone pincerna . Willelmo de Sanford . Henrico le bel . et multis aliis.

[1]   Superscript in the same hand.
[2]   **B** ends here with *et aliis.*

139. *Lifetime lease in the form of a chirograph by Abbot Henry and the convent of St. Peter's, Gloucester, of land in Twigworth to Walter Loker and Aliz his wife for 3s. 1d. annual rent. (1205 × 24)*

G.C.L., 'Deeds and Seals', xi, no. 6 (78 mm [left] × 135 mm [foot]); two seals on tags: left: white wax coloured green, round (35 mm in diam.); obverse: fleur-de-lis; legend: +SIGILL': WALTERI: LOKER; no counterseal; right: white wax painted green, repaired, round (30 mm in diam.); four oval leaves forming a Greek cross; legend: + SIGILL' . ALIZE. WACE; no counterseal; endorsements: contra Walterum locarium (s. xiii[in]), **Hand f**; Tuig(e)worth'[;] Bertona (s. xiv[in]); ad terminum vite (s. xiv); Baddeley, 'Further Early Deeds', p. 51.

. . . I R . . . G R A . . . U M

Sciant presentes et futuri quod ego Henr(icus) dei gratia abbas et conuentus sancti Petri Gloucestrie concessimus Waltero locario et Aliz uxori sue quatuor acras terre et dimidiam apud Tuig'wrd' . et dimidiam acram prati . illas scilicet quas Wacius cocus de nobis tenuit . tenendas de nobis libere et quiete quamdiu uterque uel alter eorum uixerit . pro tribus solidis et uno denario annuatim nobis in Annuntiationem beate Marie persoluendis. Post decessum uero ipsorum predicta terra sine alicuius reclamatione ad nos libere reuertetur. In cuius rei testimonium presens scriptum in modum cirographi confecimus . Cuius vnam partem sigillo ecclesie nostre munitam dictis Waltero et Aliz tradidimus⸍ alteram uero partem sigillo dicti Walteri . et sigillo dicte Aliz uxoris sue roboratam⸍ penes nos retinuimus. Hiis testibus . magistro Ricardo de Brackl' . Waltero scriptore . Mauricio marescallo . Simone De Cellario . Henrico Le bel . et multis aliis.

Walter and his wife ultimately gave their tenure to St. Peter's by a charter which he placed upon its altar in the presence of Alice his wife (*Cart. Glouc.* i, no. 86; ii, no. 890). A charter of Walter *locarius* is in G.C.L., 'Reg. B', no. 672, p. 291.

140. Conventio *in the form of a chirograph between the abbot (Henry Blont) and the convent of St. Peter's, Gloucester, and Robert son of Ruelan: Robert granted to St. Peter's the mill at* Gare *(unident.) for ten years for the annual payment of a load of grain at Christmas. Robert had held the mill of the abbot and convent for 3½ half marks a year. After ten years, Robert and his heirs were to hold the mill for the same service. In return for the grant the abbot and convent remitted to Robert the 10 marks which he owed to the abbot for a fine made with lord William Marshal for the mill.* 30 November 1212.

A. H.C.L., no. 796 (101 mm [left] × 154 mm [foot]); seal on tag, white wax, chipped, round (35 mm in diam.); obverse: a great bird (eagle?) with right wing extended facing to the left; legend: +SIGILL' ROBERTI FIL' ROWELAN; no counterseal; endorsements: de molendi[no] de gare (s. xiii[in]), **Hand f**; De molendino de Gare[;] Caps(ula) .xv. de laicis tenuris. (s. xiii[ex]); Robertum Ruelani. (s. xiv[2]); Non indiget[1] registrari (s. xiv[ex]); **B**. P.R.O., C 150/1, fol. 228; *Cart. Glouc.* ii, no. 843; cal. in Baddeley i, no. 25.

C/Y/R/O/G/R/A/P/H/V/. . .: C/Y/R/O/G/R/A/P/H/. . .

Hec est conuentio facta inter dominum abbatem et conuentum Glouc' ex una parte . et Rob(er)tum filium Ruelani ex altera[2] . Anno incarnationis domini millesimo ducentesimo duodecimo in festo sancti Andree . videlicet quod idem Rob(ertus) et heredes sui dimiserunt et concesserunt . ut predicti abbas et conuentus teneant ad firmam molendinum de Gare cum pertinentiis suis usque ad decem annos completos pro vna lada bladi peruenientis ab ipso molendino . ad Natale domini singulis annis eidem .R. persoluenda . Qvod uidelicet molendinum dictus Rob(ertus) clamat tenere de predictis abbate et conuentu Glouc' pro tribus marcis et dimidia per annum'. sicut in carta quam inde Rob(ertus) exinde habet'. plenius continetur.[3] Completis autem predictis decem annis'. predictus .R. et heredes sui predictum molendinum libere sine contradictione alicuius recipient tenendum per predictum servitium iuxta formam predicte carte sue. Pro hac autem dimissione et concessione . predicti abbas et conuentus remiserunt et quietas clamauerunt memorato .R. et heredibus suis decem marcas argenti . quas ipse .R. debebat abbati Glouc' pro fine facto cum domino Willelmo marescallo pro predicto molendino. In cuius rei testimonium'. presens scriptum in modum scriptum cyrographi confectum est . Cuius alteram partem sigillo predicti Roberti munitam'. abbas et conuentus Glouc' sibi retinuerunt . Alteram uero partem . sigillo eiusdem abbatis et conuentus roboratam . idem Robertus sibi reseruauit. Hiis testibus . magistro Ricardo de Brackel' . Waltero scriptore . Salomone Ianitore . Symone de Framilad' tunc seruiente de Bromtun' . ¶ Willelmo le franceis . Itheil de Gleaustun' . Roberto filio Bledi' . Ricardo filio Iohannnis clerici . Ricardo filio Ruelan . Gileberto filio Helye et multis aliis.

The mill of *Gare* was given to St. Peter's, a gift confirmed by King Henry II, by Alexander de Cormeilles (*Cart. Glouc.* i, p. 81; nos. 286, 288). Alexander attested Hugh de Lacy's grant of St. Peter's, Hereford, to Gloucester in 1100 (ibid. iii, no. 995).

---

[1] *indigent* in MS.   [2] *ex altera* superscript in the same hand.
[3] **B** as printed in *Cart. Glouc.* ends here.

141. *Final concord between Peter of Uley plaintiff and Henry abbot of St. Peter's,*
Gloucester, defendant concerning the advowson of the church of Uley of which the
assize of darrein presentment was summoned between them in the king's court. 8
July 1222. Canterbury.

Bodl. MS. Charters Gloucester, a.1, no. 9 (76 mm [right] × 121 mm [foot]); endorsement:
:Ewelegh' (s. xiv^ex).

C Y R O G R A . . H . . . M

Hec est finalis concordia facta in curia domini regis apud Kantuar' in crastino octaui
Petri et Pauli . anno regni regis Henrici filii regis Iohannis sexto . Coram .H. de
Burgo tunc capitali iustic' Angl' . Martino . de Pat'hull' . Radulfo Harang' .
Stephano de Seg'aue . Thoma de Haiden' . Roberto de Lexinton' . iustic(iis) et . aliis
domini regis fidelibus tunc ibi presentibus . Inter Petru(m) de Euleg' petentem . et
Henricum abbatem Glouc' deforciantem per Robertum de Gironde monachum suum
positum loco suo ad lucrandum uel perdendum de . aduocatione ecclesie de Euleg' .
vnde assisa ultime . presentationis summonita fuit inter eos in eadem . curia . Scilicet
quod predictus Petr(us) remisit et quiet(um) clamauit de se et heredibus suis ipsi
abbati et successoribus suis et ecclesie sue de Glouc' in perpetuum⁄. totum ius et
clamium quod habuit in aduocatione predicte ecclesie. Et predictus abbas recepit
eundem Petru(m) et heredes suos in singulis benefactis et orationibus que fient de
cetero in ecclesia sua de Glouc'.

This is the upper right portion of a tripartite chirograph. The second half of the word
[CYROGRA]PHU[M] is written down the left-hand side. See no. 142. On this case, see *CRR*,
x. 266–70.

142. *Another copy of no. 141.*

P.R.O., CP 25/1/73/6, no. 54 (77 mm [left] × 142 mm [foot]); Endorsements: Kant' anno .vi.
(s. xiii...^med); Glouc' .vi. (s. xiv^ex × s. xv).

This is the foot of the original tripartite document and is in the same hand as the other extant
part, no. 141. The left edge of no. 141 fits into the top right edge of this piece and thereby
completes the letters R A P H V M. The lower edge of no. 141 formed the rest of the right edge
of the original undivided document; *Glouc'* is written below the text.

143. *Grant in the form of a chirograph by Abbot Henry and the convent of St.*
Peter's, Gloucester, of land in front of the alley of Feet Lane (probably Alvin Street,
Gloucester) to Ralph Farrier for 4s. annual rent payable to the almoner.
(1205 × 24)

A. G.C.L., 'Deeds and Seals', ix, no. 19, fol. 9 (92 mm [left]; 172 mm [foot]); slit for tag on turn-up; tag and seal missing; endorsements: Contra Randulfum ferur (s. xiii$^{...med}$); Vetelone (s. xiii); Registratur (s. xiv^{ex} × s. xv^{in}); **B**. ibid. 'Reg. B', no. 557, p. 244.

CYROGRAPHVM

Sciant presentes et futuri quod ego Henric(us) dei gratia abbas et conuentus sancti Petri Glouc' concessimus Radulfo Le Ferurh terram nostram in fronte viculi de Vetelone . Illam scilicet que iacet inter terram magistri Hereberti et Vetelone . Tenendam et habendam d[ictam terram]^1 sibi et heredibus suis pro quatuor solidis annuatim elemosinario nostro qui pro tempore fuerit persoluendis . duobus anni terminis . Medieta[te ad]^2 Hockedai et alia medietate ad festum sancti Michaelis. Hec autem terra mensurata per uisum legalium uirorum continet in fronte quatuordeci[m]^3 uirgas ulnarias cum pollice interposito . In profunditate uero viginti et nouem uirgas ulnarias cum pollice interposito . In medio autem quatuordecim uirgas uno quarterio minus cum pollice interposito . Retro autem vndecim uirgas ulnarias et dimidiam et duos pollices cum pollice interposito[.] Edificium autem superpositum appreciatum est decem solidos. Et si ita contigerit quod ipse Radulfus uel heredes sui seruisiam fecerint ad uendendam soluet nobis unum denarium uel quatuor galones de meliori seruisia ad libitum elemosinarii. Si uero aliquo casu emergente predictus Radulfus uel heredes sui predictam terram reliquerint simile edificium uel pretium nobis restituet. Idem uero Radulfus iuramentum nobis prestitit quod fidelis erit ecclesie nostre de reddendo redditu nostro plenarie statutis terminis . et quod nec artem nec ingenium exquiret unde domus nostra per tenuram suam dampnum incurrat . et quod predictam terram neque uendet neque ascambiet neque in vadimonium ponet neque alicui in feudum et hereditatem tradet neque ad alium locum religionis transferet sine assensu nostro. Eandem securitatem nobis facient heredes sui cum singuli sibi succedent. In cuius rei testimonium presens scriptum diuiso inter nos cirographo confecimus . Cuius unam partem sigillo ecclesie nostre munitam ei tradidimus . Alteram uero partem penes nos retinuimus. Hiis testibus . magistro Waltero scriptore . Galfrido de Westun' . Ricardo Burg' . Dauid Dunning . Iohanne de Ludelowe . Nicholao Clerico . et multis aliis.^{4}

^{1} Hole in MS.
^{2} Hole in MS.
^{3} Hole in MS.
^{4} **B** ends with *et multis aliis*, after listing as witnesses only Master David *scriptor*, David Dunning, and John of Ludlow.

144. *Grant in fee and inheritance in the form of a chirograph by Abbot Thomas and the convent of St. Peter's, Gloucester, to Thomas Banastre of land near Kingsholm (by Gloucester) for 20d. annual rent payable to the almoner. (1224 × 28)*

A. G.C.L., 'Deeds and Seals', i, no. 36, fol. 20 (122 mm [left] × 172 mm [foot]); tag and seal missing; endorsements: Contra Thomam Banastre (s. xiii^{med}), **Hand I**; uersus aulam regis (s. xiii^{ex}); Registratur (s. xiv^{ex} × s. xv^{in}); **B**. ibid. 'Reg. B', no. 512, p. 225.

C Y R O . . . R A P H . . .

Sciant presentes et futuri quod ego Thomas dei gratia abbas et conuentus sancti Petri Glouc' concessimus Thome Banastr(e) terram nostram uersus aulam regis . Illam scilicet que iacet inter terram prioris sancti Oswaldi et terram Alexandri Brun tenendam et habendam de nobis in feudo et hereditate sibi et heredibus suis pro viginti denariis elemosinario nostro qui pro tempore fuerit annuatim duobus terminis persoluendis . Medietate ad festum sancti Michaelis . et alia medietate ad Hockeday. Predicta uero terra per uisum legalium uirorum mensurata habet in fronte septem virgas vlnarias et vnum quarterium cum pollice interposito et quatuor pollices . In profunditate´. triginta quatuor virgas vlnarias cum pollice interposito dimidio quarterio minus . In medio´. nouem virgas vlnarias et vnum quarterium cum pollice interposito et quatuor pollices . Retro´. decem virgas vlnarias cum pollice interposito vno quarterio minus. Quando uero predictus Thomas predictam terram a nobis recepit´. edificium superpositum appreciatum est quinque solidis. Si autem aliquo casu emergente ipse uel heredes sui predictam terram nobis reliquerint´. simile edificium aut pretium nobis restituent. Idem etiam .T. iuramentum nobis prestitit quod fidelis erit ecclesie nostre de soluendo redditu nostro plenarie statutis terminis . et quod nec artem nec ingenium exquiret vnde domus nostra per tenuram suam dampnum incurrat . et quod predictam terram neque vendet neque escambiet neque in vadimonium ponet nec alicui in feudum et hereditatem tradet . neque ad alium locum religionis transferet´. sine assensu nostro. Eandem securitatem facient nobis heredes sui´. cum singuli sibi succedent. In cuius rei testimonium presens scriptum sigillo ecclesie nostre munitum diuiso inter nos cyrographo´. ei tradidimus. Hiis testibus . magistro Roberto de Culn' . magistro Waltero scriptore[1] . Ricardo Burg' . Dauid Dunning . Henrico Le Bel . Drogone de pont' . Waltero de Honiton' . et multis aliis.

1 **B** ends here with *et aliis.*

145. *Grant in fee and inheritance in the form of a chirograph by Abbot Thomas and the convent of St. Peter's, Gloucester, to Adam Esgar of a tenure near the Henneride (in Kingsholm, by Gloucester) for 2s. annual rent payable to the almoner. (1224 × 28)*

A. G.C.L., 'Deeds and Seals', i, no. 35, fol. 20 (103 mm [left] × 141 mm [foot]), **Scribe 15** (below, Plate XVII); tag and seal missing; endorsements: Contra Adam Esgar (s. xiii^{med}), **Hand I**; aula regis (s. xiii^{2}); Registratur (s. xiv^{ex} × s. xv^{in}); **B**. ibid. 'Reg. B', no. 507, p. 223.

C Y R O G R A P H U M

Sciant presentes et futuri quod ego Thom(as) dei gratia abbas et conuentus sancti

Petri Glouc'. concessimus Ade Esegar terram nostram. illam scilicet que iacet inter terram infirmarie nostre. et riuulum que uocatur He'neride. Tenendam et habendam de nobis in feodo et hereditate sibi et heredibus suis pro duobus solidis. elemosinario nostro qui pro tempore fuerit annuatim persoluendis. duobus terminis. medietate uidelicet ad festum sancti Michaelis. et alia medietate ad festum sancte Marie. Predicta uero terra per uisum legalium uirorum mensurata. continet in fronte tresdecim uirgas ulnarias et dimidiam cum pollice interposito. In medietate ̓ duodecim uirgas ulnarias. et unum quarterium cum pollice interposito. In longitudine ̓ triginta vnam uirgam ulnariam. cum pollice interposito. et tres pollices. Retro ̓ tres uirgas ulnarias cum pollice interposito. Item concessimus eidem .A. vnum curtilagium pertinens ad eandam terram. quod propinquum est curtilagio abbatie nostre. quod per uisum legalium uirorum mensuratum habet in fronte viginti et octo uirgas ulnarias. et vnum quarterium cum pollice interposito. In medietate ̓ viginti et sex uirgas ulnarias et tria quarteria cum pollice interposito. In longitudine ̓ triginta et sex uirgas ulnarias cum pollice interposito. Retro ̓ novemdecim uirgas ulnarias cum pollice interposito. Idem uero .A. iuramentum nobis prestitit quod fidelis erit ecclesie nostre de soluendo redditu nostro plenarie statutis terminis. et quod nec artem. nec ingenium exquiret ̓ vnde domus nostra per tenuram suam dampnum incurrat. Et quod predictam terram neque uendet. neque escambiet. neque in uadimonium ponet. nec aliqui in feodum et hereditatem tradet. neque ad alium locum religionis transferet ̓ sine assensu nostro. Eandem securitatem facient nobis heredes sui ̓ cum singuli sibi succedent. In cuius rei testimonium presens scriptum sigillo ecclesie nostre munitum diuiso inter nos cyrographo ̓ ei tradidimus. Hiis testibus. magistro Waltero scriptore. magistro Roberto de Cul'. Ricardo Burg'. Dauid Dunning. Henrico Le Bel. Drogone de Pont'. Waltero de Honit'[1]. et multis aliis.

For Henneride, a stream, see *PNG*, ii.144.

[1] **B** ends here with *et aliis*, but omits the witnesses' names between Walter scribe and Walter of Honiton.

146. *Grant in fee and inheritance in the form of a chirograph by Abbot Thomas and the convent of St. Peter's, Gloucester, to Walter Kentwine of land by Northgate (Gloucester) for 8s. annual rent. (1224 × 28)*

G.C.L., 'Deeds and Seals', ii, no. 23, fol. 13 (114 mm [left] × 191 mm [foot]); slit for tag on turn-up; tag and seal missing; endorsements: Contra Walterum Kenwin' (s. xiii[1]), **Hand o/Scribe 17** (below, Plate XLIVf); :ii.[a] Warda (s. xiii[med]), **Hand t** (below, Plate XLIVk); Registratur[;] Infra portam borialem interiorem (xiv[ex] × s. xv[in]).

C Y R . . G R . . P H . . . M

Sciant presentes et futuri quod ego Thom(as) dei gratia abbas et conuentus sancti Petri Glouc' concessimus Waltero Kentwine terram nostram in vico uersus

Norþgate . quam Rogerus presbiter de sancto Iohanne dedit nobis que iacet inter terram quam Ricardus Pigace de nobis tenuit . et terram Ricardi filii Willelmi in eodem vico . Tenendam et habendam de nobis in feudo et hereditate sibi et heredibus suis . Reddendo nobis inde singulis annis octo solidos ad quatuor terminos . Videlicet ad festum sancti Andree⸍. duos solidos . ad Annuntiationem beate Marie⸍. duos solidos . ad festum sancti Iohannis Baptiste⸍. duos solidos . et ad festum sancti Michaelis⸍. duos solidos. Predicta uero terra per visum legalium uirorum mensurata habet in fronte uersus predictum vicum tres virgas ulnarias cum pollice interposito et tres pollices . In longitudine⸍. viginti nouem virgas ulnarias . et vnum quarterium cum pollice interposito . In medio⸍. tres virgas ulnarias . et vnum quarterium cum pollice interposito . Retro⸍. sicut in medio. Quando uero predictus .W. predictam terram a nobis recepit⸍. edificium superpositum apreciatum est decem solidos. Si autem aliquo casu contingente ipse uel heredes sui prefatam terram nobis reliquerint⸍. simile edificium aut pretium nobis restituent. Idem uero .W. iuramentum nobis prestitit quod fidelis erit ecclesie nostre de soluendo redditu nostro plenarie statutis terminis . et quod nec artem nec ingenium exquiret vnde domus nostra per tenuram suam dampnum incurrat . et quod predictam terram neque vendet necque escambiet neque in vadimonium ponet . nec alicui in feudum et hereditatem tradet . neque ad alium locum religionis transferet⸍. sine assensu nostro. Eandem securitatem facient nobis heredes sui⸍. cum singuli sibi succedent. In cuius rei testimonium⸍. presens scriptum sigillo ecclesie nostre munitum diuiso inter nos cyrographo⸍. ei tradidimus. Hiis testibus . Ricardo Burg' . Iohanne Rufo . Iohanne Draperio . Mauricio filio Durandi . Dauid Dunning' . Drogone de Pont' . Henrico Le Bel . Ricardo de Bredon' . et multis aliis.

147. *Grant in fee and inheritance in the form of a chirograph by Abbot Thomas and the convent of St. Peter's, Gloucester, to Walter Serjeant of land near Pucklane (Gloucester) for 4s. annual rent payable to the almoner. (1224 × 28)*

A. G.C.L., 'Deeds and Seals', i, no. 50, fol. 26 (exact left and right meas. unavail. because charter with turn-up folded down is glued flat in the scrapbook; based on apparent fold line of turn-up, 134 mm [left]; 143 mm [right]; foot damaged, *c*.161 mm), **Scribe 15**; slit for tag on turn-up; tag and seal missing; endorsements: Contra Walterum seriant (xiii[1]), **Hand o/Scribe 17**; de terra in Pukelane (s. xiii); **B**. ibid. 'Reg. B', no. 506, pp. 222–3.

CYROGRAPHUM

Sciant presentes et futuri quod ego Thomas dei gratia abbas et conuentus sancti Petri Glouc' . concessimus Waltero Le Seriant . terram nostram que iacet inter terram Idonee . et vicum qui dicitur Puchelana . tenendam et habendam de nobis in feodo et hereditate sibi et heredibus suis pro quatuor solidis . annuatim elemosinario nostro qui pro tempore fuerit persoluendis . Duobus terminis . videlicet ad festum Sancti Michaelis⸍. duobus solidos . et ad Annuntiationem Beate Marie⸍. duos solidos. Predicta uero terra per uisum legalium uirorum mensurata habet in fronte⸍. decem et septem uirgas ulnarias cum pollice interposito . In longitudine' sexaginta et sex uirgas ulnarias et tria quarteria cum pollice interposito . Retro autem' septem uirgas ulnarias et unum quarterium cum pollice interposito. Quando etiam predictus .W. predictam terram a nobis recepit' edificium superpositum appreciatum est'. quinque solidos. Si autem aliquo casu emergente ipse uel heredes sui nobis predictam terram reliquerint' simile edificium aut pretium resti[tuent].[1] Idem siquidem .W. iuramentum nobis prestitit . quod fidelis erit ecclesie nostre de soluendo redditu nostro plenarie statutis term[ini]s[2] . et quod nec artem nec ingenium exquiret. vnde domus nostra per tenuram suam dampnum incurrat . Et quod predictam terram neqe uendet neque escambiet . neque in uadimonium ponet . nec alicui in feodum et hereditatem tradet . neque ad alium locum religionis transferet' sine assensu nostro. Eandem securitatem facient nobis heredes sui' cum singuli sibi succedent. In cuius rei testimonium presens scriptum sigillo ecclesie nostre munitum diuiso inter nos cyrographo dicto .W. tradidimus. Hiis testibus . Dauid Dunning . Ricardo Burg' . magistro Roberto de Culn' . magistro Waltero scriptore . magistro Willelmo scriptore . Henrico Le Bel . Drogone de Pont' . Waltero de Honiton'[3]. et multis aliis.

[1] MS. stained.
[2] MS. stained.
[3] **B** ends here with *et aliis*; it omits the witnesses' names between Richard burgess and Walter of Honiton.

148. *Final concord between William de Pontdelarche and Margery his wife and Thomas abbot of St. Peter's, Gloucester, concerning 2½ virgates of land in Whaddon which the abbot holds of them. 3 February 1227. Gloucester.*

A. P.R.O., CP 25/1/73/7, no. 100 (100 mm [left] × 205 mm [foot]; endorsement: De comitatu Glouc' (s. xiii[2]); **B**. G.C.L., 'Reg. B', no. 892, pp. 347–8.

C. . .R. . .G. . .A P. . .V. . .

Hec est finalis concordia facta in curia domini regis apud Gloucest' in crastino Purificationis beate Marie . Anno regni Henrici filii regis Iohannis vndecimo . Coram Stephano de Seg'aue . Roberto de Lexinton' . Willelmo filio Warin' . Waltero de Bello Campo . Waltero le poer iustic(iis) itinerantibus et aliis domini regis fidelibus tunc ibi presentibus . Inter Will(elmu)m de Puntdelharche et Marg(er)iam vxorem eius querentes per Iohannem de Wylton' positum loco eorum ad lucrandum uel perdendum et Thomam abbatem de Gloucestr' deforciantem per Robertum de Gyrunde monachum suum positum loco suo ad lucrandum uel perdendum de consuetudinibus et seruitiis que idem Will(elmus) et Marg(er)ia exigebant ab eodem abbate de duobus virgatis terre et dimidia cum pertinentiis quas idem abbas tenet de predictis Will(elm)o et Marg(er)ia in Waddon' . Quas consuetudines et seruitia idem abbas eis non cognouit . et vnde placitum fuit inter eos in prefata curia . Scilicet quod predictus abbas recognouit et concessit se debere eisdem Will(elm)o et Marg(er)ie forinsecum seruitium de predicto tenemento . Ita quod quando scutagium uenerit et scutum fuerit ad viginti solidos⸍ idem abbas et successores facient predictis Will(elm)o et Marg(er)ie et heredibus ipsius Marg(er)ie seruitium quatuor solidorum et quatuor denariorum et ad plus plus et ad minus minus pro omni seruitio. Et pro hac recognitione concessione fine et concordia⸍ idem Will(elmu)s et Marg(er)ia dederunt abbati sex marcas argenti.

Glouc'

149. *Final concord between Thomas abbot of St. Peter's, Gloucester, and Haimo clerk of Bristol tenant concerning 15s. annual rent from Bristol. 9 February 1227. Bristol.*

P.R.O., CP 25/1/73/8, no. 116 (97 mm [left] × 186 mm [foot]); no endorsement.

C. . .R. . .G. . .A. . .P H V M

Hec est finalis concordia facta in curia domini regis apud Bristoll' in octavo Purificationis beate Marie . Anno regni regis Henrici filii regis Iohannis vndecimo [.] Coram Stephano de Seg'aue . Roberto de Lexinton' . Willelmo filio Warini . Waltero de Bello Campo . Waltero le poer iustic(iis) itinerantibus et aliis domini regis fidelibus tunc ibi presentibus . Inter Thomam abbatem de Gloucestr' petentem[1] per Nigellum de Mortun' monachum suum positum loco suo ad lucrandum uel perdendum et Hamonem clericum de Bristoll' tenentem de quindecim solidatis et quatuor denariis redditus cum pertinentiis in Bristoll' . vnde assisa summonita fuit inter eos in prefata curia ad recognoscendum utrum predictus redditus esset libera elemosina pertinens ad ecclesiam ipsius abbatis de Loringes an laicum feodum predicti Hamonis . Scilicet quod predictus Hamo recognouit predictum redditum cum pertinentiis esse ius ipsius abbatis et ecclesie sue de Gloucestr' . et pro hac recognitione fine et concordia⸍ idem abbas concessit predicto Hamoni totum predictum redditum cum pertinentiis . Habendum et tenendum Hamoni et heredibus suis de predicto abbate et successoribus suis et ecclesia sua de Gloucestr' imperpetuum . Reddendo inde annuatim septem solidos et sex denarios ad duos terminos anni . Scilicet medietatem ad Natiuitatem sancte Iohannis Baptiste et aliam medietatem ad Natale pro omni seruitio[.]

Gloucestr'

[1] *petentes* in MS.

150. *Grant in fee and inheritance in the form of a chirograph by Abbot Henry and*

*the convent of St. Peter's, Gloucester, to Matilda former wife of John Ailive of land
(in Gloucester) for 2s. annual rent payable to their almoner. (1228 × 43)*

A. G.C.L., 'Deeds and Seals', i, no. 31, fol. 18 (136 mm [left] × 164 mm]), **Scribe 16**;
fragment of tag; seal missing; endorsements: Contra Mabilliam Brond (s. xiii²); Non registratur
quia duplex (s. xiv^ex); written below the text and mostly covered by the turn-up: Her'lone et
uersus aulam Regis (s. xiv) ; **B**. ibid. 'Reg. B', no. 513, pp. 225–6.

C. . .ROGRAPHV̇M

Sciant presentes et futuri quod ego Henr(icus) dei gratia abbas et conuentus sancti
Petri Glouc' concessimus Matildi que fuit vxor Iohannis Eiliue terram nostram que
iacet inter terram Mabilie Brond . et terram Petri Eiliue . Tenendam de nobis in feodo
et hereditate sibi et heredibus suis pro duobus solidis elemosinario nostro qui pro
tempore fuerit annuatim persoluendis duobus terminis . Medietate ad
Annuntiationem beate Marie . et alia medietate ad festum sancti Michaelis. Predicta
uero Matildis et heredes sui reddent eidem elemosinario nostro vnum denarium de
qualibet ceruisia quam fecerint ad vendendum. Predicta uero terra per visum
legalium uirorum mensurata᷄ habet in longitudine quadraginta duas uirgas ulnarias
cum pollice interposito . In fronte autem quinque uirgas cum pollice interposito et
quatuor pollicibus . In latitudine retro sex uirgas ulnarias et dimidiam cum pollice
interposito. Quando uero predicta Matildis predictam terram a nobis recepit᷄
edificium superpositum appreciatum est sex solidos. Si uero aliquo casu emergente
predicta Matildis uel heredes sui predictam terram reliquerint᷄ simile edificium uel
pretium nobis restituent. Eadem uero Matildis iuramentum nobis prestitit quod fidelis
erit ecclesie nostre de soluendo redditu nostro plenarie statutis terminis . et quod
predictam terram neque vendet neque excambiet neque in vadimonium ponet nec
alicui in feodum et hereditatem tradet . neque ad alium locum religionis transferet
sine assensu nostro. Eandem securitatem facient nobis heredes sui cum singuli sibi
succedent. In cuius rei testimonium presens scriptum sigillo ecclesie nostre munitum
diuiso inter nos cyrographo ei tradidimus. His testibus . Waltero scriptore . Dauid
Dunnig' . Drogone Pincerna . Galfrido Ianitore . Willelmo de Sanford . Waltero
marescallo . et aliis.

Under the turn-up on the left is an *H* of *c.* 1220. The location of the property on Hare Lane
and towards Kingsholm is indicated by the endorsement (above).

151. *The other half of no. 150.*

G.C.L., 'Deeds and Seals', i, no. 23, fol. 14 (118 mm [left] × 162 mm [foot]), **Scribe 16**; slit
through turn-up; tag and seal missing; endorsements: Contra Matildam que fuit vxor Iohannis
Eliue (s. xiii^med), **Hand I**; Registratur (s. xiv^ex × s. xv^in).

152. *Grant in fee and inheritance in the form of a chirograph by Abbot Henry and the convent of St. Peter's, Gloucester, to Nicholas Fuke for 5s. annual rent of land (in Gloucester?) given by Richard son of Katherine to St. Peter's. (1228 × 43)*

W.S.R.O., Cap. I/17/86 (94 mm [right] × 151 mm [foot]); damaged; tag for seal; seal missing; endorsement: iii.ᵃ Warda (s. xiii^{med}).

. . .O G R A. . .H V M

[Sciant pre]sent[es et futuri quod ego] Henric(us) dei gratia abbas et conuentus sancti Petri Glouc' concessimus Nicholao Fuke [terram nost]ram [in ruta][1] f[. . .il]lam[2] scilicet quam Ricardus filius Katerine nobis dedit que iacet inter terram que fuit Danielis pisca[toris]. . .[3] eodem[4] . . .[5] . Tenendam de nobis in feodo et hereditate sibi et heredibus suis . Reddendo inde annuatim quinque solidos ad quator terminos anni . Videlicet ad festum sancti Michaelis quindecim denarios . Ad Nathale domini quindecim denarios . Ad Annuntia[tione]m beate Marie [quin]decim denarios . et ad Natiuitatem sancti Iohannis Baptiste quindecim denarios. Quando uero predictus Nichol(au)s predictam terram a nobis recepit[´.] edificium superpositum apreciatum fuit dimidiam marcam. Predicta uero terra per u[i]sum legalium uirorum mensurata habet in fronte quatuor uirgas ulnarias . et dimidiam cum pollice interposito . Retro quinque uirgas ulnarias cum pollice interposito . In profunditate sexdecim uirgas ulnarias cum pollice interposito[.] Si aliquo casu emergente contigerit quod ipse uel heredes sui terram nostram reliquerint[´.] simile edificium aut pretium nobis restituent. Idem uero Nicholaus iu[ramen]tum nobis prestitit quod fidelis erit ecclesie nostre et maxime de reddendo redditu nostro plenarie statutis terminis . et quod nec artem nec ingenium exquiret unde domus nostra per tenuram suam dampnum incurrat . et quod predictam terram neque uendet [n]eque excambiet neque in uadimonium ponet neque alicui in feodum et hereditatem tradet neque ad alium locum rel[i]gionis transferet sine assensu nostro. Eandem securitatem nobis fac[i]ent heredes sui cum singuli sibi succedent; [et u]t tam ipse quam heredes sui cur[ia]m nostram sequentur. In cuius rei testimonium prese[n]s scriptum [in] modum cyrographi inter nos confectum sigillo nostro roboratum eidem Nicholao tradidimus . Cuius alteram partem sigillo ipsius mun[i]tam penes nos retinuimus. Hiis testibus Thoma de sancto Martino . Waltero scriptore . Waltero Hoich . Galfrido Cutt. . .stuch' . F[u]lco[ne] fabro . Radulfo Dauwe . Nich[ola]o Clerico . Iohanne draperio . et multis aliis.[6]

To judge from the clauses and witnesses of this lease, the property is likely to have been in Gloucester.

---

[1] Hole in MS. The words in brackets are conjectural.
[2] Hole in MS.   [3] Hole in MS.
[4] Reading uncertain.
[5] Hole in MS.
[6] *Clerico* and the five words following it are covered by the turn-up.

153. *Grant in fee and inheritance in the form of a chirograph from Abbot Henry and the convent of St. Peter's, Gloucester, to William Hackespone of land in Kingsholm (by Gloucester) for 23d. annual rent payable to the almoner. (1228 × 43; poss. 1205 × 24)*

A. G.C.L., 'Deeds and Seals', ii, no. 24, fol. 13 (99 mm [left] × 178 mm [foot]), **Scribe 17**; slit for tag on turn-up; tag and seal missing; endorsements: Resignatio cuiusdam terre. quam Galfridus Russel aliquando tenuit. (s. xiii); W. Hackespon' (s. xiii^ex); de elemosinaria (s. xiv); versus aulam Regis (s. xiv); de Elemosinaria (s. xiv); **B**. ibid. 'Reg. B', no. 510, pp. 224–5.

CYROGRAPHUM

Sciant presentes et futuri quod ego Henr(icus) dei gratia abbas et conuentus sancti Petri Glouc' concessimus Willelmo Hackespone terram nostram uersus aulam regis . illam que iacet inter terram Ydonie vidue et terram eiusdem Willelmi . Tenendam et habendam de nobis in feodo et hereditate sibi et heredibus suis pro viginti tribus denariis elemosinario nostro qui pro tempore fuerit annuatim persoluendis ad duos terminos anni . Medietate ad Hocked(ai) . et alia medietate ad festum sancti Michaelis . saluo telonio nobis de quolibet bracino super eandem terram braciato uel vno denario. Predicta uero terra per uisum legalium uirorum mesurata. habet in fronte quatuor uirgas ulnarias cum pollice interposito et vnum quarterium . In longitudine. sexaginta uirgas ulnarias et octo cum pollice interposito et tria quarteria . Retro. quatuor uirgas ulnarias cum pollice interposito et vnum quarterium. Quando uero predictus Willelmus predictam terram a nobis recipit. edificium superpositum appreciatum est dimidiam marcam. Si uero aliquo casu emergente ipse uel heredes sui predictam terram nobis reliquerint. simile edificium uel pretium nobis restituent. Idem uero Willelmus iuramentum nobis prestitit quod fidelis erit ecclesie nostre de soluendo redditu nostro plenarie statutis terminis et quod nec artem nec ingenium exquiret vnde domus nostra per tenuram suam dampnum incurrat . et quod predictam terram neque vendet neque escambiet neque in vadimonium ponet . nec alicui in feodo et hereditate tradet . neque ad alterum locum religionis transferet sine assensu nostro. Eandem securitatem facient nobis heredes sui cum singuli sibi succedent. In cuius rei testimonium presens scriptum sigillo ecclesie nostre munitum diuiso inter nos cyrographo. dicto Willelmo tradidimus. Hiis testibus . Ricardo Burg' . Dauid Dunning . magistro Waltero scriptore[1] . Drogo de Punt' . Galfrido de Westun' . Petro Clerico et multis aliis.

[1]   **B** ends here with *et multis aliis.*

154. *The other half of no. 153.*

G.C.L., 'Deeds and Seals', i, no. 34, fol. 20 (original meas.: 113 mm [left] × 186 mm [foot]), **Scribe 17**; no turn-up; slit for tag at foot; tag and seal missing; endorsements: Contra Willelmum Hakespone. (s. xiii[1]), **Hand o/Scribe 17**; de terra uersus aulam regis; In manu nostra (s. xiii[2]); Registratur (s. xiv^ex × s. xv^in).

155. *Grant in fee and inheritance in the form of a chirograph by Abbot Henry and the convent of St. Peter's, Gloucester, to William Hackspone of land in Kingsholm (by Gloucester) for 18d. annual rent. (1228 × 43; poss. 1205 × 24)*

G.C.L., 'Deeds and Seals', i, no. 20, fol. 12 (140 mm [left] × 191 mm [foot]), **Scribe 17** (below, Plate XIX); fragment of tag for seal; seal missing; endorsements: Contra Willelmum Hakespone (erased; s. xiii^1), **Hand o/Scribe 17**; Resignatio cuiusdam terre apud aulam regis quam aliquando fuit Galfridi Russel (s. xiii^1); Willelmus Hakespone (s. xiii^{ex}); Westgatestret (c. s. xiv^1).

CYROGRAPHUM

Sciant presentes et futuri quod ego Henr(icus) dei gratia abbas et conuentus sancti Petri Glouc' . concessimus Willelmo Hakespone terram nostram uersus aulam regis . illam scilicet que iacet inter terram eiusdem Willelmi et terram que fuit Walteri þurebarn . Tenendam et habendam de nobis in feodo et hereditate sibi et heredibus suis pro decem et octo denariis nobis annuatim persoluendis ad duos terminos anni . Medietate ad Hocked(ai) . et alia medietate ad festum sancti Michaelis. Idem uero Willelmus et heredes sui de quolibet bracino super eandem terram braciato dabunt nobis vnum denarium de telonio. Predicta uero terra per uisum legalium uirorum mensurata$^\checkmark$ habet in fronte septem uirgas ulnarias cum pollice interposito et vnum quarterium et dimidium . In profunditate$^\checkmark$ sexaginta et octo uirgas ulnarias cum pollice interposito . In medium$^\checkmark$ duodecim uirgas ulnarias et dimidiam cum pollice interposito . Retro nouem uirgas ulnarias cum pollice interposito duobus pollicibus minus. Quando uero predictus Willelmus predictam terram a nobis recepit$^\checkmark$ edificium superpositum appreciatum est dimidiam marcam. Si uero aliquo casu emergente ipse uel heredes sui predictam terram nobis reliquerint$^\checkmark$ simile edificium uel pretium nobis restituent. Idem uero Willelmus iuramentum nobis prestitit quod fidelis erit ecclesie nostre de soluendo redditu nostro plenarie statutis terminis . et quod nec artem nec ingenium exquiret vnde domus nostra per tenuram suam dampnum incurrat . et quod predictam terram neque vendet neque escambiet neque in vadimonium ponet nec alicui in feodum et hereditatem tradet neque ad alium locum religionis transferet sine assensu nostro. Eandem securitatem facient nobis heredes sui cum singuli sibi succedent. In cuius rei testimonium presens scriptum sigillo ecclesie nostre munitum diuiso inter nos cyrographo dicto Willelmo tradidimus. Hiis testibus . Ricardo Burg' . David Dunning . Ricardo filio Willelmi . magistro Waltero Scriptore . Ricardo de Bred' . Galfrido de Westun' et multis aliis.

156. *The other half of no. 155.*

G.C.L., 'Deeds and Seals', v, no. 42, fol. 20 (128 mm [left] × 192 mm [foot]), **Scribe 17**; slit for tag on turn-up; tag and seal missing; endorsements: Contra Will(elmu)m Hakespon' . (s. xiii^1), **Hand o/Scribe 17**; versus aulam regis in manu nostra (s. xiii^2); Registratur (s. xiv).

157. *Grant in fee and inheritance in the form of a chirograph by Abbot Henry and the convent of St. Peter's, Gloucester, to Richard furrier of land in the pelterers' quarter of Gloucester for 12s. annual rent. (1228 × 43)*

G.C.L., 'Deeds and Seals', x, no. 24, fol. 18 (115 mm [left] × 205 mm [foot]); slit for tag on turn-up; tag and seal missing; endorsements: Contra Ricardum parmentarium (s. xiii[1]); iii. Warda (*c.* s. xiii[med]); Stephanus Broun et W. de Bokelon de tertia warda (s. xiv[1]); sc(ribitur) (s. xiv[med]); Scriptum Ric(ard)i parmentarii[;] Registratur[;] In peletria (s. xiv[ex] × s. xv[in]).

C Y R O G R A P H V M (inverted)

Sciant presentes et futuri quod ego Henr(icus) dei gratia abbas et conuentus sancti Petri Glouc' concessimus Ricardo parmentario terram nostram in pelleteria Glouc' . illam scilicet quam Willelmus de Hereford de nobis tenuit que iacet inter terram que fuit Walteri de Cyrencestr' ex una parte et terram eiusdem Walteri ex altera parte . Tenendam de nobis in feodo et hereditate sibi et heredibus suis pro duodecim solidis nobis annuatim duobus anni terminis persoluendis medietatate ad festum sancti Michaelis et alia medietate ad Hokeday[.] Quando uero predictus Ricardus predictam terram a nobis recepit edificium superpositum appreciatum fuit unam marcam. Predicta uero terra per uisum legalium uirorum mensurata habet in fronte tres uirgas ulnarias et vnum quarterium cum pollice interposito . Retro tres uirgas ulnarias et vnum quarterium et dimidium quarterium cum pollice interposito [.] In profunditate septem uirgas ulnarias uno quarterio minus cum pollice interposito. Si uero aliquo casu emergente contigerit quod ipse uel heredes sui predictam terram nobis reliquerint simile edificium aut pretium nobis restituent. Idem uero Ricardus iuramentum nobis prestitit quod fidelis erit ecclesie nostre et maxime de reddendo redditu nostro plenarie statutis terminis et quod nec artem nec ingenium exquiret unde domus nostra per tenuram suam dampnum incurrat et quod predictam terram neque uendet neque excambiet neque in uadimonium ponet neque alicui in feodum et hereditatem tradet neque ad alium locum religionis transferet sine assensu nostro[.] Eandem securitatem nobis facient heredes sui cum sibi singuli succedent et tam ipse quam heredes sui curiam nostram sequentur[.] In cuius rei testimonium presens scriptum in modum cyrographi inter nos confecimus cuius unam partem sigillo ecclesie nostre munitam ei tradidimus . alteram uero partem penes nos retinuimus. Hiis testibus . Ricardo Burgense . Waltero Hoihc . Galfrido Cuttestuchen tunc preposito Glouc' . Ricardo filio Yde . Radulfo fratre suo . Rogero parmentario . Nicholo scisore . Ada de Hereford et multis aliis.

158. *The other half of no. 157.*

G.C.L., 'Deeds and Seals', x, no. 27, fol. 20 (120 mm [left] × 205 mm [foot]); heavily stained; tag through slit on turn-up; seal missing, but residue of white wax on tag; endorsements: .iii.[a] Warda (*c.* s. xiii[med]); A (s. xiii) .iii. Warda; Ricardus parmentarius (s. xiii[ex] × s. xiv[in]); in pelleteria (uncertain date).

159. *Grant in fee and inheritance in the form of a chirograph by Abbot Henry and the convent of St. Peter's, Gloucester, to Geoffrey Scin of land (in Gloucester?) for 8s. annual rent. (1228 × 43)*

H.C.L., no. 1633 (120 mm [left] × 206 mm [foot]), **Scribe 16**; slit for tag on foot; tag and seal missing; no endorsements; cal. in Baddeley ii, no. 61, p. 25.

C Y R O G R A P H V M (*inverted*)

Sciant presentes et futuri quod ego Henr(icus) dei gratia abbas et conuentus sancti Petri Glouc' concessimus Galfrido Scin terram nostram quam Nicholaus de Infirmaria quondam de nobis tenuit . illam scilicet que iacet inter terram que fuit Radulfi Ianitoris . et terram que fuit Gilberti Gundrich'[.] Tenendam et habendam de nobis in feodo et hereditate sibi et heredibus suis pro octo solidis nobis annuatim persoluendo ad quattuor anni terminos . videlicet ad festum sancti Michaelis duobus solidis . ad Nativitatem domini duobus solidis . ad Annuntiationem beate Marie duobus solidis . et ad Natiuitatem beati Iohannis Baptiste duobus solidis. Quando uero predictus Galfridus predictam terram a nobis recepit. edificium superpositum appreciatum est quatuor marcas argenti. Si uero aliquo casu emergente ipse uel heredes sui predictam terram reliquerint. simile edificium uel pretium nobis restituent. Predicta uero terra per uisum legalium uirorum immensurata. habet in fronte sex uirgas ulnarias et dimidiam cum pollice interposito et duos pollices . In profunditate. quadraginta tres uirgas ulnarias et dimidiam cum pollice interposito . Retro. sex uirgas ulnarias et dimidiam cum pollice interposito et duos pollices. Idem uero Galfridus iuramentum nobis prestitit quod fidelis erit ecclesie nostre de soluendo redditu nostro plenarie statutis terminis . et quod nec artem nec ingenium exquiret vnde domus nostra per tenuram suam dampnum incurrat . et quod predictam terram neque vendet neque escambiet neque in vadimonium ponet . nec alicui in feodum et hereditatem tradet neque ad alium locum religionis transferet sine assensu nostro. Eandem securitatem facient nobis heredes sui cum singuli sibi succedent. In cuius rei testimonium presens scriptum sigillo ecclesie nostre munitum diuiso inter nos cyrographo dicto Galfrido tradidimus. Hiis testibus . Ricardo Burg' . Dauid Dunnig' . Iohanne Draperio, Willelmo feragu . Galfrido de Weston' . Ricardo de Bredon' . Waltero de g'aua . Nicholao clerico et multis aliis.

The land which Geoffrey received may be that belonging to him which was referred to in a charter listing a number of Gloucester tenements (*Cart. Glouc.* ii, no. 807).

160. *Lifetime lease in the form of a chirograph by Abbot Henry and the convent of St. Peter's, Gloucester, to Emma widow of Richard de la ston' of ¹/₂ virgate in Wotton (St. Mary Without) for 10s. annual rent and 2s. for the abbot's aid and two ploughing services, one in the winter and the other in summer, and three reaping services annually. (1228 × 43)*

G.C.L., 'Deeds and Seals', vii, no. 20, fol. 12 (111 mm [left] × 120 mm [foot]), **Scribe 18**; seal on tag, repaired, oval (length, unavail.; width, *c.* 25 mm); a partial cross-shaped device with fleur-de-lis at the three visible ends; legend: . . .LL.'EMME FIL' . . .; no counterseal; endorsements: Wotton' (s. xiii[ex]); .Bertona (s. xiv[1]); Registratur (s. xiv); ad terminem vite (s. xv?).

CYROGRAPHVM

Sciant presentes et futuri quod ego Henr(icus) dei gratia abbas et conuentus sancti Petri Glouc' concessimus Emme relicte Ricardi de La ston' dimidiam virgatam terre cum pertinentiis in Wotton' illam scilicet quam modo tenet . Tenendam et habendam de nobis tantum in uita sua . Reddendo nobis annuatim decem solidos de redditu et duos solidos ad auxilium abbatis et faciet nobis singulis annis duas arruras vnam scilicet in yeme et aliam in estate et tres bedripas cum vno homine pro omnibus seruitiis quam diu vixerit. Post decessum uero ipsius Emme dicta dimidia uirgata terre cum omni melioratione superposita ad nos sine alicuius contraditione libere reuertetur. In cuius rei testimonium presens scriptum diuiso inter nos cyrographo confecimus . Cuius unam partem sigillo ecclesie nostre munitam ei tradidimus . Alteram uero partem sigillo ipsius roboratam penes nos retinuimus. Hiis testibus . magistro Waltero scriptore . Roberto le sauuage . Drogone de Puntif . Galfrido de Weston' . Mauricio stabulario . Nicholao Clerico . et multis aliis.

161. Grant in fee and inheritance in the form of a chirograph by Abbot Henry and the convent of St. Peter's, Gloucester, of land in Kingsholm (by Gloucester) to Ralph Swetowe for 2s. annual rent payable to their almoner. (1228 × 43)

G.C.L., 'Deeds and Seals', viii, no. 13, fol. 7 (145 mm [left] × 246 mm [foot]); seal on tag, white wax stained green; fragment, repaired; obverse: oval (27 mm; width unavail.); fleur-de-lis; legend: +S'R. . .PI: S. . .; no counterseal; endorsements: versus Aulam Regis (s. xiii[ex] × s. xiv[in]); Registratur (s. xiv[ex] × s. xv[in]).

C. . .R O G. . .A P H U. . .

Sciant presentes et futuri quod ego Henric(us) dei gratia abbas et conuentus sancti Petri Glouc' concessimus Radulfo Swetowe terram uersus aulam regis . Illam scilicet que iacet inter terram prioris sancti Oswaldi et terram Ade de Twigeworth' . Tenendam et habendam de nobis in feudo et hereditate sibi et heredibus suis pro duobus solidis elemosinario nostro qui pro tempore fuerit annuatim duobus terminis persoluendis . Medietate ad Hock(edai) et alia medietate ad festum sancti Michaelis. Predicta vero terra per visum legalium virorum mensurata est et habet in fronte septem virgas vlnarias et vnum quarterium cum pollice interposito et quotuor pollices . In profunditate triginta quatuor virgas vlnarias cum pollice interposito dimidio quarterio minus . In medio nouem virgas ulnarias et vnum quarterium cum pollice interposito et quatuor pollices . Retro decem virgas ulnarias cum pollice interposito vno quarterio minus. Quando uero predictus Radulfus predictam terram .a. nobis recepit edificium superpositum appreciatum est quinque solidos. Si autem aliquo casu emergente ipse vel heredes sui predictam terram nobis reliquerint simile edificium aut pretium nobis restituent. Idem uero Radulfus nobis iuramentum prestitit quod fidelis erit ecclesie nostre de soluendo redditu nostro plenarie statutis terminis et quod nec artem nec ingenium exquiret . vnde domus nostra per tenuram suam dampnum incurrat et quod predictam terram neque vendet . neque excambiet . neque in vademonium ponet nec alicui in feudum et hereditatem tradet neque ad alium locum religionis transferet sine assensu nostro. Eandem securitatem facient nobis heredes sui cum singuli sibi succedent. In cuius rei testimonium presens scriptum sigillo ecclesie nostre munitum diuiso . inter nos cirographo ei tradidimus. Hiis testibus . Willelmo fatte . Henrico Ruffo . Galfrido clerico . Waltero molendinario . Ada Le Poter . Iurdano Vilatore et aliis.

162. *The other half of no. 161.*

A. G.C.L., 'Deeds and Seals', i, no. 49, fol. 26 (139 mm [right] × currently 232 mm [foot; current meas.; orig. 236 mm]); damaged; slit for tag on turn-up; tag and seal missing; endorsement: Radulfus Swetoue de terra uersus aulam regis. (s. xiii^{ex} × s. xiv^{in}); **B**. ibid. 'Reg. B', no. 514, p. 226.

163. *Grant in the form of a chirograph by Abbot Henry and the convent of St. Peter's, Gloucester, to William miller of land in Kingsholm (by Gloucester) for 7s. annual rent. (1228 × 43; poss. 1205 × 24)*

A. G.C.L., 'Deeds and Seals', i, no. 28, fol. 16 (119 mm [left] × 182 mm [foot]), **Scribe 16**; slit for tag through turn-up; tag and seal missing; endorsements: Contra Willelmum molendinarium (s. xiii^{med}), **Hand I**; versus aulam regis (s. xiii^{2}?); Registratur (s. xiv^{ex} × s. xv^{in}); Corf molendinarius tenet. Anno regis Henrici quinti quinto (s. xv); **B**. ibid. 'Reg. B', no. 508, pp. 223–4.

CYROGRAPHVM (*inverted*)

Sciant presentes et futuri quod ego Henr(icus) dei gratia abbas et conuentus sancti Petri Glouc' concessimus Willelmo molendinario et heredibus suis terram nostram que iacet inter terram Milonis de Sandhurste et terram Hugonis Greneturcel uersus aulam regis pro septem solidis elemosinario nostro qui pro tempore fuerit. annuatim persoluendis duobus terminis . scilicet ad Annuntiationem beate Marie tribus solidis et sex denariis . et ad festum sancti Michaelis tribus solidis et sex denariis. Predicta uero terra per uisum legalium uirorum mensurata habet in fronte quatuordecim uirgas ulnarias et dimidiam et dimidium quarterium pollice interposito . In profunditate uero quinquaginta uirgas ulnarias cum pollice interposito . Retro autem octodecim uirgas ulnarias et dimidiam cum pollice interposito. Quando uero Willelmus predictam terram de nobis recepit edificium superpositum appreciatum est quatuor marcas et dimidiam. Si uero idem Willelmus uel heredes sui aliquo casu emergente predictam terram reliquerint. simile edificium uel pretium nobis restituent. Idem uero Willelmus iuramentum nobis prestitit quod fidelis erit ecclesie nostre de soluendo redditu nostro plenarie statutis terminis . et quod nec artem nec ingenium exquiret vnde domus nostra per tenuram suam dampnum incurrat . et quod predictam terram neque vendet neque excambiet . neque in vadimonium ponet . nec alicui in feodum et hereditatem tradet . neque ad alium locum religionis transferet sine assensu nostro. Eandem securitatem facient nobis heredes sui cum singuli sibi succedent. In cuius rei testimonium presens scriptum sigillo ecclesie nostre munitum diuiso inter nos cyrographo ei tradidimus. Hiis testibus . Waltero scriptore . Dauid Dunnig' . Drogone Pincerna . Willelmo de Sanford . Galfrido Ianitore[1] . Petro Clerico . et aliis.

---

[1] **B** omits the witnesses' names between David Dunning and Peter Clerk.

164. *Final concord between Henry abbot of St. Peter's, Gloucester, and Rohese daughter of Henry Maloysel, Ralph of Taynton and Cecilia his wife, Thomas Dun and Hawisia his wife, and Margaret Musket, concerning one third of a knight's fee in Hope Mansell (Herefs.), which they acknowledge to be the right of the abbot and his church; for the acknowledgement the abbot gave them 4 marks. 18 November 1230. Westminster.*

P.R.O., CP 25/1/80/7, no. 121 (110 mm [left] × 189 mm [foot]); no endorsement.

CYROGRAPHVM

Hec est finalis concordia facta in curia domini regis apud West' . In octaba sancti Martini . anno regni regis Henrici filii regis Iohannis quatrodecimo . Coram Thoma de Multon' . Stephano de Seg'aue . Willelmo de Ralegh' . Roberto de Lexinton' . Willelmo de Insul' . Willelmo de Lond' . magistro Roberto de Scherdelawe . iustic(iis) . et aliis domini regis fidelibus tunc ibi presentibus . Inter Henr(icum) abbatem Gloucestr' querentem per fratrem Elyam monachum suum positum loco ipsius abbatis ad lucrandum uel perdendum et Roesiam filiam Henrici Maloysel . Radulfum de Teynton' et Ceciliam vxorem eius . Thomam Dun . et Hawisiam vxorem eius . et Margaretam Musket impedientes de tercia parte feodi vnius militis cum pertinentiis . In Oppe Maloysel . Vnde placitum warantie carte sumonita fuit inter eos in eadem curia . Scilicet quod predicta Roesia . Radulfus . Cecilia . Thomas . Hawisia . et Margareta recognouerunt totam predictam terram cum pertinentiis esse ius ipsius abbatis . et ecclesie sue Gloucestr' . Vt illam quam idem abbas habet ex dono ipsorum . Roesie . Radulfi . Cecilie . Thome . Hawisie . et Margarete . Habendam et tenendam eidem abbati et successoribus suis et ecclesie sue de Gloucestr' . de predictis Roesia . Radulfo . Cecilia . Thoma. Hawisia . et Margareta. et heredibus earundem Roesie . Cecilie . Hawisie . et Margarete . in liberam et perpetuam elemosinam . i(n)perpetuum . Faciendo inde seruitium capitalibus dominis eiusdem feodi quod ad predictam terram pertinet . pro omni seruitio et exactione. Et pro hac recognitione . fine . et concordia idem abbas dedit predictis Roesie . Radulfo . Cecilie . Thome . Hawisie . et Margarete quatuor marcas argenti.

Hereford'

165. *Lease in the form of a chirograph by Abbot Henry and the convent of St. Peter's, Gloucester, of Colethrop for thirty years to Richard of Hatherley chaplain, but reserving all rents and services owed by the land. 29 September 1234.*

H.C.L., no. 1582 (86 mm [left] × 124 mm [foot]), **Scribe 18** (below, Plate XXa); seal on tag, green wax, damaged, one large and several small fragments; obverse (below, Plate If): oval (67 mm × 37 mm [incomplete meas.]): partial image of an abbot holding a staff or crozier in the right hand; legend: +S. . . CESTRA; reverse: a counterseal, oval (44 mm × 26 mm [incomplete meas.]): an abbot standing to front in pontificals; in the right hand a staff or crozier; in the left an upraised book; legend: . . .RETVM . . .OVC. . .TRIE; endorsement: Non registratur (s. xiii^ex); cal. in Baddeley ii, no. 41, p. 21.

CYROGRAPHUM (*inverted*)

Sciant presentes et futuri quod ego Henr(icus) dei gratia abbas et conuentus sancti Petri Glouc' anno ab Incarnatione domini millesimo ducentesimo trecesimo quarto ad festum sancti Michaelis ad petitionem Hugonis Cole liberi hominis nostri concessimus et confirmauimus domino Ricardo de Heþerleye Capellano traditionem totius terre ipsius Hugonis Cole que est in Coleþrop usque ad terminum triginta annorum continue sequentium . saluis nobis redditibus . seruitiis . sectis et wardis et omnibus aliis consuetudinibus ad illam terram pertinentibus . In cuius rei testimonium presens scriptum diuiso inter nos cyrographo confecimus . Cuius unam partem sigillo ecclesie nostra munitam ei tradidimus. Alteram uero partem sigilio ipsius roboratam penes nos retinuimus.

This was the tenant's copy. Note the lack of an attestation clause. The present editor is grateful to Miss Joan Williams, Librarian of Hereford Cathedral Library, for help with the measurements of the seal.

166. *Final concord between Henry son of William and Henry abbot of St. Peter's, Gloucester, concerning ½ virgate in Hartpury; which the abbot acknowledged to be the right of Henry son of William, to hold of the abbot and his church for 5s. 10d. annual rent; for the acknowledgement Henry quitclaimed to the abbot and his church all his right and claim in the serjeanty for the forest of Wynebrugg'. 21 June 1236. Gloucester.*

P.R.O., CP 25/1/73/10, no. 170 (damaged; 103 mm [right] × 199 mm [foot]); no endorsement.

...R O...A P...U M

[Hec] est finalis concordia facta in curia domini regis apud Glouc' die sabbati proxima ante festum sancti Iohannis Baptiste anno regni regis [Hen]rici filii Iohannis vicesimo . Coram Willelmo de Ebor' . Willelmo de Insula . Radulfo de Norwic' . Thurstano le despens' . et Radulfo [d]e Chandos iustic(iis) itinerantibus et omnibus domini regis fidelibus tunc ibi presentibus . Inter Henr(icum) filium Will(elm)i petentem et Henricum abbatem Glouc' tenentem de dimidia virgata terre cum pertinentiis in Hardepyrie . vnde assisa mortis antecessoris summonita fuit inter eos in eadem curia . scilicet quod predictus abbas recognouit totam predictam terram cum pertinentiis esse ius ipsius Henr(ici) . Habendam et tenendam eidem Henr(ico) et heredibus suis de predicto abbate et successoribus suis et ecclesia sua de Glouc' inperpetuum'. reddendo inde annuatim quinque solidos et decem denarios sterlingorum ad duos terminos anni . scilicet medietatem ad festum sancte Michaelis et alteram medietatem ad Annuntiationem beate Marie pro omni seruitio et exactione. Pro hac recognitione fine et concordia'. idem Henr(icus) remisit et quietam clamauit de se et heredibus suis predicto abbati et successoribus suis et ecclesie sue de Glouc' totum ius et clam(ium) quod habuit in seriantia foreste de Wynebrugg' inperpetuum.

Glouc'

167. *Final concord between William Caperun and Henry abbot of Gloucester concerning half a messuage in Gloucester, which William quitclaimed to the abbot and his church; for the quitclaim the abbot gave William 20s. 15 July 1241. Gloucester.*

A. P.R.O., CP 25/1/73/16, no. 303 (damaged; measurements: 74 mm [left] × 181 mm [foot]); no endorsement; B. G.C.L., 'Reg. B', no. 884, pp. 381–2.

C Y R O G R A P...

Hec est finalis concordia facta in curia domini regis apud Glouc' a die sancti Iohannis Baptiste in tres [septimanas anno][1] regis Henrici filii regis Iohannis vicesimo quinto. Coram Roberto de Lexinton' . Radulfo de Sulleg' . Will[elmo de Culewurch'][2] Iollano de Neuill' et Roberto de Haya iustic(iis) itinerantibus et aliis domini regis fidelibus tunc ibi presentibus . Inter Will(elmu)m Caperun petentem et Henricum abbatem Glouc' . tenentem de medietate vnius mesuagii in Glouc' . vnde placitum fuit inter eos in eadem curia . Scilicet quod predictus Will(elmu)s remisit et quietam clamauit de se et heredibus predicto abbati et successoribus suis et ecclesie sue de

Glouc' totum ius et clamium quod habuit in medietate predicti mesuagii cum pertinentiis inperpetuum. Et pro hac remissione quieta clamantia fine et concordia.ˊ idem abbas dedit predicto Will(elm)o viginti solidos sterlingorum.

Glouc'

¹ Added from **B**.
² Added from **B**.

168. *Final concord between Roger farrier and Henry abbot of St. Peter's, Gloucester, concerning a virgate in Upleadon, which Roger quitclaimed to the abbot and his church; for the quitclaim the abbot gave him 1 mark. 22 July 1241. Gloucester.*

A. P.R.O., CP 25/1/73/15, no. 278 (damaged; 91 mm [left] × 151 mm [foot]); no endorsement; **B.** ibid. C.150/1, no. 827, fol. 224v; *Cart. Glouc.* ii, no. 830.

C Y R O G R A P H U...

Hec est finalis concordia facta in curia Domini Regis apud Glouc' . a die sancti Iohannis [Bap]tiste in vnum mensem anno regni regis Henrici filii regis Iohannis vicesimo quin[to .] Coram Roberto de Lexinton' . Radulfo de Sulleg' . Willelmo de Culewurth' . Iollano de Neuill' et Roberto de Haya iustic(iis) itinerantibus et aliis domini regis fidelibus tunc ibi presentibus [.] Inter Rog(eru)m Marescall(um) petentem et Henricum abbatem Glouc' tenentem de vna virgata terre cum pertinentiis in Leden' . vnde assisa mortis antecessoris summonita fuit inter eos in eadem curia . Scilicet quod predictus Rog(er)us remisit et quietam clamauit de se et heredibus suis . predicto abbati et successoribus suis et ecclesie sue de Glouc' . totum ius et clamium quod habuit in tota predicta terra cum pertinentiis inperpetuum. Et pro hac remissione et quieta clam(antia) fine et concordia.ˊ idem abbas dedit predicto Rog(er)o.ˊ vnam marcam argenti.

Glouc'

169. *Final concord between Robert son of Adam and Henry abbot of St. Peter's, Gloucester, concerning a virgate in Lower Ley, which Robert acknowledged to be the right of the abbot and his church; for this acknowledgement the abbot granted to Robert an annual payment for life of ½ mark and four crannocks of wheat, three crannocks of rye, and three crannocks of beans to be received at Ley from the master of the works. 29 July 1241. Gloucester.*

A. P.R.O., CP 25/1/73/13, no. 250 (91 mm [left] × 192 mm [foot]); no endorsement; **B.** G.C.L., 'Reg. B', no. 824, pp. 355–6.

C Y R O G R A P H V M

Hec est finalis concordia facta in curia domini regis apud Glouc' a die sancti Iohannis

Baptiste in quinque septimanas anno regis Henrici filii regis Iohannis vicesimo quinto coram Roberto de Lexinton' . Radulfo de Sulleg' . Willelmo de Culewrhe . Iollano Neuilla et Roberto de Haya iustic(iis) itinerantibus et aliis domini regis fidelibus tunc ibi presentibus inter Rob(ertum) filium Ade petentem et Henricum abbatem Glouc' tenentem de vna uirgata terre cum pertinentiis in Ley'a vnde assisa de morte antecessorum summonita fuit inter eos in eadem curia [.] scilicet quod predictus Rob(ertus) recognouit totam predictam terram cum pertinentiis esse ius ipsius abbatis et ecclesie sue de Glouc'[.] Et pro hac recognitione et finali concordia idem abbas concessit pro se et successoribus suis dicto Rob(erto) dimidiam marcam argenti et quatuor cronocos frumenti et tres cronocos siliginis et tres cronocos fabarum annuatim percipiendos apud Leyg' per manum magistri operis predicte ecclesie quicumque pro tempore fuerit magister tota uita ipsius Rob(erti)[.] Et post decessum ipsius Rob(erti) predictus abbas et ecclesia sua predicta quieti erint de solutione predicte dimidie marce et predicti bladi inperpetuum.

GLOVC

For the identification of Lower Ley see G.C.L., 'Reg. B', no. 815, p. 352; *PNG*, iii. 203. The text of Abbot Henry's grant of the ½ mark and the other specified items is in G.C.L., 'Reg. B', no. 821, pp. 354–5.

170. *Final concord between Hawisia de Londres and the abbot of Gloucester concerning the advowson of the church of Hannington (Wilts.), which the abbot acknowledged to be the right of Hawisia and which he rendered to her; he acknowledged also that the advowson of the church of East Garston (Berks.) which he had by the gift of Hawisia's ancestor Maurice de Londres was the right of Hawisia, and he remitted and quitclaimed both advowsons to her. For this, Hawisia granted to the abbot and his church the advowson of the church of Colwinston in the county of Cardiff (Glam.), remitted and quitclaimed the maintenance of a groom and a horse which she had at Ewenny Priory, and granted a water mill which the abbot had built in Ewenny on Hawisia's land. 16 February 1242. Reading.*

P.R.O., CP 25/1/284/18, no. 57 (145 mm [left] × 192 mm [foot]); no endorsement.

CYROGR...PH...M

Hec est finalis concordia facta in curia domini regis apud Radding' a die Purificationis beate Marie in quindecim dies . Anno regni regis Henrici filii regis Iohannis vicesimo sexto . Coram ipso domino rege . Willelmo de Ebor' preposito Beuerl' . Willelmo de Cantilupo . Bertramo de Crioll' senescallo domini regis . Henrico de Bathon' et Ieremia de Caxtan' iustic(iis) . et aliis domini regis fidelibus tunc ibi presentibus . Inter Hauwisia(m) de London' querentem et abbatem de Glouc' per Willelmum de Lastindon' positum loco suo ad lucrandum uel perdendum impediente(m) de aduocatione ecclesie de Hanedon' . vnde placitum suum fuit inter eos in eadem curia . Scilicet quod predictus abbas recognouit pro se et successoribus suis et ecclesia sua de Glouc' aduocationem predicte ecclesie esse ius ipsius Hauwis(ie) et illam ei reddidit in eadem curia. Recognouit etiam idem abbas pro se et successoribus suis et ecclesia sua predictam aduocationem ecclesie Esgarestun' quam habuit de dono Mauricii de London' antecessoris ipsius Hauwis(ie) esse ius ipsius Hauwis(ie) . et aduocationes predictarum ecclesiarum de Hanedon' et Esgareston' remisit et quietaclamauit pro se et successoribus suis et ecclesia sua predicta eidem Hauwis(ie) et heredibus suis inperpetuum. Et pro ista recognitione [.] redditione . remissione . quietaclamatione . fine et concordia⸍ eadem Hauwis(ia) concessit eidem abbati et successoribus suis et ecclesie sue de Glouc' aduocationem ecclesie de Colwinestun' in comitatu de Kaerdith . et remisit pro se et heredibus suis eidem abbati et successoribus suis et ecclesia sue predicte totum ius et clamum quod habuit in aduocatione predicte ecclesie inperpetuum. Et preterea eadem Hauwis(ia) pro se et heredibus suis remisit eidem abbati et successoribus suis et ecclesie sue predicte perhendinationem vnius garcionis et vnius equi quam habuit per annum in prioratu ipsius abbatis de Eweny inperpetuum. Concessit etiam pro se et heredibus suis quod idem abbas et successoribus sui et ecclesia sua predicta habeant et teneant quoddam molendinum aquaticum in Eweny quod idem abbas construxit super territorium ipsius Hauwisie in pace et quiete de ipsa Hauwia(ia) et heredibus suis inperpetuum.

Wilt'

171. *Grant in the form of a chirograph by Abbot John and the convent of St. Peter's, Gloucester, of two virgates in Churcham to Ernald Barun for suit of court for the abbey and Churcham manor in hundreds and shires, and for suit of court at the abbey and at its court at Churcham twice a year, and for 20s. annual rent. (1243 × 63)*

G.C.L., 'Deeds and Seals', i, no. 39, fol. 22 (122 mm [left] × 240 mm [foot]); fragment of tag; seal missing; endorsements: De terra de Chirihchom' (s. xiii^med); Caps(ula) .x. de laicis tenuris (s. xiii^2); Carta Ernaldi Barun de duabus uirgatis in Chyrcham. C. temporalium parte 2^a. (*c.* s. xiv^ex); Registratur (s. xiv^ex × s. xv^in).

C Y R O G R A P H V...

Sciant presentes et futuri quod ego Ioh(ann)es dei gratia abbas et conuentus sancti Petri Glouc' . dedimus . concessimus . et hac presenti carta nostra confirmamus Ernaldo Barun . et Matillde vxori sue duas uirgatas terre cum pertinentiis suis in manerio nostro de Chirchamm' . Illas uidelicet quas Willelmus freman de Chirchamm' de nobis aliquando tenuit . Tenendas et habendas de nobis et successoribus nostris sibi et heredibus suis libere et quiete pro sequelis faciendis ab eisdem et eorum heredibus pro nobis et manerio nostro de Chirchamm' in hundredis et comitatibus . Pro sequela etiam curie nostre in abbatia nostra cum ceteris liberis hominibus nostris quotiens eam sedere contigerit . Et sequela curie nostre de Chircham' bis per annum ab eisdem et eorum heredibus nobis similiter facienda . Et pro viginti solidis sterlingorum nobis et successoribus nostris annuatim ab eisdem et eorum heredibus ad duos terminos persoluendis . videlicet medietate ad Annuntiationem beate Marie . et alia medietate ad festum sancti Michaelis . pro omni exactione et seculari demanda saluo regali seruitio. Pro hac autem concessione et donatione nostra . dicti Ernaldus et Matillda vxor eius dederunt nobis premanibus triginta tres marcas argenti. Idem uero Ernaldus et Matillda vxor eius iuramentum nobis prestiterunt . quod fideles erint ecclesie nostre . et maxime de reddendo redditu nostro plenarie statutis terminis . et de predictis seruitiis fideliter faciendis . et quod predictam terram neque uendent . neque escambient . neque in uadimonium in judaismo ponent . neque ad alium locum religionis transferent sine assensu et uoluntate nostra. Eandem securitatem nobis facient heredes sui cum singuli sibi succedent. In cuius rei testimonium presens scriptum in modum cyrographi inter nos confectum est . Cuius unam partem sigillo ecclesie nostre munitam dictis Ernaldo et Matillde tradidimus. Alteram uero partem sigillo ipsius Ernaldi roboratam´ penes nos retinuimus. Hiis testibus . Waltero de Pulton' . Waltero de Heydon' . Helya de Heydon' . Waltero de Blakeneye . Godefrido le fauconer . Adam le fauconer . et multis aliis.

172. *Grant in fee and inheritance in the form of a chirograph by Abbot John and the convent of St. Peter's, Gloucester, to Adam son of William Brasily of land on Castle Street (Gloucester) for 3s. annual rent payable to the almoner. (1243 × 63)*

G.C.L., 'Deeds and Seals', iv, no. 23, fol. 11 (112 mm [left] × 177 mm [foot]); slit for tag on foot; tag and seal missing; endorsement: in vico cast(ri) (s. xiii[ex]?).

CYROGRAPHVM

Sciant presentes et futuri quod ego Ioh(ann)es dei gratia abbas et conventus sancti Petri Glouc' . concessimus Ade filio Willelmi Brasily quandam terram nostram in vico castri Glouc' . illam scilicet que iacet inter terram que fuit Roberti Lormarii et terram Ade carpentarii . Tenendam et habendam de nobis in feudo et hereditate sibi et heredibus suis . Reddendo inde annuatim elemosinario nostro qui pro tempore fuerit tres solidos ad duos anni terminos . Videlicet medietatem ad festum sancti Michaelis . et aliam medietatem ad Annuntiationem beate Marie. Predicta uero terra per visum legalium virorum mensurata continet in anteriori parte sex uirgas ulnarias cum pollice interposito duobus pollicibus minus . In longitudine viginti uirgas ulnarias cum pollice interposito et tres pollices . In medio sex uirgas ulnarias et dimidiam cum pollice interposito et vnum quarterium . Retro octo uirgas ulnarias et vnum quarterium cum pollice interposito. Quando uero predictus Adam predictam terram a nobis recepit´ edificium superpositum appreciatum fuit dimidiam marcam. Si uero aliquo casu emergente ipse uel heredes sui predictam terram nobis reliquerint´ simile edificium uel pretium nobis restituent. Idem uero iuramentum nobis prestitit quod fidelis erit ecclesie nostre . et maxime de reddendo redditu nostro plenarie terminis statutis. Si uero in aliquo termino defecerit in solvendo׳ licebit nobis dictam terram in manus nostras capere . et tamdiu retinere quousque nobis plenarie satisfecerit . Iuramentum etiam quod nec artem nec ingenium exquiret . vnde domus nostra per tenuram suam dampnum incurrat . et quod predictam terram neque uendet neque excambiet neque in vadimonium ponet neque alicui in feudum et hereditatem tradet neque ad alium locum religionis transferet sine assensu et uoluntate nostra. Eandem securitatem nobis facient heredes sui cum singuli sibi succedent . et tam ipse quam heredes in curiam nostram sequentur. In cuius testmonium presens scriptum in modum cyrographi inter nos confectum est . Cuius vnam partem sigillo ecclesie nostre munitam dicto Ade tradidimus. Alteram uero partem sigillo ipsius roboratam penes nos retinuimus. Hiis testibus. Willelmo de Sumery . Iohanne Symund tunc bailliuis Glouc' . Willelmo de London' . Willemino lormario . Adam carpentario et aliis.

The witness William de London' appears to be a local Gloucester figure who attested charters c. 1250 to c. 1280 (Stevenson, nos. 480, 490, 684; see also nos. 89–90).

173. *Grant in fee and inheritance in the form of a chirograph by Abbot John and the convent of St. Peter's, Gloucester, to John smith of Travel Lane of land on Longsmith Street in Gloucester for 10s. annual rent. (1243 × 63)*

G.C.L., 'Deeds and Seals', i, no. 7, fol. 4 (145 mm [left] × 178 mm [foot]), **Scribe 19**; tag for seal; seal missing, but remains of white wax on tag; endorsement: .iii.ª Warda (s. xiii^{ex} × s. xiv^{in}).

C...ROGRAPHV...

Sciant presentes et futuri quod ego Ioh(ann)es dei gratia abbas et conuentus sancti Petri Glouc' concessimus Iohanni fabro de Traueilon' terram nostram in vico fabrorum Glouc' que iacet inter terram Galfridi Cuttestuch' et terram Elye pistoris in angulo uenelle que ducit uersus ecclesiam sancte Trinitatis . Tenendam de nobis in feodo et hereditate sibi et heredibus suis . Reddendo inde nobis annuatim decem solidos ad .iiii.^{or} anni terminos . videlicet ad festum sancti Michaelis duos solidos et sex denarios . et ad Natale duos solidos et sex denarios . et ad Annuntiationem beate Marie duos solidos et sex denarios . et ad Natiuitatem sancti Iohannis Baptiste duos solidos et sex denarios . Predicta uero terra per uisum legalium uirorum mensurata continet in fronte in latitudine sexdecim virgas ulnarias cum pollice interposita . tribus pollicibus minus . In profunditate iuxta predictam uenellam septemdecim uirgas ulnarias cum pollice interposito . et dimidium quarterium. Quando uero predictus Iohannes predictam terram a nobis recepit׳ edificium superpositum appreciatum fuit decem solidos . Si uero aliquo casu emergente ipse uel heredes sui predictam terram nobis reliquirent׳ simile edificium uel pretium nobis restituent. Idem uero iuramentum nobis prestitit . quod fidelis erit ecclesie nostre . et maxime de reddendo redditu nostro plenarie terminis statutis. Si uero in aliquo termino defecerit in soluendo. licebit nobis dictam terram in manus nostras capere . et tamdiu retinere . quousque nobis plenarie satisfecerit. Iurauit etiam quod nec artem nec ingenium exquiret . vnde domus nostra per tenuram suam dampnum incurrat . et quod predictam terram neque uendet neque excambiet . neque in uadimonium ponet . neque alicui in feudum et hereditatem tradet . neque ad alium locum religionis transferet sine assensu et uoluntate nostra. Eandem securitatem nobis facient heredes sui cum singuli sibi succedent . et tam ipse quam heredes sui curiam nostram sequentur. In cuius rei testimonium presens scriptum in modum cyrographi inter nos confectum est . Cuius unam partem sigillo ecclesie nostre munitam dicto Iohanni tradidimus. Alteram uero partem sigillo ipsius roboratam penes nos retinuimus. Hiis testibus . Iohanne draperio . Gilberto aurifabro . Iohanne Walense . Symone le stempere . Iohanne Clench . Willelmo de Nortun' et multis aliis.

174. *Grant in the form of a chirograph by Abbot John and the convent of St. Peter's, Gloucester, of land on Castle Street (Gloucester) to Richard of Keynsham mason for 19s. annual rent. (1243 × 63)*

G.C.L., 'Deeds and Seals', iii, no. 1, fol. 1 (99 mm [left] × 177 mm [foot]); seal on tag; white wax, varnished, chipped; obverse (below, Plate Ih): oval (no accurate meas. avail.); an abbot or St. Benedict seated facing front; in the right hand a crozier; in the left an upraised book; legend illegible; reverse (below, Plate Ii): counterseal: pointed oval (45 mm × 26 mm); image of full-standing abbot or St. Benedict, nimbed, facing front; in the right hand a crozier, in the left an upraised book; legend: . . . SECRETVM S. . .CES. . .RIE; endorsement: iiii[a] Warda (s. xiii[ex] × s. xiv[in]).

C Y...O G R A P H V M

Sciant presentes et futuri quod ego Ioh(anne)s dei gratia abbas et conuentus sancti Petri Glouc' concessimus Ricardo de Kainesham cementario terram nostram que iacet inter terram Iohannis lorimerii et terram prioris sancti Bartholomei in vico castelli . Tenendam de nobis inperpetuum sibi et heredibus suis pro nouemdecim solidis quod nobis annuatim ad quatuor terminos persoluet . Videlicet ad festum sancti Iohannis Baptiste quatuor solidis et nouem denariis . ad festum sancti Michaelis quatuor solidis et nouem denariis . ad Natale domini quatuor solidis et nouem denariis . ad festum sancte Marie in Martio quatuor solidis et nouem denariis[.] Predicta uero terra per visum legalium virorum mensurata . continet in longitudine viginti quatuor virgas domini regis ulnarias et tres pollices cum pollice interposito . In capite versus castelli. quatuor uirgas et dimidiam . vno pollice minus . cum pollice interposito . In capite uersus magnam rutam. tres uirgas et tria quarteria cum pollice interposito. Quando uero dictus Ricardus dictam terram a nobis recepit edificium superpositum apreciatum fuit ad valorem centum solidorum. Si uero aliquo casu emergente ipse uel heredes sui dictam terram nobis reliquerint. simile edificium uel pretium nobis restituent. Idem iuramentum uero nobis prestitit quod fidelis erit ecclesie nostre et maxime de reddendo redditu nostro statutis terminis . et quod nec artem nec ingenium exquiret vnde domus nostra per tenuram suam dampnum incurrat . et quod predictam terram neque vendet neque excambiet . neque in vadimonium ponet neque alicui in feudum et hereditatem tradet neque ad[1] alterum locum religionis transferret sine assensu et voluntate nostra[.] Eandem securitatem nobis facient heredes sui cum singuli sibi succedent et tam ipse quam heredes sui curiam nostram sequentur. In cuius rei testimonium presens scriptum in modum cyrographi inter nos confectum est cuius unam partem sigillo nostro roboratam dicto Ricardo tradidimus . Alteram uero partem sigillo ipsi munitam penes nos retinuimus . Hiis testibus domino Hugone de aula regis . Iohanne filio Simonis . Willelmo de Chilteham . Ricardo de Celario . Ricardo franc' . Petro Cissore et multis aliis.

This is the tenant's copy. John son of Simon served as one of Gloucester's bailiffs *c.* 1240 × 65 (*VCH Glos.* iv. 372); in 1260 one of his fellow bailiffs was William of Cheltenham; William also served as bailiff with other colleagues in the period *c.* 1240 to perhaps 1269 (ibid.).

[1] Superscript in MS.

175. *Grant in fee and inheritance in the form of a chirograph by Abbot John and the convent of St. Peter's, Gloucester, of land on the* magna platea *below the castle lane (Gloucester) to Richard of Keynsham for 8s. annual rent. (1243 × 63)*

G.C.L., 'Deeds and Seals', ii, no. 21, fol. 11 (115 mm [left] × 170 mm [foot]), **Scribe 19**; seal on tag, white wax, fragment; obverse: portion of a seated abbot or St. Peter, facing front; reverse: lower portion of a standing abbot or St. Benedict, facing front; legend missing; endorsement: .iiii. Warda (s. xiii[med]).

C Y R [O] G R A P H [U] M (*inverted*)

Sciant presentes et futuri quod ego Ioh(ann)es dei gratia abbas et conuentus sancti Petri Glouc' . concessimus Ricardo de Keynesham' terram nostram in magna platea sub venella de Castellone . que iacet inter terram nostram et terram que fuit Willelmi Lorimarii . Tenendam de nobis in feudo et hereditate sibi et heredibus uel assignatis suis . Reddendo inde nobis annuatim octo solidos ad quatuor anni terminos . Videlicet ad festum sancti Andree duos solidos . ad Annuntiationem beate Marie duos solidos . ad Natiuitatem sancti Iohannis Baptiste duos solidos . et ad festum sancti Michaelis duos solidis. Predicta uero terra per uisum legalium uirorum mensurata . continet in fronte quatuor uirgas ulnarias cum pollice interposito . et vnum quarterium et dimidium . Retro quinque uirgas ulnarias cum pollice interposito . dimidio quarterio minus . In profunditate triginta duas uirgas ulnarias cum pollice interposito. Quando uero predictus Ricardus predictam terram a nobis recepit. edificium superpositum appreciatum fuit duas marcas. Si uero aliquo casu emergente ipse uel heredes siue assignati sui predictam terram nobis reliquerint. simile edificium uel pretium nobis restituent. Idem uero iuramentum nobis prestitit quod fidelis erit ecclesie nostre . et maxime de reddendo redditu nostro plenarie terminis statutis. Si uero in aliquo termino deficerit in soluendo. licebit nobis dictam terram in manus nostras capere . et tamdiu retinere. quousque nobis plenarie satisfecerit. Iurauit etiam quod nec artem nec ingenium exquiret . vnde domus nostra per tenuram suam dampnum incurrat . et quod predictam terram neque uendet neque excambiet neque in uadimonium ponet . neque alicui in feudum et hereditatem tradet . neque ad alium locum religionis transferet sine assensu et uoluntate nostra. Eandem securitatem nobis facient heredes uel assignati sui cum singuli sibi succedent . et tam ipse quam heredes uel assignati sui curiam nostram sequentur. Si uero aliquo processu temporis in dicta terra ius uendicare . et de eadem ipsum . heredes uel assignatos suos implacitare contingat´. non aduocabunt nos in warentum . sed ipsi suis expensis placitum sustinebunt . et dictam terram defendent. Quod si forte Ricardus . heredes uel assignati sui . eam per placitum perdiderint´. non recuperabunt super nos . neque terram . neque aliquid occasione dicte terre . expensarum . uel edificii superpositi. In cuius rei testimonimum presens scriptum in modum cyrographi inter nos confectum est . Cuius unam partem sigillo ecclesie nostre munitam dicto Ricardo tradidimus. Alteram uero partem sigillo ipsius roboratam´. penes nos retinuimus. Hiis testibus . Hugone de Kyngesham' . Adam Le Furbur . Ricardo Swift . Willelmo de London' . Willelmo Caperun . Willelmo de Norhamptun' . Henrico clerico . et aliis.

William Lorimer held land of St. Peter's on Castle Street (above, nos. 124–5). The *magna platea* may possibly have been Westgate Street or was located in the vicinity (see Lobel, *Gloucester*, 8).

176. Grant in fee and inheritance in the form of a chirograph by Abbot John and the convent of St. Peter's, Gloucester, to William of Owlpen of land in Gloucester by Southgate for 8s. annual rent payable to the almoner. (1243 × 63)

A. G.C.L., 'Deeds and Seals', vii, no. 7, fol. 4 (115 mm [left] × *c*. 169 mm [foot]); fragment of tag for seal; seal missing; endorsements: Olepenne (s. xiii^{med}); austral' (s. xiii^{med}?); Registratur (s. xiv^{ex} × s. xv^{in}); f (s. xv^{ex}); versus portam . . .Glouc' (s. xv^{ex}?)[1]; **B**. ibid. 'Reg. B', no. 664, pp. 288–9.

CYROGRAPHVM

Sciant presentes et futuri quod ego Ioh(ann)es dei gratia abbas et conuentus sancti Petri Glouc' concessimus Willelmo de Olepenn' terram nostram uersus portam australem Glouc' . Que iacet inter terram Iohannis Licoriz . et terram Iohannis blundi . Tenendam de nobis in feudo et hereditate sibi et heredibus suis . Reddendo inde annuatim elemosinario nostro octo solidos ad duos anni terminos . Scilicet unam medietatem ad festum beate Marie in Martio . et aliam medietatem ad festum sancti Michaelis. Predicta uero terra per uisum legalium uirorum mensurata continet de latitudine in fronte decem uirgas domini regis ulnarias cum pollice interposito . et vnum quarterium et dimidium . Retro uero vndecim uirgas domini regis ulnarias et dimidiam cum pollice interposito et unum pollicem . In profunditate iuxta terram Iohannis Licoriz viginti quatuor uirgas domini regis ulnarias cum pollice interposito

et unum quarterium et tres pollices . In profunditate iuxta terram Iohannis blundi
sexdecim uirgas domini regis ulnarias cum pollice interposito. Quando uero predictus
Willelmus predictam terram a nobis recepit'. edificium superpositum appreciatum
fuit decem solidos. Si uero aliquo casu emergente ipse uel heredes sui predictam
terram nobis reliquerint'. simile edificium uel pretium nobis restituent. Idem uero
iuramentum nobis prestitit quod fidelis erit ecclesie nostre . et maxime de reddendo
redditu nostro plenarie terminis statutis . et quod nec artem nec ingenium exquiret
vnde domus nostra per tenuram suam dampnum incurrat . et quod predictam terram
neque uendet neque excambiet neque in uadimonium ponet . neque alicui in feudum
et hereditatem tradet . neque ad alium locum religionis transferet sine assensu et
uoluntate nostra. Eandem securitatem nobis facient heredes sui cum singuli sibi
succedent. In cuius rei testimonium presens scriptum in modum cyrographi inter nos
confectum est . Cuius unam partem sigillo ecclesie nostre munitam dicto Willelmo
tradidimus . alteram uero partem sigillo ipsius roboratam penes nos retinuimus. Hiis
testibus . Willelmo Sumery . Iohanne Symund tunc bailliuis Glouc'[2] . Dauid Le
Taylur . Iohanne le Blunt . Waltero de sancto Dauid . Ricardo Crupel . et multis aliis.

William Somery served as one of Gloucester's bailiffs *c.* 1240 × *c.* 1265 and specifically in
1244, 1245, 1247, 1248 (*VCH Glos.* iv. 372).

[1] These words were written on each side of *austral'*.
[2] **B** ends here with *et aliis*.

177. *Grant in fee and inheritance in the form of a chirograph by Abbot John and
the convent of St. Peter's, Gloucester, of land outside Northgate (Gloucester) to
Robert rich for 5s. annual rent. (1243–63; poss. 1284 × 1307)*

G.C.L., 'Deeds and Seals', xi, no. 8 (156 mm [left] × 270 mm [foot]); tag for seal (on inside
edges, partial text of an inventory); seal missing; endorsements: Extra portam borialem (*c.* s.
xiii[ex]); ii.[a] Warda (*c.* s. xiv[ex]); Registratur (s. xiv[ex] × s. xv[in]).

CYROGRAPHVM (*inverted*)

Sciant presentes et futuri quo ego Ioh(anne)s dei gratia abbas et conuentus sancti Petri
Glouc' concessimus Roberto diuiti et heredibus suis terram nostram extra portam
borialem quam magister Rogerus cocus seruiens noster in puram et perpetuam
elemosinam nobis dedit . illam scilicet que iacet inter terra eiusdem Roberti diuitis ex
vna parte et terram Ricardi francissi ex altera . Tenendam et habendam in feudo et
hereditate de nobis sibi et heredibus suis pro quinque solidis ad quatuor terminis anni
persoluendis . Videlicet ad festum sancti Michaelis . quindecim denariis . ad Natale
quindecim denariis . ad festum beate Marie in Martio quindecim denariis et ad
Natiuitatem sancti Iohannis Baptiste quindecim denariis[.] Predicta uero terra per
uisum legalium uirorum mensurata continet in fronte octo uirgas domini regis
ulnarias et vnum quarterium cum pollice interposito[.] In longitudine uero continet
quadraginti et decem et octo uirgas domini regis ulnarias et tria quarteria cum pollice

interposito. Retro uero continet sex uirgas ulnarias et tria quarteria duobus pollicibus minus cum pollice interposito. In medio uero continet septem uirgas ulnarias et dimidiam uirgam cum pollice interposito[.] Quando uero predictus Robertus predictam terram a nobis recepit edificium superpositum appreciatum fuit duas marcas. Si uero aliquo casu emergente ipse uel heredes sui predictam terram nobis reliquerint́. simile edificium uel pretium nobis restituent. Idem uero Robertus iuramentum nobis prestitit quod fidelis erit ecclesie nostre et maxime de reddendo redditu nostro plenarie statutis terminis . Et quod nec artem nec ingenium exquiret . vnde domus nostra per tenuram suam dampnum incurrat [.] Et quod predictam terram neque uendet neque excambiet neque in uadimonium ponet neque alicui in feudum et hereditatem tradet neque ad alium locum religionis transferet sine assensu et uoluntate nostra[.] Eandem securitatem nobis facient heredes sui cum singuli sibi succedent . et tam ipse quam heredes sui curiam nostram sequantur[.] In cuius rei testimonium presens scriptum in modum cyrographi inter nos confectum est [.] Cuius vnam partem sigillo ecclesie nostre munitam dicto Roberto tradidimus. Alteram uero partem sigillo ipsius roboratam penes nos retinuimus. Hiis testibus.

Aspects of this hand make the inclusive dates of the charter's issue uncertain, because it has features which are found in *acta* both before and after 1263; and the date of the earliest endorsement cannot resolve the matter. In support of issue by Abbot John de Gamages (1284–1307) rather than John de Felda (1243–63) are parts of two lines on the inside of the tag from some kind of inventory written in a script compatible with the later abbacy (see e.g. Johnson and Jenkinson, ii, Plate XXI[a]).

178. *Grant in fee and inheritance in the form of a chirograph by Abbot John and the convent of St. Peter's, Gloucester, to Richard Woolmonger of land in Newland (by Gloucester) for 2s. annual rent. (1243 × 63)*

G.C.L., 'Deeds and Seals', v, no. 6, fol. 3 (92 mm [left] × 195 mm [foot]), **Scribe 19**; damaged; slit for tag; tag and seal missing; endorsements: contra Ricardum leWolmong' (s. xiii[2]); De terra in Neulo'de c(a)rt(a)[1] (s. xiv); Registratur (s. xiv[ex] × s. xv[in]).

. . . O G R A P H V M (*inverted*)

Sciant presentes et futuri quod ego Ioh(ann)es dei gratia abbas et conuentus sancti Petri Glouc' . concessimus Ricardo le Wolmongere terram nostram apud la Newelonde . . .[2] fuit Ade Tovi . et terram que fuit Hereberti clerici . Tenendam et habendam de nobis in feudo et hereditate sibi et heredibus suis . Reddendo inde annua[tim . . . qui pro tempore][3] fuerit duos solidos ad duos anni terminos . Videlicet medietatem ad festum sancti Michaelis . et aliam medietatem ad Annuntiationem beate Marie. Predicta uero terra per [uisum legalium uirorum][4] mensurata continet in anteriori parte septem uirgas ulnarias cum pollice interposito et vnum quarterium et dimidium . In longitudine quadraginta et sex uirgas ulnarias cum pollice interposito . In medio nouem uirgas ulnarias cum pollice interposito et unum quarterium . Retro octo uirgas ulnarias cum pollice interposito et dimidium duobus pollicibus minus.

Quando uero predictus Ricardus predictam terram a nobis recepit[1] edificium superpositum appreciatum fuit dimidiam marcam. Si uero aliquo casu emergente ipse uel heredes sui predictam terram nobis reliquerint[2] simile edificium uel pretium nobis restituent. Dabunt etiam ipse et heredes sui nobis de qualibet ceruisia quam braciauerint . quatuor lagenas ceruicie uel vnum denarium ad electionem elemosinarii nostri qui pro tempore fuerit. Idem uero iuramentum nobis prestitit quod fidelis erit ecclesie nostre . et maxime de reddendo redditu nostro plenarie terminis statutis. Si uero in aliquo termino defecerit in soluendo[3] licebit nobis dictam terram in manibus nostris capere . et tamdiu retinere[4] quousque nobis plenarie satisfecerit. Iurauit etiam quod nec artem nec ingenium exquiret . vnde domus nostra per tenuram suam dampnum incurrat . et quod predictam terram neque uendet neque excambiet neque in vadimonium ponet . neque alicui in feudum et hereditatem tradet neque ad alium locum religionis transferet sine assensu et uoluntate nostra. Eandem securitatem nobis facient heredes sui cum singuli sibi succedent . et tam ipse quam heredes sui curiam nostram sequentur. In cuius rei testimonium presens scriptum in modum cyrographi inter nos confectum est . Cuius vnam partem sigillo ecclesie nostre munitam dicto Ricardo tradidimus. Alteram uero partem sigillo ipsius roboratam penes nos retinuimus. Hiis testibus . Mauricio Symenel . Waltero le pot' . Radulfo ferratore . Nicholao Wusum . Henrico rotario . et aliis.

[1] Reading uncertain.
[2] MS. cut away; a *C* or partial *G* or *Q* remains immediately before the portion cut away.
[3] MS. cut away.
[4] MS. cut away, but fragments of minims make the reconstruction certain.

179. *Lease in fee and inheritance in the form of a chirograph by Abbot John and the convent of St. Peter's, Gloucester, of their land in Bristol across the Avon in Redcliff Street to Walter Blund for 16s. annual rent. (1244 × 45; 1250 × 51; 1250 × 60)*

H.C.L., no. 1665 (92 mm [left] × 193 mm [foot]); tag and seal missing; endorsements: de Bristoll' (s. xiv[in]); Non indiget registrari (s. xiv[1]); cal. in Baddeley ii, no. 68, p. 27.

C Y R O G R A P H V M (*inverted*)

Sciant presentes et futuri quod ego Ioh(ann)es dei gratia abbas et conuentus sancti Petri Glouc' concessimus Waltero blundo de Bristoll' terram nostram in Bristoll' ultra Abanam in Radecliuestrete . que iacet inter terram ipsius Walteri et terram que fuit Vincentii Speciarii . Tenendam de nobis sibi et heredibus suis in feodo et hereditate pro sexdecim solidis nobis annuatim soluendis . videlicet una medietate ad Pascha . et alia medietate ad festum sancti Michaelis. Preterea uero terra per uisum legalium uirorum mensurata continet in fronte .iiii.[or] uirgas ulnarias cum pollice interposito et tria quarteria. Retro uero totidem et extenditur a platea usque ad Lawedich. Idem uero Walterus iuramentum nobis prestitit quod fidelis erit ecclesie nostre . et maxime de reddendo redditu nostro plenarie terminis statutis . et quod nec artem nec ingenium exquiret . vnde domus nostra per tenuram suam dampnum incurrat . nec eandem terram ad alium locum religionis transferet sine assensu et uoluntate nostra. Eandem securitatem facient nobis heredes sui cum singuli sibi succedent. In cuius rei testimonium presens scriptum in modum cyrographi inter nos confectum est . Cuius unam parte sigillo ecclesie nostre munitam dicto Waltero tradidimus. Alteram uero partem sigillo ipsius roboratam penes nos retinuimus. Hiis testibus . Symone clerico tunc maiore Bristoll' . Thoma longo . Iacobo la Warre . Ricardo Kadifor . Willelmo de Watford' . Willelmo fader . Henrico de sancto Petro clerico et aliis.

The date of the lease is limited to three occasions when Simon clerk served as mayor of Bristol (*Cart. St. Mark's Bristol*, 283).

180. *Final concord between John of Fretherne and John abbot of St. Peter's, Gloucester, concerning a fishery in the river Severn, which John of Fretherne claimed Abbot Henry had raised to the damage of his freehold in Fretherne; he granted that the abbot might have 20 putchers, and for this the abbot gave him 20 marks. 20 January 1245. Westminster.*

A. P.R.O., CP 25/1/74/17, no. 329 (90 mm [left] × 182 mm [foot]); no endorsement; **B**. ibid.
C 150/1, fol. 241v; *Cart. Glouc.* ii, no. 892.

C Y . . . O G . . . P H U M

Hec est finalis concordia facta in curia domini regis apud Westm' in octaba sancti Hillarii . anno regni regis Henrici filii regis vicesimo nono coram Henrico de Bathonia . Rogero de Thurkelby . Roberto de Notingham . Iollano de Neuill' . Gilberto de Preston' et Iohanne de Cobeha'[1] iustic(iis) et aliis domini regis fidelibus tunc presentibus . Inter Ioh(ann)em de Frethorn querentem et Iohannem abbatem de Glou'nia deforciantem per Adam marescallum positum loco suo ad lucrandum uel perdendum . De quadam piscaria in aqua de Sabrina . Vnde idem Ioh(ann)es questus fuit quod Henricus abbas Glou'nie predecessor ipsius abbatis iniuste leuauit predictam piscariam in predicta aqua ex opposito de Puchacre ad nocumentum liberi tenementi ipsius Ioh(ann)is in Frethorn . Et vnde placitum [f]uit[2] inter eos in eadem curia . Scilicet quod predictus Ioh(ann)es concessit pro se et heredibus suis quod idem abbas et successores sui habeant in predicta aqua viginti puches sine contradict[i]one ipsius Ioh(ann)is et heredum suorum . Ita quod idem abbas uel successores sui ibidem in predicta aqua nullo alio modo poterint piscari nec plures puches habere in eodem loco nec idem Ioh(ann)es nec heredes sui decetero aliquam communam piscationis poterint clammare in predicta aqua in predicto loco inperpetuum. Et pro hac concessione [.] fine et concordia idem abbas dedit predicto Ioh(ann)i viginti marcas argenti.

[1] Omitted from text printed in *Cart. Glouc.*
[2] Hole in MS.

181. Conventio *in the form of a chirograph between Abbot John and the convent of St. Peter's, Gloucester, and Abbot William and the monks of St. Augustine's Bristol; the abbot and convent of St. Peter's granted to St. Augustine's in fee farm Patchway for 10 marks annual rent and to Avicia de Columbars and her heirs 3¼ measures of black bread and a pair of boots at St. Martin. (8 April 1246 × 27 May 1250)*

A. H.C.L., no. 1171 (163 mm [left] × 255 mm [foot]); sealed with two seals on tags; 1) on left, dark green wax, chipped; pointed oval (52 mm [length]; width unavail.); obverse: a full-standing abbot in pontificals facing front, in the left hand a crozier, in the right a book (?); legend: +SIGILL' . VILL' DEI GRATIA . ABBATIS SANCTI . AV. . . DE BRISTOLL'; reverse: a counterseal: pointed oval (30 mm × 20 mm); Christ facing left blessing a kneeling apostle Thomas with his right hand extended to the side of Christ; above the head of the kneeling figure is the legend: IMINET ET ECCE CRVOR : ET DEITATE FRVOR; 2) on right, black wax, chipped; obverse: oval (*c.* 57 mm × 42 mm); a twin-towered ecclesiastical building, the left tower taller than the right; legend: +SI. . . AP. . . AGVSTINI. . . .E. . .TOWIE.; reverse, a counterseal, pointed oval (30 mm × 20 mm); the same image and legend as above; endorsements: Carta de Pethschawe (s. xiii^med), **Hand q**; endorsement: Registratur (s. xiv^ex × s. xv^in); **B.** P.R.O. C 150/1, fol. 161v [slightly different text]; *Cart. Glouc.* ii, no. 575; **C.** 'Cart. St. Aug. Bristol', fol. 160 and v; *Cart. Bristol*, no. 465; **D.** G.C.L., 'Reg. B', no. 47, p. 19; cal. in Baddeley ii, no. 69, pp. 27–28.

C. . .R O G R A P H V M (*inverted*)

Hec est conuentio facta inter dominum Ioh(ann)em abbatem sancti Petri Glouc' et eiusdem loci conuentum ex parte una et dominum Willelmum abbatem sancti Augustini de Bristoll' et eiusdem loci conuentum ex altera . Videlicet quod predicti abbas et conuentus sancti Petri Glouc' concesserunt et in feudi firmam tradiderunt dictis abbati et conuentui sancti Augustini totam terram suam quam habuerunt apud Petschawe cum omnibus pertinentiis suis . et etiam omnes homines cum eorum sequelis dictam terram tenentes secundum hoc quod eos habuerunt et tenuerunt . Habendam et tenendam sibi et successoribus suis de supradictis abbate et conuentu sancti Petri et eorum successoribus libere pacifice quiete et integre [.] In boscis et planis . In viis et semitis . In pratis et pasturis . In frussatis et essartis . et in omnibus rebus et locis cum omnibus libertatibus et liberis consuetudinibus . Reddendo inde annuatim predictis abbati et conuentui sancti Petri et eorum successoribus in abbatia sancti Petri Glouc' decem marcas argenti . deputatas sacristarie eiusdem ecclesie ad quatuor anni terminos . scilicet in Natiuitate sancti Iohannis Baptiste duas marcas et dimidiam . In festo sancti Michaelis duas marcas et dimidiam . Ad Nathale domini duas marcas et dimidiam . et ad Pascham duas marcas et dimidiam . Et domine Auicie de Columbar' et heredibus eius singulis annis tres virgas et quartam partem unius virge nigri panni et unum par botarum in festo beati Martini pro omnibus secularibus seruitiis exactionibus et demandis ad dictam terram pertinentibus inperpetuum. Et si dictis abbati et conuentui sancti Petri loco et terminis prenominatis de dicto redditu plene satisfactum non fuerit' quotienscumque hoc continerit extunc certa conuentione hinc inde concessa liceat memoratis abbati et conuentui sancti Petri et eorum successoribus predictos abbatem et conuentum sancti Augustini et eorum successores tam apud Esseleworth' quam apud Petschawe per quascumque uiderint sibi expedire districtiones sine contraditione continue tam diu distingere et districtiones tenere donec tam de arreragio dicti redditus quam tediis dampnis et laboribus occasione dilationis solutionis eiusdem eis plene fuerit satisfactum. Dicti autem abbas et conuentus sancti Petri totam predictam terram cum omnibus suis pertinentiis prefatis abbati et conuentui sancti Augustini et eorum successoribus contra omnes gentes warantizabunt. In cuius rei testimonium presens scriptum in modum cyrographi confectum est . Cuius unam partem sigillo abbatis et conuentus sancti Augustini munitam dicti abbas et conuentus sancti Petri Glouc' sibi reseruarunt. Alteram partem sigillo dictorum abbatis et conuentus sancti Petri Glouc' dicti abbas et conuentus sancti Augustini sibi retinuerunt roboratam.[1] Hiis testibus . domino Roberto Walerand tunc vicecomite Glouc' . domino Nicholao Poinz . domino Ricardo de Cromhal' . domino Iohanne de Salso marisco[2] . Nicholao de Monte acuto . Radulfo Walense . Elia de Filton' . Petro Croc . Willelmo de Framton' . Heruico de Dalinton' . Galfrido de Weston' . Iohanne de Eldrefeld . et multis aliis.

According to the St. Peter's Calendar of Donations, the abbey acquired Patchway from Wibert of Kingsholm in 1117 (*Cart. Glouc.* i, pp. 106, 124). The witness Robert Waleran was sheriff of Gloucester in 1249, acting in person in 1249; he was sheriff also in 1246, but acted then through deputies (*List of Sheriffs*, 49; *Cart. Bristol*, no. 465 n.); the abbot of St. Augustine's was William Longe (*VCH Glos.* ii. 76, 79).

[1] **B** ends here with *T(estibus)*.
[2] **D** ends here with *et aliis*.

182. *Notification in the form of a chirograph by Abbot John and the convent of St. Peter's, Gloucester, that they had commuted the serjeanty which Richard le Bret held in Pitchcombe from the abbey; Richard and his ancestors had previously provided a squire with a horse to accompany a monk travelling on the abbey's business, but henceforth he and his heirs were to serve the first dish in the abbey's great hall on the feast of St. Peter and St. Paul (29 June), the other services and suits remaining unchanged and Richard and his heirs paying 1 mark a year. (c. 1152–3)*

A. H.C.L., no. 1638 (158 mm [left] × 212 [foot]); slit for tag on foot; tag and seal missing; endorsements: Carta contra[1] Ricardum le Bret (s. xiii[2]); Pychenecombe (s. xiv); Registratur (s. xiv[med]?); **B.** G.C.L., 'Reg. B', no. 382, pp. 63–64; cal. in Baddeley ii, no. 80, pp. 30–31.

CYROGRAPHUM

Omnibus Cristi fidelibus Ioh(ann)es dei gratia abbas sancti Petri Glouc' et eiusdem loci conuentus salutem in domino sempiternam. Sciatis quod cum Ricardus Le Bret et antecessores sui de nobis et predecessoribus nostris totum tenementum suum in Pichenecu'be cum pertinentiis suis tenuissent pro quo nobis facere debuerunt et consueuerunt esquieriam nomine seriantie . Videlicet quod cum aliquis monachus ecclesie nostre pro negotiis eiusdem ecclesie expediendis alicubi esset equitaturus⸌ prefatus Ricardus et antecessores sui nobis inuenire debebant et solebant vnum esquiertum cum uno runcino congruo eundem monachum infra regnum Anglie secuturum . et eidem seruiturum ab egressu abbatie nostre⸌ donec rediret . et deferre lectum dicti monachi super proprium equitium ipsius esquierii . videlicet vnam culcitram . duos langellos . et vnum coopertorium . Item vnum librum dicti monachi [.] Crassetum. candelas . et duos panes . et dimidiam sextarium uini uel seruisie . et ad hoc faciendum prompti et parati fuissent . et esse debuissent . per totum annum integrum quotienscumque rationabiliter summoniti fuissent ad custum domus nostre . Et cum dictus esquierius infra abbatiam ratione dicti seruitii perhendinasset . percipere solebat et debebat quolibet die duos panes esquierii cum seruisia pertinente et vnum ferculum de coquina. Si uero runcinum suum in predicto seruitio nostro mori contigisset⸌ tantum decem solidos pro dicto runcino a nobis percipere debuisset. Nos circa conuentione inter dominum Ricardum et nos inita totum seruitium predictum in subscriptum seruitium commutantes . pro nobis et successoribus nostris eidem Ricardo et heredibus suis concessimus et uolumus . quod ipsi de cetero per se ipsos pro dicto tenemento cum pertinentiis aquietando . nobis et successoribus nostris faciant hoc seruitium nomine seriantie . videlicet assedendi primum ferculum in magna aula nostra Glouc' die apostolorum Petri et Pauli coram nobis et successoribus nostris . uel coram quacumque alia digniori persona in eadem aula tunc presidente. Preterea predictus Ricardus et heredes sui facient nobis sectas ad curiam nostram Glouc' et de Stanedis . cum aliis liberis tenentibus nostris . sicut idem et antecessores sui solebant et facere debebant . Ita scilicet quod nichilominus ob mutationem predictorum seruitiorum nobis et successoribus nostris integre remaneant herieta . releuia . warde . maritagia . escaete . et cetera omnimoda quecumque ad dominos feodorum huiusmodi tenementi⸌ quibuscumque modis et formis . de tenementis seu ea tenentibus ad nos et successores nostros pertinere uel accidere poterunt uel debuerint. Reddent insuper nobis et successoribus nostris predictus Ricardus et heredes sui vnam marcam argenti annuatim ad duos terminos annni . Scilicet medietatem ad Annuntiationem beate Marie . et aliam medietatem ad festum sancti Michaelis. Et si dictum tenementum quocumque casu ad personas feminarum deuolui contigerit⸌ exclusis personis feminarum per attornatos masculos sufficientes et irreprehensibiles seruitium suppleant memoratum. Singulis autem annis die quo dictus Ricardus et heredes sui nobis et successoribus nostris seruitium fecerint prenominatum⸌ volumus ut ipsi nobiscum sint in mensa . et habeant eo die ad edendum et bibendum adeo honorifice sicut senescallus domus nostre qui pro tempore fuerit . et fenum et auena . nocte sequente ad duos equos tantum. In cuius rei testimonium presens scriptum in modo cirographi inter nos confectum est . Cuius unam partem sigillo ecclesie nostre munitam dicto Ricardo tradidimus. Alteram uero partem sigillo ipsius roboratam⸌ penes nos retinuimus. Hiis testibus . domino Henrico de Cheueringwrth' . domino Adam Mustel . militibus . domino Ricardo de Compton' clerico[2] . Reginaldo de Aclee . Roberto de Ledene . Waltero de Baus' . Iohanne Achard . et aliis.

This grant was evidently made *c.* 1252–3, like the *conventio* upon which the above terms were based (*Cart. Glouc.* ii, no. 567).

¹ Superscript in the same hand.
² **B** ends here with *et aliis*.

183. *Grant in the form of a chirograph by Abbot John and the monks of St. Peter's, Gloucester, to Richard le Bret of Pitchcombe of the wardship of the land which had been held by Henry of Avenbury in Harescombe, in Standish manor, with the marriage of his heir, for which Richard gave the abbey 50 marks and a cask of wine. 28 October 1252 × 27 October 1253.*

A. H.C.L., no. 1655 (218 mm × 130 mm); tag with residue of white wax; seal missing; endorsements: Cyrographum Ricardi le bret de warda terre et heredis Henrici de Auenebur' (s. xiii^{med}); Caps(ula) .viii. de laicis tenuris (s. xiii²); Harsecombe (s. xivⁱⁿ); ad terminum uite (s. xiv^{ex}); **B**. P.R.O., C 150/1, fols. 159v–160; *Cart. Glouc.* ii, no. 567; cal. in Baddeley ii, no. 45, p. 21.

CYROGRAPHVM

Hec est conuentio facta inter dominum Ioh(ann)em abbatem et conuentum sancti Petri Gloucestr' ex parte una . et Ricardum le Bret de Pichenecumb' ex altera . Videlicet quod iidem abbas et conuentus concesserunt et tradiderunt anno regni Regis Henrici filii regis Iohannis tricesimo septimo . eidem Ricardo de Pichenecumb' et heredibus suis uel suis assignatis gardam terre cum pertinentiis suis quam Henricus de Auenebur' aliquando tenuit in manerio de Stanedys . videlicet in Hersecumb' cum maritagio infantis et heredis eiusdem Henrici . ita quod non disperagetur . Tenendam et habendam dictam gardam dicte terre quamdiu iuxta morem Angl' debet esse sibi tutore . Ita quod nec uastum . nec destructionem nec deteriorationem in pertinentiis eiusdem faciant . Saluis tamen eis husbote et heybote. Si uero de dicto herede humanitus contigerit.́ concesserunt dicti abbas et conuentus eidem Ricardo et heredibus suis gardam dicte terre cum suis pertinentiis cum maritagio alterius existentis heredis . saluo eisdem seruitio pertinente ad dictam terram . scilicet esquieria et secta curie sue apud Glouc' et apud Stanedys cum aliis liberis hominibus suis. Pro hac autem concessione et traditione sua . dictus Ricardus dedit dictis abbati et conuentui quinquaginta marcas argenti . et vnun doleum vini. Dictus uero Ricardus et heredes sui hec omnia obseruabunt sub forisfactura centum solidorum. In cuius rei testimonium presenti scripto in modum cyrographi confecto . partes sigilla sua apposuerunt. Hiis testibus . Roberto de Felda . Roberto de Leden' . Philippo de Mattesdon' . Philippo de Hatherl' . Petro de Felda . Willelmo Geraldo . et aliis.

184. *Grant in fee and inheritance by Abbot John and the convent of St. Peter's, Gloucester, of land in the cobblery of Gloucester to Herbert mercer for 12s. annual rent payable to the prior for the repair of the glazing. (1253 × 54)*

G.C.L., 'Deeds and Seals', vi, no. 11, fol. 5 (91 mm [left] × 223 mm [foot]), **Scribe 19**; slit for seal on turn-up; tag and seal missing; endorsements: Carta terre Ph' . . . [1] rel. . . tempore Hugonis Merton' . . . ista terra in Hasti' . . .n tenuit Rob' Got et postea Byseley in tempore regis He(n)r(ici) qu. . . pertinent' i' aula' . . . (s. xv?); . . . arc' (modern?; superscript above the immediately following); in sutaria Glouc (uncertain date).

Sciant presentes et futuri quod ego Ioh(ann)es dei gratia abbas et conuentus sancti Petri Glouc' . concessimus Herberto mercerio terram nostram in sutaria Glouc' que iacet inter terram dicti Herberti et terram prioris Lantonie . Tenendam de nobis in feudo et hereditate sibi et heredibus suis pro duodecim solidis nobis annuatim ad quatuor terminos persoluendis . et per manum prioris que pro tempore fuerit recipiendis ad reparationem uitreorum . Videlicet ad festum sancti Michaelis tribus solidis ad festum sancti Andree tribus solidis . ad Annuntiationem beate Marie tribus solidis . et ad Natiuitatem beati Iohannis Baptiste tribus solidis. Predicta uero terra per visum legalium uirorum mensurata continet in fronte duas uirgas domini regis ulnarias cum pollice interposito . et unam pollicem . In longitudine uero sex uirgas domini regis ulnarias et dimidiam . et dimidium quarterium cum pollice interposito . Retro uero duas uirgas domini regis ulnarias . duobus pollicibus minus. Quando uero predictus Herbertus predictam terram a nobis recepit. edificium superpositum appreciatum fuit ad ualentiam unius marce argenti. Si uero aliquo casu emergente ipse uel heredes sui dictam terram nobis reliquerint. simile edificium uel pretium nobis restituent. Idem uero iuramentum nobis prestitit quod fidelis erit ecclesie nostre . et maxime de reddendo redditu nostro plenarie statutis terminis . et quod nec artem nec ingenium exquiret vnde domus nostra per tenuram suam dampnum incurrat . et quod predictam terram neque uendet . neque excambiet . neque in uadimonium ponet . neque alicui in feudum et hereditatem tradet . neque ad alium locum religionis transferet sine assensu et uoluntate nostra. Eandem securitatem nobis facient heredes sui cum singuli sibi succedent. In cuius rei testimonium presens scriptum in modum cyrographi inter nos confectum est . cuius unam partem sigillo ecclesie nostre munitam dicto Herberto tradimus. Alteram uero partem sigillo ipsius roboratam. penes nos retinuimus. Hiis testibus . Luca Cornubiense . Egidio piscatore tunc bailliuis Glouc' . Ricardo franceys . Roberto le mercer . Iohanne le fuster' . Willelmo le ferrur' . Iohanne Carlas . et multis aliis.

Luke of Cornwall and Egeus fisher were bailiffs in 1253/4. The charter's beneficiary Herbert mercer also served as a bailiff of Gloucester with William of Cheltenham *c.* 1240 × 65 (*VCH Glos.* iv. 372; Stevenson, nos. 428–39); he received a grant of four acres of arable in Pedmarsh and a messuage at Kingsholm *c.* 1250 from William, son of William furrier (ibid. no. 471); he was one the town's leading merchants who were located in upper Westgate Street; at his death *c.* 1268 his holdings numbered five houses and 11 shops (*VCH Glos.* iv. 28 & n.; see also Stevenson, nos. 580, 604–5).

---

[1] The script in this gap and the six following is illegible with ultra-violet light.

185. *Grant in the form of a chirograph by Abbot John and the convent of St. Peter's, Gloucester, to Roger of* Northwich *burgess of Gloucester of land in Gloucester in perpetuity for 2 marks annual rent. 28 October 1253 × 27 October 1254.*

G.C.L., 'Deeds and Seals', v, no. 3, fol. 2 (102 mm [left] × 224 mm [foot]), **Scribe 19**; tag for seal with residue of white wax; seal missing; endorsement: Ignot' . (s. xiv^{med}?)

C. . .R O G R A P H V M (*inverted*)

Sciant presentes et futuri quod ego Ioh(ann)es dei gratia abbas et conuentus sancti Petri Glouc' . anno regni regis Henrici filii regis Iohannis .xxxviii.° concessimus Rogero de Northwych' burgensi Glouc' terram nostram que iacet inter terram Walteri de Teukesbur' et terram que fuit Henrici Tycche in villa Glouc' . Tenendam et habendam de nobis in perpetuum sibi et heredibus suis pro duobus marcis quas nobis annuatim ad quatuor terminos persoluet . Videlicet ad Natiuitatem sancti Iohannis Baptiste dimidiam marcam . et ad festum sancti Michaelis dimidiam marcam . ad festum sancti Andree apostoli dimidiam marcam . et ad festum beate Marie in Martio dimidiam marcam. Predicta uero terra mensurata per visum legalium uirorum . continet in fronte quatuor uirgas domini regis ulnarias . et vnum quarterium cum pollice interposito . Et in profunditate sex uirgas ulnarias et vnum quarterium cum pollice interposito. Quando uero dictus Rogerus dictam terram a nobis recepit'. edificium superpositum appreciatum fuit ad ualorem viginti solidorum. Si uero aliquo casu emergente ipse uel heredes suis dictam terram nobis reliquerint'. simile edificium uel pretium nobis restituent. Idem uero iuramentum nobis prestitit . quod fidelis erit ecclesie nostre . et maxime de reddendo redditu nostro plenarie statutis terminis . et quod nec artem . nec ingenium exquiret . vnde domus nostra per tenuram suam dampnum incurrat . et quod predictam terram neque uendet . neque excambiet . neque in vadimonium ponet . neque alicui in feudum et hereditatem tradet . neque ad alium locum religionis transferet sine assensu et uoluntate nostra. Eandem securitatem nobis facient heredes sui cum singuli sibi succedent. In cuius rei testimonium presens scriptum in modum cyrographi inter nos confectum est . Cuius unam partem sigillo ecclesie nostre munitam dicto Rogero tradidimus. Alteram uero partem sigillo ipsius roboratam'. penes nos retinuimus. Hiis testibus . domino Ricardo de Celario . domino Hugone de aula regis . domino Iohanne filio Symonis . Henrico tunc clerico de uilla . Willelmo de Caperun et aliis.

Roger of Northwich (*Northwych*) attested local *acta* from *c.* 1240 to *c.* 1260 (Stevenson, nos. 350, 402, 415, 448, 542). The witness Richard de Celario served as one of Gloucester's bailiffs *c.* 1228 × *c.* 1240 and again *c.* 1240 × *c.* 1265 (*VCH Glos.* iv. 372); he held land on Westgate Street and appears frequently as a witness in *acta* of the period in general.

186. *Grant in the form of a chirograph by Abbot John and the convent of St. Peter's, Gloucester, of land in Gloucester in perpetuity to Roger of* Northwich *burgess of Gloucester for 40s. annual rent. 28 October 1253 × 27 October 1254.*

G.C.L., 'Deeds and Seals', ix, no. 36, fol. 19 (221 mm × 92 mm), **Scribe 19** (below, Plate XXI); seal on tag; white wax, chipped, repaired; obverse: round (23 mm in diam.); a hunting hound ? running to the left, above a bird in flight to the left); legend: . . . S' ROGERI DE NORW . . . ; no countereal; endorsements: sc(ribitur) [;] .iii.ᵃ Warda.[;] Northwich' . de quadam selda in sutaria. inter seldam Stephani Bronn in parti boriali et seldam I. le Marin' in parte australi (s. xiv²).

C Y R O G R A P H V M (*inverted*)

Sciant presentes et futuri quod ego Ioh(ann)es dei gratia abbas et conuentus sancti Petri Glouc' . anno regis Henrici filii regis Iohannis .xxxviii. concessimus Rogero de Northwych' burgensi Glouc' terram nostram que iacet inter terram Walteri de Teukesbur' et terram Ade le ferrur in villa Glouc' . Tenendam et habendam de nobis in perpetuum sibi et heredibus suis pro quatuordecim solidis quos nobis annuatim ad quatuor terminos persoluet . Videlicet ad Natale domini tres solidos et sex denarios . ad festum beate Marie in Martio tres solidos et sex denarios . ad Natiuitatem beati Iohannis Baptiste tres solidos et sex denarios . et ad festum sancti Michaelis tres solidos et sex denarios. Predicta uero terra per visum legalium virorum mensurata continet in fronte duas uirgas domini regis ulnarias cum pollice interposito et duos pollices . In profunditate sex uirgas domini regis ulnarias cum pollice interposito et quatuor pollices. Quando uero dictus Rogerus dictam terram a nobis recepit⸌ edificium superpositum appreciatum fuit ad valorem viginti solidorum. Si uero aliquo casu emergente ipse uel heredes sui dictam terram nobis reliquerint⸌ simile edificium uel pretium nobis restituent. Idem uero iuramentum nobis prestitit quod fidelis erit ecclesie nostre . et maxime de reddendo redditu nostro plenarie statutis terminis . et quod nec artem nec ingenium exquiret . vnde domus nostra per tenuram suam dampnum incurrat . Et quod predictam terram neque uendet . neque escambiet . neque in uadimonium ponet . neque alicui in feudum et hereditatem tradet . neque ad alium locum religionis transferet sine assensu et uoluntate nostra. Eandem securitatem nobis facient heredes sui cum singuli sibi succedent. In cuius rei testimonium presens scriptum in modum cyrographi inter nos confectum est . Cuius unam partem sigillo ecclesie nostre munitam dicto Rogero tradidimus. Alteram uero partem sigillo ipsius roboratam penes nos retinuimus. Hiis testibus . Willelmo de Somery . Iohanne filio Symonis . Ricardo de Celario . Hugone de aula regis . Waltero de Teukesbur' . et multis aliis.

187. *Confirmation in the form of a chirograph by Abbot John and the convent of St. Peter's, Gloucester, to William of Showle, son of William of Showle, of an exchange of nine acres at Showle (Herefs.) for nine acres in* Padhull *by the abbey's court at Monkhide (in Yarkhill, Herefs). (1254)*

A. H.C.L., no. 776 (121 mm [left] × 212 mm [foot]); fragment of brown silk or linen cord; seal missing; endorsements: scriptum W. de Solle (s. xiv²); Registratur (s. xiv × xv^in); **B**. G.C.L., 'Reg. B', no. 138, p. 48; cal. in Baddeley ii, no. 43, p. 21.

C Y R O G R A P H U. . .(inverted)

Sciant presentes et futuri quod ego Iohannes dei gratia abbas sancti Petri Clouc' et eiusdem loci conuentus tradidimus concessimus et hac presenti carta nostra confirmauimus domino Willelmo de Solle filio Willelmi de Solle et heredibus suis in exscambium quandam terram nostram in campo de Solle que iacet inter terras dicti Willelmi cum quadam acra quam aliquando tenuit de nobis Willelmus Durant et computantur nouem acre in uniuerso . pro nouem acris iacentibus in campo uocato Padehulle . que sunt site iuxta curiam nostram de Hyda. Dictus vero Willelmus faciet nobis prefatas nouem acras ita liberas et quietas uersus omnes ab omni terreno seruitio et qualibet demanda⸌ sicut libera est illa terra quam eidem tradidimus. Et de decima sancte ecclesie persoluenda et adquietanda dictus Willelmus et heredes sui pro nobis respondebunt et defendent et contra omnes mortales dictas nouem acras inperpetuum warantizabunt sicut in carta dicti Willelmi continetur. Et quia uolumus quod hoc exscambium robur optineat perpetuum⸌ presens scriptum in modum cyrographi confectum est inter nos . cuius unam partem sigillo ecclesie nostre signatam dicto Willelmo tradidimus. Alteram uero partem sigillo sepefati Willelmi roboratam⸌ penes nos retinuimus. Hiis testibus . domino Petro tunc Herefordense episcopo . domino Willelmo Tregoz tunc rectore ecclesie de Stokes[1] . domino .I. Britun tunc vicecomite Hereford' . domino Ricardo de Bachindene milite . Ricardo de Hyda . Ricardo de la Wike . Iohanne de Souuille . et aliis.

For Showle, Westhide, and its tenant family, see *Herefordshire Place-Names*, 215–16. John le Breton was sheriff of Herefordshire in 1254 (*List of Sheriffs*, 59).

[1]   **B** omits *tunc* before *rectore* and ends here with *et aliis*.

---

188. *Grant in fee and inheritance in the form of a chirograph from Abbot John and the convent of St. Peter's, Gloucester, to William Clemond of land and curtilages outside Northgate (Gloucester) for 10s. 5d. annual rent. (1255)*

A. G.C.L., 'Deeds and Seals', iii, no. 19, fol. 12 (169 mm [left] × 240 mm [foot]); slit for tag on turn-up; tag and seal missing; endorsements: Willelmus Cleimont. de diuersis tenementis extra Northgate; pro quibus reddit .x. solidos .v. denarios. (s. xiii²); Registratur (s. xiv^ex × s. xv^in); **B**. ibid. 'Reg. B', no. 586, pp. 255–6.

C A R T A C Y R O G. . .A F. . .A (inverted)

Sciant presentes et futuri quod ego Ioh(ann)es dei gratia abbas et conuentus sancti Petri Gloucestrie concessimus Willelmo Cleymund terram nostram extra Northgate illam scilicet quam Adam de nobis tenuit . que iacet inter terram prioris sancti Oswaldi et terram Roberti diuitis . que quidem terra per uisum legalium uirorum mensurata habet in fronte octo uirgas domini regis ulnarias cum pollice interposito᷍. dimidium quarterium minus . In profunditate᷍. triginta et septem uirgas et dimidiam et minus quarterium cum pollice interposito . In medio᷍. septem uirgas et dimidiam et dimidium quarterium cum pollice interposito . Retro᷍. septem uirgas et duos pollices cum pollice interposito. Quando uero predictus Willelmus predictam terram a nobis recepit᷍. edificium superpositum appreciatum fuit ad ualorem uiginti solidorum. Si uero aliquo casu emergente predictus Willelmus uel heredes sui predictam terram nobis reliquerint᷍. simile edificium uel pretium nobis restituent. Concessimus etiam predicto Willelmo quoddam curtilagium nostrum quod se extendit a predicta terra nostra usque ad terram eiusdem Willelmi Cleymund quod quidem mesuratum habet in fronte uiginti et nouem uirgas cum police interposito . et in longitudine uersus australem partem᷍. nonaginta et duas uirgas et tria quarteria cum pollice interposito . et in longitudine uersus partem aquilonarem᷍. octoginta uirgas uno quarterio minus . et in medio᷍. uiginti et septem uirgas et dimidiam cum pollice interposito . Retro uero uiginti et quinque uirgas cum pollice interposito. Preterea concessimus eidem Willelmo quamdam partem curtilagii quam dictus Adam de nobis tenuit que quidem iacet inter terram que fuit Iohannis tinctoris et terram Robert Ponlesheye[1] . que mensurata᷍. continet uersus aquilonem tresdecim uirgas et dimidiam cum pollice interposito . In longitudine uiginti et tres uirgas et vnum quarterium cum pollice interposito . In medio duodecim uirgas cum pollice interposito. Concessimus eidem Willelmo unam partem curtilagii que se extendit a terra que quondam fuit Willelmi le Riche usque ad terram Roberti tinctoris extra Norþgate et continet in parte᷍. nouem uirgas et vnum quarterium cum pollice interposito . in longitudine᷍. uiginti et quatuor uirgas et quatuor pollices cum pollice interposito . Retro᷍. iuxta terram dicti Roberti tinctoris extra Norþgate . tresdecim uirgas et tres pollices[2] cum pollice interposito . Tenendas et habendas totas predictas terras per partes superius distinctas de nobis in feodo et hereditate sibi et heredibus suis pro decem solidis et quinque denariis ad quatuor anni terminos nobis persoluendis . scilicet ad festum sancti Michaelis duos solidos et septem denarios . et vnum quadrantem . ad Natale duos solidos et septem denarios . et vnum quadrantem . Ad Annuntiationem beate Marie duos solidos et septem denarios . et vnum [quadrantem . Ad festum][3] Iohannis Baptiste᷍. duos[4] solidos et septem denarios et vnum quadrantem. Idem uero Willelmus iuramentum nobis prestitit quod fidelis erit ecclesie nostre . et maxime de reddendo redditu nostro plenarie statutis terminis . et quod nec artem . nec ingenium exquiret vnde nostra [domus][5] per tenuram suam dampnum incurret . et quod predictam terram neque vendet . neque excambiet . neque in vadimonium ponet . neque alicui in feodum et hereditatem tradet . neque ad alium[6] locum religionis tradet᷍. sine assensu et uoluntate nostra. Eandem securitatem nobis facient heredes sui cum singuli sibi succedent. In cuius rei testimonium presens scriptum in modum cirographi inter nos confectum est cuius alteram partem sigillo nostro signatam dicto Willelmo tradidimus. Alteram uero partem sigillo ipsius roboratam penes nos retinuimus. Hiis testibus . Willelmo de Chelteham . Iohanne Symund . tunc balliuis Glouc' . Ricardo Franceys[7] . Rogero len veyse . Luca Cornubiense . Hugone de la Kingesho' . Waltero de Sandun' . Iohanne Payn . Henrico clerico et aliis.[8]

For the date of the grant, see *VCH Glos*. iv. 372. William Clemond attested local *acta* between 1248 and 1261 (Stevenson, nos. 429, 523, 541, 564, 654); Roger len veyse (alias le wyse) was also an frequent witness in this period and served as a Gloucester bailiff with John son of Simon, William de Sumery, and William of Cheltenham (*VCH Glos*. iv. 372).

1   Reading uncertain.
2   *pollice* in MS.
3   MS. damaged; wording conjectural.
4   *duo* in MS.
5   *domus* omitted from MS.
6   The *l* is written over an apparent *a* as an addition in the MS.
7   **B** ends here with *et aliis*.
8   From *Payn* on is covered by the turn-up.

189. *Grant in the form of a chirograph by Abbot John and the convent of St. Peter's, Gloucester, of land on Lich Lane in Gloucester to Reginald goldsmith for 7s. 6d. annual rent payable to the sacristan. (1258)*

A. G.C.L., 'Deeds and Seals', i, no. 57, fol. 31 (142 mm [left] × 203 mm [foot]); seal on tag; white wax, fragment; obverse: two arms of a cross at 90 degree angle to each other or a fleur-de-lis; legend: . . .LDI: AV. . .; no counterseal; endorsements: Reginaldus aurifaber (s. xiii^2); in Lychlone (s. xiv^{in}); Registratur (s. xiv^{ex} × s. xv^{in}); **B**. ibid. 'Reg. B', no. 24, p. 11.

...R O G...A...H V M

Sciant presentes et futuri quod ego Ioh(anne)s dei gratia abbas et conuentus sancti Petri Glouc' concessimus et tradidimus Reginaldo aurifabro burgensi . terram nostram que iacet in cornerio propinquiori ianue cimiterii nostri in uico qui uocatur Lychlone . in villa Glouc' . inter terram sacriste[1] nostri et uiam iuxta murum cimiterii nostri . Habendam et tenendam de nobis et successoribus nostris imperpetuum sibi et heredibus suis pro septem solidis . et sex denariis . quos sacriste nostre annuatim ad quatuor terminos persoluet . Videlicet ad Natiuitatem sancti Iohannis Baptiste . uiginti duos denarios et obolum . ad festum sancti Michaelis uiginti duos denarios et obolum . ad Natale domini uiginti duos denarios et obolum . et ad festum beate Marie in Martio uiginti duos denarios et obolum. Predicta uero terra per uisum legalium uirorum mensurata continet in latitudine quatuor uirgas domini regis ulnarias et dimidiam . et quinque pollices cum pollice interposito . In longitudine uero tresdecim uirgas domini regis vlnarias de dimidiam . et tres pollices cum pollice interposito. Quando uero dictus Reginaldus a nobis dictam terram recepit edificium superpositum appreciatum fuit ad valorem viginti solidorum. Si uero aliquo casu emergente ipse uel heredes sui dictam terram nobis reliquerint́. simile edificium uel pretium nobis restituent. Idem uero iuramentum nobis prestitit quod fidelis erit ecclesie nostre et maxime de reddendo redditu nostro plenarie statutis terminis . Et quod nec artem nec ingenium exquiret . vnde domus nostra per tenuram suam dampnum incurrat . Et quod predictam terram neque uendet . neque excambiet neque in vadimonium ponet . neque alicui in feodum uel hereditatem tradet . neque ad alium locum religionis transferet . sine assensu et voluntate nostra. Eandem securitatem nobis facient heredes sui cum singuli sibi succedent. In cuius rei testimonium presens scriptum in modum cyrographi inter nos confectum est . cuius vnam partem sigillo ecclesie nostre munitam dicto Reginaldo.' tradidimus. Aliam uero partem sigillo ipsius roboratam penes nos retinuimus. Hiis testibus . Rogero Lenweise . Willelmo de Chiltheham tunc bailliuis[2] Glouc'[3] . Hugone de Kyngeshom . Iohanne filio Symonis . Luca Cornubiense . Ricardo Fraunceis . Iohanne Pain . et aliis.

For the date, see *VCH Glos.* iv. 372.

[1] Erasure.

[2] *t(em)p(or)is* in MS.

[3] **B** ends here with *et aliis.*

190. Inspeximus *of Abbot John of St. Peter's, Gloucester, of a charter of 12 January 1149 in favour of Tewkesbury Abbey by William earl of Gloucester confirming grants made by his grandfather Robert fitz Hamon. Gloucester. 6 June 1260.*

B.A.O., no. 5139 (238) (201 mm × 134 mm); tag for seal; seal missing, but a small fragment of red wax remains attached to tag; endorsement: Testificatio abbatis sancti Petri Glouc' super ecclesiis nobis collatis a domino W. comite Glouc' (s. xiii[2]); Patterson, *EGC*, no. 179 (text of William earl of Gloucester's charter only).

Vniuersis sancte matris ecclesie filiis presentem paginam inspecturis uel audituris .I. abbas sancti Petri Glouc' salutem in domino sempiternam. Litteras illustris viri domini .W. comitis Glouc' non cancellatas non abolitas in ullam sui partem[1] viciatas signo ipsius roboratas inspeximus . In hec uerba .W. comes Glouc' omnibus baronibus suis et amicis salutem. Sciatis me concessisse deo et ecclesie sancte Marie de Thekesbyr' pro anima mea et pro anima patris et matris mee omniumque parentorum meorum . omnes ecclesias illas que fuerunt Roberti capellani[2] Roberti filii Haymonis aui mei et quas dederat predicte ecclesie sancte Marie ∶ In primis ecclesiam sancti Petri de Brist' cum omnibus pertinentiis suis infra burgum et extra . Et in eadem uilla ecclesiam sancti Trinitatis . et ecclesiam sancti Michaelis . et ecclesiam sancti Iacobi extra burgum suum[3] . Ecclesiam de Tornebyr' cum pertinentiis suis . Ecclesiam de Meresf' . Ecclesiam de Sopelb' . Ecclesiam de Feirf' cum pertinentiis suis . Ecclesiam de Leche . Ecclesiam de Shened' . Ecclesiam omnium sanctorum in Lond' . Ecclesiam de Merelawe et ecclesiam de Hameld' cum pertinentiis suis . Ecclesiam de Pentrix . Ecclesiam de Essemer' . Ecclesiam de Froma . Ecclesiam de Chedesl' cum pertinentiis suis . Ecclesiam de Winkel' . Ecclesiam Edwisleya . Ecclesiam de Chetelha'pt' . Ecclesiam de Budif' . Ecclesiam de Liddeam . Ecclesiam de Kilketon' . Ecclesiam de Vmberleg' . Ecclesiam de Bechintona . Apud K'dif . ecclesiam sancte Marie et capellam de castello . cum pertinentiis suis . Ecclesiam de Landiltuto cum pertinentiis[4] suis . Ecclesiam de Nouo

Castello . Ecclesiam de Lanbled' cum pertinentiis suis. Has omnes concessi et confirmaui ecclesie sancte Mar[ie de][5] Theok' ita liberas et quietas cum omnibus appenditiis suis sicut vnquam melius et quietius et honorificentius tenuit illas [capellanus][6] Roberti filii Haymonis aui mei et temporis patris mei . et tempore Henrici regis. Testibus . Reynaldo de Chahan' . Fulcone filio Guarini . R[ualo][7] de Valuin' . Rogero de Guuiz . Radulfo de Hasting' . Agelino . Roberto filio Seward . et Warino de C'aneb' . apud Warha[m in]carnationis[8] dominice . Anno m.°.c.°.xlviii. ii. Idus Ianuarii. In cuius rei testimonium et ad perpetuam rei geste memoriam sigillum nostrum ad deuotam predicte ecclesie sancte Marie de Theok' abbatis et conuentus instantiam presentibus litteris de uerbo ad uerbum diligenter examinatis duximus apponendum. Datum Glouc' in octauo sancte Trinitatis. Anno gratie M°.CC.°.sexagesimo.

¹ *parte* in MS.
² *Rob(er)ti capellani* superscript in the same hand.
³ *suam* in MS.
⁴ *pertinentiis* blotted out by a stain.
⁵ Text blotted out by a stain; wording conjectural.
⁶ Hole in MS.; wording conjectural.
⁷ Hole in MS.; wording conjectural.
⁸ Hole in MS.; wording conjectural.

191. *Final concord between John Abbot of Gloucester and John de Cellario and Isolda his wife and William of Turkdean and Alice his wife concerning a messuage in Gloucester, which they acknowledged to be the right of the abbot and his church; for the acknowledgement the abbot gave them 33s. 3 June 1261. Bristol.*

P.R.O., CP 25/1/74/25, no. 557 (94 mm [left] × 173 mm [foot]; no endorsement.

C Y. . .O G. . .A P. . .U. . .

Hec est finalis concordia facta in curia domini regis apud Bristoll' . In crastino Ascensionis domini anno regni regis Henrici filii regis Iohannis quadragesimo quinto . Coram Gilberto de Preston' . Martino de Litlebir' [.] Wilelmo Engilfend et Galfrido de Leukenor iustic(iis) itinerantibus et aliis domini Regis fidelibus tunc ibi presentibus [.] Inter Iohannem abbatem sancti Petri Glouc' querentem et Iohannem del Celerario et Isoldam vxorem eius et Willelmum de Turkesdene et Aliciam vxorem eius deforciantes de vno mesuagio cum pertinentiis . in Glouc' vnde placitum conuentionis suum fuit inter eos in eadem curia . Scilicet quod predicti Iohannes et Isolda [.] Willelmus et Alicia recognouerunt predictum mesuagium cum pertinentiis esse ius ipsius abbatis et ecclesie sue sancti Petri Glouc' et illud remiserunt et quietumclamauerunt de se et heredibus ipsorum Isolde et Alicie predicto abbati et successoribus suis et ecclesie sue predicte inperpetuum. Et pro hac recognitione remissione [quiet]aclamatione¹ fine et concordia . idem abbas dedit predictis Iohanni et Isolde [.] Willelmo et Alicie triginta et tres solidos sterlingorum.

Glouc'

¹ Hole in MS.

192. *Final concord between John abbot of St. Peter's, Gloucester, and John Giffard concerning the services demanded by the bishop of Hereford from two-thirds of a knight's fee in Ullingswick (Herefs.) which the abbot held of John; John acknowledged that he should acquit the bishop of the services and gave him 5 marks. 22 May 1261. Gloucester.*

A. P.R.O., CP 25/1/74/26, no. 578 (114 mm [left] × 195 mm [foot]); no endorsement; **B**. ibid. C 150/1, fol. 187v; *Cart. Glouc.* ii, no. 692.

CYROGRAPHUM

Hec est finalis concordia facta in curia domini regis apud Glouc' . A die Pasche in vnum mensem . Anno regni Regis Henrici filii regis Iohannis quadragesimo quinto . Coram Gilberto de Preston [.] Martino de Litlebir' . Willelmo de Engilfend' et Galfrido de Leukenor iustic(iis) itinerantibus et aliis domini regis fidelibus tunc ibi presentibus . Inter Iohannem abbatem de Glouc' querentem et Iohannem Giffard . de hoc quod idem Iohannes acquietaret predictum abbatem de seruitiis que episcopus Herford' ab eo exigat de libero tenemento suo quod de predicto Iohanne tenet in Elli'gwyk' . scilicet de duabus partibus feodi vnius militis cum pertinentiis . Et vnde idem abbas questus fuit quod predictus episcopus Herford' distrinxit ipsum quod faceret sectam ad curiam ipsius episcopi de Herford' de mense in mensem . Et quod daret ei releuium cum contigerit de predicto tenemento de qua secta et quo releuio idem Iohannes qui medius est inter eos ipsum acquietare debet [.] Et vnde placitum fuit inter eos in eadem curia . Scilicet quod predictus Iohannes recognouit et concessit pro se et heredibus suis quod ipsi decetero acquietabunt et defendent eundem abbatem et successores suos et ecclesiam suam sancti Petri de Glouc' versus predictum episcopum et successores suos et ecclesiam suam Hereford' . de predicta secta et predicto releuio inperpetuum[.] Et predictus Iohannes dedit predicto abbati quinque marcas argenti [.] et pro hac recognitione [.] concessione [.] donatione [.] fine et concordia predictus abbas remisit et quietumclamauit de se et ecclesia sua predicta predicto Iohanni omnia dampna que dicebat se habuisse occasione quod predictus Iohannes ipsum prius non acquietauerat de predicta secta et predicto releuio vsque ad diem quo hec concordia facta fuit inperpetuum.

Glouc'

193. *Letter from the abbot and convent of St. Peter's, Gloucester, to the king concerning their church of Lampeter [?] which is unjustly occupied by Welshmen and is without a parson. (s. xiii[2])*

P.R.O., SC 1/3 (151) (195 mm × 36 mm); no mode of sealing evident; endorsement: perquira(n)t[1] super tenentes per breuia (s. xiii[2]); *Cart. Glouc.* i, p. lxxix; *Recueil des lettres anglo-francaises*, no. 4, p. 5.

Le abbe et le couent de seynt Pere de Gloucestr' prient a lur seignur le rey ke cum il autrefeiz chalangeyent le droit ke a ews apent endroit del eglyse de Lampadervaur ke la leure fut et occupe e purprys sus ews par Galeys e dunks respundu lur fut par le rey e son consoill' kil enpledassent la persone de meme leglyse. ke notre seignur lur voille fere dreyture de sa grace e pur augmone desicum leglyse est aussi cum sanz persone.

The script of the letter contains features from both before and after 1263.

[1] Reading uncertain.

194. *Grant by the Brethren of the Hospital of St. Mary Magdalen, Dudstone, to the abbot and convent of St. Peter's, Gloucester, of 4d. annual rent charged on land bought by the abbey in Newland (Gloucester), for which the abbey gave the hospital 3s. (s. xiii^{med})*

A. G.C.L., 'Deeds and Seals', i, no. 48, fol. 25 (150 mm × 71 mm); seal on tag; white wax, repaired, rubbed; obverse: round (25 mm in diam.); image(s) indiscernible; legend; + SI. . .ILLV. . . .CE MARIE . . .; no counterseal; endorsements: In Newlonde quietumclamatio iisdem abbati et conuentui sancti Petri (*c.* s. xiv^{ex}); Registratur (s. xiv^{ex} × s. xv^{in}); 10 (crossed; uncertain date); B. ibid. no. 549, p. 241.

Omnibus Cristi fidelibus presens scriptum visuris vel audituris fratres hospitalis sancte Marie Magdalene de Dodeston' salutem in domino. Nouerit vniuersitas vestra quod nos dedimus concessimus et quietumclamauimus abbati et conuentui sancti Petri Gloucestr' et eorum elemosinarie pro nobis et pro omnibus successoribus nostris totum ius et clamium quod habuimus uel aliquo modo habere potuimus in quodam redditu annuali quatuor denariorum quos habuimus ex dono Iohannis Ingulf videlicet de terra quam dicti abbas et conuentus emerunt de Alicia Tynte apud la Neulonde. Et ad maiorem securitatem dictis abbati et conuentui cartam dicti Iohannis Ingulf reddidimus. Pro hac autem donatione et quietaclamatione dederunt nobis premanibus dicti abbas et conuentus per manus elemosinarii tres solidos argenti ad urgens negotium nostrum. In cuius rei testimonium presenti scripto sigillum communitatis[1] nostre apposuimus. Hiis testibus Philippo de Mattesdon' . Willelmo de Chelteham . Iohanne de Eldesfeld' . Petro de felda . Willelmo Munetret et aliis.

The hospital of St. Mary Magdalen, Dudstone, was founded probably by Walter of Gloucester at Wotton outside Gloucester; it received the patronage of Earl Roger of Hereford in the early 1150's and came under the control of Llanthony Secunda (*VCH Glos.* iv. 15; Kealey, *Medieval Medicus*, 112; see also Knowles and Hadcock, 273 [for a different date]). Dudstone was located north of Gloucester (*PNG*, ii. 137). For John Ingulf's charter which St. Peter's acquired in the transaction recorded above see below, no. 314. St Peter's also acquired land which the hospital had quitclaimed to Ingulf (below, no. 297).

[1] Reading uncertain.

195. *Charter of Ralph of Abergavenny granting half of his land (unident.) to the Blessed Peter the Apostle and the almonry of Gloucester abbey and the custody of the other half to Geoffrey the almoner until his return from St. James (of Compostella); if he failed to return he gave that half also to the abbey. (s. xii^{ex}) Hundred and hallmoot of Dudstone and King's Barton.*

A. G.C.L., 'Deeds and Seals', ix, no. 20, fol. 9 (148 mm × 43 mm); damaged; no turn-up; slit for seal on foot; seal missing; endorsements: Radulfus . Bergeueni (s. xii[2]); Registratur (s. xiv^{ex} × s. xv^{in}); **B**. ibid. 'Reg. B', no. 560, p. 245.

Rad(ulfus) de Bergeuini dedit et concessit deo et beate Petri apostoli et elemosine abbatie Gloec'[1] medietatem terre sue . et alteram partem medietatis concessit in custodiam Galfridi elemosinarii donec redeat de Sancto Iacobo . et si non redierit^ istam medietatem cum predicta medietate dat et concedit . deo et abbatie beati Petri Gloec'. Hec donatio facta fuit et presentata in hundredo et hallemoto de Duddestana. et Bertona . His testibus Roberto Capellano de Sancto Iohanne . Ricardo clerico vicecomitis . Alexandro pincerna[2] . Alexandro de Stokes . Petro de Piritona [.] Rogero de Cherchedona . Roberto de Bertona . Morino ministro abbatis Gloec' . Iohanne de P'tona et ceteri quamplures[3] de hundredo[.]

[1] An illegible erasure precedes *medietatem*.
[2] **B** ends here with *et alii quamplures de hundredo*.
[3] Notice the change of case.

196. *Notification by Elured son of Robert of Barton that he has given to St. Peter's, Gloucester, all his right in two pieces of land in Kingsholm (by Gloucester), in free alms, saving to Elured and his heirs annual dues of 3d. at Michaelmas and 1d. at Hockday, with warranty. (c. s. xiii^{in})*

A. G.C.L., 'Deeds and Seals', vi, no. 16, fol. 8 (203 mm × 139 mm [right; orig. meas.]; no provision for sealing; endorsements: : .ii.^a Warda (s. xiii^{med}); sc(ribitur) (s. xiv^{med}); Registratur (s. xiv^{ex} × s. xv^{in}); Kyngshome; I. . .[1] (s. xv); **B**. ibid. 'Reg. B', no. 880, p. 380.

Sciant presentes et futuri quod ego Elured(us) filius Roberti de Berton' dedi et concessi et in perpetuum quietum clamaui deo et ecclesie sancti Petri Glouc' et monachis ibidem deo seruientibus totum ius quod ego et heredes mei habuimus uel habere potuimus in duabus terris versus aulam regis quas Galfridus potarius et Walterus burg' de me et heredibus meis hereditarie tenuerunt tenendas et habendas de me et de heredibus meis pro salute anime mee et omnium antecessorum meorum in liberam . puram . et perpetuam elemosinam cum omnibus pertinentiis suis saluis michi et heredibus meis pro omnibus seruitiis et secularibus demandis annuatim tribus denariis ad festum sancti Michaelis . et vno denario ad Ho(c)ked(ai). Ego uero Elured(us) et heredes mei predictis monachis et eorum successoribus predictas terras contra omnes homines et feminas warentizabimus . et de omnibus sectis et secularibus demandis et longabulo erga dominum regem et omnes homines aquietabimus. Si uero contigerit quod ego uel heredes mei predictas terras warentizare predictis monachis non poterimus.' excambium eis ad valentiam predictarum terrarum de aliis terris nostris plenarie faciemus. Et ut hec mea donatio et concessio et quieta clamantia futuris temporibus rata et stabilis perseueretur.' eam presenti carta et sigilli mei inpressione confirmaui. Hiis testibus . magistro Waltero scriptore . Petro de aula regis[2] . Herberto Walewrd' . Simone de Cellario . Willelmo de B'tona . Henrico Le Bel . Mauricio Marscallo . Ricardo de Aula . et multis aliis.

[1] Illegible with ultra-violet light.
[2] **B** ends here with *et multis aliis.*

197. *Notification by Walter son of Walter Bliss that he has given to St. Peter's, Gloucester, all his land in the girdlery (possibly Mercer Row, Gloucester) in free alms for the use of infirm monks, subject to 2s. annual rent to Richard Tirel and his heirs, and of all his right in other land there which his uncle Thomas and in succession to Thomas his father Walter had held from the abbey for 16s. (annual rent); in the hundred of Gloucester Walter surrendered to St. Peter's his uncle's charter and his own. (c. 1228 × 40)*

A. G.C.L., 'Deeds and Seals', vii, no. 16, fol. 9 (201 mm × 151 mm); seal on tag; white wax laquered light red, round (34 mm in diam.); obverse: an encircled rosette within a diamond; legend: +S': WALTERI: FILII: WALT . . .ISSE; no counterseal; endorsements: Carta Walt(er)i Bliss de terra in zonaria. (s. xiii^{ex}); in zonaria[;] Reg[istratur][1] (s. xiv^{ex} × s xv^{in}); **B.** ibid. 'Reg. B', no. 1062 (1061), pp. 460–1.

Sciant presentes et futuri quod ego Walter(us) filius Walteri Blisse dedi et concessi et presenti carta mea confirmaui deo et eccelsie sancti Petri Glouc' . et domino abbati et conuentui ibidem deo seruientibus ad usus infirmorum monachorum pro salute anime mee et patris mei et matris mee et omnium antecessorum meorum totam terram meam in zonaria que iacet inter terram Dauid scissoris et terram Ricardi Gunter cum omnibus pertinentiis suis sine aliquo retinemento ad opus meum uel heredum meorum que michi iure hereditario de Sibilla matre mea filia Helye palmeri secundum legem et consuetudine terre descendit . tenendam et habendam in liberam . puram. et perpetuam elemosinam . reddendo de ea annuatim Ricardo Tirel et heredibus suis duos solidos ad quatuor anni terminos pro omnibus seruitiis et secularibus demandis . sicut ego et antecessores mei et heredes mei reddere debebamus et solebamus . Scilicet sex denarios ad festum sancte Marie Martialis . et sex denarios ad festum sancti Iohannis Baptiste . et sex denarios ad festum sancti Michaelis . et sex denarios ad Natale domini. Concessi etiam et reddidi eisdem monachis et pro me et pro omnibus heredibus meis quietum clamaui totum ius quod ego uel heredes mei habuimus uel aliquo modo habere potuimus in quadam alia terra in zonaria quam Thomas auunculus meus de infirmaria abbatie pro sexdecim solidis hereditarie tenuit que predicto Waltero patri meo de predicto Thoma auunculo meo iure hereditario pro defectu heredum carnis sue sicut proximo heredi in hereditatem descendit. Et ad maiorem securitatem cartam conuentus Glouc' . quam Thomas auunculus meus de predicta terra habuit insimul cum carta mea coram hundredo Glouc' . eis reddidi. In cuius rei testimonium presens scriptum sigillo meo sigillatum eisdem tradidi. Hiis testibus . Ricardo Burg'nse . Ada Croc preposito Glouc' . Ricardo filio Katerine . Waltero scriptore[2] . Ada filio Rogeri . Ada Gladewine . Galfrido ianitore . et multis aliis.

[1]   Part has been lost, possibly covered by repair material.
[2]   **B** ends here with *et aliis.*

198. *Notification by William Le Breton, son of Robert of Barton, that he has sold to the abbot and convent of St. Peter's, Gloucester, his right in two pieces of land in Gloucester, saving 20s. a year from the first to the abbey's almonry, 16d. a year from the second to the canons of Llanthony, and the tenure in each of Ralph Craft; William gave the abbey his charters and seisin of the lands, and received the purchase price of 12 marks, in the full hundred of Gloucester. (1200 × c. 1228)*

G.C.L., 'Deeds and Seals', i, no. 37, fol. 21 (155 mm × 166 mm); seal on plaited cords; white wax stained green, fragment, worn; obverse: round; image illegible; legend: . . .ILLVM WILL. . .; no counterseal; endorsements: ˊiiii Warda (s. xiii[2]); versus ecclesiam sancte Trinitatis (s. xiv) [;] non in ista carta fit indicatio[1] de .xvi denariis canonicorum Lanton' solue'd' (c. s. xiv[ex]).

Sciant presentes et futuri quod ego Willelm(us) Le Breton' filius Roberti de La b'tona in magno negotio meo vendidi et quietum clamaui de me et heredibus meis abbati et conuentui sancti Petri Glouc' pro duodecim marcis totum ius et totum clamium quod ego uel heredes mei habuimus uel habere potuimus in hiis terris subscriptis . videlicet in terram quam Henricus sacrista aliquando tenuit . que iacet uersus ecclesiam sancte Trinitatis . inter terram quam Walterus Slep tenuit de ecclesia sancti Oswaldiˊ et terram quam Ydonea mater Bartholomei tenuit . Habenda et tenenda libere et quiete absque omni seruitio ad me uel ad heredes meos pertinente . saluis elemosinarie sancti Petri viginti solidis annuis de eadem terra percipiendis duobus terminis . medietate ad Hok(e)d(ai) . et alia medietate ad festum sancti Michaelis . et salua tenura Radulfi Craft sicut carta mea et heredum meorum continetˊ quam inde habet. Predicta uero terra per visum legalium virorum mensurata habet in latitudine decem virgas ulnarias . et in longitudine viginti quatuor virgas ulnarias. Cartam uero eiusdem abbas et conuentus quam inde habui resignaui. Item . In illa terra que fuit supradicte Ydonee matris supradicti Bartholomei que iacet inter terram Alexandri Tilemon . et supradictam terram quam supradictus Henricus sacrista aliquando tenuit . habenda et tenenda libere et quiete ab omni servitio ad me uel ad heredes meos pertinente . salua tenura[2] Radulfi Craft . et saluis sexdecim denariis canonicis Lanton' duobus terminis persoluendis . uidelicet ad Natale et alia medietate ad Natiuitatem sancti Iohannis Baptiste. Predicta uero terra per visum legalium virorum mensurata habet in fronte autem vnam virgam vlnariam . et tria quarteria cum pollice interposito . In longitudine uero decem virgas vlnarias cum pollice interposito. Huius uero carte mee et heredum meorum et predictarum terrarum saisinam ego predictus Willelm(us) Le Breton eidem abbati et conuentui in pleno hundredo Glouc' feci . et ibidem ab eisdem supradictis duodecim marcas recepi. Et ut supradicta omnia perpetuam optineant firmitatem . ea presenti carta sigillo meo munita confirmaui. Hiis testibus . Ricardo Burgense et Mauricio filio Durandi tunc prepositis . Henrico Burgense . Dauid Dunning . Iohanne de Gosedich' . Thoma Oye . Simone de Cellario . Henrico Le Bel . et multis aliis.

¹ Reading uncertain.   ² *tenurā* in MS.

199. *Notification by Richard Burgess that he has granted to St. Peter's, Gloucester, in free alms land in Gloucester for the use of the infirm. (c. s. xiiᵉˣ)*

A. G.C.L., 'Deeds and Seals', ii, no. 12, fol. 7 (151 mm × 120 mm); seal on green, white and brown cords; white wax stained green, fragment, repaired; obverse: oval (meas. unavail.); intaglio gem: full-standing nude male figure facing left, the right hand resting on some object, in the left hand a standard; legend illegible; no counterseal; endorsements: Carta Ric(ardi) Burgeys. (s. xiii); de quadam terra in magno uico iuxta ecclesiam beate Marie de Graslone et de quadam particulam terre in Graslone (s. xiiiᵉˣ?); Registratur (s. xiv); E (illeg. details; uncertain date); **B**. ibid. 'Reg. B', no. 1065 (1064), p. 462.

Sciant presentes et futuri quod ego Ricardus Burg' dedi et concessi et presenti carta mea confirmaui deo et ecclesie sancti Petri Gloec' . ad usum infirmorum in puram et pepetuam elemosinam terram illam quam emi de Ricardo rufo . illam scilicet qui iacet inter terram prioris de Lanton' . et terram quam Godefridus filius Esegari eisdem monachis dedit . que habet in fronte sex uirgas ulnarias cum pollice interposito . Retro. sex uirgas . In profunditate. xxi. uirgas predictas¹ mensura mensuratas. Concessi etiam prefatis monachis quandam partem terre illius quam emi de Roberto filio Meriet que iacet in uiculo iuxta prenominatam terram . que habet in latitudine tres uirgas ulnarias . Retro. quatuor et dimidiam . In profunditate nouem uirgas de dimidiam . sicut de predicta terra mensuratas. Et ut hec mea donatio rata et inconcussa in perpetuum perseueret. presenti scripto sigilli mei impressione munito eam confirmaui. His testibus . Ricardo . Petro . et Henrico filiis meis . Waltero Kadiuor² . Ricardo rufo . Ricardo filio Iordani . Radulfo de Tudeham . Waltero scriptore . et multis aliis.

¹ *uirgam predictam* in MS.
² **B** ends here with *et aliis*.

200. *Notification by Lawrence de Chandos, knight, that he has granted to Abbot John and the convent of St. Peter's, Gloucester, in free alms the wood called Buckholt (in Cranham) and annual rents of 2s. 6½d., 6d., and 1d. (c. 1260)*

A. G.C.L., 'Deeds and Seals', i, no. 27, fol. 16 (248 mm × 133 mm); turn-up repaired, sealing evidence unavail.; tag and seal missing; endorsements: Carta Laur(encii) de Chandos . . .

Domino Iohanni abbati de bosco de Bockol. . .[2] Will(elm)o de Pinecot . . .[3] . . . .[4] filius Will(elm)i de Pinecote. . . .[5] (s. xiii[med]); Caps(ula) xx de laicis tenuris (s. xiii[2]); Registratur (s. xiv?); carta Laurenc' de Chando de toto bosco suo de Bochol' (s. xv?); L(iber) Terrarum parte 2v (modern?)[6]; **B**. P.R.O., C 150/1, fol. 36; *Cart. Glouc.* i, no. 91.

Sciant presentes et futuri quod ego Laurencius de Chaundos miles dedi concessi . et hac presenti carta mea confirmaui domino Iohanni abbati sancti Petri Gloucestr' . et eiusdem loci conuentui totum boscum meum quod uocatur Bocholte cum solo et omnibus aliis pertinentiis . exceptis quinque acris quas Henricus de Drois de me tenuit . et excepta quadam parte eiusdem bosci quam Basilia que fuit uxor Roberti fratris mei tenuit in dotem . quod quidem boscum Adam de Benetham de me tenet. Dedi etiam dictis abbati et conuentui duos solidos sex denarios et vnum obolum annui redditus quos Willelmus de Pinnecote forestarius michi reddere consueuit . Et sex denarios annui redditus quos Iohannes Barcet michi reddere consueuit . et vnum denarium annui redditus quem Iohannes filius Willelmi de Pinnecote[7] michi reddere consueuit . cum homagiis . releuiis . wardis . herietis . et omnibus aliis eschaetis sine aliquo retenemento. Quare uolo et firmiter concedo pro me et heredibus meis quod dicti abbas et monachi et eorum successores habeant et teneant totum predictum boscum et redditum . cum solo et omnibus suis ubique pertinentiis in puram liberam et perpetuam elemosinam . libere . quiete et integre i(n)perpetuum ita quod nec ego nec aliquis ex parte mea aliquid iuris uel clamii in dicto bosco uel redditu cum pertinentiis durante seculo uendicare uel habere poterimus nisi tantummodo orationes. Ego uero dictus Laurenci(us) et heredes mei totum predictum boscum et redditum cum omnibus pertinentiis sicut predictum est . dictis abbati et monachis et eorum successoribus contra omnes gentes imperpetuum warantizabimus et defendemus et de omnimodis seruitiis sectis et demandis aquietabimus. In cui[us][8] rei testimonium presenti scripto sigillum meum apposui. Hiis testibus magistro Rogero de Glouc' [.] domino Ricardo de Chirchesdon [.] domino Iohanne [P][9]iriton' . Philippo de Haþerle . Philippo de Mattesdon' . Ricardo venatore . Roberto de Pinntone[10] . et aliis.

For the date of the grant see *Cart. Glouc.* i, p. 65. Lawrence de Chandos later was granted life tenure at Brockworth by Abbot Reginald de Homme (1263 × 1284) (ibid. no. 98).

[1]   Ink smudged; illegible.
[2]   Text faded; illegible.
[3]   Terminal letter faded; illegible.
[4]   Text faded; illegible.
[5]   Text faded; illegible.
[6]   Reading uncertain.
[7]   Apparently *Pintiecote* changed to *Pinncote* in MS.; reading uncertain.
[8]   Portion of MS. destroyed.
[9]   Portion of MS. destroyed.
[10]   Reading uncertain.

201. *Notification by Ranulf II earl of Chester that he has given to St. Peter's, Gloucester, 40s. revenue from the mills of Olney (Bucks.) and has confirmed his sister Alice's gift of a mill at Tathwell (Lincs.) for the soul of her husband Richard fitz Gilbert. (April × May 1153).*

A. H.C.L., no. 802 (180 mm × 61 mm); no turn-up; slit for tag in foot between last two lines of text; tag and seal missing; endorsements: Ranulf comes Cestrie (1153 × *c.* 1170); Rann(ulfus) comes Cestrie. (s. xii²), **Hand a**; De .xl. solidis in molendinis de Olneia. et de molendino de Taddewella (1153 × *c.* 1170), **Hand b**; .c(apsula) .xv. de laicis tenuris. (s. xii² × s. xiii^in); Registratur (s. xiv^ex × s. xv^in); **B.** P.R.O., C 150/1, no. 157, fol. 61; *Cart. Glouc.* i, no. 157; *Chart. Chester*, no. 116; cal. in Baddeley i, no. 6, p. 226.

Ran(ulfus)[1] comes Cest'ie conestabulis[2] suis et dapiferis suis . et omnibus baronibus Francis et Anglis et omnibus ministris suis . et omnibus fidelibus sancte ecclesie[3] . salutem. Sciatis me dedisse in elemosinam ecclesie sancti Petrie Gloucest'ie et monachis eiusdem ecclesie . quadraginta solidos in molendinis Olneie . ereditario iure. [Et vol]o et precipio ut firmiter et in pace teneant . et ut nullus eis aliquam molestiam inde illis infe[r]r[e]t. Confirmo[4] etiam per presentem hanc cartam molendinum de Taddawella quam dedit eis Aliz: soror mea pro anima Ricardi filii[5] Gilleberti . uiri sui. Et ideo uolo et precipio quod illam teneant in elemosina perpetuali de me et eredibus meis. Et si quis eis aliquam iniuriam inde faciat . super excommunicationem[6] faciat.[7] Testibus . Hugone . Wac . et castellano . et Ricardo pincerna[8] . et Radulfo marescallo.[9]

The above text was transcribed with the aid of ultra-violet light. For the probable date of the charter, see *Chart. Chester*, 131–2. The grant is noted in the abbey's Calendar of Donations (*Cart. Glouc.* i, p. 104).

[1] Printed *Rogerus* in *Cart. Glouc.*
[2] *Canostal'* in MS.
[3] *eclesie* in MS.
[4] *canfirmo* in MS.
[5] *fili* in MS.
[6] *excummunicationem* in MS.
[7] **B** as printed in *Cart. Glouc.* ends here.
[8] *pincerno* in MS.
[9] *marescello* in MS.

202. *Notification by John of Cormeilles that he has confirmed to the abbot and convent of St. Peter's, Gloucester, in free alms three virgates in Radenham (in Murcott, Minsterworth) given by Lucas of Clanfeld and his sons and has granted rents in cash and kind for 4s. a year and royal service. (c. 1225 × 35)*

A. H.C.L., no. 2174 (147 mm × 77 mm), poss. **Scribe 18**; seal on tag: green wax, rubbed; obverse: round (*c.* 30 mm); a triangular shaped shield; legend: +s' . . .; no counterseal;

endorsements: Confirmatio .I. de Cormailes de terra de Radenham; Caps(ula) .iii. de laicis tenuris (s. xiii^ex × s. xiv^in)); Registratur (s. xiv^ex × s. xv^in); **B.** P.R.O., C 150/1, fol. 237; *Cart. Glouc.* ii, no. 873; cal. in Baddeley ii, no. 148, p. 45.

Sciant presentes et futuri quod ego Ioh(anne)s de Cormal' concessi et confirmaui pro me et heredibus meis abbati et conuentui sancti Petri Glouc' in liberam puram et perpetuam elemosinam tres uirgatas terre de tenemento meo cum omnibus pertinentiis earum in Radenham quas Lucas de Clenefeld cum Roberto . Willelmo . et Waltero filiis suis eisdem abbati et conuentui imperpetuam elemosinam dedit . Et unam libram piperis de illa uirgata terre quam idem Lucas dedit Willelmo le Blund cum Annora filia sua in liberum maritagium . Et duodecim denarios quos Robertus Rufus predicto Luce et heredibus suis annuatim reddere debebat . Et etiam regale seruitium de predictis uirgatis terre et Roberto Rufo . Tenenda et habenda omnia predicta libere et quiete imperpetuum saluis mihi et heredibus meis quatuor solidis annuatim ad festum sancti Michaelis pro omnibus seruitiis exactionibus et secularibus demandis que de terra exeunt uel exire poterunt . excepto regali seruitio. Et ut hec mea concessio et confirmatio robur optineat imperpetuum[1] presens scriptum sigillo meo munitum predictis abbati et conuentui tradidi. Hiis testibus . Rogero filio Stephani de Andev'e . Ada de la spineye . Thoma Carbunel . Willelmo seruiente de Lutlintun' . et multis aliis.

The text of Lucas's charter is in *Cart. Glouc.* ii, no. 596; relevant *acta* are in ibid. nos. 870–2. Thomas Carbonel, son of Philip, received land from his sister, Edith, *c.* 1220 (Stevenson, nos. 165–6); he may have been an attesting cook (ibid. no. 164). For *Radenham*, see *Cart. Glouc.* i, p. 110; *PNG*, iii. 165.

[1] **B** as printed in *Cart. Glouc.* ends here.

203. *Alleged notification by William Devereux that he has confirmed Monkhide (in Yarkhill) in Herefordshire to the abbot and convent of St. Peter's, Gloucester, in free alms. (supposedly 1114 × 30; s. xiii[1])*

A. G.C.L., 'Deeds and Seals', xi, no. 1 (227 mm × 81 mm); seal on tag; white wax, chipped, repaired, round (approx. 50 mm orig. in diam.); obverse: a mounted equestrian figure to the right, a raised sword in the right hand, a shield on the left arm; legend: . . .IGILLVM. . .RO. . .; reverse, no counterseal; endorsements: Carta de hida ex dono Will(elm)i de Ebroicis (s. xiii^med), poss. **Hand q**; Registratur (s. xiv^ex × s. xv^in); **B.** ibid. 'Reg. B', no. 100, pp. 35–36; Baddeley, ii, p. 48.

Notum sit tam presentibus quam futuris quod ego Will(elmu)s de Ebroicis pro salute anime mee et omnium antecessorum meorum dedi concessi et hac presenti carta confirmaui deo et ecclesie sancti Petri Gloecestrie et abbati et monachis ibidem deo seruientibus in liberam puram et perpetuam elemosinam quamdam terram meam cum omnibus pertinentiis suis que uocatur Hida que est de feudo meo in H'efordsir'. tenendam et habendam de me et heredibus meis solutam quietam et liberam ab omnibus exactionibus sectis secularibus demandis consuetudinibus omnibus seruitiis domini regis et cuiuscu(m)que domini terreni et omnibus aliis que terris uel tenementis exigi poterunt uel reddi quia ego ipse eam ab omnibus ut predictum est tam per me quam per heredes meos acquietabo ac defendam[1] in perpetuum. Et ego et heredes mei predictam terram cum omnibus pertinentiis suis predictis abbati et monachis contra omnes mortales warantizabimus in perpetuum[.] In huius rei testimonium presens scriptum sigillo meo roboratum domino Willelmo abbati in pleno capitulo Gloec' tradidi et postea in presentia domini abbatis et totius conuentus et multorum aliorum super altare sancti Petri propriis manibus coram deo et omnibus sanctis eius deposui.

The text's reference to Abbot William would date the transaction 1113 × 30, but its script, suspension signs, form of tironian *con*, and warranty clause establish it as a forgery. For Monkhide, see *Herefordshire Place-Names*, 215.

[1] *deffendam* in MS.

204. *Alleged notification by William Devereux and his sons, Hugh, John, and William that they have confirmed, in the presence of Abbot Gilbert and the whole chapter, the grant by the elder William's father to St. Peter's, Gloucester, of Monkhide in Herefordshire free of all service, with acquittance of any service due to the king. (1139 × 48)*

A. G.C.L., 'Deeds and Seals', i, no. 5, fol. 3 (192 mm × 74 mm); cords, originally pink ? for seal; seal missing; endorsements: De Hida (s. xiii[med]), **Hand m**; carta W(illelmi) de Ebroicis et filiorum eius de terra de H. . .[1] (s. xiv[med]); ii (uncertain date); Registratur (s. xiv[ex] × s. xv[in]); **B**. ibid. 'Reg. B', no. 101, p. 36.

Will(el)mus de Ebroicis et Hugo et Ioh(ann)es . et Will(el)mus filii eius vniuersis matris ecclesie filiis salutem[.] Notum sit omnibus presentibus et futuris quod ego Will(elmu)s de Ebroicis . et filii mei Hugo. et Ioh(ann)es . et Will(el)mus concessimus . et presenti carta confirmauimus deo et ecclesie sancti Petri Gloec' in presentia domini .G. abbatis et totius capituli Gloec' . terram quamdam que uocatur Hida in Herefordesira que est de feudo nostro . et quam pater meus dedit eidem ecclesie in puram et perpetuam elemosinam tenendam de me et heredibus meis liberam et quietam ab omni exactione . consuetudine . et seruitio domini regis . et cuiusque domini terreni quia ego ipse eam ab omni seruitio terreno adquietabo . tam per me quam per heredes meos. Huius rei testes sunt . Rogerus comes Hereford' . Walterus frater eius . Walterus de Bello ca'po . Radulfus de Bascheuilla . Rogerus filius Picardi . Hugo de Turbeuilla . Hugo de Faleisa . Rogerus de Stantona . Alanus filius main . Radulfus Auenel . Robertus filius Hugonis . Robertus de Boudeswell' . Baldewinus de Buillero . Willelmus pauper . Philippus Alis . et Gilebertus frater eius . Willelmus Foliot . Serlo Foliot . Herebertus Quatremains.

The Devereux family were honorial tenants of the Lacy lords of Weobly (Wightman, *The Lacy*

Family, 154–5 & n.); Monkhide was given to Helewisa upon her marriage to William Devereux (ibid. 170; above, no. 48 n.); a donation to St. Peter's by William's father was confirmed in a spurious (?) charter of William I (*Cart. Glouc.* i, no. 316); Archbishop Theobald of Canterbury between 1138 and 1148, while Gilbert Foliot was abbot of St. Peter's, and later Henry II confirmed the above grant (ibid. i, nos. 130, 347; ii, no. 630); Saltman, *Theobald*, no. 111; see above, nos. 46–48).

1   Almost certainly *Hida* but illegible with ultra-violet light.

205. *Notification by Robert Chaplain son of Richard miller of Eastleach Martin that he has granted to St. Peter's, Gloucester, in free alms the land and mill which he held of the abbey in Eastleach in return for spiritual benefits. (s. xiii^{med})*

A. G.C.L., 'Deeds and Seals', vi, no. 26, fol. 13 (232 mm × 93 mm); seal on tag; green wax, fragment, chipped, repaired: obverse, oval (meas. unavail.); image indiscernible; legend: . . . IE . . . CA . . .; no counterseal; endorsements: Carta Rob(er)ti Cap(e)ll(an)i de molendino de Estlech'[;] Caps(ula) .xv. de laicis tenuris (s. xiii^{med}); E te(m)p(or)alium p(ar)t(e) Ia (s. xiv^{ex}); Registratur (uncertain date); **B**. P.R.O., C 150/1, fol. 75; *Cart. Glouc.* i, no. 220.

Sciant presentes et futuri quod ego Rob(ertu)s Capellanus filius Ricardi molendinarii de Estlech . dedi . concessi . et quietum clamaui . pro salute anime mee et animarum antecessorum meorum deo et ecclesie beati Petri Gloucest'ie et monachis ibidem deo seruientibus totam terram meam cum molendino . redditibus . seruitiis . pratis . pascuis . pasturis . eisiamentis et cum omnibus suis pertinentiis et libertatibus . quam quidem terram . et quod molendinum cum eorum pertinentiis ego ab eisdem monachis tenui in manerio de Estlech . et quarumcumque ad me et ad heredes meos aliquo modo iure hereditario accidere poterit inposterum . Tenendam et habendam in puram et perpetuam elemosinam sibi et successoribus suis imperpetuum absque aliquo retenemento ad opus meum uel heredum meorum . Reseruatis tamen michi . antecessoribus . et successoribus meis dicte ecclesie beneficiis spiritualibus.[1] In cuius rei testimonium presens scriptum sigilli mei munimine′. et inpressione roboraui. Hiis testibus . Radulfo de Lecche . Henrico Beaufiz . Willelmo de Lecch' . Simone le mascun . Martino le drap(er) . Siwat de Fifhide . Waltero bolle . et multis aliis.

1   **B** as printed in *Cart. Glouc.* ends here with *etc.*

206. *Notification by Gilbert of Eldersfield that he has granted to the abbot and convent of St. Peter's, Gloucester, the land which he held from the abbey between the bridges of Gloucester, for which the abbey has given him 1 mark. (1258)*

A. G.C.L., 'Deeds and Seals', vi, no. 9, fol. 5 (251 mm × 88 mm); tag with residue of white wax; seal missing; endorsements: Quieta clamatio .G. de Eldisfeld de domo inter pontes (s. xiii^2); Registratur (s. xiv^{ex} × s. xv^{in}); **B**. ibid. 'Reg. B', no. 812, p. 351.

Sciant presentes et futuri quod ego Gilebert(us) de Eldresfeld' reddidi . remisi . et quietam clamaui abbati et conuentui sancti Petri Glouc' illam terram quam tenui in feodo et hereditate a dictis abbate et conuentu que iacet inter pontes Glouc' videlicet inter terram Iohannis de Eldesfeld' et terram que fuit Reginaldo Badde [.] Ita quod liceat dictis abbati et conuentui dictam terram retinere uel in feudum et hereditatem cuicumque tradere . Et etiam de eadem ordinare prout voluerint absque aliqua contradictione mei uel heredum meorum nullo iure nec clamio michi nec heredibus meis in dicta terra in posterum reseruato. Pro hac autem redditione . remissione . et quieta clammatione dicti abbas et conuentus dederunt michi premanibus vnam marcam argenti . pro qua quidem pecunia eosdem abbatem et conuentum coram bailliuis Glouc' in plenam saisinam dicte terre posui. Et me et heredes meos extra posui inperpetuum. In cuius rei testimonium presenti scripto sigillum meum apposui. Hiis testibus . Rogero Ienueyse . Willelmo de Chilteham tunc prepositis Glouc' . Iohanne filio Symonis . Ricardo Hoch[1] . Petro Sewi . Ricardo de Celario . et multis aliis.

For Gilbert of Eldersfield, see no. 112 & n. The witnesses Roger le Wyse and William of Cheltenham were bailiffs of Gloucester in 1258 (*VCH Glos.* iv. 372).

---

[1] **B** ends here with *et aliis.*

---

207. *Notification by Adam Esgar that he has given to St. Peter's, Gloucester, his land outside Alvingate (Gloucester) for the support of sick monks, saving payment of ½d. a year to the prior and convent of St. Oswald; if the donor or his heirs cannot warrant the gift, a reasonable exchange will be made. (c. 1224 × 28)*

A. G.C.L., 'Deeds and Seals', v, no. 44, fol. 21 (18.5 mm × 79 mm); seal on tag; white wax, fragment, rubbed, repaired; obverse: round (*c.* 30 mm in diam.); partial image of a fleur-de-lis; legend illegible; no counterseal; endorsements: Carta de aula regis (s. xiii[1]); Priori sancti Oswaldi obolum ad Hockeday (s. xiii); Aluengate; Registratur (s. xiv[ex] × s. xv[in]); **B**. ibid. 'Reg. B', no. 1015 (1014), p. 439.

Sciant presentes et futuri quod ego Adam Esgar dedi et concessi deo et ecclesie sancti Petri Glouc' et monachis ibidem deo seruientibus in liberam puram et perpetuam elemosinam in usus egrotantium monachorum terram meam extra Eluenegathe uersus Henneride . Illam scilicet que iacet inter terram eorumdem monachorum et terram quam Mabilia Brond dedit ecclesie sancti Iohannis Baptiste in Glouc' ad luminare . Tenendam et habendam in perpetuum libere et quiete ab omni seruitio et seculari demanda ad me uel heredes meos pertinente saluo priori et conuentui sancti Osuualdi Glouc' vno obolo annuatim ad Hockeday pro omnibus seruitiis persoluendo. Ego autem predictus .A. et heredes mei predictam terram predictis monachis contra omnes homines et feminas warantizabimus in perpetuum. Si uero aliquo casu contingat quod ego uel heredes mei predictam terram predictis monachis warantizare non possimus. rationabile escambium de aliis terris nostris faciemus eisdem. In cuius rei testimonium presens scriptum sigillo meo munitum prefatis monachis tradidi. Hiis testibus . Ricardo filio Willelmi . Thoma Oye . Waltero scriptore[1] . Roberto Le sauuage . Nicholao de infirmaria . et multis aliis.

Thomas Oye, who served as one of Gloucester's bailiffs 1200 × 40, attested many local *acta* (*VCH Glos.* iv. 371–2).

[1] **B** ends here with *et aliis.*

208. *Grant in free alms to the abbot and convent of St. Peter's, Gloucester, by Gerald Farrier of all his right in land in Sidnall in Pencombe (Herefs.). (s. xiii[in])*

A. H.C.L., no. 780 (144 mm × 132 mm), **Scribe 16**; seal on tag; white wax stained dark green; obverse: round (30 mm in diam.); a large fleur-de-lis flanked by decorative leaves; legend: +SIGILL': GERALDI: MARSCALLI; no counterseal; endorsements: Carta de Suthale [;] Caps(ula) .xiii. de laicis tenuris (s. xiii[2]); Registratur (s. xiv[ex] × s. xv[in]); in parochia de Pencombe (s. xv[1]); **B.** P.R.O., C 150/1, fol. 172v; *Cart. Glouc.* ii, no. 623; cal. in Baddeley ii, no. 65, pp. 26–27.

Sciant presentes et futuri quod ego Geraldus Marescallus pro deo et salute anime mee dedi et quietum clamaui abbati et conuentui sancti Petri Glouc' inperpetuum totum ius quod ego et heredes mei habuimus uel habere potuimus in tota terra de Suthenhale cum omnibus pertinentiis suis in parochia de Pencumbe quam habui ex dono domini Martini de Pateshulle pro homagio et seruitio meo . In liberam puram et perpetuam elemosinam cum omnibus libertatibus ad eandem terram pertinentibus in uilla . et extra uillam sine aliquo retinemento ad opus meum uel heredum meorum . et ad maiorem securitatem tam presentem cartam quam omnes alias quas de predicta terra habui in pleno comitatu Herefordie dictis abbati et conuentui tradidi. Et ut hec mea donatio perpetuum robur optineat presenti scripto sigilllum meum apposui. Hiis testibus . Petro de Eggesworþe[1] . magistro Waltero scriptore . magistro Waltero de Banneburi . Waltero Biset . Hugone Giffard' . Galfrido de Morton' . Galfrido de Weston' . et multis aliis.

The text of the grant by Martin of Pattishall (d. 1229) to Gerald is in *Cart. Glouc.* ii, no. 622; it is noted in the abbey's Calendar of Donations (ibid. i, p. 114). Gerald's gift of the land to St. Peter's as recorded above is also noted in the Calendar (ibid. 114–15).

[1] **B** as printed in *Cart. Glouc.* ends here with *etc.*

209. *Notification by Ralph fitz Stephen that Patchway belongs to St. Peter's, Gloucester, and is free of scutage and hidage as a tenure in free alms. (c. 1189)*

A. H.C.L., no. 1641 (130 mm × 110 mm); seal on plaited cords, white wax, chipped; top missing; obverse: pointed oval (length unavail.; width, *c.* 25 mm); a lion ? rampant; legend:

. . .VL. . .ANE . . .; no counterseal; endorsements: De libertate de Petsage (*c.* 1200); Registratur (s. xiv^ex × s. xv^in); **B**. P.R.O., C 150/1, fol. 161; *Cart. Glouc.* ii, no. 573; cal. in Baddeley i, no. 31, p. 233 .

Omnibus ad quos presens scriptum peruenerit . Radulf(us) filius Steph(ani) salutem in domino. Vniversitati uestre[1] notum fieri uolo quod ego Rad(ulfus) filius Steph(ani) per visnetum circa Winterburnam plenarie didici quod Petsage est pertinens ad ecclesiam sancti Petri Gloec' . et quod ipsa Petsage est libera et quieta de scutagio et hidagio sicut pura et perpetua elemosina. Et quia nolo quod tractu temporis monasterium sancti Petri Gloec' . uel per me . uel per heredes meos in posterum super villa de Petsage aliquid de scutagio . uel hidagio uel de exactione aliqua patiatur grauamen uel molestiaḿ . concedo pro salute anime mee . et pro salute regis Henrici domini mei et pro salute . vxoris mee et omnium parentum meorum quod iam dictum monasterium sua in perpetuum gaudeat libertate. In cuius rei testimonium presens scriptum sigilli mei impressione roborauí . confirmaui. Hiis testibus . Willelmo fratre meo . et Willelmo nepote meo . Willelmo de Chaines[2] . Matheo clerico meo . Waltero Giffard . Waltero Tochi . Roberto de la Felde . Gaufrido de Liletona . Willelmo de Bromiard' .

Ralph fitz Stephen (d. 1202) was a *familiaris*, royal chamberlain, and itinerant justice during the reign of King Henry II from 1157 or earlier to 1189; he was sheriff of Gloucestershire from Michaelmas 1171 until Michaelmas 1175. His grant in part for the soul of King Henry suggests an occasion following the king's death. Among fitz Stephen's holdings were lands at Winterbourne valued at £22 (Lally, 'Court and Household of Henry II', 332–5). Fitz Stephen mentioned that Patchway belonged to his demesne in another grant to St. Peter's (*Cart. Glouc.* ii, no. 574). Conflicting claims to rights at Patchway between St. Peter's and St. Augustine's Bristol were resolved in a *conventio* between John and William, abbots respectively of the two houses (above, no. 181).

[1] *nostre* in MS. [2] **B** ends here with *Willelmo de Chames et aliis.*

---

210. *Notification by Eustace son of Thurstan Fleming that he has granted a hide called Sidnall in Pencombe (Herefs.) to the convent of St. Peter's, Gloucester. (c. 1200)*

A. H.C.L., no. 779 (147 mm × 40 mm); tongue apparently cut from left foot; seal missing; no provision for sealing; endorsements: De Penecumba[;] Caps(ula) .xiii. de laicis tenuris (s. xiii^ex); Penthenhala[;] Registratur (s. xiv^ex × s. xv^in); **B**. P.R.O., C 150/1, fols. 172–172v; *Cart. Glouc.* ii, no. 621; cal. in Baddeley i, no. 1, p. 224.

Sciant presentes et futuri quod ego Eustachius filius Thurstini Flandrensis ad petitionem Agnetis matris mee . dedi sancto Petro et fratribus de Gloucestra vnam hydam in Pencomba que vocatur Sudenhala solutam et quietam ab omni re . et per scriptum istud super altare sancti Petri de Glouc' posui. Huius rei testes sunt . Thurstinus Flandrensis frater meus . Willelmus presbiter eiusdem uille . Willelmus de stabulo . Wimundus . Rogerius de Kaillewi . Rogerius Castel[1] . et Radulfus dapifer.

According to the St. Peter's Calendar of Donations, Agnes, widow of Turstin Fleming, and her son Eustace granted the hide at Sidnall to the abbey during the abbacy of Reginald de Homme (1263 × 84) ('Historia', 107, 115; see also ibid. 124), but the script is of the early thirteenth century. On ibid. 124 is a notice of a joint grant from Eustace and his mother Agnes which may refer to the donation recorded in the charter above. Apparently the notices on ibid. 107 and 115 refer to a grant by Eustace, the text of which indicates that it was made after Agnes's death and in the time of Abbot Reginald.

¹ **B** as printed in *Cart. Glouc.* ends here with *etc.*

211. *Charter of William Fuket, son of William Fuket, granting to the abbot and convent of St. Peter's, Gloucester, and their almonry the four acres in Abbot's Barton outside Gloucester which his father granted to John May in free marriage with William's sister Alice; the almoner is to pay William 2d. a year. (s. xiii^{med})*

A. G.C.L., 'Deeds and Seals', ii, no. 5, fol. 3 (228 mm × 140 mm), **Scribe 32**; seal on tag; white wax stained green, chipped, repaired; obverse: round (32 mm in diam.); large fleur-de-lis; legend: + . . . WILL'I: FILII: WIL': FUKET; no counterseal; endorsements: Confirmatio et quietaclamatio Will(elm)i Foket de quatuor acris terre. F. Q.a I.I. D (s. xiii^{med}); Registratur (s. xiv^{ex} × s. xv^{in}); **B**. ibid. 'Reg. B', no. 626, p. 271.

Sciant presentes et futuri quod ego Will(elmu)s Foket filius Willelmi Foket concessi et confirmaui abbati et conuentui sancti Petri Glouc' et eorum elemosinarie illas quatuor acras terre cum pertinentiis suis in bertona dicti abbatis extra Glouc' . Quas Willelmus Foket pater meus dedit Iohanni Mey in liberum maritagium cum Alicia sorore mea . et in quas acras idem abbas et conuentus et eorum elemosinarius habuerunt ingressum per dictos Iohannem et Aliciam . Tenendas et habendas sibi et successoribus suis libere et quiete integre cum pertinentiis suis de me et heredibus meis in perpetuum . sine aliquo clamio . reuocatione uel demanda que posset per me uel per heredes meos euenire . Reddendo inde annuatim michi et heredibus meis ipsi per manum elemosinarii eorum qui pro tempore fuerit duos denarios argenti ad festum sancti Michaelis pro omnibus seruitiis et demandis . Quos duos denarios predicti Iohannes et Alicia assignauerunt michi recipiendos pro se et pro heredibus eorum. Et si forte aliquo casu emergente contigerit . quod dictus Iohannes Mey et Alicia uxor eius uel eorum heredes dictam terram cum pertinentiis . dictis abbati et conuentui warantizare non potuerint.¹ ego et heredes mei pro predicto redditu duorum denariorum michi assignato de terris nostris warantizabimus ad ualentiam et extentam dictarum quatuor acrarum . videlicet de duobus seillonibus apud Calurecrofte iuxta terram Roberti Foket . et de duobus seillonibus extendentibus ad caput longe forerde iuxta terram Roberti Foket . in campo de Truddewrth' . et de uno seillone apud Middelwey iuxta terram dicti Roberti Foket . et de una acra de tribus seillonibus iacentibus ultra Sudbrok iuxta uiam regalem . et de duobus seillonibus desuper bertonam inter terram Iohannis Peky et terram Royse Crikel' . et de una acra iacente apud Asketillespol iuxta terram Roberti Foket . et de uno seillone iacente in marisco iuxta terram Roberti Foket. Pro hac autem concessione . confirmatione et warantizatione mea'. dicti abbas et conuentus dederunt michi premanibus per manum elemosinarii eorum ad magnum negotium duodecim denarios argenti. Et quia uolo quod hec mea concessio . confirmatio et warantizatio . rata et stabilis in perpetuum perseueret'. presenti scripto sigillum meum apposui. Hiis testibus . Galfrido de Weston' . Iohanne de Eldresfeld' . Willelmo de Cheddesleye[2] . Roberto len veyse . Waltero de Snedham . Galfrido de la Graue . Willelmo Gerard(e) . Symone de Mattresdon' . et aliis.

This charter in effect confirmed John and Alice's gift to St. Peter's of her *maritagium* (below, no. 246). See below, no. 311 for William's charter to John Mey; see also no. 247.

[1] *pot(er)unt* in MS.
[2] **B** ends here with *et aliis.*

212. *Notification by Wimarc widow of John Franchevaler that she has granted in free alms to St. Peter's, Gloucester, land which she bought from Wacius Cook in Longford for shoeing the horses of visiting and poor guests at the abbey. (1179 × 1205; poss. c. 1179)*

A. G.C.L., 'Deeds and Seals', i, no. 3, fol. 2 (246 mm × 177 mm); partial tag on turn-up; seal missing; endorsements: WIMARC. FRANCHEV'. De illa terra quam Willelmus filius Siwardi tenuit in Langeford (*c.* 1179); C(apsula) .iiii. de laicis tenuris (s. xii^{ex}); **B**. P.R.O., C 150/1, fol. 111v; **C**. G.C.L., 'Reg. B', no. 426, p. 188; *Cart. Glouc.* i, no. 349 (from **B**).

Sciant presentes et futuri quod ego Wimarc relicta Iohannis francheualer dedi et concessi deo et ecclesie sancti Petri Gloec' et monachis ibidem deo seruientibus pro salute anime mee et pro animabus domini mei Iohannis francheualer . et Willelmi filii mei . et omnium parentum meorum in liberam puram et perpetuam elemosinam . terram quam emi de Wacio Coco in Longeford' . de proprio catallo meo inperpetuum libere et quiete possidendam . quam Willelmus filius Siwardi tenuit de me . scilicet quatuor acras de prato . et duas acras de terra arabili ad ferramenta emenda'. equis uirorum religiosorum hospitium scilicet superuenientium et indigentium. Ferramenta uero et emolumenta ex predicta terra peruenientia'. recipiantur . et administrentur . per manus monachi hostellarii religiosos uiros hospitandos suscipientis. Et ut hec donatio rata et inconcussa inperpetuum permaneat'. eam presenti carta sigilli mei impressione munitam roboraui. Roberto francheualer filio meo et Olimpiade filia Willelmi filii mei consentibus et presentem cartam super altare beati Petri offerentibus.[1] His testibus . Æmaldo de Walesworth' . Iocelino et Milone filiis eius . Hereberto . et Thoma . filiis Iocelini[2] . Henrico de Bares . Philippo Carbonel . Waltero Tochi . Willelmo Ianitore . Waltero de Abilad' . Salomone de Frocest'ia . Galfrido de Lilletona . Willelmo ruffo de Framilad' . Gaufrido de Merewent . Helya de Pagaham . et multis aliis.

Wimarc's gift was made during the abbacy of Thomas Carbonel and apparently after the deaths of her husband and son (*Cart. Glouc.* i, p. 95). John Franchevaler was alive possibly as late as *c.* 1170 when he attested a grant by Elias Giffard (G.R.O., GBR/J1/84; for dating comparison, see Salter, *Oxford Charters*, no. 77 (1154 × 63); Stevenson, no. 84, dated the Giffard charter *c.* 1180). Another version of Wimarc's grant is in *Cart. Glouc.* i, no. 350. Wimarc's grant above is referred to in an *inspeximus* of Silvester bishop of Worcester (1216–18) (ibid. no. 131, p. 230).

[1] **B** as printed in *Cart. Glouc.* ends here.
[2] **B** ends here with *et aliis.*

213. *Notification by Alexander Furbrich that he has quitclaimed to the abbot and convent of St. Peter's, Gloucester, all his right in land by Alvingate (Gloucester) of the fee of the earl of Gloucester and of the abbot of Gloucester, for which the abbey gave Alexander 1 mark and his daughter Margery 12d. (c. 1228 × 40)*

A. G.C.L., 'Deeds and Seals', iv, no. 22, fol. 11 (186 mm × 130 mm); seal on tag; white wax stained green, repaired; obverse: round (32 mm in diam.); large fleur-de-lis; legend: +S' ALEXSANDRI. FURBRICH; no counterseal; endorsements: Alexander furchirc (s. xiii ?); versus v[1] . . . (s. xiv?); another endorsement illegible with ultra-violet light; **B.** ibid. 'Reg. B', no. 745, pp. 321–2.

Sciant presentes et futuri quod ego Alexander Furbrich. remisi . et in perpetuum pro me . et pro omnibus heredibus meis quietaclamaui domino abbati et conuentui sancti Petri Glouc' . totum ius . et clamium quod ego uel heredes mei habuimus. vel aliquo tempore habere potuimus in quadam terra uersus portam de Eluenegate . de feodo comitis Glouc' . et abbatis Glouc' . Que iacet inter terram Iohannis Pomerai . et Iohannis Bai . Quam Thomas rector ecclesie beati Iohannis Baptiste emit de Rocelino. Pro hac autem concessione . et quietaclamatione. predicti monachi in mea magna necessitate vnam marcam argenti michi dederunt . et Margerie filie mee duodecim denarios. In cuius rei testimonium presens scriptum sigillo meo sigillatum eis tradidi. Hiis testibus . Thoma rectore ecclesie sancti Iohannis Baptiste . Waltero Pain tunc preposito . Waltero Hoch[2] . Adam filio Rogeri . Willelmo le saltere . Stephano Cornubiensi . Willelmo de Wike . et multis aliis.

On the left front of the turn-up two words, one above the other, have been erased, which ultra-violet light failed to make legible. The text of Rocelin mercer's sale of the property to Thomas as parson of St. John's Gloucester is in G.C.L., 'Reg. B', no. 447, p. 198). Walter Pain served as bailiff of Gloucester on a number of occasions 1200 × *c.* 1240 (*VCH Glos.* iv. 371–2).

[1] Reading uncertain.
[2] **B** ends here with *et aliis.*

214. *Notification by Hugh of Garn that he has granted in free alms to Abbot Henry Foliot and the convent of St. Peter's, Gloucester, three acres of meadow in Pulmede in the parish of Westbury on Severn for 1d. annual rent and an initial payment of 6 marks; if Hugh cannot warrant the land to the abbey he will give land in Garn (in Westbury) in exchange. (1228 × 43)*

A. H.C.L., no. 1662 (180 mm × 139 mm), **Scribe 16** (below, Plate XVIII); tag and seal missing; endorsements: Carta Hugonis de Gerna (s. xii^{ex}); Huge de Gern.' de prato. (c. 1225 × 50); Registratur (s. xiv^{ex} × s. xv^{in}); **B**. G.C.L., 'Reg. B', no. 92, pp. 32–33; cal. in Baddeley i, no. 30, p. 233.

Sciant presentes et futuri quod ego Hugo de Gerna pro salute anime mee et antecessorum meorum dedi et concessi deo et ecclesie sancti Petri Glouc' et domino Henrico Folet tunc abbati et monachis ibidem deo seruientibus in liberam puram et perpetuam elemosinam tres acras prati mei in Pulmede cum pertinentiis suis in parrochia de Westburi . illas scilicet que iacent inter pratum domini regis ex vna parte et terram que fuit Henrici diaconi que uocatur Newelonde ex altera parte . Habendas et tenendas de me et heredibus meis predictis abbati et monachis et eorum successoribus inperpetuum libere et quiete ab omni seruitio et ab omnibus secularibus demandis et consuetudinibus que sunt uel que euenire poterunt sicut puram elemosinam meam . Reddendo inde annuatim michi et heredibus meis vnum denarium ad festum sancti Michaelis pro omnibus seruitiis et secularibus demandis et consuetudinibus. In initio autem huius donationis mee predicti abbas et monachi pro magna necessitate mea et inopia dederunt michi premanibus sex marcas sterlingorum ad aquietanda debita mea uersus Cristianos et Iudeos. Ego uero predictus Hugo et heredes mei predictas acras cum pertinentiis suis dictis abbati et monachis et eorum successoribus contra omnes homines et feminas tam Iudeos quam Cristianos warantizabimus inperpetuum. Et si aliquo casu emergene contigerit quod ego Hugo et heredes mei predictas acras predictis monachis warantizare non poterimus.' rationabile escambium ad ualentiam predictarum acrarum de tenemento meo in Gerna siue in prato siue in terra arabili ad uoluntatem eorum per uisum legalium uirorum eis planarie faciemus. In cuius rei testimonium presens scriptum sigilli mei inpressione roboraui. Hiis testibus . magistro Waltero scriptore . Nicholao filio Yuonis . Iohanne de Staure . Mauricio marescallo . Galfrido de Weston' . Nicholao clerico . Willelmo Walense . Petro clerico . et multis aliis.

215. *Grant in the form of a chirograph by Adam son of Roger of Gloucester to the abbot and convent of St. Peter's, Gloucester, of a stall in Gloucester on the western street and land on Longsmith Street for 1d. annual rent and the remission of all Adam's debts and arrears owed to the abbey and of 10d. annual rent which Adam owes to the abbey for land by the stall. (s. xiii^{med})*

G.C.L., 'Deeds and Seals', ii, no. 14, fol. 9 (149 mm [left] × 186 mm [foot]); seal on tag; white wax stained green; fragment, repaired; round (measurements unavail.); crescent with ends pointing up; above, an eight-pointed star; legend: . . . AD'MI. F. . .; no counterseal; endorsements: .Contra .Adam. filium Rogeri. (s. xiii[1]); Caps(ula) .xviii. de laicis tenuris (s. xiii[2]); Th' Bernvode. iiii. V(ar)da (s. xiii[ex]); iiiia Warda (s. xiii[2]; poss. s. xiii[ex]); Quietacl(amatio) (s. xiv[ex]); sc(ribitur) [;] Registratur (s. xiv[ex] × s. xv[in]).

C Y R O . . .P. . .M

Sciant presentes et futuri quod ego Adam filius Rogeri de Glouc' dedi remisi et inperpetuum quietamclamaui abbati et conuentui sancti Petri de Glouc' vnam seldam meam in platea occidentali Glouc' que iacet inter seldam que fuit Dauid Donning' et seldam meam quam tenui de Ricardo burgense que continet in latitudine in anteriori parte duas virgas vlnarias et dimidiam cum pollice interposito . In posteriori . vero parte totidem. In profunditate vero continet sex virgas vlnarias et dimidiam et vnam quarterium cum pollice interposito exceptis tribus pollicibus. Preterea dedi et concessi et quietamclamaui dictis abbati et conuentui vnam terram meam in vico fabrorum que iacet inter terram que fuit Willelmi Toli et furnum que fuit Dauid Dunning quam tenui de Ricardo burgense que continet de latitudine in anteriori parte quatuor virgas vlnarias et tria quartia cum pollice interposito . In posteriori vero parte totidem . In longitudine vero continet septem virgas ulnarias cum pollice interposito exceptis tribus pollicibus tenendas et habendas dictis abbati et conuentui de me et heredibus meis libere et quiete integre cum edificiis et omnibus aliis pertinentiis suis iure et hereditarie inperpetuum . Reddendo inde annuatim michi et heredibus meis vnum denarium ad Pascham pro omnibus seruitiis et demandis. Pro hac autem donatione concessione et quietaclamatione mea dictus abbas et conuentus remiserunt michi omnia debita et areragia redditus in quibus eis tenebar soluere. Et insimile remiserunt michi in perpetuum decem denarios annualis redditus quos eis debui de terra quam de eis tenui iuxta predictam seldam. Et ego predictus Adam et heredes mei warantizabimus predictas terras cum omnibus pertinentiis suis predictis abbati et conuentui contra omnes homines et feminas inperpetuum. Et si illas warantizare non poterimus faciemus predictis abbati et conuentui rationabile excambium de aliis terris nostris in adeo bono et competenti loco per visum legalium virorum in villa Glouc' . Et ut hec mea donatio et quietaclamatio et predicta relaxatio decem denarium annualis redditus ex parte predictorum abbatis et conuentus firma et stabilie permaneat presenti cirografo inter nos diuiso sigillum meum apposui. Alteram vero partem sigillo predictorum abbatis et conuentus munitam penes me retinui. Hiis testibus . Waltero Hoich . Willelmo le Spec(iario) . Willelmo de Lond' . Stephano Cornubiense . Willelmo de Someri . Hugone de Kingesham' . Willelmo le Riche et aliis.

This is the copy provided by Adam to St. Peter's.

216. *Notification by Katherine of Gloucester widow of Walter son of Peter that she*

has confirmed in free alms to St. Peter's, Gloucester, her land on Colstalle *Street (Gloucester) and 2s. annual rent from the canons of Llanthony for land by St. Nicholas's church; the gift is for shoeing the horses of religious guests and was made in the hundred of Gloucester. (1200 × c. 1228)*

A. G.C.L., 'Deeds and Seals', vii, no. 33, fol. 19 (159 mm × 93 mm); seal on tag; white wax stained green, chipped and rubbed, repaired; oval (length unavail.; width, 32 mm); obverse: a full-standing frontal gowned female figure; legend: . . .IGILL. . .: KATERIN. . .; no counterseal; endorsements: Carta Kat(er)ine de Glouc' [;] In vico Colstalli; Registratur (s. xiv × s. xv); vico Colstalli (s. xv?); B. ibid. 'Reg. B', no. 409, p. 178.

Sciant presentes et futuri quod ego Kat(er)ina de Glouc' . relicta Walteri filii Petri pro salute anime mee . et omnium parentum et amicorum meorum dedi et hac carta mea confirmaui deo et ecclesie sancti Petri Glouc' . et monachis ibidem deo seruientibus terram meam in vico Colstalli . quam Radulfus Cope tenuit de me . quam emi de Michaele cognato meo . Tenendam et habendam in puram et perpetuam elemosinam . liberam . et quietam . ab omnibus seruitiis et secularibus demandis ad me uel ad heredes meos pertinentibus sine reclamatione mei uel heredum meorum qui fuerunt uel esse poterunt in perpetuum. Dedi etiam eisdem monachis duos solidos singulis annis de canonicis Lanton' . percipiendos statutis terminis . sex scilicet denarios ad festum sancti Michaelis . sex ad Natale domini . sex ad Annuntiationem sancte Marie . Sex ad festum sancti Iohannis Baptiste . de terra quam Willelmus Russel tenuit de me uersus ecclesiam sancti Nicholai . quam emi de prefato Michaele cognato meo. Ita ut predicta terra . et predicti duo solidi cedant in usus hospitum religiosorum per manus hostilarii qui pro tempore fuerit . ad emendum scilicet ferraturas equarum. Feci etiam prefatis monachis tam de predicta terra . quam de predictis solidis . plenam seisinam in hundredo Glouc' . Iohanne Rufo . et Adam Walense . prepositis tunc existentibus. Et quia uolo quod hec mea donatio rata et inconcussa permaneat in posterum. eam presenti scripto sigilli mei impressione munito confirmaui. Hiis testibus . Alexandro filio meo . Ricardo de Bosco . Henerico monachis Glouc'[1] . Iohanne Rufo . Adam Walense tunc prepositis . Mauricio filio Durandi . Iohanne de Gosediche . Radulfo Aurifabro . Henrico filio meo . Hugone Clerico . Symone de Celario . Waltero Longo . et Helya seruientibus de hundredo . et multis [a]liis.

For the date, see *VCH Glos.* iv. 371. For *Colstalle* Street see *PNG*, ii. 134.

[1] **B** ends here with *et aliis.*

217. *Notification by William Hairun son of Philip Hairun that he confirms his brother Walter's gift to St. Peter's, Gloucester, of a virgate and a half in Coate (in Eastleach Martin) with a third part of the chief house and 2s. 6d. annual rent which Thomas Hairun, William's nephew, owed to Walter for a virgate at Coate. (s. xii ex)*

A. G.C.L., 'Deeds and Seals', vi, no. 33, fol. 17 (106 mm × 112 mm); slit for tag on turn-up; tag and seal missing; endorsements: De Estlech'[;] .c(apsula) .xii. de laicis tenuris (s. xii x), poss. **Hand h**; Carta .W. Hayrun (s. xiv); de Est leche. E temporalium parte prima (*c*. s. xiv^ex); Registratur (s. xiv^ex × s. xv^in); **B**. P.R.O., C 150/1, fols. 77v–78; *Cart. Glouc.* i, no. 233.

Notum sit omnibus ad quos presens scriptum peruenerit. quod ego Will(el)mus Hairun filius Philippi Hairun concedo et presenti carta mea confirmo . donationem illam quam Walterus Hairun frater meus fecit deo et ecclesie sancti Petri Gloucestrie . et monachis ibidem deo seruientibus . pro salute anime sue . et omnium parentum suorum . videlicet unam virgatam terre et dimidiam a la Cote cum tertia parte capitalis mansionis . et duos solidos et sex denarios quos Thomas Hairun nepos meus eidem Waltero fratri meo annuatim debebat pro una virgata terre a la cote . Que omnia ego Will(el)m(us) eidem Waltero et heredibus suis dedi . et carta mea confirmaui . Que omnia ego Will(el)m(us) remitto et quietum clamo predictis monachis totum seruitium quod ad me et heredes meos de predicta terra pertinebat . cum homagiis . et releuiis . et omnibus aliis ad predictam terram pertinentibus. Et ut hec concessio mea et confirmatio rata sit et inconuulsa. presentem cartam sigilli mei impressione munitam. predictis monachis tradidi.[1] Hiis testibus. Ricardo burgeis . Ricardo filio Willelmi . Henrico burgeis . Ada Walense . Radulfo de Tudeha' [.] Waltero scriptore . Salomone Ianitore . Drogone pincerna . Mauricio stablario . Helia de Standeis . et multis aliis.

[1] **B** as printed in *Cart. Glouc.* ends here.

218. *Notification by William Hairun son of Phillip Hairun that he has granted to St. Peter's, Gloucester, the part which he had retained of the chief house in Eastleach, at perpetual farm for an annual rent of 1 lb. of wax. (s. xii^ex × s. xiii^in)*

A. G.C.L., 'Deeds and Seals', vi, no. 22, fol. 12 (196 mm × 83 mm), **Scribe 29** (below, Plate XXIII); tag for seal with residue of green wax; seal missing; endorsements: De Estlech' . .c(apsula) .xii. de laicis tenuris. (s. xii^ex × s. xiii^in); Carta Will(elmi) Hayrun (s. xiv); E temporalium[1] parte prima[2] de parte capitale mansionis Estlech' pro qua soluimus vnam libram cere (s. xiv^ex); Registratur (s. xv) [;] **B**. P.R.O., C 150/1, no. 226, fols. 76v–77; *Cart. Glouc.* i, no. 226.

Sciant presentes et futuri quod ego Will(el)m(u)s Hairun filius Philippi Hairun concessi et tradidi deo et ecclesie sancti Petri Glouc' et monachis ibidem seruientibus . illam partem capitalis mansionis in Estlech quam in manu retinueram . cum curtilagio et columbario meo. tenendam de me et heredibus meis ad perpetuam firmam. reddendo annuatim michi et heredibus meis vnam libram cere in festo sancti Michaelis pro omnibus seruitiis. Hiis testibus[3] . Roberto decano de Lech . Waltero de Bannebir' . magistro Ricardo de Brackel' . Waltero scriptore . Henrico de Cotes . Aluredo de Lech . Drogone Le butiller . Iohanne draperio . Radulfo de Fifhide . Salomone Ianitore . Waltero de Mora . et multis aliis.

This grant and presumably confirmations by William's brother Walter and son Thomas seem to be mentioned in an *inspeximus* of Silvester bishop of Worcester (*Cart. Glouc.* i, no. 131, p. 230; see also ibid. p. 75 in the abbey's Calendar of Donations).

¹ Reading uncertain.
² Reading uncertain.
³ **B** as printed in *Cart. Glouc.* ends here.

219. *Charter of Master Nicholas of Hatherley son of Maurice granting to St. Peter's, Gloucester, land in the girdlery (possibly Mercer Row), Gloucester, in free alms for the use of the infirmary, the infirmarian answering for the 4s. to the chief lords of the fee; Master Nicholas surrendered to the monks, with his charter, the charters of his mother Dionysia, Robert Page, Richard Francis, and Alexander son of Maurice. (1258)*

A. G.C.L., 'Deeds and Seals', vii, no. 38, fol. 22 (272 mm × 88 mm); tag for seal; seal missing; residue of white wax on tag; endorsements: Carta de zonaria (s. xiii^med), **Hand r**; zonaria (s. xiv); Registratur (s. xiv^ex × s. xv^in); **B**. ibid. 'Reg. B', no. 1063 (1062), p. 461.

Sciant presentes et futuri quod ego magister Nichol(aus) de Haytherleg' filius Mauricii . dedi . concessi . et hac presenti carta mea confirmaui deo et ecclesie beati Petri Glouc' et monachis ibidem deo seruientibus . totam terram cum domibus . edificiis . redditibus . et aliis pertinentiis suis in zonaria Gloucestr' . quam emi de Ricardo Le Franceys burgensi Glouc' pro viginti et octo marcis . in liberam et perpetuam elemosinam ad opus infirmorum fratrum in infirmaria Glouc' . pro salute anime mee . et pro salute animarum patris mei et matris . et omnium antecessorum meorum . Ita quod infirmarius qui pro tempore fuerit . respondebit capitalibus dominis dicti feudi de quatuor solidis argenti ad terminos consuetos pro omnibus seruitiis . sectis . et secularibus demandis. Ego uero magister Nichol(aus) et heredes mei totam predictam terram cum domibus . edificiis . redditibus . et aliis pertinentiis . predictis monachis contra omnes homines et feminas in perpetuum warantizabimus . defendemus . et de omnimodis secularibus demandis adquietabimus. Et ad maiorem securitatem . cartam Dyonisie matris mee . et cartam Roberti Page . et cartam Ricardi le Franceys et cartam Alexandri filii Mauricii . dictis monachis tradidi . vna cum presenti carta. Et quia uolo quod hec mea donatio . concessio . et carte mee confirmatio . perpetue firmitatis robur optineat́ huic presenti scripto sigillum meum apposui. Hiis testibus . Willelmo de Chilteham' . Rogero Lenveyse tunc bailliuis Gloucestr' . Iohanne filio Symonis . Alexandro del Broc¹ . Ricardo de Celario . Hugone de aula regis . Luca Cornubiense . Iohanne Anketil . Ricardo de Bokelinton' tunc clerico infirmarie . et multis aliis.

The abbey's Calendar of Donations records this gift for the year 1263, but the date when the attesting bailiffs were in office was 1258 ('Historia', 83–84; *VCH Glos.* iv. 372).

¹ **B** ends here with *et aliis.*

220. *Notification by Richard son of Robert of Little Hide (Monksbury Court in Yarkhill, Herefs.) that he has granted to the abbot and convent of St. Peter's, Gloucester, in free alms four and a half acres and a foreland of the arable of his fee at Monkhide (in Yarkhill, Herefs.). (s. xiii[1])*

A. G.C.L., 'Deeds and Seals', v, no. 9, fol. 3A (238 mm × 99 mm); seal on tag; white wax stained green, fragment, rubbed, repaired; round (meas. unavail.); a horse with rider (?) to the right; legend: . . . RICARDI D. . .; no counterseal; endorsements: Carta Ricardi de P'va Hyda (s. xiii[2]); Registratur (s. xiv × s. xv[in]); B. ibid. 'Reg. B', no. 112, p. 39.

Sciant presentes et futuri quod ego Ricardus filius Rob(er)ti de Parua Hyda pro salute anime mee et omnium antecessorum et successorum meorum dedi[1] concess[i] et hac presenti carta mea confirmaui deo et ecclesie sancti Petri Glouc' et abbati et monachis ibidem deo seruientibus in liberam puram et perpetuam elemosinam quatuor acras et dimidiam et vnam forerdam terre mee arabilis in Hyda de feodo meo in H'eforschyre . quarum vna acra iacet inter terram sacristarii Glouc' ex vna parte apud Padehulesiche . Dimidia uero acra iacet inter terram Elyanore de Solle et Iohanne de marisco cuius vnum capud tendit super croftum sacristarii Glouc' . Et vna acra iacet inter terram sacristarii Glouc' ex vna parte et terram que est domini Willelmi de Hyda ex altera parte . Et due acre iacent in Chauenhulle inter terram Willelmi de Solle ex parte vna et terram Willelmi Godefray ex altera . Et vna forerda iacet inter terram sacristarii Glouc' ex utraque parte et extendit se a capite terre Philippi Lyre usque ad terram dicti Ric(ardi) de Parua Hyda . Tenendam et habendam de me et heredibus meis solutam et quietam ac liberam ab omnibus sectis exactionibus secularibus demandis omnibus consuetudinibus seruitiis domini regis et cuiuscumque domini terreni et omnibus aliis que de terris uel tenementis exigi poterunt uel reddi . Quia ego ipse et heredes mei eam ab omnibus ut predictum est plenarie acquietabimus et de omnibus uersus quoscumque defendemus inperpetuum. Et ego Ric(ardus) et heredes mei totam predictam terram cum omnibus pertinentiis suis predictis abbati et monachis contra omnes mortales warantizabimus inperpetuum. In cuius rei testimonium et munimen presenti scripto sigillum meum apposui. Hiis testibus domino Willelmo de Hyda milite . Willelmo de Solle[2] . Willelmo de Huscemayne . Willelmo de Hyda clerico . Radulfo de molendino . Iohanne filio persone . et aliis.

A charter of Robert of Hide, dated 29 September 1202, is in G.C.L., 'Reg. B', no., 123, p. 43. For *Parva Hyda* and *Hyda* see *Herefordshire Place-Names*, 215–16. The Index of 'Register B' associates the donations mentioned in this charter with Gloucester abbey's manor of Monkhide (fol. v verso).

[1] Possibly tironian *et* erased; uncertain with ultra-violet light.
[2] **B** ends here with *et aliis*.

221. *Lease for ten years in the form of a chirograph by Geoffrey of Highleadon of land at* Muchelesmede *to Abbot Thomas and the convent of St. Peter's, Gloucester,*

for 60s. to acquit him of his debt to the Jewry and for 1d. annual rent. 29 September 1227.

H.C.L., no. 1644 (89 mm [left] × 151 mm [foot]); slit for tag on foot; tag and seal missing; endorsements: Carta Galfridi de Hynledene [;] Caps(ula).i.[a] de laicis tenuris (s. xiii[ex] × s. xiv[in]); Non indiget registrari (s. xiv[ex]); cal. in Baddeley ii, no. 40, pp. 20–21.

C. . .O. . .R A F. . . C I R O. . .R A F. . . *(inverted)*

Sciant presentes et futuri quod ego Galf(ridus) de Leden' anno ad incarnationis domini .M.°.CC.° vicesimo septimo . ad festum sancti Michaelis tradidi et concessi Thome dei gratia abbati et conuentui sancti Petri Glouc' duas acras prati mei in Muchelesmede iuxta pratum abbatis de Cormell' . quod uocatur Co'mede . et totum pratum meum quod uocatur Achetillesmede . cum omnibus pertinentiis suis . tenendas et habendas de me et heredibus meis sine aliqua dimunatione siue retinemento ad opus mei uel heredum meorum ad terminum decem annorum continue sequentium . pro vno denario mihi uel heredibus meis pro omnibus seruitiis et secularibus demandis in die sancti Iohannis Baptiste annuatim persoluendo. Pro hac traditione et concessione mea predicti abbas et conuentus dederunt mihi praemanibus sexaginta solidos ad adquietandum me in Iudeismo. Vt autem hec traditio et concessio mea rata et inconcussa permaneat. presenti scripto diuiso inter nos cirographo eam confirmaui . Cuius unam partem sigillo meo sigillatam. eis tradidi. Alteram vero partem sigillo ipsorum abbatis et conuentus roboratam penes me retinui. Hiis testibus . magistro Waltero scriptore . Drogone pincerna . Waltero de Hamt' . Galfrido de West' . Henrico LeBun'[1] . Rein'r[2] le schiel'r . et multis aliis.

[1] Reading uncertain.
[2] Reading uncertain.

222. *Notification by Walter of Holcombe that he has confirmed to St. Peter's, Gloucester, the mill of Wotton (St. Mary, by Gloucester) which had been given by Richard son of Nigel and Emma his wife when their sons William and Thurstan became monks. (1148 × 79)*

A. G.C.L., 'Deeds and Seals', iii, no. 28, fol. 16 (185 mm × 110 mm), **Scribe 5**; slits in foot for two tags and seals; on the left, tag and seal missing; on the right, seal on tag; white wax, chipped; round (61 mm in diam.); a helmeted equestrian figure to the right, an upraised sword in the right hand; legend: + SIGILLVM WALTERI DE HOLCVMBE; no counterseal; endorsements: de MOLENDINO de WttUNA (s. xii[ex] × s. xiii[in]), **Hand g**; c(apsula) .xv. de laicis tenuris. (s. xii[ex] × s. xiii[in]); Carta Walt(er)i de Holecumba (c. 1300); Duplicatur (uncertain date); **B**. P.R.O., C 150/1, fols. 187v–188; *Cart. Glouc.* ii, p. 693.

Sciant presentes et futuri quod ego Walt(er)us de Holecumba . concessi et confirmaui deo et sancto Petro et monachis Gloec' . molendinum de Wotona cum tota terra quam Ricardus filius Nigelli et Emma uxor eius dederunt eisdem monachis. cum filiis suis Willelmo et Thurstino . quando eos in ecclesia sua monachos fecerunt . in perpetuam elemosinam . liberam et quietam ab omni exactione et consuetudine seculari . et seruitio tam regale quam meo [.] Ita ut nullus successorum aliquam habet reclamationem . in predicta terra uel molendino. Quod quia ratum uolo et inconcussum in posterum permanere.[/] presenti carte[1] sigillum meum appono. Teste domino Nicholao Landauensi episcopo . Qui ob testimonium ueritatis huius conuentionis cui ipse interfuit.[/] sigillum etiam suum huic carte apposuit. Testibus etiam Milone de Mucegros . Walterio filio Wiberti . et Goffrido filio eius . Maugerio . et Willelmo fratribus ipsius Walt(er)ii de Holecumba . Radulfo cellerario . Willelmo cantore . Godefrido et Hugone monachis . et multis aliis . Radulfo filio Godefridi . Walterio Thochi . Roberto de Bertona . Roberto testa . Hugone de Brichmereton' . Willelmo de Heref' . Willelmo Pic . Willelmo ruffo . Goffrido de Lilletona . Radulfo ferragu.

The text of Richard son of Nigel's grant of Paygrove Farm (in Wotton St. Mary), land in the garden of the almonry, the mill at *Forde*, and tithe of Wotton to St. Peter's, dated 1126, is in *Cart. Glouc.* ii, no. 571 (see 'Historia', 118, where the gift is described as the mill of Wotton, made in 1126 on the occasion of Richard and his wife's sons' entrance into St. Peter's as monks); Earl Robert of Gloucester confirmed Richard's grant 1126 × 1131 (Patterson, *EGC*, no. 82; see also ibid. no. 262; 'Historia', 118; *Cart. Glouc.* ii, no. 572; see also 'Historia', 79, 107, which dates the grant of *Forde* during the abbacy of William Godmon [1113–30]). According, however, to the St. Peter's Calendar of Donations, King Henry I in 1109 gave the abbey a grove in King's Barton (by Gloucester) called Paygrove along with land at Abloads Court (in Sandhurst) in exchange for the land occupied by the monks' garden on which the tower of the royal castle at Gloucester had been built ('Historia', 59; see also *Regesta*, ii, no. 1008); according to the Calendar, Walter sheriff of Gloucester granted Abloads Court to St. Peter's in an exchange ordered by King Henry I ('Historia', 123). For the above locations, see *PNG*, ii. 136, 152, 158–9.

¹   **B** ends here with *etc.*

223. *Notification by Matilda, daughter of Geoffrey Hooper, that with the assent of her lord Reiner palmer she has quitclaimed to the abbot and convent of St. Peter's, Gloucester, all her right in land by the abbey's garden (in Gloucester?), for which land she had impleaded William of Clemund by a royal writ of right in the monks' court, where they gave her ½ mark for the quitclaim. (s. xiii[in])*

A. G.C.L., 'Deeds and Seals', ii, no. 18, fol. 10 (*c.* 91 mm [right]), **Scribe 30** (below, Plate XXIV); fragment; slit for tag; no turn-up; tag and seal missing; evidence of endorsements unavail. because the fragment is glued to the scrapbook page without leaving an opening on the verso; **B**. ibid. 'Reg. B', no. 585, p. 255.

[Sciant presentes et futuri quod ego Matildis filia Ga]lfridi Hoparii de assensu et voluntate Reinerii palmarii [domini mei remisi et imperpetuum pro me et omnibus heredibus] meis quietum clamaui[1] domino abbati et conuentui Gloucest' totum [ius et clamium quod ego vel heredes mei habuimus vel] aliquo tempore secundum legem terre aliquo modo habere potui[mus in quadam terra versus ortum predictorum monachorum de feodo] eorundem monachorum de qua terra inplacitaui Willelmum de Clei[munt tenentem eorundem monachorum in curia ipsorum] per breue domini regis de recto. Pro hac autem quieta clamatione [predicti monachi dimidiam marcam argenti in curi]a illorum michi dederunt. In cuius rei testimonium presens scriptum sigillo [meo sigillatum eis tradidi. Hiis testibus . magistro W]altero scriptore . Ricardo Burg'nse[2] . Iohanne Draperio . Willelmo de Sumeri . Thoma . . .

Missing portions of the text recovered from **B** are enclosed in brackets.

[1]   Two superscript words added here in **A**, *Finam prestito* (xiii ?; reading uncertain; two different hands).

[2]   **B** ends here with *et multis aliis*.

224. *Another version of no. 223, without reference to the payment of ½ mark. (s. xiii*[in]*)*

A. G.C.L., 'Deeds and Seals', ii, no. 17, fol. 10 (68 mm [rt]; only meas. avail.), **Scribe 30**; fragment; apparent slit for tag; no turn-up; tag and seal missing; evidence of endorsement unavail. because the fragment is glued to the scrapbook page without leaving an opening on the verso; **B**. ibid. 'Reg. B', no. 584, p. 254.

[Sciant presentes et futuri quod ego Matildis filia Galfridi hoparii de asse]nsu et voluntate Reinerii palmarii domini mei remisi et inperpetuum pro [me et pro omnibus heredibus meis quietum clamaui domino abbati et conu]entui Gloucest'ie totum ius et clamium quod ego uel heredes mei habuimus [vel aliquo tempore secundum legem terre aliquo modo habere potuimus in quad]am terra versus ortum predictorum monachorum de feodo eorundem monachorum [de qua terra implacitaui Willelmum Cleymunt tenentem eorundem] monachorum in curia ipsorum per breue domini regis de recto. Et ut [hec mea quietaclamatio ratam imperpetuum obtineat firmit]atem presens scriptum sigillo meo sigillatum eis tradidi. His testibus´. magistro [Waltero scriptore . Ricardo Burgense][1] . . . Draperio . Willelmo de Sumeri . Thoma Oie . Ada Gldewine . et multis aliis.

Missing portions of the text recovered from the copy in **B** are enclosed within brackets.

[1]   **B** ends here with *et multis aliis*.

225. *Notification by Matilda daughter of Geoffrey Hooper in her widowhood that she has quitclaimed to the abbot and convent of St. Peter's, Gloucester, land by the abbey's garden (in Gloucester?). The notification is similar to no. 223, but mentions the support of Matilda's children, the abbey's grant to her of a weekly loaf, and her plea against William of Clemund not in the monks' court but before a judge, and the witnesses are mostly different. (c. 1200 × 28)*

A. G.C.L., 'Deeds and Seals', ii, no. 16, fol. 10 (111 mm [left] × 171 mm [foot]; other sides damaged); seal on tag; white wax stained green; obverse: oval (38 mm × 25 mm); elongated fleur-de-lis; legend: + S' MATHILDIS F.G.: HOP.; no counterseal; endorsement(s) cannot be determined because the charter is glued to the page without an opening to show the reverse side; B. ibid. 'Reg. B', no. 499, p. 219.

Sciant presentes et futuri quod ego Matildis filia Galfridi Hoparii te[mpore viduitatis remisi et imperpe]tuum pro me et pro omnibus heredibus meis quietum clamaui domino ab[bati et conuentui Glouc' totum ius clamium] quod ego uel heredes mei habuimus uel aliquo tempore secundum [legem terre aliquo modo habere potuimus in] quadam terra versus ortum predictorum monachorum de feudo eorundem monac[horum de qua terra implacitaui Willelmum de Cle]munt tenentem eorumdem monachorum coram iusticario apud Gloc' . per preceptum domini regis. Pro hac autem mea quieta clamatione predicti monachi dimidiam marcam argenti ad sustentationem meam et puerorum meorum michi dederunt. Preterea predicti monachi michi diuine karitatis intuitu qualibet septimana vnum panem fulberti[1] tamen in vita mea concesserunt. In cuius rei testimonium presens scriptum sigillo meo sigillatum absque omni reclamatione eis tradidi. Hiis testibus . Waltero Pain tunc preposito . Ricardo de celario[2] . Adam filio Rogeri . W[a]ltero Hoyich . Adam Gladeyno . et multis aliis.

Text missing or illegible in the damaged A has been supplied from B.

[1] No explanation of the phrase has been found.   [2] B ends here with et multis aliis.

226. *Confirmation by Henry Kais son of Henry Kais to St. Bride's chapel in the infirmary of St. Peter's, Gloucester, of a rent of 2s. which William Chose used to pay for a stall in Mercer Row, Gloucester, also granting 6d. of rent owed to the donor for properties on Oxbode Lane and the Jewry; in consideration of this the abbey has advanced to Henry 20s. (c. 1228 × 40)*

A. G.C.L., 'Deeds and Seals', iv, no. 9, fol. 4 (193 mm × 112 mm), **Scribe 33**; seal on tag; white wax stained green, chipped; obverse: round (34 mm in diam.); a male bust facing left; legend: +SIGILL' HENRICI KAIS; no counterseal; endorsements: Carta[1] contra Henr(icum) Kays .ii.s' vi d'. (s. xiii^med); Registratur (s. xiv^ex × s. xv^in); B. ibid. 'Reg. B', no. 1068 (1067), pp. 463–4.

Sciant presentes et futuri quod ego Henr(icus) Kais filius Henrici Kais de Glouc' pro[2] salute anime mee et antecessorum meorum dedi et concessi et hac presenti carta mea confirmaui deo et capelle beate Brigide que est in infirmaria monachorum sancti Petri Glouc' redditum duorum solidorum quem reddet Willelmus Chose et heredes sui[3] predicte capelle annuatim duobus terminis . scilicet ad Nathale domini[4] duodecim denarios et ad Annuntiationem beate Marie duodecim denarios sicut michi reddere debebat et solebat pro selda quam de me hereditarie tenuit que est in merceria Glouc' que sita est inter seldam Roberti Gnet et seldam Nicholay Chose.

Preterea dedi et concessi predicte capelle infirmarie sex denariorum redditus quod Iohannes Draperius et heredes sui michi et heredibus meis ad festum sancti Michaelis imperpetuum reddere debebat[5] et solebat[6] de[7] terris quas de me hereditarie tenebat . Videlicet duos denarios de quadam terra in Oxebodelone que iacet inter terram Iohannis Rufi et terram predictorum monachorum . et duos denarios de selda quam Robertus Niker tenet . que iacet inter terram Nicholay Gnet . et terram que fuit Mauricii Durant . et duos denarios de quadam[8] terra[9] in Iudaismo Glouc' que iacet inter terram prioris Lanton' de Wallia et terram Felicie de Dunie. Pro hac autem donatione et concessione mea dederunt michi predicti monachi vinginti solidos premanibus. Ego uero Henr(icus) Kais et heredes mei predicte capelle totum predictum redditum contra omnes homines et feminas imperpetuum warantizabimus. In cuius testimonium presens scriptum sigillo meo sigillatum predictis monachis[10] tradidi. Hiis testibus . magistro Waltero scriptore . Ricardo Burgense . Dauid Dunning . et Waltero Pain tunc prepositis Glouc'[11] . Iohanne draperio[12] . Waltero de Theokesbur' . Nicholao Cumioc . Nicholao Treweman . Rogero mercerio . Nicholao Chose . Roberto Gnet . Nicholao de Theokesburia[13] Clerico . et aliis.

It is possible that at least 4s. of revenue was generated by the property which William Chose held of Henry Kais in Mercer Row, because *c.* 1200 × 28 Henry Kais also confirmed payment of the rent of 2s. for the same property mentioned above, but to support lamps before the altar of St. Thomas the Martyr in the abbey church (G.C.L., 'Reg B', no. 20, fol. 9); another possibility is that the rent was transferred from the altar to the chapel or vice versa. For the above charter's date, see *VCH Glos.* iv. 371.

[1] An illegible word superscript above *Carta.*
[2] *p* with the abbreviation sign omitted in MS.; *pro* in no. 227.
[3] *heredes sui* omitted in no. 227.
[4] *ad festum sancti Michaelis* in no. 227.
[5] *debebant* in no. 227.
[6] *solebant* in no. 227.
[7] *pro* in no. 227.
[8] omitted in no. 227.
[9] *que est* added in no. 227.
[10] *eis* in place of *predictis monachis* in no. 227.
[11] *Glouc'* omitted in no. 227.
[12] **B** ends here with *et aliis.*
[13] *de Theokesbur'* omitted in no. 227.

227. *Another version of no. 226.*

G.C.L., 'Deeds and Seals', iv, no. 10, fol. 4 (175 mm × 103 mm); seal on tag; white stained green, round (34 mm in diam.); obverse: a male bust facing left; legend: + SIGILL' HENRICI KAIS; no counterseal; endorsements: Carta Henrici[1] Kays. (s. xiii^{med}); de terra in merceria que est inter terram .R. gnat et Nicholai Chose (s. xiii^{ex}); magister[2] ville debet soluere .vi. denarios Inf(ir)mar(ie) .vi. denarios. (s. xiii^2); Non registratur quia duplicatur (s. xiv^{ex}).

Either this is an imperfect copy of no. 226 or vice versa.

[1] *Crarta Hanrici* in MS.   [2] Reading uncertain.

228. *Quitclaim by Henry Kais son of Henry Kais of Gloucester to St. Peter's, Gloucester, in free alms of his right to the rent of 14s. owed to him by Walter Hoic for two stalls in the stone house by the stone cross (Gloucester); Walter was to pay the 14s. to the prior who in turn was to assign 7s. to the cellarer. Henry also granted 3d. in free alms from property on St. Mary's Street before the abbey's gate. (1200 × c. 1228)*

G.C.L., 'Deeds and Seals', ii, no. 3, fol. 2 (217 mm × 95 mm); seal on green and brown(?) cords; white wax stained dark green; obverse: round (35 mm in diam.); a male bust facing left; legend: + SIGILL' HEN...S; no counterseal; endorsements: Redditus xiiii s. (s. xiv); Quietclamatio Henr(ici) Kays abbati et conuentui Glouc' de domo lapidea versus crucem[1] lapideam (uncertain date).

Sciant presentes et futuri quod ego Henricus Kais filius Henrici Kais de Glouc' pro salute anime mee et omnium antecessorum et successorum meorum dedi et quietum clamaui deo et sancto Petro et monachis Glouc' in liberam puram et perpetuam elemosinam totum ius quod ego uel heredes mei habuerunt uel habere potuimus in quatuordecim solidis quos Walterus Hoch et heredes sui michi et heredibus meis annuatim persoluere tenebantur de duabus seldis que sunt in domo lapidea eorumdem monachorum uersus crucem lapideam. Et uolo ut predictus Walterus Hoch et heredes sui predictos quatuordecim solidos annuatim persoluant Thome priori Glouc' uel cui ipse assignauerit ad utilitatem fratrum s(uorum) duobus terminis . medietatem ad festum sancti Michaelis . et aliam medietatem ad Hoked(ai). Idem uero Thomas prior uel cui ipse[2] assignauit de eisdem quatuordecim solidis . septem solidos soluet annuatim cellario eisdem terminis. Preterea dedi et concessi deo et eisdem monachis similiter in liberam puram et perpetuam elemosinam tres denarios annuos quos Robertus filius Walteri Luui annuatim debebat michi et heredibus meis ad festum sancti Michaelis . de terra que iacet inter terram Roberti filii Osmundi et terram eorumdem monachorum in vico sancte Marie ante portam abbatie. In cuius rei testimonium presens scriptum sigillo meo munitum predicto Th. priore tradidi. Hiis testibus . Mauricio Durand et Iohanne Tinctore tunc prepositis . Ricardo Rufo . Ricardo Burg'ns' . Waltero scriptore . Henrico Burgn' . Philippo Burgn' . Nicholao Gunt' . Simone de Cellario [.] Willelmo del parlur . Henrico Bæl. Mauricio marscallo seruientibus abbatie. et multis aliis.

Maurice (son of) Durand and John dyer were bailiffs of Gloucester in the period 1200 × c. 1228 (*VCH Glos.* iv. 371).

---

[1] Reading uncertain.
[2] *ipso* in MS.

229. *Lease in the form of a chirograph by Philip son of Roger of Kimsbury of land at Yendercombe (in Upton St. Leonards) to the abbot and convent of St. Peter's, Gloucester, for four years at 4s. annual rent; St. Peter's was also to pay Thomas, rector of the church of St. John the Baptist, Gloucester, 1 mark a year for three years. 1244. Gloucester.*

H.C.L., no. 1737 (78 mm [left] × 166 mm [foot]), **Scribe 35** (below, Plate XXIX); tag for seal; seal missing; stain from seal, but colour indistinguishable; endorsements: pes inter nos et Philippu(m) de Kynen'ibir' de terra in Guendercu'be (s. xiii^2); Non indiget registrari (s. xiv^{ex} × s. xv^{in}).

CYROGRAPHVM

Sciant presentes et futuri quod ego Philipp(us) de Kynem'bir' filius Rogeri de Kynem'bir' . anno domini m.° cc.° quadrigesimo quarto . concessi et presenti scripto confirmaui abbati et conuentui sancti Petri Glouc' totam terram meam de Gwendercumbe tam in bosco quam in plano . Quam Willelmus de Upton' capellanus aliquando tenuit ad firmam . Tenendam et habendam totam dictam terram cum omnibus pertinentiis suis a festo sancti Michaelis proximo sequenti usque ad terminum .iiii.^{or} annorum continue sequentium . Ita libere et quiete sicut dictus Willelmus de Vpton capellanus dictam terram tenuit . Reddendo inde tempore firme sue pro quolibet anno michi uel heredibus meis in festo sancti Michaelis quatuor solidos sterlingorum pro omni seruitio exactione et demanda . Et reddendo inde insuper domino Thome rectori ecclesie sancti Iohannis Baptiste Glouc' tribus annis vnam marcam argenti annuatim ad duos terminos . videlicet ad Purificationem beate Marie dimidiam marcam . et ad festum sancti Iohannis Baptiste dimidiam marcam. Post lapsum uero dictorum quatuor annorum predicta terra cum omnibus suis pertinentiis ad me uel ad heredes meos sine alicuius contradictione uel impedimento libere reuertetur. In cuius rei testimonium presens scriptum in modum cyrographi inter nos confectum est . Cuius vnam partem sigillo meo munitam dictis abbati et conuentui tradidi. Alteram uero partem sigillo ipsorum roboratam penes me retinui. Hiis testibus . domino Thoma de Duntesburn' . Waltero Hoch . Henrico aurifabro . Th. de Metteresdon' . Waltero de Snedham' . Galfrido de Graua . Petro le Taillur . Willelmo Venezun filio Philippi de Hocholth' . et aliis.

230. *Lease for 20 years in the form of a chirograph by Philip of Kimsbury to Abbot John and the convent of St. Peter's, Gloucester, of land at Yendercombe (in Upton St. Leonards) for 10 marks in advance to acquit Philip with the Gloucester Jewry; the annual rent was to be 10s. 29 September 1248.*

H.C.L., no. 1635 (99 mm [left] × 187 mm [foot]), **Scribe 35**; seal on tag; white wax, round (37 mm in diam.); obverse: four leaves in cross shape intersected at 45 degree angles by fleurs-de-lis; legend: +S'FILIPPI:DE KENEMARSBVRI*; no counterseal; endorsements: Carta Ph(ilipp)i de Kynemaresbur': Iondercumbe; (s. xiii^{med}); Registratur (s. xiv^{ex} × s. xv^{in}); cal. in Baddeley ii, no. 44.

CYROGRAPHVM

Sciant presentes et futuri quod ego Philippus de Kynemaresbur' anno regni regis Henrici filii regis Iohannis tricesimo secundo ad festum sancti Michaelis tradidi domino Iohanni abbati et conuentui sancti Petri Glouc' ad firmam totam terram meam que uocatur Yondercumb' cum omnibus pertinentiis suis ad terminum viginti annorum continue sequentium pro decem marcis probate monete quas mihi premanibus pacauerunt ad aquietandum me de Iudaismo Glouc' . Tenendam et habendam totam predictam terram cum suis pertinentiis de me et heredibus meis uel assignatis meis sibi et successoribus suis libere et quiete ab omni exactione et seculari demanda . Reddendo inde annuatim mihi et heredibus uel assignatis meis decem solidos argenti ad festum sancti Michaelis. Ego uero Philippus et heredes mei uel assignati mei dictis abbati et conuentui et eorum successoribus totam predictam terram cum omnibus suis pertinentiis contra omnes gentes tam Iudeos quam Cristianos usque ad predictum terminum completum warantazabimus et defendemus. Et si contingat quod pro defectu mei . heredum . uel assignatorum meorum . dicti abbas et conuentus Glouc' dampnum incurrant. volo . concedo . et firmiter promitto pro me . heredibus uel assignatis meis . quod ipsi dictam terram cum suis pertinentiis teneant sine aliquo impedimento uel calumpnia mei . heredum . uel assignatorum meorum . donec per visum legalium uirorum de exitu eiusdem terre plenam dampni sui habeant restitutionem. In cuius rei testimonium presens scriptum in modum cyrographi inter nos confectum est . Cuius unam partem sigillo meo munitam dictis abbati et conuentui tradidi. Alteram uero partem sigillo ipsorum roboratam penes me retinui. Hiis testibus . domino Henrico Ruso . Roberto de Felda . Philippo de Mattesdon' . Galfrido de la Graue . Thoma de la forge . Waltero de Snedham' . Roberto Amauri . et aliis.

231. *Grant in perpetual alms in the form of a chirograph by Henry of Leicester and Cecily his wife to St. Peter's, Gloucester, and namely to the sacristy of 17 acres for 2s. annual rent payable by the sacristan; for the gift Ralph the sacristan granted to the donors 4s. and confraternity with the churches of Gloucester and of (St. Guthlac's Priory) Hereford . (s. xii²)*

A. G.C.L., 'Deeds and Seals', v, no. 24, fol. 10 (118 mm [left] × 167 mm [foot]); tongue apparently cut from top right corner; no turn-up; three cross *signa* across foot; seal on tag; fragment, chipped, rubbed; white wax; oval (meas. unavail.); partial standing figure facing front; legend illegible; no counterseal; endorsements: .G.(s. xii²); Henrici de Leicestria. (s. xii; possibly same hand); Registratur s. xiv^ex?); **B**. ibid. 'Reg. B', no. 120, p. 42.

Sciant presentes et futuri quod ego Henric(us) de Leircestria et Cecelia uxor mea donauimus deo et ecclesie sancti Petri Gloecestrie et nominatim ad eiusdem ecclesie sacristariam .x. et vii acras tenendas inperpetuam elemosinam pro .ii. solidis reddendo nobis singulis annis. Hos .ii. solidos reddet nobis sacrista Gloecestrie quiquis fuerit .iii. terminis anni [.] ad Purificationem sancte Marie primam partem [.] ad Pentecosten secundam [.] ad festum sancti Michaelis .iii. Pro hac donatione dedit nobis Radulfus sacrista .iiii. solidos et concessit nobis societatem ecclesie Gloecestrie et ecclesie H'eford'[.] Hanc donationem fecimus concessu et testimonio domini nostri Walterii de La Hida[.] Alii testes sunt Godefridus clericus de Esp'tuna .

Patricius de Gloecestria [.] Alexander de G'desleia[1] [.] Godefridus prepositus de La Hida et .iii. fratres eius [.] Willelmus [.] Edricus [.] Durandus.

+   +   +

C I R O G R A P H [U][2] M

[1]   **B** ends here with *et alii*.
[2]   The letter is covered by the tag.

232. *Grant by Peter of Woodmanton, son of Henry of Leicester, to St. Peter's, Gloucester, of 4 acres of land in* Chevenhulle *and a fifth in Whitwick manor (in Yarkhill, Herefs.) in free alms. (s. xii[ex])*

A. G.C.L., 'Deeds and Seals', i, no. 19, fol. 11 (163 mm × 86 mm); seal on tag; white wax stained green, fragment, chipped; obverse: round (37 mm in diam.); a large fleur-de-lis, legend: +S. . . PETRI: DE: LEICESTRIA; no counterseal; endorsement: Registratur (s. xiv[ex] × s. xv[in]); **B.** ibid. 'Reg. B', no. 121, pp. 42–43.

Sciant presentes et futuri quod ego Petrus de Wodemonnetun' filius Henrici de Leircestre assensu et uoluntate Wimarc uxoris mee et heredum meorum pro salute anime mee et uxoris mee et omnium antecessorum et successorum meorum dedi et concessi deo et ecclesie sancti Petri Gloecestrie et monachis ibidem deo seruientibus quinque acras terre . .iiii.[or] scilicet que iacent in campo de Cheuenhulle . et quintam que iacet in Norfeld iuxta nemus de Witwike in puram et perpetuam elemosinam libere et quiete ab omni seruitio seculari quod est uel esse potest. Predictam uero donationem ego Petr(us) et heredes mei contra omnes homines warantizabimus. Ut et hec mea donatio in perpetuum rate permaneat′. predictas quinque acras presenti scripto sigillo meo munito confirmaui. His testibus . Adam decano de Coure . Thoma decano de Westun' . magistro Moyse de Yarehulle . Willelmo de Solle . Roberto de la Hyde . Waltero de aula . Waltero de Eiglintun' . Alexandro de Aspertun' . Aluredo de la B'etun' . Roberto clerico de Bromtun' . Philippo Carbonel . Waltero Toki . Willelmo Ianitore . Iohanne coco . R[o]gero preposito de la Hyde . Rogero clerico et multis aliis.

For Whitwick, Woodmanton, and *Cheuenhulle*, see below, no. 242; *Norfeld* was near Whitwick.

233. *Grant by William of Leighterton in perpetual alms to St. Peter's, Gloucester, of 8½ acres at Leighterton (in Boxwell) with the obligation of forinsec service. (s. xiii, –14 November 1229; prob. 1228 × 14 November 1229)*

A. G.C.L., 'Deeds and Seals', i, no. 55, fol. 29 (201 mm × 83 mm); seal on tag; white wax stained green, chipped, cracked, repaired; obverse: round (34 mm in diam.); image indiscernible; legend: +SIGILL' W. . .LMI DE LECTR. . .T. . .; no counterseal; endorsements: De terra de Leghtrint'[;] c(apsula) .i. de laicis tenuris (s. xiii[1]); Registratur (s. xiv^{ex} × s. xv^{in}); **B.** P.R.O., C 150/1, fol. 114v; *Cart. Glouc.* i, no. 358.

Sciant presentes et futuri quod ego Willelm(us) de Lehtrint' filius Willelmi de Lehtrint' dedi et concessi et hac presenti carta mea confirmaui pro salute anime mee et animarum antecessorum et heredum meorum deo et ecclesie sancti Petri Glouc' . et monachis ibidem deo seruientibus octo acras terre mee in Lehtrint' . et dimidiam cum omnibus pertinentiis suis . Quarum sex acre iacent ad grossam spinum . Due et dimidia in cultura que dicitur Stanllæ . Que scilicet octo acre et dimidia sunt de residuo terre mee que michi remansit post primam donationem quam feci predicte ecclesie et eisdem monachis . Habendas et tenendas eisdem abbati et conuentui et eorum successoribus de me et heredibus meis in perpetuam elemosinam faciendo forinsecum seruitium quantum ad tantam terram pertinet.' pro omni seruitio. Et ego et heredes mei warentizabimus eisdem abbati et conuentui et eorum successoribus totam predictam terram cum pertinentiis quam eis dedi contra omnes homines in perpetuum. Et ut mea donatio et concessio rata sit . et inconcussa permaneat.' eam sigilli mei munimine roboraui. Hiis testibus[1] . domino Martino de Pateshull' . Ylberto de Greinuill' . Humfrido Le Bret . magistro Ricardo de Brackel' . Drogone Pincerna . Waltero de mora . et multis aliis.

In the abbey's Calendar of Donations, the donor of this charter is listed as having given 8 acres at Leighterton, but with no mention of the half acre, in the time of Abbot Henry Foliot (*Cart. Glouc.* i, p. 97). Martin of Pattishall's date of death is the *terminus ad quem* for the recorded transaction (Turner, *English Judiciary in the Age of Glanville*, 194).

[1]   **B** as printed in *Cart. Glouc.* ends here.

234. *Grant by William of Leighterton son of William of Leighterton in free alms to St. Peter's, Gloucester, of 22 acres in Leighterton (in Boxwell) with the obligation of forinsec service. (s. xiii^{1})*

A. H.C.L., no. 1669 (153 mm × 127 mm); slit for tag; tag and seal missing; endorsements: C(apsula) .i. a de laicis tenuris de Lectrint'. (s. xiii[2]); Registratur (s. xiv^{ex} × s. xv^{in}); **B.** P.R.O., C 150/1, fols. 116–116v; *Cart. Glouc.* i, no. 365; cal. in Baddeley ii, no. 146, p. 45.

Sciant presentes et futuri quod ego Will(elmu)s de Lechtrint' filius Willelmi de Lechtrinton' dedi et concessi et hac presenti carta mea confirmaui pro salute anime mee et animarum antecessorum meorum et heredum meorum deo et ecclesie sancti Petri Gloec' et monachis ibidem deo seruientibus viginti duas acras terre mee in Lechtrinton' cum omnibus pertinentiis suis . Quarum nouem acre iacent ad Grossam spinam . et vna acra ad caput earundem . et vna acra se habet ex transuerso duodecim acrarum apud grossam spinam . et due acre et dimidia in Trenleyshulle . et due acre et dimidia in cultura que dicitur Stonleia . et sex acre in Suthfelde apud Greneweie . Que scilicet viginti due acre sunt de residuo terre mee que michi remansit post primam donationem quam feci predicte ecclesie et predictis monachis [.] Habendas et tenendas eisdem monachis et eorum successoribus de me et heredibus meis in liberam . puram . et perpetuam elemosinam . faciendo forinsecum seruitium quantum ad tantam terram pertinet. pro omni seruitio. Et ego Will(elmu)s et heredes mei warantizabimus eisdem monachis et eorum successoribus predictas viginti duas acras cum pertinentiis quas eis dedi contra omnes homines et feminas in perpetuum. Et vt hec mea donatio et concessio rata sit et inconuulsa permaneat. eam sigilli mei munimine roboraui. His testibus . domino Martino de Pateshull' . Ylberto de Greinuil' . Hunfrido Le Breth . magistro Ricardo de Brakel' . magistro Waltero scriptore . Iohanne Capellano eiusdem . Henrico de Leigraua . Drogone de Ponteise . Waltero de mora . Henrico Bel et multis aliis.

A virgate of William's land, or that of his namesake father, was bought by Alfred *de Hungrie* and subsequently given to St. Peter's ('Historia', 97).

235. *Grant by William de (la) Mare in free alms to St. Peter's, Gloucester, of 12 acres of land and 2 acres of meadow at Murcott (in Minsterworth) worth 7s. a year; the donor and his heirs were to be responsible for all service due to the king; if the donation could not be warranted, an exchange would be made. (1165 × c. 1197; poss. 1165 × 83)*

A. K.C.C., Rochester upon Medway Studies Centre, DRc/T660 (218 mm × 115 mm); seal on tag; green wax, chipped, damaged, round (48 mm in diam.); an equestrian figure with a sword raised in the right hand facing right; legend: . . .MARA; endorsements: Will(elm)i de La Mara de terra de Morcota (s. xii^{ex}); c(apsula) .ii.a de laicis tenuris (s. xii^{ex} × s. xiii^{in}); Caps(ula) .ii.^{a} de laicis tenuris (s. xiii^2); Registratur (s. xv); **B**. P.R.O., C 150/1, fol. 139v; *Cart. Glouc.* ii, no. 473.

Sciant presentes et futuri quod ego Will(elmu)s de Mara dedi et concessi deo et ecclesie sancti Petri Gloec' . et monachis ibidem deo seruientibus pro salute anime mee et patris et matris mee et antecessorum meorum et pro anima Willelmi filii Ricardi in puram et perpetuam elemosinam .xii. acras terre et duas acras prati in Morcota . que ualent per annum .vii. solidos quas Aewlf et Eurard tenent. Et uolo quod predicti monachi teneant terram illam quietam ab omni seruitio . et ab omni exactione. Et ego et heredes mei pro me terram illam aquietabimus in perpetuum de omni seruitio uersus dominum regem et uersus omnes alios homines. Si uero forte contigerit quod ego uel heredes mei non possumus eis guarantizare predictam terram. nos in terris uel in redditibus eisdem monachis rationabile escambium ad ualentiam faciemus. Et ut hec donatio et concessio nostra rata et inconcussa permaneat. sigilli nostri inpressione presens scriptum roboramus.[1] His testibus . magistro Petro de Lech . Iohanne decano . Godefrido filio Geraldi . sacerdotibus . Ricardo Murdac . Helia Kokerel . Baderun de Blechesduna . Alexandro pincerna . Henrico fratre abbatis militibus . Roberto de Bulesduna . Roberto de Slohtres . Walterio Thoki . Roberto portario . Iohanne de Mareis . Roberto teste . Nicholao de Rudes . Ricardo de Custance.

The abbey's Calendar of Donations recorded this gift ('Historia', 99–100). It was confirmed 1165 × c. 1197 by Margaret de Bohun, one of the heirs to the earldom of Hereford, of which de la Mare held two knight's fees (ibid. 100; Walker, 'Earldom of Hereford Charters', no. 121; *Cart. Glouc.* ii, no. 474); but since King Henry II, with Earl William of Gloucester attesting (arrested 1183; d. 1183), confirmed an exchange of land at Murcott which St. Peter's made with Roger Walensis, it is possible, assuming de la Mare's gift was involved, that the above charter should be dated c. 1165 × 83 (*Cart. Glouc.* i, p. 353, ii, p. 129, where Walensis is erroneously called Reginald). The charter's reference to William son of Richard appears to be to a son of Richard son of Pons, lord of Clifford.

[1] **B**. ends here with *etc.*

236. *Grant by Thomas son of Maurice of Matson and parson of the church of St. John the Baptist, Gloucester, in free alms to St. Peter's, Gloucester, for the almonry of land in the suburb of Gloucester by Alvingate belonging to the fees of the earl of Gloucester and of the abbot of Gloucester, paying annually through the almoner ¼d. to the earl and 2d. to the abbot (s. xiii; c. 1230 ?)*

A. G.C.L., 'Deeds and Seals', viii, no. 22, fol. 12 (264 mm × 88 mm); fragment of tag for seal; seal missing; endorsements: Thom(as) filius Mauricii. (s. xiii[1]); De terra quam Iohannes Le suthperne tenet. (c. xiii[ex]?); versus portam Aluengate[1] (s. xiii[2]); . . .ta Thome[2] rectoris ecclesie sancti Ioh(annis) Baptiste[3] (s. xiv[ex]); versus Aluengate (s. xiv[ex])[;] Registratur (s. xiv[ex] × s. xv[in]); **B**. ibid. 'Reg. B', no. 744, p. 321.

Sciant presentes et futuri quod ego Thom(as) filius Mauricii de Mathesd' persona ecclesie sancti Iohannis Baptiste que sita est infra portam aquilonarem Glouc' . dedi . et concessi . et hac presenti carta confirmaui pro salute anime mee et antecessorum meorum deo et ecclesie beati Petri Glouc' . et monachis ibidem deo seruientibus quandam terram meam in suburbio Glouc' . Quam emi de Rocelino le[4] mercer que iacet uersus Eluenestret[5] . Inter terram Iohannis Bay . et terram Iohannis Pomerai . que est de feodo comitis Glouc' . Et de feodo eiusdem abbatis Glouc' . Tenendam et habendam in liberam . puram . et perpetuam elemosinam ad augmentum elemosine ipsorum . Reddendo per manum elemosinarii ipsorum . annuatim domino comiti Glouc' ad festum sancti Oswaldi vnum quadrantem pro parte illa que est de feodo ipsius comitis . Et domino abbati Glouc' ad Hokedai duos denarios . pro parte illa que est de feodo ipsius abbatis pro omnibus seruitiis . et secularibus demandis. Predicta uero terra per uisum legalium uirorum mensurata . Que est ex parte feodi comitis. continet in fronte octo uirgas ulnarias cum pollice interposito . et tres pollices . In longitudine viginti et septem virgas ulnarias cum pollice interposito . et dimidiam . et dimidium quarterium . Retro uero sex virgas vlnarias cum pollice interposito . Et tria quarteria. Ex parte uero feodi abbatis continet autem quadraginta duas uirgas ulnarias cum pollice interposito . et dimidiam . In longitudine . triginta uirgas ulnarias cum pollice interposito . et vnum quarterium . et dimidium quarterium . Retro uero triginta et quinque uirgas ulnarias cum pollice interposito . et dimidiam. In cuius rei testimonio presens scriptum sigillo meo sigillatum predictis abbati . et conuentui tradidi. Et ad maiorem securitatem cartam quam habui de Rocelino le mercer qui michi eandem terram uendidit in simul cum carta ista eis reddidi. Hiis testibus . magistro Waltero scriptore . Ricardo Burg' . Waltero Hoch[6] . Galfrido Ianitore . Galfrido Cutesting' . Iohanne drapario . Willelmo le saler . Hugone cissore . et multis aliis.

A Thomas son of Maurice of Matson granted to St. Peter's land on Grace Lane in Gloucester in 1229 (G.C.L., 'Reg. B', no. 691, p. 299). He may be one of the Thomases who appear in local *acta c*. 1230 × 45 (Stevenson, nos. 226–7, 229, 315, 422).

[1]   Reading uncertain with ultra-violet light.
[2]   Superscript in the same hand.
[3]   *Baptistite* in MS.
[4]   *la* in MS.
[5]   Reading uncertain.
[6]   **B** ends here with *et aliis*.

237. *Grant by Henry Mercer to St. Peter's, Gloucester, of land in the suburb of Gloucester. (1200 × c. 1228)*

A. G.C.L., 'Deeds and Seals', ix, no. 18, fol. 9 (109 mm [right] × 207 mm [foot]); damaged; slit for tag on turn-up; tag and seal missing; endorsements: Contra Henricum Le m(er)cer (s. xiii); de omnibus istis ignoratur locus p' dilige(n)t(er) i(n)q(ui)ritur; Registratur (s. xiv?); **B**. ibid. 'Reg. B', no. 558, pp. 244–5.

[Scia]nt presentes [et futuri] quod ego Henr(icus) Le m(er)cer dedi et concessi deo et ecclesie sancti Petri Glouc' et monachis ibidem deo seruientibus pro salute [anime] mee et antecessorum[1] meorum quamdam terram meam in suburbio Glouc' que est de feodo eiusdem ecclesie illam scilicet que iacet inter capi[tale] mesuagium[2] meum et terram Stephani monachi . et continet in anteriori parte vndecim uirgas regis ulnarias et quatuor pollices cum pollice [interposit]o . In posteriori parte nouem uirgas regis ulnarias et unum quarterium cum pollice interposito . In profunditate quadraginta et septem [uirgas et d]imidiam cum pollice interposito. Dedi etiam eidem ecclesie totam terram quam Martinus Le sauun' de me tenuit in feodo fir(ma) [salu]is elemosinar(io) eiusdem ecclesie quatuor sol(idis) per annum. Dedi etiam eidem ecclesie unum curtillagium quod iacet retro terram [dicti Ma]rtini et continet in parte uersus terram dicti Martini vndecim uirgas regis ulnarias et dimidium quarterium cum pollice interposito . In [poster]iori parte decem uirgas et dimidiam cum pollice interposito . In profunitate triginta septem uirgas et dimidiam cum pollice interposito. [Te]nendas et [haben]das predictas terras et curtillag(ium) libere et quiete in perpetuum ab omnibus seruitiis et secularibus demandis sine omni [impe]dimento quod possit de me uel de heredibus meis euenire. Et ego Henr(icus) et heredes mei predictam donationem et concessionem dicte ecclesie contra omnes homines et feminas warantizabimus. Et ut hec mea donatio et concessio firma et stabilis sit in perpetuum presenti scripto sigillum meum apposui. Hiis testibus . Ricardo burgense .

Thoma Oie tunc preposito in Glouc' . [Waltero ?] Hoich . Willelmo de Churchesdun' . Hugone Keutwan'[3] . Drogone pincerna . Willelmo Walense et aliis.[4]

Portions of the text in brackets are from **B**. For the date see *VCH Glos.* iv. 371.

[1]   *anticessorum* in MS.

[2]   *mesiagium* in MS.

[3]   Reading uncertain; possibly *keucwan*'.

[4]   **B** lists as witnesses only Richard Burgess, Thomas Oye, and William Walensis.

238. *Grant by Herbert Mercer to the abbot and convent of St. Peter's, Gloucester, and their almoner of ½ acre in Pedmarsh in return for an advance of 8s. and an annual payment by the almoner of ½d. (s. xiii^{med})*

A. G.C.L., 'Deeds and Seals', i, no. 42, fol. 23 (240 mm × 125 mm), **Scribe 37** (below, Plate XXXI); fragment of tag; seal missing; endorsements: C (s. xiii^{in}); Herebertus Le mercer (s. xiii^{med}); quia ista dimidia acra terre continetur infra ortum monachorum (s. xiii^{ex} × xiv); Pedemarsfeld' (s. xiii^{ex} × s. xiv^{in}); Registratur (c. s. xiv^{ex}); **B**. ibid. 'Reg. B', no. 471, pp. 207–8.

Sciant presentes et futuri quo ego Herebertus Le mercer dedi . concessi et hac presenti carta mea confirmaui abbati et conuentui sancti Petri Glouc' et eorum elemosinario pro viginti solidis sterlingorum quos michi premanibus pacauit dimidiam acram terre mee lucrabilem videlicet illam que iacet in Pedem'esfeld' inter terram que fuit Baldwini Tod et terram Walteri de La Felde . Tenendam et habendam predictis abbati et conuentui et eorum elemosinario qui pro tempore fuerit libere et quiete integre cum pertinentiis suis in perpetuum . Reddendo inde annuatym michi et heredibus meis vel meis assignatis per manum elemosinarii eorum vnum obolum argenti ad Pascha pro omnibus seruitiis et secularibus demandis. Et ego predictus Hereb(er)tus et heredes mei . vel mei assignati predictis abbati et conuentui et eorum elmosinario qui pro tempore fuerit predictam dimidiam acram terre cum pertinentiis contra omnes homines et feminas in perpetuum warantizabimus et de omnibus seruitiis sectis et secularibus demandis ad dictam terram pertinentibus aquietabimus. Et quia volo hanc meam donationem. concessione . et confirmationem ratam et stabilem inperpetuum permanere presens scriptum sigilli mei inpressione roboraui. Hiis testibus . Willelmo capellano de Duddestan . Roberto Le mercer[1] . Thoma tabernario . Henrico Ruffo . Galfrido clerico . Iohanne de Aula Regis . Andr(eo) capellano de Glouc' . Waltero clerico et aliis[.]

[1]   **B** ends here with *et aliis*.

239. *Grant by John Mey and his wife Alice to the abbot and convent of St. Peter's, Gloucester, and its almonry of 4 acres in Barton outside Gloucester for payments by the almoner of 4 marks in advance and of ¼d. annually to John Mey and 2s.*

annually to William Foket; the land was the maritagium *which William gave John with his daughter Alice. (s. xiii^med)*

A. G.C.L., 'Deeds and Seals', ii, no. 1, fol. 1 (22 mm × 144 mm), **Scribe 32** (below, Plate XXVI); two seals on tags; 1) left, dark green wax; obverse: round (28 mm in diam.); a fish, head pointing to top of seal; legend: + S' IOHANNIS: LE MEY; no counterseal; 2) right, dark green wax; obverse: oval (33 mm × 23 mm); a stylized tree or plant pointing downwards; legend: + S.' ALICIE: FILIE: W. . .OK' . . .; no counterseal; endorsements: Carta Ioh(ann)is Mey et Alic(ie) vxoris eius de quatuor acris terre. In Berth'i'. (s. xiii^med) abbatis (s. xiii^ex?); Registratur (s. xiv^ex × s. xv^in); **B**. ibid. 'Reg. B', no. 627, p. 272.

Sciant presentes et futuri quod ego Ioh(ann)es Mey et Alicia vxor mea . dedimus . concessimus . et hoc presenti scripto confirmauimus abbati et conuentui sancti Petri Glouc' et eorum elemosinarie pro quatuor marcis argenti quas per manum elemosinarii eorum ipsi nobis ad magnum negotium nostram premanibus pacauerunt . Quatuor acras terre nostre in Bertona dicti abbatis extra Glouc' . Illas scilicet quatuor acras quas Willelmus Foket dedit mihi in liberum maritagium cum predicta Alicia filia sua . De quibus acris duo seillones iacent in R'uecroft inter terram abbatis predicti⸴ et terram Osberti Foket . Et unus seillo iacet contra Aldefeldesbrugg' . et extendit ex una parte apud Wetrugg'. Et duo seillones iacent inter terram sancti Leonardi et terram Osberti Foket . Et quinque seillones iacent in Sudhanleg' inter terram Thome de Mattresdon' et terram Osberti Foket . Et tres seillones iacent inter terram Walteri Schyrreue et terram Osberti Foket . Et tres seillones iacent inter terram Walteri Trikefeyd et terram Osberti Foket . et extendunt ex vna parte super Middelweye . Tenendas et habendas sibi et successoribus suis qui pro tempore fuerint . libere et quiete integre cum pertinentiis suis sine aliqua clamatione . vexatione uel demanda per nos uel per heredes nostros inperpetuum . Reddendo inde annuatim per manum elemosinarii eorum Willelmo Foket et heredibus suis duos denarios argenti ad festum sancti Michaelis pro nobis et heredibus nostris sicut reddere debuimus et consueuimus . et nobis et heredibus nostris vnum quadrantem argenti ad predictum terminum sancti Michaelis pro omnibus seruitiis . sectis . exactionibus et demandis. Et nos uero predicti Iohannes et Alicia vxor mea et heredes nostri dictis abbati . et conuentui . dictis quatuor acras terre cum omnibus suis pertinentiis contra omnes homines et feminas tam Iudeos quam Cristianos in perpetuum warantizabimus. Et quia uolumus quod hec nostra donatio . concessio et confirmatio . rata et stabilis in perpetuum perseueret⸴ tam dicta Alicia vxor mea quam ego dictus Ioh(ann)es presenti scripto sigilla nostra apposuimus . et cartam quam per predictum Willelmum de eadem terra habuimus⸴ dicto elemosinario liberauimus. Hiis testibus . Galfrido de Weston' . Ioh(ann)e de Eldresfeld'[1] . Willelmo de Cheddesleye . Rogero len veyse . Waltero de Snedham . Galfrido de La Graue . Willelmo Gerard' . Symone de Mattresdon' . et multis aliis.

---

[1]   **B** ends here with *et aliis.*

240. *Confirmation by Alice widow of John Mey in her free power and widowhood of the previous grant (no. 239) for the support of the almonry of St. Peter's, Gloucester; for her confirmation Alice received 3 crannocks of corn. (s. xiii^{med})*

A. G.C.L., 'Deeds and Seals', ix, no. 23, fol. 11 (235 mm × 97 mm), **Scribe 34** (below, Plate XXVIII); fragment of tag; seal missing; endorsements: Carta confirmationis Alicie vxoris Iohannis Mey (s. xiii^{med}), **Hand p/Scribe 34** (below, Plate XLIVg); Registratur (s. xiv^{ex} × s. xv^{in}); B. ibid. 'Reg. B', no. 628, p. 272.

Sciant presentes et futuri quod ego Alicia quondam vxor Iohannis Mey in libera potestate et viduitate mea dedi . concessi . et confirmaui et hoc presenti scripto pro me et omnibus heredibus meis quietas clamaui abbati et conuentui sancti Petri Glouc' ad augmentum elemosinarie eorumdem quatuor acras terre cum pertinentiis in Berton' ipsorum quas predictus Iohannes quondam vir meus et ego eis dedimus et carta nostra confirmauimus . Illas scilicet quatuor acras quas Willelmus Foket pater meus predicto Iohanni mecum dedit in liberum maritagium . Tenendas et habendas quatuor acras terre cum suis pertinentiis libere . quiete . integre . et pacifice sine aliquo clamio . vexatione uel demanda per me uel per heredes meos imperpetuum . Reddendo inde annuatim per manum elemosinarii eorum qui pro tempore fuerit Willelmo Foket et heredibus suis duos denarios argenti ad festum sancti Michaelis pro me et heredibus meis sicut dictus Iohannes quondam vir meus et ego eidem reddere debuimus et consueuimus . et michi et heredibus meis vnum quadrantem argenti ad predictum festum sancti Michaelis pro omnibus seruitiis . sectis . exactionibus . et omnimodis secularibus demandis. Pro hac autem donatione . concessione . confirmatione . et quieta clamatione mea . dederunt michi predicti abbas et conuentus per manum elemosinarii eorum tres cronnocos bladi ad magnum negotium meum. Ego uero Alicia et heredes mei predictas quatuor acras terre cum suis pertinentiis predictis abbati et conuentui contra omnes homines et feminas imperpetuum warantizabimus. Et quia volo quod hec mea donatio . concessio . confirmatio et quieta clamatio rata et stabilis imperpetuum perseueret. presens scriptum sigilli mei impressione roboraui. Hiis testibus . Philippo de Mattesdon' . Willelmo Gerand[1] . Waltero de Snedham . Roberto Keys . Symone de Mattesdon' . Iohanne de Eldresfeld' . Henrico forestario de Maysemor . et multis aliis.

[1]   B ends here with *et multis aliis*.

241. *Grant by Henry of Minsterworth son of William of Minsterworth in free alms to St. Peter's, Gloucester, of all his right to rent of 8s. 3d. from three tenants for meadows. (8 July 1215 × 1225)*

A. G.C.L., 'Deeds and Seals', v, no. 4, fol. 2 (185 mm × 140 mm); fragment of tag; seal missing; endorsements; . . .wrthe (uncertain date); [non i]nd[i]get r[e]gistrari (s. xiv); one other endorsement illegible with ultra-violet light; B. P.R.O. C 150/1, fols. 138–138v (slightly different text); *Cart. Glouc.* ii, no. 466.

Sciant presentes et futuri quod ego Henr(icus) de Munstrewr*þ*' filius Willelmi de Munstrewr*þ*' assensu et uoluntate Agathe vxoris mee et heredum meorum pro salute anime mee et uxoris mee et omnium antecessorum nostrorum dedi et concessi in liberam puram et perpetuam elemosinam deo et ecclesie sancti Petri Glouc' et monachis ibidem deo seruientibus totum ius quod ego uel heredes mei habuimus uel habere potuimus in redditu octo solidorum et trium denarium quem Hugo Marescallus Glouc' et Helyas de Perches et Rogerus Clericus filius Rogeri filii Cecilie michi annuatim certis terminis soluebant pro pratis que de me in feudo et hereditate tenebant . Scilicet dictus Hugo marescallus pro prato quod tenet in Sciremed . . . tres solidos et sex denarios duobus terminis anni . medietatem ad festum sancti Michaelis . et aliam medietatem ad Annuntiationem beate Mari[e] . . . Prenominatus Helyas pro pratis quorum una pars iacet in furlungo inter pratum de R. clerici et dominicam culturam meam . Alteram partem in Hibeching' . que fuit Roberti Ca. . . triginta denarios ad Natiuitatem beate Mar[e] . Sepedictus uero Rogerus clericus pro tribus acris . . . iacent in furlungo inter pratum supradicti Helie de Purchas et pratum Rogeri Cleri. . . septem denar(ios) ad eund. . . redditu predicti Hug' . Helyas et Rogerus et eorum heredes*'*. abbati et monachis sancti Petri Glouc' sine aliqua reclamatione . . . meorum supradictis terminis decetero plenarie respondebunt. Et tam ipsi quam heredes eorum facient homagia sua . . . tempore fuerint et dabunt heredes eorum rationabile releuium . Sicut michi et heredibus meis facere debuerunt. Et ego Hen. . .ctos octo sol(idos) et tres denar(ios) predictis abbati et monachis Glouc' contra omnes homines et feminas warantizabimus et . . . et exactione tam regali quam alio*'*. adquietabimus. Si uero ita contigerit quod ego .H. uel heredes mei predicto octo solidos et tres denarios dictis abbati et monachis Glouc' warantizare non possimus*'*. faciemus eis rationabile escambium siue in terris siue in redditu ad ual. . .iam octo solidorum et trium denarium. Quod quia ratum esse uolo*'*. presens scriptum sigillo meo munitum . eis tradidi. Hiis testibus Radulfo Musard tunc vicecomite Glouc' . Radulfo de Wiletun . Petro de Eggeswr*þ*' . Stephano de Harenhull' . Petro de aula regis . magistro Reginaldo de Hamine . Henrico capellano de Munstrewr*þ*' . magistro Waltero Scriptore . Ricardo Burgeis . Waltero de Bannebir' . Dauid Dunning . Iohanne de Gosedich . et multis aliis.

Ralph Musard served as sheriff of Gloucestershire after 8 July 1215, in 1220, and in 1221 (Stevenson, p. 90; Foss, *Judges*, ii. 419; *List of Sheriffs*, 49); he attested several local *acta* before his death in 1225 (Stevenson, nos. 125, 182, 204).

242. *Confirmation by Walter of Monkhide (in Yarkhill, Herefs.) of the grant in free alms by Henry of Leicester and Cecily his wife to St. Peter's, Gloucester, and its sacristy of 17 acres in Monkhide and to St. Guthlac's Priory of the 2s. rent which Henry and Cecily received from the sacristan; in addition Walter confirmed to St. Guthlac's 4 acres in* Cheuenhulle *and 1 acre in* Northfeld' *by the wood of Whitwick (in Yarkhill, Herefs.) granted by Henry of Woodmanton; the priory was to pay an annual rent of 1 lb. of cumin to Walter. (s. xiii[in])*

A. G.C.L., 'Deeds and Seals', i, no. 18, fol. 11 (182 mm × 124 mm); seal on tag; white wax lacquered green; obverse: round (33 mm in diam.); a large fleur-de-lis; legend: +SIG'LL'.WALTERI: DE HIDA; no counterseal; endorsements: Walt(er) De Hida (s. xiii^{med}), **Hand m** (below, Plate XLIVd); Registratur (s. xiv^{ex} × s. xv^{in}); **B**. ibid. 'Reg. B', no. 122, p. 43.

Sciant presentes et futuri quod ego Walter(us) de Hida pro salute anime mee et omnium antecessorum meorum concessi et hac presenti carta mea confirmaui deo et ecclesie beati Petri Clouc' in liberam puram et perpetuam elemosinam decem et septem acras terre apud Hidam sancti Petri Clouc' quas Henricus de Leicestria et Cecilia uxor eius donauerunt in liberam puram et perpetuam elemosinam sacristarie dicte ecclesie sancti Petri Glouc'. Concessi etiam prioratui Apostolorum Petri et Pauli et sancti Guthlaci Hereford' et presenti carta confirmaui duos solidos quos idem Henricus pro salute anime sue dicto prioratui in liberam puram et perpetuam elemosinam donauit quos percipere consueuit annuatim de sacrista Glouc' pro predictis decem et septem acris. Preterea concessi et confirmaui dicte ecclesie Glouc' quatuor acras qui iacent in Cheuenhulle et vnam in Northfeld' iuxta nemus de Witewike quas Petrus de Wodemoneton' in liberam puram et perpetuam elemosinam eis donauit. Et uolo ut monachi Glouc' habeant et teneant omnes predictas acras cum omnibus pertinentiis suis et libertatibus . libere et quiete et pacifice et integre de me et heredibus meis in perpetuum pro vna libra cimini a monachis dicti prioratus Hereford' michi et heredibus meis in festo sancti Michaelis pro omnibus rebus et demandis que ad terras illas poterunt pertinere'. annuatim soluenda. In cuius rei testimonium presens scriptum sigillo meo munitum monachis dicte ecclesie Glouc' tradidi. Hiis testibus . Nicholao Le seculer . Willelmo de solla . Symone de Weston'[1]. Ricardo de Esthida . Thoma de Weston' . Waltero de Asperton . et multis aliis.

For the texts of Henry of Leicester's and Peter of Woodmanton's grants to St. Peter's see above, nos. 231–2. Walter of Monkhide (*de hida*) or possibly a namesake predecessor attested Peter's grant to St. Peter's as his lord (above, no. 231). *Cheuenhulle* and *Northfeld* were located in Whitwick manor, in Yarkhill (Herefs.) according to the context of the above charter (*Herefordshire Place-Names*, 216); but Gloucester's 'Register B' associates the grants with its manor at Monkhide (fol. v verso).

[1] B ends here, adding *et multis aliis*.

243. *Declaration in the form of a chirograph by Abraham son of Moses that the abbot and convent of St. Peter's, Gloucester, had repaid in full the loan made to the community by his father. 1195.*

H.C.L., no. 1323 (163 mm × 57 mm); three small slits at foot; another slit by the top of *A* in *ABRAHE* along the top; no medieval endorsements; Walker, 'Gloucester Charters', no. 12; facsm. facing p. 265; cal. in Baddeley ii, no. 144, p. 44.

CYROGRAPHUM : ABRAHE : FILII : MOSSEI

Ego qui sum subtus sigillatus recognosco uera recognitione quod abbas Gloec' et totus conuentus sunt quieti de omnibus debitis que debebant patri meo Mosseo Iudeo a die quo seculum fuit creatum usque ad die .xvii. in mense quem Hebrei uocant Elul . anno circuli lunaris Hebrei .ix.[1] centum. et lv. Et si quis a .iiii.^{or} mundi partibus uenerint filius uel filia . uel aliquis Iudeus et calumpniet et aportet sigillum super abbatem et conuentum Gloec' sub nomine patris mei[.] ego debeo facere pacem toti abbatie contra eos . et quod cognoui scripsi et sigillaui. Abram filius Mossei.

In 1192 Abraham son of Moses owed the king 300 marks for the right to the debts owed to his father (*VCH Glos.* iv. 15; *P.R.* 1191 & 1192, P.R.S. N.S. ii. 292).

[1] An empty space follows created by an erasure.

244. *Grant by Nicholas Mueth in free alms to St. Peter's, Gloucester, of 15s. rent owed by Maurice Durand for land which Nicholas and Maurice bought from Henry Kais, for a bakehouse outside Eastgate, and for land on the great road by Northgate (Gloucester); the abbot and convent were to pay an annual rent of ½ lb. of cumin to Henry Kais. (c. s. xiii^{in})*

G.C.L., 'Deeds and Seals', ix, no. 42, fol. 22 (179 mm × 107 mm); seal on tag; dark green wax, fragment, cracked, rubbed, repaired; obverse: round (*c.* 30 mm in diam.); possible partial figure of a sagittarius facing to the right; legend: + ...MOWIET.; no counterseal; endorsements: .iii.^{a} (uncertain date); Carta Nicholai Mueth. (s. xiii^{in}); ii^a et iii^a Warda. (*c.* s. xiii^2?); caps(ula) .xviii. de laicis (s. xiii^{ex} × s. xiv^{in}); Registratur (s. xiv^{ex} × s. xv^{in}).

Sciant presentes et futuri quod ego Nicholaus Mueth dedi et concessi et hac presenti carta mea confirmaui deo et ecclesie sancti Petri Glouc' et monachis ibidem deo seruientibus in liberam puram et perpetuam elemosinam quindecim solidos annuos quos Mauricius Durand' et heredes sui michi et heredibus meis annuatim debent pro portionibus meis de illis terris quas idem Mauricius et ego emimus de Henrico Kais . scilicet de quodam furno extra Eilesgathe et de quadam terra in magna ruta uersus Northgath' que iacet inter terram ipsius Henrici et terram predicti Mauricii . quas portiones ipse Mauricius de me et heredibus meis per cartam meam iure hereditario tenet . salua dimidia libra cimini quam predicti abbas et conuentus Henrico Kais et heredibus suis pro predictis portionibus predictarum terrarum annuatim ad festum sancti Michaelis pro omnibus seruitiis persoluent. Quod quia ratum esse uolo. presentem cartam sigilli i(m)pressione confirmaui. Hiis testibus . Ricardo Burg' . Ricardo Rufo . Henrico Burg' . Dauid Dunning . Willelmo de Samford . magistro Waltero scriptore . Drogone pincerna . Waltero de mora . Henrico Le Bel . et multis aliis.

Nicholas Mueth witnessed several local *acta* from *c.* 1190 to *c.* 1230 (Stevenson, nos. 86, 115, 241, 246, 272); property of his was located on Walkers Lane in the parish of St. Nicholas, Gloucester (ibid. no. 271).

245. *Confirmation by Ralph Murdac to St. Peter's, Gloucester, of the grants in free alms of Monkhide (in Yarkhill, Herefs.) by William Devereux senior, William his son, and the younger William's son Roger, Ralph's cousin. (s. xiii^{med})*

A. G.C.L., 'Deeds and Seals', v, no. 7, fol. 3 (96 mm × 94 mm); tag torn from turn-up; seal missing; endorsements: .R. Murdac de Hida (s. xiii^{med}); iiii. (poss. same date and hand); Carta Rad(u)l(fi)[1] Murdac de terra Hyda; Registratur (s. xiv^{ex}?); **B**. ibid. 'Reg. B', no. 103, p. 36.

Notum sit tam presentibus [quam futuris] quod ego Rad(ulfu)s Murdac pro animabus omnium antecessorum et successorum meorum dedi concessi ratificaui et presenti carta confirmaui deo et ecclesie sancti Petri Gloecestrie et monachis ibidem deo seruientibus ac eorum successoribus concessionem et donationem quam Willelmus de Ebroicis senior et Willelmus filius eius et Rogerus filius Willelmi secundi cognatus meus eisdem fecerunt de quadam terra cum pertinentiis suis que vocatur Hyda in Herefordsira . tenendam et habendam de me et heredibus meis . in liberam puram et perpetuam elemosinam solutam quietam et liberam ab omnimoda exactione sectis consuetudinibus servitiis regalibus et omnibus aliis que quocumque modo de terris uel tenementis exigi poterunt uel reddi. Et ego et heredes mei totam terram predictam cum omnibus pertinentiis suis in omnibus vt predictum est contra omnes mortales predictis monachis et eorum successoribus warantizabimus et vt puram et perpetuam elemosinam acquietabimus et defendemus in perpetuum. Et vt hec mea donatio concessio ratificatio et confirmatio perpetue firmitatis robur optineant cartam presentem sigilli mei inpressione corroboraui. Hiis testibus . Rogero Oilli . Willelmo de Tracy[2] . Galfrido Murdac . Ricardo Murdac . Radulfo de Lechelade clerico[3] de Estleche . Waltero de Boywell' . et aliis.

The text of the elder William Devereux's grant referred to above seems to be no. 203 above. See also 'Reg. B', fol. v verso.

[1] Reading uncertain.
[2] **B** ends here with *et aliis*.
[3] *l* possibly originally *R*.

246. *Grant by Richard de Mucegros to Abbot Henry and the convent of St. Peter's, Gloucester, of Sheldon (Devon), which Richard held at farm from the abbey for life, and quitclaim of all his right in the vill, for which the abbot and convent remitted all arrears of the farm. 6 May 1216.*

H.C.L., no. 1678 (221 mm × 112 mm), **Scribe 31** (below, Plate XXV); seal on tag; green wax, fragment; obverse: round (*c.* 35 mm in diam.); partial equestrian figure facing right; legend: . . .DI: DE: MVS. . .; no counterseal; endorsements: De Seldene .R. de Muchegros. (s. xiii^{in}); c(apsula) .vii.a de laicis tenuris (s. xiii^{in}), poss. **Hand h**; Registratur (s. xiv^{ex} × s. xv^{in}); cal. in Baddeley ii, no. 62, p. 26.

Omnibus Cristi fidelibus ad quos presens scriptum pervenerit . Ricard(us) de Mucegros salutem. Noverit vniversitas vestra quod anno dominice incarnationis

millesimo . ducentesimo . sextodecimo . in festo sancti Iohannis ante portam
Latinam . in abbatia Glouc' reddidi Henrico abbati et monachis sancti Petri Glouc'
villam de Schelden' cum pertinentiis quam tenui de eis ad firmam tantum in vita
mea . et vnam cartam eorum habui quam similiter eis eadem die reddidi . et omne ius
et clamium quod in terra illa siue firma predicta umquam habui: remisi . et eis
omnino de me et heredibus meis quietum clamaui. Et pro hac quieta clamatione:
predicti abbas et monachi omnia arreragia que debui eis de predicta firma et omnes
demandas quas habuerunt uersus me de firma illa: mihi remiserunt . et cartam suam
de quieta clamantia: mihi fecerunt. In cuius testimonium perpetuum presentem
cartam sigillo meo signatam sepe dictis abbati et monachis tradidi . et fide interposita
me obligaui per me et pro heredibus meis quod numquam contra cartam illam
molestiam eis inferamus uel gravamen. Hiis testibus . Nicholao filio Pontii . Martino
de Pateshull' clerico . Hugone Mustel' . Hereberto de Mucegros . Reginaldo de
Piriton' . Ricardo Burgeis . Rogero de Barris . Roberto de Montana . Drogone
Pincerna . Waltero de Mora . Simone de Aula . Waltero Mariscallo . Simone de
Matresdon' . Gaufrido de Matresdon' . Roberto de Baiocis . Roberto de Felda .
Waltero Croylin' . et multis aliis.

247. *Grant in writ form by Roger Parvus and his heir Hugh to St. Peter's,
Gloucester, of 8 acres at Whaddon in the presence of Abbot Hamelin and the entire
community. (1148 × 55)*

A. H.C.L., no. 1602 (225 mm × 49 mm), **Scribe 2** (below, Plate IV); tongue and tie; seal,
dark red wax, in fragments; partial lion rampant to the right; legend: . . . ROGE. . .; no
counterseal; endorsements: Rogerii parui (1148 × 55+), **Hand c/Scribe 2** (below, Plate
XLIIIc); de viii.° acris (s. xii^2); c(apsula) .x. de laicis. tenuris. (s. xii^{ex} × s. xiii^{in}), poss. **Hand h**;
.Waddon' (s. xiii); Registratur (s. xv); **B**. P.R.O., C 150/1, fol. 183; *Cart. Glouc.* ii, no. 673;
cal. in Baddeley i, no. 10, p. 227.

Sciant presentes et futuri quod ego Rogeri(us) paruus et Hugo heres meus dedimus
deo et sancto Petro et monachis Gloec' in perpetuam elemosinam octo acras de
Wedduna que iacent iuxta curtem de Brotrop pro salute anime nostre et
antecessorum nostrorum et in presentia Hamelini abbatis et totius conuentus eiusdem
ecclesie et multorum aliorum qui affuerunt: super altare sancti Petri posuimus. Quod
quia firmum et stabile esse uolumus ego Rogeri(us) predictam donationem huius
carte mee et sigilli mei atestationem confirmaui et Hugo filius et heres meus proprio
assensu et quod magis est fidei sue interpositionem communiuit. Huius rei testes
sunt[1] . Willelmus de Hereford . Gaufredus Gernun . Robertus . et Willelmus . et
Simon . sacriste . et Robertus lebret . et Rogerius Clalluel . et Robertus Scardein . et
multi alii.

For the dating of this charter, see 'Historia', 62. Another charter of Roger in favour of St.
Peter's, given with the assent of his lord Gilbert de Miners, is in *Cart. Glouc.* ii, no. 586; see
also ibid. no. 799.

[1] **B** as printed in *Cart. Glouc.* ends here.

248. *Confirmation in writ form by Rotrou (II) count of Perche to St. Peter's, Gloucester, of donations by Ernulph de Hesding and Patrick de Chawarth in Kempsford. (c. 1130 × 43)*

A. H.C.L., no. 798 (134 mm × 69 mm), **Scribe 21** (below, Plate XXb); seal on tongue with tie; white wax, small fragment of possibly round seal; obverse: possible hind legs of a horse belonging to an equestrian figure facing to the right; legend . . .DEL. . .; reverse: fragment of counterseal; possible front legs of a horse belonging to an equestrian figure; legend: . . .SA. . .; endorsements: Rotro comes de P'tico . de Kinem' (*c.* s. xii[med]), **Hand a** (below, Plate XLIIIa); .c(apsula) .xi. de laicis tenuris. (s. xii[ex] × s. xiii[in]); Registratur (s. xiv[ex] × s. xv[in]); **B.** P.R.O., C 150/1, fol. 106; *Cart. Glouc.* i, no. 329; cal. in Baddeley i, no. 5, pp. 225–6.

Ego .R. consul de P'tico concedo monachis ecclesie[1] sancti Petri de Gloecestria res illas quas audiui esse datas in uilla de Chinemeresford ab Ernulfo de Hesding et Patricio de Cadurcis liberas et quietas . sicutt eis existentibus habuerunt . Teste[2] .R. comite de Uuiareuuic . Waltero de Salesb' . et Sibilla uxore[3] sua . et Meinfelin . britone . et Waltero de Maheruto . capellano qui hanc chartam scripsit . et Waltero de Aldeburne.

The charter is written in two different modified bookhands (*Ego ... res*; and *illas ... Aldeburne*) within the period 1130 × 43 (above, p. xl). Inclusive dates for the recorded transaction are established by, respectively, the succession of the witness Walter of Salisbury to the Chitterne barony and the death of the donor Rotrou II of Perche (Sanders, *English Baronies*, 112; *Regesta*, ii, no. 834 n). The confirmation pertains to previous grants made to St. Peter's by *antecessores* of Walter of Salisbury and his wife Sibyl, Ernulph I de Hesding, and Patrick de Chawarth. The lordship of Kempford had passed by the marriages of Ernulph's daughter Maud to Patrick and of their daughter Sibyl to Walter (Sanders, *English Baronies*, 112 & n., 124–5 & nn.). Ernulph's original grant appears to be included in a *pancarta* (*Cart. Glouc.* i, no. 325; ibid. nos. 332–5 for Patrick de Chawarth's).

[1] *eclesie* in MS.; terminal *s* changed to *e*.
[2] **B** as printed in *Cart. Glouc.* ends here with *Hiis testibus*.
[3] *e* superscript in the same hand.

249. *Remise and quitclaim by Herbert son of Henry Piterich of Wotton St. Mary Without in free alms to the abbot and convent of St. Peter's, Gloucester, of land within the monks' garden and without (at Gloucester) in perpetual alms and remitting all right and claim upon it. (1248/9)*

G.C.L., 'Deeds and Seals', v, no. 40, fol. 19 (234 mm × 134 mm); seal on tag; cream coloured wax, with traces of dark stain; obverse: round (20 mm in diam.); a bearded male bust to the right; legend: . . .E. . .E LAWOOT. . .; no counterseal; endorsements: Quieta clamatio Hereb(er)ti filii Henrici[1] Pit(er)ich (s. xiii[2]); Infra ortum monachorum[2] et extra .I. (s. xiii[ex]); Registratur (s. xiv[ex]); .I. (s. xiv[ex]).

Sciant presentes et futuri quod ego Herebertus filius Henrici Piterich de Wotton' remisi et in perpetuum pro me et omnibus heredibus meis quietam clamaui domino abbati et conuentui sancti Petri Glouc' in puram et perpetuam elemosinam pro salute anime mee et omnium antecessorum et successorum meorum . totam illam terram cum pertinentiis suis que iacet inter terram que fuit Baldewini Tod et terram que fuit Walteri de Longeford' infra ortum eorum et extra . Remisi etiam et in perpetuum pro me et omnibus heredibus meis dicto abbati et conuentui quietum clamaui totum ius et clamium quod in dicta terra habuimus . vel aliquo modo habere poterimus . Tenendam et habendam dicto abbati et conuentui qui pro tempore fuerint . libere et quiete . integre cum pertinentiis suis in perpetuum sine aliqua reclamatione . iure . vel demanda . per me vel per heredes meos. Et ut hec mea remissio et quieta clamatio pro me et omnibus heredibus meis in perpetuum firma et stabilis vt predictum est permaneat in presenti scripto sigillum meum apposui[.] Hiis testibus Waltero Hoich' . Willelmo de Sumery . Ricardo Franceys tunc bailliuis Glouc' . Ricardo Blundo . Galfrido de graua [.] Ada de Twigeworth' . Ricardo de Celario et aliis.

William de Sumery and Richard Francis were bailiffs at Gloucester in 1248/9 (*VCH Glos.* iv. 372).

---

¹ Superscript.
² Superscript in modern (?) hand.

250.   *Grant by Hugh de Plucknett in free alms to St. Peter's, Gloucester, of messuages in Lambourn (Berks.) for the monks to find a lamp to burn night and day in the chapel of St. Mary of Lambourne and at masses to be sung there, for the soul of his son Alan; grant also that the monks or the tenants of the messuages might put their draught animals in Hugh's pastures free of pannage and herbage. (1179 × 1205)*

A. W.S.R.O., Cap. I/17/85; (149 mm × 114 mm); seal, detatched from tag, chipped, worn, and broken pieces rejoined; white wax, round (*c.* 57 mm in diam.); image of large winged bird possibly facing front; legend: . . . SIG. . .VGO[NIS] DE . . .AI; no counterseal; endorsements: Carta Hug(onis) de Pluggleni de Lamb'[1] (s. xii^{ex} × s. xiii^{in}), **Hand f**; c(apsula) .viii. de ecclesiasticis et laicis tenuris (s. xii^{ex} × s. xiii^{in}); Registratur (s. xiv^{ex} × s. xv^{in}); B. P.R.O., C 150/1, fols. 117v–118; *Cart. Glouc.* i, p. 374.

Sciant presentes et futuri quod ego Hugo de Plugenai dedi . et concessi . et presenti carta mea confirmaui pro salute anime mee et Sibille uxoris mee . et pro anima Alani filii mei . et omnium heredum meorum deo et ecclesie sancti Petri Gloc' . et monachis ibidem deo seruientibus mesagium . quod Aldwinus claudus tenuit et mesagium quod Edwinus Smuri tenuit in Lamburn' . cum omnibus pertinentiis et libertatibus suis in liberam puram et perpetuam elemosinam . Ita tamen quod predicti monachi pro anima predicti Alani filii mei singulis noctibus per annum inuenient unam lampadem ardentem inperpetuum in capella beate Marie de Lambur' . et similiter ad omnes horas diurnas . et ad missas que in eadem capella cantabuntur. Concedo etiam quod predicti monachi uel qui predicta mesagia de eis tenuerint . habeant aueria sua in paschiis meis quieta de pannagio et herbagio. Quia uero hanc concessionem meam stabilem et firmam . esse . uolo[2] presenti carta sigilli mei impressione munita eam confirmaui. His testibus . Anfrido et Henrico . tunc capellanis de Lamburn' . Eustachio diacono . Rogero de Heddel' . Iozone de la leia . Osmundo clerico . Ernaldo clerico . Reginaldo le Sir' . Eluredo Seuesot . Euerard[o] Seuesot . magistro Adam de Frowec . Philippo Carbun' . Willelmo de Bromiard . Mauricio marescallo . Thoma de Bromt' . Galfrido de Frowec' .

For the date, see 'Historia', 95–96; regarding this grant, see *Cart. Glouc.* ii, no. 833. For Hugh, his second wife Sibyl, son Alan, and Lambourne, see Salter, *Oxford Charters*, no. 50 n.

[1]   *iam* added in a different hand; date uncertain.
[2]   **B** as printed in *Cart. Glouc.* ends here with *carta, etc.*

251. *Notification by Henry (II) de Pomeroy of an agreement made in his presence between the monks of St. Peter's, Gloucester, and William son of Walter regarding Sheldon (Devon): William surrendered his claim to Sheldon and granted that a mill be built and land; the monks granted William and his men pasturage for their cattle, but they were not to mow or cut without the monks' permission; William gave himself, his wife, and his heirs to St. Peter's; if he wished, he might join the community; if he did not do so before his death, his body would be received there. (c. 1165 × 1207)*

H.C.L., no. 1609 (277 mm × 79 mm); slit in turn-up for tag; tag and seal missing; on left side of turn-up, fragment of tongue; seal missing; endorsements: De Seldene. (*c.* s. xii[ex]); c(apsula) .vii. de laicis tenuris. (s. xii[ex] × s. xiii[in]); Carta Henr(ici) de Pomerya [;] Registratur (s. xiv); cal. in Baddeley ii, no. 141, pp. 43–44.

H. de Pom' omnibus suis hominibus et amicis tam presentibus quam futuris salutem. Hoc est pactum quod fuit factum et concessum in mea presentia inter monacos Gloecestrie et Willlelmum filium Walterii. Ille Willelmus pro dei amore dimisit calumpniam quam habebat in terra Sildene et concessit bene et in pace ad faciendum molendinum et terram ad lucrandum per diuisam inter certam terram et moram sicut fuit perambulata recte ad Canutam spinam in Tib'ha.. . .[1] de spina'. recte ad fontem Dudebroc. Monaci autem concesserunt Willelmo et suis hominibus pasturam in mora pecoribus[2] eorum . tali tenore quod Willelmus et homines eius nec debent falcare in mora nec s[. . .]iare[3] nisi concessu monachorum uel ministrorum eorum. Idem Willelmus dedit se et suam uxorem et heredem suum sancto Petro Gloec'. Si uoluerit uitam suam mutare ibi mutabit . si uero non mutauerit priusquam moriatur corpus eius ibi recipietur. Teste . Hugone de Boll'. Teste . Rodberto Russel . Teste . Osmundo clerico . Teste . Rogero filio Etardi . Teste . Radulfo Coffin . Teste . Pagano de Ceorratune . Teste . Ricardo filio Thome . Teste . Radulfo de Hamb'.

A William son of Walter appears as a witness in a charter dated 1196 in favour of St. Peter's, but there is no way to identify this individual with the William of the above text (*Cart. Glouc.* i, no. 240). The angularity of the script establishes that the above text was written in the late twelfth century and thus that the text's Henry de Pomeroy was very likely Henry (II) (see below, no. 252 n.).

[1] Hole in MS.; partial *m* or *n* cut off by the hole.
[2] *pecuniis* in MS.
[3] Hole in MS.

252. *Confirmation by Henry (II) de Pomeroy to St. Peter's, Gloucester, of Sheldon (Devon) quit of all secular service except for what was due the king. Henry also granted in free alms the 2s. which he used to receive annually in recognition of his right over the land, offering them on the altar of St. Peter's for his soul and those of his parents. (c. 1165 × 80)*

H.C.L., no. 1604 (197 mm × 89 mm); seal on tag; green wax, large fragment, chipped, round (*c.* 65 mm in diam.); obverse: a helmeted equestrian figure to the right, a raised sword in the right hand; legend: . . .IGIL. . . POM. . .; no counterseal; endorsements: De Sceldena. (s. xii²), **Hand b** (below, Plate XLIIIb); c(apsula) .vii.ᵃ de laicis tenuris (s. xii² × s.xiiiⁱⁿ); carta Henr(ici) de Pomeria [;] Registratur (s. xivᵉˣ × s xvⁱⁿ); cal. in Baddeley ii, no. 139, p. 43.

Sciant presentes et futuri quod ego Henric(us) de Pom'ia concessi et confirmaui terram de Seldena in Devenesira que est de feudo meo deo et ecclesie sancti Petri Gloec' et monachis ibidem deo seruientibus cum omnibus pertinentiis suis et libertatibus et liberis consuetudinibus tenendam de me et heredibus meis liberam et quietam ab omni servitio et exactione seculari . excepto servitio regali sicut unquam melius et quietius et liberius eam tenuerunt tempore antecessorum meorum. Duos etiam solidos quos in recognitionem iuris mei de eadem terra annuatim recipere solebant pro salute anime mee et anime patris et matris mee . et pro animabus antecessorum meorum eidem ecclesie dedi et concessi et super altare beati Petri Gloec' in puram et perpetuam elemosinam optuli. Quod quia ratum et inconvulsum manere uolo´ presenti scripto sigilli mei inpressione munito confirmaui. His testibus . magistro Reginaldo de Ernleia . Roberto de Bucherel clericis . Baldwino filio Roberti . Radulfo de Bascheruilla iuniore . Iohanne Franccheualer . Hereberto de Boslai . Radulfo de Hambiri . Roberto de Euerci militibus . Iohanne de Bellomonte . Oliver de Karruges hominibus meis . Walterio Toki . Roberto Ianitore . Radulfo Albo . Galfrido de Lilletun' . Halmone Karbonel . Ricardo Le grant servientibus abbatis.

The grantor of the above text was Henry (II) de Pomeroy (d. 1207) (Sanders, *English Baronies*, 106–7; see also Green, *The Government of England under Henry I*, passim, esp. 266–7). According to the abbey's Calendar of Donations, St. Peter's originally acquired Sheldon in an exchange with William de Pomeroy's brother Jocelin for Berry Pomeroy, which William had given to the abbey in 1102, and the abbey in turn obtained Hope Mansell for

Sheldon ('Historia', 12, 88). Later, however, the Calendar contradicts itself, attributing the grant of Sheldon to William de Pomeroy (ibid. 123), and recording that Henry (I) de Pomeroy gave back Sheldon but retained 2*s.* a year in recognition of his grant (ibid. 113, erroneously attributing the grant to the abbacy of Serlo).

253. *A copy of no. 252, with minor variations in the list of witnesses. (s. xii^2; s. xii^{ex}?)*

H.C.L., no. 800 (161 mm × 120 mm); seal on tag; white wax, chipped, rubbed; obverse: round (c. 67 mm in diam.); an equestrian figure to the right, a raised sword in the right hand; legend: SI. . . HENRI. . . DE POM. . .; no counterseal; endorsements: De Sceldena (s. xii^2), **Hand b**; c(apsula) .vii.^{a} de laicis tenuris (s. xii^{ex} × s. xiii^{in}); dupplicetur[;] Registratur (s. xiv^{ex} × s. xv^{in}); cal. in Baddeley ii, no. 140, p. 43.

. . . His testibus . magistro Reginaldo de Arnleia . Roberto de Bukerel clericis . Baldwino filio Roberti . Radulfo de Bascheuilla iuniore . Iohanne Franc cheualer . Herberto de Boslai . Radulfo de Hamburia . Roberto de Euerci . militibus [.] Iohanne de Bello monte . Oliuer de Karruges hominibus meis . Roberto ianitore . Waltero Tochi . Radulfo Albo . Gaufrido de Wottesduna . Hamone Carbunel . Ricardo le grant . seruientibus abbatis.

Geoffrey de Lilletun' in no. 252 has become Geoffrey de Wottesduna, and the order in which Walter Toki and Robert Ianitor are named is reversed.

254. *Confirmation by Henry (III) de Pomeroy son of Henry (II) to St. Peter's, Gloucester, of Sheldon (Devon), which his father and grandfather Henry (I) had given. (1207 × 16)*

H.C.L., no. 1636 (149 mm × 105 mm), **Scribe 28** (below, Plate XXII); four slits on turn-up for cords; seal and cords missing; endorsements: .H. de Pomeria Seldena (s. xiii^{in}); c(apsula) .viia de laicis tenuris. (s. xiii^{in}); dupplicata (s. xiv^{med}); Registratur (s. xiv^{ex} × s. xv^{in}); cal. in Baddeley ii, no. 142.

Sciant presentes et futuri quod ego Henricus de Pomeria filius Henrici de Pom'ia pro salute anime mee et anime patris et matris mee . et pro animabus antecessorum meorum dedi et concessi in puram et perpetuam elemosinam . et presenti carta mea confirmaui deo et ecclesie sancti Petri Gloec' . et monachis ibidem deo seruientibus totam terram de Seldena quam pater meus Henricus de Pom'ia et auus meus Henricus de Pom'ia eis dederunt concesserunt . et cartis suis confirmauerunt . tenendam de me . et heredibus meis in perpetuum . liberam . solutam . et quietam sicut puram et perpetuam elemosinam. Ego autem et heredes mei de cetero adquietabimus eam ab omni seruitio et exactione seculari. Concessi etiam eis et presenti carta mea confirmaui duos solidos . quos pater meus Henricus de Pom'ia filius Henrici de Pom'ia in recognitione iuris sui de eadem terra annuatim percipere solebat . Quos pro salute anime sue . et pro animabus patris . et matris sue . et antecessorum suorum eidem ecclesie dedit . et concessit . et super altare beati Petri Gloec' in puram et perpetuam elemosinam optulit. Quod quia ratum et inconuulsum manere uolo in perpetuum⸍. presenti scripto sigilli mei impressione munito⸍. confirmaui. Hiis testibus . Waltero archidiacono Cornub' . Ricardo Reuel . Ogero filio Ogeri . Ricardo Flammeng . Symone filio Roges[1] . Ricardo de Greinvill' . Roberto de Champaus . Pagano clerico . Ricardo de Muchegros . Odone fratre eius.

This charter was issued before the death of Walter archdeacon of Cornwall in 1216 and very close to the date of no. 255, which has a similar witness-list (cf. Morey, *Bartholomew of Exeter*, 127). While no. 254 was classified by its fourteenth-century endorser as a duplicate, it is likely to have been written before no. 255, which appears to improve on the word-order and the wording and has as witness a second brother for Richard de Mucegros.

[1] *Sic* in MS.

255. *Another version of no. 254. (1207 × 22)*

G.C.L., 'Deeds and Seals', xi, no. 2 (148 mm × 134 mm), **Scribe 28**; seal on tag; white wax, round (52 mm in diam.) obverse: a lion rampant(?) to the right; behind, a tall three-pronged fleur-di-lis; legend: + SIGILL' HENRICI D. . .MERIA; no counterseal; endorsement: De Seldena c(apsula) .vii.[a] de laicis tenuris. (s. xiii[in]); carta Henrici Pomeroy (*c.* xiv[ex]); Registratur (s. xiv); another endosement illegible with ultra-violet light; imperf. transcr. in Baddeley, ii, pp. 49–50.

Sciant presentes et futuri quod ego Henric(us) de Pom'ia filius Henrici de Pom'ia pro salute anime mee . et anime patris et matris mee . et pro animabus antecessorum meorum dedi et concessi in puram et perpetuam elemosinam . et presenti carta mea confirmaui deo et ecclesie sancti Petri Gloec' . et monachis ibidem deo seruientibus terram de Seldena cum omnibus pertinentiis suis . et libertatibus . et liberis consuetudinibus suis . quam pater meus Henricus de Pom'ia et auus meus Henricus de Pom'ia eis dederunt . concesserunt . et cartis suis confirmauerunt . tenendam de me et heredibus meis in perpetuum . liberam . solutam . et quietam sicut puram et perpetuam elemosinam. Ego autem et heredes mei de cetero warentizabimus eam predictis monachis sicut liberam elemosinam nostram . et adquietabimus eam de seruitio regali . et de omni seruitio . et consuetudine . et exactione seculari. Concessi etiam eis et presenti carta mea confirmaui duos solidos . quos pater meus Henricus de Pom'ia filius Henrici de Pom'ia in recognitione iuris sui de eadem terra annuatim percipere solebat . Quos pro salute anime sue . et pro animabus patris et matris sue et antecessorum suorum eidem ecclesie dedit . et concessit . et super altare beati Petri Gloec' in puram et perpetuam elemosinam optulit. Quod quia ratum et inconuulsum manere uolo in perpetuum . presenti scripto sigilli mei impressione munito⸍. confirmaui. Hiis testibus . Waltero archideacono Cornub' . Ricardo Reuel . Ogero filio Ogeri . Ricardo Flammeng . Symone filio Reges[1] . Ricardo de Greinuill' . Roberto de Champaus . Pagano clerico . Ricardo de Mucheg'os . Hereberto . et Odone fratribus eius.

The description of his grandfather as Henry establishes the donor's identity as Henry (III).

[1] *Sic* in MS.

256. *Grant by Gilbert of Great Rissington and his wife Emma to Abbot Thomas and the convent of St. Peter's, Gloucester, of a meadow in Great Rissington, Emma's maritagium, to hold during Gilbert's and Emma's life for an annual rent of 7s. and a cheese, and an entry payment of 4s. (1179 × 1205)*

A. H.C.L., no. 1677 (136 mm × 101 mm), **Scribe 11** (below, Plate XIII); tag and seal missing; endorsements: Contra Gileb(ertum) de Risenduna (s. xii^{ex} × s. xiii^{in}); De prato iuxta molendinum de Risend' (s. xii^{ex} × s. xiii^{in}); .c(apsula) .xv. de laicis. tenuris. (s. xii^{ex} × s. xiii^{in}); non indiget registrari (s. xiv); **B**. P.R.O., C 150/1, fol. 158; *Cart. Glouc.* ii, no. 561; cal. in Baddeley i, no. 21, p. 230.

Notum sit omnibus quod ego Gilb(er)tus de Risindona et Emma uxor mea. concessimus domino Thome abbati et ecclesie sancti Petri Gloec' . pratum nostrum in Risindona illud uidelicet . quod Andreas de Cotes dedit eidem . Emme uxore mee in matrimonium . tenendum quamdiu ego Gilb(er)tus et predicta Emma uxor mea uixerimus. pro septem solidis et uno caseo nobis singulis annis ad festum sancti[1] Iohannis Baptiste persoluendis. Et pro hac concessione prefatus abbas dedit nobis[2] in ingressu quatuor solidos. Quod ut ratum et inconuulsum permeneat . presenti scripto sigilli nostri inpressione munito . confirmauimus. His testibus . Waltero blundo de Risindona . Philippo blundo . Galfrido clerico . Rogero persona . Waltero scriptore . Samsone de Clifford . Waltero Toki . Thoma de Bro'tuna[3] . Rogero mareskallo . Petro burg' . Philippo Carbonel . Durand de Hauuill' et multis aliis. Et hanc conuentionem quam diu ego .G. et .E. uxor mea uixerimus . fideliter tenendam. fide interposita confirmauimus.[4]

The date of the charter is indicated by the character of the script and the reference to Abbot Thomas.

[1] Erasure, apparently correcting *sanctum*.
[2] Erasure, apparently correcting *michi*.
[3] Reading uncertain.
[4] **B** continues with *Hiis testibus*.

257. *Quitclaim by Nicholas of St. Bride's to the abbot and convent of St. Peter's, Gloucester, of his right in a virgate in Standish. (1179 × 1205)*

A. H.C.L., no. 778 (140 mm × 98 mm); seal on tag; white wax, chipped; obverse: oval (length unavail.; width 27 mm); a winged man riding a horse bare-back to the right, in intaglio; legend: . . . NICHOLAI DE SCA BRIGIDA; no counterseal; endorsements: Carta Nicholai d[e] sancta Brigida de una uirgata terre in Staned'[;] c(apsula) .viii.^{a} de laicis tenuris (s. xii^{ex} × s. xiii^{in}), poss. **Hand h**; Stanedisch' (c. s. xiii^{exa}?); Standis[;] Registratur (s. xiv^{ex} × s. xv); **B**. P.R.O., C 150/1, fol. 170v; **C**. G.C.L., 'Reg. B', no. 249, p. 101; *Cart. Glouc.* ii, no. 610; cal. in Baddeley i, no. 17, p. 229.

Sciant presentes et futuri . quod ego Nicholaus de sancta Brigida dedi et concessi et quietum clamaui deo et ecclesie sancti Petri Gloec' . et abbati et monachis ibidem deo seruientibus totum ius quod habebam in uirgata terre . quam Gaufridus Dispensator tenebat in Stanedis . ut habeant et teneant eam in perpetuum liberam et quietam ab omni reclamatione mei et heredum meorum . et per textum super altare sancti Petri optuli in presentia domini Thome abbatis et totius conuentus. Quod quia ratum et inconuulsum manere uolo . presenti scripto et sigilli mei impressione munito confirmaui. His testibus . Waltero Giffard . Waltero Bloet . Alexandro pincerna . Waltero de Side . Henrico le droeis[1] . militibus . Waltero Tochi . Roberto de Bertuna . et Roberto filio eius . Roberto Croili . Wimundo de Ældesword' . Roberto teste . Nicholao de Rudes . Willelmo tunc pincerna abbatis . Iohanne de Mareis . Gaufrido de Liletuna . Willelmo de Londoniis . Helya de Stanedis . Wigot de Froecest' . Petro de Fromilad' . Gaufrido de Bromtuna . Ricardo Ruffo de Framilade.

This original adds significantly to the list of witnesses, obtained from **C**, which is printed in *Cart. Glouc.* Nicholas's grant is noted in the abbey's Calendar of Donations ('Historia', 111).

[1]   **B** ends here with *etc.*; **C**, with *et aliis multis.*

---

258.   *Grant by Miles of Sandhurst in free alms to St. Peter's, Gloucester, and its almoner of land outside Alvingate (Gloucester), subject to 2¾d. annual rent to the king's barton. (s. xiii[1]; poss. c. 1225 × 50)*

A. G.C.L., 'Deeds and Seals', ii, no. 30, fol. 16 (177 mm × 134 mm); seal on tag; white wax stained green; obverse: round (27 mm in diam.); fleur-de-lis; legend: + SIGILLV . . . MILONIS; no counterseal; endorsements: Milo de Sandhirste (s. xiii^{med}); de quadam terra extra Aluenegate (s. xiii^2); Registratur (s. xiv?); **B**. ibid. 'Reg. B', no. 463, p. 205.

Sciant presentes et futuri quod ego Milo de Sondhurste dedi et concessi et hac presenti carta mea confirmaui et pro me et pro omnibus heredibus meis quietam clamaui deo et ecclesie sancti Petri Gloucest' et elemosinario eiusdem domus ad pauperum sustentationem quandam terram meam extra portam de Aeluenegate illam scilicet que iacet inter terram eorumdem monachorum et terram Willelmi Holdeburg de feudo Bertone domini regis tenendam et habendam in liberam puram et perpetuam elemosinam reddendo inde annuatim [apud] Berton' domini regis ad Hockedei . tres obolos . et ad Natiuitatem beate Marie unum obolum . et ad festum sancti Andree . tres quadrantes[1] . sicut ego et antecessores mei et heredes mei reddere debebamus et solebamus[.] Predicta uero terra per visum legalium virorum mensurata continet in fronte tresdecim virgas ulnarias domini regis cum pollice interposito . duobus pollicibus minus . In profunditate autem quadraginta et octo . et dimidium quarterium cum pollice interposito . In medio autem decem et octo virgas . et vnum quarterium cum pollice interposito . In posteriori parte viginti . virgas cum pollice interposito. Ego vero Milo et heredes mei predictam terram predictis monachis contra omnes homines et feminas warantizabimus saluo seruitio domini regis. Et vt hec mea donatio et quieta clamantia ratam inperpetuum obtineat firmitatem presens scriptum sigillo meo sigillatum eis tradidi. Hiis testibus . domino Radulfo de Wilitun' . magistro Waltero scriptore[2] . Roberto Le sauuage . domino Petro de aula regis . Galfrido de Westun' . Amari de Bares . Radulfo filio Herberti de Waleswurþe . et multis aliis.

---

[1]   *quadrentes* in MS.
[2]   **B** ends here with *et aliis.*

259. *Remise and quitclaim by Petronilla, widow of Miles of Sandhurst, in free alms to the abbot and convent of St. Peter's, Gloucester, of the land which she held in dower outside Alvingate (Gloucester) in return for ½ mark. (c. s. xiii[1])*

A. G.C.L., 'Deeds and Seals', ii, no. 15, fol. 9 (160 mm × 63 mm); seal on tag; green wax, chipped; obverse: oval (*c.* 33 mm × 25 mm); a standing falcon or hawk to the right; on the left a vine with stylized leaves or flowers; legend: + S' PETRON. . .ARES[1]; no counterseal; endorsements: Pet(r)onilla de Sendurste de tercia parte terre Milonis de eadem extra Aluenegate (s. xiii[2]); Registratur (s. xiv[ex] × s. xv[in]); **B.** ibid. 'Reg. B', no. 464, p. 205.

Sciant presentes et futuri . quod ego Pet(ro)nilla relicta Milonis de Sendurste . remisi . et in perpetuum quietamclamaui . et hac presenti carta mea confirmaui domino abbati et conuentui sancti Petri Glouc' . totam tertiam partem cum omnibus pertinentiis suis in quadam terra extra portam de Aluenegate . que iacet inter terram eorum monachorum et terram Willelmi de Ildeburche . de feodo Berton' domini regis . que me contigebat nomine dotis . Tenendam et habendam . in liberam . puram . et perpetuam elemosinam . Quam dominus meus . Milo de Sendurste predictis monachis dedit et concessit . et carta sua confirmauit. Pro hac concessione . et quietaclamatione . predicti monachi dederunt michi premanibus dimidiam marcam argenti in magna necessitate mea. In cuius rei testimonium presens scriptum sigillo meo sigillatum eis tradidi. Hiis testibus . Adam filio Rogeri . Adam Gladewino . Roberto Le Feorrer' . Henrico Le Lokere . Galfrido Clerico . Henrico de Orto . Rogero de Stanedis . et multis aliis.

---

[1]   The reading ARES is uncertain.

260. *Confirmation by Jordan of Sanford in free alms with the assent of his wife to St. Peter's, Gloucester, of two assarts, a wood in their midst with adjacent small meadows, and common of pasture in Chelworth (Wilts.). (s. xii^{med}; poss. 1154 × 72)*

A. H.C.L., no. 1603 (195 mm × 65 mm); no turn-up; slit for seal at foot; tag and seal missing; endorsements: In domo Godwini fabri in eadem tenura manentis . fuit hoc breue sigillatum (s. xii^{med}); De essartis in Cheleswrd'a (s. xii^2?); c(apsula) .viii.^{a} de ecclesiasticis tenuris (s. xiii^2); Carta Iordani de Sanford de duabus assartis silue et pratellis[;] C. temporalium parte 2.^{a} (s. xiv); Registratur (s, xiv^{ex} × s. xv^{in}); B. P.R.O., C 150/1, fol. 60v; *Cart. Glouc.* i, no. 152; cal. in Baddeley i, no. 4, p. 225.

Sciant presentes et futuri quod ego Iordan(us) de Sanford assensu uxoris mee et heredum meorum concedo et confirmo in elemosinam perpetuam deo et sancto Petro et monachis Gloec' duo essarta in Cheleswrda . et siluam que est in medio eorum . cum adiacentibus pratellis libere et quiete ab omni exactione et consuetudine tenenda . et communionem pasture in bosco et in plano.^{1} Huius rei؛ testes sunt Aluredus decanus Cirec' . Henricus presbiter de Pult' . et Ger' Capellanus de Bisel' . Goodwinus faber . Iordanus Basset tunc dapifer . Robertus de Maisil . Walerand de Crikel' . Reinaldus de Widef . Hubertus de Cernai . et aliis multis.

Jordan's confirmation may have been a response to a writ from Henry II, apparently issued 1154 × 72, commanding him to support St. Peter's with regard to his ancestors' grants to the abbey in free alms in Chelworth (*Cart. Glouc.* i, no. 155). The abbey's two assarts there came from William II, and both Henry I and Stephen confirmed the grant (*Regesta*, i, no. 472; ii, nos. 673, 1937; iii, nos. 351 [below, no. 41], 352).

1 **B** as printed in *Cart. Glouc.* ends here.

261. *Quitclaim by Robert the serjeant son of Adam the serjeant in free alms to St. Peter's, Gloucester, of a virgate in the hamlet of (Lower) Ley in the parish of Westbury (on Severn), which his father had held from Henry de Miners for 10s. annual rent which Henry's daughter Isabel gave in her widowhood to the abbey. (s .xiii^1; poss. 1224 × 28)*

A. W.S.R.O., Cap. I/17/87; (178 mm × 88 mm), **Scribe 33** (below, Plate XXVII); seal on brown cords (orig. brown and pink?), green wax, round (31 mm in diam.); image of a lamp, cup, or covered dish crowned with a fleur-de-lis with flanking stars(?), one in each of the four fields into which the image is divided; legend: + S' ROBERTI: SERVIENTIS; no counterseal; endorsements: Carta Rob(er)ti Seruientis de terra in Leye. (s. xiii^1); Registratur (s. xiv^{ex} × s. xv^{in}); B. G.C.L., 'Reg. B', no. 818, pp. 353–4.

Sciant presentes et futuri quod ego Rob(er)tus sergeant filius Ade sergeant dedi et concessi et imperpetuum pro me et omnibus heredibus meis quietam clamaui deo et ecclesie beati Petri Glouc' et abbati et conuentui ibidem deo seruientibus pro salute anime mee et omnium antecessorum meorum unam uirgatam terre cum omnibus pertinentiis suis que iacet in hameleto de Leye in parochia de Westbur' quam Adam sergeant pater meus in feodo et hereditate pro decem solidis pro omnibus seruitiis de Henrico de Min'iis hereditarie tenuit . Quos decem solidos redditus mei et omnia alia seruitia mea Ysabel filia predicti Henrici de Min'iis primogenita tempore uiduitatis sue ad sustentationem operis ecclesie sancti Petri Glouc' in liberam elemosinam dedit et carta sua confirmauit et in saisinam in ligia potestate sua eos posuit . Tenendam et habendam totam predictam terram cum omnibus pertinentiis suis in liberam puram et perpetuam elemosinam sine aliquo retinemento ad opus meum uel heredum meorum nisi solummodo predicte domus orationes. In cuius rei testimonium presens scriptum sigillo meo sigillatum predictis monachis tradidi. Hiis testibus . domino Henrico de Bathon' . domino Petro de Eggeswrþe . Willelmo de Helyun[1] . Galfrido de Weston' tunc ianitore abbatie Glouc' . Waltero de la graue . Nicholao clerico . et multis aliis.

For Robert and Lower Ley see esp. G.C.L., 'Reg. B', nos. 815, 819–20, pp. 352, 354. In 1241 Robert acknowledged the abbey's right to the virgate in Lower Ley in return for annual rents in cash and kind (above, no. 169; see also G.C.L., 'Reg. B', no. 821, pp. 354–5). The scribe who wrote this charter was active 1224 × 28.

1 **B** ends here with *et aliis.*

262. *Grant by William of Showle in free alms to St. Peter's, Gloucester, with the consent of his wife Idonea of three headlands in* Solcrofte *and a spring and the stream at* Homgate *and confirming his father Hugh's gift of rent for pasture from the men of Monkhide (in Yarkill, Herefs.). (1174 × 1213/14)*

A. H.C.L., no. 1605 (220 mm × 105 mm); fragment of tag; seal missing; endorsements: Will(elmu)s de Soll'. (s. xii[ex] × xiii[in]), **Hand k** (below, Plate XLIVb); Registratur (s. xiv[ex] × s. xv[in]); **B**. G.C.L., 'Reg. B', no. 133, p. 47; cal. in Baddeley i, no. 34, p. 234.

Sciant presentes et futuri quod ego Will(elmu)s de Solle assensu et uoluntate Idonie vxoris mee et heredum meorum pro salute anime mee et uxoris mee et omnium antecessorum et successorum meorum dedi et concessi deo et ecclesie sancti Petri Gloucestrie et monachis ibidem deo seruientibus tres forerdas que iacent in capite de Solcrofte et fontem et cursum fontis qui est apud Homgate in perpetuam elemosinam . libere et quiete ab omni seruitio seculari quod est uel esse potest. Confirmaui etiam assensu et uoluntate predicte uxoris mee et heredum meorum eidem ecclesie et eisdem monachis donationem Hugonis patris mei . scilicet pasturam que est in exitu hominum de la Hide . ut habeant et teneant eam similiter in puram et perpetuam elemosinam liberam et quietam ab omni seruitio et exactione seculari. Predictam uero donationem et predictam confirmationem. ego predictus Will(elmu)s et heredes mei contra omnes homines warantizabimus. Et ut hec mea donatio et confirmatio inperpetuum rate permaneant. eas presenti scripto sigillo meo munito confirmaui. Hiis testibus . Ada capellano de Coure . Thoma decano de Weston'[1] . magistro Moyse . Yarculle . Waltero filio Aliz . Odone preposito de Weston' . Roberto de la Hide . Alexandro de Asperton' . Ernaldo Molendinario . Rogero preposito de la Hide . Waltero Thoki . Willelmo Ianitore . Galfrido de Mattresdon' . Phillippo Carbonel . Willelmo sacrista . et multis aliis.

Aside from the evidence of its script, the date of this charter is established by the attestation of Adam chaplain of Much Cowarne. Apparently he was admitted to the church on the presentation of Abbot Hamelin of St. Peter's between 6 October 1174 and 10 March 1179 by Bishop Robert Foliot and died in 1213/14 (Barrow, *Hereford Episcopal Acta*, no. 144 & n.; cf. G.C.L., 'Reg. B', no. 169, p. 59, recording the grant of the church to Adam on 13 September 1174 but either naming Abbot Henry, in error for Abbot Hamelin, or giving 1174, in error for 1184).

[1] **B** ends here with *et multis aliis.*

263. *Grant by William of Showle with the consent of his wife Idonea to the abbot and convent of St. Peter's, Gloucester, of 4 acres of land with a meadow below the moor of Monkhide (in Yarkhill, Herefs.) for a payment of 2 marks and for 2s. annual rent. In addition William gave ½ acre by* Stapela *in free alms for the salvation of his soul and those of his predecessors. (1174 × 1213/14)*

A. H.C.L., no. 1628 (162 mm × 102 mm); fragment of tag for seal; seal missing; endorsements: Will(elmu)s de Soll'. (s. xii^ex × s. xiii^in), **Hand k**; Registratur (s. xiv^ex × s. xv^in); B. G.C.L., 'Reg. B', no. 132, pp. 46–47; cal. in Baddeley i, no. 33, p. 234.

Sciant presentes et futuri quod ego Will(elmu)s de Solla assensu et uoluntate Ydonee uxoris mee et heredum meorum concessi deo et beato Petro et abbati Gloecestrie et monachis ibidem deo seruientibus quatuor acras terre arabilis que iacent iuxta terram Ærnaldi et tendunt ad mersam cum quodam prato quod uocatur Cuttimede quod iacet subtus moram de Hida . tenendas et habendas de me et heredibus meis inperpetuum libere et quiete ab omni seruitio seculari quod est uel esse potest . pro duobus solidis ad festum sancti Iohannis Baptiste . annuatim persoluendis. Hanc autem conuentionem et concessionem ego et heredes mei contra omnes[1] homines et omnes feminas warantizabimus. Preterea ego et heredes mei seruitia regalia et alia quecumque ad predictam terram cum prato pertineant adquietabimus pro predictis duobus solidis mihi et heredibus meis annuatim persoluendis. Pro hac uero concessione et warantizatione predictus abbas et conuentus dederunt mihi duas marcas argenti. Concessi etiam caritatis intuitu pro salute anime mee et animarum predecessorum meorum dimidiam acram terre que fuit Radulfi albi iuxta Stapelam in liberam et perpetuam elemosinam. Et ut hec conuentio inperpetuum rata et inconuulsa permaneat*. eam presenti scripto sigillo meo munito confirmaui. Hiis testibus . Adam tunc decano de Coura . Roberto de Solla fratre meo[2] . Waltero de Eglint' . Waltero filio Aliz . Rogero de Weston' . Petro de Wudemont' . Alexandro de Asperton' . Waltero de Aspert' . Ærnaldo molendinario . Rogero tunc preposito de Hida . Waltero fratre eius et multis aliis.

For the date see above, no. 262.

[1]   Initial *o* replaces *b*, which has been erased.
[2]   **B** ends here with *et multis aliis*.

264. *Grant by William of Showle with the consent of his wife Idonea to the abbot and convent of St. Peter's, Gloucester, of his pasture at Monkhide (in Yarkhill, Herefs.) for the use of the sacristy, for 2s. annual rent. (c. 1174 × 1213/14; possibly c. 1203)*

A. H.C.L., no. 1894 (188 mm × 92 mm); fragment of tag for seal; seal missing; endorsements: Will(elmu)s de Soll'. (s. xii^{ex}; poss. xiii^{in}), **Hand k**; Registratur (s. xiv^{ex} × s xv^{in}); **B.** G.C.L., 'Reg. B', no. 131, p. 46; cal. in Baddeley i, no. 32, p. 234.

Sciant presentes et futuri quod ego Will(elmu)s de Solla assensu et consensu Idonee uxoris mee et heredum meorum dedi et concessi abbati et conuentui Glouc' ad opus sacristarie eiusdem loci pasturam meam apud Hyda' que iacet inter moram et Chutmedam in escambium terre sue que dicitur Solmeda tenendam de me et heredibus meis inperpetuum libere et quiete . integre et plenarie ab omni seruitio . consuetudine . et exactione . Excepto quod sacrista qui in eadem ecclesia pro tempore fuerit*. persoluet michi et heredibus meis singulis annis inperpetuum pro eadem pastura duos solidos ad festum sancti Iohannis Baptiste. In cuius rei testimonium presens scriptum sigilli mei appositione munitum confirmaui. Hiis testibus . Henrico priore Herefordie . Willelmo de Cirenc' . priore de Stanleia[1] . Thoma decano de West' . Adam decano de Cowra . Petro capellano de Archilla . magistro Moyse de Archilla . Viuiano et Luciano fratribus eius . Rogero de West' . Roberto de Hida . Rogero preposito de Hida . Willelmo Coco Herefordie . Pontio clerico fratre eius . Stephano Ianitore . et multis aliis.

For the date see above, no. 262. The possible date *c.* 1203 is based on the attestations of Henry prior of Hereford and William of Cirencester prior of Leonard Stanley (*HRH*, 91, 93).

[1]   **B** ends here with *et multis aliis*.

265. *Grant by William of Showle son of William of Showle in free alms to St. Peter's, Gloucester, of various lands associated with Monkhide (in Yarkhill, Herefs.). (c. s. xiii^{in})*

A. H.C.L., no. 1637 (202 mm × 75 mm); fragment of tag on foot; seal missing; endorsements: Will(elm)i de Solle (s. xiii^in), **Hand k**; Registratur (s. xiv^ex × s. xv^in); **B**. G.C.L., 'Reg. B', no. 136, p. 48; cal. in Baddeley ii, no. 37, pp. 19–20.

Sciant presentes et futuri quod ego Will(elmu)s de Solla filius Willelmi de Solla pro salute anime mee et omnium antecessorum meorum dedi et concessi et hac presenti carta mea confirmaui deo et ecclesie sancti Petri Glouc' et monachis ibidem deo seruientibus duos seillones terre arabilis de terra mea de Solla . illos scilicet qui iacent inter terram meam ex una parte et moram dictorum monachorum ex alia parte cum forertha que est ad capud predictorum seillonum et terram illam que iacet inter pratum dictorum monachorum quod uocatur Cuttemede . et terram quam Godefridus homo ipsorum tunc de eisdem monachis tenuit . Et dimidiam acram que iacet inter terram dictorum monachorum. et cheminum regale uersus Eglinton' . Et aliam dimidiam acram que iacet inter terram sepedictorum monachorum et cheminum regale uersus uiam que uocatur La Lane. tenendas et habendas omnes predictas terras cum omnibus pertinentiis earum in liberam . puram . et perpetuam elemosinam liberas et quietas ab omni demanda et seculari seruitio quod est uel esse potest. Ego uero Will(elmu)s de Solla et heredes mei omnes predictas terras cum omnibus pertinentiis earum predictis monachis contra omnes homines et feminas inperpetuum warantizabimus. Et ut hec mea donatio et concessio rata et inconcussa inperpetuum permaneat. presens scriptum sigillo meo munitum predictis monachis tradidi. Hiis testibus magistro Moyse tunc rectore ecclesie de Gerchull' . Ricardo de La Hyde[1] . Waltero Palmario . Iohanne de La Hide . Rogero Champeneis . Thoma et Randulfo tunc famulis sacriste . et multis aliis.

For Eggleton, see *Herefordshire Place-Names*, 81. See G.C.L., 'Reg. B', fol. v verso for the association of William's grants with Monkhide.

[1] **B** ends here with *et multis aliis.*

---

266. *Confirmation by William of Showle son of William of Showle to the abbot and convent of St. Peter's, Gloucester, of the donations of his father and ancestors. (c. 1225 × c. 1231)*

A. H.C.L., no. 1629 (157 mm × 87); slit for tag; tag and seal missing; endorsements: Confirmatio Will(elm)i de Solle (s. xiii^in), **Hand k**; Registratur (s. xiv^ex × s. xv^in); **B**. G.C.L., 'Reg. B', no. 134, p. 47; cal. in Baddeley ii, no. 35, p. 19.

Sciant presentes et futuri quod ego Will(elmu)s de Solle filius Willelmi de Solle . concedo et confirmo deo et ecclesie sancti Petri Glouc' et abbati et monachis ibidem deo seruientibus . omnes donationes et concessiones quas pater meus Willelmus de Solle et antecessores mei predicte ecclesie et monachis predictis dederunt et concesserunt . sicut in cartis eorum quas penes se hunc continentur . scilicet pasturam apud Hyda' . que iacet inter moram et Cottemeda' . Et quatuor acras terre arabiles que iacent iuxta terram Hernaldi . et tendunt ad mersam . Et quoddam pratum quod vocatur Cottemede quod iacet subtus moram de Hyda . Et dimidiam acram terre arabilis que fuit Radulfi albi iuxta Stapela' . Et tres forerdas que iacent in capite de Solcrofte . Et fontem et cursum fontis . qui est apud Homgate . Et pasturam que est in exitu hominum de La Hyde . Tenendas et habendas omnes predictas donationes et concessiones . in liberam puram et perpetuam elemosinam ab omni seruitio et seculari demanda de me et heredibus meis secundum tenorem cartarum ipsorum. Quod quia ratum esse volo presens scriptum sigillo meo munitum' eis tradidi. Hiis testibus . Matheo Britole . Stephano de Neuwinton'[1] . magistro Moyse . Ricardo de La Hyd' . Rogero Champeneis . et multis aliis.

The witness Master Moses had died by *c*. 1231 (Barrow, *Hereford Episcopal Acta*, no. 348 & n.). The charter's hand suggests the 1220's.

[1]   **B** ends here with *et multis aliis*.

267. *Grant by William of Showle son of William of Showle to the abbot and convent of St. Peter's, Gloucester, of 9 acres in Padehulle field near the abbey's court of Monkhide (in Yarkhill, Herefs.) in exchange for land in Showle (in Yarkhill, Herefs.) free of service. (1254 × 57)*

A. H.C.L., no. 1630 (177 mm × 92 mm); seal on green cloth cords; red wax; obverse: pointed oval (34 mm × 20 mm); an eight-petalled flower, four large petals separated by smaller ones in saltire; legend: + S'WILELMI: DE SOLE.; no counterseal; endorsements: Will(elmu)s de Scholle (s. xiii^{med}), **Hand q** (below, Plate XLIVh); Registratur (s. xiv^{ex} × s. xv^{in}); **B**. G.C.L., 'Reg. B', no. 137, p. 48; cal. in Baddeley ii, no. 38, p. 20.

Sciant presentes et futuri quod ego Willelmus de Solle filius Willelmi de Solle tradidi concessi et hac presenti carta mea confirmaui dominis abbati et conuentui Clouc' nouem acras meas terre arabilis in campo de Padehulle que iacent iuxta curiam suam de Hyda in exscambium pro nouem acris in campo de Solle . que iacent inter terras meas ibidem. Et faciam illas acras quas tradidi dictis dominis abbati et conuentui ita liberas et quietas ab omni terreno seruitio et qualibet demanda sicuti est illa terra quam ab eisdem recepi. Et de decima ecclesie persoluenda similiter de omni terreno seruitio et de qualibet demanda pro predicta terra adquietanda uersus omnes pro predictis abbate et conuentu' ego et heredes mei respondebimus defendemus et contra omnes inperpetuum warantizabimus. Et quia uolo quod hoc exscambium iugiter perseueret' huic carte mee sigillum meum apposui. Hiis testibus . domino Petro Hereford' episcopo . domino .W. de Tregoz tunc rectore ecclesie de Stokes[1] . domino .I. Britun tunc vicecomite Hereford' . domino Ricardo de Bachindene milite . Ricardo de Hyda . Ricardo de Wyka . Iohanne de Souuille et aliis.

The date is indicated by the shrievalty of John Britun (*List of Sheriffs*, p. 59.)

[1]   **B** ends here with *et multis aliis*.

268. *Remise and quitclaim by William of Showle son of William of Showle in free alms to Abbot John and the convent of St. Peter's, Gloucester, of lands at* Chuttemede, Stapela, Humgate, *and Monkhide (in Yarkhill, Herefs.). (c. 1259)*

A. H.C.L., no. 1668 (198 mm × 198 mm); seal on tag; white wax stained green; obverse: oval (40 mm × 25 mm); an up-turned crescent with a curved four-pointed star above; legend: +S'WILELMI.DE.CHOL; no counterseal; endorsements: Will(elmu)s de Scholle (*c.* 1259+), **Hand q**; Registratur (s. xiv × s. xv^{in}); **B**. G.C.L., 'Reg. B', no. 135, pp. 47–48; cal. in Baddeley ii, no. 36, p. 19.

Omnibus Cristi fidelibus presens scriptum visuris uel auditurus Will(elmu)s de Solla filius Willelmi de Solla salutem in domino. Noverit vniuersitas vestra me dedisse concessisse et pro me et heredibus meis remisisse et quietum clamasse domino .I. abbati sancti Petri Glouc' et monachis deo ibidem seruientibus et eorum successoribus quandam pasturam cum pertinentiis que iacet inter moram et Chuttemede . et quatuor acras terre arabilis que iacent iuxta terram Ærnaldi et extendunt ad mersam . et quoddam pratum quod vocatur Chuttemede quod iacet subtus moram de Hyda . et dimidiam acram terre arabilis que fuit Radulfi albi iuxta Stapelam . et tres forerdas que iacent in capite de Solcrofte . et fontem et cursum fontis qui est apud Humgate . et pasturam que est in exitu hominum de Hyda. Quare volo et firmiter concedo pro me et heredibus meis quod dicti abbas et monachi et eorum successores habeant et teneant omnia predicta tenementa cum suis ubique pertinentiis bene et in pace in puram et perpetuam elemosinam . libere . quiete . et integre sine aliquo retinemento ita quod nec ego nec aliquis ex parte mea aliquid iuris uel clamii in predictis tenementis cum pertinentiis vendicare uel habere poterimus in perpetuum. Ego etiam dictus Will(elmu)s et heredes mei omnia predicta tenementa cum pertinentiis predictis abbati et monachis et eorum successoribus omnibus contra omnes gentes warantizabimus . defendemus . et acquietabimus in perpetuum. In cuius rei testimonium presenti scripto sigillum meum apposui. Hiis testibus . domino Waltero de Muchegros . domino Roberto de Meysi tunc vicecomite Hereford'[1] . domino Willelmo de Hyda . Ricardo de Wyke . Ricardo de Hyda . Thoma filio Odonis . Roberto de Trynleck' . et multis aliis.

1 **B** ends here with *et multis aliis.*

269. *Grant by William* rich *son of William* rich *of Sneedham to St. Peter's, Gloucester, and the almoner of land at* Fulunham *for the use of the poor; the almoner gave William 2 marks and was to pay annually a pair of gloves or ½d. to Philip de Ockold's heirs. (s. xiii[1])*

A. G.C.L., 'Deeds and Seals', iii, no. 8, fol. 5 (203 mm × 151 mm); seal on tag; white wax varnished brown, repaired; obverse: pointed oval (24 mm × 15 mm); a long-tailed animal to the right; legend: + S'WILL'I LE RICHE DE SNEDHAM; no counterseal; endorsements: Fuleham (s. xiii^ex); Carta Will(elmi) Le Riche de Snedham de terra in Fulhom. pro qua. ob(olum). ad Pascham (s. xiii^med); Registratur (s. xiv^ex × s. xv^in); **B**. ibid. 'Reg. B', no. 706, pp. 303–4.

Sciant presentes et futuri quod Ego Will(elmu)s le riche filius Willelmi le riche de Snedham dedi et concessi . et hac presenti carta mea confirmaui deo et ecclesie beati Petri apostoli Gloucest'ie et elemosinario eiusdem loci interiori. qui ibidem pro tempore fuerit ad usus pauperum quamdam particulam terre mee que dicitur Fulunham . que iacet inter terram Roberti Keys et terram Iohannis Daubeney in latitudine . Cuius vna pars se extendit uersus aquilonem usque ad terram dicti Iohannis Daubeney . Altera uero pars se extendit uersus partem australem usque ad terram Ricardi Crikefeld . et continet nouem decim seylones . Tenendam et habendam prenominatam terram . cum omnibus suis ubique pertinentiis de me et heredibus meis uel meis assignatis . sibi et heredibus siue succesoribus suis . libere quiete integre bene et in pace in perpetuum . ad usus pauperum per dispositionem dicti elemoninarii . Reddendo inde annuatim heredibus Philippi de Hocholte unum par cirotecarum uel unum obolum ad Pasca . pro omnibus seruitiis sectis curiarum uel hundredis tallgiis exactionibus consuetudinibus et omnibus aliis demandis secularibus que de liberis terris exeunt uel exire poterunt . saluo seruitio domini regis . pro tanto tenemento . nichil michi nec heredibus meis retinentes nisi tantummodo orationes que fiunt in predicta ecclesia inperpetuum. Pro hac autem donatione et presentis carte mee confirmatione. dedit michi supradictus elemosinarius. ad meum urgentissimum negotium . duas marcas argenti premanibus. Ego uero dictus Will(elmu)s le riche. et heredes mei uel mei assignati . prenominatam terram cum omnibus suis ubique pertinentiis sepedicto elemosinario et successoribus in officio illo commorantibus. inperpetuum warantizabimus defendemus . et acquietabimus contra omnes mortales . inperpetuum. In cuius rei testimonium huic presenti carte sigillum meum apposui. Hiis testibus Iohanne Daubeney . Roberto Keys[1] . Henrico de Rues . Willelmo de Ruun . Philippo de Haƥerleye . Roberto de Kimeresburi . Roberto de Ledene [.] Henrico de Marwent . Waltero de La graue . Ricardo Toki . et multis aliis.

Sneedham is represented by Sneedham's Green (*PNG*, ii. 171); *fulunham* apparently was located in the vicinity; see below, no. 329.

[1] **B** ends here with *et multis aliis.*

270. *Grant by Edith daughter of Walter Thurbarn in her liege power to St. Peter's, Gloucester, of all her land outside Alvingate (Gloucester). (s. xiii^in)*

A. G.C.L., 'Deeds and Seals', vii, no. 6, fol. 4 (154 mm × 69 mm); fragment of tag for seal; seal missing; endorsements: Edith filia Walt(er)i Ƥurbari de terra extra Aluenegate; y (s. xiii^ex); Registratur (s. xiv^ex); **B**. ibid. 'Reg. B', no. 466, p. 206.

Sciant presentes et futuri quod ego Edith filia Walt(er)i Þurbarn in ligio potestate mea reddidi et imperpetuum pro me et omnibus heredibus meis quietam clamaui abbati et conuentui sancti Petri Glouc' totam terram meam extra Aluenegate . Illam scilicet quam de eis hereditarie pro octo denariis tenui annuatim eisdem monachis persoluendis . Illam scilicet terram que iacet inter terram ex utraque parte eorum monachorum. Concedo etiam quod predicti monachi de predicta terra sine omni conditione mei et heredum meorum de predicta terra ad profectum et uoluntatem eorum faciant et disponant. In cuius rei testimonium presens scriptum sigillo meo sigillatum confirmaui. Hiis testibus . magistro Waltero scriptore . Ricardo burgens' . Dauid Dunning[1] . Iohanne Draperio . Thoma Oye . Iohanne de Ludelowe . Galfrido de Westune . Nicholao Clerico . et multis aliis.

[1] B ends here with *Dauid Dunyng' et multis aliis.*

271. *Grant by Thurevia to the almonry of St. Peter's, Gloucester, of her land (unident.) free of all service except the rent of 2d. owed to the canons of Llanthony. (c. 1175)*

G.C.L., 'Deeds and Seals', ix, no. 13, fol. 6 (128 mm × 72 mm [right]); no turn-up; no provision for sealing; endorsements: Thureuia (s. xiii^ex?); Registratur (modern?).

Notum sit omnibus quod ego Thureuia dedi et concessi elemosine sancti Petri Gloec' pro anima mea et pro animabus omnium amicorum meorum terram meam liberam et quietam ab omni seruitio excepto hoc quod reddet duos denarios canonicis Lantonie ad Hockedei. His testibus . Waltero de Kinemeresford et Waltero Abetot monachis . Hernaldo Cutelberni [.] Alberto Poli . Radulfo aurifabro . Ricardo drapario . Bricio . Ricardo de Charesi . Iohanne Eilwini . Ricardo famulo Iohannis de Mareis . Willelmo Thurebern . Haþewlfo palmario.

272. *Confirmation by William de Tracy to Abbot Gilbert and the convent of St. Peter's, Gloucester, of the donation of Yanworth made by his brother Ralph of Sudeley. (1139 × 48)*

A. P.R.O., C 150/2/[1] (198 mm × 73 mm); seal on tag: white wax, round, broken in three pieces (principal fragment *c.* 70 mm in diam.); obverse: an image of a large, long-knecked, four-legged animal facing right; legend: . . . SIG. . .LVM W. . .RAC. . .; reverse: counter-seal; round (25 mm in diam.); image indistinguishable, possibly a bird facing left; legend: +SECRETVM SALOMONI; endorsements: De Ianwrde. (s. xii[2]); c(apsula) .vii.[a] de laicis tenuris. (s. xii[2] × s. xiii^in); Registratur (s. xiv^ex × s. xv^in); **B.** ibid. C 150/1, fol. 195; *Cart. Glouc.* ii, no. 727.

.G. uenerabili Gloec' abbati totique conuentui Will(el)m(us) de Traceio salutem . et seruitium. Notum habeatur uobis et omnibus sancte ecclesie filiis . quod benigno animo concedo donationem illam quam Radulfus de Sullea frater meus fecit uobis de Ianwrda manerio nostro. Volo siquidem et firme concedo ut pro animabus nostris et pro animabus patrum et antecessorum nostrorum habeatis idem manerium in elemosinam . sit que ęcclesie de Gloec' inperpetuum datum et super altare fixe attitulatum. Huius autem donationis ita a me et a Radulfo fratre meo concesse testes sunt[1] . Henricus de Traceio . Iordanus de Cambernun . Willelmus de Monte acuto . Hugo de Ralea . Willelmus de Munceaus[2] . Radulfus de Munpinceun . Ricardus capellanus . Thomas famulus Osberni monaci . Robertus[3] de Culna . Robertus de Camrepuls.

The charter's tag is a strip cut from another twelfth-century charter. Its partial text, on the tag's inside surface, reads: . . . *uenerabili abbati totique conuentui Will. . .tu' habeatur uobis . . . omnibus sancte ęcclesie filiis. quod donationem illam quam R. . .* The words *da nobis* written in a different twelfth-century hand also appear on the outside of the tag on the left-hand end below the seal. So close are the first group of the above words to the first line of William de Tracy's charter that the fragment may well have been from a rejected earlier draft.

[1] **B** as printed in *Cart. Glouc.* ends here with *etc.*
[2] Corrected in MS. from *munccaus* in an apparently contemporary hand.
[3] A space of 26 mm was left between the *punctus* and the *R* of *Rob(er)t(us)* in MS. An *R* has been erased in this space.

273. *Grant by Robert farrier, son of William farrier of Wall to Abbot John de Felda and the convent of St. Peter's, Gloucester, of ½ virgate at Aldsworth for a payment of 40s. and an annual rent of a pair of gloves or ½d. (1243 × 63)*

A. H.C.L., no. 1676 (165 mm × 97 mm), **Scribe 19**; fragment of tag for seal; seal missing; endorsements: carta (s. xiii[2]) Rob(er)ti Le marescall' de Walle (s. xiii[med]); Caps(ula) .i. de laicis tenuris. (s. xiii[...med]; poss. same hand as *Rob(er)ti . . .*); .Aldesworth'. (s. xiv[in]?); Registratur (s. xiv[ex] × s. xv[in]); Registratur (s. xiv[ex] × s. xv[in]); de dimidia virgata terre cum messuagiis; Aldisworþe (s. xv); **B**. P.R.O., C 150/1, fols. 22–22v; *Cart. Glouc.* i, no. 26; cal. in Baddeley ii, no. 46, pp. 21–22.

Sciant presentes et futuri quod ego Rob(er)tus le mareschal filius Will(elm)i marescalli de Walle . dedi et concessi et hac presenti carta mea confirmaui domino Iohanni de la Felde abbati sancti Petri Glouc' et eiusdem loci conuentui pro quadraginta solidis quos mihi premanibus pacauerunt . totam illam dimidiam virgati terre cum mesuagiis . redditibus . et omnibus aliis pertinentiis suis . Quam antecessores mei et ego de eisdem abbate et conuentu in manerio suo de Aldeswrth' tenuimus . Tenendam et habendam sibi et successoribus suis libere . quiete et integre in perpetuum . Reddendo inde annuatim mihi et heredibus meis unum par cyrotecarum uel unum obolum ad Pascha pro omni seruitio et demanda. Ego uero predictus Rob(er)tus et heredes mei totam predictam terram cum omnibus pertinentiis suis . predictis abbati et conuentui contra omnes homines et feminas in perpetuum warantizabimus . defendemus et adquietabimus. In cuius rei testimonium[1] presenti scripto sigillum meum apposui. Hiis testibus . Henrico de Auenebur' .

Roberto de Ledene . Ricardo Barbe . Willelmo de Colethrop' . Roberto de la Sale . et multis aliis.

Wall is represented by Wall Farm in Aldsworth (*PNG*, i. 23).

¹ **B** ends here with *etc.*

274. *Grant by Walter Loker with the assent of his wife Alice to St. Peter's, Gloucester, of land on Castle Street (Gloucester) in free alms; the abbey's refectioner was to pay the earl of Gloucester 6d. landgabel due from the land. (s. xiii^{in})*

A. G.C.L., 'Deeds and Seals', x, no. 22, fol. 17 (122 mm × 103 mm); two tags through slits on foot: on left, residue of white wax on tag; on right, fragment of tag; endorsements: De terris in vico castelli (s. xiii^{ex}?); Castelstret[;] Registratur (s. xiv^{ex} × s. xv^{in}); **B**. ibid. 'Reg. B', no. 1012 (1011), p. 437.

Sciant presentes et futuri quod ego Walt(erus) locarius assensu et uoluntate Alicie uxoris mee pro salute animarum nostrarum et omnium antecessorum nostrorum dedi et concessi et presenti carta confirmaui deo et ecclesie sancti Petri Glouc' in puram et perpetuam elemosinam terram meam in vico castelli illam scilicet quam Willelmus de Saldford' de me tenuit secundum dispositionem refectorarii predicte ecclesie qui de tempore fuerit in usus refectorii necessarios´. specialiter conuertendam. Predictus autem refectorarius dictam terram de longabulo sex denariorum uersus comitem Glouc' annuatim adquietabit. In huius rei testimonium presens scriptum sigillo meo et sigillo dicte Alicie uxoris mee munitum monachis ecclesie predicte ad perpetuam securitatem commisi. Hiis testibus . Ricardo Burg' . Dauid Dunning¹ . Mauricio Durand' . Waltero scriptore . Willelmo de Saldford' . Drogone pincerna . Mauricio stabulario . Willelmo Pigace . Nicholao de infirmario . et multis aliis.

¹ **B** ends here with *et aliis.*

275. *Grant by Ralph of Willington in free alms to St. Peter's, Gloucester, of 2 hides at Wallhope (in Tidenham), given to him by King Henry III, for 2s. annual rent, for which Ralph and his heirs were to acquit the land of the rent of an unmewed sparrow-hawk and all other service due to the king and were to warrant the land to the abbey, and if they failed in the warranty were to make a reasonable exchange within a year of the abbey's losing the land or to pay compensation to the full value of the land. (1224 × 28)*

A. H.C.L., no. 1166 (169 mm × 141 mm), **Scribe 36**; seal on tag; green wax, triangular shield-shaped (at top, *c*. 34 mm; length, *c*. 40 mm); a heater-shaped shield; legend: +SIGILL': RADVLFI: DE WILINTVN; no counterseal; endorsements: de Welhope (s. xiii^{med}); Registratur (c. s. xiv^{ex}?); **B**. P.R.O., C 150/1, fol. 182; *Cart. Glouc.* ii., no. 667; cal. in Baddeley ii, no. 64, p. 26.

Sciant presentes et futuri quod ego Rad(ulfu)s de Wilinton' dedi concessi et hac presenti carta mea confirmaui deo et ecclesie sancti Petri Gloucestr' . et monachis ibidem deo seruientibus duas hidas terre cum omnibus pertinentiis . quas habui ex dono Henrici regis filii regis Iohannis in Welhop' . Habendas et tenendas de me et heredibus meis predicte ecclesie . in liberam . puram et perpetuam elemosinam imperpetuum . vt in releuiis homagiis et seruitiis . cum omnibus libertatibus et exitibus que de terra predicti peruenire poterunt . libere . quiete . et in pace . Reddendo inde annuatim mihi et heredibus meis . pro omni seruitio . consuetudine et demanda´. duos solidos esterlingorum ad festum beati . Michaelis . pro quibus duobus solidis . Ego Rad(ulfu)s et heredes mei predictam terram cum pertinentiis´. uersus dominum regem de vno esperuario soro vna cum omnibus aliis regalibus seruitiis acquietabimus . Et predicte ecclesie´. contra omnes gentes. warentizabimus. Et si forte contingat quod ego Rad(ulfu)s uel heredes mei predictam terram prenominate ecclesie warentizare non poterimus´. infra primum annum quo ipsa ecclesia de prefata terra fuerit dissesita´. presenti scripto tenemur facere rationabile escambium predicte ecclesie´. ad valentiam dicte terre in omnibus in tuto loco et competenti in comitatu Gloucestr'. Et si non feceremus escambium predicte ecclesie ipso anno sicut predictum est´. de perditione ipsius anni ad valentiam totius predicte terre prenotate ecclesie´. rationabiliter tenemur facere restaurationem. Et quia volo quod hec mea donatio . concessio et presentis carte mee confirmatio et warentizatio[1] perpetuam optineat firmitatem´. presens scriptum sigilli mei inpressione duxi roborandum. Hiis testibus . Radulfo de Channdos . Almarico de parco . Petro de Eggeworth' . Radulfo de Redleg' . Roberto le sauuag' . Iohanne Pay' . Milone de Sandhurst' . et multis aliis.

The abbey's Calendar of Donations dates this grant during the abbacy of Thomas of Bredon ('Historia', 120). For Henry III's grant of the 2 hides to Ralph of Willington, see *Cart. Glouc.* ii, no. 668. Abbot John de Felda in turn granted the 2 hides to Henry of Reigate (ibid. no. 724).

[1]   **B** as printed in *Cart. Glouc.* ends here with *etc.*

276. *Grant by Olympias of Willington, for the salvation of her soul and those of her husband Ralph, her ancestors, and successors, to the Lady Chapel at St. Peter's, Gloucester, of 2s. annual rent to find a lamp for the altar of St. Petronilla in that chapel. (s. xiii^{med})*

A. G.C.L., 'Deeds and Seals', i, no. 40, fol. 22 (152 mm × 110 mm), **Scribe 36** (below, Plate XXX); fragment of tag; seal missing; endorsements: Carta Olimpiad(e) vxoris Radulfi de Wilintag'. (s. xiii¹); Tertia carta de ii. solidis (s. xiii¹); Registratur (s. xiv^{ex} × s. xv^{in}); **B**. ibid. 'Reg. B', no. 1110, p. 485.

Sciant omnes tam presentes quam futuri quod ego Olimpias de Wilinton' pro deo et salute anime mee et Radulfi de Wilinton' viri mei [et] antecessorum et successorum nostrorum . dedi concessi et hac presenti carta mea confirmavi . deo et capelle beate Marie iuxta magnam ecclesiam sancti Petri Gloucestr' duos solidos annui redditus soluendos ad festum beati Michaelis in manus monachi qui pro tempore fuit custos predicte capelle . videlicet ad inueniendam vnam lampadem ad missam beate Marie cotidie coram altari sancte Petronille in eadem capella . et ad missam duorum capellanorum coram dicto altari ministrantium . Et insuper per omnes dies integras et vigilias omnium festorum beate Marie per annum . scilicet Natalis domini . Purificationis[1] . Annuntiationis . Assumptionis . Nativitatis et Conceptionis et per diem integrum et vigil(iam) sancte Petronille . Habendos et tenendos predicto capellano liberam . puram et perpetuam elemosinam . quiete et in pace. Ego uero Olimp(ias) et heredes mei uel assignati mei predictos duos solidos predicte capellano ad predictam officium perficiendum . Contra omnes gentes warentizabimus in perpetuum. Et cum in fata decessero᷈. heredes mei uel assignati mei qui quatuor acras terre tenebunt quas iure hereditario habui de Milone de Sandhurst de feodo Walteri de Coluirden'᷈. dictos duos solidos annuatim ad predictum terminum prefate capelle soluere tenentur. Vt hac autem mea donatio et concessio . robur perpetue firmitatis optineat᷈. presenti scripto sigillum meum feci apponi. Hiis testibus . Almarico de parco . Radulfo de Redleg' . Roberto Le sauuag' . Milone de Sandhurst . Almarico de Bar' . Iohanne de Bar' . Alano de Waldis qui presentes litteras scripsit . et aliis.

See also *Cart. Glouc.* iii, no. 1029.

[1] *Purifificationis* in MS., the word running across a break in the line, *Purifi / ficationis.*

277. *Grant by John Ailive with the assent of his wife Matilda to Henry de Curtilagio of land by Alvingate (Gloucester) in the fee of the almoner of St. Peter's, Gloucester, for 4d. annual rent, 7s. 8d. in advance, and a piece of white wool worth 12d. for his wife. (c. 1230 × 50)*

A. G.C.L., 'Deeds and Seals', ix, no. 28, fol. 13 (22.5 mm × 122 mm); seal on tag: dark green wax, chipped, repaired; obverse: pointed oval (length, 31 mm; width, unavail.); a fleur-de lis in the form of a cross; legend: +S. . .ANIS: AILIVE; no counterseal; endorsements: :De terra quam dedit Iohannes de ort . . .[1] (s. xiii[1]); vi (s. xiii); Aluenegat' (s. xiv?); Registratur (s. xiv[ex] × s. xv[in]); Y (uncertain date); B. ibid. 'Reg. B', no. 443, pp. 196–7.

Sciant presentes et futuri quod ego Ioh(ann)es Ayliue de Glouc' . de assensu et mera uoluntate Matillidis vxoris mee dedi . concessi . et hac presenti carta mea confirmaui Iohanni filio Henrici de Curtilagio quandam terram meam iacentem inter terrram meam . et terram dicti Henrici patris dicti Iohannis quam dictus Henricus tenet in feodo de elemosinario sancti Petri Glouc' uersus Aluenegate habendam et tenendam de me et heredibus meis uel assignatis sibi et heredibus suis uel assignatis libere . quiete . integre . bene . et in pace cum edificiis . et aliis pertinentiis suis in feodo et hereditate i(n)perpetuum . Reddendo inde annuatim mihi et heredibus meis uel assignatis . ipse et heredes sui siue assignati sui quatuor denarios argenti ad quatuor anni terminos . scilicet ad Natiuitatem beati Iohannis Baptiste unum denarium . ad festum beati Michaelis vnum denarium . ad Natale domini vnum denarium . et ad Annuntiationem beate Marie unum denarium . pro omnibus seruitiis et secularibus demandis. Pro hac autem donatione et concessione mea᷈. dedit michi predictus

Iohannes septem solidos et octo denarios sterlingorum ad urgens negotium meum premanibus . et Matillidi vxori mee vnam peciam de alba lana pretii duodecim denariorum. Et ego Ioh(anne)s Ayliue et heredes mei predictam terram cum omnibus pertinentiis suis prefato Iohanni et heredibus suis siue assignatis suis contra omnes homines et feminas imperpetuum warantizabimus. Terra uero mensurata per visum legalium uirorum[1] continet de latitudine in anteriori parte duas uirgas domini regis vlnarias cum pollice interposito et vnum quarterium . Retro uero eandem mensuram . In profunditate continet tresdecem uirgas ulnarias cum pollice interposito et sex pollices. Vt hec autem mea donatio . concessio . et presentis carte mee confirmatio perpetue firmitatis robur optineat[1] presens scriptum sigilli mei impressione roboraui. Hiis testibus . Iohanne filio Symonis . Hugone Bagge[2] . Thoma filtore . Willelmo Acelyne . Hugone Bulger . Alano de Theokesbur' . Gilberto de Hanleg' . Waltero Bay . Radulfo clerico et aliis.

[1] The terminal letter is blurred and illegible.   2 **B** ends here with *et aliis*.

---

278. *Grant by Matilda Ailive in her widowhood and liege power to Henry Ailive of part of her land by Alvingate, Gloucester, in hereditary tenure for ½d. annual rent and 5s. in advance. (1263–4)*

A. G.C.L., 'Deeds and Seals', ix, no. 33, fol. 17 (254 mm × 124 mm), **Scribe 46**; seal on tag; white wax stained green, chipped, cracked, repaired; obverse: round (26 mm in diam.); an eight-pointed flower or rosette; legend: +S'MATILL'E: AILI. . .; no counterseal; endorsements: Matilda Eyliue (s. xiii[2]); Aluenegat' (*c.* s. xiii[ex]); I (s. xiii); Registratur (s. xiv × s. xv[in]); vii (s. xv); x (uncertain date); **B**. ibid. 'Reg. B', no. 444, p. 197.

Sciant presentes et futuri quod ego Matildis Elyue in mea pura viduitate ac mea ligea potestate dedi . concessi et hac presenti carta mea confirmaui Henrico Eyliue Glouc' quamdam partem terre mee cum domibus edificiis et cum omnibus aliis pertinentiis suis iacentem versus Haluengathe Glouc' inter terram meam et terram quondam Henrici de la Leytone . et extendit se a regia strata super terram meam. Terra vero prefata per visum legalium virorum mensurata continet in parte anteriori de latitudine vnam virgam domini regis vlnariam et dimidiam virgam . In medio uero tantum . Retro continet tres virgas domini regis vlnarias cum pollicibus interpositis . et vnum quarterium et vnum pollicem . In longitudine continet quinque decem[1] virgas domini regis vlnarias cum pollicibus interpositis excepto dimidio quarterio . Habendam et tenendam de me et heredibus meis sibi et heredibus suis ac quibuscumque assignatis suis libere . solute . integre . quiete . bene . pacifice iure hereditario inperpetuum . Reddendo inde annuatim michi et heredibus meis ipse et heredes sui seu sui assignati vnum obolum argenti ad festum sancti Michaelis pro omnimodis seruitiis . sectis . querelis . consuetudinibus et demandis secularibus. Pro hac autem donatione concessione et carte mee confirmatione dedit michi predictus Henricus quinque solidos sterlingorum premanibus ad meum magnum negotium. Ego uero Matildis et heredes mei prefato Henrico et heredibus suis ac suis assignatis totam memoratam terram cum omnibus pertinentiis suis contra omnes mortales inperpetuum warentizabimus adquietabimus et defendemus. In cuius rei testimonium hanc presentem cartam sigilli mei munimine confirmaui. Hiis testibus . Willelmo de Chilteham . Philippo le Spicer . tunc balliuis Glouc'[2] . Luca Cornubiense . Iohanne Cornubiense . Willelmo Cleymond . Willelmo Asseline . Willelmo Sage . Willelmo Bay . Alano de Theokebur' . Gilberto de Henleya . Hugone Le bulcher . Iohanne de la Leyton' . Iohanne clerico . et aliis.

The attestations of William of Cheltenham and Philip the spicer as baillifs establish the charter's date of issue (*VCH Glos.* iv. 372).

¹ *decim* in MS.
² **B** ends here with *et aliis*.

279. *Confirmation by Mabel daughter of John Ailive to Henry Ailive of Gloucester of land by Alvingate Gloucester for 2d. annual rent and 10s. in advance. (1263–64)*

A. G.C.L., 'Deeds and Seals', vii, no. 39, fol. 23 (208 mm × 139 mm; damaged), **Scribe 46**; seal on tag, green wax, fragment, repaired; round or oval; obverse: eight-pointed rosette or star; legend: . . . MA.. . .; original state of reverse, unknown due to repair; endorsements: I (s. xiii[med]); Aluenegat' (*c.* s. xiii[ex])[;] Registratur (s. xiv[ex] × s. xv[in]); iii (uncertain date); **B**. ibid. 'Reg. B', no. 440, p. 195.

Sciant presentes et futuri quod ego Mabelia filia Iohannis Eyliue dedi concessi et hac presenti carta mea confirmaui Henrico Eyliue Glouc' quandam partem terre mee cum domibus edificiis et cum omnibus aliis pertinentiis suis . iacentem versus Halvengath' Glouc' inter terram quam Matildis mater mea tenet ratione franci banci sui . et terram quam Henricus de La Leytone quondam emit de Iohanne Eyliue patre meo. Terra vero prefata per visum legalium virorum mensurata᷎. continet in parte anteriori de latitudine duas virgas domini regis vlnarias cum pollicibus interpositis . In medio continet vnam virgam domini regis vlnariam . et tria quarteria et tres pollices . Retro enim continet tres virgas domini regis vlnarias cum pollicibus interpositis et vnam quarterium et duos pollices . In longitudine vero continet quindecim virgas domini regis vlnarias cum pollicibus interpositis excepto dimidio quarterio . Habendam et tenendam de me et heredibus meis sibi et heredibus suis ac quibuscumque assignatis suis libere . [solut]e . [i]ntegre [.] quiete . bene . pac[ifice . iure] hereditario im[perpetuum . Reddendo inde ann]uatim michi et heredibus [meis ipse et heredes sui seu sui] assignati duos denarios argenti ad [du]os anni terminos . Videlicet [ad festum sancti Mich]aelis vnum denarium . et ad Ho[ckedai vnum denarium] pro omnimodis seruitiis . sectis . querelis . consuetudinibus et demandis secularibus ad predictam terram contingentibus. Pro hac autem mea donatio[ne c]oncessione et carte mee confirmatione dedit michi predictus Henricus decem solidos sterlingorum premanibus ad meum magnum negotium. Ego vero Mabelia et heredes mei predicto Henrico et heredibus suis ac assignatis suis totam memoratam terram cum omnibus pertinentiis suis contra omnes mortales inperpetuum warentizabimus et pro predicto redditu adquietabimus et defendemus. In huius rei testimonium hanc presentem cartam sigilli mei munimine confirmaui. Hiis testibus . Willelmo de Chelteham . Philippo Le spicer tunc balliuis Glouc' . Luca Cornubiense . Iohanne Cornubiense . Willelmo Cleymond . Willelmo Asseline .

Laurencio Trewemon . Willelmo sage . Willelmo Bay . Alano de Thekebur' . Gilberto de Henleya . Iohanne clerico . et aliis.

Damaged and illegible portions of the text have been added from **B**. Date as no. 278.

280. *Grant by Richard of Alderton to Thomas son of Grisolita of 9 acres in* Oldland *and 9 acres in* Bencroft *with a messuage held by Robert Bat and with meadow belonging to ½ virgate of land in* Muclemede *(all in Alderton). (c. 1170 × 90)*

A. H.C.L., no. 575 (202 mm × 82 mm); seal on tag: red wax; obverse: round (41 mm in diam.); a lion facing right; legend: + SIGILLVM: RICARDI: DEWESTTONE[1]; no counterseal; endorsements: De Aldrinton' [;] .C(apsula) .iiii.^{a} de laicis tenuris. (s. xiii^{in}?); Registratur (s. xiv^{ex} × s. xv^{in}); Carta Ric(ardi) de Aldrinton' de ix acris terre in Oldlond et ix acris in Bencroft cum messuagio et dimidia virgata prati;.A. temporalium part(e) 2^a (c. 1400); **B**. P.R.O., C150/1, fol. 24v; *Cart. Glouc.* i, no. 38.

Sciant qui sunt et qui futuri sunt quod ego Ricard(us) de Aldrintuna dedi et concessi Thome filio Grisolite pro homagio et seruitio suo nouem acras in Oldelonde . et nouem acras in alio campo in Bencrofte cum mesuagio quod Robertus Bat tenuit . et cum prato ad dimidiam terre uirgatam pertinente in Muclemede tenendas de me et heredibus meis sibi et heredibus quos constituere uoluerit inperpetuum libere et quiete et honorifice in pratis et pascuis et omnibus aliis libertatibus reddendo singulis annis michi et heredibus meis ille uel heredes sui tres solidos . ad festum sancti Kenelmi . scilicet die sancti Eadwardi pro omni seruitio et consuetudine ad me uel ad meos pertinente. Et pro hac concessione et donatione dedit michi predictus Thomas .xii. denarios. Et ut hec donatio mea rata et inconcussa permaneat sigilli mei[2] impressione roboraui. His testibus . Willelmo Capellano de Kenemertune . Philippo de Tudentuna . Roberto de Diclesdune et Ricardo filio suo . Bertram de Aldri'tune . Thurefrido filio eius . Philippo clerico . Hugone drapar(io) . Philippo et Iohanne et Hugone filiis Grisolite . Ricardo et Iohanne de Gretaine . et multis aliis.

The text of a charter of the donor's son Robert confirming this grant by quoting part of it verbatim appears in *Cart. Glouc.* ii, no. 748. For Alderton and the field-names mentioned, see *PNG*, iii. 48–50. Note the difference between the name of the donor in the text and that on the seal. The reference to St. Edward's day in relation to the feast of St. Kenelm is unexplained.

[1] Reading of the second *T* uncertain.   [2] **B** as printed in *Cart. Glouc.* ends here with *etc.*

281. *Grant by Simon son of Alfred of land between the bridges of Gloucester to Peter son of Thomas clerk and his sister Joan, with the obligation of paying the king's landgabel of 4d. (c. 1230)*

A. G.C.L., 'Deeds and Seals', ix, no. 37, fol. 19 (184 mm × 82 mm); seal on tag; brown wax stained dark green; obverse: round (28 mm in diam.); a large fleur-de-lis; legend: +SIGILL'. SIMONIS. FIL. ALVREDI; no counterseal; endorsements: carta Symon(is) (s. xiii); mag(istro) [o]peris[1] (s. xiii[2]); iiii Warda (s. xiv); Registratur (s. xiv^{ex} × s. xv^{in}); **B**. ibid. 'Reg. B', no. 813, pp. 351–2.

Sciant presentes et futuri quod ego Symon filius Aluredi dedi et concessi et presenti carta mea confirmaui Petro filio Thome clerici et Iohanne sorori sue quandam terram meam inter pontes Glouc' . illam . scilicet . que iacet inter terram Reginaldi de Heldesfelde et terram eam quam dedi Hawyse vxori mee ad dotem suam . Tenendam et habendam in feudo et hereditate sibi et heredibus suis uel assignatis suis . et eorum heredibus ab omnibus seruitiis . saluo tantum modo londgabulo regis . videlicet quatuor den(ariis) . ad Hok(edai) quolibet anno sicut ego reddere debui et consueui pro omnibus seruitiis et consuetudinibus. Predicta vero terra mensurata per visum legalium virorum continet in parte anteriori in latitudine quatuor virgas domini regis vlnarias et tria quarteria cum pollice interposito . In parte autem posteriori eandem habet mensuram et extendit in longitudine a vico usque ad Sabrinam. In cuius rei testimonium presentem cartam sigillatam sigillo meo predictis Petro et Iohanne tradidi. Hiis testibus Ricardo burgens' . Dauid Dunnig[2] . Willelmo de Sanford' . Reginaldo de Heldesfeld . Ada Tinctore . Radulfo Tinctore et multis aliis.

For mention of Simon son of Alfred and his property, see *Cart. Glouc.* i. 186; Stevenson, nos. 162 & n., 179–80, 222.

[1] Reading uncertain, even aided by ultra-violet light.   [2] **B** ends here with *et aliis*.

282. *Fragment of a grant by Walter Barbe son of Walter Barbe to John Barbe. (c. s. xiii^{med})*

G.C.L., 'Deeds and Seals', viii, no. 20 (e), fol. 11; damaged fragment; no details available.

. . . [Walterus filius] Walt(er)i Barbe concessi dedi et . . . [Johanni] Barbe totam terram ill. . . [que ex]tendit se in longitudine ab ori. . . viam que ducit de Tib'ton . . . Habendam et tenendam de me et [heredibus meis] . . . quiete ab omni seruitio secular. . .is predictus Iohannes Barbe et heredes sui . . . exactione consuetudine et demanda . . . [conc]essione donatione et carte me. . . de . . . Et ego predictus Walt(er)us . . . suis uel suis assignatis totam . . . [imper]petuum warantizabimus defend[emus] . . . [In cu]ius rei testimonium presentem cartam . . . Ledene . Galfrido Elwi . Willelmo de . . .elleris . Iohanne Dobin . Ricardo de Tal. . .

283. *Sale by William of Becland farrier of Gloucester to Nicholas of Hereford of the land which he held of the prior of Llanthony Secunda on Southgate Street (Gloucester) for 15s. (c. 1240 × c. 1265)*

A. G.C.L., 'Deeds and Seals', ii, no. 4, fol. 2 (201 mm × 129 mm), **Scribe 42**; seal on tag; white wax stained green, rubbed, broken, repaired; obverse: possibly oval (length, 32 mm; width unavail. due to repair); a cross-shaped fleur-de-lis, arms of equal length separated by smaller leaves in saltire; no counterseal; endorsements: quietaclamatio Will(elm)i de Boclond quam fecit Nicholao de Herford' de terra versus venellam fabrorum (s. xiii^{med}); Smyzthstr'te; Registratur (s. xiv^{ex} × s. xv^{in}); **B**. ibid. 'Reg. B', no. 1054 (1053), pp. 458–9.

Notum sit vniuersis tam presentibus quam futuris quod ego Will(elm)us de Beclande marescallus de Glouc' vendidi et inperpetuum pro me et pro heredibus meis quiet(um)clamaui Nicholao de Hereford' et heredibus suis uel quibuscunque asignatis suis totam illam terram cum edificiis et cum omnibus aliis pertinentiis suis quam tenui de priore et conuentu Lanthonie iuxta Glouc' in platea australi . illam scilicet que iacet inter terram eiusdem Nicholai quam tenet de priore et conuentu Lanthonie et venellam fabrorum tenendam et habendam totam illam predictam terram cum omnibus pertinentiis suis sibi et heredibus uel quibuscunque asignatis suis libere et quiete integre et pacifice absque clamio . vexatione . uel demanda per me uel per heredes meos inperpetuum. Et pro hac venditione et quietaclamantia mea dictus Nicholaus dedit michi quindecim solidos argenti. Ego autem dictus Will(elm)us de Beclande ad maiorem securitatem huius venditionis et quietaclamantie cartam quam habui de prior et conuentu Lanthonie de illo tenemento coram probis hominibus dicto Nicholao quiete liberaui. In huius rei testimonio huic presenti scripto sigillum meum apposui. Hiis testibus . Willelmo de Sumer' . Stephano Cornubiense tunc bailliuis in Glouc' . Ricardo de cellario. Laurencio le mercer[1] . Willelmo le loker . Ricardo le loker . Waltero Haym . Ricardo le symphenur . Laurencio filio Ricardi . et aliis.

William de Sumery and Stephen of Cornwall were bailiffs of Gloucester between *c.* 1240 × *c.* 1265 (*VCH Glos.* iv. 372).

[1]   **B** ends here with *et aliis*.

284. *Grant by Benedict chaplain to Henry goldsmith, burgess of Gloucester, of land belonging to the fee of the abbot and convent of St. Peter's, Gloucester, located by the wall of the abbey's cemetery (Gloucester). (c. 1228 × c. 1240)*

G.R.O., GBR/J1/355 (162 mm × 106 mm); seal on tag, chipped and rubbed; oval (23 mm × 20 mm); [image illegible]; legend: [illegible]; no counterseal; endorsement: iuxta murum cimiterii abbatis. (s. xv^{ex}?); cal. in Stevenson, no. 355.

Sciant presentes et futuri quod ego B(e)n(e)dict(us) capellanus tradidi et concessi Henrico aurifabro burgensi Glouc' quandam terram meam que me contigit de morte Cristiane sororis mee que fuit uxor Ricardi filii Katerine . illam scilicet que iacet uersus murum cimiterii abbatie de Glouc' inter terram Rogeri Le Wise et terram Roberti de Theokeb' que est de feudo abbatis et conuentus Glouc' . et continet in fronte nouem uirgas vlnarias et dimidiam quarteriam cum pollice interposito . In posteriore parte continet septem uirgas ulnarias et tria quarteria cum pollice interposito . In longitudine continet . viginti et vnam uirgam ulnariam et tria quarteria cum pollice interposito . Tenendam et habendam de me et heredibus meis sibi et heredibus suis uel cui eam dare uel assignare uoluerit libere et quiete in perpetuum . pro omnibus seruitiis et demandis quoad me uel ad heredes meos pertineat. Pro hac autem concessione et dimissione predictus Henricus aurifaber dedit michi de introitu predicte terre sex marcas esterlingorum. Ego etiam predictus B(e)n(e)dict(us) capellanus et heredes mei predicto Henrico aurifabro et heredibus suis uel assignatis suis predictam terram contra omnes homines et feminas in perpetuum warantizabimus. Et ut hec mea concessio et dimissio perpetuam optineat

stabilitatem. presenti scripto et sigilli mei impressione confirmaui. Testibus hiis .
Ricardo Burg' maiore Glouc' . Henrico Burg' fratre suo . Waltero Hoihc tunc
preposito . Iohanne draperio [.] magistro Rogero de Sixtune . Henrico Bretun .
Willelmo de Fro'tune . Radulfo Crafet . et pluribus aliis.

The charter was issued when Richard Burgess was mayor and Walter Hoic a bailiff of
Gloucester (*VCH Glos.* iv. 371–2).

285. *Grant by Roger of Berkeley with the assent of his wife Margery to John son of Roger son of Simon of land at Hyde (by Gloucester) for 35s. 7d. entry. (c. s. xiii^{med})*

A. H.C.L., no. 2196 (*c*. 237 mm × *c*. 139 mm); slits for three seals on turn-up; tags and seals
missing; endorsements: Carta Rog(er)i de Berkeley et Margerie vxoris [;] Registratur (s.
xiv^{med}); **B**. G.C.L., 'Reg. B', no. 758, fols. 327–8.

Sciant presentes et futuri quod ego Rog(erus) . de Berkeleye assensu et bona
voluntate Margerie vxoris . mee dedi et concessi et hac presenti carta nostra
confirmaui . Iohanni filio Rogeri filii Symonis totam terram nostram cum domibus
edificiis et cum curtilagiis et cum omnibus pertinentiis suis que eidem Margerie iure
hereditario descendebant per Rogerum de La strode fratrem suum . Videlicet totam
illam terram que iacet inter terram abbatis et conuentus sancti Petri Glou' . et terram
predicti Iohannis quam emit de Nicholao Morin . et totam terram arabilem que iacet
inter stangnum molendini dicti Morin . et terram Ricardi Le blunt[1] . ex parte australi .
et totam terram que iacet inter stangnum molendini et regalem uiam in Hyda .
Habendam et tenendam de me et heredibus meis sibi et heredibus suis uel suis
assignatis et eorum heredibus . libere . et quiete . integre . in perpetuum cum haycis .
fossatis silicibus . vinariis . stangnis molendinis et cum omnibus aliis pertinentiis suis
faciendo inde capitalibus dominis seruitium debitum et consuetum pro omnibus
seruitiis et omnimodis secularibus demandis . ad eandem terram spectantibus. Pro
hac autem donatione et concessione nostra dedit nobis predictus Iohannes . ad
magnum negotium nostrum triginta et quinque solidos sterlinguorum et septem .
denarios . de introitu. Et ego predictus Rog(erus) et Margeria . vxor mea et heredes
nostri . predicto Iohanni et heredibus suis uel assignatis suis et eorum heredibus
predictam terram cum omnibus pertinentiis suis ut predictum est contra omnes
gentes . in perpetuum warentizabimus defendemus et aquietabimus. Et ad maiorem
securitatem dicta Margeria . fidem suam affidauit . quod numquam contra presentis
carte tenorem venire presumet. In cuius rei testimonium . ego Rog(erus) de
Berkeleye . et Margeria vxor mea . hanc presentem cartam sigillorum nostrorum
inpressione confirmauimus. Hiis testibus . Iohanne filio Galfridi le mercer [.] Helya
Textore[2] . Nicholao Le Lorimer . Hugone Tinctore . Iohanne Geyderhom . Waltero
Le Bukeler . Iohanne Mercatore . Iohanne . Asse . Waltero fowel . et aliis [.]

---

[1] Reading of *blunt* from B.
[2] **B** ends here with *et aliis.*

286.   *Sale and quitclaim by Geoffrey Brewer to William of Samford of land (probably at Gloucester) for 9½ marks, saving the landgabel owed to the abbot of Gloucester. (1200 × c. 1228)*

G.R.O., GBR/J1/272 (187 mm × 144 mm), **Scribe 40** (below, Plate XXXIV); seal on tag; dark green wax; round (39 mm in diam.); a great long-necked bird facing to the left; legend: +SIGILLVM GALFRID LE BRAZVR (the S, D, and Z reversed); no counterseal; no endorsement; cal. in Stevenson, no. 272.

Sciant presentes et futuri quod ego Galfridus Le brazur vendidi et in perpetuum quietam clamaui quandam terrram meam Willelmo de Samfordia et heredibus suis de me et heredibus meis . Illam scilicet quam ego emi de Isabele filia Radulfi Chechel et de heredibus suis tempore viduitatis sue de libero maritagio suo que iacet inter terram quam ego Galfr(idus) vendidi Willelmo de Lilitona et terram quam Meifelinus tenuit . pro nouem marcis argenti et dimidiam quas idem Willelmus de Samford michi et vxori mee Edit et heredibus meis pro magna inopia nostra subleuanda premanibus pacauit . saluo abbati Glouc' longabulo sicut ego reddere consueui. Terra vero illa mensurata per visum legalium virorum continet in parte anteriori nouem uirgas regis vlnarias preter dimidium quarterium pollicibus interpositis . In longitudine continet sexaginta sex virgas regis vlnarias et dimidiam pollicibus interpositis et in parte posteriori decem virgas regis vlnarias et unum quarterium pollicibus interpositis. Et ego predictus Galfr(idus) et heredes mei predicto Willelmo et heredibus suis predictam terram contra omnes homines et feminas warantizabimus. Et vt hec uenditio mea rata et inconcussa perseueret: ego et vxor mea Edit fide nostra affidauimus et presens scriptum sigillo meo sigillatum predicto Willelmo tradidi. Hiis testibus . Rogero capellano de sancto Nicholao . Ricardo burg' . Mauricio Durand tunc prepositis Glouc' . Ricardo rufo . Dauid Dunning . Henrico burg' . Nicholao Muet . Iohanne tinctore . Ada filio Rogeri . Ada Walense . Ada Croc . Stephano filio Aþelini . Philippo clerico qui hanc cartam scripsit . et multis aliis.

The charter is dated by the attestations of the bailiffs (*VCH Glos.* iv. 371). Philip clerk, who identified himself as the writer of this charter, was a prolific local *scriptor* (see G.R.O., GBR/249–50, 266, 269, 271, 273–4, 300–2, 331, 339; see also below, no. 291 n.); he is included in the present editor's forthcoming study of local Gloucester scribes. He evidently served the Gloucester hundred court.

287.   *Grant by Henry Bruton of Gloucester with the assent of his wife Felicia to Richard dyer, burgess of Gloucester, of 2 acres of his meadow at Minsterworth for a pair of white gloves or ½d. annual rent to Henry and 20d. annual rent to the abbot and convent of St. Peter's, and as entry 3 marks and 6s. to Henry and 4s. to Felicia. (c. 1258 × 62)*

H.C.L., no. 671 (173 mm × 140 mm), **Scribe 48** (below, Plate XLII); seal on tag; dark green wax, round (25 mm in diam); obverse: a lion rampant to the right; legend: +SIGILL. HENRI. . .RITVN; no counterseal; endorsement: Carta Henr(ici) Bruton' de prato de Cornham; Registratur (s. xiv[ex] × s. xv[in]).

Sciant presentes et futuri quod eo Henr(icus) Bruton' de Glouc' assensu et voluntate
Felicee vxoris mee et heredum meorum dedi concessi et hac presenti carta mea
confirmaui . Ricardo tinctori burgensi Glouc' duas acras prati mei in Minist'wrth' in
Hommehiþefurlong' que iacent inter pratum Radulfi Dawe et pratum quod fuit
aliquando Michaelis Cavel . Habendas et tenendas de me et heredibus meis sibi et
heredibus suis uel assignatis suis . libere et quiete integre pacifice et plenarie cum
omnibus pertinentiis suis in feodo et hereditate inperpetuum . Reddendo inde
annuatim michi et heredibus meis ipse et heredes sui uel assignati vnum par
cyrotecarum albarum uel vnum obolum ad Pascha . Et abbati et conuentui sancti
Petri viginti denarios argenti ad Natiuitatem beate Marie pro omnimodo seruitio
curiarum sectis consuetudinibus exactionibus et secularibus demandis . saluo regali
seruitio quantum pertinet ad tantum pratum de eodem tenemento. Pro hac donatione
et concessione mea dedit michi predictus Ricardus tres marcas et sex solidos
sterlingorum et Felicie vxori mee quatuor solidos de introitu. Et ego uero dictus
Henr(icus) et heredes mei prefato Ricardo et heredibus suis uel assignatis suis
predictas duas acras prati cum omnibus pertinentiis suis contra omnes homines et
feminas in perpetuum warantizabimus . et per predictum seruitium aquietabimus et
defendemus. Et quia volo quod hec mea donatio concessio et confirmatio perpetue
firmitatis robur optineat. presentem cartam sigilli mei inpressione roboraui. Et
Felicia vxor mea se obligauit fide media quod dictum Ricardum nec heredes suos de
dicto prato vexabit quamuis in dote sibi succederent. Hiis testibus Willelmo de
Boifeld' . Waltero de Ministrwrth' . Willelmo Koch' . Rogero homine Petri .
Henrico de Boifeld' . Hugone Le cent' . Willelmo Lovetot' . Roberto Le Wise .
Waltero tinctore . Ricardo clerico.

288. *Grant by Richard burgess to William son of Godric of the land between the
two bridges of Gloucester, which he bought from Ernesius son of Wulfwin, for
3s. 3d. annual rent. (c. 1175 × 92)*

A. G.C.L., 'Deeds and Seals', iv, no. 1, fol. 1 (156 mm × 57 mm); fragment of tag in turn-up;
seal missing; endorsements: Carta R(icardi) buries (s. xiii[1]); Carta Ric(ardi) Burgeys (c. 1230);
De terra quam Robertus tinctor tenet (s. xiii[ex]); quam dictus Ric(ardu)s emit de Ernesio filio
Wlw(in)i[1] (s. xiii[ex]); Inter duos pontes (s. xiii[ex]?); Inter pontes (s. xiv[ex]); Registratur (c. s.
xiv[ex]).[2] **B**. ibid. 'Reg. B', no. 1073 (1072), p. 466.

Notum sit presentibus et futuris quod ego Ric(ardus) burgensis concessi terram inter
duos pontes Gloec' quam emi de Ernis filio Wl[fwini][3] Willelmo filio Godrici
tenendam sibi et heredibus de me et heredibus meis . reddendo singulis annis iii
solidos et iii denarios . xix denarios et obolum ad festum sancti Michaelis et xix
denarios et obolum ad Pascham. De conuentione exequenda dedi ei cartam et
sigillum in hundredo Gloec'. Et edificia terre illius appreciata sunt per uisum
legalium hominum xx solidis . Ideo quod si casu aliquo domus deciderent aut
peiorantur et Willelmus hanc conuentionem exequi nollet aut non posset redderet
michi terram [et] domos quales eas recepit aut pretium. Huius conuentionis sunt
testes . Walterus Hut . Morin . H' filius Osmundi . Adam ruffus[4] . Ricardus draper [.]

Ernald filius Dunning . Elured filius[5] Horm . Willelmus Uuenad . Walterus child [.] Eluredus filius[6] Seuare frater eius . Ricardus filius Beatricis . Nicolaus filius Wlthert . Ricardus albus[7] [.] Ernald aurifaber . Nicolaus aurifaber . Robertus filius Faremon . Walterus Wise . Rogerus filius Mald [.] Robertus tailur . Walterus filius Petri.

Abbot Thomas Carbonel confirmed the above grant to William (above, no. 79). The witness William Uuenat (or Ovenad) became a canon at Llanthony Secunda before 1192 (*Cart. Glouc.* ii. 6; Stevenson, no. 83 n., p. 70 n.); he held land in the parish of St. Nicholas near the lane which goes to the house of the archdeacon. (Stevenson, no. 370).

[1] The terminal letter and abbreviation are uncertain because the rest of the line is not visible through the 'window' of the scrapbook page to which the charter is glued, but the name *Ernis filio Wulfwini* is established from its mention in no. 79. *Ernesio filio Wlw(in)i* has apparently been written over another endorsement which is illegible with ultra-violet light.
[2] Two other endorsements are illegible with ultra-violet light.
[3] See n. 1 above.
[4] **B** ends her with *et aliis.*
[5] *fulum* in MS.
[6] *fulu'* in MS.
[7] *albo* in MS.

---

289. *Grant by Mary daughter of Elias Calveswombe of Gloucester to Mabel widow of Walter son of Drogo of land on Longsmith Street (Gloucester) for 5d. annual rent payable to the prior of Llanthony Secunda and a premium of 3 marks to Mary. (c. 1228 × 1240)*

G.C.L., 'Deeds and Seals', x, no. 7, fol. 5 (162 mm × 106 mm); slit for tag on turn-up; tag and seal missing; no endorsements.

Sciant presentes et futuri quod ego Maria filia Elye Calueswombe de Glouc' concessi et confirmaui et pro me et hominibus meis quietum clamaui Mabille vidue Walteri filii Drogonis illam terram in vico fabrorum de Glouc' que iacet inter terram Alexandri Cantil . et terra que fuit Ade Berte quam terram habui de dono Nicholai CaluesWombe . fratris mei et quam terram predictus Walterus aliquando tenuit conditionaliter . vt michi necessaria inueniret. Vnde volo et concedo ut predicta Mabillia et heredes sui siue assignati sui habeant et teneant predictam terram cum edificiis et omnibus aliis pertinentiis suis libere . et quiete . integre . in feodo et hereditate sine aliquo clamio uel impedimento siue retinemento ad opus meum uel heredum meorum inposterum . Reddendo inde annuatim priori et conuentui de Lanton' quinque denarios ad Pentecosten pro omnibus seruitiis et secularibus demandis . sicut ego soluere debui. Et pro hac concessione et quieta clamatione mea predicta Mabillia dedit michi tres marcas argenti in gersumnia. In huius rei testimonium presens scriptum sigillo meo sigillatum eidem .M. vidue tradidi. Hiis testibus . domino Ricardo Burgens' . Waltero Payn . tunc preposito . Hugone de aula regis . Waltero Hoch . Dauid Dunning . Nicholao Cumioch . Henrico Birton' . Radulfo Yde . Willelmo B'reton' . et multis aliis.

Walter Payn was a bailiff of Gloucester c. 1228 × 1240 (*VCH Glos.* iv. 371–2). It is not certain that St. Peter's held this property before 1264.

290. *Sale by Mary daughter of Elias Calveswombe in her widowhood and liege power to Walter Mary, her son, of land on Longsmith Street (Gloucester) for 4½ marks to her and 5d. annual rent to the prior of Llanthony Secunda. (c. 1228 × 1240)*

G.C.L., 'Deeds and Seals', x, no. 8, fol. 5 (162 mm × 142 mm), **Scribe 43**; seal on tag; white wax stained green; obverse: oval (39 mm × 25 mm); a large elongated fleur-de-lis; legend: +S' MARIE: FIL': ELIE: CALVESWOMB'; no counterseal; endorsements: E.[1] . . .[2] in Brod . . .[3] s . . .[4] stret (s. xiv?); Brod smythstreete (s. xv × s. xvi?).

Sciant presentes et futuri quod ego Maria filia Elie Calueswonbe . tempore viduitatis mee et in ligea potestate mea . vendidi et inperpetuum pro me et pro heredibus meis quietam clamaui . Waltero Marie filio meo pro seruitio suo et pro quatuor marcis et dimidiam sterlingorum quas michi pre manibus pacauit . totam terram meam cum pertinentiis suis in vico fabrorum que iacet✓ inter terram Alexandri Sautel et terram que fuit Ade Berte . Et que mensurata est per uisum legalium hominum . et continet in anteriori parte in latitudine octo virgas domini regis vlnarias cum pollice interposito et dimidium quarterium . Retro uero continet octo uirgas domini regis vlnarias cum pollice interposito et dimidiam . In profunditate continet triginta quatuor virgas domini regis vlnarias cum pollice interposito vno quarterio minus . Tenendam et habendam sibi et heredibus suis . siue assignatis suis . libere . et quiete inperpetuum . sine aliquo retinemento ad opus meum uel heredum meorum . Reddendo inde annuatim . domino priori . Lonthon' quinque denarios sterlingorum ad Pentecosten pro omnibus seruitiis et demandis . sicud ego reddere solebam et debebam. In cuius rei testimonium hanc cartam sigillo meo sigillatam✓ dicto Waltero coram hundredo Glouc' . tradidi. Hiis testibus . Galfrido Cuttestuche . Waltero Hoyhc . tunc prepositis Glouc' . Rogero La Wise . Henrico Brutun . Iohanne de La stouwe . Radulfo Dauwe . Reginaldo de La Bertunn' . et aliis.

The names of the bailiffs indicate the date of this charter (*VCH Glos.* iv. *372)*. It is not certain that St. Peter's held this land before 1264. The endorsements suggest that the land was on Broadsmith Street.

[1] Reading uncertain.
[2] Illegible with ultra-violet light.
[3] Part of the word may be obscured by being covered by the window of the scrapbook page.
[4] Letter illegible with ultra-violet light.

291. *Sale in the form of a chirograph by Emma de celario to Pain Chaver of a messuage (Gloucester) for 7s. and grant to him of the land belonging to the messuage for 2s. annual rent. (s. xii^{2})*

A. G.C.L., 'Deeds and Seals', viii, no. 16, fol. 8 (177 mm × 107 mm); no turn-up; slit for tag on foot; tag and seal missing; endorsements: Aluenegate (s. xv)[;] Registratur (s. xiv^{ex} × s. xv^{in}; poss. in previous hand); **B**. ibid. 'Reg. B', no. 1017 (1016), p. 338.

C I R O G. . .[1] U M (*inverted*)

Sciant omnes tam presentes quam futuri quod ego Eme de celario vendidi Pain Cheuer pro septem solidis . mesagium meum quod mercaui de Alurico filio Orbi . pro .vii. solidis de meo proprio catallo. Preterea ego Ema[2] tradidi et concessi predicto

Pain totam terram illam que pertinet ad predictum mesagium super quam ipsum extat situm in feudum et hereditatem . tenendam de me et heredibus meis sibi et heredibus suis . libere et quiete . pro duobus solidis . reddendis annuatim . pro omni seruitio . ad duos scilicet anni terminos .xii. denarios ad Hokadai . reliquos .xii. ad festum sancti Mykaelis. Vt autem hanc pactionem fideliter obseruaremus⸴ hanc pactionem fideliter tenendam⸴ nec nos artem uel ingenium constituros quibus nullus meorum perderet⸴ ex hutraque parte affidauimus. Hec autem conuentio concessu nostrum et pretio pactato coram hundredo de Glouc'⸴ extitit iterata . et hoc presenti cyrographo presentata et confirmata. Hii sunt testes Ernaldus tunc prepositus . Galterus Hut . Willelmus burg'nsis[3] . Rogerus filius Matilldi . Henricus sacrista . Robertus filio Selewinne . Henricus mercator . Radulfus aurifaber . Radulfus albus . Ricardus ruffus . Haraldus lorimer . Willelmus Brutun . Ricardus filius Beatriz . Helias paumer . Robertus de la B'tune . Petrus clericus . Rogerus p'co . Galterus p'co et multi alii.

[1] Two majuscules, without abbreviation signs, occupy this space, but cannot be read because of the cutting of the chirograph.

[2] *Eme* in MS.

[3] B ends here with *et multi alii.*

292. *Sale by Pain Chaver of Gloucester to William chaplain of St. Aldate's of his land outside Northgate, Gloucester, for 3 marks. (1200 × c. 1228)*

A. G.C.L., 'Deeds and Seals', v, no. 30, fol. 13 (192 mm × 57 mm), **Scribe 38**; seal on tag, white wax; obverse: round (30 mm in diam.); large bird with wings extended to the left front; legend: . . .IGILL' PAGANI CHEV. . .; no counterseal; endorsements: Pagan(us) Cauer uendidit Villelmo capellano (*c.* s. xiii^med); Langahal' (s. xiii^ex?); Aluengate (s. xiv^ex?); Registratur (s. xiv^ex × s. xv^in); **B.**, ibid. 'Reg. B', no. 1016 (1015), pp. 439–40.

Sciant presentes et futuri quod ego Pagan(us) Chauer Glouc' vendidi et concessi Willelmo capellano de sancto Aldato quamdam terram meam extra ianuam aquilonalem Glouc' pro tribus marcis esterlingorum . Videlicet illam quam ego iamdictus Pagan(us) tenui de Emma de celario . quam etiam terram Alfricus filius coci tenuit ante me de eadem Emmo predicta . tenendam et habendam quietam inperpetuum sibi uel cui illam asignare uoluerit. Et ego sepedictus Pagan(us) et heredes mei warentizabimus predictam terram predicto Willelmo uel aturniato suo contra omnes homines et feminas . saluo langablo eiusdem terre. Et quia volo quod hec uenditio mea firma sit et stabilis⸴ presenti carta et sigilli mei inpressione confirmaui. His testibus . Ricardo filio Willelmi . Mauricio palmario . tunc prepositis Glouc'[1] . Iohanne ruffo . Waltero Scriba . Henrico mercerio . Gileberto cissore . Iohanne Oie et aliis.

[1] **B** ends here with *et aliis.*

293. *Grant by Richard Clerk son of Brictmer of* Bodenscumba *to Reginald of Brecon and Felicia (his wife), Richard's daughter, of his land by the church of St.*

*Martin in Gloucester in hereditary right for 1 mark annual rent to his son Henry,
and saving the rent and service owed to the prior and brothers of the Hospital of
Jerusalem. (1205 × 24)*

A. G.C.L., 'Deeds and Seals', v, no. 27, fol. 11 (180 mm × 74 mm), **Scribe 29**; seal on tag,
green wax; obverse: oval (38 mm × 28 mm); a large bird to the front with wings extended;
legend: +SIGILL' RI. . .IO; no apparent counterseal[1]; endorsements: Registratur (s. xiv?); prope
ecclesia Sancti Martini in Gloc(estria) (s. xv or later?); **B**. ibid. 'Reg. B', no. 13, pp. 6–7.

Sciant presentes et futuri quod ego Ricard(us) Clericus filius Brictmeri de
Bodenescumba dedi et concessi et presenti carta mea confirmaui Reginaldo de
Breken' et Felicie filie mee et heredibus de ea exeuntibus terram meam prope
ecclesiam sancti Martini in Glouc' . quam tenui de priore et fratribus Hospitalis
Ierosolimitanorum in Anglia . tenendam et habendam sibi et heredibus suis iure
hereditario ita libere et quiete sicut ego eam unquam liberius tenui et habui . saluo
redditu et seruitio prioris et fratrum Hospitalis Ierosolimitanorum in Anglia . sicut
carta eorum de predicta terra protestatur. Idem etiam Reginald(us) predictam terram
de longabulo adquietabit . et Henrico clerico filio meo unam marcam argenti
annuatim persoluet. duobus terminis . Medietatem ad Pascha . et medietatem ad
festum sancti Michaelis. Quod quia ratum esse uolo et stabile. presenti carta et sigilli
mei impressione confirmaui. Hiis testibus . domino Henrico abbate Glouc' et Thoma
suppriore . et Willelmo filio meo et Ioscelino monachis Glouc' . Waltero de
Bannebur' . Waltero scriptore clericis . Ricardo Burgeis . Henrico Burgeis . Ricardo
filio Willelmi Burgeis . Radulfo de Brochamtuna . Waltero de Caudicota et multis
aliis.

St. Peter's may not have acquired this property before 1264, although the attestation by so
strong a St. Peter's contingent suggests a proprietary interest.

[1] The tag is stitched to the page just above the seal, making it impossible to turn the seal, but the
reverse side is smooth, which suggests that no counterseal is there.

---

294. *Confirmation by Richard of Coleford to Henry de Suthalre of 2½ acres of land
in* Longecroft *for a payment of 23s. 8d. and 5d. annual rent. (s. xiii[1])*

G.C.L., 'Deeds and Seals', ii, no. 6, fol. 3 (228 × 93 mm); seal on tag: white wax stained dark
green; chipped, repaired; oval (38 mm × 23 mm); an elongated fleur-de-lis; legend: +S'
RICARDI . . .E COLEFORD; no counterseal; no medieval endorsement.

Sciant presentes et futuri quod ego Ricardus de Coleford dedi et concessi et hac
presenti carta mea confirmaui Henrico de Suþalre pro homagio et seruitio suo duas
acras et dimidiam terre mee cum pertinentiis suis . scilicet duas acras iacentes in
longecroft iuxta terram Godefredi porcarii et exstendunt se uersus terram Reginaldi
de Suþalre . et dimidiam acram iacentem iuxta dictas duas acras et exstendit se in
longitudine a terra Reginaldi de Suþalre usque fossatum Rogeri bedelli . Tenendas et
habendas de me et heredibus meis sibi et heredibus suis uel assignatis suis libere et
quiete in feodo et hereditate . Reddendo inde annuatim michi et heredibus meis ipse
et heredes uel assignati sui quinque denarios ad duos terminos anni . scilicet ad

festum sancti Michaelis duos denarios et obolum . et ad festum sancte Marie in Martio duos denarios et obolum . pro omni seruitio consuetudine et exactione . saluo regali seruitio quantum pertinet ad tantum tenementum in eadem uilla et de eodem feodo. Pro hac autem donatione et concessione mea dedit michi predictus Henricus viginti et tres solidos et octo denarios sterlingorum. Ego vero predictus Ric(ardus) et heredes mei predicto Henrico et heredibus uel assignatis suis totam predictam terram cum omnibus pertinentiis contra omnes homines et feminas imperpetuum warantizabimus et defendemus. In cuius testimonium . presenti carte sigillum meum apposui. Hiis testibus . Roberto de Stanlenhc . Roberto de Gardino . Reginaldo de Suþalre . Waltero le hore . Reginaldo de Olebroc . Willelmo de Coleford . Godefrido porcario . et aliis.

295. *Grant by Dionisia widow of Reginald of Devonshire in her liege power to John Page of two pieces of land in the girdlery (possibly Mercer Row), Gloucester, for 38s. annual rent and 1 mark for entry. (c. 1240 × c. 1265)*

A. G.C.L., 'Deeds and Seals', vi, no. 39, fol. 21 (228 mm × 180 mm); seal on cords faded white, repaired; white wax stained green, fragment, repaired; obverse: oval (meas. unavail.); image indiscernible; legend: . . .RAN. . .DI. . .; reverse indiscernible; endorsements: Carta de zonaria (s. xiii^ex); zonaria[;] Registratur (s. xiv^ex); **B**. ibid. 'Reg. B', no. 1055 (1054), p. 459.

Sciant presentes et futuri quod ego Dionisia que fui vxor Reginaldi le Deueneis tempore viduetatis mee et in ligia potestate mea dedi et concessi et hac presenti carta mea confirmaui Iohanni Page burgensi Glouc' . vnam terram meam in zonaria Glouc' super quam quatuor selde aliquando site fuerunt et iacet inter terram ipsius Iohannis et terram que fuit Walteri Toky [.] Et mensurata fuit per visum legalium virorum et continet de latitudine interiori parte septem virgas domini regis vlnarias cum pollice interposito [.] Retro totidem . In profunditate tres virgas cum pollice interposito et tria quarteria et dimidium quarterium. Dedi etiam et concessi eidem Iohanni vnam terram meam in eadem zonaria Glouc' super quam due selde aliquando site fuerunt et iacet inter terram ipsius Iohannis et terram que fuit Elie le Paumer . Et mensurata fuit per visum legalium virorum et continet de latitudine in anteriori parte tres virgas domini regis vlnarias cum pollice interposito . Retro totidem . In profunditate tres virgas cum pollice interposito et vnum quarterium . Habendas et tenendas sibi et heredibus suis vel assignatis suis de me et heredibus meis vel assignatis meis libere et quiete integre cum omnibus pertinentiis suis in feudo et hereditate inperpetuum . Reddendo inde annuatim michi et heredibus meis vel assignatis meis triginta et octo solidos ad quatuor anni terminos . Videlicet ad Nathale domini nouem solidos et sex denarios . ad festum beate Marie in Martio . nouem solidos et sex denarios . ad Natiuitatem sancti Iohannis Baptiste nouem solidos et sex denarios . et ad festum sancti Michaelis . nouem solidos et sex denarios pro omni seruitio seculari consuetudine exactione et demanda. Et ego Dionisia et heredes mei siue assignati mei predicto Iohanni et heredibus suis vel assignatis suis predictas terras cum omnibus pertinentiis suis contra omnes gentes in perpetuum warantizabimus et de longabulo‿ et omnibus aliis seruitiis defendemus et adquietabimus. Pro hac autem donatione concessione ac presentis carte confirmatione dedit michi dictus Iohannes vnam marcam argenti de introitu. Et quia volo quod hec mea donatio et concessio ac presentis carte confirmatio perpetue firmitatis robur optineat presenti carte sigillum meum apposui. Hiis testibus . Iohanne Simond . Rogero le Enueise . tunc balliuis Glouc' . Willelmo de Teokebur' . Ricardo franceis[1] . Iohanne le Fuster . Iohanne Monitod . Waltero de Pinnecot . Mauricio Siminel . Henrico clerico et aliis.

For the bailiffs' dates, see *VCH Glos.* iv. 371. It is not certain that St. Peter's held this property before 1264.

[1] **B** ends here with *et aliis.*

296. *Sale by Emma daughter of Henry Dorilot of Gloucester to Stephen of Cornwall of Gloucester of her land on Hare Lane (Gloucester) for 3 marks and 40d. entry and ¼d. annual rent. (c. 1240 × c. 1265)*

A. G.C.L., 'Deeds and Seals', ix, no. 22, fol. 10 (198 mm × 139 mm); seal on tag; dark green wax, broken, repaired; obverse: pointed oval (*c.* 35 mm × *c.* 25 mm); image indiscernible; legend: . . .S'. EME. . .RIC. . . DORI. . .; no counterseal; endorsements: Herlone; E (s. xiii^{med}); iiii (uncertain date); Registratur (s. xiv^{ex} × s. xv^{in}); **B.** ibid. 'Reg. B', no. 441, pp. 195–6.

Sciant presentes et futuri quod ego Emma filia Henr(ici) Dorilot de Glouc' dedi et concessi et hac mea presenti carta confirmaui Stephano Cornubiensi de Glouc' pro tribus marcis argenti . et quadraginta denariis quos michi dedit de introitu⸍ totam terram meam in Herlone . Illam scilicet que iacet inter terram Thome Vlger . et terram Willelmi Asselin . quam Henricus Dorilot pater meus quondam tenuit . et que michi hereditarie post heredes Rogeri Dorilot fratris mei descendebat . Tenendam et habendam de me et heredibus meis⸍ sibi et heredibus suis . vel assignatis suis . In feodo et hereditate . libere et quiete . integre cum omnibus pertinentiis suis in perpetuum . Reddendo inde annuatim ipse et heredes sui vel assignati sui michi et heredibus meis vnum quadrantem argenti ad festum sancti Michaelis pro omni seruitio seculari . consuetudine et demanda. Ego uero Emma et heredes mei predicto Stephano et heredibus suis . vel assignatis suis predictam terram cum pertinentiis contra omnes homines et feminas warantizabimus . et per predictum redditum acquietabimus et defendemus. Et ut hec mea donatio et concessio perpetue firmitatis robur optineat⸍ huic presenti carte sigilli mei impressionem apposui. Hiis testibus . Iohanne filio Symonis . Rogero li enueise tunc bailliuis Glouc'[1] . Hugone de La Kyngeshom' . Luca Cornubiense . Iohanne Manitot tunc bailliuo domini archiepiscopi Eboracensis . Willelmo Gille . Willelmo Asselin . Willelmo Bay . Laurencio Triwenian . Henrico clerico . et aliis.

Date as no. 295. It is not certain that St. Peter's held this property before 1264.

[1] **B** ends here with *et aliis.*

297. *Quitclaim by the brethren of the hospital of St. Mary Magdalen of Dudstone to John Ingulf of a house in Newland (Gloucester). (s. xiii^{med})*

A. G.C.L., 'Deeds and Seals', i, no. 47, fol. 25 (213 mm × 75 mm); seal on tag; white wax, rubbed, chipped; obverse: oval (orig. meas. of length unavail.; width, 33 mm); two figures facing to the front, the left one with a halo; perhaps Christ and Mary Magdalen; legend: . . .LL' FRA. . .; no counterseal; endorsements: Registratur (s. xiv); In Newlonde (s. xv?); **B**. ibid. no., 548, p. 240.

Sciant presentes et futuri quod nos omnes fratres hospitalis beate Marie Magdalene de Dodestan' pari concordia communi assensu et una uoluntate nostra renuntiauimus et quiete clamauimus Iohanni Iggulf quamdam domum in la Newelo'de cum pertinentiis suis que sita est inter terram Willelmi le chesmu(n)gar' et terra Ricardi tinte illam scilicet domum quam Ioannes halfclar' aliquando tenuit iure hereditario et eandem domum quam Royz vxor dicti Iohannis halfclar' post decessum eiusdem Iohannis viri sui in manibus nostris tradidit et i(m)pignorau' pro neccessis victus sui eidem Royz . a nobis omnibus diebus vite sue inueniendis. Pro hac autem renuntiatione et quieta clamatione nostra dedit nobis predictus Iohannes Iggulf decem solidos esterlingorum premanibus. Et vt hec nostra renuntiatio et quieta clamatio c(er)te firmitudinis inperpetuum robur optineat . presentem cartam sigilli nostri communis munimine et impressione roborauimus. Hiis testibus . Ricardo clerico de Cu'thou'[1] . Henrico de Holecu'b' . Waltero Durand del Elbrigge . Willelmo Gerand . Iohanne tunc capellano[2] de Berwod' . et aliis.

It is not certain that St. Peter's held this property before 1264.

[1]   The horizontal suspension sign is above the *cu* which makes it difficult to determine the reading.

[2]   **B** ends here with *et aliis*, having omitted the names of Henry, Walter, and William.

298. *Sale by Alexander son and heir of Maurice Durand of Gloucester to Richard Francis of Gloucester of the annual rent of 38s. which John Page owed for a tenement in the girdlery (possibly Mercer Row), Gloucester, for 22½ marks. (1258)*

G.C.L., 'Deeds and Seals', vii, no. 22, fol. 12 (173 mm × 99 mm), **Scribe 44**; seal on tag, dark green wax, rubbed; obverse: an oval (*c.* 33 mm × 22 mm); a large bird, wings folded, facing left; legend: +S' ALEX . . .A . . .I: FIL' MAVRICI; no counterseal; endorsements: Carta de zonaria (s. xiii^{med}), **Hand r**; Registratur (s. xiv^{ex} × s. xv^{in}); zonaria (s. xv?).

Sciant presentes et futuri quod ego Alexander filius et heres Mauricii Durand de Glouc' assignaui . remisi . et dedi . et hac presenti carta mea confirmaui Ricardo frannceys de Glouc' illos triginta et octo solidos annualis redditus quod Iohannes Page michi reddere consueuit de tenemento quod tenuit in zonaria Glouc' . Habendos et tenendos eidem Ricardo ut assignato meo et heredibus suis uel suis assignatis et eorum heredibus . libere . et quiete . solute . et integre . iure hereditario in perpetuum . sine aliqua reclamatione seu retenemento mei uel meorum inposterum . Faciendo inde annuatim capitalibus dominis feodi illius seruitium debitum et consuetum prout facere debui et consueui pro omni seruitio . exactione . et demanda. Pro hac autem assignatione . remissione et donatione mea'. dedit michi predictus Ricardus viginti duas marcas et dimidiam in gersummam. In huius rei testimonium carte presenti sigillum meum apposui. Hiis testibus . Rogero le Enueyse . Willelmo de Chiltenham tunc balliuis Glouc' . Iohanne Simund . Willelmo de Toek' . Luca Cornubiense . Iohanne Sage . Alexandro del Broc . Willelmo de Watfortd . Roberto de Putteleg' . Willelmo de Sondhurste . Herberto le mercer . Willelmo le marscal . Vincentio Chose . et aliis.

Alexander seems to have been the brother of Master Nicholas of Hatherley who gave St. Peter's his rents in Gloucester in 1263 (*Cart. Glouc.* i. 83–84; see above, no. 227). The endorsement in **Hand r** shows that St. Peter's was one of the chief lords of the tenement on which the rent was payable.

299. *Grant by John of Easton with the assent of his son Thomas and his other children to his daughter Lyana in free marriage of 4 virgates of land, one ·1 Easton (in Thornbury), one in Morton, and two in Tormarton. (s. xii^{ex})*

H.C.L., no. 1651 (*c.* 194 mm × *c.* 73 mm); seal missing from cords; endorsements: Estone (s. xiii); Carte de Torm'ton (s. xiv^{med}); non indiget registrari (s. xiv).

Sciant presentes et futuri quod ego . Iohannes de Estona concessu . et assensu . Thome . filii mei . et ceterorum liberorum meorum . dedi . et concessi . in liberum maritagium . Lyane . filie mee . et heredibus eius . vel assignatis . quotuor virgatas terre . cum omnibus pertinentiis suis . et libertatibus et liberis consuetudinibus . tenendas de me et heredibus meis . sibi . et heredibus suis . vel cuicumque dare . vel . assignare voluerit . libere . et quiete . in bono . et in pace . ab omni seruitio . et demanda seculari . ad me vel heredes meos pertinente⸍. saluo forinseco seruitio . vnam scilicet virgatam terre . in Estona . de dominico meo . ad valorem vnius alicuius virgate terre . de vilenagio que de me tenetur . et vnam virgatam terre in Mortona quam Iohannes filius Alwi tenuit . et duas virgatas terre . in Torm'ton' . vnam . scilicet . quam Willelmus Cappe tenuit . et vnam quam Iohannes filius Gunnilde . tenuit. Et ego Iohannes et heredes mei . dictas . quatuor virgatas terre cum omnibus pertinentiis . et libertatibus et liberis consuetudinibus suis . dicte Lyane filie mee . et heredibus suis . vel eius assignatis . warantizabimus . adquietabimus . et defendemus . contra omnes homines . et feminas . pro predicto seruitio. Et ut hec mea donatio et concessio . et warantizatio rata sit imperpetuum et stabilis presenti scripto sigillum meum apposui. Hiis testibus . Roberto de Haseloure . Simone de Cocton' . Hamone falconario . Radulfo Le poer . Henrico de Beninton' . Ernaldo tunc decano de Blockele . Rogero de stabulo . Frankelario de Estona . Waltero spensario de Wileia . et multis aliis.

300. *Grant in the form of a chirograph by Mabel Farrier to her brother Maurice of the land of Cleymond willed to her by her father, located by the abbot's garden, and the part which she bought from her sister Matilda (Gloucester); Maurice was to pay to Mabel one bezant for entry and 3s. 9d. annual rent and to the archbishop of York 3s. 3d. for landgabel. (c. 1200 × 28)*

A. G.C.L., 'Deeds and Seals', v, no. 34, fol. 15 (67 mm [left] × 197 mm [foot]), **Scribe 38** (below, Plate XXXII); seal on tag; green wax, fragment, chipped, repaired; obverse: pointed oval (meas. unavail.); a bird with wings extended facing front; legend: . . .ARESCA. . .; no counterseal; endorsements: de terra in Cleymond que iac[et][1] ante ortum abbathie Gloucest[rie][2] (s. xiii^{ex} × s. xiv^{in}); Aluengate; Registratur (s. xiv^{ex} × s. xv^{in}); **B**. ibid. 'Reg. B', no. 1019 (1018), p. 440.

C Y R O G R A P H U M[3] (*inverted*)

Sciant presentes et futuri quod ego Mabil(ia) Marscall(us) tradidi et concessi Mauricio fratri meo . totam terram meam de Cleimu'd' quam pater meus michi legauit . Scilicet illam que iacet ante ortum abbatie sancti Petri Glouc' . et totam illam partem quam emi de Matillda sorore mea . tenendam et habendam in feodo et hereditate . libere et quiete ab omni seruitio . et exactione . Reddendo inde annuatim michi uel heredibus meis ad duos terminos tres solidos . et nouem denarios . Ad festum sancti Michaelis . viginti et duos denarios et obolum . Ad Hockedai . viginti et duos denarios et obolum. Et sciendum quod predictus Mauricius aquietabit predictam terram de langablo uersus archiepiscopum Eboracensem . Videlicet de tribus solidis . et tribus denariis. Et pro hac concessione mea predictus Mauricius dedit michi vnum besantium auri de introitu. Et quia volo quod hec concessio mea rata sit et stabilis . illam fideliter tenendam . presenti cyrographo inter nos diuiso confirmaui. Hiis testibus . Ada Gladuwin' . Thoma Oie . Roberto diuite[4] . Ada Esgard . Iohanne Le Eueske . et omni halimoto et aliis.

It is not certain the St. Peter's held this property before 1264.

[1]   Word ending obscured by overlap of scrapbook opening edge.
[2]   The same.
[3]   The penultimate letter is possibly *V*.   [4] **B** ends here with *et aliis*.

301.   *Grant by Richard Francis burgess of Gloucester to Master Nicholas of Hatherley of all his land in the girdlery (possibly Mercer Row), Gloucester, for 4s. annual rent to the chief lords of the fee and 28 marks in cash. (1258)*

A. G.C.L., 'Deeds and Seals', vii, no. 11, fol. 6 (271 mm × 124 mm), **Scribe 45** (below, Plate XXXIX); fragment of tag; seal missing; endorsements: Caps(ula) .xix. de laicis tenuris (s. xiii^2); Carta Ric(ard)i Fraunceys de terra in zonaria[:] .N. de Hatherl' (s. xiii^2); iii Warda (s. xiv); sc(ribitur) (s. xiv^{med}); Registratur (s. xiv^{ex} × s. xv^{in}); **B**. ibid. 'Reg. B', no. 1102 (1101), pp. 478–9.

Sciant presentes et futuri quod ego Ricardus Franceys burgensis Glouc' dedi concessi et hac presenti carta mea confirmaui magistro Nicholao de Hetherl' totam terram cum domibus et edificiis redditibus et aliis pertinentiis suis in zonaria Glouc' quam habui de Roberto Page et quam terram Iohannes Page frater dicti Roberti aliquando tenuit de Dyonisia matre dicti magistri Nicholai . Tenendam et habendam de me et heredibus meis sibi vel cuicumque assignare voluerit . libere quiete bene et in pace integre . Reddendo inde annuatim pro me et heredibus meis vel assignatis quatuor solidos argenti capitalibus dominis dicti feodi ad terminos consuetos pro omnibus seruitiis et secularibus demandis. Pro hac autem donatione concessione et carte mee confirmatione dedit michi dictus magister Nicholaus viginti et octo marcas argenti premanibus. Et ego dictus Ricardus franceis et heredes mei dicto magistro Nicholao et suis assignatis totam predictam terram cum domibus edificiis redditibus et aliis pertinentiis contra omnes homines et feminas inperpetuum warantizabimus et defendemus. Et quia volo quod hec mea donatio concessio et carte mee confirmatio perpetue firmitatis robur optineat. huic presenti scripto sigillum meum apposui. Hiis testibus . Willelmo de Chylteha' . Rogero Lenveyse tunc balliuis Glouc' . Iohanne Symun . Alexandro del broc . Ricardo de Celario . Hugone de aula regis . Luca Cornubiensi . Iohanne Anketyl . Ricardo pictore . Willelmo de Cokebyr' Capellano huius carte scriptore . et aliis[1].

On the basis of the first endorsement, St. Peter's may have held this property by 1264. The charter can be dated by the attestations of the two bailiffs, William of Cheltenham and Roger le Wyse (*VCH Glos.* iv. 372). Master Nicholas was the son of Maurice of Gloucester, as he states in a grant of various Gloucester properties, apparently including the subject of this charter, to St. Peter's in 1263 (*Cart. Glouc.* ii, no. 758; see also i. 84).

[1] **B** skips from *balliuis Glouc'* to William of Cockbury in listing witnesses.

302. *Quitclaim by Richard Francis burgess of Gloucester to Master Nicholas of Hatherley of all his rights in land in the girdlery (possibly Mercer Row), Gloucester, for 28 marks. (1258)*

A. G.C.L., 'Deeds and Seals', vii, no. 2, fol. 1 (220 mm × 127 mm), **Scribe 17**; fragment of tag for seal through single slit; seal missing; endorsements: .sc(ribitur) (s. xiii?); Quietaclamatio Ric(ardi) fraunceys de terris in zonaria[;] .N. de Hatherl' (s. xiii); Caps(ula) .xix. de laicis tenuris (s. xiii^{ex} × s. xiv^{in}); iii Ward' (s. xiv^{in}?); In zonaria Glouc'; Registratur (s. xiv^{ex} × s. xv^{in}); **B**. ibid. 'Reg. B', no. 1103 (1102), p. 479.

Vniuersis Cristi fidelibus Ricardus franceys burgensis Glouc' salutem eternam in domino. Noueritis me remisisse et in perpetuum pro me et heredibus meis quieteclamasse magistro Nicholao de Haytherleg' et eius assignatis totum ius et clamium quod habui seu habere potui in tota terra cum domibus . edificiis . redditibus et aliis pertinentiis suis in zonaria Glouc' quam habui de Roberto Page et quam terram Iohannes Page aliquando tenuit de Dyonisia matre ipsius magistri Nicholai . Ita quod ego et heredes mei exclusi simus inperpetuum ab omnimodo iure et clamio iuris ad nos inde pertinentibus. Et si quocumque tempore me uel heredes meos seu alios nomine iuris nostri contra predictum magistrum Nicholaum uel eius assignatos de predicta terra cum omnibus supradictis exactionem uel fatigationem mouere contigerit. ad hoc eidem magistro Nicholao teneri concedimus et volumus obligari et eius assignatis quod sine contradictione et dilatione mox eisdem teneamur in solutione quadraginta marcarum argenti nomine restitutionis fatigationum et expensarum predictis omnibus nichilominus in suo robore precise remanentibus . Concedentes et voluntates quod nullum breue domini regis seu aliud quodcumque remedium in facto uel in iure consistens nobis contra predicta possit prodesse . uel predicto magistro Nicholao seu eius assignatis in aliquo obesse. Pro hac autem remissione et quietaclamantia mea dedit michi predictus magister Nicholaus premanibus viginti et octo marcas argenti. Et ad maiorem securitatem omnes cartas et instrumenta que de predicta terra cum pertinentiis suis habui. eidem magistro Nicholao liberaui. In cuius rei testimonium huic scripto presenti sigillum meum apposui. Hiis testibus . Rogero le Enueyse . Willelmo de Chiltenham tunc balliuis Glouc' . Iohanne S[ym]und[1] . Will(elm)o de Toek' . Luca cornubiensi . Alexandro del Broc . Ricardo de Celar' . Iohanne Anketil . Ricardo clerico . et aliis.

This charter completed the transaction begun in no. 301. For the date see *VCH Glos.* iv. 372.

[1] Hole in MS.; missing portion supplied from **B**, which ends here with *et aliis.*

303. *Grant in the form of a chirograph by Wimarc wife of John Franchevaler, with the permission of her son William, to William son of Siward for term of his life of her meadow of Longford in* Druimede *and 2 acres of arable land in* Otfeld *for an annual rent of 3s. 8d. and two capons and single payments of 7s. to Wimarc and 12d. to her son; made in the hall-moot of her lady. (s. xii^2; poss later than no. 212)*

G.C.L., 'Deeds and Seals', iv, no. 27, fol. 13 (139 mm × 80 mm); no provision for sealing; no seal; endorsement: Scriptum Wymarc vxoris Iohannis Francheual' de prato in Longeford' (s. xiv^{ex} × s. xv^{in}) Registratur (s. xiv^{ex} × s. xv^{in}).

CIROGRAPVM

Sciant tam presentes quam futuri quod ego Wimarc uxor Iohannis franc cheualer concessione Willelmi filii mei concessi et tradidi Willelmo filio Siwardi totum pratum meum de Longeford in Druimede et duas acras de terra colenda in Otfeld tenenda de me uel heredibus suis. tota uita ipsius Willelmi filii Siwardi . reddendo inde michi uel heredibus meis per annum pro omni seruitio. tres . solidos . et octo . denarios . et duos capones. Et pro hac concessione dedit michi prefatus Willelmus filius Siwardi septem . solidos . et filio meo Willelmo duodecim .denarios. Preterea affidauit michi quod non queret super hoc pactum artem uel ingenium mali erga me uel heredes meos. His testibus . Alexandro pincerna . Roberto franccheual'[1] . Henrico des Bares . Willelmo fratre suo . Gocelino de Walesw' . Iohanne fratre suo et halimoto domine quod bene sciuit hanc conuentionem.

Longford was held of Ralph of Willington (*Cart. Glouc.* i, no. 348). Since Ralph and his wife were supposedly alive *c.* 1228 × 43, it is strange that the court in Wimarc's lease should be described as her lady's, unless there was a mesne lady between her and Ralph (ibid. iii, no. 529). Possibly the *domine* of the text is a mistake for *domini.*

[1] **B** ends here with *et aliis.*

304. *Grant in the form of a chirograph by Osbern son of Osmund Fuket to William son of Ernald, Osbern's uncle, of the land which Ernald held of him. (1220 × 43; prob. c. 1220 × 24)*

A. G.C.L., 'Deeds and Seals', ix, no. 14, fol. 6 (112 mm × 79 mm); seal on tag; dark green wax, chipped, rubbed, repaired; obverse: round (32 mm in diam.); a large bird facing left, wings extended, head turned to the right; legend: + . . .IGILL'. WILLI' FILII ARNULFI[1]; no counterseal; endorsement: Registratur (s. xiv^{ex} × s. xv^{in}); **B**. ibid. 'Reg. B', no. 624, p. 270.

C Y R O G R A P H U M (inverted)

Sciant presentes et futuri quod ego Osb(er)n(nus) filius Osmundi Fuket concessi . et presenti carta mea confirmaui Willelmo filio Ernaldi auunculi mei totam terram quam Ernaldus pater eius de me tenuit . Tenendam de me et heredibus meis sibi et heredibus suis in perpetuum libere et quiete ab omni seruitio . saluo toto seruitio domini abbatis et conuentus Cloucestr' . de quo seruitio predictus Willelmus et heredes sui me et omnes meos heredes plenarie adquietabunt.[2] Et si forte aliquod regale seruitium uel exactio aliqua super domuum Gloucestr' contigerit. predictus[3] Willelmus et heredes sui . me et heredes meos de eodem seruitio et exactione plene adquietabunt.[4] Quod quia ratum esse uolo presenti carta sigilli mei impressione munita. confirmaui. Hiis testibus . Thoma de Berkel' . Gileberto de Ledebir' . Thoma de Hauuill' monachis de Glouc' . Simone de Matresdun' . Galfrido de Matresdun' . Waltero scriptore . Willelmo de Oura[5] . et multis aliis.

Date based on the attestation of Thomas of Berkeley, who was lord of Berkeley 1220–43 (Sanders, *English Baronies*, 13); the script appears to belong to the abbacy of Henry Foliot (compare with **Scribe 14**).

[1] Reading uncertain.
[3] *predictos* in MS.
[5] **B** lists only Thomas of Berkeley, Gilbert of Ledbury, and William *de Oura* as witnesses.
[2] *adquietabi(n)t* in MS.; corrected in **B**.
[4] *adquietabi(n)t* in MS.; corrected in **B**.

305. *Grant by William Fuket to John Mey of Gloucester of 4 acres of arable comprising 16 sellions in Ryecroft (by Gloucester) and elsewhere, in free marriage with Alice his daughter, for 2d. annual rent. (c. 1225 × 50)*

A. G.C.L., 'Deeds and Seals', ii, no. 2, fol. 1 (159 mm × 129 mm), **Scribe 42** (below, Plate XXXVI); seal on tag; white wax stained dark green; rubbed; obverse: round (28 mm in diam.); an eight-pointed flower; legend: + SIGILLVM . . .UCKE . . .; no counterseal; endorsements: Registratur; W. fuket (s. xiv^{ex} × s. xv^{in}); **B**. ibid. 'Reg. B', no. 625, pp. 270–1.

Notum sit vniuersis presentibus et futuris quod ego Will(elm)us Fuket dedi et concessi et hac presenti carta mea confirmaui Iohanni Mey de Glouc' quatuor acras terre arabilis cum Alicia filia mea in liberam maritagium scilicet duos seillones in Ruecroft inter terram abbatis Glouc' et terram Osberti Fuket . et unum seillonem contra Aldeneldebrugge extendentem ex vna parte apud Wedrugge . et duos seillones iacentes inter terram sancti Leonardi et terram Osberti Fuket . et quinque seillones in Sudhaneleye iacentes inter terram Thome de Mattresdune et terram Osberti Fuket . et tres seillones iacentes inter terram Walteri schireue et terram Osberti Fuket . et tres seillones extendentes ex vna parte super Middelweye iacentes inter [terram][1] Walteri Cricfeyd et terram Osberti Fuket habendas et tenendas de me et de heredibus meis sibi et heredibus suis de predicta Alicia exeuntibus libere et quiete integre cum omnibus pertinentiis reddendo inde annuatim ipse et heredes sui de dicta Alicia procreati mihi et heredibus meis duos denarios argenti scilicet ad festum sancti Michaelis pro omnibus seruitiis sectis et demandis secularibus et consuetudinibus[.] Et ego dictus Will(elm)us Fuket et heredes mei warentizabimus predictas quatuor acras terre cum omnibus pertinentiis dicto Iohanni Mey et heredibus suis de predicta Alicia procreatis contra omnes homines et feminas inperpetuum . et de omnibus seruitiis et demandis sectis et consuetudinibus pro predicto redditu inperpetuum . aquietabimus. Quod quia ratum fieri uolo huic presenti scripto sigillum meum apposui. Hiis testibus . Galfrido de la graue . Reginaldo Le Deueneis[2] . Waltero de Snedham . Willelmo Gerard . Willelmo de Chirchesdun' . Osberto Fuket . Laurencio filio Ricardi . et aliis.

For the field-names, see *PNG*, ii. 143–4. 'South Hanley' appears to have been in the vicinity. The witness Reginald of Devonshire may have been dead by 6 June 1255 (Stevenson, no. 496, a charter of his son Philip).

[1] Omitted by scribe.

[2] **B** ends here with *et aliis*.

306. *Grant by Sibyl daughter of William Girdler to Alice her niece of the land (unident.; prob. Gloucester) which Helias dean of Hamme gave to her; Alice was to pay 2s. annual rent to St. Peter's, Gloucester, and 1d. a year to the church of St. Nicholas for Sibyl's soul, saving royal service of 7d. a year, and Alice gave Sibyl 2s. for entry. (1200 × c. 1228)*

G.R.O., GBR/J1/86 (167 mm × 61 mm), **Scribe 39**; seal on tag; obverse: round (33 mm in diam.); chipped; dark green; a fleur-de-lis; legend: +SIGILL' . . .IBILLE . . .LL' LE SEITE; no counterseal; endorsement: nota pro Rege (s. xiv); cal. in Stevenson, no. 86.

Sciant tam presentes quam futuri quod ego Sibilla filia Willelmi le seinter dedi et concessi Alicie nepti mee . quamdam terram que iacet inter terram Arnaldi filii Dunning . et terram Nicholai le seinter . scilicet illam quam Helyas decanus de Hamme dedit michi pro meo seruitio . Tenendam et habendam ineternum de me . sibi et heredibus suis . libere et quiete . reddendo inde annuatim abbatie sancti Petri Glouc' .duos. solidos . argenti . ad duos terminos . scilicet ad Hockedei .xii. denarios . Et ad festum sancti Michaelis .xii. denarios . Et ecclesie sancti Nicholai annuatim pro anima mea .vnum. denarium pro omni seruitio . saluo regali seruitio . scilicet .septem. denarios . annuatim ad Hockedei. Et ego predicta Sibilla . dicte Alicie et heredibus suis predictam terram contra omnes homines et feminas warantizabo. Pro hac concessione mea predicta Alicia dedit michi .duos. solidos . argenti . de introitu predicte terre. Et ut hec concessio mea rata sit et inconcussa permaneat. eam presentis carte mee testimonio . et sigilli mei i(m)pressione confirmaui. Hiis testibus . Thomas illuminatore . Nicholao le seinter . Offre aurifabro . Nicholao Muet . Waltero le mercer . Steph(ano) filio Atheline . Waltero filio Rogerii . Waltero filio Walteri . Iohanne le seinter . David parmentario . et multis aliis.

Another charter written by this scribe establishes dating limits for this grant (below, no. 316).

307. *Grant by Nicholas son of Humphrey of Gloucester to David Dunning of Gloucester of his land on Longsmith Street (Gloucester) for 1d. annual rent and 8 marks entry to acquit Nicholas and the land from the Jewry of Gloucester. (c. 1228 × 40)*

A. G.C.L., 'Deeds and Seals', vi, no. 18, fol. 9 (196 mm × 168 mm); slit for tag on turn-up; tag and seal missing; endorsements: [Car]ta[1] Nich(ola)i filii Hunfridi (s. xiii[1]); In uico Fabrorum[.] Infirmar(io) istius terre langabul(um) non adquietabat (s. xiii[med]); Smythstr'te; Registratur (s. xiv[ex] × s. xv[in]); B. ibid. 'Reg. B', no. 1048 (1047), p. 453.

Sciant presentes et futuri quod ego Nicholaus filius Hunfr(idi) de Glouc' assensu et voluntate heredum meorum tradidi et concessi Dauid Dunning de Glouc' terram meam cum domibus et edificiis et aliis pertinentiis suis . videlicet illam que iacet in vico fabrorum . inter terram ipsius Dauid . et terram que fuit Siluestri Poli . que terra mensurata per uisum proborum hominum continet in latitudine in anteriori parte octo uirgas domini regis ulnarias cum pollice interposito . et tria[2] quarteria et vnum pollicem . In posteriori parte continet septem uirgas domini regis ulnarias cum pollice interposito et vnum quarterium . In longitudine uero continet viginti quatuor uirgas domini regis ulnarias cum pollice interposito . Tenendam et habendam sibi et heredibus suis de me et heredibus meis libere et quiete in feudo et hereditate in perpetuum reddendo inde annuatim michi uel heredibus meis vnum denarium argenti ad festum sancti Michaelis pro omnibus seruitiis et demandis. Pro hac autem donatione et concessione mea predictus Dauid dedit michi octo marcas argenti de introitu ad magnum negotium meum . videlicet ad me et ad terram illam adquietandam de Iudaismo Glouc' . que ibi inuadiata fuit. Et ego predictus Nicol(aus) et heredes mei predicto Dauid et heredibus suis predictam terram cum pertinentiis suis contra omnes homines et feminas warantizabimus. Et quia volo quod hec mea traditio et concessio rata sit et stabilis presenti carta mea[3] . sigilli mei inpressione confirmaui. Hiis testibus . Ricardo burg' maiori Glouc' [.] Iohanne draperio et Willelmo de Saunford' tunc prepositis Glouc' . Henrico burg' . Ricardo filio Willelmi . Iohanne de Gosedich',[4] . . .[5] Le ferun' . Nicolao Comioc . Ricardo Kadifer . Hugone clerico . W. . .[6] Sumeri . . .[7] aliis multis.

The charter is dated by the known chronology of the bailiffs (*VCH Glos.* iv. 371). The only Sumery who is appears in Gloucester borough charters in this period is William, who may thus be the Sumery in the witness-list. David Dunning in turn granted St. Peter's 9s. from his rent from the Longsmith Street property (*Cart. Glouc.* i. 125).

[1] Beginning of word obscured by overlap of scrapbook window.   [2] *tres* in MS.

[3] *et* erroneously written here by the scribe.

[4] The witness-list in B contains only the names of Richard burgess (without the designation of mayor), Richard son of William, and John of Gosedich and ends here with *et aliis.*

[5] Damage and stain prevents reading.

[6] Hole in MS.   [7] Hole in MS.

308. *Confirmation by Henry son of Nicholas son of Humphrey of Gloucester to David Dunning of the land (in Gloucester) which Nicholas sold to him, for 40s. (c. 1228)*

A. G.C.L., 'Deeds and Seals', vi, no. 12, fol. 6 (173 mm × 122 mm); seal on tag, white wax, fragment, repaired; obverse: original shape uncertain; meas., image, legend, unavail.; reverse: no apparent sign of a counterseal; endorsements: de[1] terra Poly (s. xiii[:med]); .G. (s. xiii); Smythstr'ta; Registratur (s. xiv[ex] × s. xv[in]); **B**. ibid. 'Reg. B', no. 1049 (1048), p. 454.

Sciant presentes et futuri quod ego Henr(icus) filius Nicol(ai) filii Hunfridi Glouc' concessi[2] et in perpetuum de me et de heredibus meis quietam clamaui Dauid Dunning Glouc' et heredibus suis uel assignatis suis . terram illam quam Nicolaus pater meus sibi vendidit . scilicet illam que iacet inter terram que fuit Silvestri Poly et terram Dauid . Tenendam et habendam sibi et heredibus uel assignatis suis libere et quiete in perpetuum absque omni clamio quod possit de me uel de heredibus meis in processu temporis euenire . pro quadraginta solidis esterlingorum quos michi ad meum magnum negotium pacauit . Ego uero predictus[3] Henr(icus) et heredes mei. predicto Dauid et heredibus suis uel assignatis suis predictam terram contra omnes homines et feminas in perpetuum warantizabimus. Et ut haec concessio mea stabilis et rata permaneat'. presens scriptum sigillo meo roboratum predicto Dauid tradidi. Hiis testibus . Ricardo burg' . Thoma Oye tunc prepositis Glouc' . Iohanne de Gosedich[4] . Henrico burg' . Iohanne draperio . Waltero Hoch . Ricardo Kadif' . Willelmo fader . Henrico clerico et multis aliis.

This charter, later than no. 307, was made in or close to the year 1228 (see *VCH Glos.* iv. 371).

[1]   Superscript above *de* are six dots : : : forming a pattern.
[2]   *cincesci* in MS.
[3]   *predictos* in MS.
[4]   **B** ends here with *et aliis.*

309. *Chirograph recording the sale in the full hundred of Barton by Adam God with the agreement of his wife Cecily and his heirs to William Teoc of two messuages outside Alvingate (Gloucester), for 22s. 6d. subject to 1½d. annual rent to the king. (c. 1175)*

G.C.L., 'Deeds and Seals', i, no. 44, fol. 24 (149 mm × 93 mm); tongue torn away from lower left foot; seal missing; endorsements: CYROGRAPHUM Willelmi Theoc contra Adam god (s. xii[ex]), **Hand g**; iiia Warda (s. xiii[med]); sc(ribitur) (s. xv[in]).

CYROGRAPHUM

Cirographum istud testatur . quod ego Adam God uendidi Willelmo Teoc in pleno hundredo de Bertona . duo masagia extra Aluinegate . de .lxiiii. pedibus in longitudine . et xxxiii. pedibus in latitudine . prope terram Radulfi de B'geuenni . pro .xxii. solidis . et .vi. denariis . concessione Cecilie vxoris mee et heredum meorum . reddendo domino regi singulis annis .iii. obolos . pro omnibus seruitiis. Et ego et vxor mea predicta tactis sacrosanctis . abiurauimus totum ius quod habere credebamus in predicta terra pro nobis et heredibus nostris . ita quod de cetero placitum non mouebimus Willelmo uel heredibus suis . de terra illa . nec aliquod eis inde fiet grauamen per nos uel heredes nostros. Et si nos uel heredes nostri terram hanc warantizare non poterimus . Willemo uel heredibus suis . predictos .xxii. solidos . et .vi. denarios. eis retornabimus. Testibus . Willemo filio Stephani tunc vicecomite . Pagano Haket . Petro de P'itona . Elia Drocis . Roberto de Muceg'os . Mauricio de Mat'sdona . Roberto de B'tona . Roberto filio suo . Ada filio Fulconis . Guthwi.

Endorsement by **Hand g** indicates that this property belonged to St. Peter's long before 1264.

310. *Grant by Henry Halfknight to Maurice farrier of land between his house and the land which belonged to Hugh Le Blond in the parish of St. Oswald (Gloucester) for 1¾d. annual rent; and grant by Henry to Maurice of another parcel of land between his house and the land of the canons of St. Oswald for an advance of 28s. (c. 1225 × 40)*

A. G.C.L., 'Deeds and Seals', viii, no. 15, fol. 8 (171 mm × 169 mm); seal on tag, dark green wax, rubbed; obverse: round (34 mm in diam.); a large bird facing to the left with wings partly extended; legend: SIGIL. . . HENRICI HALF. . .; no counterseal; endorsements: :ii.[a] Warda (s. xiii[2]?), **Hand t**; Wat(er)strete[;] Registratur (s. xiv[ex] × s. xv[in]); sc(ribitur) (s. xv[in]); **B**. ibid. 'Reg. B', no. 1099 (1098), p. 477.

Sciant presentes et futuri quod ego Henr(icus) Halfcnit dedi et concessi et presenti carta mea confirmaui Mauricio marescallo quandam partem terre mee in parochia sancti Oswaldi . illam scilicet que iacet inter mansionem meam et terram que fuit Hugonis Le Blunt . Tenendam et habendam de me et heredibus meis sibi et heredibus suis siue assignatis suis . libere et quiete pro duobus denariis dempto vno quadrante pro omnibus seruitiis et secularibus demandis annuatim ad Hockeday persoluendis. Predicta uero terra per uisum legalium uirorum mensurata. habet in fronte duodecim uirgas ulnarias cum pollice interposito . In longitudine. uiginti uirgas ulnarias et dimidiam cum pollice interposito . Retro. quindecim uirgas ulnarias cum pollice interposito. Item concessi eidem Mauricio aliam particulam terre mee . illam scilicet que iacet inter mansionem meam et terram canonicorum sancti Oswaldi et habet in fronte duodecim uirgas ulnarias cum pollice interposito . In longitudine triginta tres uirgas ulnarias cum pollice interposito . Retro. vndecim uirgas ulnarias cum pollice interposito. Ego uero Henr(icus) et heredes mei predicto Mauricio et heredibus suis siue assignatis pro predicto seruitio contra omnes homines et feminas inperpetuum warantizabimus et de omnibus seruitiis adquietabimus. Pro hac autem donationem et concessione mea predictus Mauricius dedit michi premanibus ad magnum negotium meum . viginti octo solidos esterlingorum. In cuius rei testimonium presens scriptum sigillo meo sigillatum ei tradidi. Hiis testibus . magistro Henrico de P'tona[1] . Thoma Oya[2] . Ada Gladewine . Rogero de Thekesburi . Iohanne Monitot . Galfrido Cupe et multis aliis.

Endorsement by **Hand t** places this property in St. Peter's possession before 1263.

---

1 *Partona* in **B**.

2 **B** ends here with *et aliis*.

311. *Confirmation by Henry Halfknight to John son of Maurice farrier of lands which his father held in St. Oswald's parish (Gloucester). (after no. 310; prob. before 1240)*

A. G.C.L., 'Deeds and Seals', viii, no. 25, fol. 14 (201 mm × 121 mm); seal on tag; dark green wax; obverse: round (34 mm in diam.); a large bird facing front, head turned to the right, wings partly extended; legend: +SIGIL'VM. HENRICI. HALFKNIHT; no counterseal; endorsements: A (s. xiii²); ii.varda (*c.* s. xiii^med); Infirmarie . uel Elemosinarie (s. xiii); Carta Henr(ici) Halfcnith[;] Caps(ula) .xviii. del laicis tenuris (s. xiii^ex × s. xiv^in); sc(ribitur) (s. xiv^med); Waterstrete (s. xiv^ex); Registratur (s. xiv^ex × s. xv^in); **B.** ibid. 'Reg. B', no. 1101 (1100), p. 478.

Sciant presentes et futuri quod ego H(e)nric(us) Halfcnith . concessi et presenti carta mea confirmaui Iohanni filio Mauricii marescalli . totam terram illam quam pater eius de tenuit . in parochia sancti Oswaldi . sicut carta sua proportat . Illam . scilicet . que iacet inter mansionem meam . et terram que fuit Hugonis Blunt . et quandam aliam terram totam que iacet inter mansionem predictam et curtilagium canonicorum sancti Oswaldi . Tenendam et habendam de me et heredibus meis . sibi et heredibus suis uel assignatis suis . libere et quiete inperpetuum pro duobus denariis'. vno quadrante minus . pro omnibus seruitiis et secularibus demandis . annuatim ad Hock(edai) persoluendis. Prima uero particula terre per uisum legalium uirorum mensurata'. habet in fronte . duodecim uirgas ulnarias cum pollice interposito . In longitudine . uiginti uirgas ulnarias et dimidiam . cum pollice interposito . Retro'. undecim¹ uirgas ulnarias cum pollice interposito. Item . alia particula terre que iacet uersus curtilagium canonicorum habet in fronte . duodecim uirgas ulnarias cum pollice interposito . In longitudine . triginta tres uirgas ulnarias cum pollice interposito . Retro'. vndecim uirgas ulnarias cum pollice interposito. Ego uero H(e)nric(us) et heredes mei predicto Iohanni et heredibus suis siue assignatis . dictam terram expensis propriis pro predicto seruitio contra omnes homines et feminas imperpetuum warantizabimus . et de omnibus seruitiis acquietabimus. Pro hac autem concessione et confirmatione mea predictus Iohannes et Mauricius pater eius dederunt michi premanibus ad meum magnum negotium viginti et octo solidos esterlingorum. In cuius rei testimonium presens scriptum sigillo meo sigillatum'. ei tradidi. Hiis testibus [.] magistro Henrico de Parton' . magistro Waltero scriptore . Thoma Oye² tunc p(re)tore Glouc' . Ada Gladewine . Rogero de Theokesbir' . Iohanne Monitot . Galfrido Cupe . et multis aliis.

Note the unusual use of *pretor* for 'bailiff.' Thomas Oye served in this capacity at Gloucester several times between *c.* 1200 and 1240 (*VCH Glos.* iv. 371–2). Given the attestation of Walter *scriptor* and the vintage of the charter's script, *c.* 1230 is a reasonable date for its issue. The close resemblance of its witness-list to that of no. 310 suggests proximity in date.

¹ *quindecim* in **B.**   ² **B** ends here with *et aliis.*

312. *Confirmation by William Halfknight, son of John and Margaret Halfknight, of the pieces of land granted in no. 310, for 5s. (s. xiii^med)*

A. G.C.L., 'Deeds and Seals', viii, no. 14, fol. 7 (245 mm × 115 mm); seal on tag; dark green wax, obverse: round (30 mm in diam.); a large bird, wings folded back, facing right with head turned back to the left; legend: +S' WILLELMI HAL. . . [and ending with a small fleur-de-lis design]; no counterseal; endorsements: A (s. xiii); .ii.a varda (s. xiii^ex); Carta Will(elm)i Half cnith[;] Caps(ula) .xviii. de laicis tenuris (s. xiii^ex × s. xiv^in); Wat(er)strete[;] Registratur (s. xiv^ex × s. xv^in); another endorsement is hidden by overlap of edge of scrapbook window; **B**. ibid. 'Reg. B', no. 1100 (1099), pp. 477–8.

Sciant presentes et futuri quod ego Will(elmu)s Halfcnit filius Iohannis et Margarite Halfcnit concessi et hac presenti carta mea confirmaui Mauricio marescallo quamdam partem terre mee in parochia sancti Oswaldi Glouc' . illam scilicet que iacet inter mansionem meam et terram que fuit Hugonis le Blunt . tenendam et habendam de me et heredibus meis sibi et heredibus suis siue assignatis suis libere et quiete pro duobus denariis dempto vno quadrante pro omnibus seruitiis et secularibus demandis annuatim ad Hockeday persoluendis. Predicta uero terra per uisum legalium uirorum mensurata . habet in fronte: duodecim uirgas ulnarias cum pollice interposito . In longitudine: uiginti uirgas ulnarias et dimidiam cum pollice interposito . Retro: quindecim uirgas ulnarias cum pollice interposito. Item concessi eidem Mauricio aliam particulam terre mee et confirmaui . illam scilicet que iacet inter mansionem meam et curtilagium canonicorum sancti Oswaldi et habet in fronte duodecim uirgas ulnarias cum pollice interposito . In longitudine triginta tres uirgas ulnarias cum pollice interposito . Retro: vndecim uirgas ulnarias cum pollice interposito. Ego uero Will(elmu)s et heredes mei predicto Mauricio et heredibus suis siue assignatis pro predicto seruitio contra omnes homines et feminas predictas terras imperpetuum warentizabimus . et de omnibus seruitiis adquietabimus. Pro hac autem concessione et confirmatione mea . predictus Mauricius dedit michi premanibus ad magnum negotium meum quinque solidos sterlingorum. In cuius rei testimonium presens scriptum sigillo meo sigillatum ei tradidi. Hiis testibus . Ricardo de Cum'tun'[1] . tunc senescallo de Churchesdun' . Iohanne Monitot[2] . Ada Gladewine [.] Iohanne filio Rogeri . Iohanne filio Roberti . Petro Cupe . Ada Wade . Thoma Bedello . et multis aliis.

[1] Reading uncertain; *Cumpton'* in **B**.   [2] **B** ends here with *et aliis.*

313. *Confirmation by Joan daughter of Reginald Hopper with the assent of her husband Nicholas and her mother Joan to Adam Trol of Haydon of part of a house (in Gloucester) for 16d. annual rent to the almonry of St. Peter's, Gloucester, and 11s. to Joan in advance. (s. xiii^med)*

A. G.C.L., 'Deeds and Seals', ix, no. 34, fol. 17 (160 mm × 102 mm); seal on tag; dark green wax; obverse: oval (36 mm × 22 mm); a large elongated fleur-de-lis; legend: +S' IOH'NE: FIL: REGN: MERC. . .R; no counterseal; endorsements: Herlone de terra Stephani Brn' (s. xiii^2); Z (s. xiv); Registratur (s. xiv^ex × s. xv^in); Redditus ob(lati) elemosinario xvi d(enariorum). (s. xv^in); **B**. ibid. 'Reg. B', no. 439, p. 195.

Sciant presentes et futuri quod ego Iohanna filia Reginaldi le Hopere consensu et assensu Nicholai mariti mei et Iohanne matris mee et heredum meorum dedi et concessi et hac presenti carta mea confirmaui Ade Trol de Heydone et heredibus suis uel cui assignare uoluerit totam partem meam cuiusdam domus que quidem fuit Reginaldi patris mei . videlicet que est inter terram Stephani Cornubiensis et terram

Willelmi de Twigewrthe . Reddendo inde annuatim pro omni seruitio exactione et demanda sexdecim denarios elemosinario sancti Petri Gloucest'ie ad duos terminos . Scilicet octo denarios ad Hockedai et octo denarios ad festum sancti Michaelis. Ego vero dicta Iohanna et heredes mei dictam partem predicte domus predicto Ade et heredibus suis uel assignatis suis contra omnes homines et feminas warantizabimus. Pro hac autem donatione et concessione mea dedit michi predictus Adam Trol premanibus ad magnum negotium meum vndecim solidos esterlingorum. Vt autem hec donatio et concessio mea rata stabilis inperpetuum permaneat presenti scripto sigillum meum apposui. Hiis testibus . Stephano Cornubiense . Nicholao le Reue[1] . Willelmo de Twigewurth' . Helya le teler . Ricardo de Wika . Iohanne le lorimer cum filio suo Ada le lorimer . Iordano le loker . Iohanne le bonere . Roberto le peintur . Heremon le hopere . Henrico le hopere [.] Luca Cornubiense . Roberto tinctore et aliis.

The endorsement *Herlone* . . . establishes the Gloucester location.

[1] **B** ends here with *et aliis,* having rendered *Reue* as *Dene.*

314. *Grant by John Ingulf to the brethren of St. Mary Magdalen, Dudstone, of his right in land (in Newland, Gloucester) and of 4d. annual rent from the land. (s. xiii^{med}, before c. 1260)*

A. G.C.L., 'Deeds and Seals', i, no. 25, fol. 15 (208 mm × 127 mm); seal on tag; green wax; obverse: very rubbed and chipped, round (*c.* 34 mm in diam.); image indiscernible; legend: +S' IOHANNIS . . .GULF . . .; no counterseal; endorsements: contra Ioh(ann)is Ingulf, (s. xiii^{med}); de terra de La Newelo'de (s. xiii^{med}); Carta Fratrum Sancte Marie Magdalene (s. xiii^{ex}?); Registratur (s. xiv^{ex} × s. xv^{in}); 10 (0 cancelled; uncertain hand and date); **B.** ibid. 'Reg. B', no. 547, p. 240.

Sciant presentes et futuri quod ego Ioh(anne)s Ingulf dedi concessi et quietum clamaui deo et fratribus sancte Marie Magdalene de Dudeston pro anima mea et pro animabus patris mei et matris mee in puram et perpetuam elemosinam totum ius et clammum meum quod habui uel aliquo modo habere potui sine aliquo retinemento ad opus meum uel heredum meorum in quadam parte terre me videlicet de terra illa que iacet inter terrram Willelmi Salice et terram meam. Preterea quietos clamaui eisdem fratribus . quatuor denarios annualis redditus annuatim percipiendos de predicta terra ad quatuor anni terminos videlicet ad festum sancti Michaelis vnum . denarium . Ad Natale domini vnum denarium . Ad festum sancte Marie in Martio vnum denarium . Ad festum sancti Iohannis Baptiste vnum denarium . sicut Iohannes Halfclarc inde recipere consueuit . Tenendam et habendam sibi et successoribus suis libere quiete et integre inperpetuum cum omnibus pertinentiis suis et eschaetis et cum omnibus aliis consuetudinibus que de predicta terra accidere possint saluo tunc regali seruitio quantum pertinet ad tantam partem terre. Ego predictus Iohannes et heredes mei predictis fratribus et successoribus suis dictam terram cum quatuor denariis annualis redditus contra omnes homines et feminas inperpetuum warentazabimus. In huius rei testimonium huic presenti scripto sigillum meum apposui. Hiis testibus Willelmo Capellano de Dudeston . Waltero de Bannebur' . Waltero Durant .

Willelmo clerico senescallo de Chirchisdun' . Henrico Clerico de Luttletun' et aliis.

Acta mentioning the donor's widow date from *c.* 1260 (Stevenson, nos. 514–16).

315. *Grant in fee and inheritance by Henry Kais to Thomas of Evesham of land with a messuage by the bridge in Gloucester for 10s. annual rent and 1 mark for entry, with restrictions on the right to devise, to sell, or to exchange. (1200 × c. 1228)*

G.C.L., 'Deeds and Seals', iv, no. 8, fol. 3 (154 mm × 119 mm); seal on tag; white wax, chipped, repaired; obverse: round (35 mm in diam.); large bust facing to the left; legend: +SIGILL. . . HE. . .I K. . .I. . .; no counterseal; endorsement: De terra versus pontes; Redditus .x s (s. xv).

Sciant presentes et futuri quod ego Henr(icus) Kais tradidi et concessi Thome de Euesham quamdam terram in Glouc' cum mesuagio videlicet illam que iacet inter terram Galfridi Geuelot et terram Helie Iudei uersus pontem tenendam et habendam de me et heredibus meis sibi et heredibus suis in feodo et hereditate inperpetuum libere et quiete . Reddendo inde annuatim michi uel heredibus meis decem solidos argenti pro omnibus seruitiis et demandis . Videlicet ad festum sancti Michaelis duos solidos . et sex denarios . ad Natiuitatem domini duos solidos . et sex denarios . ad festum sancte Marie Martialis duos solidos . et sex denarios . ad Natiuitatem sancti Iohannis Babtiste duos solidos et sex denarios. Ego autem predictus Henric(us) et heredes mei predicto Thome et heredibus suis predictam terram contra omnes homines et feminas warentizabimus. Pro hac concessione mea predictus Thomas michi dedit premanibus vnam marcam argenti de introitu. Predicta uero terra mensurata est per uisum legalium hominum et continet in parte anteriori quatuor uirgas vlnarias et tria quarteria cum pollice interposito . In profunditate uero viginti et quatuor virgas vlnarias et tria quarteria cum pollice interposito . In parte uero posteriori . quatuor virgas vlnarias et dimidiam cum pollice interposito. Edificia autem super inuenta apreciata fuerunt pro tres martis argenti . quando predictus Thomas predictam terram recepit. Vnde si aliquo casu contingente predictus Thomas uel heredes sui᷉ . predictam terram dimittere uoluerint᷉ . predictus Thomas vel heredes sui dabunt michi uel heredibus meis tres marcas argenti . et ita licebit illis illam resignare. Sciendum insuper quod predictus Thomas et heredes sui predictam terram nec uendent uel escambient sine consilio et assensu meo uel heredum meorum . Quia ego Henr(icus) et heredes mei propinquiores erimus omnium aliorum . hominum et feminarum si uolumus ad illam emendam uel escambiendam[.] Et vt hec concessio mei rata sit et stabilis illam presentis carte mee testimonio et sigilli mei appositione confirmaui. Hiis testibus . Ricardo filio Willelmi . et Mauricio palmario . tunc prepositis Glouc' . Mauricio filio Durandi . Henrico mercerio . Iohanne Ruffo . Nicholao de Crikelade . Galfrido mercerio . Alexandro Ruffo . Rocelino mercerio . Willelmo Pauone . Hugone lob[1] [.] Nicolao filio Nicolai . Ricardo socio suo . Osberto clerico et aliis.

Richard son of William and Maurice palmer were bailiffs of Gloucester 1200 × *c.* 1228 (*VCH Glos.* iv. 371). It is not certain that St. Peter's held this property before 1264.

---

[1] Reading uncertain.

316. *Sale by Isabel daughter of Ralph Kechel and her son William to Geoffrey Brewer of land given to her in free marriage by Richard burgess by the archdeacon's house (Gloucester) for 10d. annual rent to St. Peter's, Gloucester, and for 5 marks to Isabel and William, with 2½ marks of which they bought land from Adam son of Gunwhat. (1200 × c. 1228)*

G.R.O., GBR/J1/115 (170 mm × 87 mm), **Scribe 39** (below, Plate XXXIII); two seals on tags: 1) dark green wax; obverse: round (31 mm in diam.); a great bird of prey with tufted head piece (an eagle?) to the right; legend: +SIG'LLVM ISABEL KECHEL; no counterseal; inside surface of tag appears to contain some wording of a deed in a similar, poss. the same, hand; 2) dark green wax; obverse: round (31 mm in diam.); a lion rampant to the right; legend: +SIGILLVM: VVILL'MI: FILII GVNVVAH; no counterseal; endorsement: .ante domum archidiaconi (*c*. s. xiii^ex); cal. in Stevenson, no. 115.

Sciant tam presentes et futuri quod ego Ysabele filia Rad(ulfi) Kechel et Will(elmu)s filius meus assensu et uoluntate heredum nostrorum uendidimus et quiete clamauimus de nobis et heredibus nostris . Galfrido de Bracino et heredibus suis totam terram nostram cum pertinentiis suis . que iacet ante domum archidiaconi . scilicet inter terram Willelmi le secrestein et terram Thome filii Willelmi filii Vuenat . illam scilicet quam Ricardus burg' dedit michi Ysabele in liberum maritagium . habendam inperpetuum sibi et heredibus suis . reddendo inde annuatim abbatie Glouc' decem .denarios. argenti pro omni seruitio ad Hockedei. Ego autem predicta Ysabele et Will(elmu)s filius meus et heredes nostri predicto Galfrido et heredibus suis . predictam terram contra omnes homines et feminas warantizabimus. Pro hac enim uenditione et quieta clamantia nostra predictus Galfridus dedit nobis premanibus quinque marcas argenti . de quibus denariis emimus quamdam terram de Ada filio Gunwhat . scilicet pro duobus marcis et dimidia argenti. Et quia hanc venditionem nostram et quietam clamantiam uolumus ratam fore et inconcussam. eam presentis carte nostre testimonio et sigillorum nostrorum impressionibus confirmauimus. Hiis testibus . Ernisio decano Glouc' . Henrico fratre suo . Waltero Kadifor . Roberto diuite . Helya palmario . Willelmo Russel tunc prepositis Glouc' . Henrico Kais . Ricardo burg' . Philippo burg' . Willelmo le secrestein . Nicholao Muwet . Thoma filio Vuenat . Henrico fratre suo . Ada Boterel . Mauricio marescallo . Dauid de Celario . Rogero clerico . et multis aliis.

Geoffrey Brewer *c*. 1230 granted the land bought from Isabel to William of Samford, saving the landgabel owed to the abbot of St. Peter's (Stevenson, no. 286). As Stevenson observed, the second seal was evidently used by Isabel's son (p. 85 n.). Mention of the Gloucester bailiffs establishes the inclusive dates for the charter (*VCH Glos.* iv. 373).

317. *Grant by Richard of Kidderminster with the assent of Edith his wife to Nicholas son of Ivo of Newnham and to Ralph vintner of Gloucester of land in Gloucester which he received with his wife belonging to the fee of St. Peter's, Gloucester; annual rents of 2s. were payable to Richard and 5s. 6d. to St. Peter's; for the lease Nicholas and Ralph gave Richard 2 marks, to the Jews of Gloucester 20s. 3d. of his debt, to Richard Bat 3s. 4d. for an agreement with him, to Richard's*

wife 5s. for entry, and to Richard's son 6d; Richard was to give Nicholas and Ralph the deed for the property which he received from the abbey in court. (1200 × c. 1228; c. 1210?)

G.R.O., GBR/J1/137 (208 mm × 111 mm); seal on tag; dark green wax; rubbed; round (40 mm in diam.); a fleur-de-lis; legend: +S'GILL' RICARDI DE KIDEREMVNSTRIA; no counterseal; no endorsement; cal. in Stevenson, no. 137.

Sciant presentes et futuri quod ego Ricardus de Kideremunstria assensu et voluntate Edith vxoris mee et heredum meorum tradidi et concessi Nicholao filio Yuonis de Neweham et Radulfo vinitori de Glouc' quandam terram meam in Glouc' que est de feudo ecclesie beati Petri Glouc' videlicet illam quam cepi cum Edith vxore mea videlicet illam que iacet inter terram Willelmi Algar et venellam qua itur ad abbatiam . Tenendam et habendam de me et heredibus meis illis et heredibus suis in feudo et hereditate inperpetuum libere et quiete ab omni seruitio . Reddendo inde annuatim michi uel heredibus meis duos solidos argenti et ecclesie beati Petri de Glouc' quinque solidos et sex denarios pro omnibus seruitiis et demandis . videlicet ad Hokeday duodecim denarios michi uel heredibus meis . et ecclesie beati Petri duos solidos et nouem denarios . Et ad festum sancti Michaelis duodecim denarios michi uel heredibus meis et ecclesie beati Petri duos solidos et nouem denarios. Ego autem predictus Ric(ardus) et heredes mei predictis Nicholao et Radulfo predictam terram contra omnes homines et feminas warantizabimus . pro qua liberatione mea predicti Nicholas et Radulfus dederunt michi duas marcas argenti et Iudeis Glouc' viginti solidos et tres denarios de debito meo . et Ricardo Bat tres solidos et quatuor denarios de quadam conditione facta inter me et dictum Ricardum . et Edithe vxori mee quinque solidos de introitu . et Roberto filio meo sex denarios. Ego uero dictus Ric(ardus) predictis Nicholao et Radulfo cartam meam quam recepi de ecclesia beati Petri de predicta terra coram visu legalium uirorum tradam. Et ut hec conuentio mea rata sit et stabilis' illam presentis carte mee testimonio et sigilli mei appositione confirmaui . et fideliter vna cum predicta Editha vxore mea tenendam affidaui. Hiis testibus . Ricardo Rufo . Ricardo filio Willelmi . Iohanne Rufo et Ada Walense tunc prepositis de Glouc' . Iohanne draperio . Ada aurifabro . Alexandro aurifabro . Willelmo Algar . Waltero Slep . Iohanne Monitwot . Willelmo de Alecestr' . Roberto palmario . Reginaldo Sapiente . Elya palmario . Thoma Scriptore . Henrico damisele . Mauricio filio Durandi . et aliis.

John Rufus and Adam Welshman were bailiffs of Gloucester between 1200 and 1228 (*VCH Glos.* iv. 371).

318. *Grant in the form of a chirograph by John son of Henry of Leighton of Gloucester with the assent of his wife Matilda to Henry Ailive of land by Alvingate in the suburb of Gloucester for 2s. annual rent. (1263/4)*

G.C.L., 'Deeds and Seals, ix, no. 31, fol. 15 (168 mm [left] × 199 mm [foot]), **Scribe 46** (below, Plate XL); seal on tag; white wax stained green, cracked, chipped, repaired; obverse:

round (36 mm in diam.); eight spokes of a wheel without the rim; legend: +S'I. . .ANNIS: FIL'I: EN. . .I. . .: L. . .; no counterseal; endorsements: Henr' Eylliue (s. xiii²); versus Aluengat' (s. xiii²); Registratur (s. xiv^{ex} × s. xv^{in}); viii (s. xiv^{ex} × s. xv^{in}); in suburbio Glouc' (s. xvi?); X (uncertain date).

CYROGRAPHVM

Sciant presentes et futuri quod ego Iohannes filius Henrici de la Leyton' Glouc' assensu et bona voluntate Matildis matris mee dedi et concessi et hac presenti carta mea confirmaui Henrico Eylyue quandam particulam terre mee quam emi de Iohanne Eylyue cum quodam mesuagio desuper constructo . Iacentem versus Haluenghat' in suburbio Glouc' inter terram meam et vna parte . et terram dicti Henrici ex altera . et extendit se a regia strata super terram meam. Terra vero prefata per visum legalium virorum mensurata᷄. continet de latitudine in parte anteriori duas virgas domini regis vlnarias cum pollicibus interpositis et vnum quarterium . Retro vero᷄. eandem mensuram continet . In profunditate etiam continet quinque et decem[1] virgas domini regis vlnarias cum pollicibus interpositis . Habendam et tenendam de me et heredibus meis᷄. sibi et heredibus suis ac suis assignatis libere . solute . integre . quiete . bene . pacifice . iure hereditario inperpetuum . Reddendo annuatim inde michi et heredibus meis ipse et heredes sui seu sui assignati duos solidos argenti ad quatuor anni terminos . Videlicet ad Nathale domini sex denarios . ad Annuntiationem beate Marie sex denarios . ad Natiuitatem beati Iohannis Baptiste sex denarios . et ad festum sancti Michaelis sex denarios pro omnimodis seruitiis . sectis . querelis . consuetudinbus et demandis secularibus. Ego vero Iohannes et heredes mei prefato Henrico et heredibus suis siue suis assignatis memoratam terram cum dicto mesuagio et cum omnibus pertinentiis suis contra omnes mortales inperpetuum warentizabimus adquietabimus et defendemus. Quando vero prefatus Henricus prenotatam terram a me recepit᷄. edificium superappositum fuit per visum proborum virorum propter octodecim solidos sterlingorum. Et si ita contingat quod idem Henricus vel heredes sui siue assignati dictam terram casu aliquo mihi vel heredibus meis relinquere voluerint᷄. simile edificium aut pretium nobis restituent. In cuius rei testimonium presenti scripto ad modum cyrograpi inter nos confecto sigilla nostra sub alternatione apposuimus . Cuius vnam partem sub sigillo meo dicto Henrico tradidi munitam. Alteram vero partem sub sigillo suo penes me retinui signatam. Hiis testibus . Willelmo de Chelteham . Philippo le Spicer . tunc balliuis Glouc'[2] . Willelmo Cleymond . Iohanne Cornubiense . Willemo Bay . Willelmo Sage . Laurencio Trewemon . Willelmo Asseline . Gilberto de Hanleya . Alano de Thekebur' . Hugone Le bulcher . Iohanne clerico . et aliis.

This is the tenant's copy; its date is established by the attestation of the baliffs (*VCH Glos.* iv. 372).

---

[1]   *et decem* superscript possibly in the same hand; it is not added in the other half of the chirograph, no. 319.

[2]   **B** ends here with *et aliis*.

319. *The other half of no. 318. (1263/4)*

A. G.C.L., 'Deeds and Seals', vii, no. 4, fol. 3 (157 mm × 194 mm), **Scribe 46**; seal on tag, white wax; obverse: round (29 mm in diam.); image not clear; legend: +S' HENRICI . . .; no counterseal; endorsements: :Cyrographum de terra quam Ioh(anne)s de orto dedit. (*c.* 1263/4); Aluenegat' (s. xiii^{ex}); y (s. xiii^{ex}?); Registratur (s. xiv^{ex} × s. xv^{in}); v (s. xiv^{ex} × s. xv^{in}); . . . Alvengate in suburbio Glouc' (s. xvi?); **B**. ibid. 'Reg. B', no. 442, p. 196; no. 444, pp. 197–8.

This is the donor's copy of the lease. The first endorsement makes it possible that St. Peter's held the property by 1264.

320. *Confirmation by Geoffrey son of Maurice of Matson with the assent of his wife Matilda, his son Thomas, and his lord, Abbot Thomas, to Waleran chaplain of Bourton on the Water of a messuage with 4 acres in Saintbridge (in Abbot's Barton, by Gloucester) for 2s. annual rent and 14s. entry to Geoffrey, 12d. to Matilda, and 6d. to his son Thomas. (1199–1200)*

G.R.O., GBR/J1/88 (267 mm × 90 mm); seal on tag; white wax lacquered brown; fragment; obverse: oval (at middle, 30 mm; only meas. avail.); legend: +SIGIL'M GALF. . .RES. . .V. . .E; no counterseal; no endorsement; cal. in Stevenson, no. 88.

Sciant tam presentes quam futuri quod ego Galfrid(us) de Mett'esdune filius Mauricii de Mett'esd' . assensu et petitione Matill(dis) uxoris mee . et concessu Thome filii et heredis mei . et Thome Carbunel domini mei tunc temporis abbatis Glouc' . dedi et concessi et hac presenti carta ea confirmaui Walerano Capellano de Burctune pro seruitio et homagio suo illud messagium apud Sandebruge quod Iohannes de La Lane tenuit cum eisdem quatuor acris terre . quas idem .I. tenuit de me cum eodem mesagio . et cum omnibus aliis pertinentiis . Tenendum de me et heredibus meis sibi et heredibus suis in feudo et hereditate . libere . et quiete . integre . et honorifice . ab omnibus seruitiis . et secularibus exactionibus . et cum omnibus libertatibus . et liberis consuetudinibus . Annuatim reddendo michi et heredibus meis duos solidos ad duos terminos . Scilicet ad Annuntiationem sancte Marie . duodecim denarios . et ad sanctum Michaelem . duodecim denarios . pro omni seruitio . Tali conditione quod prefatus .W. faciat heredem suum de illo mesagio et de illis quatuor acris terre quemcu(m)que uoluerit absque clamo et omni calumpnia de me uel heredibus meis saluo redditu meo et heredum meorum . Sed ad locum religionis terram illam transferre non tenetur. Ego autem .G. prefatus et heredes mei .W. prefato et heredibus suis illam terram et illam conuentionem contra omnes homines et feminas warantizabimus pro qua conuentione et donatione prefatus .W. dedit michi de introitu illius terre quatuordecim solidos . et .M. uxori mee . duodecim denarios . et .T. heredi meo sex denarios anno primo regni Iohannis regis. Vt autem hec mea carta et donatio rata sit et inconcussa permaneat imperpetuum' fide mea afidaui et sigillo meo confirmaui. Hiis testibus . Iohanne Decano Glouc' . Ernisio capellano . Henrico capellano de sancta Trinitate . magistro Edmundo . magistro Thoma . Simone de Matt'esdun' . Thoma de Matt'esd' . Waltero Thoki . Galfrido de Liletun . Philippo Carbunel . Osberto de La graue . Mauricio de Snedha' . Rogero Burdin . et multis aliis.

321. *Confirmation by Simon lord of Matson to William son of William Le Budel of 1 acre by Saintbridge (in Abbot's Barton, by Gloucester) for the annual rent of one pair of gloves or 1d. and 20s. for entry. (c. 1228 × 40)*

G.C.L., 'Deeds and Seals', iv, no. 26, fol. 13 (173 mm × 117 mm), **Scribe 43**; seal on tag, green wax; obverse: round (*c.* 25 mm in diam.); a bird with wing(s) extended to the right; legend: + SIGIL' SIM. . .IS DE . . .AT. . .SDVN'; no counterseal; no endorsement.

Sciant presentes et futuri quod ego Simon dominus de Matresdunn' dedi et concessi et hac presenti carta mea confirmaui . Willelmo filio Willelmi Le Budel . pro homagio et seruitio suo . vnam acram terre . iuxta Sondebrug' . Scilicet . sex seillones . cum pertinentiis suis . que iacent inter terram Rogeri Bancnotte . de Wuttunn' . et regale iter . Tenendam et habendam de me et heredibus meis . sibi et heredibus suis . libere . et quiete . integre . inperpetuum . Sine clamo et calumpnia . et omni exactione quod possit per me uel per heredes meos aliquo modo euenire . Reddendo inde annuatim michi uel heredibus meis . vnum par cyrotecarum. uel vnum denarium ad Pasca pro omnibus seruitiis et demandis. Pro hac autem donatione et concessione mea᷇. predictus Willelmus dedit michi viginti solidos sterlingorum de introitu . et ipse et heredes suis quietum clamauerunt me . Simone(m) . et heredes meos . de omnibus calumpniis terre . et demandis inperpetuum. Et ego sepe dictus Simon et heredes mei predicto Willelmo et heredibus suis . siue asignatis suis predictam terram cum pertinentiis suis . contra omnes homines et feminas inperpetuum warentazabimus . et aquietabimus. Et vt hec mea donatio et concessio . firma et stabilis inperpetuum permaneat᷇. presens scriptum sigillo meo sigillatum᷇. predicto Willelmo᷇. coram legalibus hominibus tradidi. Hiis testibus . Petro de Eggewurþe . magistro Waltero Scriptore . Thoma de Matresdunn' . Willelmo . Geraldo . Ernulfo filiis Sim(onis) de Matresdunn' . Waltero Pain . et . aliis.

Without an endorsement that can be dated, there is no certainty that St. Peter's held this land before 1264; the phrase *coram legalibus hominibus tradidi* suggests that the transaction occurred in the Gloucester borough court. On the ends of the tag are portions of script which are illegible and cannot be dated because only portions of the letters have survived. The parchment on which they were written had been cut into strips. On the right tag end the top of an early 13th-century *M* survives. Saintbridge belonged to Abbot's Barton (*Cart. Glouc.* ii, no. 768; see also *PNG*, ii. 141).

322. *Grant in fee and inheritance by Thomas son of Geoffrey of Matson to Walter son of Gilbert of Dickley of ½ virgate at Sneedham for 4s. annual rent. (c. 1230)*

A. G.C.L., 'Deeds and Seals', x, no. 2, fol. 1 (210 mm × 87 mm); seal on tag; white wax laquered; obverse: round (28 mm in diam.); an eagle with wings extended facing right with its head turned to the left; legend: +S' THOME: DE MATRESDONE; no counterseal; endorsements: Carta Th(ome) filii Galfridi de Mattesdon' de dimidia virgata terre in Snedham. pro. qua. iiii. s'. (s. xiii^ex); Registratur (s. xiv^ex × s. xv^in); **B**. ibid. 'Reg. B', no. 709, p. 305.

Sciant presentes et futuri quod ego Thom(as) filius Galfridi de Mat'esdon' dedi et concessi . et hac presenti carta mea confirmaui Waltero filio Gileberti de Dickeleya pro seruitio et homagio suo illam dimidiam virgatam terre mee de Snedham quam pater suus tenuit . Tenendam et habendam de me . et de heredibus meis illi . et heredibus suis . in feudo et hereditate . libere . et integre . cum omnibus pertinentiis suis . et cum omnibus libertatibus suis et liberis consuetudinibus suis . Reddendo inde annuatim michi uel heredibus meis quatuor solidos sterlingorum ad duos terminos anni . videlicet ad sanctam Mariam Martialem duos solidos . et ad sanctum Michaelem duos solidos pro omnibus seruitiis et demandis . saluo seruitio domini regis quantum pertinet ad illam dimidiam virgatam terre. Pro hac autem donatione et confirmatione mea predictus Walterus dedit michi dimidiam marcam argenti. Et ego predictus Thom(as) et heredes mei predicto Waltero . et heredibus suis illam predictam dimidiam virgatam terre cum pertinentiis suis contra omnes homines et feminas imperpetuum warantizabimus . et de omnibus seruitiis et demandis acquietabimus . saluo seruitio domini regis vt predictum est. Et quia volo quod hec mea donatio et concessio rata sit et stabilis . hoc presens scriptum sigilli mei impressione confirmaui. Hiis testibus . Symone de Matresdon' . Filippo et Arnulfo filiis suis[1] . Filippo filio Ade . et Willelmo fratre suo . Mauricio de Snedham . Waltero filio suo . Galfrido de la graua . Filippo de Hocholt . Thoma de Hauekescu'b' [.] Rogero de Kinem'esb'r' . Willelmo clerico . et aliis.

[1] **B** ends here with *et aliis*.

323. *Confirmation by Henry Mercer, a tenant of St. Peter's, Gloucester, to William cheesemonger of land on Feet Lane (Gloucester) for annual rents of 1d. to Henry, 1d. to the king, and 1½d. to the abbot of Gloucester and 6 marks for entry. (1200 × c. 1228; prob. c. 1228)*

G.C.L., 'Deeds and Seals', vi, no. 28, fol. 15 (174 mm × 176 mm); seal on tag, dark green wax, chipped; obverse: round (31 mm in diam.); a fleur-de-lis; legend: + SIGILL' HEN. . .ICI LE MERCER; no counterseal; endorsements: W. le Glouar (s. xiii); Henrici Le m[erce]r de terra . . .[1] (uncertain date); Willelmi Le Chesmongre (s. xiii^{med}); A (s. xiii^2); Caps(ula) .xviii. de laicis tenuris. (s. xiii^{ex} × s. xiv^{in}); Fotelone; Isabella Stowd[2] quod tenuit id' ob' advok[3] [;] Registratur (s. xiv × s. xv^{in}); .ii.^{a} (uncertain date); sc(ribitur) (s. xv^{in}).

Notum sit vniuersis quod ego Henric(us) le Mercer tradidi et concessi et hac presenti carta confirmaui Willelmo chesmongere quandam terram meam in Fetelone illam scilicet que iacet iuxta terram abbatis Glouc' et terram elemosinarii [.] Habendam et tenendam de me et heredibus meis sibi et heredibus suis uel asignatis suis libere et quiete in feudo et hereditate inperpetuum reddendo inde annuatim ipse uel heredes uel assignati sui michi et heredibus meis vnum denarium argenti ad Hocday . et domino regi vnum denarium . ad eundem terminum . et abbati sancti Petri Glouc' . tres obolos ad eundem terminum pro omnibus seruitiis et demandis secularibus ad dictam terram spectantibus. Pro qua concessione mea dictus Willelmus dedit michi sex marcas argenti ad magnum negotium meum de introitu. Terra autem mensurata per visum virorum legalium habet in fronte versus viam domini regis .xx.^{ti} tres ulnas domini regis . et tres pollices cum pollice interposito . Media vero pars habet de latitudine .xxii.^{ti} ulnas domini regis et tria[4] quarteria et dimidiam[5] cum pollice interposito . Posteriora uero pars apud austrum habet de latitudine .xxiiii.^{or} ulnas domini regis et vnum quarterium et tres pollices . In profunditate habet quinquaginta et vnam virgam domini regis et vnum quarterium cum pollice interposito. Et ego dictus Henricus Le merc(er) et heredes mei totam dictam terram dicto Willelmo et heredibus uel assignatis suis contra omnes homines et feminas imperpetuum warentizabimus et de omnibus seruitiis pro predicto redditu aquietabimus. Et quia uolo quod concessio mea perpetue firmitatis robur obtineat huic presenti scripto sigillum meum apposui. Hiis testibus . Ricardo Burgensi . Thoma Oye . tunc prepositis . Hereberto fratre . H(e)nrici merc(er) . Waltero Hoch . Ricardo Hoch . Mauricio Iu'ien'^{6} . Nicholao Gunt' . Holekin tinte . Ricardo filio Katerine . Laurencio . et aliis.

Although the bailiffs' names establish the charter's general limiting dates, the scribe employed suspension signs more characteristic of the following three decades.

^{1} Wording illegible with ultra-violet light.
^{2} Reading uncertain.
^{3} Reading uncertain.
^{4} *tres* in MS.
^{5} *demidiam* in MS. ^{6} Reading uncertain.

324. *Sale and quitclaim by Rocelin Mercer to Thomas parson of St. John's church, Gloucester, of land by Alvingate (Gloucester), of which one part belonged to the abbot of Gloucester's fee and the other to the earl of Gloucester's fee; Thomas paid 5½ marks to Rocelin and 12d. to his son Thomas and was to owe ¼d. a year to the earl of Gloucester and 2d. a year to the abbot of Gloucester. (c. 1216 × 20)*

A. G.C.L., 'Deeds and Seals', viii, no. 21, fol. 12 (181 mm × 82 mm), **Scribe 31**; seal on tag; green wax, chipped, repaired; obverse: round (33 mm in diam.); a large fleur-de-lis; legend: . . .IL' ROCELINI: MERCER. . .; no counterseal; endorsements: Contra Roceli[num] Le mercer (s. xiii?); versus Eluenegat' x^1 (s. xiii^{ex} × s. xiv?); **B**. ibid. 'Reg. B', no. 447, p. 198.

Sciant presentes et futuri quod ego Rocelin(us) Le mercer dimisi . uendidi et quietam clamaui de me et de heredibus meis Thome persone ecclesie sancti Iohannis Glouc' totam terram meam . videlicet que iacet inter Iohannis Bay et terram Galfridi Pomeray uersus Heluene gate . vna quedam pars est de feodo abbatis Glouc' et altera pars de feodo comitis Glouc' . cum omnibus pertinentiis sine aliquo retenemento . Habendam et tenendam sibi inperpetuum uel cui eam assignare uoluerit libere et quiete . Reddendo inde annuatim pro omni seruitio et omnibus demandis comiti Glouc' .i. quadrantem pro parte illa que est de feodo ipsius comitis . et duos denarios abbati Glouc' ad Hockeday pro parte illa que est de feudo ipsius abbatis[.] Hanc autem uenditionem et quietam clamacionem uersus omnes homines et feminas ego et heredes mei dicto Thome et cuicu(m)que predictam terram assignauerit inperpetuum warantizabimus. Et pro hac uenditione et quieta clamatione et warantisatione dictus Thomas dedit michi quinque marcas et dimidiam . et Thome filio meo .xii. denarios. In cuius rei testimonium perpetuum huic scripto sigillum meum apposui . et sepedicto Thome persone tradidi. Hiis testibus . Gilberto Capellano . Adam Golde^2 .

Henrico Le mercer . Radulfo et Iohanne filiis suis . Iohanne Bay . Odone Ruffo . Henrico Cays . Ada Botild' . Rogero Sewy . Hugone Asse . et multis aliis.

Scribe 31 who wrote this charter was active in 1216; Thomas of Matson was rector of St. John's, Gloucester, *c.* 1220 (Stevenson, nos. 164, 190).

[1] Possible endorsement by another, later hand.
[2] **B** ends here with *et multis aliis.*

325. *Grant by Richard de Mewissint' son of Richard to Hathewy of Ledbury* ham *of 6 acres with houses in Ockeridge (Herefs.) for 2s. annual rent, 2s. entry, a pair of cordovan boots for his wife, and an undershirt for his heir. (c. 1200)*

H.C.L., no. 2201 (*c.* 221 mm × *c.* 65 mm); slit for tag on turn-up; tag and seal missing; endorsements: sc(ri)bitur (s. xiii[ex]); Alkruge (s. xiv[ex]?).

Sciant presentes et futuri quod ego Ric(ardus) de Mewissint' filius Ricardi dedi et concessi in feodo et hereditate Haþewy de hamma de Ledeb'r' pro homagio et seruitio suo sex acras terre cum domibus quas Yselia tenuit in dote in willa de Alcr' . Habendas et tenendas dicto Haþewy et heredibus suis de me et heredibus meis libere et quiete et integre ab omni seruitio consuetudine et exactione . Reddendo inde annuatim michi et heredibus meis ipse et heredes sui duos solidos ad quatuor vsuales per episcopatum Herefordensem terminos . pro omni seruitio saluo regali seruitio quantum pertinet ad terram tenementi. Pro qua concessione et donatione mea dedit michi predictus Haþewy duos solidos in gersum[a] et vxori mee duas[1] botas de cordiwano et heredi meo vnam camisiam. Et ego Ric(ardus) et heredes mei debemus warantizare supradictam terram cum domibus predictis prefato Haþewy et heredibus suis contra omnes viros et feminas. Quod quia firmum et stabile volo permanere' presenti id carta et sigilli mei inpressione confirmare curaui. Hiis testibus . Alano de Walint' . Willelmo de Alcr' . Waltero Rudduc . Ricardo falkenario . Eluredo pistore . Willelmo de Meuissint' . Alexandro mareskallo . Ricardo Coco . Adam de Stret' . et multis aliis.

St. Peter's may not have held this property before 1264.

[1] *vnas* in MS.; an error for *duas.*

326. *Grant in fee and inheritance by Richard of Hyde to William son of Joan of his part of 1 acre of meadow belonging to Monkhide (in Yarkhill, Herefs.) for ½d. annual rent and 13s. in advance. (s. xiii[med])*

A. G.C.L., 'Deeds and Seals', viii, no. 17, fol. 9 (229 mm × 82 mm), **Scribe 47** (below, Plate XLI); seal on tag; white wax stained green, rubbed, chipped; obverse: oval (32 mm × *c.* 26 mm); possible intaglio; image indiscernible; legend: + . . . RICARDI: DE: HIDA; no counterseal; endorsement: Hida (s. xiii[med]), **Hand s** (below, Plate XLIVj); Carta Ric(ard)i de hida[;] Registratur (s. xiv[ex] × s. xv[in]); **B.** ibid. 'Reg. B', no. 130, p. 46.

Sciant presentes et futuri quod ego Ricardus de Hyda dedi et concessi et hac presenti carta mea confirmaui Willelmo filio Ioane pro seruitio suo et pro tresdecim solidis argenti quos michi dedit premanibus totam partem meam vnius acre prati cum Rosa child quod iacet in Vildenebrugesmedue inter pratum Willelmi Godefray' ex vna parte et pratum sacriste et Willelmi Godefrai ex altera parte . et extendit ex vno capite uersus Vildenebruge . et ex alio capite uersus hayciam sacriste . Habendam et tenendam de me et heredibus meis sibi et heredibus suis vel suis assignatis . vel cuicunque in sanitate vel egritudine voluerit dare . legare [.] vendere vel assignare salua religione et Iudayismo . In feodo et hereditate . libere . et quiete . integre . bene . et in pace cum omnibus libertatibus . Reddendo inde annuatim michi et heredibus meis ipse et heredes sui vel sui assignati vnum obolum videlicet ad festum beati Michaelis . pro omnibus seruitiis [.] exactionibus . consuetudinibus . querelis . sectis curiarum . wardis . releuiis . herietis . auxiliis . et demandis omnimodis que de terra exeunt vel exire poterunt saluo regali seruitio ad tantum tenementum pertinente. Ego vero Ricardus de Hyda et heredes mei predicto Willelmo et heredibus suis vel suis assignatis totam predictam partem meam predicti prati sicut in singulis articulis prenotatum est contra omnes homines et feminas Cristianos inperpetuum warantizabimus et defendemus. Et quia volo quod hec mea donatio et concessio rata sit et stabilis huic presenti scripto sigillum meum apposui. Hiis testibus . Willelmo de Solle . Iohanne de Sewalle[1] . Petro Le Wyte . Thoma de Wyke . Hugone de molindino de Weston' . Rogero de Sewalle . Radulpho palmario de Charcull' et aliis.

For the association with Monkhide, see G.C.L., 'Reg. B', fol. v verso.

[1] **B** ends here with *et aliis multis.*

327. Grant in fee and inheritance by Robert son of Richard of Hyde to William son of Joan of Hyde of two butts of land near Yarkhill (Herefs.) for two roots of ginger annually and 7s. in advance. (c. 1230)

G.C.L., 'Seals & Deeds', i, no. 12, fol. 7 (187 mm × 110 mm), **Scribe 47**; seal on tag, white wax, fragment, round, chipped; obverse: an eight-pointed rosette; legend: . . . RI. . . DE HIDA; reverse: possible counterseal, but illegible; endorsement: .Hyda. (s. xiii^{med}), **Hand s**.

Sciant presentes et futuri quod ego Rob(er)tus filius Ricardi de Hyda dedi et concessi et hac presenti carta mea confirmaui Willelmo filio Ioane de Hyda pro seruitio suo et pro septem solidis argenti quos michi dedit premanibus duas buttas terre mee iacentes in Stanbald inter terram Willelmi de Solle et gardinum Ioane de Hyda et extendentes se usque terram persone de Varcullne . Habendas et tenendas de me et heredibus meis sibi et heredibus suis vel suis assignatis . vel cuicunque in sanitate vel egritudine . voluerit . dare . legare . vendere . vel assignare sine aliqua contradictione mei vel heredum meorum . In feodo et hereditate . libere et quiete . integre . bene . et in pace . cum omnibus libertatibus . Reddendo inde annuatim mihi et heredibus meis ipse et heredes sui vel sui assignati duos rascinos gingeberis . scilicet ad festum beati Michaelis . pro omnibus seruitiis . exactionibus . consuetudinibus . sectis curie . wardis . releuiis . herietis. auxiliis et demandis que de terra exeunt vel exire poterunt. Ego vero Rob(er)tus et heredes mei dicto Willelmo et heredibus suis vel suis assignatis predictas duas buttas terre cum pertinentiis suis contra omnes homines et feminas in perpetuum warantizabimus. Et quia volo quod hec mea donatio et concessio rata sit et stabilis huic presenti carte sigillum meum apposui. Hiis testibus . Willelmo de Solle . Iohanne de Sewalle . Rogero de Sewalle . Petro le Wyte . Thoma de Wyke . Radulfo palmerio . Rogero Ianci . et aliis.

Portions of script, illegible because they have been cut through, appear in the top right and left corners of the parchment. This charter relates to Monkhide: see G.C.L., 'Reg. B', fol. v verso.

328. *Confirmation by Nicholas Morin to Richard White of Gloucester of a half croft in Hyde (by Gloucester) for 5 marks to acquit his debt to the Jews of Gloucester and ½d. annual rent; in addition Nicholas acquitted Richard of all heriots, wardships, suits of court, reliefs, and all other escheats. (1230 × 60)*

A. G.C.L., 'Deeds and Seals', vii, no. 10, fol. 5 (202 mm × 146 mm); seal on tag: dark green wax, obverse: round (28 mm in diam.); a fleur-de-lis; legend: +S': NICOLA. . .: MORIN; no counterseal; endorsement: Carta Nicholai Moryn de terra in La Hyda (s. xiv[in]); Registratur (s. xiv[ex] × s. xv[in]); B. ibid. 'Reg. B', no. 697, pp. 300–1.

Sciant presentes et futuri quod ego Nicholaus Morin dedi et concessi et hac presenti carta mea confirmaui Ricardo Albo de Glouc' pro homagio et seruitio suo pro quinque marcis sterlingorum quas michi dedit ad debita mea aquietanda uersus Iudeos Glouc' . medietatem crofti que extendit a prato molendini Morin vsque ad Goswitelon' . Scilicet illam medietatem ex parte australi uersus terram abbatis Glouc' . et medietatem terre que iacet apud la sondputte ex parte orientali que extendit del broc vsque ad semitam que iacet iuxta terram fratrum sancti Bartholomei . Tenendam et habendam sibi et heredibus suis vel assignatis suis de me et heredibus meis libere et quiete integre cum fossatis et medietate salicium assistentium et cum omnibus aliis pertinentiis suis [.] Reddendo inde annuatim michi et heredibus meis vnum obolum ad festum sancti Michaelis pro omnibus seruitiis et secularibus demandis ad me vel heredes meos pertinentibus inperpetuum saluo regali seruitio quantum pertinet ad tantum tenementum. Preterea concessi predicto Ricardo et heredibus suis vel assignatis suis singulis sibi succedentibus quod per predictum redditum quieti sint inperpetuum de herietis [.] wardis . sectis et releuiis et de omnimodis aliis eschaetis que de terra exeunt vel exire poterunt in posterum. Ego uero Nicholaus et heredes mei predicto Ricardo et heredibus suis vel assignatis suis predictas terras cum omnibus pertinentiis suis inperpetuum contra omnes gentes warantizabimus et de omnibus seruitiis sectis et demandis aquietabimus saluo regali seruitio vt predictum est. Et quia volo quod hec mea donatio . concessio et warantizatio perpetue firmitatis robur optineant presentem cartam sigilli mei appositione confirmaui. Hiis testibus . Iohanne Draperio . Thoma persona de sancto Iohanne[1] . Waltero Fouel . Rogero Ace . Waltero de Tekebur' . Rogero de Nortwich [.] Roberto de Tekebur' . Willelmo vaginatore . Iohanne de Chiu[2] et aliis.

Identifiable sites mentioned in the charter make it clear that the half croft, located according to the endorsement at *La Hyda*, was at Hyde by Gloucester.

[1] **B** ends here with *et aliis.*
[2] Reading uncertain.

329. *Confirmation by Philip of Ockold to William le Riche of Sneedham of his land at* Fuldhome *for an annual rent of ½d. or a pair of gloves of that value and ½ mark for entry. (c. s. xiii^{in})*

A. G.C.L., 'Deeds and Seals', iii, no. 9, fol. 5 (169 mm × 82 mm), **Scribe 41**; seal on tag: white wax stained brown, chipped, repaired; obverse: round (30 mm in diam.); a large fleur-de-lis: legend: S' PHILIPPI DE OCHOLTTE; no counterseal; endorsements: Fulehom (s. xiii^{med}), **Hand s**; Carta Philippi de Ocholte (s. xiii^{ex}); Registratur (s. xiv^{ex} × s. xv^{in}); **B**. ibid. 'Reg. B', no. 705, p. 303.

Sciant presentes et futuri quod ego Philipp(us) de Hocholte dedi . et concessi . et hac presenti carta mea confirmaui Willelmo le Riche de Snedham' pro seruitio et homagio suo totam illam particulam terre mee de Fuldhome . que iacet inter terram Walteri Crikefedt . et Ricardi Sing' . Tenendam . et habendam de me . et de heredibus meis . illi et heredibus suis . uel suis assignatis . in feudo . et hereditate . libere . quiete . et integre . Reddendo inde annuatim michi . uel heredibus meis vnum obolum . ad Pasca . uel vnum par cirotecarum ad valorem vnius oboli . pro omnibus seruitiis . sectis . consuetudinibus . et secularibus demandis saluo seruitio domini regis pro tanto tenemento. Pro hac autem donatione et confirmatione mea . predictus Willelmus dedit michi de introitu dimidiam marcam argenti. Et ego predictus .P. et heredes mei . predicto Willelmo et heredibus suis . uel suis assignatis illam particulam terre contra omnes homines et feminas imperpetuum warantizabimus. In cuius uero rei testimonium hoc presens scriptum sigilli mei impressione confirmaui. Hiis testibus . domino Symone de Matresdone . domino Guiberto de Rues[1] . Thoma de Matresdon' . Willelmo Kerald . Galfrido de la graue . Thoma de fabroca . Waltero de Snedham' et aliis.

[1] **B** ends here with *et aliis*.

330. *Grant and quitclaim by Robert Page mercer of Gloucester to Richard Francis of Gloucester of all his right to lands in the girdlery (possibly Mercer Row), Gloucester, held formerly by his brother John from Dionisia of Devonshire, for an advance of 40s. (1258)*

A. G.C.L., 'Deeds and Seals', vii, no. 35, fol. 21 (183 mm × 132 mm), **Scribe 44**; slit for tag on foot; tag and seal missing; endorsements: Carta de zonaria (s. xiii^{med}), **Hand r** (below, Plate XLIVi); zon[ar]ia (1258+); Registratur (s. xiv^{ex} × s. xv^{in}); **B**. ibid. 'Reg. B', no. 1056 (1055), pp. 459–60.

Vniuersis Cristi fidelibus presens scriptum visuris uel audituris Rob(er)tus Page mercenarius Glouc' salutem eternam in domino. Noueritis me remisisse et inperpetuum quieteclamasse Ricardo Fraunceys de Glouc' pro quadraginta solidis argenti quos michi premanibus pacauit‹ totum ius et clamium quod habui uel habere potui in totis terris cum earumdem pertinentiis in zonaria Glouc' quas Ioh(ann)es Page frater meus tenuit aliquando de Dionisia le Deueneys . Ita quod ego et heredes mei exclusi simus inperpetuum ab omnimodo iure et iuris clamio quod in predictis terris cum earumdem pertinentiis habuimus uel habere possumus inposterum. Et si quocumque tempore me uel heredes meos contra predictum Ricardum uel heredes suos seu assignatos de predictis terris cum earumdem pertinentiis fatigationem uel exactionem mouere contigerit. ad hoc eisdem teneri concedimus et volumus obligari . quod mox eisdem teneamur in solutione quadraginta marcarum nomine clari et puri debita. Nec volumus quod aliquod remedium quodcumque fuerit uel esse poterit nobis contra predicta possit prodesse . et eidem Ricardo et suis in aliquo obesse. Et ad maiorem securitatem et euidentiorem cartam quam predictus Iohannes frater meus de predictis terris de feffamento habuit. eidem liberaui. In huius rei testimonium scripto presenti sigillum meum apposui. Hiis testibus . Rogero le Enueyse . Willelmo de Chiltenham tunc balliuis Glouc' . Willelmo de Toek'[1] . Luca cornubiense . Iohanne Simund . Alexandro del Broc . Roberto de Putteleg . Willelmo de Sondhurste . Iohanne Payn . Hugone le Enueyse . Ricardo clerico . et aliis.

The names of the bailiffs establish the date (*VCH Glos.* iv. 372).

[1]   **B** ends here with *et aliis.*

331. *Lease in the form of a chirograph by John Poli of Gloucester to Nicholas of Hereford of land in Gloucester on South(gate) Street, which John held as tenant of St. Peter's, Gloucester, and on which his stone house stood, for eight years from 20 May 1238, for 20s. 6d. in advance and 32d. annual rent. (c. 1238)*

G.C.L., 'Deeds and Seals', iii, no. 16, fol. 10 (219 mm [left] × 171 mm [foot]); fragment of tag on turn-up; seal missing; endorsement: Vacat (s. xiv).

C Y R . . . G R A P H U M

Notum sit vniuersis quod ego Ioh(annes) Poli de Glouc' . tradidi et concessi Nicolao de Herford' . vnam terram meam in Glouc' . quam teneo de abbate de Glouc' . qui iacet infra terram meam in platea australi de Glouc' iuxta terram ipsius Nicolai . super quam domus mea lapidea sita est . Tenendam et habendam . sibi et heredibus suis . uel assignatis suis . de me et heredibus meis . ad firmam . Libere et quiete integre cum domo lapidea et puteo et cum omnibus aliis pertinentiis suis et edificiis . quantum teneo de feudo abbatis Glouc' . ibidem . videlicet a festo sancti Auberti regis . anno regni domini regis Henrici filii regis Iohannis . vicesimo secundo . usque ad terminum octo annorum sequentium . pro viginti solidis et sex . denariis argenti . quos michi premanibus pacauit . Et soluendo inde annuatim michi et heredibus meis . triginta et duos denarios . ad duos terminos anni . pro omnibus seruitiis et demandis . scilicet ad Hockeday sexdecim denarios . et ad festum sancti Michaelis sexdecim denarios. Et si ita contigerit quod post predictum terminum . uel infra predictum terminum terram illam uel domum uendere uel in uadiare voluero . uel alicui in feodo tradere ipse Nicolaus et heredes sui . siue assignati sui . propinquiores erint ad illam terram uel domum eamdem[1] uel altero modo recipiendam quam aliquis alius . Et pro tali pretio. sicut aliquis alius michi certissime et legaliter offerret. Et quicquid ipse Nicolaus uel heredes sui siue assignati sui inposuerint per concessum meum et uisum meum . in sustentatione et commodatione[2] edificiorum. ad finem predicti termini satisfaciam eis plenarie . uel . ipsi omnia que inposuerint sine contraditione asportabunt. Et ego uero predictus Iohannes et heredes mei predicto Nicolao et heredibus suis siue assignatis suis . predictam terram et domum cum pertinentiis suis . usque ad finem predicti termini contra omnes homines et feminas warantizabimus . et de omnibus seruitiis aquietabimus. Hanc uero concessionem et conuentionem fide mea affidaui . et presens scriptum inter nos diuisum sigillo meo confirmaui. Hiis testibus . Iohanne Longe . Waltero Haym . Willelmo Le Loker . Willelmo de Bocklond . Iohanne debonhure[3] . et Willelmo de Sumery et aliis.

'St. Aubert' is Ethelbert, king of the East Angles, who was venerated at Hereford.

[1] *eamdam* in MS.   [2] Reading uncertain.   [3] Reading uncertain.

332. *Grant by John son of Silvester Poli of Gloucester to Nicholas of Hereford, burgess of Gloucester, of land on Longsmith Street (Gloucester) belonging to the abbot of Gloucester's fee and formerly held by David Dunning and of another parcel of land of which Nicholas had possession earlier, for 2s. annual rent and 2 marks for making the grant, with the promise of compensation should John fail to pay the rent due to the abbot. (s. xiii^med^)*

G.C.L., 'Deeds and Seals', ix, no. 38, fol. 20 (225 mm × 168 mm); seal on tag; white wax stained dark green; obverse: round (33 mm in diam.); a large fleur-de-lis; legend: +SIGILLVM. IOHANNIS. POLI; no counterseal; endorsements: carta Nycholai de Herford' de terra Iohannis Poly in vico fabrorum. (*c*. s. xiii ex); Smyzthstr'te [;]; Registratur (s. xiv^ex^ × s. xv^in^).

Sciant presentes et futuri quod ego Ioh(annes) filius Siluest(e)r Poly de Glouc' . tradidi et concessi Nicholao de He'eford' . burgensi de Glouc' . vnam partem terre meę . que est de feudo abbatis Glouc' . et iacet in vico fabrorum iuxta terram abbatis Glouc' . quam Dauid' Dunning quondam tenuit . que continet de latitudine in anteriori parte uersus vicum . quinque uirgas domini regis vlnarias . cum pollice interposito . et vnum quarterium . et duos pollices . In posteriori uero parte continet de latitudine totidem . In profunditate continet decem uirgas et dimidiam cum pollice interposito . et dimidium quarterium . et duos pollices. Preterea concessi et pro me et pro heredibus meis hac presenti carta confirmaui . dicto Nicholao de H'eford' . vnam aliam partem terram quam tenui de eodem feudo eiusdem abbatis de Glouc' . que iacet iuxta predictam terram . et iuxta terram quam Willelmus de Boclonde tenuit de priore Lanton' extra Glouc' . In quam ipse Nicholaus prius habuit ingressum per Iohannem de Wydicumb' virum Edithe Poly matris mee . Tenendas et habendas illas duas parcellas terre sibi et heredibus suis . uel assignatis suis . de me et heredibus meis . libere . et quiete . integre . cum medietate putei . et cum edificiis et omnibus aliis pertinentiis . suis . in feudo et hereditate . Reddendo inde annuatim michi et heredibus meis duos solidos . ad duos terminos . videlicet ad Hockeday. duodecim denarios . et ad festum sancti Michaelis duodecim denarios . pro omnibus seruitiis et demandis. Ego uero predictus Ioh(annes) Poly et heredes mei warantizabimus predictas parcellas terre cum medietate putei et cum omnibus aliis pertinentiis . suis . predicto Nicholao et heredibus suis uel assignatis suis . contra omnes homines et feminas . Et de londogabulo et redditu abbatis Glouc' aquietabimus. Et si aliquo casu contigerit quod ego predictus Ioh(annes) uel heredes mei non soluerimus redditum abbatis Glouc' . ad terminos statutos . et ipse Nicholaus . vel heredes sui uel assignati sui . uexati et districti sint ad soluendum per terram suas per defaltam nostram . concessi pro me et pro heredibus meis ut ipse Nicholaus et heredes sui uel assignati sui intrent in aliam partem terre meę de feudo ipsius abbatis Glouc' . supra quam domus lapidea sita est . et illam teneant et habeant cum domibus et edificiis et omnibus aliis pertinentiis suis . sine aliqua vexatione uel aliquo impedimento per me uel per heredes meos quousque eis satisfactum fuerit plenarie de toto dampno quod pro defalta nostra habuerint . et de toto redditu quem pro nobis pacauerint . et antequam terram illam michi uel heredibus meis reddant uel in aliqua curia de terra illa respondeant. Pro hac autem traditione . concessione . confirmatione . et conuentione mea predictus Nicholaus dedit michi duas marcas argenti. Quod quia uolo ratum fieri presentem cartam sigilli mei impressione confirmaui. Hiis testibus . Ricardo de Celario . Nicholao Cumiock . Ada Longo . Willelmo le Loker . Waltero Haym . Iohanne Longo . Roberto filio Eue . Willelmo de Boclonde . Willelmo de Sum'y . et aliis.

The names in the witness-list argue for the proximity of the charter's issue to nos. 333–4, especially no. 333.

333. *Grant by John son of Silvester Poli of Gloucester to Nicholas of Hereford, burgess of Gloucester, of land with buildings on Longsmith Street (Gloucester) and another parcel, for 2s. annual rent and 4 marks and 2s. for entry, with promises of compensation should John fail to pay the rent owed to the abbot of Gloucester and of first refusal should he wish to sell the adjacent land on which his own house stood. (1200 × 43, prob. c. 1230)*

G.C.L., 'Deeds and Seals', ii, no. 28, fol. 15 (252 mm × *c*. 137 mm (glueing created a fold which makes the edge slightly shorter than the actual measurement); slit on turn-up; tag and seal missing; endorsements: . . . Ioh(ann)e Poli de terra in vico fabrorum (s. xiii?); Registratur (s. xiv[ex]).[1]

Notum sit vniuersis quod ego Ioh(anne)s filius Siluest(r)i Poli de Glouc' dedi et concessi et hac presenti carta confirmaui Nicholao de Hereford' burgensi de Glouc' quamdam terram meam cum edificiis desuper [constructis] in vico fab[rorum] illam scilicet que iacet inter terram que fuit cuiusdam[2] Dauid Dunning et terram Will(elm)i de Boclande.' et quamdam parcellam terre retro super quam quedam domus necessaria adia. . .[3] [camere] mee [lapidee] sita . . .[4] illam scilicet que iacet inter predictam cameram et terram predicti Dauid.' habendam et tenendam de me et heredibus [meis sibi et heredibus] suis libere et quiete in feudo et hereditate inperpetuum . Reddendo inde annuatim ipse uel heredes sui uel asignati sui michi et heredibus [meis] duos solidos argenti ad duos terminos scilicet ad Hocday duodecim denarios et ad festum sancti Michaelis duodecim denarios pro omnibus seruitiis et demandis et consuetudinibus ad me et heredes meos spectantes . Pro qua concessione mea predictus Nicholas dedit michi quatuor marcas argenti et duos solidos de introitu ad magnum negotium meum. Terra autem mensurata per uisum proborum hominum continet in anteriori parte de latitudine decem virgas domini regis ulnarias et vnum quarterium et dimidium et duos pollices cum pollice interposito . Retro uero continet de latitudine decem uirgas et tres quarterios et duos pollices cum pollice interposito . In profunditate iuxta terram Dauid Dunning continet viginti et duas uirgas et tres quarterios et duos pollices cum pollice interposito . In profunditate fere . In medio continet decem uirgas et tres quarterios cum pollice interposito . scilicet ex fronte autem usque ad corneram camere lapidee ex una parte . et altera parte erga puteum continet in profunditate ex fronte vsque ad medietatem putei. Et ego predictus Ioh(anne)s Poli et heredes mei totam predictam terram cum omnibus pertinentiis suis predicto Nicholao et heredibus suis uel asignatis suis contra omnes homines et feminas in perpetuum warentizabimus et de omnibus seruitiis et demandis pro predicto redditu inperpetuum aquietabimus. Et si in aliquo casu [contigerit] quod ego Ioh(anne)s uel heredes mei non soluerimus redd[itum abbatis Glouc'] ad terminos statutos uel alium seruitium uel demandam si exigetur et ipse Nicholaus uel heredes seu assignati sui uexati et destricti [sint] ad soluendum per defaltam [nostram] *concessi pro me et pro* heredibus meis ut ipse Nicholaus et heredes sui uel asignati sui *intrent in aliam partem* terre mee de feudo abb[atis] Glouc' *et illam teneant et habeant* cum domibus et edificiis et omnibus aliis pertinentiis suis sine aliquo [inpedimento] *per me uel* per heredes meos quousque eis *satisfactum fuerit plenarie de toto dampno quod pro* defalta nostra habuerint. Et si ego Ioh(anne)s uel heredes mei uoluerimus . . .[5] uel terram super quam domus sita est uend. . .[6] bene [uolumus et concedimus] . . .[7] Nich' omnibus hominibus uenditioni illi sit propinquior. Quod quia ratum fieri volo huic presenti scripto sigillum meum apposui. Hiis testibus . Waltero Hoch tunc [preposito] . [Ri]cardo de cellario . Willelmo de Boclande . Nicholao de Cumyoc . Ada Longo . Willelmo le loker . Waltero Haym . Iohanne Longo . et aliis.

Words in brackets have been read with ultra-violet light or have been added from formulas in common use; those in italics derive from no. 332 above. Dating limits for the charter are the periods in which Walter Hoic or Hoth was bailiff (*VCH Glos.* iv. 371–2), the script favouring a date *c*. 1230.

[1] Another endorsement possibly written in the same hand as *Registratur* is illegible due to a stain on the MS.　　[2] *quidam* in MS.　　[3] MS. damaged.　　[4] MS. damaged.
[5] MS. damaged.　　[6] MS. damaged.　　[7] MS. damaged.

334. *Grant by Nicholas son of Walter Potter of Feet Lane (Gloucester) to Nicholas Lorimer, smith, of land in Newland (by Gloucester) in free marriage with his sister Edith, for annual rents of 2s. to the almonry of St. Peter's, Gloucester, and ½d. to Nicholas son of Walter. (s. xiii^{med})*

A. G.C.L., 'Deeds and Seals', x, no. 20, fol. 16 (240 mm × 151 mm), **Scribe 37**; fragment of tag; seal missing; endorsements: N (s. xiii[2]); Neueland' (s. xiii); Elem. . .[1] (s. xiii); .ii s'. ista terra iacet in Herlone . . .[2] parte orientali fer' ex. . .[3] (s. xiii[2]?); Carta Nich(ola)i le poter (s. xiv^{in}); Registrat. . .[4] (s. xiv^{ex} × s. xv^{in}?); M. (uncertain date); **B**. ibid. 'Reg. B', no. 515, p. 227.

Sciant presentes et futuri quod ego Nichola[us] filius Walt(e)r(i) Le pot(er) de Fetelon' dedi et concessi et hac presenti carta mea confirmaui Nicholao Lormario fabro in liberam ma[rita]gium cum Editha sorore mea . quandam terram meam cum edificiis et omnibus aliis pertinentiis suis videlicet illam que [iacet inter] terram que fuit Roberti Le Riche quam dedit Thome filio suo et terram Henrici focarii in Noua Landa . Tenendam [et] habendam sibi et heredibus suis de predicta Editha exeuntibus et eorum heredibus vel assignatis libere et quiete integre cum pertinent[iis suis] inperpetuum . Reddendo inde annuatym elemosinarie sancti Petri Glouc' duos solidos sterlingorum ad duos terminos anni vide[licet ad Hoc]keday duodecim denarios . et ad festum sancti Michaelis duodecim denarios sicut antecessores mei reddere solebant et debebant et mi[chi et heredibus] meis vel meis assignatis vnum obolum argenti ad Pascha pro omnibus seruitiis . exactionibus et demandis. Predicta uero terra per visum prob[orum virorum] mensurata continet in fronte de latitudine octo uirgas et dimidiam domini regis ulnarias cum pollicibus interpositis . In medio⸝ continet [octo virg]as domini regis cum pollicibus interpositis et duos pollices . Retro⸝ uero continet octo uirgas et vnum quarterium cum pollicibus interpositis . et duos pollices . In profunditate continet quinquaginta et quinque uirgas et dimidium quarterium cum pollicibus interpositis. Et ego dictus Nicholaus filius Walt(er)i Le pot(er) et heredes mei siue mei assignati dicto Nicholao Lormario fabro et heredibus suis de predicta Editha exeuntibus et eorum heredibus vel assignatis predictam terram cum edificiis et omnibus aliis pertinentiis suis contra omnes homines et feminas in perpetuum warantizabimus. Et quia [volo] hanc meam donationem concessionem et confirmationem ratam et stabilem in perpetuum permanere presens scriptum sigilli mei inp[ressione] roboraui[.] Hiis testibus . Rogero de Northwiz . Henrico Ruffo de Orto . Ricardo Le Wlmongare[5] . Henrico Rotario . N[?]. . .eylur[6] . Iordano Le Naillare et aliis[.]

Missing portions from the badly damaged text have been supplied from **B**.

[1] Hole in MS.   [2] Hole in MS.   [3] Illegible.   [4] Hole in MS.
[5] **B** ends here with *et aliis*.   [6] A large hole in MS. makes reading of *N* uncertain.

335. *Grant by Quenilda widow of Ralph farrier in her liege power with the assent of her son Robert to Walter farrier, burgess of Gloucester, of land by Feet Lane in Gloucester, for annual rents of ½d. to Quenilda and 16d. to the almoner of St. Peter's, Gloucester, and for an advance payment of 8s. 8d. and the pardoning of 18s. owed by Ralph. (c. 1250)*

G.C.L., 'Deeds and Seals', iii, no. 4, fol. 3 (214 mm × 135 mm), **Scribe 44**; seal on tag: white wax stained green, broken, repaired: obverse: oval (35 mm × 23 mm); a decorated standard topped by a fleur-de-lis; legend: . . .S'Q. . .ENILDE FILIE RA. . .VLFI; no counterseal; endorsements: iuxta Fetelane; A (s. xiii[ex]); Carta Quenilde ferr[;] Elemosin(ie) .xvi. d(enarii) (s. xiv[ex]); Registratur (s. xiv[ex] × s. xv[in]).

Sciant presentes et futuri quod ego Quenilda que fui vxor Radulphi le Ferrur assensu et voluntate Roberti filii et heredis mei tempore viduitatis mee et ligia potestate mea dedi et concessi et hac presenti carta mea confirmaui Waltero le Ferun burgensi Glouc' quandam partem terre iuxta Vetelon' quam predictus Radulfus quondam vir meus et ego⸝ tenuimus de abbate et conuentu sancti Petri Glouc' . que iacet inter terram meam ex vna parte . et Vetelon' ex altera . Que mensurata est per visum proborum hominum [et] continet de latitudine in fronte quinque uirgas domini regis ulnarias et dimidiam cum pollice interposito . Residua uero pars quatuor uirgas ulnarias et tria quarteria cum pollice interposito . In profunditate triginta et vnam virgam ulnariam cum pollice interposito . Habendam et tenendam de me et heredibus meis sibi et heredibus suis uel suis assignatis . libere . et quiete . integre . bene et in pace . in feodo et hereditate inperpetuum . Reddendo inde annuatim michi et heredibus meis ipse et heredes sui uel sui assignati vnum obolum argenti ad festum sancti Michaelis et elemosinario sancti Petri Glouc' sexdecim denarios ad terminos debitos et consuetos pro omni seruitio et demanda. Ego uero predicta Quenilda et heredes mei predicto Waltero et heredibus suis uel suis assignatis predictam terram cum omnibus pertinentiis suis contra omnes gentes inperpetuum warantizabimus . et defendemus. Pro hac autem donatione et concessione mea dedit mihi predictus Walterus ad magnum negotium meum octo solidos et octo[1] denarios et perdonauit michi octodecim solidos quod ei debui de debito predicti Radulphi viri mei. In huius rei testimonium[2] carte presenti sigillum meum apposui. Hiis testibus . Mauricio Simenel . Henrico le Roer . Roberto Cluse . Iurdano le Nayllare . Iohanne de Brokampton' . Iohanne Sage . Willelmo mil(it)e . Henrico clerico . Ricardo clerico . et aliis.

[1] *et octo* erased in MS.   [2] *ei te* of *rei testimonium* erased in MS.

336. *Confirmation by Robert son and heir of Ralph farrier of the grant by his mother Quenilda to Walter farrier. (c. 1250)*

A. G.C.L., 'Deeds and Seals', iii, no. 5, fol. 3 (195 mm × 85 mm), **Scribe 44**; seal on tag: white wax stained green, obverse split off and lost; repaired; no counterseal; endorsements: Fetelone (*c.* s. xiii^{ex}); b (*c.* s. xiii^{med}, poss. in same hand); Carta Rob(er)ti filii et heredum Radulphi ferrun (s. xiv^{in}?); Registratur (s. xiv^{ex} × s. xv^{in}); **B**. G.C.L., 'Reg. B', no. 521, p. 229.

Sciant presentes et futuri quod ego Rob(er)tus filius et heres Radulphi le Ferrur concessi et hac presenti carta mea confirmaui Waltero le Ferun omnem illam donationem et concessionem quam Quenilda mater mea ei fecit de quadam terra iuxta Vetelone . Habendam et tenendam in omnibus secundum tenorem carte quam predictus Walterus habet de predicta Quenilda matre mea de dicta terra sine aliquo retenemento ad me uel ad heredes inposterum. Pro hac autem concessione et confirmatione mea dedit predictus Walterus predicte Quenilde matri mee octo solidos et octo denarios ad comune negotium nostrum et perdonauit nobis octodecim solidos quos debuimus de debito predicti Radulphi patris mei. In huius rei testimonium presenti scripto sigillum meum apposui. Hiis testibus . Edrich' tunc balliuo Glouc' . Mauricio Simenel . Henrico le Roer . Roberto Cluse . Iurdano le Naillar' . Iohanne de Brokampton' . Iohanne Sage[1] . Ricardo clerico . et aliis.

The witness-lists of this and no. 335, which was written by the same scribe, show that the two were written either on the same occasion or very close to each other.

[1] **B** omits the six witnesses' names from Maurice Simenel to John Sage.

337. *Fragment of a deposition mentioning Mabel wife of Robert baker. Friday . . .
1254.*

G.C.L., 'Deeds and Seals', xi, no. 24; no turn-up; seal on tag sewn to fragment, white wax,
rubbed, round (30 mm in diam.); obverse: a fleur-de-lis; legend: + S . . .; no counterseal; no
visible endorsement.

. . . quod anno gratie .M.° cc.° l.° iiii.ᵒʳ die Veneris prima ante festum . . . fidauit
Mabilia vxor Roberti pistoris quod nunquam . . . Robertus vir suus Iohanni de sancto
Pat'no capellano ven. . .are presentibus. Hiis testibus Galfrido capellano . . . .
Walt(ero) Fowel . Hugone . . . Nicholę Rich. . . .in' clet' . Roberto clet' . [et mu]ltis
aliis.

This transaction appears to relate to land which John of St. Padern chaplain bought from
Robert baker and gave to support a lamp for the Lady chapel in St. Peter's, Gloucester
(G.C.L., 'Reg. B', no. 1122 (1123), pp. 493–4; see also ibid. no. 1124 (1125), pp. 494–5).
Mabel may be the widow of the Robert baker who was a tenant of St. Peter's on Brook
Street, Gloucester, *c.* 1265 (*Cart. Glouc.* iii. 154).

338. *Sale and quitclaim by Robert vintner of Gloucester to William of Samford
of land which he held of the abbot of Gloucester on Ebridge Street (Gloucester)
and of land which he held from Alice and Agnes of Abergavenny; William gave
21 marks and a blue robe to Robert, and a green cloak, a scarlet tunic, and a
veil to his wife Matilda, and was to pay annual rents of 1 mark to the abbot
and convent of St. Peter's, Gloucester, 12d. to Alice and Agnes, 5d. to the king,
and 12d. to the church of St. Nicholas (Gloucester) for a mass of St. Mary. (c. 1228
× 40)*

G.R.O., GBR/J1/248 (170 mm × 161 mm); seal on tag; dark green wax; obverse: round (30
mm in diam.); a fleur-de-lis; legend: +SIGILL': ROBERTI: VINITORIS; no counterseal; no
medieval endorsement; cal. in Stevenson, no. 248.

Sciant presentes et futuri quod ego Rob(er)tus vinitor de Glouc' vendidi et quietum
clamaui Willelmo de Samford' et heredibus suis siue assignatis suis totum ius quod
ego uel heredes mei habuimus uel habere poterimus in terra quam tenui de abbate
Glouc' que iacet iuxta terram que fuit Roberti Le Riche in Ebrugestreta Glouc'.
Vendidi etiam et quietum clamaui eidem Willelmo et heredibus suis siue assignatis
suis totum ius quod ego uel heredes mei habuimus uel habere poterimus in terra
quam tenui de Alicia et Agneta filiarum Alani de Bergeueni que iacet inter predictam
terram quam tenui de abbate et terram que fuit Reginaldi de Brekeneoch' . pro viginti
et vna marca argenti quas idem Willelmus michi ad meum magnum negotium
premanibus pacauit . et vnam robam de blu . et Matildi vxori mee vnum pallium de
viridi . et vnam tunicam de scarleta et quandam peplum[.] Et ego predictus
Rob(ertus) et heredes mei warantizabimus hanc predictam venditionem et quietam
clamantiam predicto Willelmo et heredibus suis siue assignatis suis contra omnes
homines et feminas inperpetuum . ita scilicet quod ipse Willelmus et heredes sui siue

assignati sui sint respondentes annuatim abbati et conuentui sancti Petri Glouc' de una marca argenti . et predicte Alicie et Agnete et heredibus eorum annuatim de duodecim denariis . et domino regi per annum de quinque denariis . et ecclesie sancti Nicholai de duodecim denariis annuatim ad missam de sancta Maria celebrandam. Ego uero predictus Rob(ertus) affidaui quod ego et heredes mei hanc predictam venditionem et quietam clamantiam fideliter et sine dolo tenebimus et quod nec artem nec ingenium exquiremus per nos nec per aliquem alium vnde predictus Willelmus uel heredes sui siue assignati sui de predictis terris in processu temporis sint uexati uel perdentes. In huius rei testimonium presens scriptum sigillo meo munitum predicto Willelmo tradidi . et ad maiorem securitatem cartas quas de predictis tenementis habui coram hundredo Glouc' eidem Willelmo reddidi. Hiis testibus Ricardo burg' tunc maiore Glouc' . Hugone scisore . Waltero Kentwin tunc prepositis Glouc' [.] Dauid Dunning . Ricardo rufo . Iohanne drapario . Iohanne de Gosedic . Ricardo filio Willelmi . Ada filio Rogeri . Ada Croc . Mauricio filio Dura[n]di [.] Thoma Oye . Ricardo filio Walteri . Ada Gladwin [.] Hugone clerico [.] magistro Waltero scriptore [.] Philippo clerico et aliis.

Above the first line of text is a line drawn in pencil to guide the writer. Above that line are the ends of writing, indicating how texts might be written continuously on parchment strips and cut off at appropriate points. The charter is dated by the attestation of the bailiffs (*VCH Glos.* iv. 372). Robert vintner apparently received land from the two sisters in the same period (G.R.O., GBR/J1/247), possibly one of the properties referred to in his sale to William.

339. *Sale and quitclaim by Robert Rufus, dyer, to David Dunning of Gloucester of land by Walkers Lane (Gloucester), for 43s. and saving annual rents of 8d. to the hospital of St. Bartholomew, Gloucester, and of 2½d. to the abbot of St. Peter's, Gloucester. (1200 × c. 1228)*

G.R.O., GBR/J1/243 (165 mm × 142 mm); seal on tag; obverse: oval (34 mm × 29 mm); dark green; poss. fleur-de-lis; legend: + SIGILL: ROBERTI: RUFFI; no counterseal; endorsement: .Dauid Dunning[;] Iuxta Walkareslone[;] .domino abbati Glouc' de longabula .iid ob.' (s. xiii[2]); cal. in Stevenson, no. 243.

Sciant presentes et futuri quod ego Rob(er)t(us) Rufus tinctor vendidi et inperpetuum de me et de heredibus meis quietam clamaui Dauid Dunning Glouc' et heredibus suis uel assignatis suis quamdam terram meam . scilicet illam que iacet inter terram Willelmi Le chalumier et vicum fullonum. Tenendam et habendam sibi et heredibus suis uel assignatis suis . libere . et quiete . absque omni seruitio et demanda . saluis annuatim capitalibus dominis decem denariis et obolo argenti . scilicet ad hospitalle beati Bartholomei Glouc' octo denariis ad festum sancti Oswaldi . et domino abbati[1] sancti Petri Glouc' duobus denariis et obolo ad festum sancti Michaelis . Pro quadraginta et tribus solidis argenti . quos premanibus michi ad meum magnum negotium pacauit. Ego vero predictus Rob(ertus) et heredes mei predicto Dauid et heredibus suis uel asignatis suis predictam terram contra omnes homines et feminas in perpetuum warantizabimus. Et ut hec venditio mea stabilis et rata permaneat' presens scriptum sigilli mei inpressione confirmaui. Hiis testibus . Thoma Oye tunc preposito Glouc' . Ricardo burg' . Willelmo de Samphord . Iohanne tinctore . Willelmo tinctore . Willelmo Le chalumier . Thoma Ouenad . Willelmo fader et multis aliis.

The date is indicated by the attestation of the bailiff (*VCH Glos.* iv. 371). For the location see *PNG*, ii. 133.

[1] *abati* in MS.

340. *Grant by William of Showle to William son of Joan of Hyde two sellions of land at* Hanbald *(near Yarkhill, Herefs.) for an annual rent of a root of ginger and 7s. in advance. (c. 1230)*

A. G.C.L., 'Deeds and Seals', viii, no. 18, fol. 9 (243 mm × 119 mm), **Scribe 47**; seal on tag; white wax, rubbed, repaired; obverse: oval (*c.* 24 mm × 17 mm); an elongated eight-pointed flower or star; legend: . . . .S' WILL. . . DE S. . .LL. . .; no counterseal; endorsements: .Hida. (*c.* s. xiv[in]); Carta W. de Solle; Registratur (s. xiv[ex] × s. xv[in]); **B.** ibid. 'Reg. B', no. 127, p. 45.

Sciant presentes et futuri quod ego Will(elmu)s de Scolle dedi et concessi et hac presenti carta mea confirmaui Willelmo filio Ioane de Hyda pro seruitio suo et pro septem solidis argenti quos michi dedit premanibus duos seyllones terre mee iacentes apud Hanbald' inter terram Willelmi Godefray et terram dicti Willelmi filii Ioane . et extendentes se a terra persone de Varcull' usque gardinum quod[1] Iohannes clericus aliquando tenuit . Habendam et tenendam de me et heredibus meis sibi et heredibus suis vel suis assignatis . vel cuicunque in sanitate vel egretudine voluerit dare . legare . vendere vel assignare . In feodo et hereditate libere et quiete . integre . bene . et in pace cum omnibus libertatibus . Reddendo inde annuatim michi et heredibus meis ipse et heredes sui vel sui assignati vnum racynum gingiberis . videlicet ad festum beati Michaelis . pro omnibus seruitiis . exactionibus . consuetudinibus . sectis . auxiliis et demandis omnimodis que de terra exeunt vel exire poterunt saluo regali seruitio ad tantum tenementum pertinente. Ego vero Will(elmu)s de Solle et heredes mei dicto Willelmo filio Ioane et heredibus suis vel suis assignatis predictos duos seylliones terre cum omnibus pertinentiis suis contra omnes homines et feminas in perpetuum warantizabimus et defendemus. Et quia volo quod hec mea donatio et concessio rata sit et stabilis huic presenti carte sigillum meum apposui. Hiis testibus . Iohanne de Sewalle . Rogero de Sewalle . Thoma de Wyke[2] . Radulpho palmario . Petro Le Wyte de Vareu'll' . Roberto Ustrid . Thoma P(er)trihc de Hyda . et aliis.

[1] *quam* in MS.   [2] **B** ends here with *et aliis.*

341. *Grant in the form of a chirograph by Sigar priest and all the parish of St. Nicholas (Gloucester) to Roger Weaver of half the land which was Alward Capie's, sc. the half which Alward bought from Baldwin the priest's son, for annual rents of 8d. to St. Nicholas and 3d. to the abbot (of Gloucester) and 6s. for entry. (s. xii[ex])*

G.R.O., GBR/J1/85 (127 mm × 104 mm); no provision for sealing; no endorsement; cal. in Stevenson, no. 85.

CIROGRAPHVM

Sciant presentes et futuri quod ego Sigar(us) . sacerdos et omnis parrochia sancti . Nicholai . concessimus . Rogero Telatori et heredibus suis medietatem terre que fuit Alwardi . Capie . illam medietatem . scilicet terre⸴ quam predictus Alwardus emit de Baldewino filio sacerdotis [.] Tenendam in feudo et hereditate dando sancto . Nicholao singulis annis⸴ .viii.^{to} denarios duobus terminis . scilicet .iiii.^{or} denarios . ad festum sancti . Michaelis et iiii.^{or} denarios ad Anuntiationem sancte . Marie . et preterea .iii. denarios domino abbati . scilicet ad terminum Hocgthedai. Predictus uero Rogerus dedit predicto Sigario . pro hac liberatione[1] et concessione .vi. solidos . pro introitu pro parte illa que est iuxta domum . Godid filie Baldwini. Huius pactionis testes sunt . Iordanus vltra pontem . Ærnaldus filius Dunnig . Ernisius filius Thured . Ælueredus ultra pontem . Wlierdus ultra pontem . Osmundus fullo . Nicholaus filius Seuare . Tomas filius Ernisii . Ernaldus aurifaber . Willelmus unibonarius . Mauricius . Augustinus telator . Aluredus Telator.

[1] *lib(er)cone* in MS.

342. *Grant by Richard Symphanur to Master John Mason of a shop on Draper Street, Gloucester, for a payment of 40s. to Richard and 2s. annual rent to the abbot of Gloucester. (1258)*

G.C.L., 'Deeds and Seals', ix, no. 5, fol. 2; (199 mm × 125 mm); seal on tag; white wax, rubbed; obverse: round (26 mm in diam.); an eight-pointed flower or rosette; legend: +S' RICARDI . . .IMPA. . .; no counterseal; endorsements: iiia Ward' (s. xiii^{med}); In peleteria. iii v(arda) (s. xiii); ; Carta Ricardi Le Symphan(ur); Caps(ula) .xviii. de laicis tenuris (*c*. 1265); Registratur[;] In draperia (s. xiv^{ex} × s. xvⁱⁿ); sc(ribitur) (s. xvⁱⁿ).

Sciant presentes et futuri quod ego Ricardus Le symphanur de Gloucestr' dedi et concessi et hac presenti carta confirmaui magistro Iohanni Cementario vnam soppam in vico draperie de Gloucestr' ex opposito soppe Rogeri Lenveyse . sitam inter soppam Roberti de Puttheleye ex parte occidentali et soppam Roberti Sely ex parte orientali . Que illa soppa mensurata per visum proborum et legalium hominum continet in latitudine in fronte autem tres vlnas ferreas domini regis et vnum quarterium cum pollicibus interpositis . et retro habet eandem latitudinem . In profunditate uero continet duas vlnas ferreas domini regis et tres quarterias et dimidiam . cum pollicibus interpositis . Habendam et tenendam de me et heredibus meis predicto magistro Iohanni et heredibus suis uel cuicumque eamdem soppam dare . vendere uel assignare voluerint siue in sanitate siue in egritudine . Libere quiete pacifice iure hereditario imperpetuum . Reddendo inde annuatim abbati et conuentui sancti Petri Gloucestr' duos solidos argenti ad terminos debitos et consuetos. Et ego predictus Ricardus et heredes mei predictam soppam cum pertinentiis predicto magistro Iohanni et heredibus suis uel assignatis sicut predictum est contra omnes gentes Cristianas et Iudeas warantizabimus defendemus et acquietabimus imperpetuum. Et pro hac concessione donatione et warantizatione defensione et acquietantione dedit michi predictus magister Iohannes quadraginta solidos argenti premanibus. Quod autem hec mea concessio donatio warantizatio defensio et acquietantio et presentis carte confirmatio pro me et heredibus meis rata et stabilis imperpetuum permaneat . presenti scripto sigillum apposui. Hiis testibus . Willelmo de Chiltenham . Rogero Lenveyse tunc balliuis Gloucestr' . Willelmo de Teukesbir' . Ricardo de Celario . Iohanne filio Simonis . Iohanne de Eldresfeud . Iohanne Le Blund [.] Hugone le Seynter . Petro Le taylur . et aliis.

The attestation of the bailiffs fixes the date of the charter (*VCH Glos.* iv. 372).

343. *Grant by William son of Warin to Ellen daughter of his wife Dionysia of a property in Weibrugstret (Westgate Street?, Gloucester) which he bought from Margery Clambred, for annual rents of 18d. to Hugh of Kilpeck and a pair of gloves to Margery. (c. s. xiii^{in})*

G.C.L., 'Deeds and Seals', i, no. 30, fol. 17 (199 mm × 82 mm), damaged; seal on tag; white wax stained green, repaired; obverse: round (31 mm in diam.): a tree of life (?); legend: . . .GILL' WILL'MI FIL' WARI. . .; no counterseal; endorsements: Carta Will(elm)i filii Warini (s. xiii^1), **Hand n** (below, Plate XLIVe); iiii W(arda) (s. xiii^{med}?); iiii Warda (c. s. xiii^{ex}; poss. xiv^{in}); Caps(ula) .xviii. de laicis tenuris (s. xiii^2); A (s. xiv); sc(ribitur) (s. xv^{in}).

Sciant presentes et futuri quod ego Will(elmus) filius Warini dedi et concessi Elene filie uxoris mee Dionisie pro servitio suo quand. . . que dicitur Weibrugstrete scilicet illam quam emi de Marger(ia) Clambred . Tenendam et habendam sibi et heredibus . . . dicta Marger' et heredibus suis libere quiete integre et plenarie [.] Reddendo inde annuatim . . . et heredes sui . . . domino Hug(oni) de Kilp[ec] decem et octo denarios . Et predicte Marger' et heredibus suis vnam^1 cyro. . . singulas . . . denarii . . . seruitio exactione consuetudine et demanda quod ad tantum tenementum pertinet uel pertinere possit. Et ut hec mea donatio et concessio firma sit et stabilis inperpetuu[m] ego eam hac presenti carta mea et sigilli mei inpressione . . .aui. Hiis testibus . . . Warini . Hugone filio Ail. . . . Henrico Craft . Willelmo palmario . Willelmo filio Symonis . Radulfo filio Reginaldi . Iohanne clerico . Waltero Sauuage . Gileberto Ywein . Ricardo de Haya . Waltero pict . . . . et multis aliis.

^{1} *vnas* in MS.

344. *Grant by Alice daughter of Reginald Welbert of Gloucester to Hugh Girdler of land in the parish of St. Mary (de Lode, Gloucester), for ½d. annual rent to Alice and ½d. for landgabel to the abbot of Gloucester and for payment of 4s., a blue tunic, and a pair of shoes to Alice for entry. (c. 1228 × 43)*

G.R.O., GBR/J1/329 (183 mm × 156 mm); seal on tag; white wax painted green, chipped; round (30 mm in diam.); a cross with four arms of equal length ending as fleurs-de-lis; legend: +S' ALIS. . . FILIE: REINAL. . .: WELBERT; no counterseal; no endorsement; cal. in Stevenson, no. 329.

Sciant presentes et futuri quod ego Alic(ia) filia Regin(aldi) Weyberd' . de Glouc' . tradidi et concessi Hugoni le Seinter de Glouc' quandam^1 terram meam . in parochia sancte Marie ante portam abbastie in parua venella que ducit uersus Sabrinam . que iacet inter terram ipsius Hugonis et terram Duce Carbunel . Tenendam et habendam sibi et heredibus suis et cuicumque uel . quibuscumque dare . vendere . uel assignate uoluerit . de me et heredibus meis . libere et quiete . integre . in feudo et hereditate . cum pertinentiis suis . Reddendo inde annuatim michi et heredibus meis unum obolum ad Pasca . et soluendo inde abbati Glouc' . per annum . vnum obolum . ad Hockeday de londogabulo . pro me et heredibus meis . Vnde uolo quod ipse Hugo et heredes sui . uel assignati sui aquietent me et heredes meos de seruitio illo uersus dominum abbatem Glouc'. in perpetuum. Terra uero mensurata . continet in latitudine in anteriori parte . septem virgas domini regis vlnarias et vnum quarterium . et duos pollices . cum pollice interposito . In longitudine. quinquaginta duas virgas domini regis vlnarias . et vnum quarterium . cum pollice interposito . In latitudine in posteriori parte sex virgas domini regis vlnarias . et dimidiam de quatuor pollices . cum pollice interposito. Pro hac autem traditione et concessione mea predictus Hugo dedit michi quatuor solidos . argenti de introitu . vnam tunicam de blu . et vnum par sotolarum. Edificia que tunc super predictam terram erant inuenta. apreciata fuerunt pro duobus solidis. Ego uero predicta Alic(ia) et heredes mei predictam terram predicto Hugoni . et heredibus suis uel assignatis suis contra omnes gentes . warantizabimus. Et quia uolo quod hec mea traditio et concessio rata sit stabilis. presens scriptum sigilli mei impressione confirmaui. Hiis testibus . Thoma Oye tunc preposito Glouc' . Willelmo Feragu . Waltero de Oxonhale . Willelmo marescallo . Petro de Maresfeld' . Ada Cuperich' . Willelmo de Sumery . Ada de Herefordia . et aliis.

Thomas Oye served as bailiff of Gloucester in 1200 × c. 1228 and c. 1228 × 40 (*VCH Glos.* iv. 371–2); the script of the charter clearly belongs to the latter period.

¹ *quandami* in MS.

---

345. *Grant by Ralph son of Robert White of Sneedham to Master Henry of five sellions of arable and a gore with their headlands and ditch in Bulfercherl for ¼d. for a paschal candle for (Upton) St. Leonard's and 4s. to Ralph in advance. (s. xiii^in)*

A. G.C.L., 'Deeds and Seals', vi, no. 40, fol. 21 (137 mm × 92 mm), **Scribe 41** (below, Plate XXXV); seal on tag; cream coloured wax laquered, chipped; obverse: round (29 mm in diam.); a bird of prey with wings closed to the right; legend: +S' RADULFI WYTE DE SNEDAM.; no counterseal; endorsement: Registratur (s. xiv^ex); z (s. xiv); **B**. ibid. 'Reg. B', no. 707, p. 304.

Sciant presentes et futuri quod ego Radulph(us) filius Rob(er)ti albi de Snedham dedi . et concessi . et hac presenti carta mea confirmaui magistro Henrico vicino meo quinque sellones terre mee arabilis . et vnam goram cum forardis suis et fossato in Bulfercherl iacentes inter terram suam ex utraque parte iuxta pratum Walteri de Snedham . et extendentes super pratum meum et predicti magistri . Tenendas . et habendas sibi et heredibus suis . uel cuicumque dare . uendere . uel assignare uoluerit de me . et heredibus meis libere . quiete . et integre cum pertinentiis suis iure hereditario cum omnibus libertatibus suis et liberis consuetudinibus suis [.] Reddendo inde annuatim michi et heredibus meis ipse et heredes sui . uel sui assignati vnum quadrantem ad cereu(m) pascale(m) sancti Leonardi . pro omnibus seruitiis . herietis . sectis . et secularibus demandis. Pro hac autem donatione et concessione mea predictus magister dedit michi .iiii. solidis sterlingorum premanibus. Et ego predictus Radulph(us) et heredes mei predicto magistro .H. et heredibus suis uel suis assignatis contra omnes homines et feminas inperpetuum warantizabimus predictos seillones per predictum seruitium . et de omnibus seruitiis et secularibus demandis acquietabimus. In cuius rei testimonium sigillum meum proprium presentibus apposui. Hiis testibus [.] Philippo de Matresdon' . Symone de Mat'esdon'[1] . Willelmo Gerald . Roberto Keys . Waltero de Snedham . Roberto Cortoys . et aliis.

[1] **B** ends here with *et multis aliis*.

346. *Grant by of William White to John de Capelore of three sellions of arable in Marcombe field (in Upton St. Leonards), for a rose annual rent and 10s. in advance. (s. xiii[2]; poss. xiii[ex])*

A. G.C.L., 'Deeds and Seals', vii, no. 17, fol. 11 (250 mm × 132 mm); seal on tag; white wax, chipped, rubbed; obverse: round (*c.* 29 mm in diam.); leaves or cones forming a cross; legend: +S. . . WILL'LE W. . .M; no counterseal; endorsements: de terra quam Ioannes de . . .[1] . . .ore[2] emit de Will(elm)o le Wite[3] de Snedham (s. xiii[2]); Registratur (s. xiv[ex] × s. xv[in]); **B**. ibid. 'Reg. B', no. 726, p. 312.

Sciant presentes et futuri quod ego Will(elmu)s le Wyte de Snedham dedi concessi et hac presenti carta mea confirmaui . Iohanni de Capelore tres selliones terre mee arabiles iacentes in campo quod uocatur Marcumbe inter terram Iohannis de Snedha' et terram abbatis Gloucest' in[4] longitudine . et extendunt se ad vnum capud super terram abbatis Gloucest' et ad aliud super terram domini Philippi de Mattesdon' militis . Et duas particulas terre mee iacentes in quodam campo quod uocatur Witecroft quarum vna particula iacet inter terram abbatis Gloucest' in longitudine extra utraque parte . Et alia particula inter terram dicti abbatis ex utraque parte in longtudine et extendunt se super terram domini Philippi de Mattesd' militis . in vtroque capite . Habendam et tenendam totam dictam [terram][5] dictus Iohannes et heredes sui siue sui assignati de domino feodi libere . quiete . bene et in pace hereditarie imperpetuum . . . inde annuatim dictus Iohannes et heredes sui siue sui assignati vnam rosam in festo Natiuitatis sancti Ioannis Baptiste domino feodi pro omnibus seruitiis . consuetudinibus . releuiis excaetis sectis curie cuiuscunque et omnibus aliis[6] demandis que de terra exigi possunt. Pro hac autem donatione concessione et presenti carta confirmatione dedit michi predictus Iohannes decem solidos argenti premanibus in magno urgenti meo negotio. In cuius rei testimonium hanc presentem cartam sigilli mei inpressione roboraui. Hiis testibus . Germano de Tonebrigge . Philippo de Mattesdon' [.] Willelmo Geraud[7] . Waltero le pope . Roberto Curteys . et aliis.

[1] Illegible with ultra-violet light.
[2] The letter before *ore* may be an *l* and may be part of a longer word which cannot be read due to damage.
[3] The second letter may be *e* not *i*.
[4] Tironian *et* in MS.
[5] Read with ultra-violet light.
[6] *Alis* in MS.
[7] **B** ends here with *et aliis*.

347. Grant by John of Great Witcombe and his wife Edith to Nicholas of Hereford burgess of Glouceser of land in Longsmith Street (Gloucester) for 2s. annual rent and 20s. entry. (c. 1228 × 40)

A. G.C.L., 'Deeds and Seals', xi, no. 7 (192 mm × 94 mm), **Scribe 43**; two tags with seals: left: white wax coloured green, obverse: round (28 mm in diam.); a fleur-de-lis in a cross with arms of equal length; legend: + S' IOHANIS: DE WIDICUMB; no counterseal; right: white wax stained green, chipped; obverse: round (32 mm in diam.); four standards ending in fleurs-de-lis crossed with four standards ending with pinecones or leaves; legend: . . . SIGI. . . EDIA. . .; no counterseal; endorsements: . . . de Wide. . .be . . . de Herford' . . . in vico fabrorum. (s. xiii); 1.ª; Smythstr'te (uncertain date); 3) Registratur (s. xiv^{ex} × s. xv^{in}); **B**. ibid. 'Reg. B', no. 1054 (1053), p. 456; Baddeley, 'Further Early Deeds', pp. 52–53.

Sciant presentes et futuri quod ego Ioh(anne)s de Widecumb' et Ediht(a) vxor mea que fuit filia Iohannis [Donsiþ]et de Glouc' concessimus . et tradidimus et hac presenti carta nostra confirmauimus . Nicholao de H'eford' . burgensi de Glouc' quandam partem terre nostre in vico fabrorum . illam . scilicet . que iacet inter terram domini prioris de Lanthon' . et terram nostram ex alia parte . Et que mensurata est per uisum legalium hominum,́ et continet in anteriori parte . in latitudine quinque virgas domini regis vlnarias . cum pollice interposito et dimidium quarterium . Retro uero continet in latitudine quinque virgas domini regis vlnarias cum pollice interposito et dimidiam . In profunditate iuxta terram predicti prioris de La'thon' continet nouem virgas domini regis vlnarias et dimidiam . cum pollice interposito et dimidium quarterium . In profunditate uero iuxta terram nostram continet usque^1 ad medietatem putei . Tenendam et habendam de nobis et heredibus nostris sibi et heredibus suis siue assignatis suis libere . et quiete . integre cum edificiis inperpetuum . Reddendo inde annuatim nobis uel heredibus nostris duos solidos argenti ad duos terminos anni . Scilicet ad Hockeday duodecim denarios . et ad [festum sancti Michaelis] duodecim denarios . pro omnibus seruitiis et demandis. Pro hac autem concessione et traditione nostra predictus Nicholaus [dedit nobis vigi]nti solidos sterlingorum premanibus de introitu. Et Ego Ioh(anne)s predictus et vxor mea Edihta et [heredes] nostri [predicto Nic]holao et heredibus suis siue assignatis suis predictam terram contra omnes homines et feminas inperpetuum wa[rantizabimus et] de londgabulo^2 aquietabimus. Et vt nostra concessio et traditio firma et stabilis inperpetuum per[maneat pre]sentem cartam sigilli nostri inpressione confirmauimus et predicto Nicholao coram legalibus hominibus [tradidimus.] Hiis testibus . Willelmo Loker' . Willelmo marescallo . Waltero Haym^3 . Ada Coperyhc . Roberto Peppe . Iohanne mercatore . . .iis[.]

The parts within square brackets have been supplied from **B**. A Nicholas of Hereford attested a local Gloucester charter *c.* 1240 (Stevenson, no. 374).

^{1} Initial *a* changed to *u*.
^{2} *longabl'o* in MS.
^{3} **B** ends here with *et aliis.*

348. Grant by Peter Wodie son and heir of Nicholas Wodie of Wotton to John of the wood of Hatherley of land in Wotton (St. Mary Without, Gloucester?) and a messuage on Barton Street outside Gloucester belonging to the land, for annual rents of 5s. payable to the abbot of St. Peter's, Gloucester, and 1d. to John of Holcomb. (s. xiii^med)

G.R.O., GBR/J1/531 (223 mm × 114 mm); seal on tag; possibly white wax painted green; chipped; obverse: oval (35 mm × 21 mm); an eight-pointed rosette or flower; legend: +S' PET. . .I: WODIE . . .; no counterseal; endorsement: carta Ad(e) d(e) Ardern'. de terra de Wtthone que Iahan(nes)[1] de Kerwerþin tenuit (c. s. xiii^ex); cal. in Stevenson, no. 531.

Sciant presentes et futuri quod ego Petrus Widie filius et heres Nicholai Wydie de Wotton' concessi dedi quietaclamaui et hac presenti carta mea pro me et heredibus meis confirmaui Iohanni de boscho de Hayþerleya pro homagio suo et seruitio totam terram meam cum edificiis desuper constructis pratis . pasturis . redditibus . et cum omnibus allis suis pertinentiis . Videlicet illam que michi decendebat in hereditate in villa de Wotton' per predictum Nicholaum Wydie de Wotton' . Preterea vnum mesuagium quod iacet in la bertonestrete extra Glouc' ad prefatam terram pertinens cum omnibus suis pertinentiis . Habendam et tenendam de me et heredibus meis sibi et heredibus suis siue suis assignatis libere . solute . integre [.] quiete [.] bene . pacifice . iure hereditario et inperpetuum absque omni clamio seu vexatione mei vel heredum meorum inposterum . Reddendo inde annuatim ipse et heredes sui vel sui assignati domino abbati sancti Petri Glouc' quinque solidos argenti ad tres terminos . videlicet ad festum sancti Michaelis viginti denarios . ad Purificationem beate Marie viginti denarios . et ad Pentecosten viginit denarios . Et preterea Iohanni de Holecumbe vnum denarium ad festum sancti Michaelis . pro omnimodis seruitiis . sectis . querelis . consuetudinibus et demandis secularibus ad me siue ad heredes meos inde pertinentibus . saluo regali seruitio ad eandem terram pertinente. Et quia volo quod hec mea concessio . donatio et mea quietaclamantia et huius presentis carte confirmatio perpetue firmitatis robur obtineat῾ hoc presens scriptum sigilli mei impressione roboraui. Hiis testibus . Philippo de Heyþerleya . Philippo de Mattresdon' . Hugone de Brichamton' . Nicholao Sygrit . Henrico Passemer . Gilberto de Syde . Henrico Peticler . Iohanne clerico . et aliis.

[1] Reading uncertain.

349. *Fragment of a charter of unknown donor(s) in favour of Robert of Upleadon (?) and possibly of another beneficiary or beneficiaries. (s. xiii²)*

G.C.L., 'Deeds and Seals', viii, no. 20 (c), fol. 11; potential endorsement evidence unavailable due to mounting.

. . .d' et tenere de me et . . . pratum cum pertinentiis tam in firmitate quam in sanitate. dare vendere . legare in na. . .a mei vel heredum meorum inperpetuum . Reddendo inde annuatim michi et heredibus meis . . . obolum ad Anuntiationem beate Marie in Martio et Roberto de Ledene uel eius assignatis vnum . . . seruitiis . sectis curie . releuiis . escaetis. et omnibus . et omnibus secularibus . . .tinet ad tantum tenementum in eadem uilla et de eadem tenura. Et ego vero predictus Wal. . . assignatis . . . Et cum . . .

350. *A fragment in the same hand as no. 349; possibly in favour of an Adam. (s. xiii²)*

G.C.L., 'Deeds and Seals', viii, no. 20 (d), fol. 11; potential endorsement evidence unavailable due to mounting.

. . . et cum omnibus aliis pertinentiis Ba. . .bene et in pace cuicumque uel quandocumque d. . .dare uel assignare voluerit . absque omni c. . . ipse et heredes sui uel eius assignati vnum . . . denarium ad festum sancti Michaelis pro o. . . demandis saluo regali seruitio quantum . . . heredes mei prenominato Ade . . . pertinentiis contra . . . tam sigilli mei . . .

351. *A fragment. (s. xiii²)*

G.C.L., 'Deeds and Seals', viii, no. 23 (b), fol. 13; potential endorsement evidence unavailable due to mounting.

. . .pa . . Iohanne de Brichampton' et . . . et terram que fuit Willelmi . . . fuit dicti Willelmi fabri . . . ville de Dunhetherl' et . . . que fuit Will(elm)i gule . et . . . parte occidentali vertit super . . . W. . .gew. . .th' et tres acras in campo . . . et vnam dimidiam acram in . . .wtined. . .

HEREFORD: PRIORY OF ST. GUTHLAC

352. *Confirmation by King Henry II to St. Guthlac's, Hereford, of the chapel of St. Martin in Hereford Castle which Hugh de Lacy had given in the king's presence to endow the church. (c. 1179 × 82)*

A. H.C.L., no. 2178 (162 mm × 83 mm); tag and seal missing; endorsements: Carta regis de capella sancti Martini de Castello.[;] .D. (s. xii^{ex} × s. xiii^{in}); Caps(ula) iiii (s. xiii²?); GH; (notarial *signum*; uncertain date); **B**. Balliol Coll. MS. 271, no. 410, fol. 93; Capes, *Hereford Charters*, 22; Bishop, *Scriptores Regis*, no. 230; Holt and Mortimer, no. 131.

Henr(icus) rex Anglorum . dux Normannorum et Aquitanorum . et comes Andegauorum . archiepiscopis . episcopis . comitibus . baronibus . iusticiis . vicecomitibus . et omnibus ministris suis Francis et Anglis salutem. Sciatis me concessisse et presenti carta confirmasse . abbati Glouc' . et priori et monachis H'eford' . capellam sancti Martini de castello meo de H'eford' quam Hugo de Laci me presente et concedente dedit in puram et perpetuam elemosinam predictis monachis ad dotandam ecclesiam apostolorum Petri et Pauli et sancti Gudlaci H'eford'. Quare uolo et firmiter precipio . quod predicti monachi habeant et teneant predictam ecclesiam sancti Martini cum omnibus pertinentiis suis . scilicet ecclesia de Maneshull' cum terris et decimis ad eam pertinentibus . et cum duabus partibus decime dominii de Iagosoure . et duabus partibus decime dominii de Iarehull' . et de Hugetun' . et de Archelestun' . et de Wirmetun' . et tota decimo gardini Hugonis de Laci ultra Waiam . et omnibus obuentionibus castelli mei de Hereford'. T(estibus) Roberto episcopo Herefordensi . Radulfo archidiacono Herefordensis . Rannulfo Poer [*ending with three dots in a vertical line*].

A modified bookhand, which Mr. Bishop has not identified, the charter's script, suggestive of ecclesiastical origin, coupled with the anomalous absence of *dei gratia* and *et*, respectively before and after *rex Angl'* in the royal title, suggest that it was probably written by a St. Peter's or a St. Guthlac's scribe. There is no reason, other than the omission in the title, to believe it to be spurious (see Barrow, *Hereford Episcopal Acta*, no. 154 & n.).

353. *Alleged confirmation by King Henry III to the monks of St. Guthlac's, Hereford, that they, their tenants, and tenements should have in Hereford all the liberties and free customs enjoyed by freemen. (s. xiii²) Gloucester.*

P.R.O., E 40/14281 (171 mm × 70 mm), damaged; no turn-up and no certain provision for sealing; endorsements: Clamatio monachorum ecclesie apostolorum Petri et Pauli H'eford' per cartam (s. xiii²); Ext'a[1] (s. xiii²; poss. same hand).

.H. dei gratia rex Angl' et dux Norm' et Aquitannie et comes And' archiepiscopis episcopis abbatibus comitibus baronibus[2] iustic(iis) vicecomitibus et omnibus ministris et fidelibus suis Francis et Anglicis totius Angl' salutem. Sciatis[3] me concessisse et presenti carta mea confirmasse . quod monachi ecclesie apostolorum Petri et Pauli et sancti Gutlaci[4] H'ford' et omnes tenentes et tenementa eiusdem ecclesie in ciuitate mea de H'ford' habeant omnes libertates et liberas consuetudines quas liberi homines mei habent uel habere possunt in eadem ciuitate. Quare[5] uolo et firmiter precipio ut predicti monachi et homines eorum in prefata ciuitate habeant omnes libertates eo modo quo liberi homines mei eas melius habent sine vexatione et contradictione aliqua super forisfacturam decem librarum. Teste . magistro Anselmo Byset[6] apud Glouc'.

The charter is not authentic. There seems to have been no provision for sealing; and aside from the lack of appropriate punctuation and capitalization, the title most importantly lacks the *dominus Hibernie* which followed *rex Anglie* in the king's *acta* (Chaplais, 'The Making of the Treaty of Paris and the Royal Style', 248, 251–3). Along the left edge of the foot are the upper ends of writing which has been cut through, suggesting that the text may possibly have been cut from a roll of copies. The endorsement *Clamatio . . . per cartam* indicates that the charter's preparation may have been associated with a royal inquest or suit.

[1] The reading of superscript *t'* is uncertain due to loss of part of the slanting cross-bar.
[2] *Barronibus* in MS.   [3] *sciatis* in MS.   [4] *Gutlacii* in MS.
[5] *quare* in MS.   [6] The editor is indebted to Dr. David Crook for this reading.

354. *Mandate from the official of the court of Canterbury to the dean of Hereford to consider an appeal by the abbot and convent of St. Peter's, Gloucester, in a dispute about the tithes of the mills of Hinton (in Felton, Herefs.) between John, rector of Hinton, and Henry, chaplain of the same. 25 January 1255. London.*

H.C.L., no. 1893 (63 mm × 64); no turn-up; no provision for sealing; endorsements: .Commissio. sed h(oc) reportetur (*c.* s. xiii^ex); Hinetone (s. xiii^ex × s. xiv^in?); Non indiget registrari (*c.* s. xiv^ex); cal. in Baddeley ii, no. 47, p. 22.

Officialis curie Cantuariensis discreto viro decano Hereford' salutem in domino. Querelam abbatis et conuentus sancti Petri Glouc' accepimus continentes quod cum magister Iohannes rector ecclesie de Hynet' Henricum capellanum eiusdem loci super decimis molendinorum de Hynet' coram officiali archidiaconi Glouc' auctoritate ordinaria (in)cognoscente traxisset in camera'. iidem abbas et conuentus rem suam agi conspicientes et metuentes s(ibi) ex h(oc) preiudicium grauari pro eo quod dicte decime per priuilegium eis a sede apostolica indultum eisdem fuerint concesse ad docendum de iure suo coram eodem humiliter admitti postular(un)t. Et quia contra iusticiam eos audire recusauit'. sentientes ex hoc indebite se grauari . dominium proprium et ad tuitionem sue apellationis sedi Cantuariensi prout assertentes apellarunt. Quocirca[1] vobis mandamus quatinus vocatis qui fuerint euocandi c(aus)am tuitionis apellationis eorum summarie discutiatis. Et si inueneritis eos apellasse'. ipsos conseruetis in statu in quo fuerint tempore apellationis intellecte . prefigentes eisdem spatium vnius mensis infra quod iter arripiant ad prosequendam suam apellationem. Datum Lond' in festo conuersionis sancti Pauli . anno domini M.° CC.° L.° quinto.

[1] Reading uncertain due to stain on MS.

355. Conventio *in the form of a chirograph by Robert bishop of Hereford between Hamelin abbot of Gloucester and a knight S(imon) de Freine regarding a mill at Ocle Pychard (Herefs.). (6 March 1174 × 10 March 1179)*

H.C.L., no. 1525 (172 mm × 88 mm); tongue and tie torn away; seal missing; no endorsements; Walker, 'Gloucester Charters', no. 7; Barrow, *Hereford Episcopal Acta*, no. 145.

C I R O G R A P H . . . (inverted)

R. dei gratia Herefordensis episcopus omnibus fi[d]el[i]b[us] ad quos littere iste peruenerit'. eternam salutem. Noverit universitas uestra . conuentionem inter abbatem Gloecest' .H. et .S. de Fraxino militem habitam super molendino de Acle de quo multo tempore inter eos controuersia extiterat'. utraque parte in presentia nostra constituta. ex eorum relatione[1] audiuimus. Quare etiam se perpetua et fideliter obseruaturum'. predictus miles tactis sacrosanctis ewangeliis in multis consentientibus iurauit . Neque in posterum aliquomodo possit in irritum deuocari'. eandem conuentionem confirmamus . et presenti scripto et sigilli nostri appositione communimus . statuentes ut ita inter eos de cetero observetur'. quemadmodum in cyrographo inter eos descripto continetur . quod inspeximus et legimus. T(estibus) . Iohanne canonico et Iohanne presbitero capellanis meis . Nicholao de Leueken' . Willelmo de Stoches . magistro Eustachio . Roberto de la Landa . Theodbaldo'.

[1] In MS., an empty space contains a hole under which the scribe has drawn a line to link the wording of the text.

356. *Letter in writ form from Peter bishop of Hereford declaring that the patronage of the vicarages of St. Peter's, Hereford, and Ocle Pychard (Herefs.) belongs to the abbot and convent of St. Peter's, Gloucester, not to the bishop. 26 May 1247.*

A. H.C.L., no. 1411 (176 mm × 39 mm); tongue and fragment of tie; seal on tongue; white wax stained green, fragment; obverse: the partial torso of a bishop, with the lower part of a crozier held in the left hand visible; no counterseal; endorsements: Acle Pichard (s. xiii^{ex}); Caps(ula) .viii. de ecclesiasticis tenuris (s. xiii^{ex}); Registratur (s. xiv^{ex} × s. xv^{in}); Quid ius patronatus d[e] Acle Pichard nobis pertineat. A. Spiritualium parte prima (s. xv); **B**. P.R.O., C 150/1, fol. 234v; *Cart. Glouc.* ii, no. 867; Capes, *Hereford Charters*, 82.

Vniuersis Cristi fidelibus presentes litteras inspecturis uel' audituris Petrus diuina miseratione Herefordensis ecclesie minister humilis salutem in domino sempiternam. Nouerit vniuersitas uestra quod iura patronatus beati Petri Hereford' et de Acle Pichard uicariarum quas qualitercumque contulimus non ad nos uel ad ecclesiam nostram Herefordensem sed ad abbatem et conuentum sancti Petri Glouc' spectare noscuntur . In cuius rei testimonium vt ius ipsorum in dictis vicariis per istam nostram confessionem satis clarum efficiatur in posterum . presenti scripto sigillum nostrum una cum sigillo decani Herefordensis fecimus appendi.[1] Datum anno gratie m cc xlvii. die sancte Trinitatis. Valete.

On the churches of St. Peter, Hereford, and of Ocle Pychard (Herefs.) see Barrow, *Hereford Episcopal Acta*, nos. 7 & n., 17, 21 & n., 22 & n., 23–24, 87, 151 & n., 155 & n., 204, 260–1); see also *Regesta*, ii, no. 602 & p. 308, pp. 403, 410; Brooke, 'St. Peter of Gloucester', 55 n., 60 n.; Brett, *English Church under Henry I*, 142 n.

[1] **B** as printed in *Cart. Glouc.* ends here with *apponi.*

357. Conventio *between Abbot Thomas and the convent of St. Peter's, Gloucester, and Gilbert de Lacy. The monks were to pay Gilbert an annuity of 20 marks until they provided him with a benefice of 10 marks or more. Gilbert renounced all right which he claimed in their church of Holme Lacy in Herefordshire. (c. 1189 × 1203)*

H.C.L., no. 733 (215 mm × 85 mm); four tags; from left: seals on 1), 2), 4); 1) white wax, chipped and rubbed, round (61 mm in diam.); obverse: an equestrian figure to the right, a raised sword in the right hand, a shield on the left arm; legend: +SIGILLVM WALTERI DE LAC. . .; no counterseal; 2) white wax, fragment, chipped, round (57 mm in diam.); obverse: an equestrian figure facing right wearing a surcoat, a sword raised in the right hand, a shield on the left arm; legend: . . .GONIS DE . . .A. . .; no counterseal; 4) white wax, badly rubbed, oval (19 mm × 18 mm); image and legend illegible; endorsements: Conuentio inter nos et Gilebertum de Laceio; .c(apsula) .viii. de laicis tenuris. (s. xii^{ex} × s. xiii^{in}), **Hand h**; Hamme Lacy (s. xiii^{ex} × s. xiv^{in}).

Sciant presentes et futuri quod ego Thom(as) abbas et conuentus sancti Petri Glouc' . concessimus divine pietatis intuitu . dilecto clerico et amico nostro Gileberto de Laceio viginti solidos annuos ad festum sancti Michaelis percipiendos'. donec providamus ei in beneficio decem marcatas vel supra. Idem Gilebertus renuntiauit totum ius[1] quod clamavit se habere in ecclesia nostra de Ha'me in H'efordsir' que pertinet ad prioratum H'eford'. Iuramentum etiam nobis prestitit in capitulo nostro apud Glouc' . quod fidelis erit ecclesie nostre et dicto prioratui H'eford' . Et quod nec artem nec ingenium exquiret . neque per se . neque per inpositam personam'. unde domus nostra uel predictus prioratus H'eford'. dampnum uel uexationem incurrat super prenominata ecclesia de Ha'me . aut aliis donationibus et elemosinis'. nobis ab antecessoribus suis collatis'. et instrumentis eorum confirmatis. Quod quia ratum esse uolumus'. in cyrographum redegimus . Cuius unam partem sigillo nostro munitam'. ei tradidimus. Alteram partem eiusdem Gileberti et domini Walteri et Hugonis fratrum ipsius . et Willelmi de Saucei sigillis roboratam'. penes nos retinuimus. Hiis testibus . Gaufrido priore Lanton' . Osberto capellano eius . Willelmo de Warewic . Gaufrido Bidun . Philippo de Ruissebir' . Willelmo de Laceio . Henrico de Lungchaump iuniore . Roberto clerico . Radulfo de Saucei . Adam capellano de Heghamstade . Symone clerico . magistro Ambrosio . magistro Adam . Waltero Toki . Willelmo Ianitore . Philippo Carbunel.

For the text of Hugh (II) de Lacy's confirmation of his ancestors' grant of the church and appurtenant lands to St. Guthlac's, see Balliol Coll. MS. 271, no. 210, fol. 53v; Wightman, *The Lacy Family*, 176 & n. Hugh (II)'s predecessor Hugh (I) de Lacy's grant of the church of Holme Lacy to St. Guthlac's is recorded in ibid. no. 413, fols. 93v–94; see Barrow, *Hereford Episcopal Acta*, p. lxiii & n., nos. 7 & n., 16, 22, 87, 204, 260.

1 *toti iuri* in MS.

358. *Final concord between Osbert of Avenbury and Thomas abbot of St. Peter's, Gloucester, concerning the advowson of the church of Avenbury (Herefs.). 11 September 1199. Hereford.*

P.R.O., CP 25/1/80/1, no. 11 (182 mm [foot] × 85 mm [right]); damaged); no endorsement.

...YROGRAPHUM

H[ec][1] est finalis concordia facta in curia domini regis apud H'eford' die Sabat' proxima post Natiuitatem sancte Marie anno regni regis Iohannis primo coram Alano abbate Teokesbir' . Henrico archidiacono[2] Stafford' . Simone de Pateshill' . Iohanne de Gestliges . Ricardo Flandrense . Willelmo de Faleis' iustic(iis) et aliis baronibus domini regis tunc ibi presentibus inter Osbertum de Auenbir' petentem . Et Thomam abbatem Glouc' tenentem . de aduocatione ecclesie de Auenebir' . vnde recognitio summonita fuit inter eos in prefata curia . Scilicet quod predictus abbas Glouc' remisit et quiet(um)clamauit predicto Osberto et heredibus suis totum ius et clamium quod habuit in aduocatione predicte ecclesie de se et successoribus suis Inperpetuum[.] Et pro hac fine et concordia et quiet(a)clamatione predictus Osbertus et heredes sui dabunt predicto abbati et successoribus suis vnam marcam argenti per annum . per manum suam inperpetuum . Scilicet ad festum sancti Michaelis donec ipse Osbertus uel heredes sui assignauerint predicto abbati uel successoribus suis predictam marcam . in reddit'.

H'eford'

On the church of Avenbury, see Barrow *Hereford Episcopal Acta*, nos. 87, 260.

1 MS. torn away.   2 *Arched(iacono)* in MS.

359. *Final concord between Thomas abbot of St. Peter's, Gloucester, and Hugh de Freine concerning the advowsons of the churches of Moccas and of Sutton St. Michael (Herefs.), which the abbot remitted and quitclaimed to Hugh in return for*

20s. annual rent charged on Sutton mill and payable to St. Peter's and the monks of St. Guthlac's. 23 February 1226. Westminster.

P.R.O., CP 25/1/80/6, no. 76 (111 mm [left] × 165 mm [foot]); no endorsement.

CYROGRAPHM[1]

Hec est finalis concordia facta in curia domini regis apud Westm' . a die Purificationis beate Marie in tres septimanas . Anno regni regis Henrici filii regis Iohannis decimo . Coram Martino de Pat'hill' [.] Thoma de Muleton' . Thoma de Heiden' [.] Roberto de Lexinton' [.] Galfrido le Sauuag' [.] Garino filio Iohel' iustic(iis) et aliis domini regis fidelibus tunc ibi presentibus . Inter Thom(am) abbatem Glouc' petentem per Galfridum de Weston' positum loco suo ad lucrandum uel perdendum . Et Hugonem de Fraxino deforciantem de aduocationibus ecclesiarum de Mocres et de Sutton' . Vnde placitum fuit inter eos in eadem curia . Scilicet quod predictus abbas remisit et quietum clamauit de se et successoribus suis ipsi Hugoni et heredibus suis. totum ius et clamium quod habuit in aduocationibus predictarum ecclesiarum cum pertinentiis imperpetuum. Et predictus Hugo pro deo et salute anime sue et heredum suorum . dedit et concessit pro se et heredibus suis ipsi abbati et successoribus suis et monachis sancti Gutlaci de Hereford' i(m)perpetuum. singulis annis viginti solidatas redditus de molendinis de Sutton' percipiendas ipsis monachis sancti Gutlaci ad duos terminos anni scilicet ad festum sancte Marie in Martio. decem solidos . et ad festum sancti Michaelis. decem solidos. Et predictus Hugo et heredes sui warantizabunt predicto abbati et successoribus suis et predictis monachis sancti Gutlaci. predictum redditum viginti solidorum. contra omnes gentes i(m)perpetuum. Et si forte predictus Hugo uel heredes sui defecerint [de][2] solutione viginti solidorum ad aliquem predictorum terminorum . secundum quod predictum est. bene licebit ipsi abbati et successoribus suis destringere ipsum Hugonem et heredes suos per catalla inuenta in predictis molendinis. usque ad plenam solutionem predictorum viginti solidorum. Et sciendum quod si idem abbas uel successores sui aliquas cartas de cetero protulerint de predictis aduocationibus. pro nullis habebuntur quantum ad predictas aduocationes.

Hereford'

St. Guthlac's held the church of Sutton St. Michael and the chapel of Sutton St. Nicholas (Barrow, *Hereford Episcopal Acta*, nos. 55 n., 126, 260, 346). Since Sutton St. Nicholas was a chapelry the advowson was evidently that of Sutton St. Michael.

[1] No space for *U*; perhaps in the **V**-shaped cut there was a suspension sign.
[2] Hole in MS.

360. *Final concord between Walter de Mucegros and Jocelin prior of St. Guthlac's, Hereford, concerning 4 acres of land and 16 acres of meadow in Cobhall (Herefs.), which Walter acknowledged to be the right of the prior. 26 September 1227. Hereford.*

P.R.O., CP 25/1/80/6, no. 97 (90 mm [left] × 200 mm [foot]); no endorsement.

CYROG...RAPHVM

Hec est finalis concordia facta in curia domini regis apud Hereford' die dominica proxima post festum sancti Mathaei . anno regni Henrici filii regis Iohannis vndecimo . Coram Mauric(io) de Gaunt . Roberto de Lexinton' et Radulfo Musard iustic(iis) itinerantibus et aliis domini regis fidelibus tunc ibi presentibus [.] Inter Walt(eru)m de Mucegros petentem et Iocelinum priorem Herford' tenentem de quatuor acris terre et sexdecim acris prati cum pertinentiis in Cobbenhal' . Vnde assisa mortis antecessoris sumonita fuit inter eos in prefata curia . Scilicet quod predictus Walt(eru)s recognouit totam predictam terram et pratum cum pertinentiis esse ius ipsius prioris . Habend(am) et tenend(am) eidem priori et successoribus suis et ecclesie sue de Hereford' in liberam et perpetuam elemosinam . Faciendo inde seruitium capitalibus dominis feodi illius quantum ad terram illam pertinebit. Et pro hac recognitione [.] fine et concordia: idem prior recepit ipsum Walt(eru)m et heredes suos in singulis benefactis et orationibus que decetero fient in ecclesia sua de Hereford'.

Hereford'

361. *Final concord between between Robert prior of St. Guthlac's, Hereford, and Roger of Hereford and Henry of Monmouth concerning woodland common to them which the prior said Roger and Henry had laid waste; Roger and Henry gave 30 acres of the woodland to the prior in severalty, for which he gave them 10 marks and relinquished his claim to the rest of the wood. 20 January 1249. Worcester.*

P.R.O., CP 25/1/80/12, no. 228 (102 mm [left] × 258 mm [foot]); no endorsement.

C...ROGR...PHUM

Hec est finalis concordia facta in curia domini regis apud Wygorn' . in octabis sancti Hillarii . anno regni regis Henrici filii regis Iohannis tricesimo tercio . Coram Rogero Thurkelby . Gilberto de Preston' . magistro Simone de Wanton' . Iohanne de Cobbeh' iustic(iis) itinerantibus et aliis domini regis fidelibus ibi presentibus . Inter Rob(ertu)m priorem Hereford' querentem Rogerum de Hereford' et Henricum de Munemue de hoc quod idem prior questus fuit quod predicti Rogerus et Henricus prostrauerunt [.] destruxerunt et aspertauerunt boscum de Hasserugge qui communis est inter predictum priorem et predictos Rogerum et Henricum sine licentia et voluntate ipsius prioris . Et vnde placitum fuit inter eos in eadem curia . Scilicet quod predicti Rogerus et Henricus dederunt et concesserunt predicto priori et successoribus suis et ecclesie sue de Hereford' triginta acras bosci cum pertinentiis de predicto bosco . per diuisas et metas subscriptas . scilicet incipiendo ab aqua que vocatur Sindreford' sicut se extendit in latitudine usque ad boscum ipsorum Rogeri et Henrici et in longitudine sicut se extendit a bosco Iohannis de Stapelton' usque ad viam que ducit uersus Hudeslegh' . Habendas et tenendas eidem priori et successoribus suis et ecclesie sue predicte in puram et perpetuam elemosinam . liberam et quietam ab omni seculari seruitio et exactione imperpetuum . Ita quod bene licebit eidem priori et sucessoribus suis predictas triginta acras bosci includere fossato et haya . et illas in defensum ponere . et assartare . et proficuum suum pro voluntate sua inde facere imperpetuum. Et predicti Rogerus et Henricus et heredes ipsorum warantizabunt acquietabunt et defendent predicto priori et successoribus suis et ecclesie sue predicte predictas triginta acras bosci cum pertinentiis vt liberam puram et perpetuam elemosinam suam contra omnes homines imperpetuum. Et preterea idem prior dedit predictis Rogero et Henrico decem marcas argenti. Et pro hoc donatione concessione warantizatione acquietantia defensione fine et concordia‑ idem prior remisit [et] quiet(um)clamauit de se et successoribus suis et ecclesia sua predicta predictis Rogero et Henrico et heredibus ipsorum totum ius et clamium quod habuit in superplusagio totius predicti bosci cum pertinentiis imperpetuum.

Hereford'

362. *Relaxation by Nicholas son of Herbert and his wife Dionisia to the hospital of St. Ethelbert (Hereford) of 2s. 4d. of the 14s. 10d. annual rent owed by the hospital; as a guarantee Nicholas surrendered his charter from St. Guthlac's for land at (Upper) Lyde (Herefs.) to Reginald, master of the hospital, who gave 2 marks for the relaxation. (c. 1225 × 30)*

H.C.L., no. 838 (176 mm × 93 mm); in the centre of the turn-up, a single slit for a tag; tag and seal missing; on the right end of the turn-up, a seal on a tag; dark green wax; obverse: round (35 mm in diam.); a fleur-de-lis; legend: +SIGILL': DIONISIE :VXORIS: NICOL': FIL': H'R'I.; no counterseal; endorsement: Carta Nichol(ai) filii Hereberti (s. xiii[1]).

Sciant presentes et futuri quod ego Nicholaus filius Hereberti et Dionisia vxor mea relaxauimus et remisimus inperpetuum deo et beate Marie et domui elemosinarie sancti Ethelberti et eiusdem domus custodibus duas solidas redditus et quatuor denariatas de quatuordecim solidatis redditus et de decim denariatis quas dicta domus et eius custodes nobis annuatim reddere consueuerunt . Ita scilicet quod de cetero dicta domus et eius custodes nec nobis nec heredibus nostris in nullo respondeant nisi de duodecim solidis et sex denariis . annuatim nobis et heredibus nostris persoluendis. Et ad maiorem securitatem predicte domui et eius custodibus prestandam‑ ego Nichol(aus) tradidi magistro Reginaldo tunc custodi illius domus cartam meam quam habui de priore et conuentui sancti Guthlaci Hereford' de duodecim acris terre apud Lud' . Ita quod si vxor mea Dionisia vel heredes nostri aliquam vexationem vel inquietationem predicte domui et eius custodibus super predictam relaxationem facere voluerint . custos domus illius predictas acras cum fructibus suis habeant et teneant quousque vxor mea Dionis(ia) et heredes nostri predictam domum et eius custodes securos fecerint de predicta relaxatione quam eis fecimus firmiter obseruanda. Pro hac autem relaxatione dedit nobis magister Reginaldus tunc custos illius domus duas marcas argenti. Et vt hec nostra relaxatio firma et stabilis permaneat‑ nos eam presenti carta nostra sigillorum nostrorum appositione confirmauimus Hiis testibus Henrico Craft . Hugone filio Ailmundi . Waltero Sauuage . Willelmo palmerio . Willelmo Wiþir . Willelmo de pipa . Nicholao cantore . et multis aliis.

St. Guthlac's had various proprietary interests at Upper Lyde (Herefs.); land there was given in 1148 × *c.* 1155 by Alberada de Loges (Barrow, *Hereford Episcopal Acta*, nos. 86B, 125; *LCGF*, no. 319). Nicholas, as the above text indicates, was a tenant of the priory. St. Ethelbert's Hospital was founded *c.* 1225 by a canon of Hereford, Elias of Bristol (Barrow, no. 344 n.); this date and the vintage of the script of Nicholas's charter suggest its date. Its scribe also endorsed it, which means that he was bureaucratically associated with the hospital or cathedral chapter.

363. *Sale and quitclaim by Stephen son of Mary to Elias of Bristol, canon of Hereford, of his right to 32d. annual rent from a tenement in the parish of St. Owen (Hereford), for 20s. to Stephen and 7d. annual rent to be paid to the prior and convent of St. Guthlac's Priory. (c. 1200 × c. 1225)*

H.C.L., no. 734 (146 mm × 138 mm); seal on tag; white wax; round (39 mm in diam.); a lion rampant to the right; legend: +SIGLL' STEFANI FILII MARIE; no counterseal; endorsement: H'eford' (s. xiv); f (uncertain date); other endorsements are illegible.

Sciant presentes et futuri quod ego Steph(anu)s filius Marie vendidi et quietum clamaui totum ius meum quod habui in tenemento illo quod Philippus filius Henrici tenuit de me in parochia sancti Audoeni quod iacet inter terram Adam filii Edit et inter terram Rogeri canonici. Elye de Bristoll' canonico H'eford' sine retenemento mihi uel heredibus meis scilicet triginta duos denarios annuatim per manum Philippi filii Henr(ici) recipiendos. tenendos et habendos[1] sibi cuicumque uel ubicumque illos assignare uoluerit . Reddendo inde annuatim septem denarios priori et conuentui[2] sancti Guthlaci scilicet tres denarios et obolum ad Annuntiationem beate Marie . et tres denarios et obolum ad festum sancti Michaelis pro omni seruitio et demandis. Et pro hac uenditione et quieta clamantia dedit mihi predictus Elyas uiginti solidos esterlingorum et ad maiorem securitatem predicto Elye prestandam . Ricardus filius meus et heres meus et Sibilla uxor mea propria sua uoluntate iurauerunt et affidauerunt . quod quando de me humanitus contingerit . numquam aliquid in predicto tenemento clamabunt . contra predictam Eliam uel suos assignatos. Ego siquidem predictum tenementum et heredes mei predicto Elye et suis assignatis contra omnes homines et feminas warentizabimus. Et ut hec mea uenditio rata sit et stabilis . ego eam presenti carta mea et sigilli mei inpressione confirmaui. Hiis testibus . Nicholao filio Hereberti . Iohanne clerico . Willelmo Seisil : Rogero filio Vthredi . Willelmo nobili . Randulfo clerico . Willelmo amiz . Ricardo palmario . et multis aliis.

Elias of Bristol's foundation charter for St. Ethelbert's gave the hospital the 32d. annual rent out of which the hospital was to pay the 7d. annual rent charged by this charter (H.C.L., no. 2001; Capes, *Hereford Charters*, 57–59; see also above, no. 362 n.). The foundation charter is the *terminus ad quem* for this charter, whose script appears to be of *c.* 1200.

---

[1] *tendendas et habendas* in MS.   [2] *conuentu* in MS.

KILPECK PRIORY

364. *Receipt in the form of a letter patent from John prior of Kilpeck for 10s. from master Richard de Montvernier, canon of Hereford, being a pension from Baysham church (in Sellack, Herefs.). 25 March 1262.*

H.C.L., no. 725 (146 mm × 56 mm); tongue and tie missing; endorsement: Quitantiam priorie de Kilpec (s. xiii²?).

Omnibus Cristi fidelibus presentes literas visuris uel audituris . Ioh(annes) prior de Kilpec salutem eternam in domino. Nouerit vniuersitas uestra . nos anno . domini .M°.cc. Sexagesimo Secundo . in festo beate Marie . in Martio . recepisse a delecto viro domino Ricardo de Monte G'nerio canonico Herfordie .decem. solidos sterlingorum . de pencione de ecclesia de Baysham. In cuius testimonium . has literas sigillo nostro s[i]ngnatas[1] ei fecimus patentes.

St. David's, Kilpeck, along with the chapel of St. Mary in the adjacent castle and other churches, chapels, and lands was given to St. Peter's, Gloucester, by Hugh fitz William, son of Norman, in 1134 (*Cart. Glouc.* i, pp. 16, 91; see above, p. xxix). For master Richard see Chapuisat, 'Le chapitre savoyard de Hereford', 45, 47, 51 (for which I am indebted to Dr. Julia Barrow).

[1] A stain on the MS. makes the reading of *i* uncertain.

365. *Letter patent from Thomas dean of Gloucester to Stephen dean of Hereford to the effect that master John, a monk of Gloucester and former rector of St. Nicholas, Hereford, said on oath that in the first year after his institution he received 13 marks from the issues of the church and in the following year 14 marks. (c. 1250)*

H.C.L., no. 1897 (132 mm × 57 mm); tongue and tie cut or torn; seal missing; endorsement: Non indiget registrari (s. xiv^ex × s. xv^in).

Viro venerabili et discreto domino .S. decano Herford' Th(omas) decanus Glouc' salutem . et sinceram in domino karitatem. Nouerit discretio uestra quod dominus Iohannes . monachus Glouc' . quondam rector ecclesie sancti Nicholai Herford' iuratus dicit . quod primo anno post institutionem suam in eadem recepit tresdecim marcas de prouentibus eiusdem ecclesie . In sequenti uero anno quatuor decim marcas recepit . et amplius᷉. nescit quot solidos. In cuius rei testimonium presentes litteras patentes uobis transmitto. Valete.

Master Thomas was archdeacon of Gloucester in 1248–53 (*Fasti*, ii. 107). Pension from the church of St. Nicholas was part of Kilpeck's endowment (Barrow, *Hereford Episcopal Acta*, no. 73).

LEONARD STANLEY PRIORY

366. *Grant by King Henry II to Leonard Stanley Priory of the church of St. Mary, Arlingham, confirming also Roger (III) of Berkeley's gift of a virgate at Maisemore and 60s. of his rents of* Hardacre. *(January 1156) Dover.*

Bodl. MS. Charters Gloucester, a.1, no. 20 (195 mm × 156 mm), **Scribe 25**; tag and seal missing; endorsement: De Herlingeh'. (*c.* 1156 × 80); facsm. in *Archaeologia*, vol. 71, p. 203; Delisle and Berger, i, no. 10, p. 105; Bishop, *Scriptores Regis*, no. 584; Holt and Mortimer, no. 154.

H. rex Anglorum et dux Normannorum et Aquitanorum et comes Andegauorum . I. episcopo Wigorniensi . et omnibus baronibus et iustic(iis) et vicecomitibus et omnibus fidelibus suis de Gloec'scyr' et de honore de Berchelaio Francis et Anglis⸵ salutem. Sciatis me concessisse in liberam et perpetuam elemosinam ecclesie sancti Leonardi de Stanlegha ecclesiam sancte Marie de Erlingeha' cum omnibus decimis eiusdem ville . in pratis et bladis et piscaturis . et omnibus rebus . et vnam virgatam terre apud Maismora' . quam Rogerus de Berchelaio dedit predicte ecclesie in elemosinam . liberam et quietam de geldo et omni consuetudine. Preterea concedo eidem ecclesie sexaginta solidos . per annum . scilicet Hardacr' de Berchelaio quam idem Rogerus ei dedit de redditibus suis . sicut carte regis H. aui mei testantur. Quare volo et firmiter precipio quod predicta ecclesia sancti Leonardi et monachi ibidem deo seruientes⸵ hec predicta libere et quiete et honorifice teneant . cum omnibus . libertatibus et liberis consuetudinibus suis. Testibus . T. cancellario. comite Reginaldo . Ricardo de Humet constabulario . M. Biset dapifero . W. filio Geroldi camerario . Apud Dour' in transitu regis.

For the dating see Delisle and Berger, i, no. 10 n., p. 105. The abbey's Calendar of Donations recorded Roger's gift of the church of Arlingham (*Cart. Glouc.* i, p. 106). *Hardacre* may have been in Nympsfield (*PNG* ii. 244).

367. *Confirmation by King Henry II of an agreement between the convent of St. Peter's, Gloucester, and Reading Abbey and the canons of St. Augustine's Bristol concerning the church of Cam, made before Bartholomew bishop of Exeter and John bishop of Chichester, papal judges delegate; St. Peter's was to hold the church, paying 6 marks a year to Reading, of which St. Augustine's was to receive half from Reading. (c. 28 July 1177). Woodstock.*

A. B.L. Add. Ch. 19606 (160 mm × 225 mm), **Scribe 27**; seal on plaited green and brown silk cords; red wax, fragment; obverse: majesty side, round (meas. unavail.); legend illegible; reverse: equestrian, round (meas. unavail.); legend illegible; endorsement: Carta regis H. secundi de pace et fine inter monachos Rading' et monachos Gloecestrie super ecclesia de Cham'a . et eius pertinentiis. (*c.* 1170); **B**. ibid. Egerton MS. 3031, fol. 24; **C.**, ibid. Harl. MS. 1708, fols. 24v–25; *Cart. Reading*, i, no. 285; Delisle, *BEC* 68 (1907), no. 41, p. 285; Hurry, *Reading Abbey*, 169–70; Morey, *Bartholomew of Exeter*, Appendix I, no. 19; Bishop, *Scriptores Regis*, no. 303; Holt and Mortimer, no. 244.

[H.] dei gratia rex Anglorum et dux Normannorum et Aquitanorum et comes

Andegauorum̄. archiepiscopis . episcopis . ab[batibus] . comitibus . baronibus . iustic(iis) . vicecomitibus . ministris . et omnibus fidelibus suis Francis et Anglis totius Angl'[. salutem.] Sciatis me concessisse et presenti carta mea confirmasse pacem et finem factum coram B. et I. Exoniensi et Cicestrensi episcopis inter monasterium et monachos de Rading' et monasterium et monachos Gloe[c'] de controversia et lite quam assistentibus canonicis sancti Augustini de Bristow' et aliis competitoribus monachorum de Rading' uertebatur inter eadem monasteria et eosdem monachos de ecclesia de Ca'ma et omnibus eius pertinentiis . Videlicet quod assensu meo et predictorum episcoporum qui ex mandato domini papę Alexandri tertii inde controuersia illa fuerant iudices delegati . Inter predicta monasteria et monachos in eis deo seruientes ita conuenit . quod monasterium Gloec' pro bono pacis et nomine transactionis pro memorata controuersia et querela perpetuo terminandā. soluet annuatim monasterio de Rading' s[e]x [marcas] argenti . tres ad Pascha et tres ad festum sancti Michaelis . quarum medietatem perci[pient canoni]ci [sanc]ti Augustini de Bristowa per manus monachorum de Rading'. Tenebit autem m[onasterium Gloec'] predictam ecclesiam de Ca'ma cum omnibus pertinentiis suis de me in capite sicut propriam elemosinam mea[m] salua monachis de Rading' predicta sex marcarum solutione a monasterio Gloec' facienda . Ita quod et monachi de Rading' sex illas marcas tanquam propriam elemosinam meam perpetuo percipiant et possideant. Id etiam compositionis tenori adiectum est ut ad prenominatę ecclesie de Camma pertinentias reuocandas qui ei subtracte sunt aut a quibuscumque detentē. monachi de Rading' coadiuuantibus canonicis sancti Augustini . consilium et auxilium monachis Gloec' karitatiue et sociali[ter impen]dant. Debent etiam monachi Gloec' predictorum canonicorum sancti Augustini de Bristow' super [memo]rata compositione quantum in eis est fideliter firmiterque seruandā. cartam confirmationis [habere.] Qvare uolo et firmiter precipio quod hec pax et concordia et finis factus inter supradicta m[onasteria] et monachos de prefata ecclesia de Ca'ma et omnibus pertinentiis suis . stabilis sit̄. et incon[cusse teneatur.] T(estibus) . comite Willelmo de Mann' . Roberto comite Legr' . Fvlcone Paienell' . Rogero d[e] S[tut' . Roberto de] Stut' . Willelmo de Stut' . Gaufrido Pertic' . Willelmo filio Aldelini dapifero . Apud [Wodest'].

Sections of the text enclosed in square brackets have been supplied from **B**. Walter de Gray Birch considered the seal appended to be an example of Henry II's second (*Catalogue of Seals*, i, no. 71, p. 12). The tenurial dispute between the two abbey's resulted from contradictory donations made apparently during the 'Anarchy' of King Stephen's reign (Kemp, 'The Churches of Berkeley Hernesse', 96–110). The terms of Henry's confirmation appear almost verbatim in a letter of Bartholomew bishop of Exeter and of John bishop of Chichester, announcing the agreement reached in the king's presence at Woodstock 28 July 1177 (Mayr-Harting, *Chichester Episcopal Acta*, no. 69; Morey, *Bartholomew of Exeter*, Appendix I, no. 18; see also *Cart. Bristol*, no. 15 & n.).

368. *Ratification by Baldwin archbishop of Canterbury of the settlement by William bishop of Worcester of the dispute between St. Peter's, Gloucester, and Leonard Stanley Priory on one hand and William of Berkeley on the other concerning the* *advowson of the church of Coberley; St. Peter's and the priory remitted their right to William, and the priory was to receive, in place of the 5s. pension formerly paid by Coberley church, half the tithes of William's demesne and of his cottars in Coberley. (February × May 1188)*

Bodl. MS. Charters Gloucester, a. 1, no. 22 (161 mm × 181 mm); damaged; fragment of tag; seal missing; no endorsement; Swynnerton, 'Stanley St. Leonards', 267–8 with facsm.; Cheney and Jones, *Canterbury Acta*, no. 276.

B. dei gratia Canturiensis archiepiscopus totius Angl' primas . Omnibus Cristi fidelibus ad quos presens scriptum peruenerit⸱ salutem in domino. Notum sit uniuersitati uestre . literas venerabilis fratris nostri Willelmi Wigorniensis episcopi nobis exhibitas fuisse in hec uerba. Vniuersis sancte matris ecclesie filiis . Willelmus diuina miseratione Wigorniensis ecclesie minister⸱ salutem in domino. Ad uniuersitatis uestre uolumus peruenire notitiam . quod controuersia que uertebatur inter abbatem et conuentum ecclesie sancti Pe[tri] Gloecestrensis . et priorem et monach[o]s de Stanleia⸱ et Willelmum de Berchelai super iure aduocationis ecclesie de Cutberl' . ex utraque parte in nos compromissione facta⸱ nostra dispositione de consilio prudentum uirorum qui nobis asistebant consentiente magistro Petro de [L]e[c]h tunc temporis persona ipsius ecclesie . hoc modo finem sortita est. P[re]f[ati] siquidem abbas et conuentus [Gloec]estr' et [p]rior de Stanl' quicquid iuris in aduocatione predicte ecclesie de Cutberleia se habere proposuerant . [prenom]ina[to] Willelmo de Berkel' qui eam clamabat et heredibus suis in perpetuum remiserunt. Quia [vero ecclesia sancti Leona]rdi de Stanleia ad uirorum religiosorum ibi existe[nt]ium sust[e]n[ta]tionem de prelibata [ecc]l[esi]a [de Cudberleia quinque] solidos quos ulterius[1] non est perceptura nom[ine pension]is [percipere solebat ne suo penitus commodo] frustraretur [nos statui]mus [v]t ipsam medieta[tem] decim[arum frugum terre totius dominii eiusdem Willelmi de Be]rk[eleia et omnium cotariorum suorum in Cutberleia quicumque] terras excoluerit⸱ per m[anus propriorum seruientium in perpetuam] elemosinam per[ci]pia[t. Ut hoc statum sicut coram nobis][2] c[om]positio facta est perpetuum et incon[vulsum perm]aneat eum presenti scri]pto commendare [et] testium su[b]scriptione sigillique nostri appos[itione con]firmare dignum duximus. Hiis testibus . magistro P[e]tro de [Lech' .] magistro Godefrido de Lanton' [.] magistro Willelmo de Tunebrig' . Roberto de Bellocampo . Roberto de Lech' [. Willelmo] filio Godefridi . Iohanne de Draiton' [.] Hugone pincerna . Walterio nepote magistri Petri . Galfrido filio Restwoldi [. . . .] Mainard'. Nos igitur quod a prefat[o episcopo i]n hac parte statutum est ratum hab[en]tes et gratum⸱ illud quod [iuste] et canonice factum est presentis scripti attestatione[3] et sigilli nostri appositione communiuimus. Hiis te[stibus Gi]raldo archidiacono Meneuensi . magistro Petro Blesensi Bathoniensi archidiacono . magistro Siluestro . magistro Alexandro Walensi . Ricardo de Umfranuill' . Reginaldo de Oilli . Nicholao de Lideford' . magistro Michaele de Buk. . . . . magistro Reginaldo de Hamme . Willelmo de Botinton' . Eustachio de Wilton' . et multis aliis . et . . .

Words in square brackets have been supplied editorially and from below, no. 370. For the dating, see Cheney and Jones, *Canterbury Acta*, no. 276 n.

[1] Reading uncertain.

[2] *Ut . . . nobis* is the conjectural reconstruction in *Canterbury Acta*; given the space and hints which fragments of the script provide, that seems preferable to *Vt autem hec . . .* as below, no. 370.

[3] *attestione* in MS.

369. *Testimony of two chaplains of Slimbridge and others concerning the division of tithes between the rector of Slimbridge and St. Peter's, Gloucester. (s. xiii^med)*

Worcester Cathedral Dean & Chapter, B. 784 (124 mm × 125 mm); no seal and no provision for a seal; no turn-up; endorsement: a: Slymbrigge (s. xiv^in).

R. capellanus de Slimbrig' iuratus dicit quod tres acre infra limites parochie de Sl'mbr' a quibus acris recepit magister R. rector ecclesie de Sl'mbr' decimam quotiens seminate sunt faba uel auena seu alio blado quam de frumento. Quando autem frumentum seminatur. abbas et conuentus Glouc' integre fructum dictarum acrarum asportant[.] Et si videret uel sciret dictum rectorem unquam fuisse in possessione fructuum dictarum acrarum frumenti seminatarum dicit quod non. Adicit etiam quod ministrauit in dicta ecclesia tempore antecessoris istius ecclesie. videlicet tempore magistri R. de Sl'mbr'e et semper vidit dictos monachos frumentum capere plenarie de tribus acris vbiqumque iacebant in diuersis campis [.] De alia uero manerie bladi. semper recepit rector ecclesie decimam dictarum acrarum. Robertus capellanus sancte Marie de Sl'mbr' iuratus dicit idem per omnia quod R. capellanus preiuratus. Willelmus Le buteler iuratus dicit de predictis acris quotiens seminate sunt frumento. sed fecerunt abbas et conuentus suam voluntatem tanquam de re sua propria cum vero alio grane bladi seminarentur semper precepit rector ecclesie qui pro tempore fuerit decimas dictarum acrarum. Andreas cleri[c]us[1] iuratus dicit idem quod preiuratus Willelmus de mora concordat cum prius iuratis.[2]

In 1225, after a dispute over Slimbridge church between Thomas of Berkeley and Abbot Thomas of Bredon, Thomas of Berkeley granted Lorridge (in Stinchcombe) to Leonard Stanley Priory and Abbot Thomas remitted the advowson of Slimbridge to Thomas of Berkeley (see below, no. 372). The above testimony may have been associated with the settlement.

[1] *cap(e)llan(us)* interlined with *cleri[c]us* superscript.

[2] *Andreas . . . iuratis* in a different hand.

370. *Agreement in the form of a chirograph between the abbot and convent of St. Peter's, Gloucester, and Leonard Stanley Priory on one hand and William of Berkeley on the other concerning the advowson of the church of Coberley, in similar terms to no. 368. (1186 × 1190)*

Bodl. MS. Charters Gloucester, a.1, no. 21 (199 mm × 149 mm); fragment of tag; seal missing; endorsement: Cuthberleye (s. xiii^ex); Swynnerton, 'Stanley St. Leonards', 266.

CYROGRAPHUM

Notum sit omnibus sancte matris ecclesie filiis quod controuersia que uertebatur inter abbatem et conuentum ecclesie sancti Petri Gloec' et priorem et monachos de

Stanleia et Willelmum de Berkeleia super iure aduocationis ecclesie de Cudb'leia facta ex utraque parte compromissione in dominum Willelmum Wigorniensem episcopum ipso dictante et ordinante et magistro Petro de Lech tunc persona ipsius ecclesie presente et assensum prebente. sub tali pacis forma sopita est. Prefati siquidem abbas et conuentus Gloec' . et prior de Stanleia . quicquid iuris in aduocatione predicte ecclesie de Cudberl' se h[a]bere proponebat prenominato Willelmo de Berkel' qui eam clamabat et heredibus suis in perpetuum remiserunt. Quia uero ecclesia sancti Leonardi de Stanl' ad uirorum religiosorum ibi existentium sustentationem de prelibata ecclesia de Cudberl' quinque solidos nomine pensionis annuatim percipere solebat ne suo penitus commodo frustraretur. statuit memoratus episcopus assensu et uoluntate sepedicti Willelmi de Berkel' . ut ipsam medietatem decimarum frugum terre totius dominii eiusdem Willelmi de Berkel' et omnium cotariorum suorum in Cudberl' quicu(m)que terras ipsas extoluerit. per manus propriorum seruientium in perpetuam elemosinam percipiat. Vt autem hec concordia rata et inconuulsa inter eos in posterum permaneat diuiso inter eos cyrographo sigillisque suis appositis . hinc inde confirmata est. His testibus . Radulfo abbate de Winchec' . magistro Petro de Lech . Iohanne decano Gloec' . magistro Godefrido de Lanton' . magistro Willelmo de Tunebrug' [.] Roberto de Bellocampo . Ricardo de Wiretceb' . Willelmo filio Stephani vicecomite Gloec' . Rogero de Berkel' . et Rogero . et Philippo . et Oliuero militibus et Roberto clerico filiis suis . Ricardo de Aldrintuna . Ricardo clerico v[icec']¹ Gloec' . Arnaldo Dunning . Arnaldo filius eius . Adam rufo . Waltero Toki . Willelmo de Botint' . Roberto de b'tuna . Gaufrido de Lillet' . Hamone Carbunel et Roberto fratre eius . Nicholao de Rudes . Roberto Testard.

The limiting dates of this chirograph are the consecration of William of Northolt as bishop of Worcester and the end of William fitz Stephen's tenure as sheriff of Gloucester (*HBC*, 278; Walker, 'Earldom of Hereford Charters', no. 103 n).

¹ MS. damaged and reading uncertain.

371. *Grant in the form of a chirograph by Abbot Thomas and the convent of St. Peter's, Gloucester, to Robert clerk, nephew of Peter of Leche, archdeacon of Worcester, for term of his life of tithes in Coberley (as awarded to Leonard Stanley Priory in nos. 368 and 370) for ½ mark a year payable to the priory. (1189 × c. 1198)*

Bodl. MS. Charters Gloucester, a.1, no. 23 (179 mm × 88 mm); damaged; fragment of tag; seal missing.

CYROGRAPHUM (*inverted*)

Notum sit omnibus quod ego Thom(as) dei gratia abbas et conuentus ecclesie sancti Petri Gloec' . concessimus Roberto clerico nepote Petri [d]e Lech archidiaconi Wigorniensi medietatem decimarum dominii Willelmi de Berkelai et cotariorum suorum¹ in Cudberl' . que pertinet ad ecclesiam sancti Leonardi de [S]tanleia. tenendam de nobis [i]n uita sua terram² pro dimidia marca arg[enti] priori de Stanl' reddenda his terminis . Ad festum sancti Micha[el]is .xl. d(enariis) . Ad Annunt[iatio]nem b[eat]e [Ma]r[ie] .xl. d(enariis). Idem uero Robertus iurauit nobis [quod] fidelis erit ecclesie nostre [d]e [predi]cto tenemento . Et quo[d ne]c ar[t]em n[ec] i[n]ge[nium ex]q[ui]ret unde [e]cclesia sancti L[eo]nardi de Stanl' de prefatis decimis [dam]pnum aut impedimentum [i]ncurra[t. I]n [cu]iu[s] r[e]i testimonium [pre]sentis cyrographi [unam] partem sigillo nostro munitam [ei] tradidimus. Alteram uero pa[r]tem sigill[o] p(re)f[ati] a[rc]hidiaconi r[o]b[or]atam penes nos [retinuim]us.

The text has been read with ultra-violet light. Words in square brackets have been added editorially. Master Peter of Leche became archdeacon of Worcester in 1189/90 and died *c.* 1198, possibly 1195 × 98 (*Fasti*, ii. 105, 107 n.).

1 Reading uncertain.   2 Reading uncertain.

372. *Final concord between Thomas of Berkeley and Thomas abbot of St. Peter's, Gloucester, concerning the advowson of the church of Slimbridge; the abbot remitted the advowson to Thomas of Berkeley, who gave all his land in Lorridge for the monks of St. Peter's serving at (Leonard) Stanley Priory. 20 January 1225. Westminster.*

P.R.O., CP 25/1/73/7, no. 85 (106 mm [left] × 173 mm [foot]); no endorsements.

. . .YROGRAPHVM

Hec est finalis concordia facta in curia domini regis apud Westm' in octavo sancti Hillarii . anno regni regis Henrici filii regis Iohannis nono . Coram Martino de Pateshill' . Thoma de Muleton' . Thoma de Haiden' Roberto de Lexinton' . Gaufrido Le Sauuag' iustic(iis) et aliis domini regis fidelibus tunc ibi presentibus . Inter Thom(am) de Berkel' petentem et Thomam abbatem de Glouc' deforciantem per Henricum le Bel positum loco suo ad lucrandum uel perdendum de aduocatione ecclesie de Slimbrig' . vnde assisa ultime presentationis summonita fuit inter fuit inter eos in prefata curia . Scilicet quod predictus abbas recognouit aduocationem predicte ecclesie esse ius ipsius Thom(e) . et illam remisit et quietam clamauit de se et successoribus suis ipsi Thom(e) et heredibus suis imperpetuum. Et predictus Thom(as) pro deo et salute anime sue dedit et concessit predicto abbati et monachis de Glouc' deo seruientibus in prioratu de Stanleye totam terram de Lorhinges cum omnibus pertinentiis suis . Scilicet quicquid idem Thomas uel eius antecessores ibidem habuerunt . In dominicis et redditibus . In vilenagiis . In homagiis et seruitiis liberorum hominium . In boscis . pratis et pasturis . et in omnibus aliis rebus ad eandem terram pertinentibus sine aliquo retinemento . Habendam et tenendam predicto abbati et monachis et eorum successoribus de predicto Thom(a) et heredibus suis in puram et perpetuam elemosinam'. liberam et quietam ab omni seculari seruitio . consuetudine et exactione. Et predictus Thom(as) et eius heredes warantizabunt predicto abbati et monachis et eorum successoribus totam predictam terram cum pertinentiis contra omnes gentes et illam de omnibus seruitiis acquietabunt et defendent'. ut puram et perpetuam elemosinam suam. Et si forte predictus Thom(as) uel eius heredes predictam terram cum pertinentiis eisdem abbati et monachis uel eorum successoribus warantizare non poterunt. idem Thom(as) uel eius heredes facient eis escambium in eodem comitatu . in loco competenti ad ualentiam totius predicte terre . in omnibus rebus. Et sciendum quod si predictus abbas uel eorum successores de cetero aliquam cartam protulerint de predicta ecclesia uersus ipsum Thom(am) uel heredes suos pro nulla(m) habebitur quantum ad ecclesiam illam[.]

Glouc'

References to a settlement in 1224 are probably to this final concord (*Cart. Glouc.* i, p. 106; *CRR*, xi, no. 2870.

373. *Final concord between Thomas abbot of Gloucester and Robert son of Robert of Horcott, whom Isabel of Horcott called to warrant, concerning a virgate and a mill in Horcott; the abbot granted the virgate and mill to Robert for 2 marks annual rent. 9 February 1225. Westminster.*

A. P.R.O., CP 25/1/73/7, no. 84 (80 mm [left] × 175 mm [foot]); no endorsement; **B**. ibid. C150/1, fol. 223v; *Cart. Glouc.* ii, no. 828.

C Y R O [G] R . . . P H U M

Hec est finalis concordia facta in curia domini regis apud Westm' in octabis Purificationis beate Marie . Anno regni regis Henrici filii regis Iohannis nono . Coram Martino de Pat'hill' . Thoma de Meleton' . Thoma de Heyde[n] . Roberto de Lexinton' . Galfrido le Sauuag' iustic(iis) et aliis domini regis fidelibus tunc ibi presentibus . Inter Thoma(m) abbatem Gloucestr' petentem per Henricum le Bel positum loco suo ad lucrandum uel perdendum . et Rob(er)tum filium Rob(erti) de Horcote quem Isabella de Horcote uocauit ad warantum et qui ei warantizauit tenentem de una virgata terre et vno molendino cum pertinentiis in Horcote . vnde placitum fuit inter eos in eadem curia . Scilicet quod predictus Robertus recognouit predictam terram et molendinum cum pertinentiis. esse ius ipsius abbatis et ecclesie sue de Gloucestr'. Et pro hac recognitione fine et concordia. idem abbas concessit eidem Roberto et heredibus suis totam predictam terram et molendinum cum pertinentiis . tenenda et habenda de predicto abbate et successoribus suis inperpetuum . Reddendo inde annuatim duas marcas argenti ad quatuor terminos . scilicet in vigilia Pasche. dimidiam marcam [.] In vigilia sancti Iohannis Baptiste . dimidiam marcam . In vigilia sancti Michaelis . dimidiam marcam . In vigilia Natalis domini . dimidiam marcam pro omni seruitio[.]

Glouc'

374. *Final concord between Thomas abbot of St. Peter's, Gloucester, and William de Pontdelarche and his wife Margery concerning two cartloads of hay from the meadow of Moreton (Valence); William and Margery acknowledged the loads to be the abbot's right to the use of the church of (Leonard) Stanley, for which the abbot gave them 4 marks. 3 November 1225. Westminster.*

P.R.O., CP 25/1/73/7, no. 88 (96 mm [left] × 141 mm [foot]); endorsement: Et sciendum quod predicti Will(elmu)s et Marg(er)ia et heredes sui war(antizabunt) eidem abbati Glouc' et successoribus suis predictas duas carratas feni percipiendas de predicto prato eorum in Morton' secundum quod predictum est contra omnes homines ut liberam puram et perpetuam elemosinam suam (s. xiii^{med}).

CYROGRAPHVM

Hec est finalis concordia facta in curia domini regis apud Westm' a die sancti Michaelis in quinque septimanas anno regni regis Henrici filii regis Iohannis decimo [.] Coram Martino de Pat'hill' [.] Thoma de Muleton' [.] Thoma de Heiden' [.] Roberto de Lexinton' [.] Gaufrido le Sauuag' iustic(iis) et aliis domini regis fidelibus tunc ibi presentibus . Inter Thom(am) abbatem Gloc'[1] petentem per Henricum le Bel positum loco suo ad lucrandum uel perdendum . et Willelmum de Puntdelarche et Margeriam vxorem eius tenentes . per Galfridum de Setmeis positum loco ipsius Willelmi ad lucrandum uel perdendum . et Rogerum Walensem positum loco ipsius Margerie ad lucrandum uel perdendum de duabus carratis feni annuatim percipiendis in prato de Morton' . vnde placitum fuit inter eos in eadem curia . Scilicet quod predicti Willelmus et Margeria recognouerunt duas carratas feni esse ius abbatis et ecclesie sue de Glouc' . scilicet singulas carratas de tractu octo boum percipiendas annuatim in prato de Morton' ad opus ecclesie de Stanleg' que est cella predicte ecclesie Glouc'. Et pro hac recognitione fine et concordia . predictus abbas dedit predictis Willelmo et Margerie . quatuor marcas argenti. Et sciendum quod predicti Willelmus et Margeria et heredes sui warantizabunt eidem abbati Glouc' et successoribus suis predictas duas carratas feni percipiendas de predicto prato eorum in Morton' secundum quod predictum est contra omnes homines vt liberam puram et perpetuam elemosinam suam[.]

Glouc'[2]

---

[1] u overstruck by o in Gluc'.   [2] Preceded by Heford', crossed out.

375. *Letter from Roger (III) of Berkeley to Theobald archbishop of Canterbury asking him to confirm the foundation of Leonard Stanley Priory. (1146 × 48)*

H.C.L., no. 775 (190 mm × 141 mm); seal on tongue; white wax laquered; chipped; obverse: round (65 mm in diam.); a standing knight facing to the right, a raised sword in the right hand, and a kite shaped shield on the left arm, warding off an attacking lion with front feet against the shield; legend: . . .IGILLV. . . . . .ER.. . . . .CKEL. . .; no counterseal; endorsement: De Stanl'. (s. xii[2]); A. Prima Carta (s. xv).

Domino suo karissimo .T. Cantuariensi archiepiscopo . et apostolico dei gratia legato . fidelis suus amicus et seruiens Rog(erus) de Berch'l' . salutem. Sciatis karissime domine quod Stanleia quẹdam uilla patris mei fuit . quẹ adhuc de patrimonio meo est . in uilla illa est ẹcclesia sancti Leonardi quam pater meus quantum ad eum pertinuit . dedit cuidam clerico suo Sabricto nomine . et eum Theoldo episcopo presentauit . qui ei personatum in ẹcclesia illa concessit. Sabrictus uero illam plusquam .xxx. annis sicut ẹcclesiam suam parrochialem tenuit . Qui licet clericos sibi assumpserit quandoque in habitu religioso quandoque in alio . nunquam tamen alicui eorum de iure quod habebat in ęcclesia quicquam concessit . nec pater meus nec ego aliquem eorum episcopo presentauimus . nec episcopus aliquem eorum in ęcclesia illa uel in toto uel in parte inuestiuit . sed Sabrictus eos sicut uoluit de suo sustinuit. Sabrictus autem paucis annis ante mortem suam requisiuit me ut ęcclesiam predictam quantum pertinebat ad me ęcclesię beati Petri Gloec' concederem . et de hoc dominum Wigornensem episcopum requireret. Ipse uero locum quendam nomine Winecroft quem sibi dederam ad ducendam uitam solitariam pro sufficientia habebat. Requisitus ab ipso dominum Wigornensem requisiui una cum Sabricto ut ęcclesiam illam Gloec' ęcclesię concederet . et in ea monachorum ordinem institueret. Ipse sui gratia petitioni nostrę assensum prebens . ęcclesiam de manu Sabrictu susceptam . et ęcclesię Gloec' in perpetuum habendam concessit . et ea Gislebertum abbatem per decanum suum Walterium inuestiuit. Sciatis uero quod Walterius clericus Sabricti licet in ęcclesia illa nichil habet nisi quod ex gratia Sabricti habebat´. tamen ne monachi eum suspectum haberent antequam ęcclesiam susciperent . iurauit eis super secundum euangelium . quod eis in re ista nunquam impedimentum quereret . nec contra eos in aliquo staret. Rogerus uero socius Walterii quod in re ista actum est per omnia gratum habens . inclusum sibi fieri petiit . in quo postea quia ad libitum suum ostium grande habere non potuit´. quo uoluit gratis abscessit . Quod si Hugo de Cotes qui sicut fere omnibus in partibus nostris notissimus est a seruitio Sabricti in quo eodem modo quo Walterius et Rogerus aliquando fuerat . transactis iam plusquam .xx. annis discessit . si ipse inquam uel socii eius scriptum aliquod sub meo nomine et sigillo presentibus litteris contrarium produxerunt iam . aut amodo produxerint´. fraudulentum utique est. Et quia me ignorante factum fuit´. fidem huic obsecro nullatenus adhiberi. Paternitatem itaque uestram supplex imploro . ut quod a nobis sane et simpliciter actum est . iuste sustineatis . nec dolo reclamantium clericorum beato Petro quod iuste possidet´. auferri sinatis. Si enim sciret uestra sanctitas . quantum ęcclesia illa sub manu monachorum honestata et ampliata sit´. gratias eis potius referretis´. quam quicquam auferri permitteretis. Valete.

For the foundation date, see *Cart. Glouc.* i, p. 113. Roger of Berkeley's letter was written between 1146, the year in which this occurred, and the end of the abbacy of Gilbert Foliot, mentioned in the letter. Archbishop Theobald confirmed the priory's possessions in a notification to Bishop Simon of Worcester datable to 1149 × 50 (Saltman, *Theobald*, no. 254 [listed as *Ex ipso autographo in Bibl. Cottoniana*, but with text based upon other printed transcriptions]). By mentioning Sabrict's presentation to Theulf bishop of Worcester (1115–23) as parson of Leonard Stanley and his tenure of the church for more than thirty years, the letter also establishes *c.* 1116 × 48 as the period in which Leonard Stanley was transformed from a parish church into a monastery (*Fasti*, ii. 99). Roger also gave the churches of Coaley, Ozleworth, Arlingham, Slimbridge, and Uley, with appurtenant lands and tithes (*Cart. Glouc.* i, p. 106; *VCH Glos.* ii. 73; above, p. xxix).

376. *Grant by Robert of Berkeley, son of Maurice of Berkeley, in free alms to Leonard Stanley Priory of a portion of his wood at Coaley. (1191 × 1220; prob. 1216 × 20)*

H.C.L, no. 797 (196 mm × 103 mm); damaged; seal on tag; white wax stained green; chipped; obverse: round (67 mm in diam.); a helmeted equestrian figure to the right, a raised sword in the right hand, a shield on the left arm; legend: + SIGILLV. . .BERT. . . :DE BERCHELAIA; reverse: counterseal; rubbed; round (37 mm in diam.); a small equestrian figure to the left, an upraised lance in the right hand; legend: + SIGILLVM: ROBERTI: DE BERKELAI; endorsement: Carta Rob(er)ti de Berkel' de bosco de Couel' apud Stanl' (s. xii^{ex} × s. xiii ^{in}?).

Sciant presentes et futuri quod ego Rob(er)tus de Berkel' . filius Mauricii de Berkel' pro amore dei et pro salute anime domini mei regis Henrici et heredum suorum et pro salute anime mee et pro salute anime Iuliane uxoris mee et omnium antecessorum meorum et heredum meorum . dedi et concessi et hac presenti carta mea confirmaui deo et ecclesie sancti Leonardi de Stanl' et monachis Gloucr' ibidem deo seruientibus . in liberam puram . et perpetuam elemosinam . quandam partem de bosco meo de Covel' cum terra . que uidelicet pars'. est iuxta boscum abbatis Gloucr' et conuentus . apud Froucr' . per has diuisas . videlicet a uia que exit ab ipso bosco abbatis que dicitur Rodwei . usque ad ueterem et cauam uiam que dicitur Lomwei . et ab ipsa uia que dicitur Lomwei'. usque ad summitatem montis . sicut ipsa uia se ascendendo extendit . et a summitate ipsius uie iterum usque ad boscum predicti abbatis . Habendum et tenendum de me et de heredibus meis . libere et quiete . integre et honorifice ab omnibus seruitiis secularibus et demandis . in perpetuum . sicut puram et perpetuam elemosinam meam. Et licebit eisdem monachis sine contradictione alicuius . ad uoluntatem suam eundem boscum cum terra'. includere et fossare . ita quod nullus eis communicet. Ego uero et heredes mei predictum boscum per predictas diuisas distinctum'. dictis monachis de Stanl' . contra omnes homines et feminas warantizabimus. Et ut hec mea donatio . rata et inconuulsa sit'. eam presenti carta sigillo meo roborata'. confirmaui. Hiis testibus . Rogero de B'kel' . Iohanne de Balun' . Iohanne Lupo . Osberno Giffard' . Gileberto Giffard' . Swigino et Helia tunc capellanis . Bernardo de Cromhal' . Ricardo de Cromhal' . Ricardo de Couel' . Thoma de Tiringeh' tunc senescallo . Roberto Cniuet . Henrico filio Rogeri de Berkel' . Thoma de Luuent . Helia de Slimbrug' . et multis aliis.

Robert of Berkeley (d. 1220) was the grandson of Robert Fitz Harding and the first cousin of the witness Roger (V) of Berkeley, lord of Dursley (Sanders, *English Baronies*, 13, 114; Barkly, 'Earlier House of Berkeley', 193–223, *caute legendum*; see also *Cart. Glouc.* i, no. 163).

377. *Grant in the form of a chirograph by Thomas of Berkeley to Leonard Stanley Priory of land (unident.) held by John Blond with a house on it. (1220 × 43)*

B.C.M., Select Chart. no. 346 (c. 113 mm [left]; no other meas. avail.); damaged; mode of sealing not evident on the surviving portion of the single turn-up; cal. in Jeayes, no. 436.

. . .P. . .U M^1 *(inverted)*

Sciant presentes et futuri quod ego Thomas de Berkelei pro deo et s. . . carta mea confirmaui deo et ecclesie sancti Leonardi de Stanl' et mona[chis] . . . Iohannes Blundus de me tenuit cum mansione superposita . Et q. . . in aquis uiis et semitis et omnibus rebus ad eandem terram pertinenti. . . de me et heredibus meis sibi et successoribus suis in puram et perpet[uam elemosinam] . . . . . .ne . et exactione . et omni demanda. Et ego .Th(omas). et heredes mei predi[ctis . . . mona]chis contra omnes gentes warrantizabimus . Et illam de omnibus servitiis et . . . [adquie]tabimus in omnibus rebus secularibus . et defendemus aduersus omnes homines u[el feminas] . . . aliquod grauamen uel demandam aliquam pro qualiqumque re eisdem mon[achis] . . . . . .diderint faciemus . uel fieri per aliquem ex nostris permittemus . Nec . . . sancti Petri Glouc' remiserunt et qui[e]tos clamauerunt pro se et s. . . . potuerunt in redditu uiginti quatuor solidorum in uilla de B. . . [Mau]ricii de Berkelai patris mei . Ita tunc quod si ego Th(omas) uel h[er]edes warantizare non possemus. licebit eisdem recurrere ad predictum redd. . . In cuius rei testimonium presens scriptum in modum cirographi conf. . . [tra]didi. Alteram uero. sigillo abbatis et conuentus Glouc' munitam. pen[es] . . . filio Ricardi . Petro de Stintescumbe[2] . Ricardo de Covel' . Thoma de . . . . Roberto de Couel' . Roberto de La planke . Hugone pistore . . . .

The donor, lord of Berkeley 1220–43, was the son of Maurice of Berkeley and the brother of Robert (Sanders, *English Baronies*, 13). The entire right side of the chirograph has been destroyed as well as smaller portions of the surviving part. Editorially reconstructed parts are enclosed within square brackets.

[1] Ending with four dots in a vertical line   [2] Reading uncertain due to damage.

378. *Grant by Henry Clerk, son of Robert Cook of Hereford, to Leonard Stanley Priory of 10s. annual rent (from Clehonger, Herefs.) to provide for a lamp before St. Mary's altar; any remainder was to be spent to improve the ornaments of the church. (c. 1230)*

G.C.L., 'Deeds and Seals', v, no. 2, fol. 1 (176 mm × 114 mm); seal on green and white cords; dark green wax; broken, repaired; obverse: round (30 mm in diam.); a large bird with wings partially extended to the front; legend: + S.'HENR' FI. . . ROB COCI DE HEREFORD. . .; no counterseal; endorsement: .: Clehungre (s. xiv); also reproduced on photographic negative, G.R.O., P.201/MI/1.

Sciant presentes et futuri quod ego Henr(icus) Clericus filius Roberti Coci de Hereford' pro salute anime mee et patris mei et matris mee et omnium antecessorum meorum dedi et concessi et presenti carta mea confirmaui deo et ecclesie sancti Leonardi de Stanl' decem solidos annuas quos percipere consueui de Iohanne de Suthwell' de terra quam idem Iohannes de me emit et in extremis suis prioratui de Stanl' legauit recipiendos de priore de Stanl' pro tempore fuerit et fideliter expendendos per manum alicuius monachi apud Stanl' commorantis ad inueniendam vnam lampadem iugiter arsuram coram altari beate Marie in maiori ecclesia de Stanl'. Et si quid residuum fuerit de predictis decem solidis quod non oporteat expendi in predicta lampade inuenienda. ad melioranda ornamenta dicte ecclesie per manum dicti monachi expendatur et non in aliis usibus. Vt igitur hec mea donatio futuris temporibus rata permaneat. presenti scripto sigillum meum apposui in testimonium. Hiis testibus . Petro tunc priore de Stanl' . Thoma de Hauuil' [.]

Waltero de Lemen' . Thoma de Stowa . Symone de feld' monachis ibidem tunc commorantibus . Roberto persona de Oslewrþ tunc capellano de Stanl' . Thoma de Samford' . Petro de feld' et multis aliis.

The witness Peter prior of Stanley occurs *c.* 1230 (*HRH*, 93).

379. *Grant by Richard Murdac of Alkerton in free alms to Leonard Stanley Priory of 4 acres by the little wood called* Five acre *(near Alkerton). (s. xii^{med})*

H.C.L., no. 791 (158 mm × 94 mm); seal on tag; dark green wax; cracked; obverse: round (60 mm in diam.); a civilian riding figure to the left, a the hawk in left hand; legend: SIGILLVM: RICARDI: DE: ALCRINTVN; no counterseal; endorsements: Carta Ric(ardi) Murdac' de quatuor acras terre iuxta siluulam Fife ac'; A. temporalium parte 2^a (*c.* 1400); Aⱡcrintone (uncertain date).

Sciant presentes et futuri quod ego Ric(ardus) Murdac de Alcrintuna assensu Willelmi heredis mei pro anima Dionisii uxoris mee . et pro salute anime[1] mee . et animabus patris . et matris mee . et omnium parentum . et antecessorum meorum . dedi et concessi deo et ecclesie sancti Leonardi de Stanleia et monachis ibidem deo servientibus et propria manu in eadem ecclesia super altare eiusdem sancti optuli .iiii.^{or} acras terre iuxta silvulam que vocatur Fifacra in perpetuam elemosinam . liberas et quietas ab omnibus servitiis . et consuetudinibus . et exactionibus. Quod quia ratum et inconvulsum semper manere uoluiⱡ presenti carta et sigilli mei contestatione confirmavi. His testibus Radulfo eiusdem loci priore . Ambrosio . Lvca . Osberto monachis . Henrico capellano . Roberto de Lecc . Rogero clericis . Roberto et Ada filiis Edrici . Petro Blundo . Iohanne ruffo . Hereberto de Barnavilla . et aliis pluribus.

[1] *anime* superscript.

380. *Grant by Richard Murdac of Alkerton with the assent of his wife Dionisia in free alms to Leonard Stanley Priory, by his hand upon the church's altar, of the mill of Alkerton and all the arable of his demesne which is by the grove called* Five acre *and a cartload of hay drawn by eight oxen in* Brademede. *The prior by the consent of the abbot and convent of Gloucester is to take Richard's son Richard to be raised, and a mass is to be sung daily for the souls of the donor and members of his family. (c. 1165 × c. 1197; before c. 1220)*

H.C.L., no. 740 (199 mm × 128 mm); seal on tag; white wax, varnished or stained brown; obverse: oval (35 mm × 32 mm); a great bird to the right; legend: + SIGILLVM RICA. ⸱ .: MV. . .THET; no counterseal; endorsements: Carta Ric(ardi) Murdac de molendino in Alcrinton'; A. temporalium parte 2^a.(*c.* 1400); Alcrintone. (uncertain date).

Sciant presentes et futuri quod ego Ricard(us) Murdac de Alcretone . assensu . et concessu uxoris mee . et heredum meorum pro salute anime mee . et animarum patris . et matris mee . et omnium parentum . et antecessorum meorum . dedi . et concessi deo . et ecclesie sancti Leonardi de Stanlee . et monachis ibidem deo servientibus . et propria manu in eadem ecclesia super altare eiusdem obtuli . Scilicet molendinum de Alcretune . cum omnibus pertinentiis . et totam culturam de dominio meo . que est iuxta gravam . que vocatur Fifaker . et unam chaream feni . tractu octo boum in Brademede in perpetuam elemosinam . libere . et quiete ab omnibus seruitiis . et consuetudinibus . et exactionibus[.] Ipse uero prior eiusdem ecclesie caritatis intuitu . concessu domini abbatis . et conventus Glocest'ie accipiet filium meum . Ricardum῎. ad nutriendum. Et insuper concesserunt mihi quod singulis anni[1] diebus quamdiu domus stabit῎. unam missam in eadem domo . pro anima mea . et pro anima uxoris mee Dionisie . et patris . et matris mee . et antecessorum meorum facient de cantaria. Quod quia ratum inconvulsum in perpetuum manere uolo῎. presenti carta . et sigilli mei atestatione confirmaui. Hiis testibus Rogero de Berkelai . Roberto de Berkel' . Filippo de Berkel' . Olivero . de Berkel' . Henrico de Coueleia . Iohanne lupo . Amaric despensatore . Willelmo de parc . Roberto de Baieus . Salomone . Iohanne roffo . Elia de Stanidis [.] Hereberto de Barnewilla . Henrico Wace . Willelmo clerico . Iohanne coco . Waltero de Owere . et multis aliis.

For the dating see below, no. 381 n.; Barkly, 'Earlier House of Berkeley', 214, 223.

[1] *annis* in MS.

381. *Grant by Richard Murdac to Herbert de Barneville of a virgate in Alkerton with a meadow for an annual rent of 1 lb. of pepper. (c. 1165 × c. 1197)*

H.C.L., no. 548 (145 mm × 97 mm); seal on tag: dark green wax, chipped; obverse: round (34 mm in diam.); a snipe ? with curved beak, wings folded to the right; legend: + SIGILLVM. RICA. . .VRTAGT; no counterseal; endorsements: .A. temporalium parte .2.[a] (c. 1400); Alcrintone (uncertain date).

Sciant presentes et futuri quod ego Ricard(us) Murdac dedi et concessi et hac presenti carta confirmaui Hereberto de Barnewila et heredibus suis unam uirgatam terre in Alcrintona pro seruitio suo et homagio cum prato et omnibus ad illam pertinentibus illam scilicet quam Willelmus filius Godwini tenuit [.] Habendam et tenendam de me et heredibus meis sibi et heredibus suis libere et quiete ab omni seruitio et seculari exactione cum omnibus libertatibus et liberis consuetudinibus in uiis et semitis et in omnibus aliis locis et in omnibus rebus saluo regali seruitio reddendo inde michi uel heredibus meis annuatim unam libram piperis ad festum sancti Michaelis. His testibus . Gilibert[o] capellano de Alcrintona . Robert[o] capellano de Estenest' . Willelmo de Sauceto . Amis de Wdestoche . Radulfo de Sauceto . Galtero de Sauceto . Henrico de Chouel' . Ricardo de Cro'hale . Bernard[o] de Cro'hale . Willemo de Lund' . Geruasio de Baudint' . Iohanne Russel . Salomone de Froucestre . Robert[o] de Burc . Elia de Stanesd' . Ricardo Carpenter . et multis aliis.

The donor was active during the second half of the twelfth century (*Cart. Glouc.* i. 74; Walker, 'Earldom of Hereford Charters', no. 122; above, nos. 379–80), and the script belongs to that period.

GLOUCESTER ABBEY: WELSH POSSESSIONS

382. *Mandate from Henry bishop of Winchester, papal legate, to Uchtred bishop of Llandaff, who was not to allow divine service in chapels recently built in the parish of Llancarfan (Glam.) or to allow further chapels to be built without the agreement of Gilbert abbot of Gloucester, to whom the church of Llancarfan belonged. (c. 29 April 1139 × 25 Sept 1143)*

A. G.C.L., 'Deeds and Seals', x, no. 4, fol. 3 (183 mm × 65 mm); tongue and tie, torn or cut from lower left corner; seal missing; endorsements: De Lancaruan (s. xii), poss. **Hand a**; de Trigot [crossed out] (s. xii?); .c(apsula) .iii. de ecclesiasticis tenuris (s. xiii?); Registratur (s. xiv^ex^); **B.** P.R.O., C150/1, fols. 132v–133; *Cart. Glouc.* ii, no. 446; Franklin, *Winchester Episcopal Acta*, no. 47; cal. in *EAWD*, ii, no. L.106.

.H. Wintoniensis dei gratia episcopus et sancte sedis apostolice legatus'. dilecto filio suo Vthtredo Landauensi epsicopo'. salutem . gratiam . et benedictionem. Dilectus filius noster Gilebertus abbas Gloec' conquestus est nobis quod in parrochia ecclesie sue de Lancaruan capelle nouiter ipso reclamante constructe sunt . Vnde uobis mandamus et mandando precipimus ut in illis diuina celebrari officia non sinatis . nec alias ulterius in eadem parrochia nisi ipso uolente edificari permittatis. Nam ecclesias eius omnes quas in uestra diocesi habet . illam scilicet de Lancaruan et alias quas ex dono Mauricii de Lond' suscepit[1] uidelicet ecclesiam sancti Michaelis et ecclesiam sancte Brigide cum omnibus pertinentiis et additamentis earum in protectione nostra suscipimus et earum subiectione ecclesie Gloec' in perpetuum presenti scripto assignamus. Valete.

Robert Fitz Hamon gave the church of Llancarfan along with 15 hides of land at Penhow to the abbey before 1100 (*Cart. Glouc.* i. 93). The limiting dates of this letter are those of Henry of Winchester's legateship (Saltman, *Theobald*, 15, 19).

[1]   Initial *a* overstruck with *s*.

383. *Examination of witnesses on behalf of Margam Abbey in its appeal to the papal court from a hearing in its dispute with St. Peter's, Gloucester, concerning tithes from the parish of Llancarfan (Glam.), heard in the church of St. John Cardiff. 8 February 1262. Cardiff.*

B.L. Harl. Ch. 75.A.40 (192 mm × 121 mm); cut in the form of a writ; tongue but no tie; seal missing; no endorsement; Clark, *Cartae et alia*, ii, no. 621.

¶ Examinatio testium productorum ex parte abbatis et conuentus de Margan et eorum depositio facta die Mercurii proxima post festum beate Agathe virginis . Anno domini .m.° c°c°.lx°. secundo . in ecclesia beati Iohannis de Kaerdif per dominum priorem de Talelecho commissarium abbatis de Wygemor et magistri Galfridi de Burgo canonici Landauensis . iudicum a domino papa delegatorum in causa appellationis mota inter abbatem et conuentum de Margan ex parte una . et abbatem et conuentum monasterii sancti Petri Gloucest'e ex altera. ¶ Frater Iohannes Comyn monachus de Margan iuratus et examinatus dicit . quod uidit et audiuit et presens fuit in ecclesia cathedrali Landauensi in crastino sancti Hyllarii . Anno domini .m°.c°c°.lx°. primo . ubi frater Philippus de Lulliwelle procurator abbatis et conuentus de Margan . Cisterciensis ordinis Landauensis dyocesis comparuit coram decano Cristianitatis Landauensis et magistro Rogero de Stauntone clerico vices officialis domini Landauensis episcopi gerentibus in causa tunc mota inter abbatem et conuentum sancti Petri Gloucest'ie ex parte vna . et abbatem et conuentum de Margan ex altera super decimis prouenientibus de terris eorumdem abbatis et conuentus de Margan consistentibus in parochia ecclesie de Lankaruan Landauensis dyocesis . Qui quidem procurator humiliter ac instanter petiit ut ipsi acta iudicii ,coram eis habita in causa ipsa tam eadem die quam in vigilia beati Nicholai proximo preterita⸴ per que causa ipsa instruebatur et processu temporis instrui poterat redigi facerent in auctenticam scripturam et eadem acta in scriptis redacta sigillis suis signarent . ut per ea in auctenticam scripturam redacta tam eorumdem abbatis et conuentus de Margan pro loco et tempore instrui possit et iuuari. Sed ipsi decanus et Rogerus hoc ei facere pretise denegarunt. Propter quam idem procurator de Margan nomine suo et dominorum suorum predictorum ad sedem apostolicam in scriptis appellauit et apostolos instanter petiit . quos ipsi decanus et Rogerus eidem procuratori concedere denegauerunt. Requisitus de hora diei quando hoc statum fuit⸴ dicit quod circa horam tertiam. Requisitus qui fuerunt presentes . dicit quod ipse et predictus frater Philippus de Lulliwelle . et fratres Iohannes de Noua villa . Willelmus Sortes . Philippus de Kaermardin monachi de Margan . magister Nicholaus Kaenetona phisicus . Iohannes Peruat . Iohannes Du . et multi alii tam clerici quam laici quia consistorium fuit ea die. Requisitus quare non fuit causa appellationis ipsius infra annum terminata a tempore appellationis ipsius interposite . dicit quod hoc stetit per curiam Romanam siue per nuntios eorumdem quos ad eandem curiam miserant ad impetrandum super eadem appellatione. Miserunt enim predictos nuntios suos uersus curiam Romanam infra octavas predicti sancti Hyllarii et neminem eorum receperunt ante vigiliam beati Vincentii martiris . anno domini m.° c°c°. lx.° secundo . eo quod impediti erant ut dicebant per viam . et etiam in predicta curia propter audientiam et bullam in eadem curia diu suspensam ut dicebat. ¶ Frater Willelmus Sortes monachus de Margan iuratus et examinatus super predicta appellatione et eius causa et aliis circumstantiis suprascriptis idem dicit et concordat cum fratre Iohanne preconiurato suo. ¶ Frater Philippus de Kaermardin monachus de Margan iuratus et examinatus super predicta appellatione et eius causa et aliis circumstantiis suprascriptis idem dicit et concordat cum fratre Iohanne preconiurato suo . adiciens quod ipse propria manu scripsit tenorem appellationis predicte quam predictus pro[cu]rator de Margan in predicto crastino sancti Hyllarii interposuit ab audientia dictorum decani et Rogeri. ¶ Magister Nicholaus de Kanetone phisicus iuratus et examinatus super predicta appellatione et eius causa et aliis circumstantiis memoratis idem dicit et concordat cum fratre Iohanne preconiurato suo . excepto quod missioni nuntiorum predictorum non interfuit . bene tamen scit litteram super dicta appellatione impetratam fuisse a sede apostolica ad quam fuit appellatum. ¶ Frater Iohannes de Noua villa monachus de Margan iuratus et examinatus super predicta appellatione et eius causa et aliis circumstantiis memoratis idem dicit et concordat cum fratre Iohanne preconiurato suo. ¶ Magister Rogerus de Staunton' clericus iuratus et examinatus super dicta appellatione et eius causa et aliis circumstantiis predictis idem dicit et concordat cum fratre Iohanne primo iurato . adiciens et iurans quod inuitus et coactus huiusmodi testimonium dixit.

384. *Mandate from Theobald archbishop of Canterbury to Uchtred bishop of Llandaff, who was not to allow divine service to be held in chapels recently built in the parish of St. Cadoc of Llancarfan (Glam.) without the abbot of Gloucester's agreement. (1139 × 48)*

A. G.C.L., 'Deeds and Seals', i, no. 4, fol. 3 (216 mm × 77 mm); tongue and fragment of tie; seal missing; endorsements: Archiep(iscopal)i de confirmatione ecclesiarum pertinentium ad Vgemara . et ecclesie de Lancarua. (s. xii^{med}); de . . .ig. . . (erased; uncertain reading with ultra-violet light; s. xii?); c(apsula) .iii. de eccclesiasticis tenuris (s. xii); Registratur (s. xiv^{ex} × s. xv^{in}); **B**. P.R.O., C150/1, fol. 132v; *Cart. Glouc.* ii, no. 445; Clark, *Cartae et alia*, i, no. 96; Saltman, *Theobald*, no. 113; cal. in *EAWD*, ii, no. L.116.

Theobaldus dei gratia Cantuariensis archiepiscopus Vchtredo dilecto fratri eadem gratia Landauensi episcopo salutem et benedictionem. Mandamus uobis atque mandando precipimus . ut in capellis que in parrochia sancti Cadoci de Lancaruan absque assensu et uoluntate abbatis Gloecestrie nuper constructe sunt⁊. diuinum officium fieri nec sinatis . nec amplius alias fieri . aut in aliquo ius prefate ecclesie minui permittatis . et parriochianos redditus et decimas persoluere rigore iusticie coerceatis. Illam namque et alias quas habent ex dono Mauricii de Londonia . uidelicet ecclesiam sancti Michaelis . et ecclesiam sancte Brigide cum omnibus rebus eis pertinentibus in tutelam et protectionem nostram suscipimus . et presenti scripto ecclesie Gloecestrensi in perpetuum assignamus. VALETE.

Cf. no. 382.

385. *Grant by Theobald archbishop of Canterbury of an indulgence of 15 days from penance to those who visit or benefit the church of St. Gwynlyw of Newport (Mon.). (1138 × 62)*

A. B.L. Cott. Ch. XVI. 38 (130 mm × 72 mm); no turn-up; a slightly jagged edge to the left foot suggests that a tongue or tie was torn off; endorsement: Registratur (s. xiv^{ex} × s. xv^{in}); **B**. P.R.O., C 150/1, fol. 150v; *Cart. Glouc.* ii, no. 526; Saltman, *Theobald*, no. 114; cal. in *EAWD*, ii, no. L.143.

T. dei gratia Cantuariensis archiepiscopus Angl' primas . vniuersis sancte ecclesie fidelibus⁊. salutem. Penitentibus et peccata confessis . et ecclesiam dei deuota mente uenerantibus pietatis instinctu admonemur misericordie solatium retribuere . et indulgentie remedium compensare. Inde est quod omnibus Cristianis qui deuotionis intuitu ecclesiam sancti Gunlei de Nouo burgo requisierint . et in aliquo beneficio pro dei amore . et animarum suarum salute eam honorauerint⸴ quindecim dierum indulgentiam de penitentia sua facimus . et omnium orationum ac beneficiorum Cantuariensis ecclesie eos perpetuo participes constituimus. Valete.

For a slightly different text, see *Cart. Glouc.* ii, no. 526.

386. *Mandate from Nicholas bishop of Llandaff to I(saac) dean of Penychan and others; they were to go to Llancarfan (Glam.), the archdeacon having demised the church there to the bishop and the abbot of Gloucester, and to put the representatives of the abbot and monks of Gloucester in seisin of the church of St. Cadoc. (1172 × 79)*

A. G.C.L., 'Deeds and Seals', ii, no. 89, fol. 16 (151 mm × 59 mm); seal on tongue, fragment, repaired, white wax, oval; meas. unavail.; the upper torso of a figure facing the front possibly holding a crozier or staff in the right hand, the left hand missing; legend missing; no counterseal; endorsement: de Lancauan;[1] c(apsula) .iii. de ecclesiasticis tenuris (s. xii^{med}); Registratur (s. xv); B. P.R.O., C 150/1, fol. 132v; *Cart. Glouc.* ii, no. 444; Crouch, *LEA*, no. 17; cal. in *EAWD*, ii, no. L.171.

Nich(olas) dei gratia Landauensis episcopus .I. decano de Penn' . Waltero de Meth' . et O[.] de Landr' et W. de sancto Hylar' salutem. Mandamus uobis et in ui obedientie iniungimus . quatinus proxima die Iouis post Pascha omni occasione remota ad Lancaruan ueniatis. Sciatis enim quod Willelmus archidiaconus ecclesiam de Landcaruan in manu mea et abbatis Gloec' . liberam et quietam absque omni calumpnia tradidit et se demisit. Inde est quod mandamus uobis et mandando precipimus . quatinus nuntios abbatis et monachorum Gloec' . de predicta ecclesia sancti Cadoci cum omnibus ad eam pertinentibus⸴ uice mea seisiatis . et si qui aliquam uobis uim fecerint⸴ sententiam ecclesiasticam auctoritate mea in illos exerceatis. Valete.

For the date, see Crouch, *LEA*, no. 17 n. Related charters of Nicholas are in *Cart. Glouc.* ii, nos. 442–3.

[1]   The mounting of the document hides the top of a superscript *r* or suspension sign after the second *a* of *Lancauan*.

387. *General confirmation by Geoffrey bishop of St. David's of gifts in his diocese to the abbot and convent of St. Peter's, Gloucester. (1203 × 14)*

G.C.L., 'Deeds and Seals', iv, no. 21, fol. 10 (238 mm × 352 mm); seal on woven white wool cords through three slits; wax, black, broken, repaired; obverse: pointed oval (*c.* 73 mm × *c.* 43 mm); a full standing bishop in pontificals facing the front, the right hand raised in blessing; the left hand indiscernible, flanked on each side by a six-pointed star; legend: +. . . DEI GRAC. . .ENEVENSIS: EPISCOPVS; reverse: counterseal: pointed oval (40 mm × 24 mm); a full standing bishop with a crozier in the left hand; legend: + GAV. . .DVS: MENEVENSIS: . . .; cal. in *EAWD*, i, no. D.406.

Vniuersis matris ecclesie filiis ad quod presens scriptum peruenerit . Galfridus diuina permissione Meneuensis episcopus . salutem et benedictionem. Vniuersitati uestre notum facimus quod nos ad petitionem dilectorum fratrum nostrorum abbatis et monachorum sancti Petri Glouc' . attendentes eorum honestatem et religionem inspectis etiam cartis donatorum suorum. et confirmatorum . Ex dono scilicet Bernardi de Nouo M'cato . et confirmatione Rogeri comitis et Walteri de Hereford' ecclesiam sancti Kenedri in uilla de Glasb'r' . cum omnibus conuentionibus . et oblationibus . terris . et decimis . et omnibus ad eam pertinentibus . ex utraque parte Waie tam de dominico quam de vilenagio . Et insuper ex dono Ricardi de Clifford' decimam de omnibus assartis factis uel faciendis de dominico de Glasb'r' . et totam decimam molendinorum . et anguillarum . Ex dono autem Radulfi de Bufford' . et confirmatione Milonis Le Brut totam decimam dominii de Pip'ton' cum decima totius vilenagii eiusdem ville . et cum omnibus aliis rebus de quibus decime dari debent . Et capellam eiusdem ville cum omnibus oblationibus . et consuetudinibus que matrici ecclesie de Glasb'r' parochiali iure debentur . Item ex dono Milonis Le Brut duodecim acras terre quas dedit predictus Milo Le Brut ad celebranda diuina ter in septimana in capella ibidem per prouisionem precentoris Glouc' qui pro tempore fuerit . Et tres solidos percipiendos a priore . et monachis de Brech' pro parrochia de Menelioch . Et quatuor solidos percipiendos a priore . et monachis de Clifford' pro decimis . et oblationibus parrochie de Porthamal . Pontithael . sicut in transactionibus hinc inde factis continetur . Item duas partes decimarum bladi de dominico de Talgard' . et medietatem omnium minutarum decimarum solo feno excepto quod ecclesia percipit . Ex dono Rogeri comitis unam virgatam terre in eadem uilla . Et medietatem omnium decimarum prouenientium de foresta de Werfinam . et totam decimam uenationis vbicumque capta fuerit in predicta foresta . et decimam de omnibus assartis factis uel faciendis de dominico de Talgard' . Et decimam dominii de Brekenoc illius scilicet terre que dicitur . Wentorf . Et totam decimam anguillarum absque alicuius participatione . scilicet de mara . Quatuor etiam solidos . et unum porcum pinguem siue duodecim denarios pro porco . quos filii Seissil Bras pro melle domini annuatim reddunt. Item confirmamus duas partes decime totius dominii de Lanmeys ultra Vscam infra limites ecclesie de Lanmeys . scilicet Bladi . et omnium de quibus decime debent dari . De quibus decimis lis aliquando mota fuit et controuersia inter monasterium sancti Petri Clouc' . et Iohannem tunc capellanum de Lanmeys . coram venerabili nostro domino Roberto tunc Herefordens(e) episcopo cui causa delegata fuit a domino papa . et possessio dicte decime de iure abbati et monachis Glouc' adiudicata'. ita tunc quod Iohannes capellanus in vita sua dictas decimas possidere sub annua pensione duodecim denariorum monachis Glouc' infra octauas Natalis domini apud Glasbur' dum uixerit soluendorum pro decima de Lanmeys supradicta . Et post obitum eius memorata decima ad prefatos monachos absque alicuius contradictione libere reuertetur . Item totam decimam totius occasionis dominii de castello de Brek' . a festo sancti Michaelis usque ad Natale domini . siue sit ex proprio siue ex empto . seu quolibet alio modo adquiesita fuerit . Item decimam totius venationis totius anni ubicumque capta fuerit in terra domininii de Brek' . infra forestam uel extra . et decimam mellis . Item medietatem omnium prouentuu(m) ecclesiasticorum prouenientium[1] ex foresta de Brek'. Item confirmamus eis medietatem ecclesie de Deuatinoc cum capellis et decimis ad eandem ecclesiam pertinentibus dictis monachis quoad omnes decimas que dari debent ecclesie . scilicet . bladi . feni . pecorum . agnorum . vitulorum . porcellorum . pannagii . caseorum . lane . et lini . Et medietatem decime herbagii uel eius pretii de tota predicta foresta . et omnium aliarum rerum de quibus decime dari debent . Item ex dono Radulfi Baskevill' .duos. solidos . et vnum salmonem annuatim . Item ex dono Bernardi de Nouo M'cato libertatem eundi . ac redeundi . uendendi et emendi . et quietantiam ab omni theloneo . et consuetudine per totam terram de Brek' . hominibus monachorum et rebus eorum. Omnes etiam compositiones inter predictos monachos . et alios tam religiosos quam seculares . siue ecclesiasticas personas amicabiliter factas. ratas habemus . et eas episcopale autoritate confirmamus. Omnes igitur prefatas possessiones predictorum monachorum . et res tam mobiles quam immobiles cum libertatibus ad easdem pertinentibus in episcopatu Meneuens(e) constitutas sub protectione dei . et sancti Dauid . et nostra suscepimus sub int(er)minatione excommunicationis districte inhibentes . ne quis in aliquo molestiam . aut grauamen . damnum . aut iniuriam eis inde presumat inferre. Que omnia ne processu temporis ualeant infirmari . aut in obliuionem deduci. presenti scripto sigillo nostro munito duximus roborare. Hiis testibus [.] Osberno tunc capellano nostro canonico Lanton' . Iohanne priore de Breck' . magistro Waltero precentore nostro . Canigano capellano . Dauid de lan Du . et multis aliis.

For Robert bishop of Hereford's hearing of the dispute between St. Peter's and John priest of Llanvaes, see Barrow, *Hereford Episcopal Acta*, no. 119.

[1]   The letter *B* is interlined, with a line drawn to the words *ex Foresta*, of uncertain date, in the margin.

388. *Letter from William dean of Gronydd (Glam.) to Hamelin abbot of St. Peter's, Gloucester, and R(oger) prior of Llanthony concerning parochial rights in the church of Stormy (Glam.). (c. 1174 × 79)*

B.L. Harl. Ch. 75.B.3 (186 mm × 45 mm); writ with tongue, stained, possibly from red wax, but no tie; seal missing; no endorsement; Clark, *Cartae et alia*, i, no. 152; cal. in *EAWD*, ii, no. L.154.

Venerabilibus patribus Ham(elino) dei gratia abbati Gloec' . et .R. priori Lant' Will(elmu)s decanus de Wrenid . salutem. Quod in nostra decania uidimus et audiuimus hoc fideliter et t[e]st[amur][1] . Quod illam ecclesiam de uilla Sturmi de qua controuersia fuit inter Rogerum Sturmi et Gilebertum presbiterum de Nouo Castello . Gaufridus Sturmi pater illius Rogeri construxit in uilla sua quam fecerat in solitudine in terra quam nemo unquam prius arauerat . et ex illius Gaufridi donatione et presentatione recepit eam Tomas presbiter et cunctis diebus uite sue possedit. Et ut uerum fateamur illa ecclesia non de ecclesia de Noui Castelli set de nobis crisma recepit . et in tempore tam .G. quam .R. ibi baptizabantur infantes et mortui sepeliebantur. Valete.

This *actum* was written by Glamorgan Scribe 3 (see above, comment on no. 13). The letter's limiting dates are Roger of Norwich's move as prior from Llanthony Prima to Llanthony Secunda and the end of Hamelin's abbacy (*HRH*, 172–3).

[1] Letters in square brackets from Clark, *Cartae et alia*, i, no. 152 because of the current poor state of the MS.

389. *Record of the gift by Philip de Braose to the church of St. Peter and the monks of Gloucester of a burgess at Radnor (Brecon) and of 12d. a year from the town to buy hay for their horses. (c. 1095 × 1139; c. 1100?)*

A. H.C.L., no. 1513 (167 mm × 66 mm); slit for tag on foot; tag and seal missing; endorsements: De Redenoure. (s. xii[2]), **Hand a**; c(apsula) .xv. de laicis tenuris. (s. xii[2] × s. xiii[in]); Registratur (s. xiv[ex]); **B**. P.R.O., C 150/1, no. 594, fol. 166; *Cart. Glouc.* ii, no. 594; cal. in Baddeley i, no. 7, p. 226.

Notum sit tam presentibus quam futuris[1] Ph. de Braiosa ęcclesię sancti[2] Petri et monachis Gloicestrę quemdam burgensem[3] apud Radenova' in elemosina dedisse . solutum et quietum ab omnibus querelis et consuetudinibus preter de excubia ac de clamore cum omnibus suis rebus et terra . et xii. denarios de pretore eiusdem uillę ad terminum festi sancti Iohannnis annuatim unde emant fenum ad equos pascendos dum ibunt ac redibunt. Hęc autem concessio facta est[4] presentibus uxore sua . et militibus et eiusdem uille pluribus[5] burgensibus . Adam de Carnelia . Willelmo . de Mesnilio'. Willelmo dapifero . et Romoldo . et .W. de Bascheuilla . Roberto de Ca'posecreto . et Gautero . de Putanglo'. Ernulfo de Louentonia . et Roberto pincerna . et Roberto dispensatore . et Edwino pistore . et Odone capellano et Radulfo clerico . et pluribus aliis quos enumerare longum est. Adhuc etiam illis concessit totas suas consuetudines eundi ac[6] reundi uendendi[7] et emendi per totam suam terram.

This form in the third person is unusual. For Philip de Braose see Sanders, *English Baronies*, 21, 108, and for the terminal date of issue, Salter, *Oxford Charters*, no. 5 n. Philip's gift is noted in the abbey's List of Donations (*Cart. Glouc.* i, p. 110). The Norman hand of this charter reflects characteristics described by Ker, *English Manuscripts*, 22–23, which makes a terminal date of *c.* 1100 quite possible; for comparison see Bishop and Chaplais, *English Royal Writs*, Plate X (1096–7); Salter, *Oxford Charters*, no. 1 (*c.* 1105 × 1115).

[1] Superscript.
[2] Originally *sancto*, but *i* overwritten.
[3] From this point on the text is completed in another hand.
[4] **B** ends here with *etc.*
[5] *plurebus* in MS.
[6] Erased.
[7] *den* superscript.

390. *Alleged* conventio *in the form of a chirograph between the abbot and convent of St. Peter's, Gloucester, and Robert Fitz Harding, by which the abbey mortgaged to Robert the manor of Tregoff with lands in Pennon and other lands and revenues*

belonging to the church of Llancarfan (Glam.) for five years for £80, allowing the
abbot the option of earlier repayment. 1146 (Written c. 1200). Cardiff.

A. P.R.O., C 150/2/[4] (84 mm [left] × 190 mm [foot]); seal on tongue with tie at top; white
wax, chipped and worn; obverse: round (*c.* 57 mm in diam.); a large animal facing left with
neck and head bent below its front legs ?; legend: . . .VM RO. . . F. . .DING;[1] no counterseal;
endorsements: Rob(ertus) filius Harding (s. xii[2]); c(apsula) ii[a] de laicis tenuris (s. xii[ex] × s.
xiii[in]); De Treigof (*c.* 1200); non indiget registrari (*c.* s. xv[in]); B. ibid. C 150/1, fol. 179; *Cart.*
Glouc. ii, no. 653; *LCGF*, Appendix VII, no. 4.

Sciant presentes et futuri quod hec est conventio facta inter abbatem et conventum
sancti Petri Glouc' et dominum Robertu(m) Harding anno incarnationis dominici
millesimo . centesimo .xl.vi. in festo beati Michaelis quod ego Robert(us) Harding
recepi manerium de Tregof' in Glamorgan cum terra de Pennum et cum aliis terris et
redditibus omnibus ad dictam manerium pertinentibus ad ecclesiam de Lancarvan
cum domibus et curtilagiis et decimis ad dictam ecclesiam spectantibus de dictis
abbate et monachis usque ad terminum quinquienii sequentis pro quatuor viginti
libris argenteis [.] Ita quod si memoratus abbas possit vel velit dictam pecuniam
michi vel uxori mee vel heredibus meis ante prefatam terminum persolvere'.
computato rationabiliter commodo rerum receptarum ex parte mea'. dum modo
fuerit michi vel meis satisfactum'. ego vel heredes mei absque omni difficultate
dictum manerium de Tregof et prefatam ecclesiam cum omnibus prenominatis dictis
abbati et conventui restituemus.[2] Huius conventionis testes sunt . dominus Willelmus
comes Glouc' et totus comitatus de Kairdif.

CYROGRAPHVM

Several anomalies undermine the authenticity of this document. The hand is transitional
twelfth- to thirteenth-century. The use of *dominus* with *Willelmus Comes* was not usual in
1146. William could not have attested as earl of Gloucester in 1146 because he succeeded to
the earldom (which included the lordship of Glamorgan) only in 1147. Robert Fitz Harding did
not style himself *Robertus Harding* as the text does (e.g. B.C.M., nos. 11, 14; G.R.O.,
D.471/T.1/1). The seal would have been either the abbot of Gloucester's or Fitz Harding's: it
cannot have been the abbot's, and it is not certain that it was Fitz Harding's (see P.R.O., DL
25/218; B.C.M., Select Ch. no. 14). Serious doubts also have been expressed about St. Peter's
ability to use the estates as security for a loan (*LCGF*, Appendix VII, no. 4 n.). Nevertheless
there may have been an actual transaction between the two parties of which the above text is a
carelessly crafted forgery. A copy of a charter of Earl William of Gloucester (albeit defective)
confirms Robert Fitz Harding's tenure of the Welsh lands of St. Peter's (*Cart. Glouc.* ii,
no. 803; also Patterson, *EGC*, no. 85, an imperfect text).

[1] Reading uncertain.
[2] **B** ends here.

391. *Grant in the form of a chirograph by Abbot Henry and the convent of St.*
Peter's, Gloucester, to Maurice of Llancarfan changing the dates on which he is to
pay the annual rent of 100s. for the church of Llancarfan (Glam.) from two, as
under his charter from Abbot Thomas, to three. (1205 × 24)

G.C.L., 'Deeds and Seals', v, no. 14, fol. 5 (103 mm [left] × 124 mm [foot]); **Scribe 14**; slit for tag on turn-up; tag and seal missing; endorsements: Contra Mauricium de Lankaruan'; iiii (s. xiii^{in}); Non indiget registrari quia (s. xiv × s. xv^{in}).

C Y R O G R A P H . . . C Y R O G R A . . . (*inverted*)

Sciant presentes et futuri quod ego Henr(icus) dei gratia abbas et conuentus sancti Petri Glouc' concessimus Mauricio de Lankaruan clerico nostro ad petitionem ipsius et amicorum suarum. ut centum solidos quod reddidit nobis singulis annis de ecclesia nostra de Lankaruan ad duos terminos . scilicet ad festum sancti Michaelis et ad Pascha sic[ut]^1 carta nostra tempore bone memorie Thome abbatis confecta testatur . quam idem Mauricius habet. reddat nobis de cetero singulis annis. ad tres terminos . videlicet ad Clausum Pasche quadraginta solidos . in Natiuitate sancti Iohannis Baptiste. viginti solidos . et ad festum sancti Michaelis quadraginta solidos. Idem uero .M. iuramentum corporale nobis prestitit quod fidelis erit ecclesie nostre de soluendis predictis centum solidis plenarie. ad predictos terminos . et quod nec artem nec ingenium exquiret. per se uel per alium. vnde domus nostra dampnum per tenuram suam incurrat. In cuius rei testimonium. presens scriptum sigillo ecclesie nostre munitum. predicto Mauricio diuiso inter nos cyrographo. tradimus. Hiis testibus . Adam priore . Thoma suppriore . Radulfo precentore . Ricardo capellano nostro . magistro Ricardo de Brack' et multis aliis.

^{1} Portion of MS. torn away.

---

392. *Lease in the form of a chirograph from Abbot John and the convent of St. Peter's, Gloucester, to Maurice of Llancarfan clerk of Tregoff manor (Glam.) for twenty years at an annual farm of 18 marks, of which Maurice paid 100 marks in advance for the first five years and part of the sixth, and was to pay the farm thereafter at Ewenny Priory; if he died within the term he might assign the issues of the manor. The abbey's cellarer was to hold the manorial court when he wished. If the manor fell into the earl's wardship Maurice would be compensated. 29 September 1260.*

G.C.L., 'Deeds and Seals', ix, no. 10, fol. 5 (207 [left] × 226 mm [foot]); fragment of tag; seal missing; endorsements: De firma de Treygof tradita magistro Mauricio de Lancaruan.[;] Caps(ula) .iii.^{a} de ecclesiasticis tenuris (s. xiii^{ex} × s. xiv^{in}); non indiget registrari (s. xiv).

C Y R O G R A P H V M

Omnibus Cristi fidelibus presens scriptum visuris uel auditurus . Ioh(ann)es dei gratia abbas sancti Petri Glouc' . et eiusdem loci conuentus salutem . eternam in domino. Nouerit vniuersitas vestra quod hec est conuentio facta . inter nos et dominum Mauricium de Lancaruan clericus . Anno domini .M.^{o}.C^{o}C^o. sexagesimo in festo sancti Michaelis . Videlicet quod idem Mauricius soluet annuatim decem et octo marcas sterlingorum pro manerio nostro de Treygof . quod ei tradidimus ad firmam dicto anno et dicto termino. cum decimis garbarum et feni eiusdem ville . et omnibus aliis pertinentiis . vsque ad terminum viginti annorum plene completorum . E quibus denariis pacauit nobis pre manibus centum marcas argenti pro quinque primis annis . et pro decem marcis in sexto anno . in quo quidem anno soluet nobis octo marcas argenti . que residue sunt de eodem anno in prioratu de Ewenny ad Pascha . et deinceps annuatim in eodem loco usque ad terminum suum plene completum . decem et octo marcas duobus terminis . videlicet medietatem in festo sancti Michaelis . et aliam medietatem in Annuntiationem beate Marie. Si vero de dicto Mauricio infra predictum terminum humanitus contigerit⸴ licebit ei omnes prouentus dicti manerii assignare a prenotato festo sancti Michaelis . anno domini .CC⁰. sexagesimo in decem[1] annos continue sequentes . salua tunc nobis solutione decem et octo marcarum ab assignatis suis terminis predictis soluendarum . Quod nisi dictus Mauricius et assignati sui si quos fecerit⸴ ad predictos terminos de prefato redditu nobis plenarie satisfecerit⸴ licebit nobis omnes prouentus dicti manerii nostri integre recipere . absque alicuius condictione . uel calumpnia vel clamio . assignatorum . executorum . uel legatoriorum suorum. Idem uero prefatus Mauricius iuramento prefato se obligauit . quod fidelis erit ecclesie nostre . et quod nec artem nec ingenium exquiret vnde domus nostra occasione firme sue dampnum incurrat . Et quod curiam et domos nostras de Treygof cum omnibus pertinentiis suis in adeo bono statu nobis relinquere termino suo completo⸴ sicut fuerunt quando ea recepit. Preterea celerarius noster tenebit curiam nostram in dicto manerio quandocumque voluerit . vt si que forte hominibus nostris illate fuerint iniurie . per ipsum Mauricium uel per alium occasione eius in presentia celerarii per visum legalium virorum iniuriam passis satisfaciet. Hoc idem facient assignati sui si quos fecerit . saluis tunc predicto Mauricio uel assignatis suis omnibus amerciamentis et prouentibus duratione dicto termino suo. Et si aliquo casu contigerit quod garda dicti manerii in manus domini comitis uel eius qui pro tempore fuerit dominus de Glamorg' ceciderit⸴ nos eundem .M. uel assignatos suos indemptiones conseruabimus. Quia uero predictus Mauricius totum manerium cum wareto ad predictum terminum sancti Michaelis a nobis recepit vna cum redditu . auxilio . et omnibus aliis pertinentiis suis⸴ eodem modo in fine viginti annorum ipse uel assignati sui . totum prefatum manerium cum wareto . redditu . auxilio . et omni melioratione superposita ac omnibus aliis pertinentiis suis integre nobis relinqueret. In cuius rei testimonium presens scriptum in modum cyrographi inter nos confectum est . Cuius vnam partem sigillo ecclesie nostre signatam predicto Mauricio tradidimus . Alteram vero partem sigillo ipsius signatam penes nos retinuimus. Hiis testibus . dominis Waltero de Sulye . Gilberto de Umframuilla . Roberto de Sumery [.] Willelmo Flandrens(e) . Philippo de Nerbert . Iohanne de sancto Iohanne . Henrico Odyn . domino .N. archideacono Landauens(e) . magistro Simone de Radenore eiusdem loci canonico . Patricio de Aldrinton' . Willelmo Heyru(n) . et aliis.

For an earlier lease of the manor in similar terms see above, no. 21.

[1] Evidently in error for *viginti*.

393. *Letter from William of Cardiff addressed to the sheriff of Glamorgan and the barons and knights of the shire court of Cardiff, undertaking on behalf of Griffith ap Kneith and his brothers that no harm be suffered by the abbot and convent of St. Peter's, Gloucester, or their men, and that should Griffith and his brothers do wrong to the abbey William would give to it the tenement which Griffith held of him in Llantrithyd (Glam.). (1207 × 31)*

A. H.C.L., no. 2309 (165 mm × 50 mm); fragments of tongue and tie at left foot; seal missing; endorsements: Littera Will(elm)i de Keyrdif; Caps(ula) ii. de laicis tenuris (s. xiii^ex × s. xiv^in); **B.** P.R.O., C 150/1, fol. 108; *Cart. Glouc.* i, no. 342; Clark, *Cartae et alia*, i, p. 57; cal. in *JNLW* 3 (1943–4), Appendix 1, C, pp. 133–4; cal. in Baddeley ii, no. 143, p. 44.

Karissimis amicis suis vicecomite Glamorg' et omnibus baronibus et militibus comitatus de K'dif Will(elmu)s de K'dif salutem. Noueritis quod manucapio pro Griffino filio Kneith' et fratribus suis quod nullum dampnum uel grauamen inferetur domino abbati et conuentui Glouc' uel hominibus eorum de terris rebus et posessionibus suis per eos nec per suos. Et si forte contigerit quod ipsi dicto abbati et conuentui uel suis in aliquo forisfecerint. ego Will(elmu)s tradam tenementum eorum quod de me tenent in uilla de Landrired' liberum et quietum in perpetuum dicto abbati et conuentui Glouc' saluo seruitio meo ad eandem terram pertinente. In huius rei testimonium litteris istis sigillum meum apposui[1]. Hiis testibus Hoel' filio Mereduth' . Reimondo de Sulie [.] Gileberto de Turb'uill' [.] magistro Radulfo Mailoch' . Iohanne capellano et multis aliis.

For the date, see Conway Davies, 'Ewenny Priory', 126 & nn.; Nicholl, *Normans in Glamorgan*, 93; Ralph Mailoc, a canon of Llandaff, died in 1231 (Patterson, *EGC*, 11–12); the script is of that vintage.

[1] **B** as printed in *Cart. Glouc.* ends here with *etc.*

INDEX OF PERSONS AND PLACES

Numbers in romans refer to pages of the Introduction, those in arabic to the numbers of the *acta*. Persons are indexed by surname where possible; 'de' is translated to 'of' where the identity of the English or Welsh place from which the surname comes is reasonably certain. Unidentified place-names are in italic. The variant spellings of the MSS. are given selectively where they are thought to be helpful.

SELECTIVE INDEX OF SUBJECTS

Numbers in romans refer to pages of the Introduction, those in arabic to the numbers of the *acta*.

Plate I.   Abbatial Seals: *a.* Abbot Hamelin, obverse (no. 70). *b* and *c.* Thomas Carbonel, obverse and reverse, counterseal (no. 84). *d* and *e.* Henry Blont, obverse and reverse, counterseal (no. 112). *f* and *g.* Henry Foliot, obverse (no. 165) and reverse (no. 37). *h* and *i.* John de Felda, obverse and reverse, counterseal (no. 174)

ANNO AB INCARNATIONE ... m̄ c̄ lxiii xp̄i. Millesimo. Centesimo. xxxviii.

Ego Stephs rex anglor ... m̄ ter̃cio · Peticione Walteri de lan Abbr Gloec̃
& quorundam baronu ... regū men ter̃cio · Peticione Walteri de lan Abbr Gloec̃
& dcr̃nas & om̃s donaco ... con̄cess̃ & cōfirmau̅ ecc̃t̃ s̄ ā pr̃ de gloec̃ · Terras · ecc̃las
reges · p̃ suas carras cōfirmatas ... tiones angl̃ie p̃d̃cq; ecc̃e dederunt · & antecessor̃ in
de Wart̃hoia cū filia & t̃r̃ ... eb; · & dono h̄enr̃ra regis · O m̃num̃ · Ō ā nā t̃ū
brau̅ · Colna s̄ andree ... ex dono henr̃ra regis · D̃ brocarop̃domo Ihesu ac
ndr̃mi · & dono Rogeri de ... q̄ sī iatbuh̄ōd · & una ecc̃am cū una hida t̃re · & una p̄̃o
us̃ & om̃ib; · ib · : cū a lea ... P̃ ecc̃am s̄ā pē de herford̃ q̄ i b̄ensis̃ · & t̃rs̃ · & der̃
in q̄ xut̃rs̃ gloec̃ ... he vt iter̃i uic̃comes̃ et ... t̃s̄ cadoc̃ de lan
us t̃m que uoca ... r̃ dono Rodb̄a fili̅ ... t̃mq̄ i de beͷim̄

N PRINCIPIO ERAT VERBVM. Huius uerbū uocat̄.
qa p eū patr mundo innotuit ut qa ipsū dicendo
id est generando dſ pat omia creauit. Ipse e. enim
dictio & uerbū & sermo patrſ. Pater est p̄ncipiū ex
q̄ omia. filius e. p̄ncipiū p qd̄ omia. Alu euāgliste
describunt xp̄m natū ex tēpore. ioħes affirmat eū
in p̄ncipio fuisse. id e. in patre. Qd̄ erat in p̄ncipio.
n sine tēpore. ni preuento p̄ncipio. n fuit pat ante
filiū. Est q̄ pat principiū non de p̄ncipio. filiū autē
p̄ncipiū sed de p̄ncipio. Vel uerbū erat in p̄ncipio
omiū creaturarū ut tēporū; q̄cqd̄ eni creaturarū qd̄
cunq; p̄ncipiū habuit ut esset. erat tc p uerbū dı.
pqd̄ facta ſō omia. Ideo quar pono substantiū
uerbū. erat. erat. erat. erat. ut intelligeres omia tēpora p̄uenisse
coeternū dō patri uerbū. Verbū dicat ut ſon q̄ de ore loquentꝭ
emitat & audit. ut ipse intellect q̄ in corde audientꝭ p̄ditū
sonū generat. Cū pſer hec uox. dſ ut uerbū. intelligim q̄n
dā substantiā ineffabile. incomutabile. incogitabile. que n
transit cū plata uoce. hoc uerbū e. patri coeternū. & eidem es
sentie. Et ne q̄s putaret filiū ita in patre subsistere ut nulla
differentia credat inesse. subiungit. Et uerbū erat apud dı̄m.
Q̄ ac sifili subsistit in patre. in unitate essentie. & pſonali diuisio
ne. Alu mo homines subito apparuisse dicunt dı filiū. ioħes apud
dı̄m sep fuisse dicit. Et uerbū erat ap dı̄m. id e. filiū apud patrem.
Alu uerū hominē. ioħes ipsū uerū dı̄m confirmat. Et ds erat uerbū.
id e. ipse filiū erat ds. Alu hominē eū apud homines tēporalit con
uersatū. ioħes in p̄ncipio apud dı̄m manentē ostendit. Hoc erat
in p̄ncipio apud dı̄m. Ita apud patrē erat unū cū ipso patre. ut
omē p̄ncipiū creaturarū sua essentia p̄iret. Alu dicunt q̄n
miracula fecit in mundo. iste omia p ipsū facta esse testatur.

Plate III. Scribe 1 (part of a commentary on St. John's Gospel)

Sciant presentes 7 futuri qd ego Rogerus paruus 7 Hugo baruf ms dedim? deo 7 sco petro 7 coouadis g'soo in pecuua' elemosina' octo
acras de weddina quᵉ iacent iux̄ra aulee de Brocrop? p̄ salute a̅i̅a̅ng nr̄g 7 a̅ntecesso₂ uro₂ 7 i̅n pr̄senꝛa hamelini abbis
7 totī conuentī eidᵉ eccl̄e 7 mutor̄ aliog qui assuⁿꝛ. Sup altare sꝯ petri posuim? qd qᵃ firma 7 stabilꝭ eꝛ. uolumus
Ego Roger? predictā donatioē huᵫ carte meᵉ 7 sigilli mei a̅ttacoē confirmaui 7 Hugo fil? baruf ms pprio assensu
eᵃ qd magir? e. fidᵉ suᵃ i̅n possaoē co̅mmuni. Huᵫ rei testeᵽ ꝝ. Willᵐ dᵉ stetford. Gaufred? germin. Robᵗ 7 Willᵗ. 7 Simon.
sacrista. 7 Robᵗ lebret. 7 Roger? clallud. 7 Robᵗ feardan. 7 mulᵗa alij.

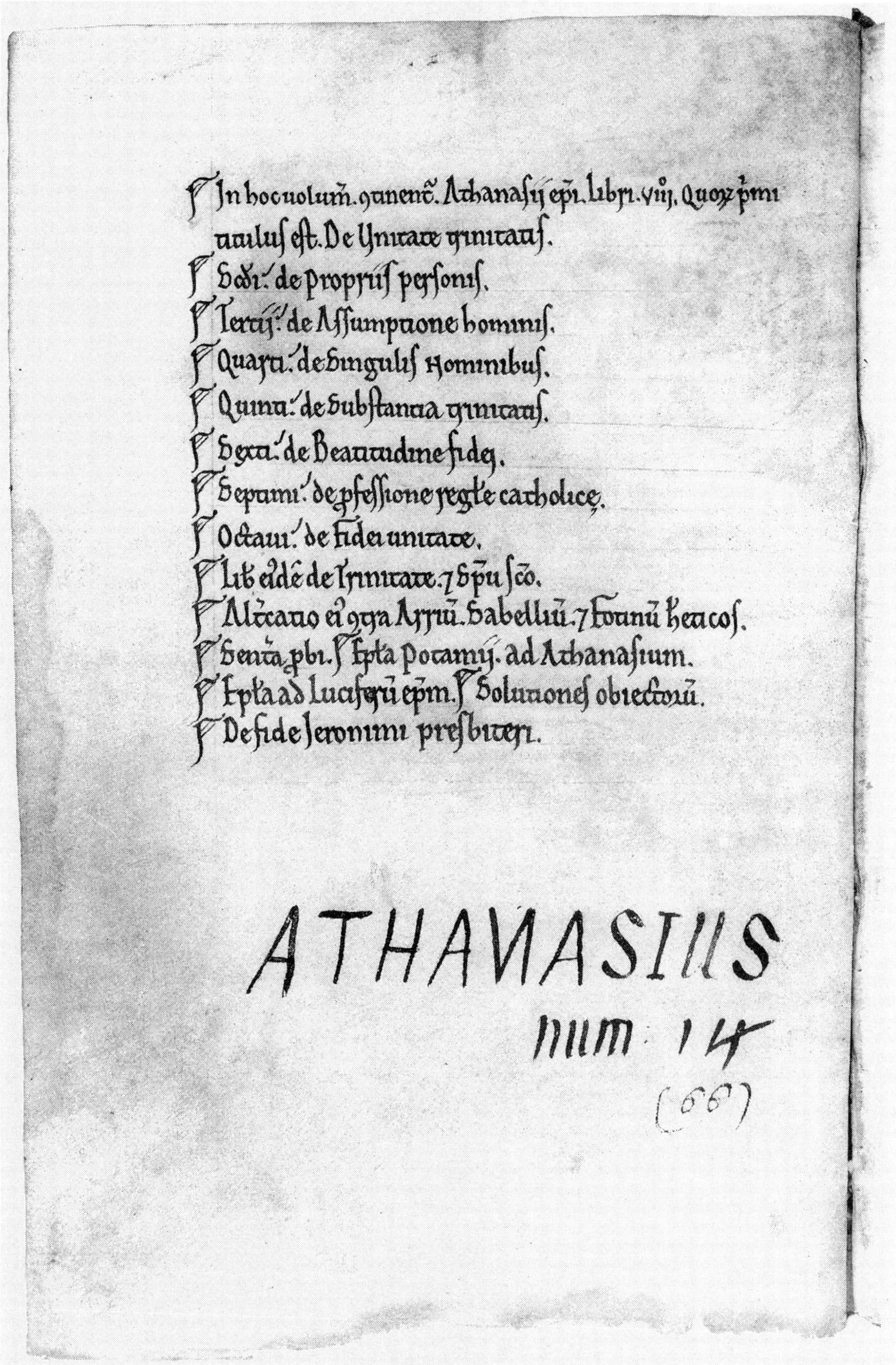

¶ In hoc uolum̄. ꝗnenē. Athanasij epi. libri. viij. Quoᵖ pm̄i

ꝯulus est. De Unitate ṫrinitatis.

¶ Sc̄di. de proprijs personis.

¶ Tertij. de Assumptione hominis.

¶ Quarti. de singulis Hominibus.

¶ Quintu. de substantia ṫrinitatis.

¶ Sexti. de Beatitudine fidei.

¶ Septimi. de pfessione regte catholice.

¶ Octaui. de fidei unitate.

¶ Lib eādē de trinitate. 7 Spu sc̄o.

¶ Altcatio eu ꝯra Arriu. babelliu. 7 ḟounu heticos.

¶ Senta. pbi. ¶ Epta potamij. ad Athanasium.

¶ Epta ad Luciferu epm. ¶ Solutiones obiectoru.

¶ De fide Jeronimi presbiteri.

Plate V. Scribe 2 (part of a volume of St. Athanasius)

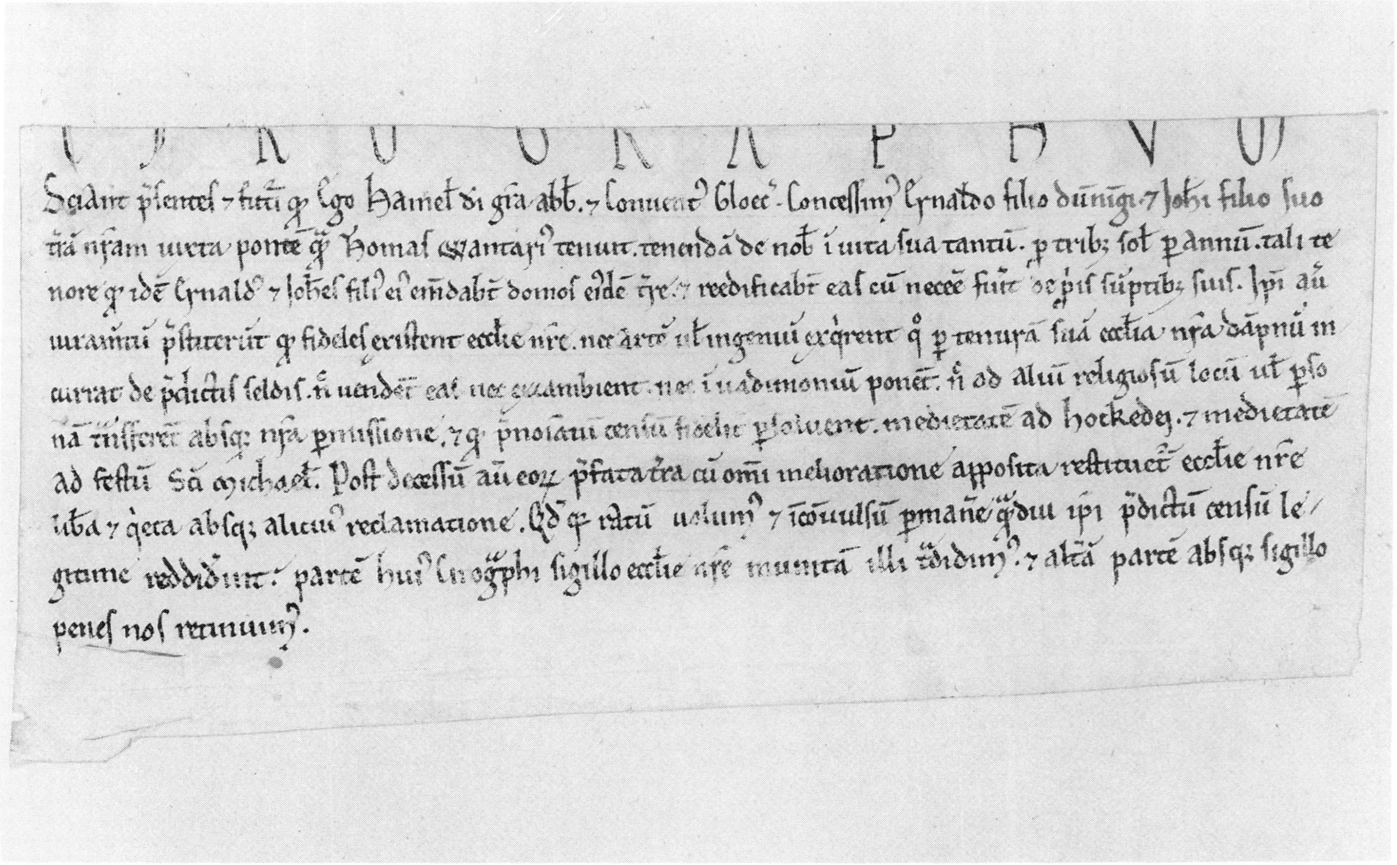

Plate VI. Scribe 3 (no. 60)

Plate VIIa. Scribe 4 (no. 61)

Plate VIIb. Scribe 8 (no. 36)

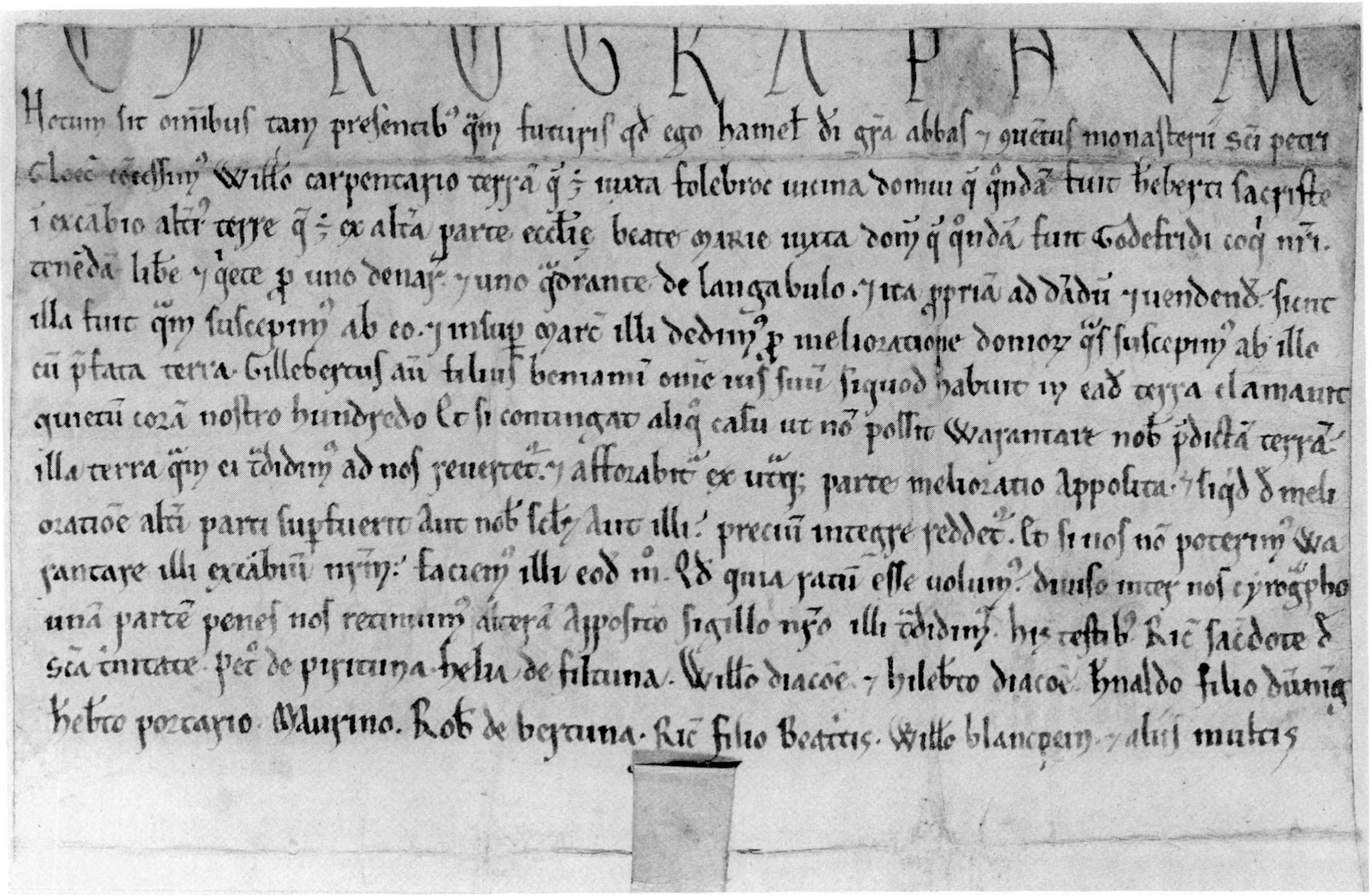

Plate IX. Scribe 6 (no. 70)

Notum sit Omnib[us] q[uo]d Ego thomas d[e]i g[rat]ia Abbas 7 Conuentus S[an]c[t]i Pet[r]i Gloec. gard[?]
[d]im[us] in pura[m] elemosina[m] Waltero filio [?] Waltri Birt tagstam ng[?]am de Miereysbu[ry]
[re]nd sub Annual pensione Sex sol[idorum]. [?] q[uo]d pa[r]... 7 i[n]comissa man[er]e uolum[us] Siu[m]...
... n[ost]ro cyrographo sigilla n[ost]ra i[m]pressione munito. aff[i]rma[n]di[mus] [?] de[m]i no Walt[ero]
... n[on] i[n]fecit q[uo]d ... q[uo]d Fidelis s[ecun]d[u]m ei[us] ecc[lesi]e n[ost]re de soluendo redditu n[ost]ro plenarie...
q[uo]d nec dya[m] nec ingeniu[m] exqui[re]t. u[n]de som[m]a mea g p[er]p[etu]a s[u]a ta[m]q[uam] i[n]cu[n]dit...

CYROGRAPHVM

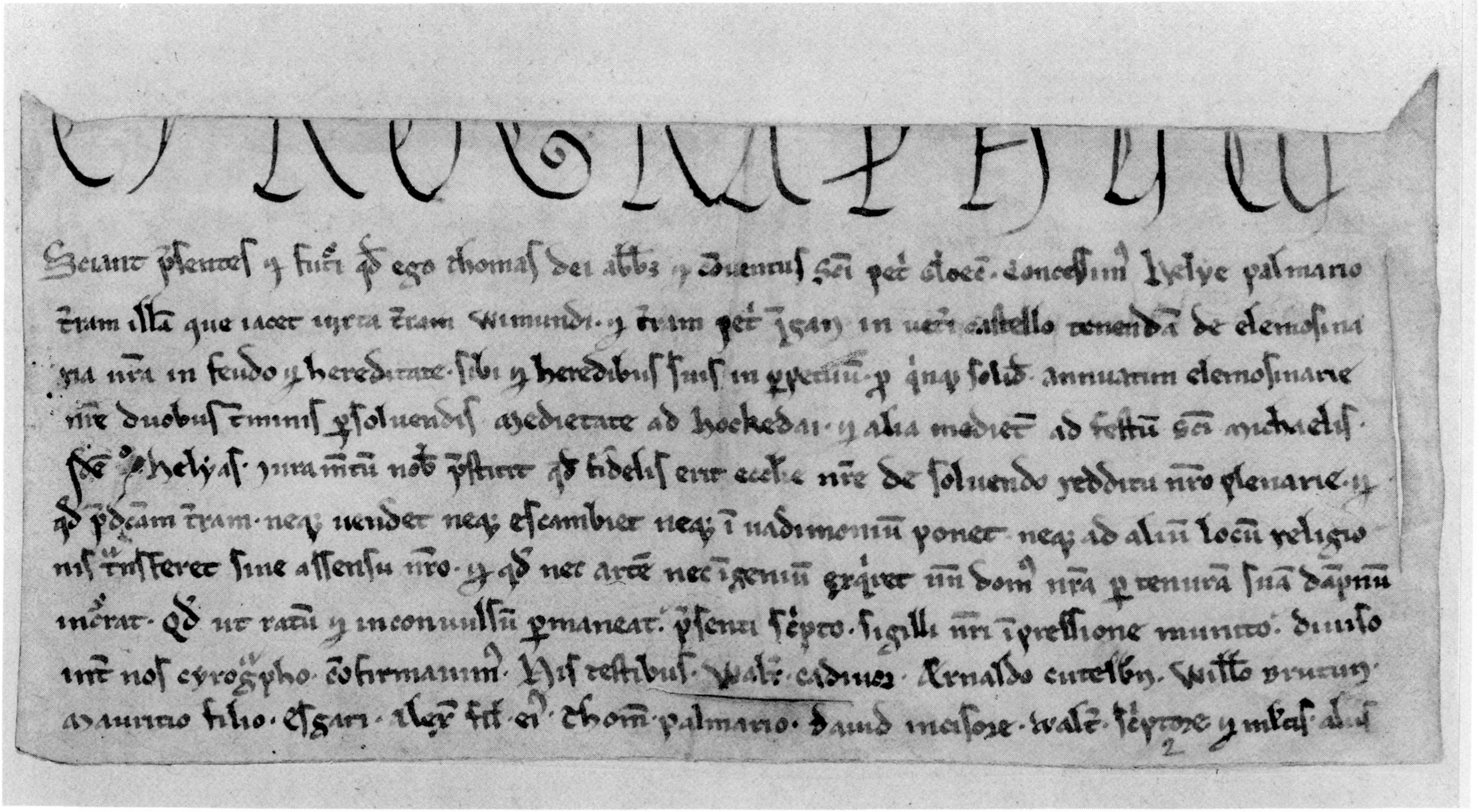

Plate XII. Scribe 10 (no. 80)

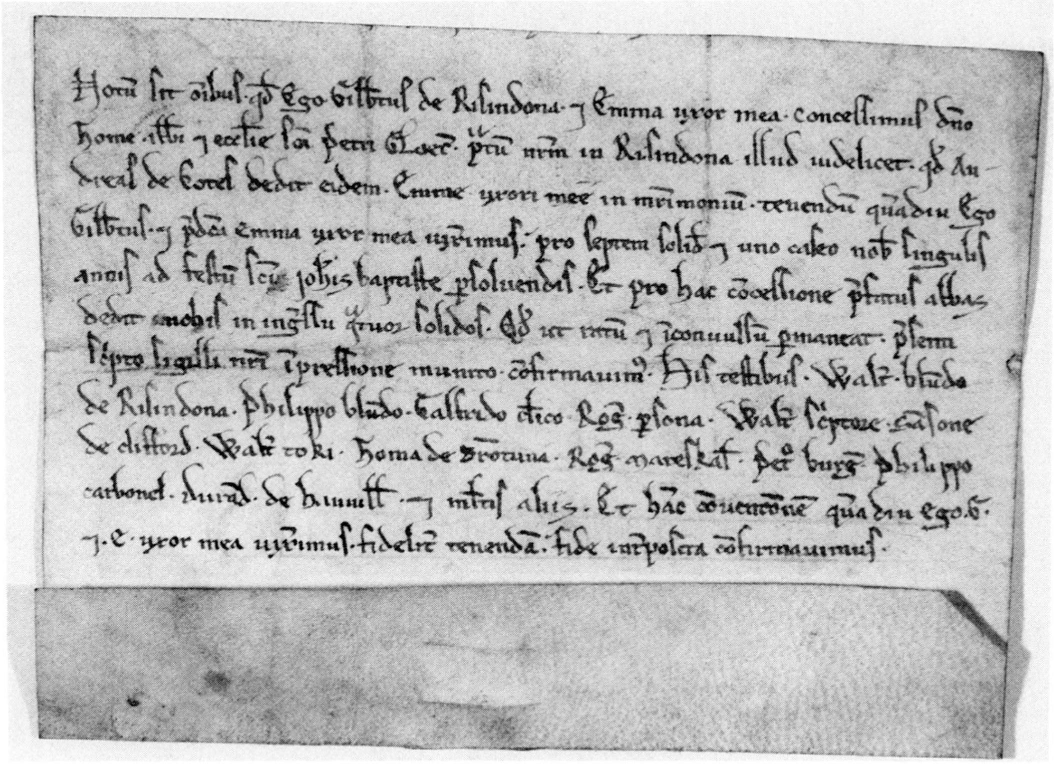

Plate XIII. Scribe 11 (no. 256)

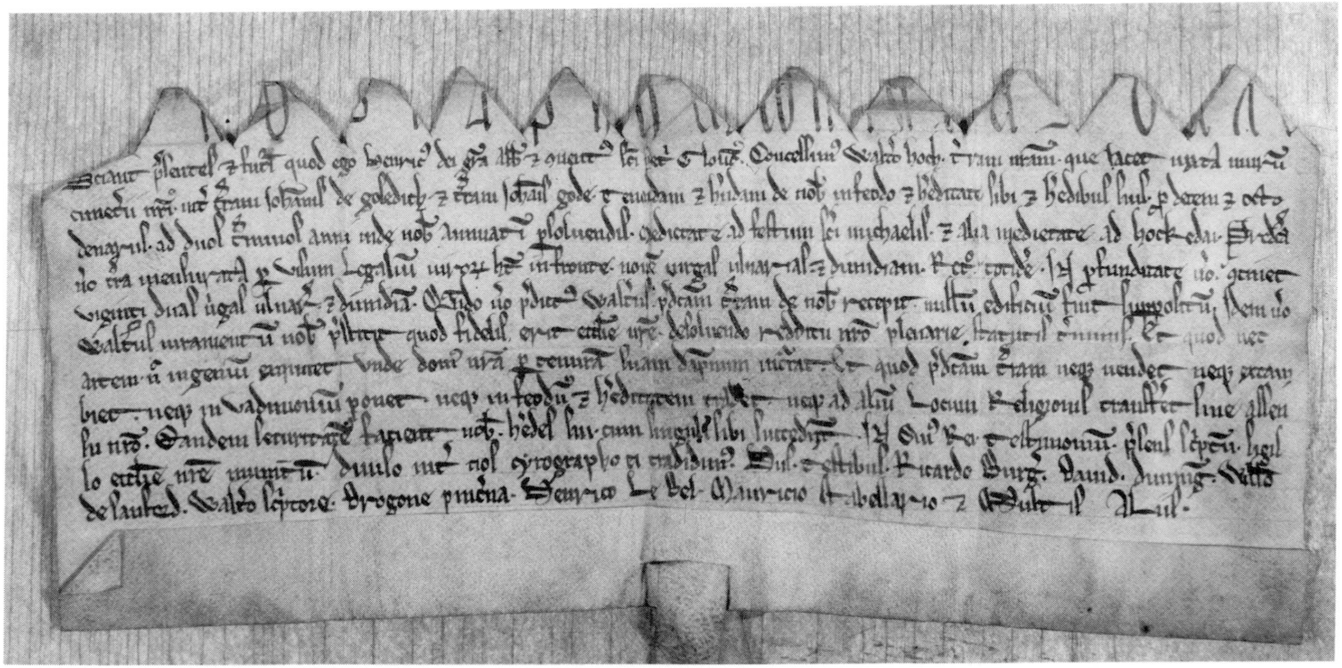

Plate XIV. Scribe 12 (no. 120)

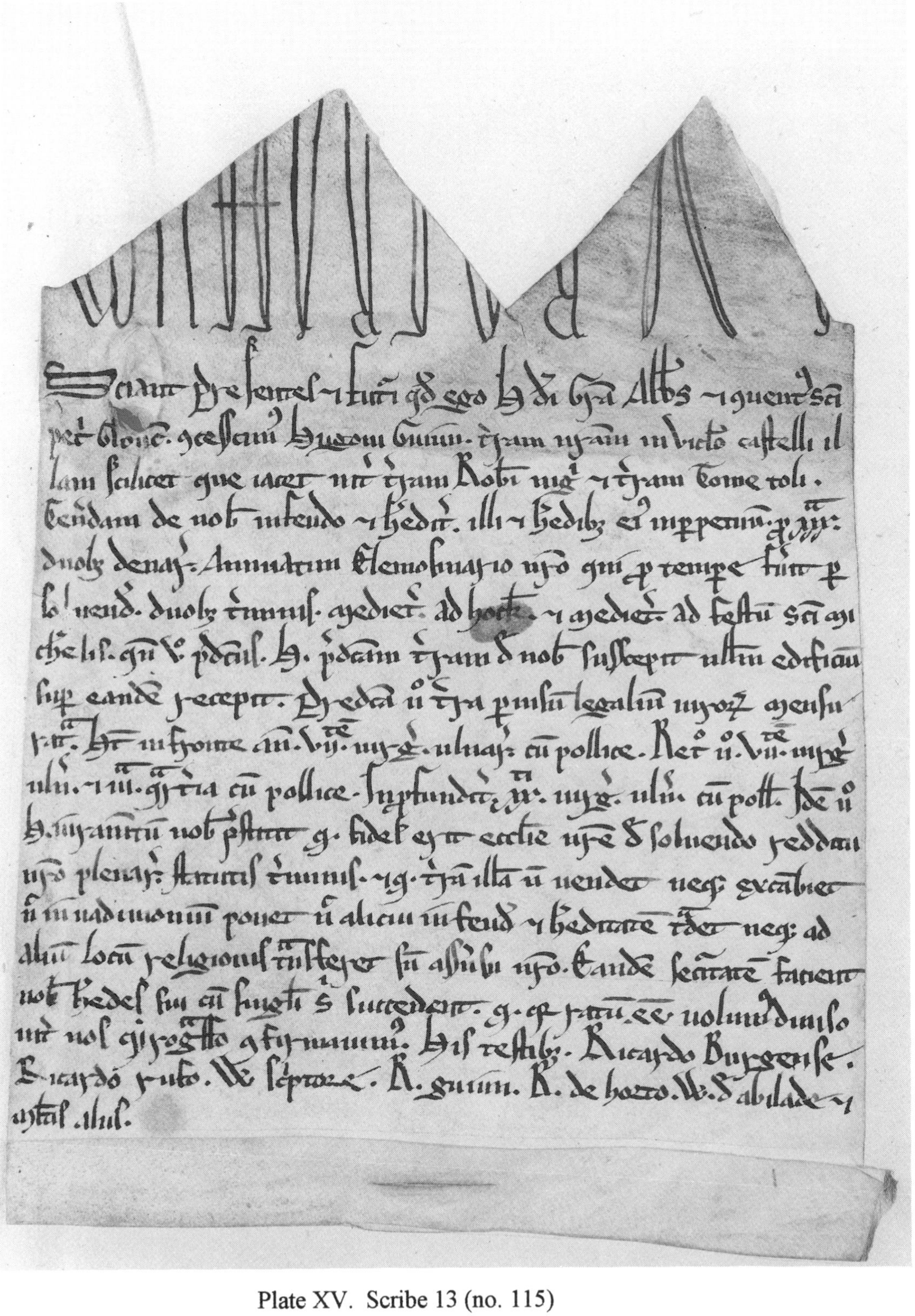

Sciant presentes et futuri quod ego H. dei gratia Abbas et Conventus de
... Glouc̄. concessimus Hugoni Burum. terram ... in Veteri Castelli il
lam scilicet que iacet ... terram Roberti ... et terram Thome Toli.
tenendam de nobis in feudo et hereditate illi et heredibus et imperpetuum. ... iiij.
duobus denariis. Annuatim elemosinario nostro qui pro tempore fuerit p
solvend. duobus terminis. medietatem ad hoc ... et medietatem ad festum sancti ...
the lis. qui ... H. predictam terram de nobis suscepit ... edificia
sup eandem ... recepit. ... hereditare ... terra ... legalem ... mensu
... Et in fronte ... vij. ... ulnas cum pollice. Retro ... vij. ...
ulna. et iiij ... cum pollice. Infundit ... iij. ... ulna cum pott. ...
H. ... nobis presentavit ... fidei et ... ecclesie ... de solvendo reddant
... plenam. terminis. ... terram illam ... vendet ... excambiet
... in vadimonium poner ... alicui ... et hereditate ... neque ad
aliud locum religionis transferet ... assensu nostro. Eandem ... tamen
nobis heredes sui ... sancti successerit. ... voluntatem diuiso
... nos ... affirmavimus. His testibus. Ricardo Burgense.
Ricardo ... W. ... R. ... R. de hecc. W. ... et
aliis.

Plate XV. Scribe 13 (no. 115)

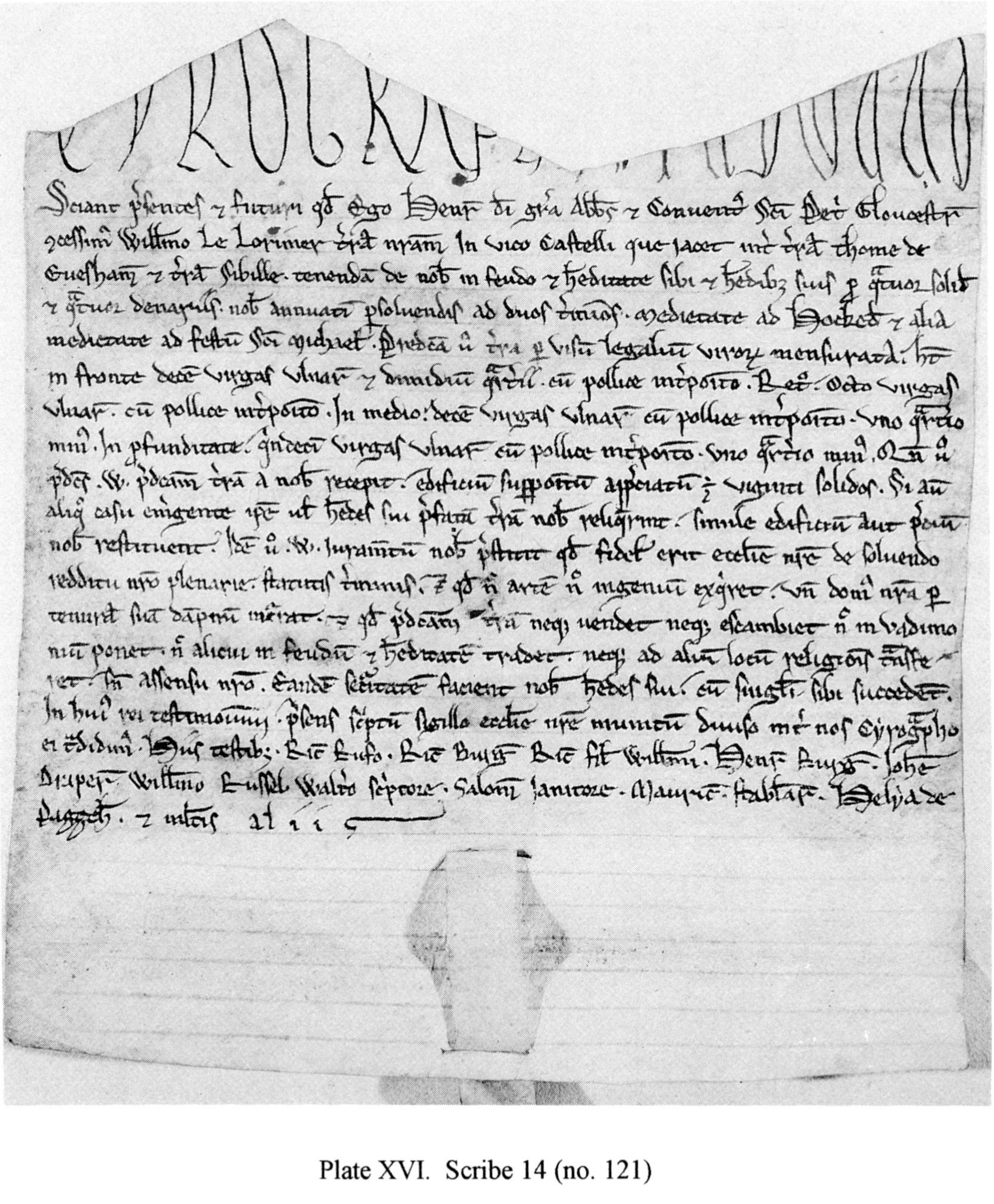

Plate XVI. Scribe 14 (no. 121)

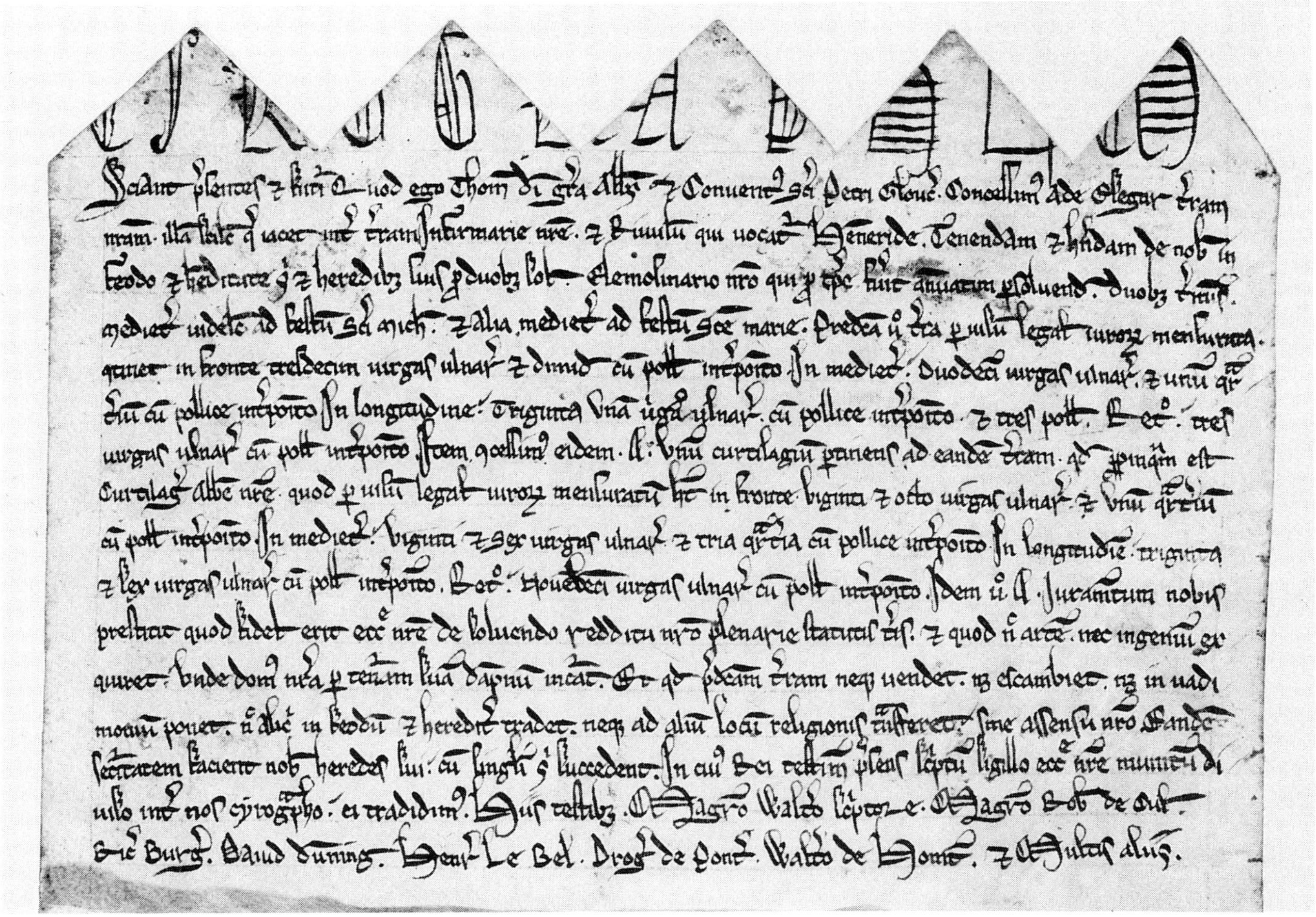

Plate XVII.   Scribe 15 (no. 145)

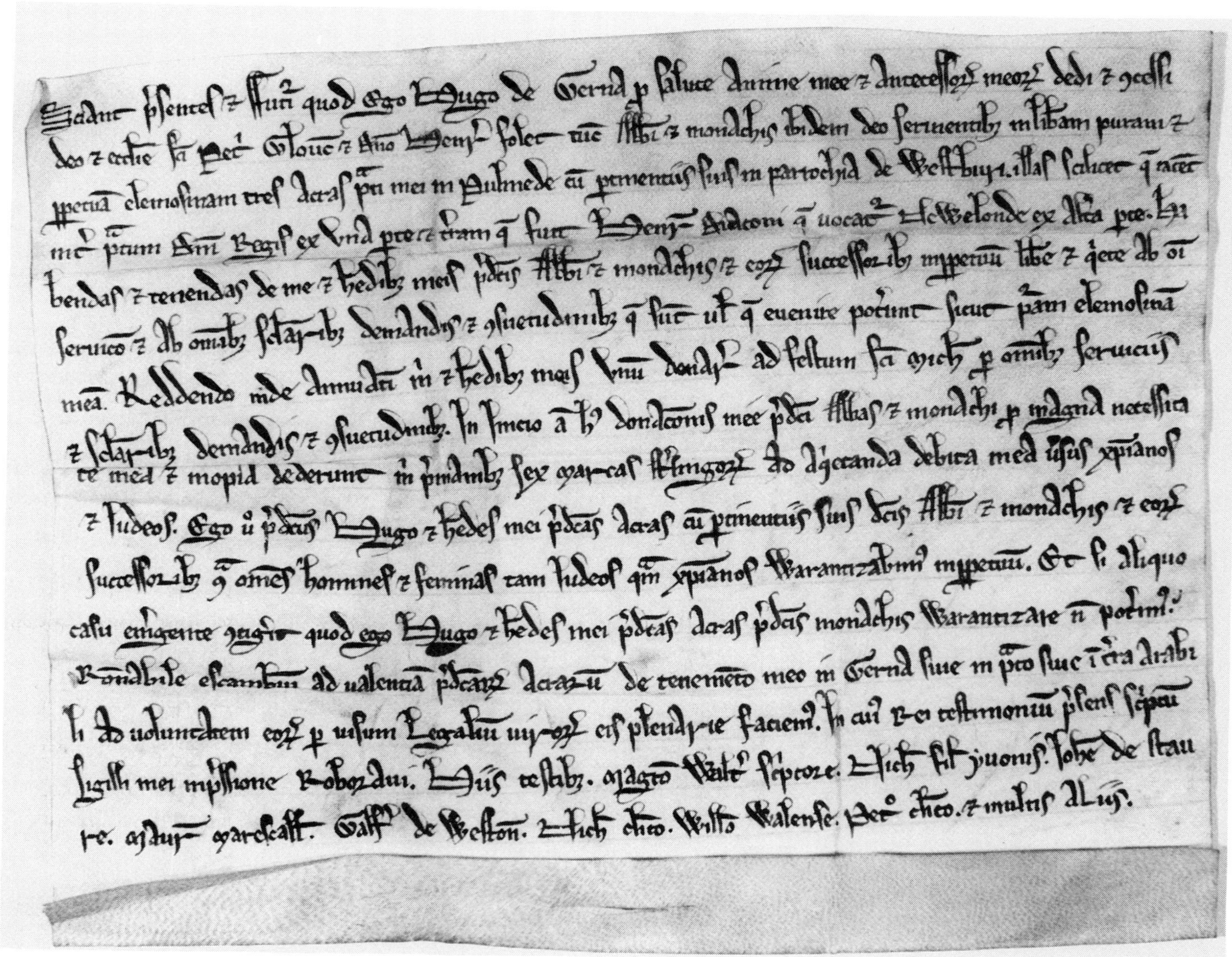

Plate XVIII.
Scribe 16
(no. 214)

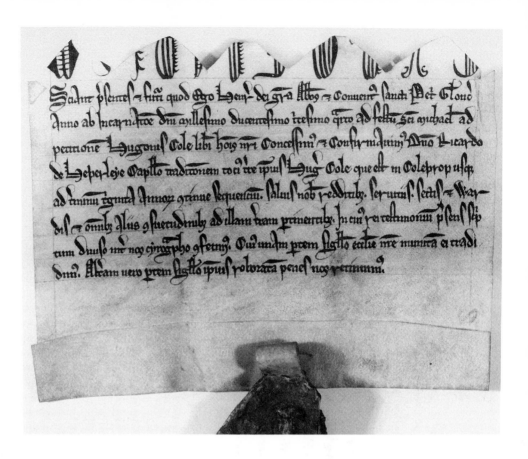

Plate XXa. Scribe 18 (no. 165)

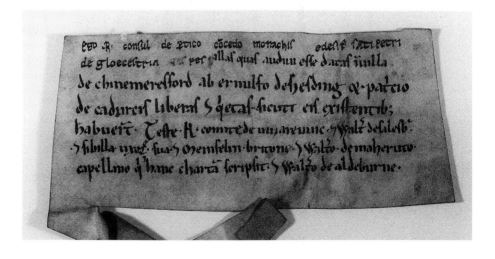

Plate XXb. Scribe 21 (no. 248)

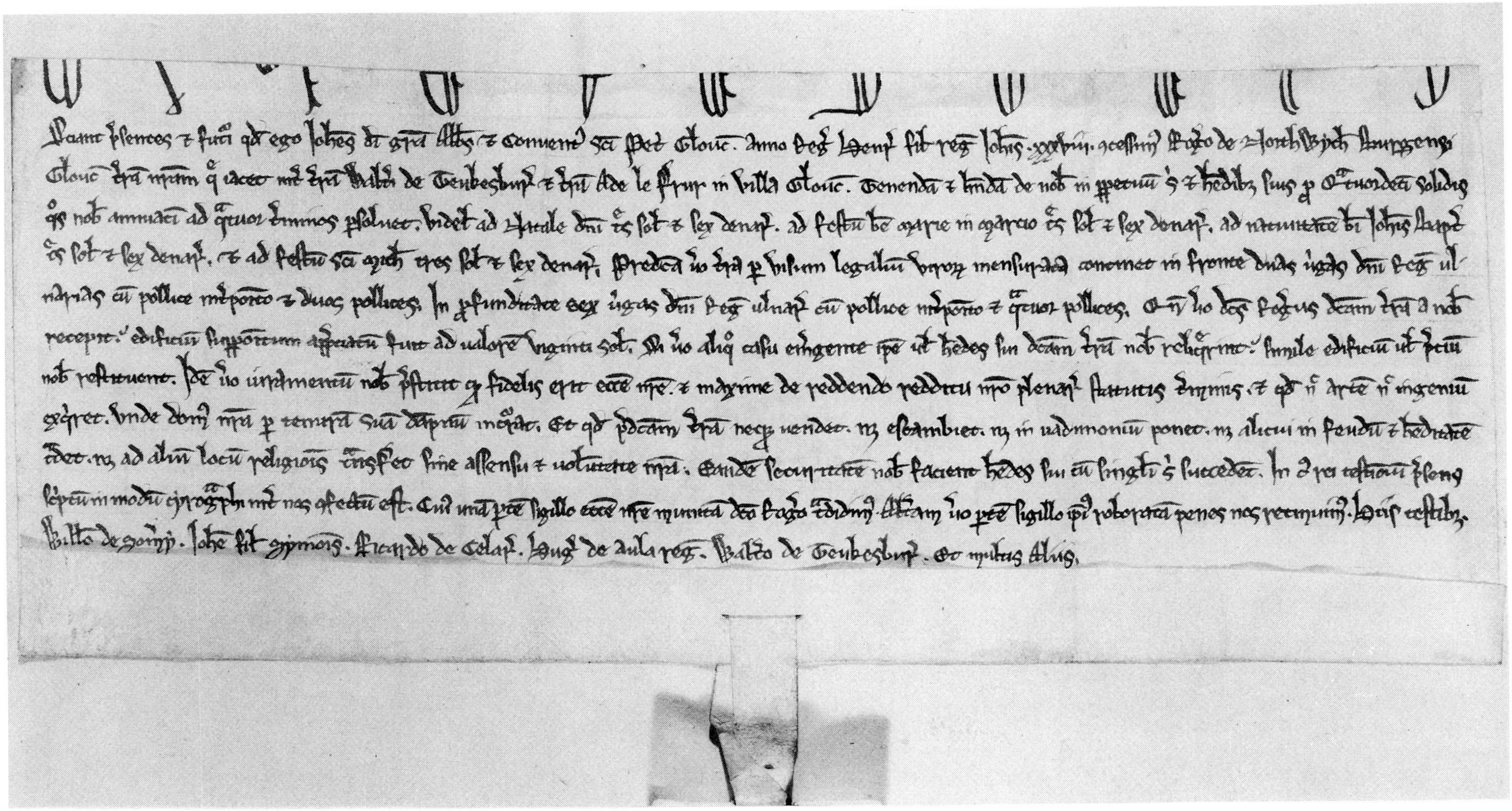

Plate XXI. Scribe 19 (no. 186)

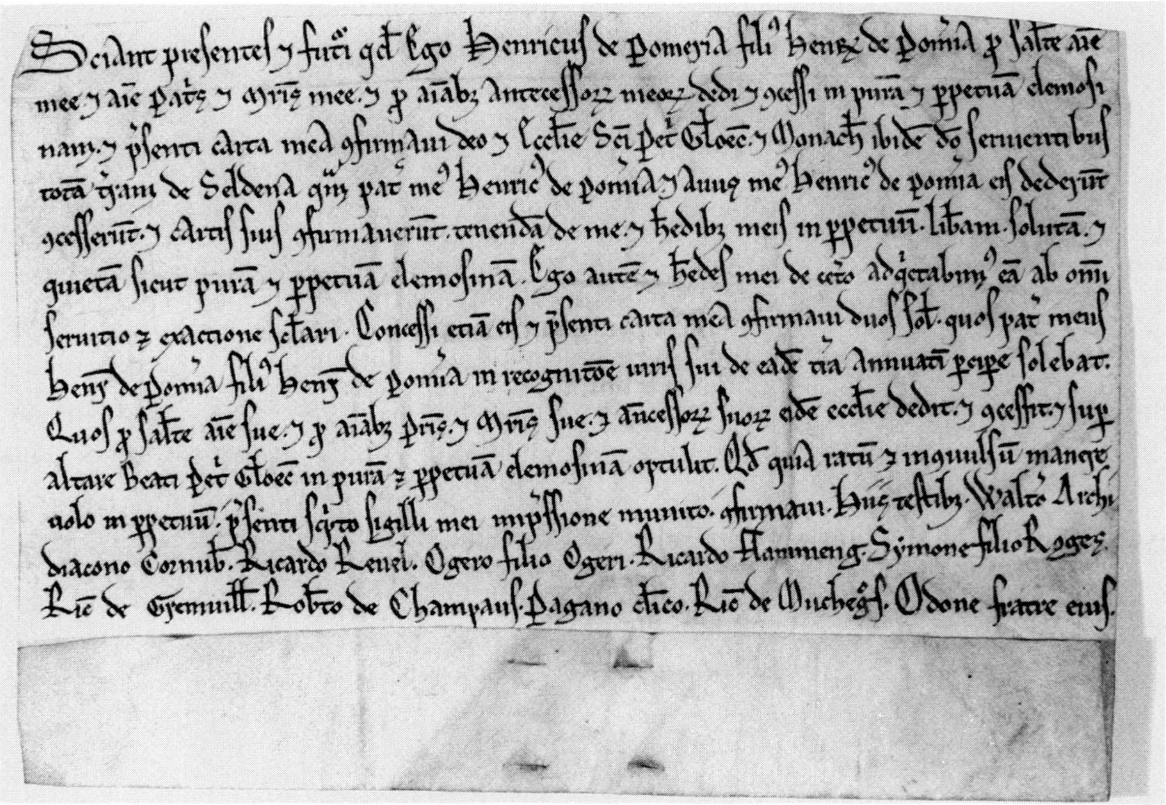
Sciant presentes et futuri quod Ego Henricus de Pomeria filius Henrici de Pomeria pro salute anime
mee et anime patris et matris mee et pro animabus antecessorum meorum dedi et concessi in puram et perpetuam elemosinam et presenti carta mea confirmavi deo et ecclesie Sancti Petri Gloec' et Monachis ibidem deo servientibus
totam terram de Seldena quam pater meus Henricus de Pomeria et avunculus meus Henricus de Pomeria eis dederunt
concesserunt et cartis suis confirmaverunt. tenendam de me et heredibus meis in perpetuum. liberam. solutam. et
quietam sicut puram et perpetuam elemosinam. Ego autem et heredes mei de certo adquietabimus eam ab omni
servitio et exactione seculari. Concessi etiam eis et presenti carta mea confirmavi duos solidos. quos pater meus
Henricus de Pomeria filius Henrici de Pomeria in recognitione iuris sui de eadem terra annuatim percipere solebat.
Quos pro salute anime sue et pro animabus patris et matris sue et antecessorum suorum eidem ecclesie dedit et concessit et super
altare beati Petri Gloec' in puram et perpetuam elemosinam optulit. Quod quidem ratum et inconvulsum manere
volo in perpetuum. presenti scripto sigilli mei impressione munito. confirmavi. Hiis testibus. Waltero Archidiacono Cornub'. Ricardo Revel. Ogero filio Ogeri. Ricardo Flammeng. Symone filio Rogeri.
Ricardo de Grenvill'. Roberto de Champaus. Pagano clerico. Ricardo de Muchegros. Odone fratre eius.

Plate XXII. Scribe 28 (no. 254)

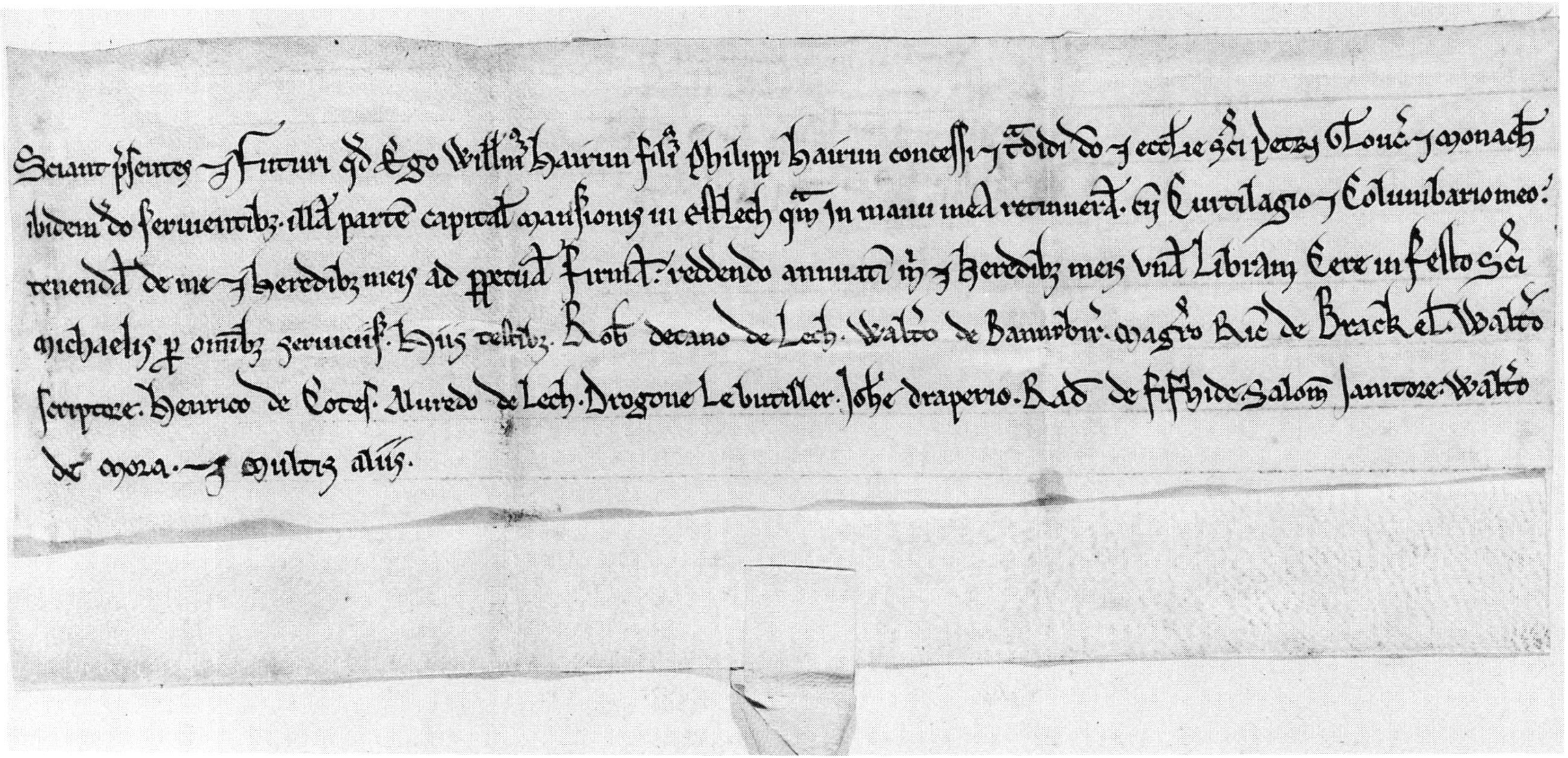

Plate XXIII. Scribe 29 (no. 218)

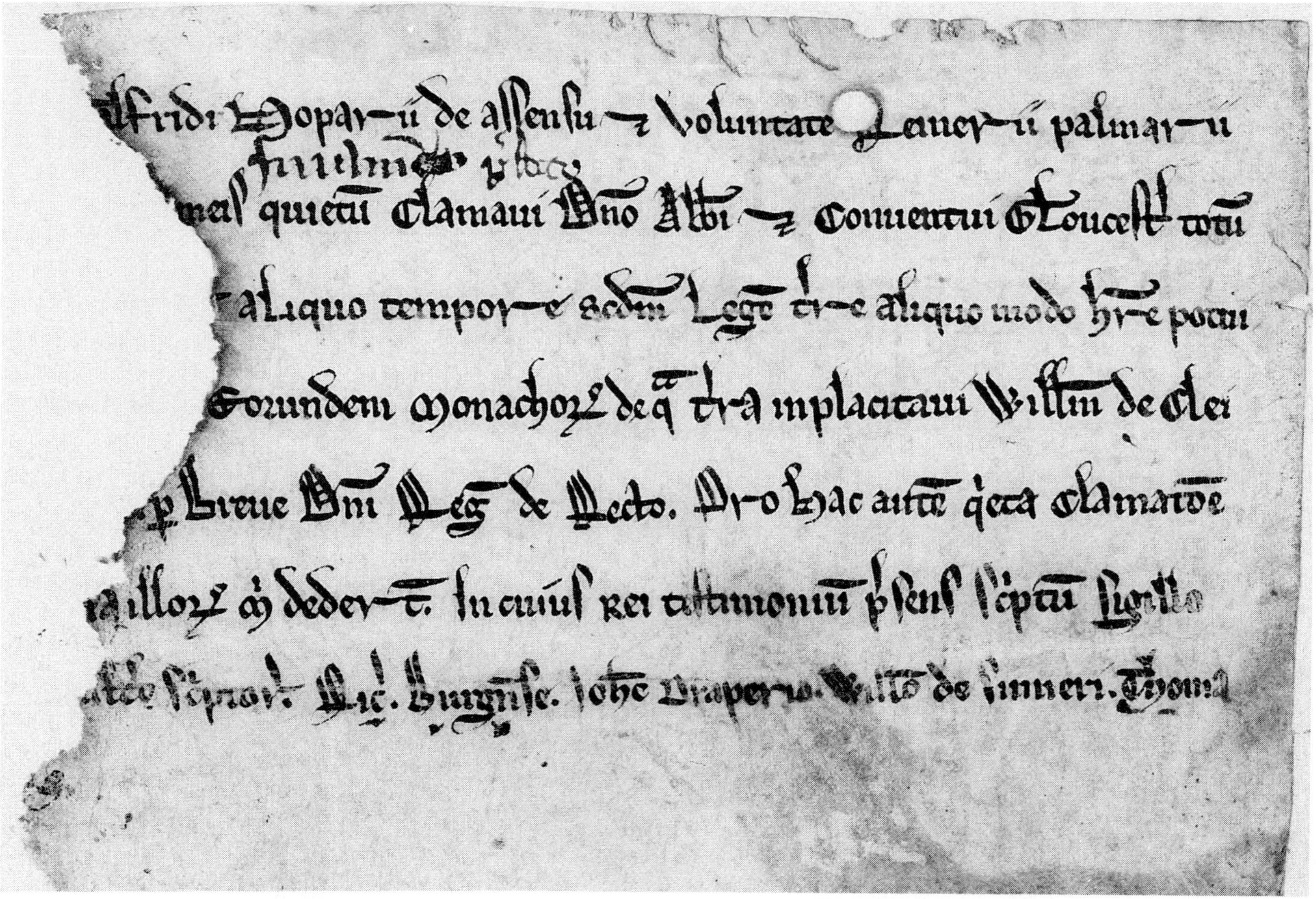

Plate XXIV. Scribe 30 (no. 223)

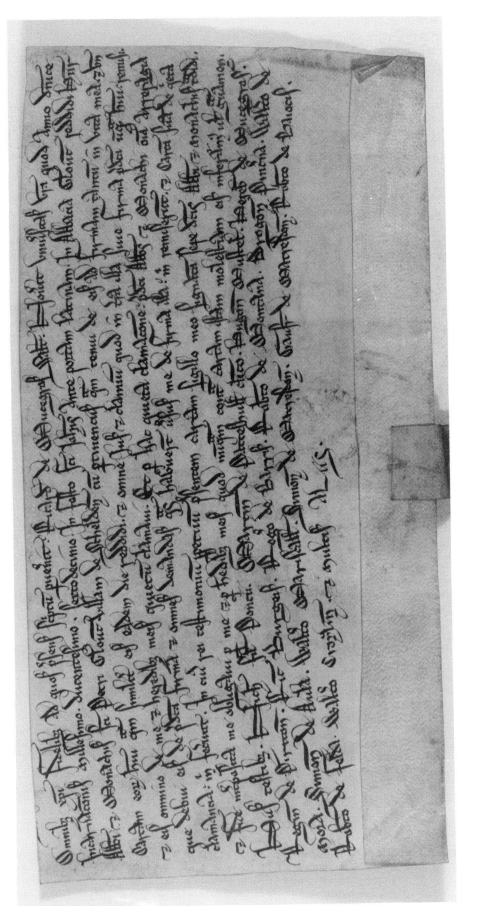

Plate XXV. Scribe 31 (no. 246)

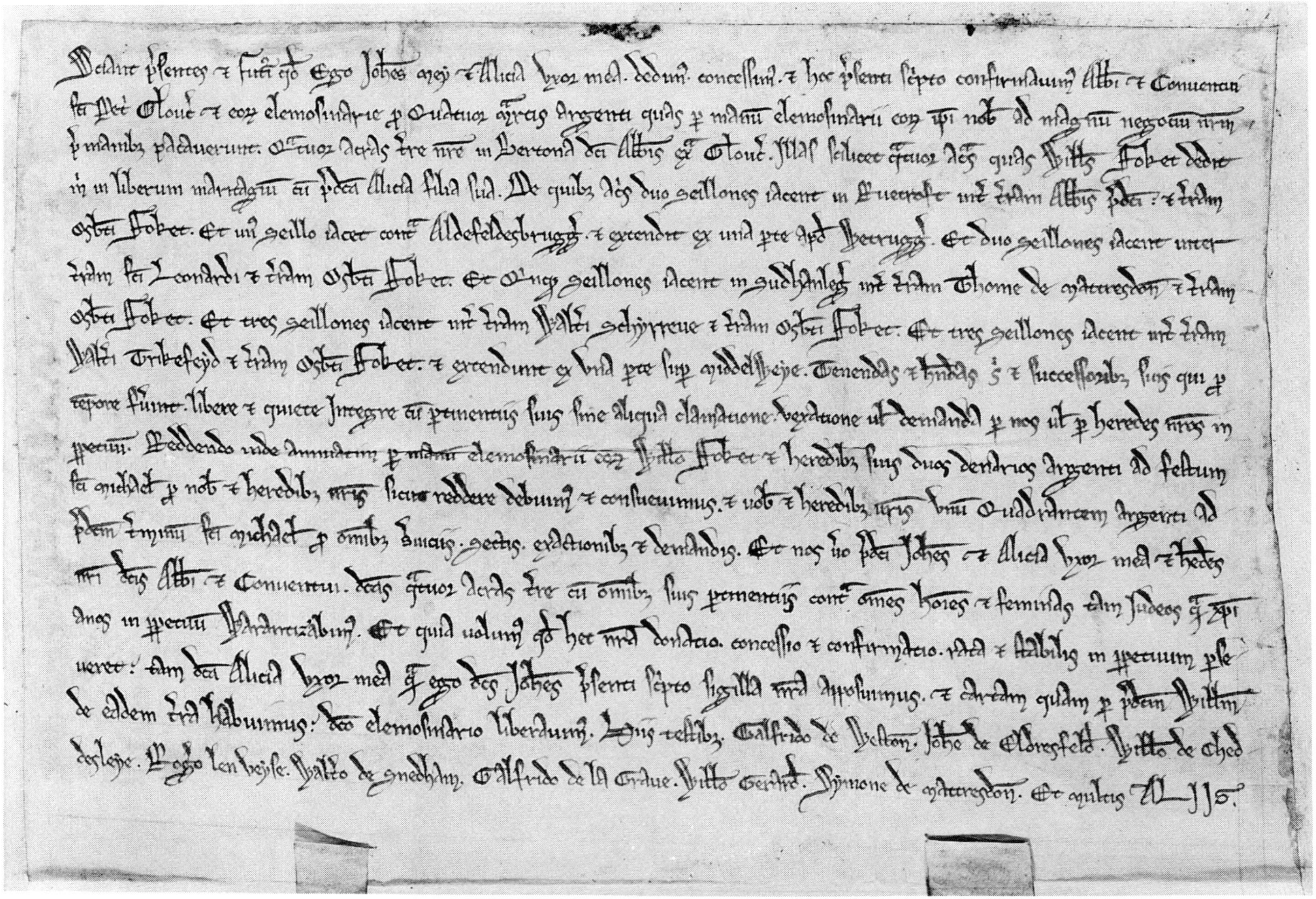

Plate XXVI. Scribe 32 (no. 239)

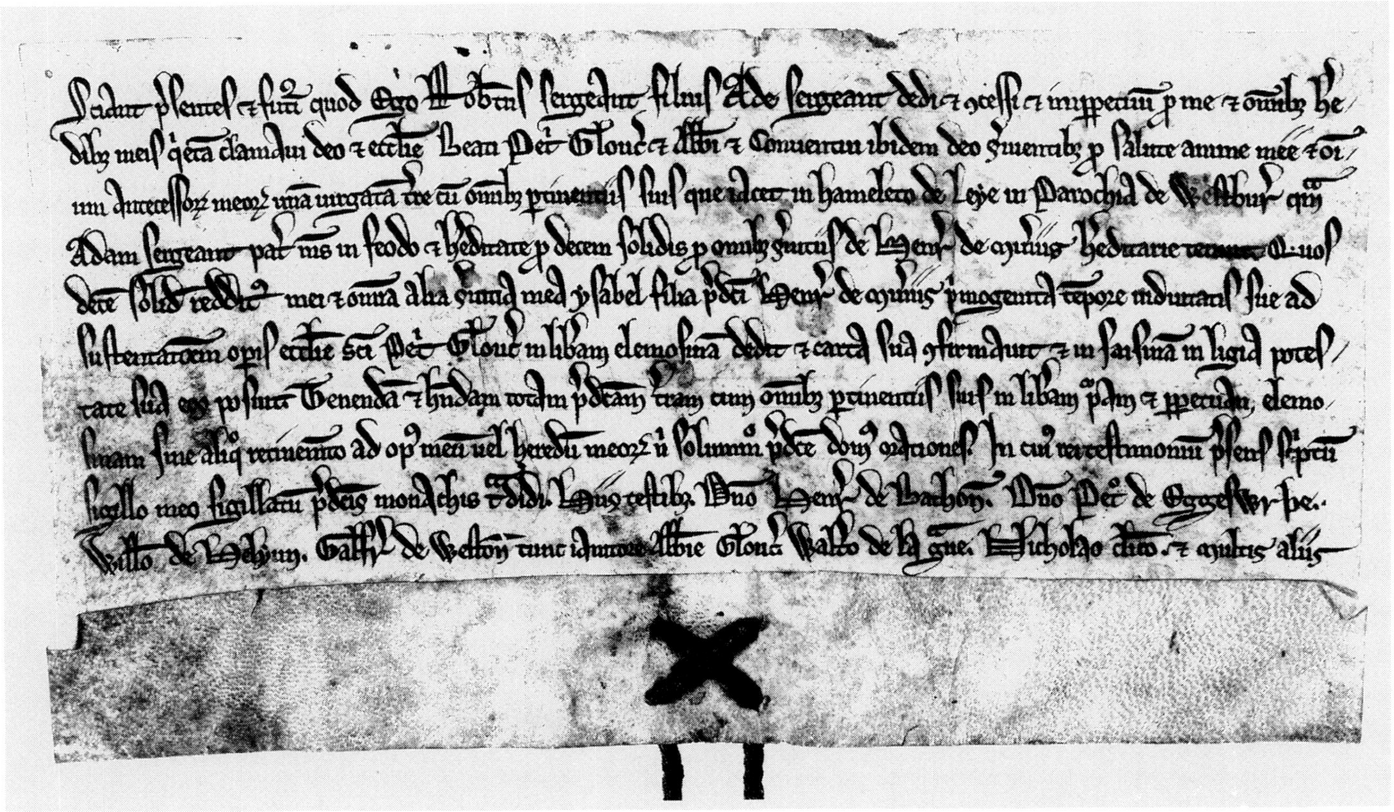

Plate XXVII. Scribe 33 (no. 261)

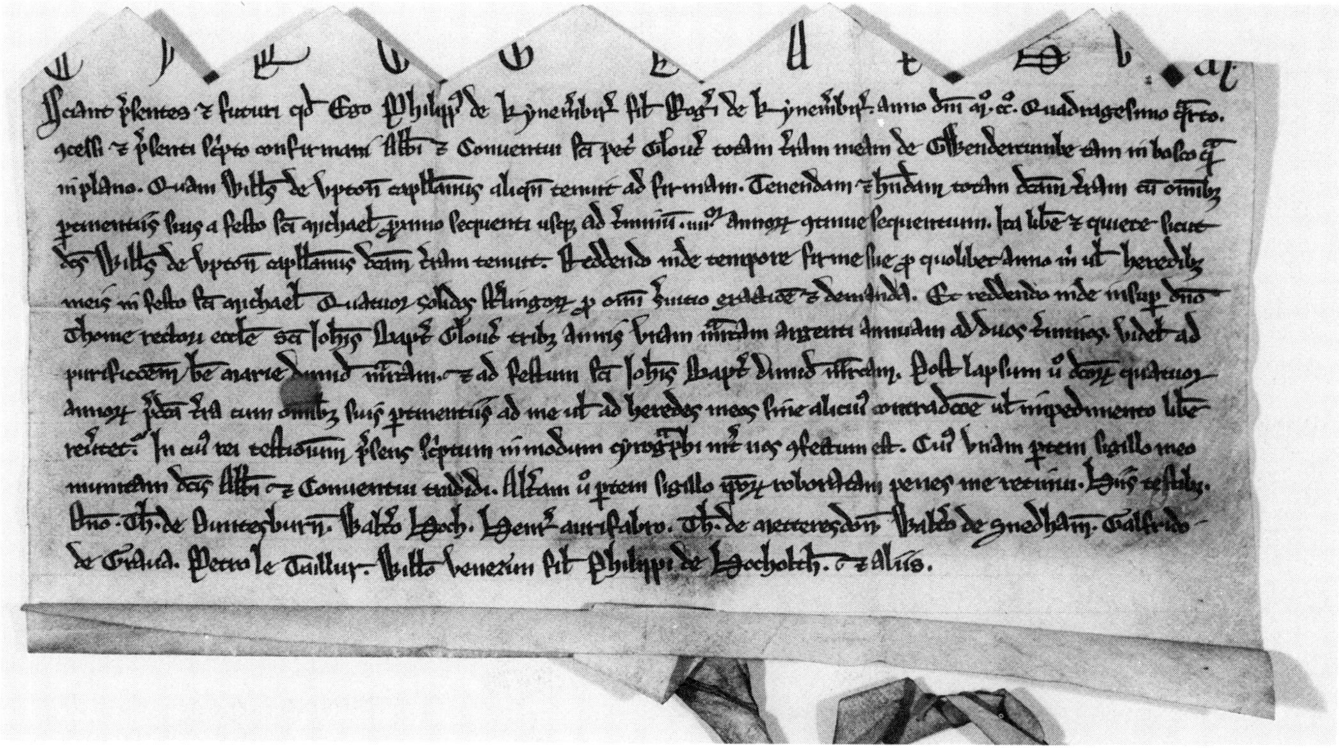

Plate XXIX. Scribe 35 (no. 229)

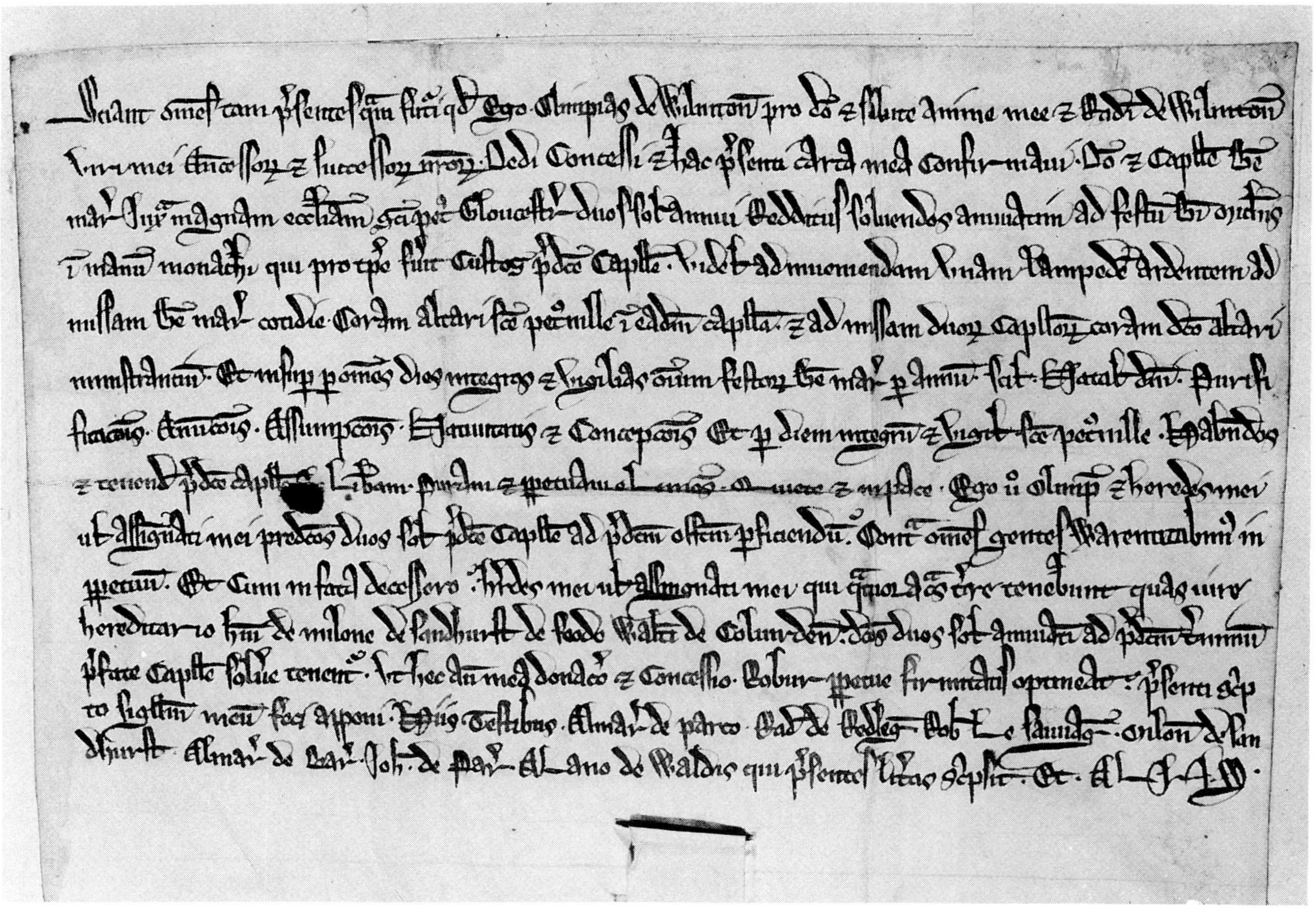

Plate XXX. Scribe 36 (no. 276)

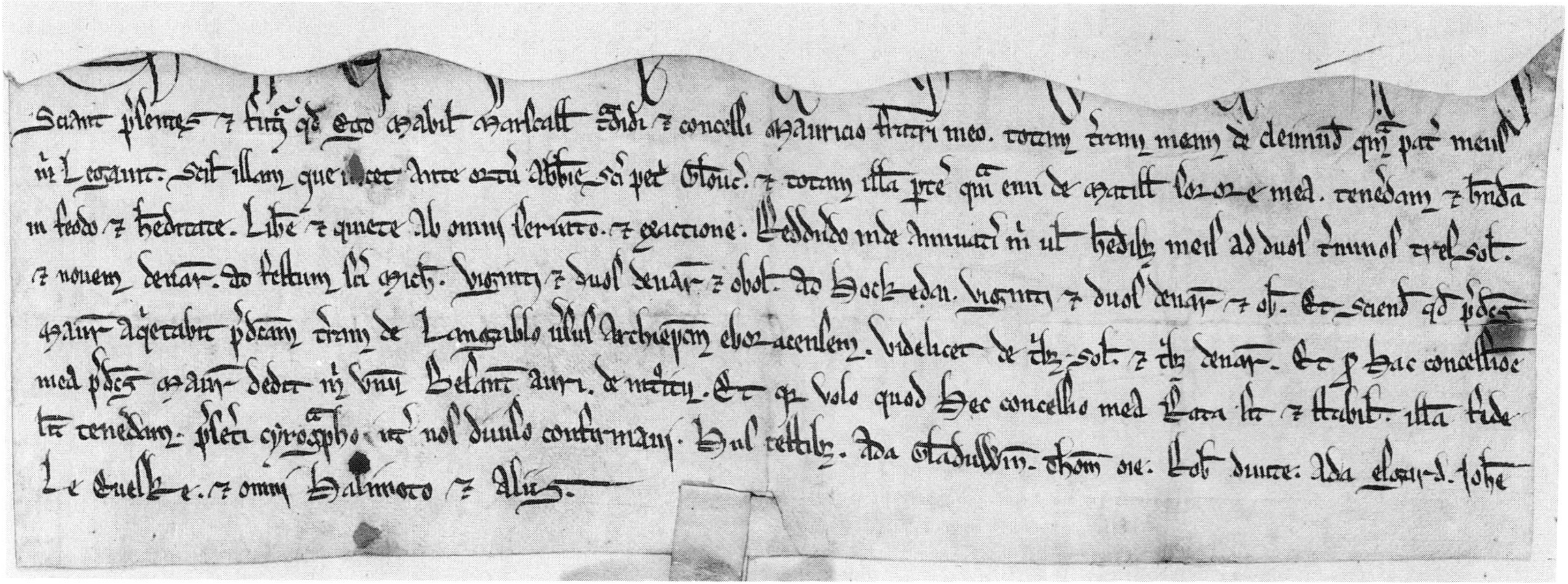

Plate XXXII. Scribe 38 (no. 300)

Sciant tam presentes quam futuri qd ego Isabelle filia Radi Bechet et Willus filius meus assensu et uoluntate horum meorum uoluntatibus et istorum clamauimus de nobis et herede nostro quietum de Gracumo et herede suo totam terram nram cū ptinentis suis que iacet inter domū Drchid Sellate meretram Willi le Seruestam et terram Thome filii Willi filii Roberti filius Willi fit Iuenat illam fit qm Ric burgensis lodit in istabele in istam marragiu. habindam in perpetuū sibi et herede suis. reddend nob Annuatim Abbatie et toue dte d. Algũ pr or ferruato ad Hockseder. Ego dicta psca Isabele et Willus filius meus et herede nri pdco castro et herede suis. pdcam terram cum omng hominus et feminus Warantizabimus. Et pro hac cū nendicone et quieta clamancia nra pdca castra ded nob pmamibus quinqz argineas Algeū de qualibet donar. enim quidem tram de dia fit Grimilsha fit et duab ouarus et omnd Arger Et qd hanc bendicone nram et quietam clamancia et uolumz racedm fore et monenisum cam phoraus carte nre testimonio et sigilloz nroz impssione cõfirmauimus. Hiis testibz Psonilio decano atoue. Thom frē suo. Walto E.d.fm. Robto saur ce. Robta palm. Walto russfd ce. ipi otoue. Thom Rans. Ric burg. philipp burg. Walt le Percettam. Walto russet mulote Thom fit Iuenat. Thom frē suo. Ala boverd. mauzo mandath et de cetaro Rogo deo. et mtis aliis.

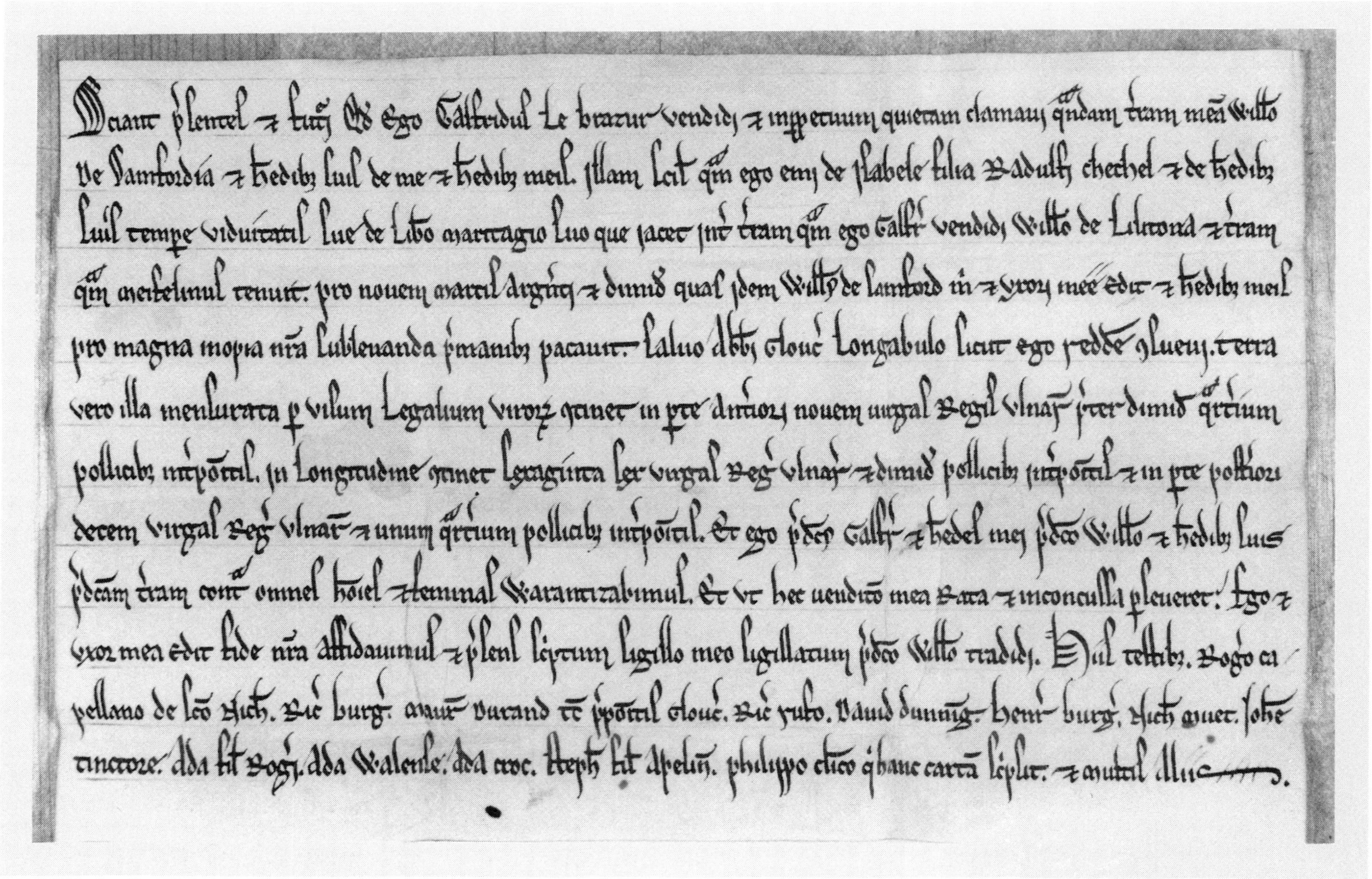

Plate XXXIV. Scribe 40 (no. 286)

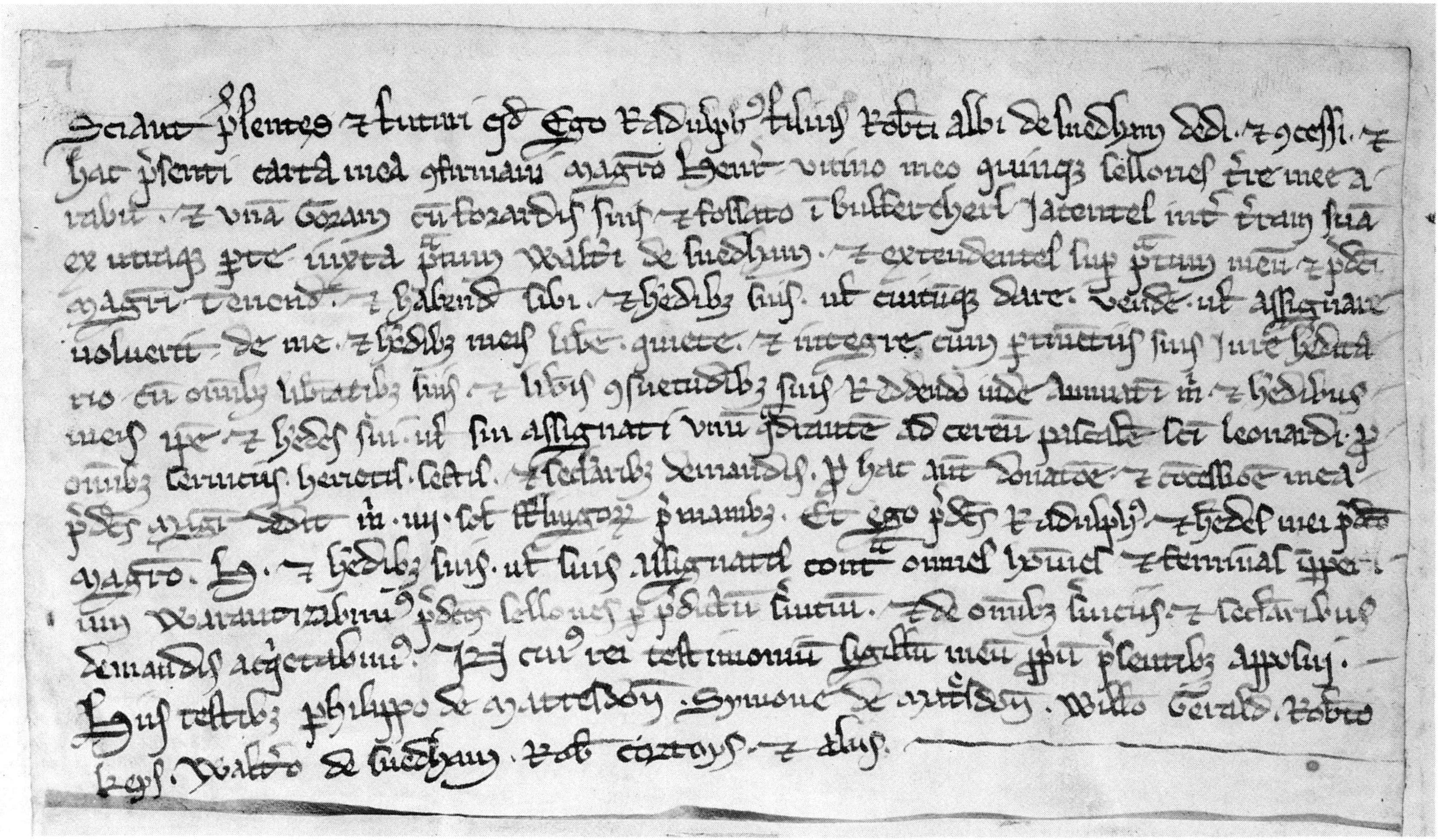

Plate XXXV. Scribe 41 (no. 345)

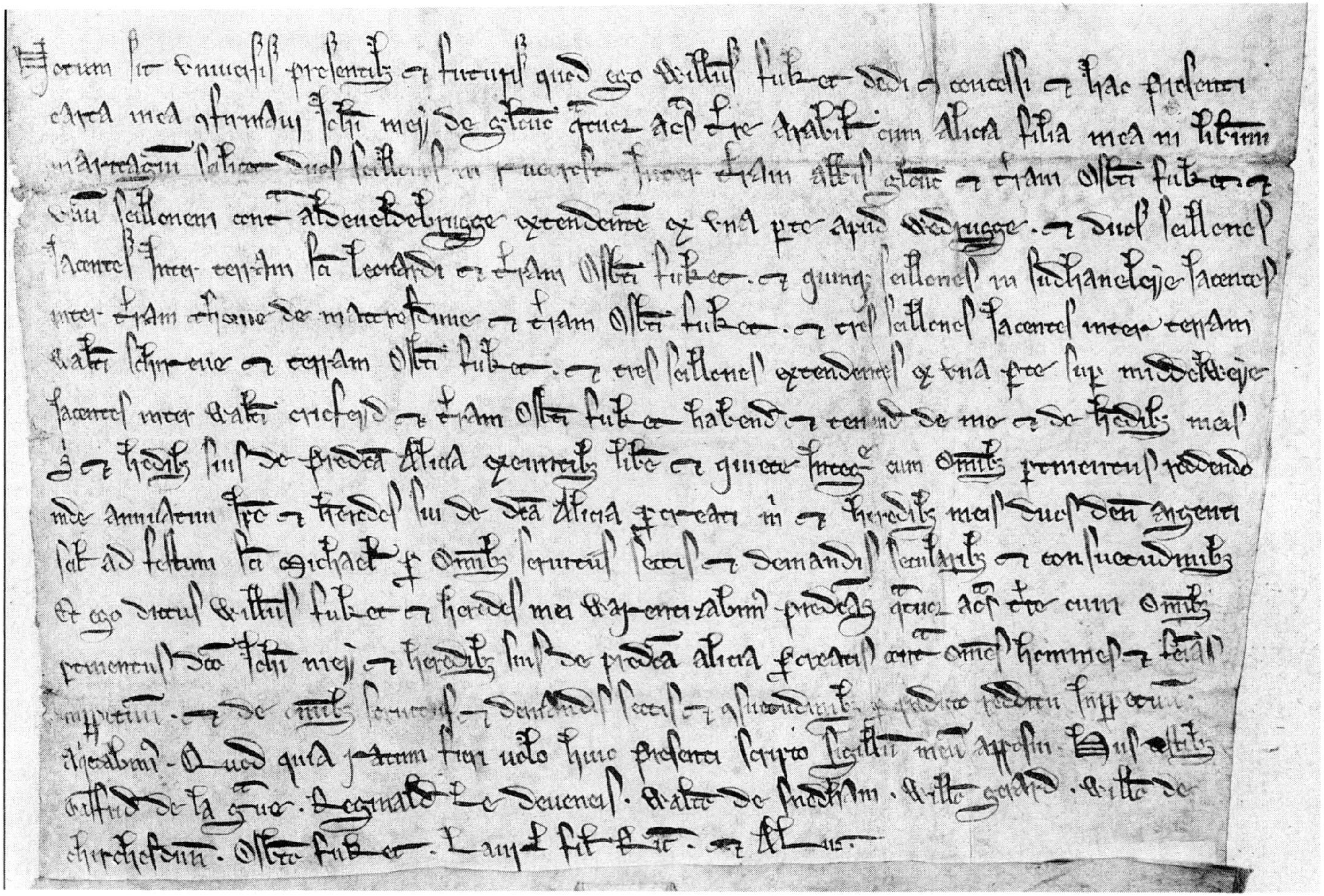

Plate XXXVI. Scribe 42 (no. 305)

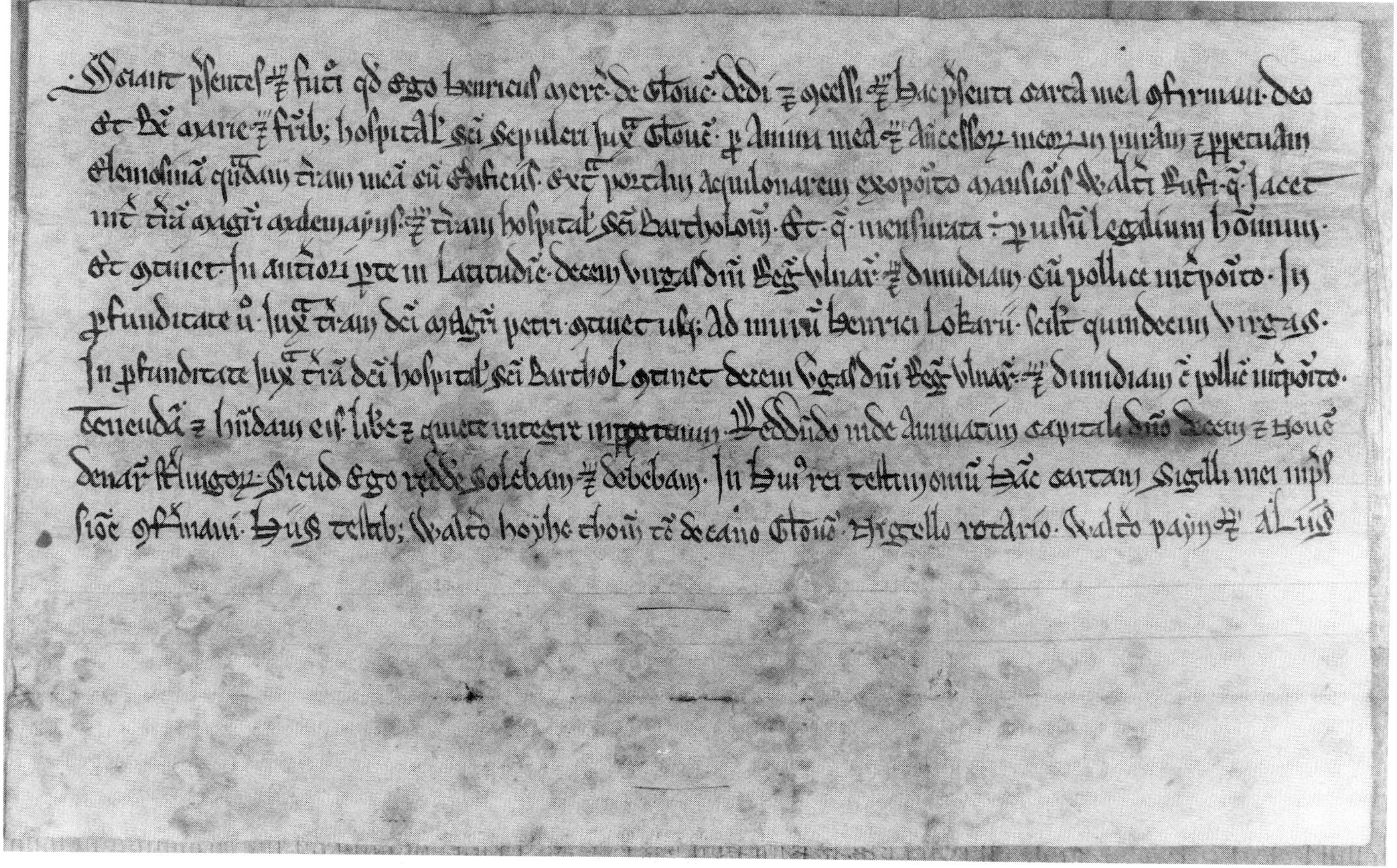
Sciant presentes et futuri quod ego Henricus Merc' de Stoue dedi et concessi et hac presenti carta mea confirmavi deo
et Beate Marie et fratribus hospitalis sancti Sepulcri iuxta Stoue pro anima mea et antecessorum meorum in puram et perpetuam
elemosinam quandam terram meam cum edificiis extra portam aquilonarem ex opposito mansionis Walteri Rufi que iacet
inter terram magistri [illegible] et terram hospitalis sancti Bartholomei. Et que mensurata est per visum legalium hominum
et continet in anteriori parte in latitudine decem virgas domini Regis ulnarias et dimidiam cum pollice interposito. In
profunditate vero iuxta terram dicti magistri Petri continet usque ad murum Henrici Lokarii scilicet quindecim virgas.
In profunditate iuxta terram dicti hospitalis sancti Barthol' continet decem virgas domini Regis ulnarias et dimidiam cum pollice interposito.
Tenendam et habendam eis libere et quiete integre in perpetuum. Reddendo inde annuatim capitali domino decem et novem
denarios sterlingorum sicud ego reddere solebam et debebam. In huius rei testimonium hanc cartam sigilli mei impressione
confirmavi. Hiis testibus: Waltero [illegible] tunc temporis decano Stoue, [illegible] rotario, Waltero Payn et aliis.

Plate XXXVII. Scribe 43

Plate XXXVIII. Scribe 44

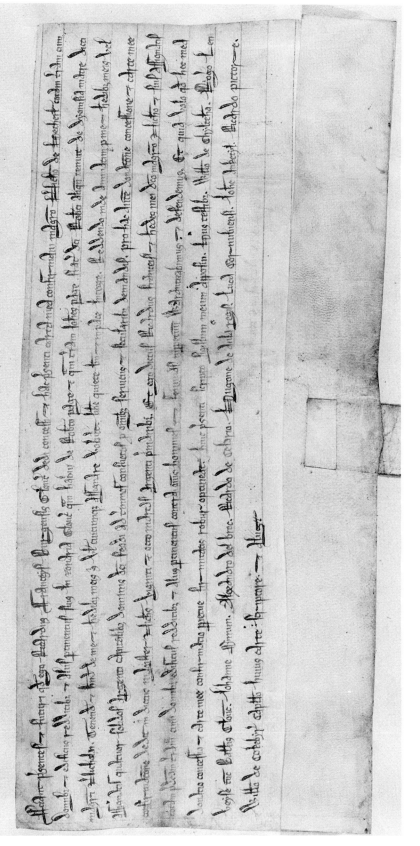

Plate XXXIX. Scribe 45 (no. 301)

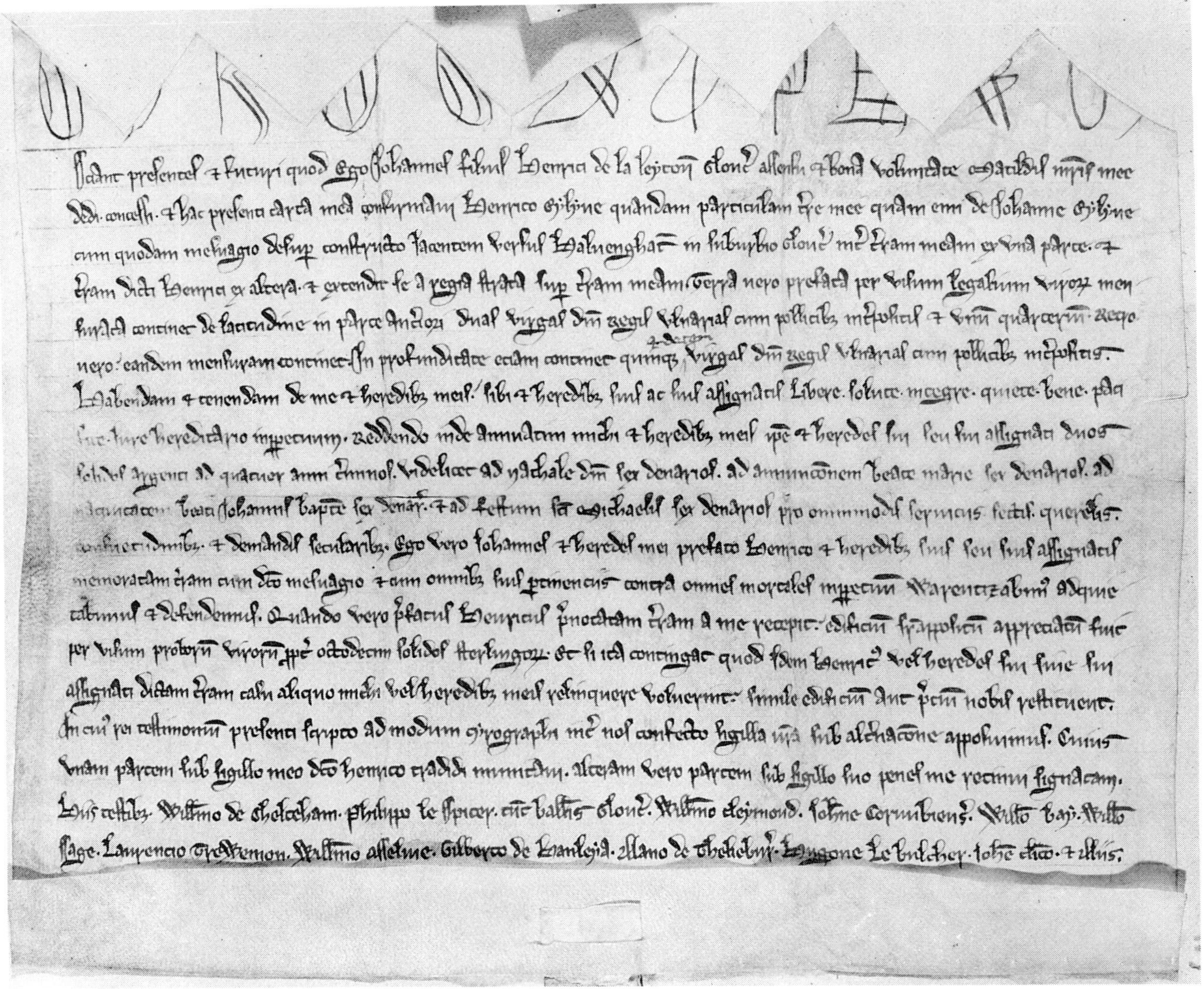

Plate XL.
Scribe 46
(no. 318)

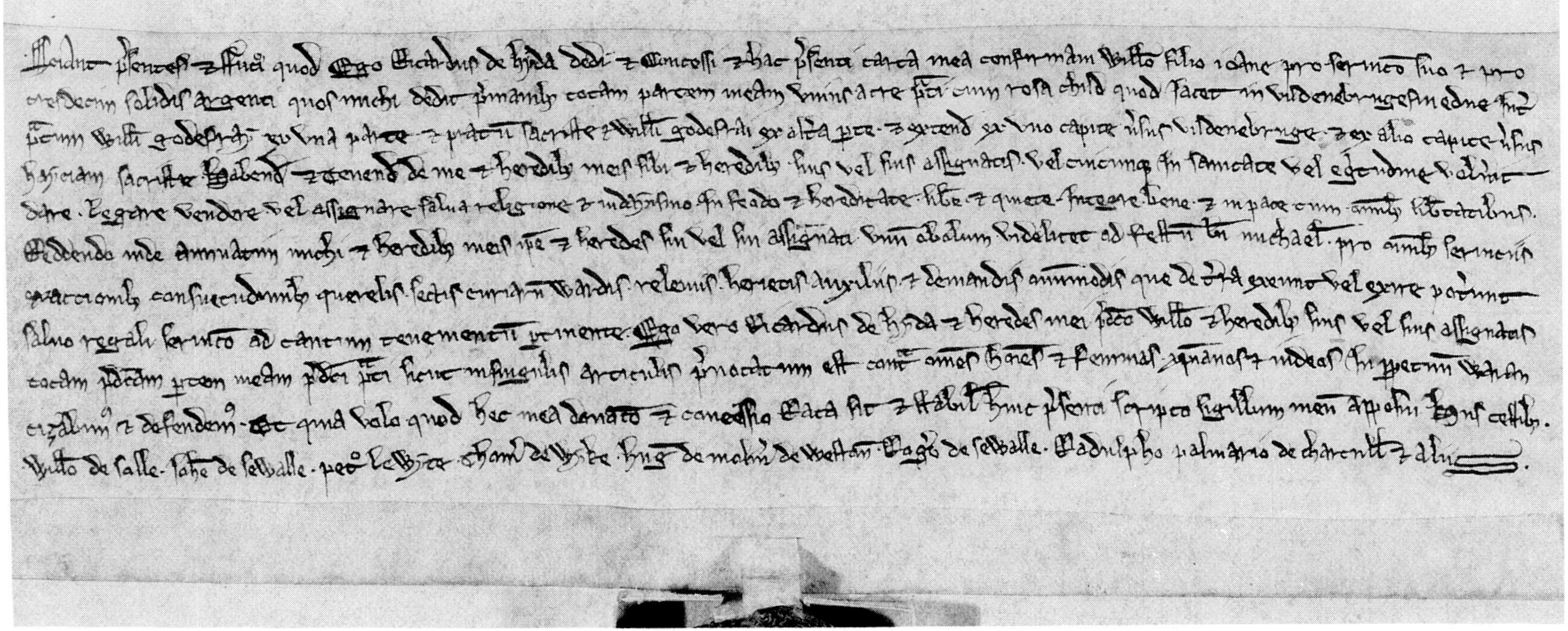

Plate XLI. Scribe 47 (no. 326)

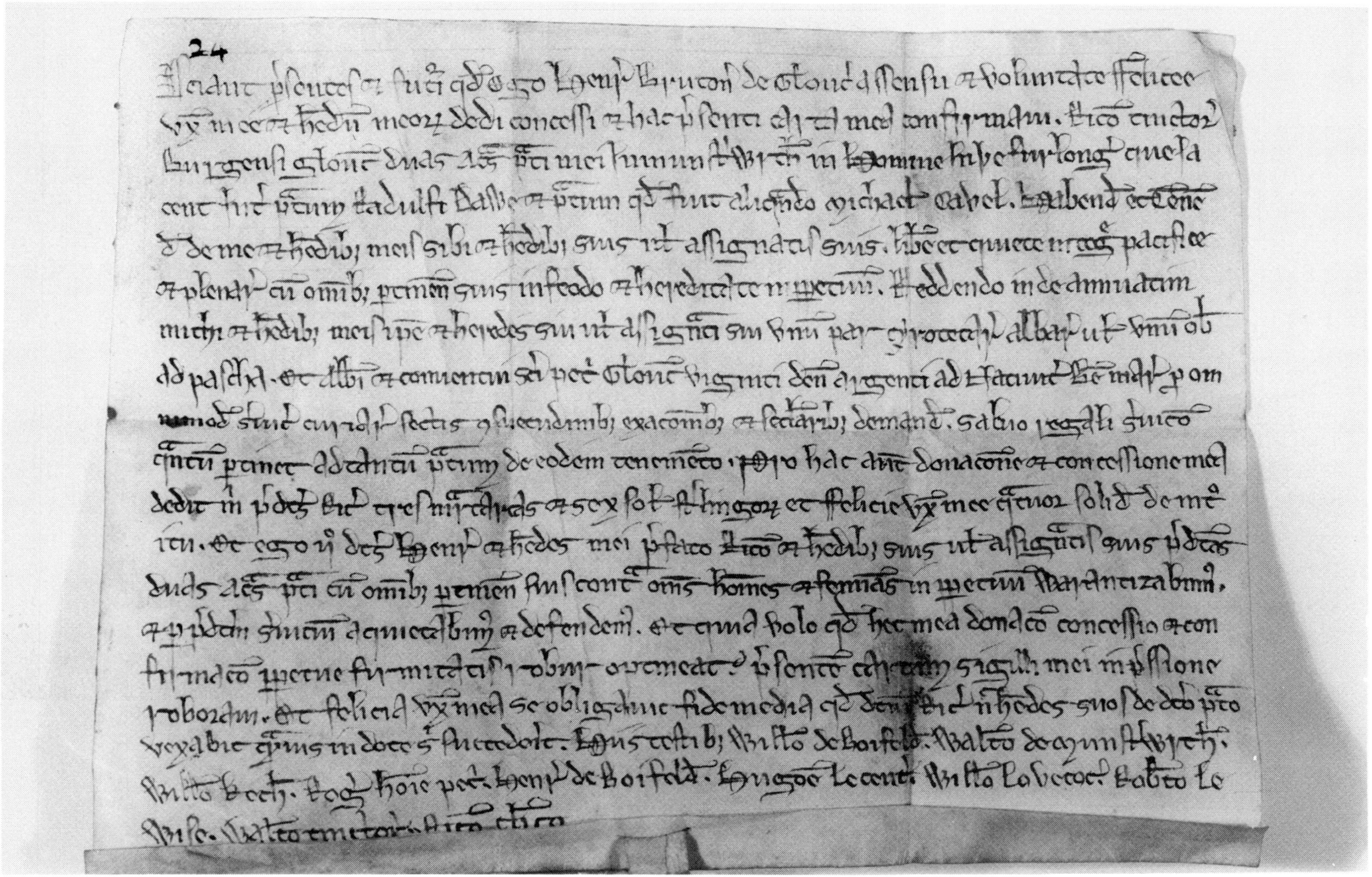

Plate XLII. Scribe 48 (no. 287)

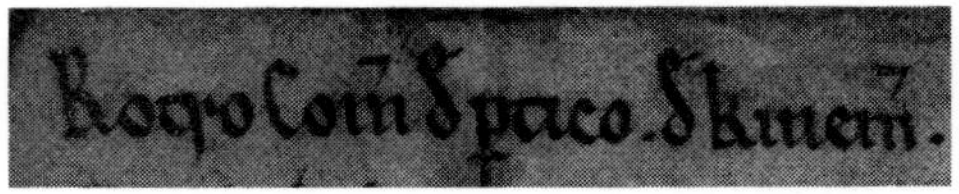

Rogero Cotii Spaco Skuueri.

a. Hand a (no. 248)

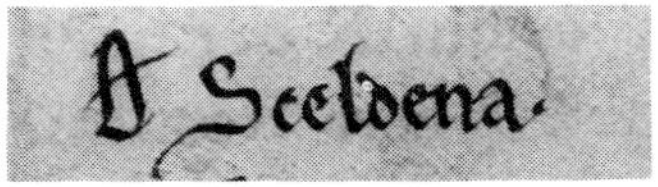

Å Scelbena.

b. Hand b (no. 252)

Rogeri parus.

c. Hand c/Scribe 2 (no. 247)

Rosedin fil'etarld.

Cont Ernaldii filii duunign.

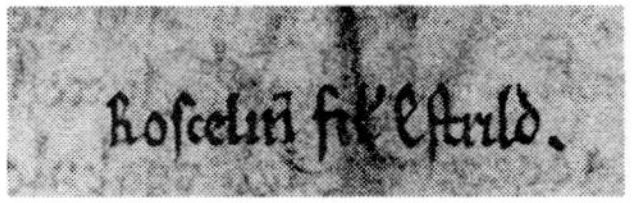

d. Hand d/Scribe 4 (no. 61) 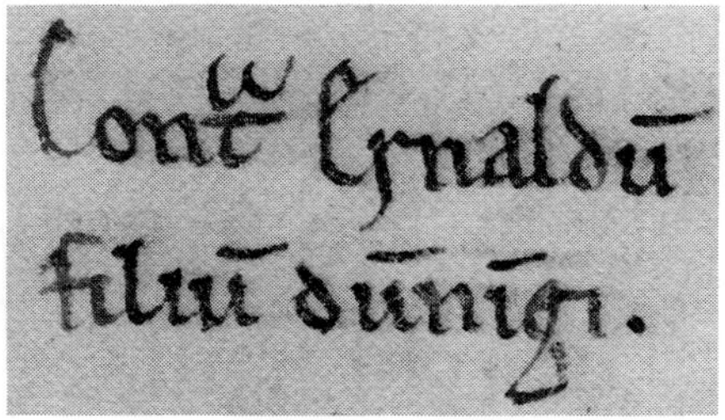   e. Hand e (no. 60)

g. Waltriii godheorce

f. Hand f (no. 114)

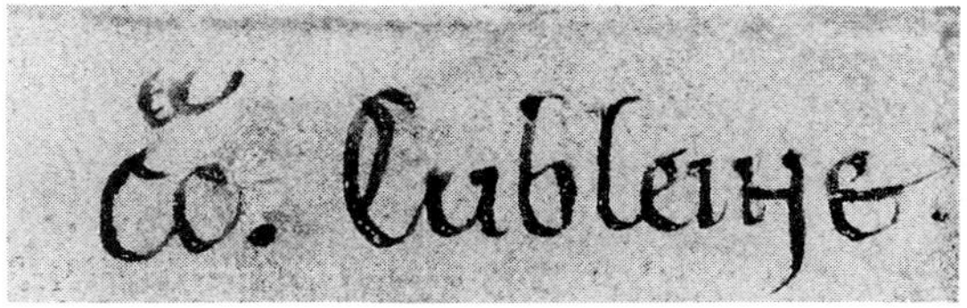

Co. Clablerye.

g. Hand g (no. 75)

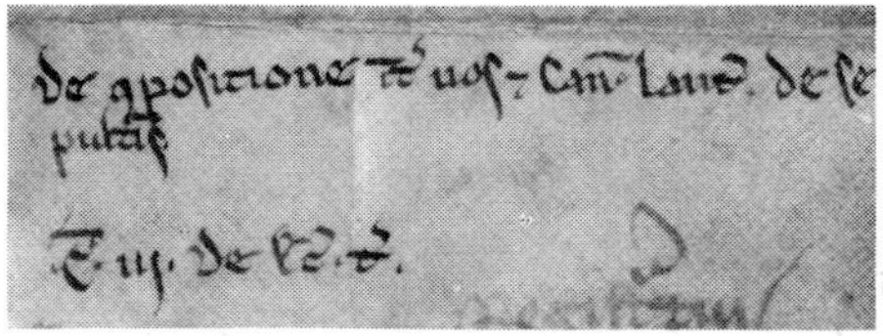

de apostoriones uof~ Cntu Luue, de le puntasi
t: iii. de Fi: Fz.

h. Hand h (no. 105)

et Coure Johan ber

i. Hand i/Scribe 7 (no. 74)

Plate XLIII

a. Hand j (no. 89)

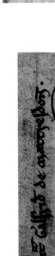

b. Hand k (no. 262)

c. Hand l (no. 95)

d. Hand m (no. 242)

e. Hand n (no. 343)

f. Hand o/Scribe 17 (no. 146)

g. Hand p/Scribe 34 (no. 240)

h. Hand q (no. 267)

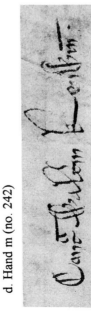

i. Hand r (no. 330)

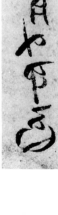

j. Hand s (no. 326)

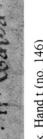

k. Hand t (no. 146)

Plate XLIV